Applied International Trade Analysis

STUDIES IN INTERNATIONAL TRADE POLICY

Studies in International Trade Policy includes works dealing with the theory, empirical analysis, political, economic, legal relations, and evaluations of international trade policies and institutions.

General Editor: Robert M. Stern

John H. Jackson and Edwin Vermulst, Editors. *Antidumping Law and Practice: A Comparative Study*

John Whalley, Editor. *Developing Countries and the Global Trading System*. Volumes 1 and 2

John Whalley, Coordinator. *The Uruguay Round and Beyond: The Final Report from the Ford Foundation Project on Developing Countries and the Global Trading System*

Jagdish Bhagwati and Hugh T. Patrick, Editors. *Aggressive Unilateralism: America's 301 Trade Policy and the World Trading System*

Alan V. Deardorff and Robert M. Stern, *Computational Analysis of Global Trading Arrangements*

Ulrich Kohli. *Technology, Duality, and Foreign Trade: The GNP Function Approach to Modeling Imports and Exports*

Stephen V. Marks and Keith E. Maskus, Editors. *The Economics and Politics of World Sugar Policies*

J. Michael Finger, Editor. *Antidumping: How It Works and Who Gets Hurt*

Horst Herbert and Ngo Van Long, Editors. *Trade, Welfare, and Economic Policies: Essays in Honor of Murray C. Kemp*

Robert M. Stern, Editor. *The Multilateral Trading System: Analysis and Options for Change*

David Schwartzman. *The Japanese Television Cartel: A Study Based on* Matsushita v. Zenith

Barry Eichengreen. *Reconstructing Europe's Trade and Payments: The European Payments Union*

Alan V. Deardorff and Robert M. Stern, Editors. *Analytical Perspectives and Negotiating Issues in the Global Trading System*

Edwin Vermulst, Paul Waer, and Jacques Bourgeois, Editors. *Rules of Origin in International Trade: A Comparative Study*

Alan V. Deardorff and Robert M. Stern, Editors. *The Stolper-Samuelson Theorem: A Golden Jubilee*

Kent Albert Jones. *Export Restraint and the New Protectionism: The Political Economy of Discriminatory Trade Restrictions*

Alan V. Deardorff, James A. Levinsohn, and Robert M. Stern, Editors. *New Directions in Trade Theory*

Robert Baldwin, Tain-Jy Chen, and Douglas Nelson. *Political Economy of U.S.–Taiwan Trade*

Danny M. Leipziger, Editor. *Lessons from East Asia*

Bernard M. Hoekman and Petros C. Mavroidis, Editors. *Law and Policy in Public Purchasing: The WTO Agreement on Government Procurement*

Tamim Bayoumi. *Financial Integration and Real Activity*

Harry P. Bowen, Abraham Hollander, and Jean-Marie Viaene. *Applied International Trade Analysis*

APPLIED INTERNATIONAL TRADE ANALYSIS

Harry P. Bowen
University of California at Irvine

Abraham Hollander
University of Montreal and Centre de Recherche
et Développement en Economique

and

Jean-Marie Viaene
Erasmus University Rotterdam and Tinbergen Institute

Ann Arbor

THE UNIVERSITY OF MICHIGAN PRESS

Published in the United States of America by
The University of Michigan Press

2001   2000   1999   1998   4   3   2   1

Library of Congress Cataloging-in-Publication Data.

Bowen, Harry P.
    Applied international trade analysis / Harry P. Bowen, Abraham
Hollander, and Jean-Marie Viaene.
        p.   cm. — (Studies in international trade policy)
    Includes bibliographical references and index.
    ISBN 0–472–09670–2 (cloth). — ISBN 0–472–06670–6 (paper)
    1. International trade.   2. Commercial policy.   3. International
economic relations.   4. International economic integration.   5. Free
trade.   6. Foreign trade and employment.   7. Competition,
International.   I. Hollander, Abraham.   II. Viaene, Jean-Marie.
III. Title.   IV. Series.
HF1379.B68 1998
382—dc21   97–26326
                                                            CIP

Printed in Hong Kong

To Anne, Arnaud, Charlotte, Elodie and B. Patricia

Contents

List of Figures

List of Tables

Preface

In the past twenty years international trade has been among the more active fields of research in economics. Developments include the analysis of good and factor flows across national boundaries when markets are imperfectly competitive, examination of causal links between trade and growth, and the study of international exchange in multidimensional settings. In large measure, this activity sprang from contemporaneous efforts to confront and then reconcile the predictions of the theory with empirical facts. Assisting the latter activity has been the clarification of methods for conducting formal tests of trade theory as well as significant efforts to broaden the scope and availability of internationally comparable data. These advances in theory and empirical methods have deepened our understanding of the factors determining the volume and composition of trade, challenged conventional wisdom about the effects of trade policies, and injected new arguments into discussions about the merits of free trade.

This book was written with two objectives in mind. First, to give students, practitioners and researchers a text that encompasses the important theoretical and applied developments in the field and brings to the fore those questions, left unanswered by traditional trade models, which the more recent models have sought to address. Second, to provide the student of international trade with a single text that integrates theory, applied analysis and the formal testing of theory.

The design of the book reflects our conviction that linking theory and data during the learning process is key. Throughout the book, theory is interwoven with empirical analysis, the latter stressing methodology as well as results. Positive analysis is followed by a presentation of policy issues. In this regard, the discussion of trade policy instruments is not limited to the derivation of qualitative results; proper attention is also paid to the partial and general equilibrium techniques used to measure the welfare and resource allocation effects of policy interventions. In addition, sprinkled throughout the book are exercises designed to deepen the students' understanding of the material and to cast light on issues glanced over in the body of the text. Each chapter concludes with a list of suggested additional readings intended to complement the main textual material.

Organization

The book comprises four parts. Part I (2 chapters) provides a road map for the remainder of the book. Chapter 1 introduces key concepts and provides background data on patterns of trade and factor flows in order to motivate and orient the reader regarding the central issues addressed by the theory. Chapter 2 introduces the subject of trade policy and includes discussion of the institutional framework for administered protection. Part II (6 chapters) covers the main theoretical aspects of the Ricardian and Heckscher–Ohlin models as well as in depth presentation and discussion of the methodologies used to formally test the theory. Also covered are the effects of policy interventions in the setting of perfectly competitive markets. The latter includes discussion of the applied methods, including general equilibrium modeling, that are used to measure the welfare and other effects of trade policy. Part III (3 chapters) presents models of imperfect competition as a means of explaining the volume and composition of trade. A chapter on positive analysis is followed by a chapter on policy which explores the effects of tariffs, quotas and contingent protection. The final chapter of Part III discusses the multinational firm and the implications of foreign direct investment for the pattern of production and international specialization. Part IV is devoted to three selected topics: regional economic integration, the relationship between exchange rates and trade, and trade and growth. A final appendix discusses the data common in applied analyses of trade and indicates sources, many of them on the Internet.

Prerequisites

The book is intended as a core text for an advanced undergraduate or graduate course in international trade. Prerequisites are an intermediate undergraduate course in microeconomics and an introductory (perhaps intermediate) course in econometrics. The mathematical tools used in this book are basic calculus and linear algebra. A few chapters make use of some elementary notions in game theory. Some facility with computer programming or a spreadsheet program is necessary to work out some of the exercises.

Acknowledgments

It is appropriate to acknowledge first our debt to teachers and colleagues who introduced us to the field and taught us many tricks of the trade: Robert E. Baldwin, Wilfred J. Ethier, Herbert Glejser, Lawrence R. Klein,

Anne O. Krueger, Edward E. Leamer, Robert Lipsey, Richard C. Marston, Ivor Pearce and Robert M. Stern. The body of applied and theoretical work undertaken by these individuals and their students continues to forcibly shape the field.

We would also like to extend special thanks to several groups of students who were exposed to successive drafts. They have been a continuing source of inspiration and friendship and their numerous reactions led to more lucid exposition and many corrections. We in particular would like to thank those who helped with research assistance at various stages: Mike Dell, Jeroen Hinloopen, Paul Kofman, Tomas Kögel, Nora Plaisier, Joachim Stibora, Albert de Vaal and Rien Wagenvoort.

We are indebted to the Tinbergen Institute and Erasmus University Rotterdam for their constant financial and logistical support at various stages of the project. Harry Bowen further acknowledges the support of both the Department of Economics and the Graduate School of Management, University of California at Irvine. Abraham Hollander also thanks the Centre de Recherche et Développement en Economique and the Social Sciences and Humanities Research Council of Canada for financial support. Jean-Marie Viaene thanks the Bank of Finland for its hospitality which enabled him to 'Finnish' his work on Chapter 13.

We would like to extend special thanks to colleagues who have been generous in their willingness to read and offer helpful comments on the manuscript: Robert E. Baldwin, Alan Deardorff, Harris Dellas, Leonard Dudley, Wilfred J. Ethier, Rob Feenstra, Switgard Feuerstein, Sanjeev Goyal, James Harrigan, James Levinsohn, Charles van Marrewijk, Joe Pelzman, Santanu Roy, Teun Schmidt, Robert M. Stern, Leo Sveikauskas, Frans van der Toorn and Casper de Vries. In addition, the past and current members of the International Studies Program of the National Bureau of Economic Research have been significant in shaping ideas and a continuing source of encouragement.

Finally, we are indebted to Mrs A. Bogaards-Kok and S. Brewer who suffered through many drafts and somehow remained cheerful despite the obstacles.

HARRY P. BOWEN (CALIFORNIA)
ABRAHAM HOLLANDER (MONTREAL)
JEAN-MARIE VIAENE (ROTTERDAM)

Glossary

AGE	applied general equilibrium
AMS	aggregate measure of support
ANZCERTA	Australia–New Zealand Closer Economic Relations Trade Agreement
ASEAN	Association of South-East Asian Nations
BTN	Brussels Tariff Nomenclature
CCCN	Customs Cooperation Council Nomenclature
CES	constant elasticity of substitution
CET	common external tariff
CGE	computable general equilibrium
CRS	constant returns to scale
CRS/PC	constant returns to scale and perfect competition
CU	customs union
CUSTA	Canada–US Free Trade Agreement
CV	compensating variation
DCR	domestic content requirement
DPMC	differentiated product–monopolistic competition
DRAM	dynamic random access memory
DSPs	dispute settlement procedures
EAP	economically active population
EC	European Community
EEC	European Economic Community
EFTA	European Free Trade Area
EOS	economies of scale
EPT	exchange rate pass-through
ERP	effective rate of protection
EU	European Union
EV	equivalent variation
FAO	Food and Agriculture Organization
FDI	foreign direct investment
FPE	factor price equalization
GATS	General Agreement on Trade in Services
GATT	General Agreement on Tariffs and Trade
GDI	gross domestic investment
GIRS	globally increasing returns to scale
GL	Grubel–Lloyd

GTAP	Global Trade and Analysis Project
H–D	Harrod–Domar
H–O	Heckscher–Ohlin
H–O–S	Heckscher–Ohlin–Samuelson
H–O–V	Heckscher–Ohlin–Vanek
ICPSR	Inter-University Consortium for Political and Social Research
IIAS	intra-industry affiliate sales
IIFDI	intra-industry foreign direct investment
IIT	intra-industry trade
ILO	International Labour Office
IMF	International Monetary Fund
I–O	input–output
IRS	increasing returns to scale
IRS/IP	increasing returns to scale and imperfect (monopolistic) competition
ISCO	International Standard Classification of Occupations
ISIC	International Standard Industrial Classification
ITO	International Trade Organization
MERCOSUR	Southern Common Market
MFA	Multi-fibre Arrangement
MITI	Ministry of International Trade and Industry (Japan)
MNE	multinational enterprise
NACE	Nomenclature des Activités de la Communauté Européenne
NAFTA	North American Free Trade Agreement
NTB	non-tariff barrier
ODA	official development aid
OECD	Organization for Economic Cooperation and Development
OPEC	Organization of Petroleum Exporting Countries
OLI	ownership, location and internalization
PCM	price–cost margin
PPF	production possibility frontier
PPP	purchasing power parity
R&D	research and development
RCA	revealed comparative advantage
RE	Ricardian equilibrium
RTA	regional trade agreement
SAM	social accounting matrix
SDR	special drawing right
SF	specific factor
SIC	Standard Industrial Classification
SITC	Standard International Trade Classification
TFP	total factor productivity

TPRM	Trade Policy Review Mechanism
TRIPs	Trade-related Aspects of International Property Rights
UNCTAD	United Nations Council on Trade and Development
UNIDO	United Nations Industrial Development Organization
VER	voluntary export restraint
VRA	voluntary restraint agreement
WE	wage equalization equilibrium
WTO	World Trade Organization

Acknowledgements

The authors and publishers wish to thank the following for permission to use copyright material:

American Economic Association for **Table 8.7** from D. Trefler, 'The Case of the Missing Trade and Other Mysteries', *American Economic Review*, 85:5 (1995) 1029–46; **Table 8.8** from R.E. Baldwin, 'Determinants of the Commodity Structure of US Trade', *American Economic Review*, 61 (1971) 126–46; **Tables 8.2, 8.3, 8.4, 8.5** from H.P. Bowen, E.E. Leamer and L. Sveikauskas, 'Multicountry, Multifactor Tests of the Factor Abundance Theory', *American Economic Review*, 77:5 (1987) 791–809.

Blackwell Publishers for **Table 1.15** from T. Straubhaar, 'International Labour Migration with a Common Market: Some Aspects of EC Experience', *Journal of Common Market Studies*, 27:1 (1988) 45–62; **Table 3.3** from G.D.A. MacDougall, 'British and American Exports: A Study Suggested by the Theory of Comparative Costs, Part 1', *Economic Journal*, 61 (1951) 487–521; **Tables 1.11, 1.18** from D. Greenaway and C. Milner, 'On the Measurement of Intra-industry Trade', *Economic Journal*, 93 (1983) 900–8, **Table 11.1** from D.L. Hummels and R.M. Stern, 'Evolving Patterns of North American Merchandise Trade and Foreign Direct Investment, 1960–90', *World Economy*, 17:1 (1994) 5–31; **Table 12.7** from D.K. Brown, A.V. Derdorff and R.M. Stern, 'A North American Free Trade Agreement: Analytical Issues and a Computational Assessment', *World Economy*, 15 (1992) 11–30; **Table 2.5** from B. Balassa and C. Balassa, 'Industrial Protection in the Developed Countries', *World Economy*, 7 (1984) 179–96; and **Table 12.3** from H.C. Petith, 'European Integration and the Terms of Trade', *Economic Journal*, 87 (1997) 262–72.

Elsevier Science-NL for **Table 11.5** from I.B. Kravis and R.E. Lipsey, 'Sources of Competativeness of the Limited States and of it's Multinational Forms', *Review of Economics and Statistics*, 74:2 (1992) 193–201; **Table 3.4** from J. McGilvary and D. Simpson, 'The Commodity Structure of Anglo-Irish Trade', *Review of Economics and Statistics*, 55 (1973) 451–8; **Table 1.9** from H.P. Bowen, 'Changes in the International Distribution of Resources and their Impact on US Comparative Advantage', *Review of Economics and Statistics*, 65:3 (1983); **Table 13.1** from D.O. Cushman, 'US Bilateral Trade

Flows and Exchange Risk during the Floating Period', *Journal of International Economics*, 24 (1988) 317–30; **Trade 8.9** from R.M. Stern and K.V. Maskus, 'Determinants of US Foreign Trade, 1958–76', *Journal of International Economics*, 11:2 (1981) 207–24; **Table 12.1** from J.-M. Viaene, 'A Customs Union between Spain and the EEC', *European Economic Review*, 18 (1982) 345–68; and **Table 6.4** from J.K. Hill and J.A. Mendez, 'The Effect of Commercial Policy on International Migration Flows: the Case of the United States and Mexico', *Journal of International Econdomics*, 17 (1984) 41–53.

Harwood Academic Publishers GmbH for **Table 2.6** from L. Schunecht, *Trade Protection in the European Community* (1992).

International Monetary Fund for **Table 12.5** from V. Tanzi and A.L. Bovenberg, 'Is There a Need for Harmonizing Capital Income Taxes within EC Countries?', mimeo (1989).

Kiel Institute of World Economics for **Table 2.8** from J.M. Finger and A. Olechowski, 'Trade Barriers: Who Does What to Whom', in *Free Trade in the World Economy*, ed. H. Giersch, J.C.B. Mohr (1987) 37–71; **Table 2.7** from S. Laird and A. Yeats, 'Trends in Non-tariff Barriers of Developed Countries, 1966–86', *Weltwirtschaftliches Archiv*, (1990) 299–325; **Table 1.17** from G. Norman and J.M. Dunning, 'Intra-industry Foreign Direct Investment', *Weltwirtschaftliches Archiv*, 120 (1984) 522–39; **Table 1.18** from D. Greenaway, 'Intra-industry and inter-industry Trade in Switzerland', *Weltwirtschaftliches Archiv*, 119 (1983) 109–21; **Table 12.2** from A. Jacquemin and A. Sapir, 'European or World Integration', *Weltwirtschaftliches Archiv*, 124:1 (1988) 127–38; and **Tables 1.12**, **1.14** from C. Culem and L. Lundberg, 'The Product Pattern of Intra-industry Trade: Stability among Countries and over Time', *Weltwirtschaftliches Archiv*, 122 (1986) 113–30.

Kluwer Law International for **Tables 2.2**, **2.3** from J.M. Finger and S. Laird, 'Protection in Developed and Developing Countries: An Overview', *Journal of World Trade Law*, 21 (1987) 9–23.

Office of Official Publications of the European Communities for **Table 2.9** from F. Abraham, 'The Effects of Intra-Community Competition on Export Subsidies to Third Countries: The Case of Export Credits, Export Insurance and Official Development Assistance', CM 59 90 281 EN C (1990); and **Table 2.11** from 'Fourth Survey from the Commission on State Aid in the European Union in the Manufacturing and Certain Other Sector', COM(95) 365 (1995).

Organisation for Economic Co-operation and Development for **Table 2.10** for J. Melitz and J. Messerlin, 'Export Credit Subsidiaries', in *The Export Credit Financing Systems in OECD Member Countries* (1987). Copyright © OECD 1987.

Oxford University Press for **Table 8.6** from W. Kohler, 'How Robust are Sign and Rank Order Tests of the Heckscher–Ohlin–Vanek Theorum', *Oxford Economic Papers*, 43:1 (1991) 158–71.

The University of Chicago Press for **Table 8.1** from E.E. Leamer, 'The Leontief Paradox Reconsidered', *Journal of Political Economy*, 88:3 (1980) 495–503; and **Table 2.4** from B. Balassa, 'Tariff Protection in Industrial Countries: An Evaluation', *Journal of Political Economy*, 73:6 (1965) 573–94.

World Trade Organization for **Tables 1.3**, **1.4** and **Figs 1.2**, **1.3**, **1.4** from *International Trade, Trends and Statistics*, Geneva (1995).

Every effort has been made to trace all the copyright-holders, but if any have been inadvertently overlooked the publishers will be pleased to make the necessary arrangement at the first opportunity.

PART I
The Trading World: Patterns and Policy

■ *Chapter 1* ■

The Pattern of International Trade and Factor Flows

1.1 A preview of trade theory	*1.3* International factor movements
1.2 Patterns of international trade	*1.4* Concluding remarks

Since the late 1970s the field of international trade has been one of the fastest growing areas of research and theoretical discovery in economics. In part, this growth reflects changes begun in the early 1970s including the movement of countries to floating exchange rates, oil price shocks, widespread trade liberalization and rapid increases in trade and growth. Such changes served to place international trade issues high on the agenda of academic economists and policy makers. Igniting the growth of academic inquiry has also been an unprecedented movement in the field of international trade to match theory and data, with the former increasingly directed toward reconciling itself with the realities of the latter. In recognition of the interplay between theory and data, this chapter first introduces the main themes of international trade theory and then presents data on the patterns of trade and international factor movements. The data presentation is meant to highlight empirical regularities and to orient the reader to the data and measures commonly used in applied analyses of international trade.

1.1 A preview of trade theory

International trade theory is fundamentally the extension and application of microeconomic theories of production and exchange to the study of economic transactions between agents in different countries. In this regard, international trade theory utilizes and enriches the fundamental paradigms of profit and utility maximization to explain why countries trade, what goods they will export and import, how trade affects resource allocation within and between nations, and whether a country benefits from international trade. Two characteristics that distinguish theoretical analyses of international trade issues from those of traditional microeconomics are its predominant use of general equilibrium analysis and a focus on the role of the nation-state as a facilitator or inhibitor of economic transactions. The latter brings into consideration the question of the benefits, if any, a country receives from international trade and whether there exist economic policies that could increase this benefit.

Does a country gain from trade?

This is a key question addressed by the theory of international trade and its answer will be a recurrent theme throughout this book. The essence of how trade may benefit a nation was eloquently stated by Adam Smith (1776) in his attack on Mercantilist doctrine. Specifically, Smith noted that international trade can benefit a nation by extending its opportunities for consumption beyond those available to it in isolation:

> The importation of gold and silver is not the principal, much less the sole benefit which a nation derives from its foreign trade. Between whatever places foreign trade is carried on, they all of them derive two distinct benefits from it. It carries out that surplus part of the produce of their land and labour for which there is no demand among them, and it brings back in turn for it something else for which there is a demand. It gives a value to their superfluities, by exchanging them for something else, which may satisfy a part of their wants, and increase their enjoyments. By means if it, the narrowness of the home market does not hinder the division of labor in any particular branch of art or manufacture from being carried to the highest perfection. By opening a more extensive market for whatever part of the produce of their labour may exceed the home consumption, it encourages them to improve its productive powers, and to augment its annual produce to the utmost, and thereby to increase the real revenue and wealth of the society. (Smith, 1776, p. 326)

David Ricardo (1817) recast and amplified Smith's observations on the benefits of trade into the now famous *principle of comparative advantage*. A country is said to have a 'comparative advantage' in a good if the country's pre-trade relative price of that good is lower than abroad. In its modern form, comparative advantage reflects differences in opportunity costs between countries. In using the principle of comparative advantage to demonstrate the potential for all countries to gain from trade, Ricardo indirectly enunciated a theory of the composition of trade: a country will export those goods in which it has a comparative advantage and import those goods in which it has a comparative disadvantage. Since a country can benefit from trade when its trade pattern reflects its comparative advantage, it is crucial to understand what determines comparative advantage and how it might change over time.

What determines comparative advantage?

Theories of trade based on the principle of comparative advantage are effectively theories of relative price determination. Since 'supply and demand' determine price, these theories derive their predictions about differences in pre-trade relative prices across countries, and hence the pattern of trade that will result from these differences, from the fundamental determinants of supply and demand. Figure 1.1 provides a stylized schematic of the supply and demand elements underlying the determination of relative prices.

Chapters 3 and 4 develop the theoretical arguments of the two prominent theories of trade based on comparative advantage: the Ricardian theory and the Heckscher–Ohlin–Samuelson (H–O–S) theory. With reference to Figure 1.1, these theories assume perfectly competitive markets and homogeneous goods and focus on supply side determinants of relative prices, namely, factor prices and technology. Briefly, the Ricardian theory explains comparative advantage in terms of cost (supply) differences that arise from differences in technology across countries. In contrast, the H–O–S theory assumes technologies are the same across countries and so instead ascribes comparative advantage to cost (supply) differences arising from differences in factor prices across countries. These factor price differences are in turn related to the more fundamental difference in the relative supplies of productive factors across countries.

As Figure 1.1 indicates, differences in demand can also give rise to relative price differences across countries. However, trade models typically assume away demand differences as a source of comparative advantage. One reason

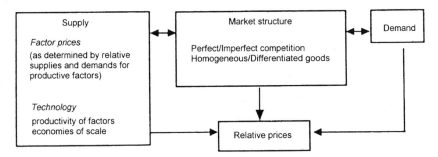

Figure 1.1 *Determinants of relative prices: a stylized view*

for ignoring demand differences is that, if demand differences were the basis of comparative advantages, then a fuller account would require one to state why demands differ; a task perhaps better suited to psychologists than economists.[1]

Figure 1.1 indicates that another possible supply side explanation for comparative advantage is economies of scale.[2] That is, even if demands and all remaining supply elements were identical across countries, relative prices could still differ between countries due to economies of scale. Since in this case industry size is a determinant of production costs, the goods in which a country has a comparative advantage would be determined by the size of its domestic industries compared to the size of these industries abroad. Chapters 3 and 9 examine scale economies as a determinant of trade and its implications for the benefits derived from trade.

Market structure and differentiated goods

Reflecting their neoclassical lineage, formal models of the Ricardian and H–O–S theories assume perfectly competitive markets and homogeneous goods. However, as explored in Chapters 9, 10 and 11, relaxing these assumptions leads to reasons for trade other than relative price differences between countries, that is, rather than comparative advantages. For example, if goods are differentiated rather than homogeneous, and consumers have a preference for variety, then trade can arise even if countries are identical in every respect. To see this, take the simple case where wine produced in France and wine produced in the United States are imperfect substitutes. It is then easy to imagine trade in 'wine' taking place between these countries, even if these countries have identical preferences, technology and factor prices. Tautologically, we might say France has a comparative advantage in 'French' wine while the United States has a comparative advantage in 'US' wine. However, the source of trade in this case is not relative price differences but rather that consumers in each country, since they have a preference for variety, wish to consume some of each type of wine.[3] Note also a special feature of the trade that results in this case: each country is both an exporter and an importer of 'wine'. This type of trade is called intra-industry trade (IIT), as distinguished from inter-industry trade, the latter being trade in goods produced by different industries. Below we consider data on the prevalence of intra-industry trade. Chapter 9 discusses theoretical models which predict the existence of intra-industry trade.

Imperfectly competitive market structures can be another source of trade, and gains from trade, independent of comparative advantages. For example, gains from trade can arise in the simplest framework of homogeneous goods and Cournot rivalry among firms because the larger market afforded by the opportunity to trade increases rivalry among firms which results in lower product prices and increased output. Models in which competition is imperfect often predict that trade between countries will be intra-industry trade. As discussed in Chapter 9, further predictions about the nature of trade and the benefits of trade are possible when models combine the assumptions of imperfect competition, economies of scale at the firm level, and consumer demands that exhibit a preference for variety.

We now turn to look at data that can elucidate the nature and significance of international trade flows. In conducting this examination of the data we will have occasion to consider if actual trade patterns reflect any of the elements that our brief overview of international trade theory suggests would determine these patterns.

1.2 Patterns of international trade

Globalization

In 1994, the value of world merchandise exports was approximately 4.2 trillion US dollars. As chronicled in Figures 1.2–1.4, world trade has grown steadily since the 1950s and this growth has generally exceeded the growth in world output.[4] This relatively rapid growth in trade compared to output is popularly referred to as 'globalization'.

Looking at data for selected subperiods, Figure 1.3 indicates that the decade from 1974 to 1984 was one of relatively slower growth compared to

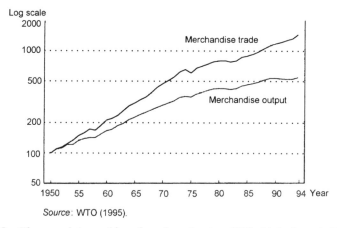

Source: WTO (1995).

Figure 1.2 *The growth in world trade and production, 1950–94 (volume indices, 1950 = 100)*

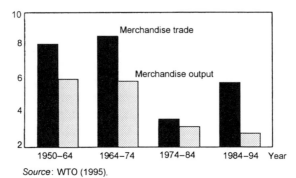

Source: WTO (1995).

Figure 1.3 *Average annual changes in world merchandise trade and world merchandise production, 1950–94*

other recent decades, but that since 1984 the growth in trade has increasingly exceeded the growth in output.

Figure 1.4 indicates that an important component of globalization has been the growth in trade of manufactured goods. The growth in this aggregate category of goods reflects, but also masks, an important feature of globalization: trade is increasingly in intermediate rather than final goods. One explanation for globalization is therefore the growing use of foreign out-sourcing made possible by relatively recent advances in telecommunications and generally lower transport costs.

As discussed in Chapter 2, another explanation for globalization is the steady reduction, since the early 1950s, of tariffs and other trade barriers facilitated by the General Agreement on Tariffs and Trade (GATT). Still another explanation is the shift since the 1970s in the development strategy

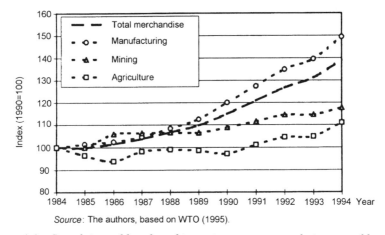

Source: The authors, based on WTO (1995).

Figure 1.4 *Growth in world trade and its major components relative to world output, 1984–94 (ratio of volume indices, 1990 = 100)*

of many developing countries, notably in Asia. Broadly speaking, many developing countries began to 'liberalize' their trade in the 1970s. This involved reducing levels of protection that shielded domestic industries from import competition while emphasizing export activities as a source of development. Last, but not least, has been the accumulation of physical and human capital, and transfers of technology,[5] which have increased the capacity for trade and also altered its composition.

Finally, an increasingly important yet difficult to measure component of world trade is trade in services. Table 1.1 shows data on the exports and net exports (exports minus imports) of commercial services for selected countries.

Table 1.1   *Trade in commercial services, selected economies, by sector, 1992 (US$ billion)*

	United States		European Union[a]		Japan		Hong Kong	
	Exports	Net exports	Exports	Net exports	Exports	Net exports	Exports	Net exports
Total	163.1	57.0	202.0	11.3	49.4	−48.0	24.3	9.9
Transport	40.1	5.7	58.2	3.2	19.9	−9.3	9.5	5.3
Maritime freight	3.9	−5.4	13.4	−2.2	9.9	2.6	1.8	−
Air passenger	17.1	6.5	12.5	0.3	1.3	−7.3	−	−
Other	19.1	4.6	32.3	5.1	8.7	−4.6	−	−
Travel	53.9	14.0	61.2	9.0	3.6	−23.2	6.9	0.7
Other services	69.1	37.3	82.7	−0.9	26.0	−15.5	7.9	3.8
Insurance	1.1	−0.3	3.2	−0.9	−	−	0.3	−0.2
Banking	5.4	2.0	8.8	4.6	−	−	1.2	0.8
Communications	3.3	−3.2	3.9	−0.2	−	−	0.0	−0.1
Other	59.2	38.8	66.8	−4.5	−	−	6.4	3.3

Note:
[a] Excludes intra-EU trade.
Sources: Adapted from WTO (1995).

Trade volumes and trade dependence

Trade volumes

Changes in the overall volume of trade mask changes in the volume of trade between regions. Table 1.2 lists intra-regional and inter-regional trade as a share of world trade for seven regions in 1979 and 1994. Diagonal entries are

Table 1.2   *Regional trade^a as % of world trade, 1979^b and 1994*

Destination / Origin	North America	Latin America	Western Europe	C/E Europe^c	Africa	Middle East	Asia
North America	6.11						
	(4.6)						
Latin America	2.34	0.91					
	(4.0)	(1.1)					
Western Europe	3.13	0.80	29.93				
	(6.6)	(2.6)	(28.8)				
C/E Europe^c	0.14	0.04	1.84	0.46			
	(0.5)	(0.6)	(4.1)	(4.3)			
Africa	0.25	0.05	1.25	0.05	0.22		
	(1.9)	(0.3)	(5.0)	(0.3)	(0.3)		
Middle East	0.42	0.05	1.31	0.05	0.03	0.27	
	(1.9)	(0.5)	(5.7)	(0.5)	(0.2)	(0.4)	
Asia	4.18	0.42	4.16	0.40	0.27	1.34	13.08
	(6.4)	(0.9)	(5.0)	(1.0)	(0.7)	(3.8)	(6.3)

Notes:

^{a} Figures for the trade of origin region *A* with destination region *B* are the sum of the value of *A*'s exports to *B* and the value of *B*'s exports to *A* divided by world exports *plus* world imports.

^{b} 1979 values are in parentheses.

^{c} Central and Eastern Europe and the former USSR.

Sources: GATT (1990); WTO (1995).

intra-regional trade, off-diagonal entries are inter-regional trade. Adding these trade shares across regions reveals that the six trade flows within and between North America, Western Europe and Central and Eastern Europe accounted for 48.9% of world trade in 1979 and 41.6% in 1994. Trade among Western European countries is by far the largest intra-regional trade flow and reflects the importance of the Common Market among EC (European Community) member countries and the trade agreements of EFTA (European Free Trade Area) countries.

Table 1.3 shows average annual compound rates of growth in the value of regional trade between 1992 and 1994.[6] The diagonal terms for North America, Latin American and Asia indicate rapid increases in intra-regional trade, partly reflecting the new and renewed implementation of regional agreements that lower intra-regional trade barriers (i.e. the NAFTA (North American Free Trade Agreement), MERCOSUR (Southern Common Market) and ASEAN (Association of South-East Asian Nations)). Trade among African countries has also seen positive growth while intra-Western European trade actually declined between 1992 and 1994.

Table 1.3 *Growth in intra-regional and inter-regional trade, 1992–4 (average annual rate of growth, %)*

Destination Origin	North America	Latin America	Western Europe	C/E Europe[a]	Africa	Middle East	Asia
North America	12.6						
Latin America	11.2	13.5					
Western Europe	4.3	6.5	−0.1				
C/E Europe[a]	13.5	8.5	11.4	4.5			
Africa	−2.6	4.3	−4.5	1.6	6.7		
Middle East	−1.0	−8.2	−5.2	−8.6	−8.2	−0.2	
Asia	9.4	11.2	7.5	13.8	5.9	−1.4	15.3

Note:
[a] Central and Eastern Europe and the former USSR.
Source: The authors, based on data in WTO (1995).

Trade between the 'North' and the 'South' (Africa, Latin America and the Middle East) grew more slowly than the trade within these regions, a trend evident since the late 1970s. Another trend that continues from the 1970s is the general decline in the trade of Africa and of the Middle East with other regions. Declines in fuel and primary commodity prices, debt-related economic difficulties and political difficulties explain a part of these declines. One fact made evident by these data is that trade between distinct but 'similar' regions tends to be higher, and to grow at higher rates, than does trade between 'dissimilar' regions.

Table 1.4 gives further information about trade by showing the twenty-five leading exporters and importers in 1984 and 1994. Over this period, China and Thailand show the largest increase in rank among exporters; China, Hong Kong and Thailand show the largest increase in rank among importers. As noted previously, the increased trade of such countries is due, in part, to a change in their development strategy from one of high import barriers (and hence low export volumes) to one of import liberalization and export promotion. In general, the changes in rankings evident in Table 1.4 attest to the rapid changes in trade that have accompanied globalization.

Two additional facts evident in Table 1.4 are (1) the largest exporters are also the largest importers, and (2) the trade imbalance of most countries is relatively small. The latter situation is not peculiar to 1994 nor is it accidental; it instead most likely reflects the actions of governments who often interpret such imbalances as a source of their internal economic problems.

Table 1.4   *Leading exporters and importers in world merchandise trade, 1984 and 1994*[a]

	1984		1994			1984		1994	
Exporter	*Rank*	*Share*	*Value*	*Share*	*Importer*	*Rank*	*Share*	*Value*	*Share*
1 USA	1	11.5	512.5	12.2	1 USA	1	17.2	689.2	15.9
2 Germany	2	10.1	424.0	10.1	2 Germany	2	8.7	378.0	8.7
3 Japan	3	8.7	397.0	9.4	3 Japan	3	6.8	275.2	6.4
4 France	4	5.0	234.8	5.6	4 France	5	5.2	228.8	5.3
5 UK	5	4.8	205.0	4.9	5 UK	4	5.2	227.2	5.2
6 Italy	8	3.8	189.5	4.5	6 Italy	6	4.2	167.5	3.9
7 Canada	7	4.6	165.4	3.9	7 Hong Kong	13	1.5	165.9	3.8
8 Netherlands	9	3.4	155.1	3.7	8 Canada	8	3.9	155.1	3.6
9 Hong Kong	16	1.5	151.5	3.6	9 Netherlands	9	3.1	139.4	3.2
10 Belgium–Lux.	10	2.7	140.1	3.3	10 Belgium–Lux.	10	2.8	131.0	3.0
11 China	19	1.3	121.0	2.9	11 China	18	1.3	115.7	2.7
12 Singapore	20	1.2	96.8	2.3	12 Singapore	16	1.4	102.7	2.4
13 Rep. of Korea	15	1.5	96.0	2.3	13 Rep. of Korea	12	1.5	102.3	2.4
14 Chinese Taipei	12	1.6	92.9	2.2	14 Spain	15	1.4	92.2	2.1
15 Spain	21	1.2	73.1	1.7	15 Chinese Taipei	20	1.1	85.5	2.0
16 Switzerland	18	1.3	70.3	1.7	16 Mexico	25	0.8	81.5	1.9
17 Former USSR	6	4.7	63.9	1.5	17 Switzerland	14	1.5	67.9	1.6
18 Sweden	13	1.5	61.3	1.5	18 Malaysia	29	0.7	59.6	1.4
19 Mexico	14	1.5	60.8	1.4	19 Austria	21	1.0	55.3	1.3
20 Malaysia	27	0.8	58.8	1.4	20 Thailand	38	0.5	54.5	1.3
21 Australia	22	1.2	47.6	1.1	21 Australia	19	1.3	53.4	1.2
22 Thailand	46	0.4	45.3	1.1	22 Sweden	17	1.3	51.7	1.2
23 Austria	31	0.8	45.2	1.1	23 Former USSR	7	4.0	46.6	1.1
24 Brazil	17	1.4	43.6	1.0	24 Brazil	28	0.8	36.0	0.8
25 Denmark	30	0.8	41.2	1.0	25 Denmark	23	0.8	35.1	0.8
Country total		77.2	3592.4	85.2	Country total		78.0	3597.3	83.0
World total		100	4215.0	100	World total		100	4333.0	100

Note:
[a] Countries are ordered by 1994 rank. Shares are world shares (%). Values in billion $US.
Source: Adapted from WTO (1995).

Trade dependence

Another indicator of a country's involvement in trade is its trade dependence, as measured by the ratio of its exports *plus* imports to its GDP (or GNP). Table 1.5 lists the average trade dependence of selected countries over the decades 1960–70 and 1982–92. The countries are ranked in descending order of their average trade dependence during 1982–92. Note first that the trade dependence of several countries exceeds 100%. This reflects that these countries engage primarily in entrepôt (warehouse) trade – that is, these countries are primarily conduits for the trans-shipment of goods from the country of production to the country of consumption.[7]

Table 1.5 *Trade dependence^a, selected countries, 1960–70 and 1982–92 (%)*

Country	1960–70^b	1982–92^b	% Change	Country	1960–70^b	1982–92^b	% Change
Singapore	265	350	32	Paraguay	30	55	86
Hong Kong	172	235	37	Malawi	59	55	−7
Malta	128	160	26	Mali	25	54	121
Belgium	87	144	67	Philippines	34	54	61
Namibia	77	130	69	Greece	28	53	91
Malaysia	79	127	61	Ecuador	34	53	55
Botswana	69	123	79	Finland	44	53	22
Mauritius	75	121	62	Nicaragua	56	53	−5
Jordan	53	115	115	Kenya	59	53	−10
Ireland	77	114	47	Morocco	39	52	35
Gambia	64	113	77	Canada	40	52	31
Jamaica	75	110	47	United Kingdom	42	52	25
Seychelles	51	107	109	Central African Republic	68	51	−24
Cyprus	78	106	35	South Africa	53	50	−5
Netherlands	84	105	24	Indonesia	22	49	118
Taiwan	42	96	127	Algeria	48	48	−1
Cape Verde Is.	119	96	−19	Nigeria	21	47	124
Papua New Guinea	54	94	73	Zaire	22	47	111
Congo	97	94	−3	Niger	23	47	102
Gabon	89	88	−1	Venezuela	43	47	9
Suriname	104	87	−16	Burkina Faso	20	46	126
Liberia	86	86	−1	Cameroon	43	46	7
Saudi Arabia	81	85	5	El Salvador	51	46	−10
Oman	84	85	0	Romania	27	45	68
East Germany	43	84	97	France	27	45	67
Norway	84	81	−4	Uruguay	28	44	57
Tunisia	49	80	65	Syria	40	44	9
Austria	50	76	51	Italy	28	42	48
Portugal	51	75	47	Turkey	14	41	189
Hungary	63	74	18	Spain	23	40	73
Israel	55	73	34	Haiti	32	39	20
Costa Rica	55	73	33	Poland	40	38	−6
Switzerland	60	72	20	Burundi	22	36	67
Iceland	83	72	−13	Pakistan	25	36	40
Panama	76	71	−6	Madagascar	38	36	−6
Trinidad and Tobago	102	71	−30	Guatemala	33	35	7
Rep. of Korea	28	69	150	Bolivia	54	35	−35
Zambia	94	69	−26	Sierra Leone	68	35	−50
Czechoslovakia	31	67	119	Ethiopia	23	34	47
Denmark	60	67	13	Australia	30	34	13
Ivory Coast	63	67	8	Tanzania	56	32	−43

Table 1.5 (*continued*)

Country	1960–70[b]	1982–92[b]	% Change	Country	1960–70[b]	1982–92[b]	% Change
Angola	42	66	58	Nepal	16	31	92
Senegal	54	65	20	Ghana	42	31	−26
Sri Lanka	75	65	−14	Mexico	17	30	71
Benin	29	63	115	Colombia	26	30	15
Sweden	44	63	44	Rwanda	27	30	13
Thailand	38	62	63	Peru	36	30	−17
Guinea	28	61	119	Uganda	24	27	14
Egypt	37	60	61	Bangladesh	25	26	1
Chad	38	60	59	China	7	23	239
Comoros	51	60	17	Sudan	31	23	−25
Guinea–Bissou	34	59	72	Japan	20	22	11
Dominican Rep.	40	59	46	Iran	36	22	−37
New Zealand	46	59	27	United States	10	20	101
Honduras	53	59	10	USSR	6	17	201
Iraq	60	59	−2	India	10	17	62
Zimbabwe	75	58	−23	Brazil	13	17	28
West Germany	36	57	58	Argentina	14	16	9
Chile	29	56	97	Myanmar	29	13	−57

Notes:
[a] Defined as a country's total exports *plus* total imports divided by nominal GDP.
[b] Unweighted average of annual trade dependence ratios over indicated period.
Source: 'Penn World Tables 5.6' (Summers and Heston, 1991).

Whereas Table 1.4 lists the United States as the world's largest trader, Table 1.5 indicates that the United States has relatively low trade dependence (an average of 20% during 1982–92). By comparison, the trade dependence of the former West Germany was 57% while Switzerland's trade dependence was 73% during this period. Whether trade dependence is high or low can reflect a number of factors. For example, low trade dependence may indicate significant restrictions on trade (e.g. Myanmar) or that non-traded sectors (e.g. services) are an important source of a country's value added (e.g. services account for over 70% of US value added). Finally, the changes over time in each country's trade dependence underscore rising globalization and interdependence. For example, the United States doubled its average trade dependence between 1960–70 and 1982–92.

The increase in trade dependence that has accompanied globalization is further indicated in Table 1.6 which shows the average trade dependence of major regions during 1960–70 and 1982–90 and its change over time. Oceania (mostly Australia) and Eastern Europe show the highest increases in trade dependence whereas Africa shows the smallest increase.

Table 1.6 *Regional trade dependence, 1960–92 (%)*

Region	1960–70[a]	1982–92[b]	% Change	Std dev. 1960–70[b]	Std dev. 1982–92[b]
Oceania	55	90	65	24	30
Eastern Europe	34	54	60	19	24
Middle East	57	82	45	18	41
North America	25	36	45	21	23
Latin America	54	77	43	33	45
Asia	55	77	38	69	86
Europe	60	82	35	35	41
Africa	55	68	24	28	32
All Regions	54	74	36	36	46

Notes:
[a] Unweighted average of annual trade dependence during indicated period.
[b] Standard deviation of trade dependence ratios across countries within indicated region.
Source: The authors, based on data from Summers and Heston (1991).

Trade patterns and revealed comparative advantage

As noted in Section 1.1, a key question addressed by the theory of international trade is what determines the pattern of goods exported and imported, that is, the commodity composition of trade. One explanation has already been suggested, comparative advantage, which in turn derives from differences across countries in the fundamental determinants of supply and demand. But to which of these possible fundamental determinants are trade patterns systematically related? Sorting out which influences are important, or which are the relatively more important, in determining trade patterns is properly the task of empirical tests of trade theory. Chapter 8 considers in detail the issues involved in testing the H–O–S theory while the empirical merits of other trade theories are discussed in the chapters where they are developed. Here we briefly consider data on the composition of trade to motivate thinking about what may lie behind observed patterns and to further introduce concepts commonly used in empirical studies of trade.

Revealed comparative advantage

Due to the overriding importance of the theoretical concept of comparative advantage its empirical measurement is crucial. However, this theoretical concept relates to patterns of pre-trade relative prices which are not observable. Applied work must therefore devise measures on the basis of observables that can be used to infer what would be the pattern of pre-trade prices. Inferring comparative advantage from observed data is called 'revealing' comparative advantage. For example, theories of comparative advantage (e.g. the H–O–S model) normally predict the pattern of a country's net exports across goods. Applied work therefore uses actual data on a country's net exports to reveal those goods in which the country presumably had a pre-trade comparative advantage.

Table 1.7 illustrates this type of analysis by showing the commodities that are the ten largest net exports and ten largest net imports of selected countries.[8] Also listed for each commodity is the value of another measure of comparative advantage, the revealed comparative advantage (RCA) index. The particular RCA index shown in Table 1.7 is computed as:[9]

$$RCA = (X_{ij}/X_{wj})/(X_{i.}/X_{w.}) \tag{1.1}$$

where X_{ij} denotes country i's exports of commodity j, X_{wj} is world exports of commodity j, $X_{i.}$ is country i's total exports and $X_{w.}$ is total world exports. When the value of (1.1) exceeds (is below) unity country i is said to have a revealed comparative advantage (comparative disadvantage) in good j. Expression (1.1) is only one of many RCA indexes that have been devised for applied work.[10] The appropriateness of most RCA indices, including (1.1), for indicating the theoretical concept of comparative advantage has been questioned in the literature.[11] But despite theoretical concerns, RCA indices continue to be used in applied work.

The data in Table 1.7 can be used to suggest similarities among the commodities in which a country has a RCA and thereby also suggest the characteristics of a country that would give rise to its comparative advantage in the indicated goods. In looking at the patterns of RCA in Table 1.7 one explanation that comes to mind is differences in factor prices. For example, Germany's RCA lies in commodities such as synthetic dyes, paints and similar chemical products, various types of machinery, and certain basic iron and steel products whereas Germany's revealed disadvantage is mostly in vegetables and vegetable products and certain natural resource products. If chemical and machinery production are thought to require mostly physical capital and skilled workers then one might conjecture that Germany's trade pattern reflects that capital and highly skilled labor are relatively cheap in Germany while land suitable for growing vegetables is relatively expensive (when the prices of these factors are compared to their prices in other countries). Conversely, the kinds of goods comprising the RCA of countries such as Hong Kong, Spain and Mexico suggest that capital and skilled labor are expensive in these countries when compared to unskilled

Table 1.7 *10 largest net exports and net imports, selected countries, 1985–7 (based on averages of net trade values over the period 1985–7)*

Country		10 largest net exports[a]	RCA index	10 largest net imports[a]	RCA index
Germany	1	531-synthetic dyes	2.50	025-eggs	0.42
	2	532-dyes n.e.s.,[b] tanning products	2.39	281-iron ore, concentrates	0.00
	3	717-textile, leather machinery	1.90	054-vegetables fresh, simply preserved	0.19
	4	675-iron & steel hoop & strip	2.16	051-fruit fresh nuts fresh dry	0.14
	5	533-pigments, paints, etc.	1.78	285-silver and platinum ores	0.07
	6	554-soaps, cleaning, etc. preparations	1.72	341-gas natural and manufactured	0.14
	7	679-iron & steel castings, unworked	1.54	055-vegetables etc. preserved, prepared	0.31
	8	022-milk & cream	1.91	221-oil seeds, nuts and kernels	0.19
	9	718-machines for special industries	1.59	292-crude vegetable materials n.e.s.[b]	0.40
	10	715-metal working machinery	1.70	121-tobacco, unmanufactured	0.11
Hong Kong	1	842-clothes & products made of fur	17.47	261-silk	1.13
	2	894-toys, sporting goods, etc.	12.08	653-woven textiles non cotton	2.17
	3	841-clothing not of fur	11.16	613-fur skins tanned or dressed	0.39
	4	285-silver and platinum ores	4.82	651-textile yarn and thread	0.81
	5	897-gold & silver wares & jewelry	6.06	212-fur skins, undressed	0.00
	6	725-domestic electric equipment	4.42	025-eggs	0.00
	7	697-base metal household equipment	4.81	571-explosives, pyrotechnic products	0.03
	8	351-electric energy	1.44	831-travel goods, handbags	4.79
	9	893-articles of plastic n.e.s.[b]	3.51	265-vegetable fibre, not cotton or jute	0.02
	10	892-printed matter	1.82	263-cotton	0.16

Table 1.7 (continued)

Country		10 largest net exports[a]	RCA index	10 largest net imports[a]	RCA index
Japan	1	891-sound recorders, producers	4.10	242-wood, rough	0.03
	2	735-ships & boats	2.05	281-iron ore, concentrates	0.00
	3	724-telecommunications equipment	2.67	045-cereals n.e.s.,[b] unmilled	0.00
	4	678-iron & steel tubes, pipes, etc.	1.85	283-non-ferrous base metal ore	0.01
	5	732-road motor vehicles	2.16	031-fish fresh, simply preserved	0.21
	6	674-iron & steel, plate, sheet	2.21	261-silk	2.87
	7	715-metal working machinery	2.03	341-gas natural and manufactured	0.00
	8	861-instruments & apparatus	2.26	321-coal, coke, and briquettes	0.17
	9	733-road vehicles non-motorized	1.87	265-vegetable fiber, not cotton or jute	0.00
	10	676-railway rails etc. iron & steel	1.23	044-maize, unmilled	0.00
Mexico	1	331-crude petroleum, etc.	13.06	045-cereals n.e.s.,[b] unmilled	0.01
	2	681-silver, platinum, etc.	5.84	676-railway rails, etc.	0.00
	3	274-sulphur etc.	3.78	221-oil seeds, nuts and kernels	0.24
	4	685-lead	3.67	091-margarine, shortening	0.00
	5	679-iron & steel castings, unworked	2.79	044-maize, unmilled	0.00
	6	071-coffee	3.97	411-animal oils and fats	0.00
	7	054-vegetables fresh, preserved	3.90	731-railway vehicles	0.15
	8	686-zinc	2.28	211-hides and skins, not fur, undressed	0.01
	9	031-fish fresh, simply preserved	2.19	675-iron & steel hoop & strip	0.05
	10	661-cement, etc. building products	1.88	022-milk and cream	0.00

Spain				
1	244-cork, raw & waste	26.57	282-iron and steel scrap	0.06
2	613-fur skins tanned or dressed	12.44	271-fertilizers, crude	0.01
3	421-fixed vegetable oils, soft	7.81	267-waste of textile fabrics	0.11
4	055-vegetables, etc., prepared	7.17	121-tobacco unmanufactured	0.17
5	051-fruit fresh nuts fresh dry	10.85	211-hides and skins, not fur, undressed	0.59
6	633-cork manufactures	6.35	331-crude petroleum, etc.	0.00
7	661-cement, etc., building products	4.79	221-oil seeds, nuts and kernels	0.15
8	241-fuel wood & charcoal	5.39	411-animal oils and fats	0.19
9	673-iron & steel shapes	3.61	285-silver and platinum ores	0.16
10	851-footwear	4.17	071-coffee	0.57
United States				
1	044-maize, unmilled	4.31	666-pottery	0.12
2	221-oil seeds, nuts & kernels	4.72	831-travel goods, handbags	0.11
3	734-aircraft	4.31	851-footwear	0.11
4	411-animal oils & fats	3.17	894-toys, sporting goods, etc.	0.64
5	045-cereals n.e.s.,[b] unmilled	3.75	681-silver, platinum, etc.	0.62
6	122-tobacco manufactured	2.99	071-coffee	0.19
7	041-wheat etc., unmilled	2.15	896-works of art etc.	1.13
8	263-cotton	4.53	688-uranium, thorium alloys	3.68
9	211-hides/skins, not fur, undressed	2.58	897-gold & silver wares & jewelry	0.34
10	267-waste of textile fabrics	2.23	841-clothing not of fur	0.15

Notes:
[a] Rankings based on ratio of net exports to world exports *plus* imports in each of 103 3-digit SITC categories.
[b] n.e.s. = not elsewhere specified.
Source: Computed by the authors from UN trade data.

labor. Also, with the exception of Hong Kong, each of these countries possesses the land suitable for growing agricultural products.

Whereas the patterns of RCA in Table 1.7 seem to suggest that factor price differences may lie behind the observed trade patterns, one could think of other influences. For example, with Figure 1.1 in mind, Germany's RCA in chemicals and machinery may instead derive from superior technology, economies of scale or even market power due to patents. As noted, sorting out these various influences is properly the task of empirical tests of trade theory.

Finally, note that the RCA index usually exceeds one when net exports are positive and is less than one when net exports are negative (i.e. net imports) but this is not always the case (e.g. Hong Kong). This points to the concerns raised in the literature about the appropriateness of RCA indexes as indicators of underlying 'true' comparative advantages.

Similarity of trade patterns and country characteristics

If trade patterns are systematically related to comparative advantages derived from differences in supply side characteristics of countries, then countries with similar characteristics should have similar trade patterns. Conversely, countries with similar trade patterns should have similar characteristics. Hence, observing which countries have similar trade patterns may suggest the country characteristics (e.g. factor prices, etc.) most important in determining trade patterns.

This type of thinking is utilized in Table 1.8 which shows, for each country in Table 1.7, the ten countries whose pattern of net exports across goods is the most similar and the least similar. Here similarity is measured by the correlation between the net trade vectors of each pair of countries. For example, Japan, the United Kingdom and Switzerland (as well as Hungary and Poland) are among the ten countries with trade patterns most similar to Germany's. Among the countries with trade patterns most dissimilar to Germany's are Turkey, Chile and Greece. What characteristics do these countries share that would imply similar or dissimilar trade patterns? Again, factor prices might come to mind or, more directly, skilled labor in the form of engineers. For the United States, the countries most similar include Argentina, Paraguay, France, Israel, New Zealand and Canada; all countries with suitable arable land. Further perusal of these listings suggests other common factors among the characteristics of the most similar, and the least similar, countries, but there are also a number of puzzling exceptions.

Table 1.8 *Countries whose net trade pattern is the most and the least similar to that of selected countries, 1985–7 (based on averages of net trade values over the period 1985–7)*

Rank	Most similar[a]	Least similar	Most similar[a]	Least similar
	to GERMANY		to HONG KONG	
1	Japan	Turkey	Macao	Netherlands
2	UK	Chile	South Korea	Belgium-Lux.
3	Switzerland	Greece	Malta	Paraguay
4	Belgium-Lux.	Indonesia	Greece	USA
5	Austria	Norway	Italy	Spain
6	France	Cyprus	Canada	Hungary
7	Italy	Philippines	Oman	Pakistan
8	Sweden	Colombia	Algeria	Finland
9	Hungary	India	Uruguay	Switzerland
10	Poland	Mexico	Singapore	Madagascar
	to JAPAN		to MEXICO	
1	Germany	Indonesia	Colombia	USA
2	South Korea	USA	Trinidad–Tobago	Argentina
3	Italy	Australia	Canada	Austria
4	Austria	Canada	Israel	Germany
5	Belgium-Lux.	Malaysia	Indonesia	France
6	Switzerland	Norway	Poland	Sweden
7	UK	Iceland	Spain	Tunisia
8	Spain	Argentina	Turkey	New Zealand
9	Yugoslavia	Paraguay	Cyprus	Morocco
10	France	Singapore	Norway	Switzerland
	to SPAIN		to the UNITED STATES	
1	Portugal	USA	Argentina	South Korea
2	South Korea	Jordan	Paraguay	Mexico
3	Yugoslavia	Switzerland	France	Italy
4	Austria	Canada	Israel	Germany
5	Italy	Morocco	New Zealand	Japan
6	Belgium-Lux.	Chile	Canada	Macao
7	Japan	Norway	Guadeloupe	Colombia
8	Mexico	Hong Kong	Oman	Algeria
9	Tunisia	Paraguay	Chile	Trinidad–Tobago
10	Thailand	Israel	Switzerland	Indonesia

Note:

[a] Similarity is measured by the correlation between the net trade vectors of the indicated pair of countries. Most similar countries have the largest positive correlation while least similar countries have the smallest negative correlation.

Source: The authors, based on UN trade data.

Relative resource supplies

The search for country characteristics that might help to explain trade patterns typifies the search for the determinants of comparative advantage. In this context, it was noted in Section 1.1 that the H–O–S theory of trade focuses on factor price differences, or more directly, differences in relative factor supplies, as the source of comparative advantages across countries. In the H–O–S framework differences in relative factor supplies are characterized in terms of the 'abundance' or 'scarcity' of factors. These terms are defined more carefully in Chapter 4, but roughly speaking, a country's abundant factors are cheaper, and its scarce factors more expensive, than are these factors in other countries. The following briefly considers this aspect.

Table 1.9 shows the distribution of physical capital, three classes of labor categorized by skill level, and arable land for selected countries or regions in 1966 and 1986, respectively.[12] For example, in 1966, the United States was the location of almost 35% of the world's physical capital. By 1986 the US share had fallen to just over 25%. Japan's share of the world's physical capital increased 33% between 1966 and 1986. In both 1966 and 1986, the United States and the EC held almost half of the world's stock of highly skilled labor whereas the world's stock of unskilled labor was located mostly in developing countries.

As discussed in Chapters 6 and 8, the ranking of a country's world resource shares indicates their relative abundance within the country. For

Table 1.9   *Country/region world resource shares, 1966 and 1986ᵃ (%)*

Country/region	Physical capital 1966	Physical capital 1986	High skilled labor 1966	High skilled labor 1986	Medium skilled labor 1966	Medium skilled labor 1986	Unskilled labor 1966	Unskilled labor 1986	Arable land 1966	Arable land 1986
Africa/Middle East	6.88	4.50	2.74	5.22	1.69	1.66	4.69	5.47	3.21	2.88
Asia	2.29	8.97	5.45	7.82	11.95	17.34	13.44	12.36	6.67	7.45
EC-12	27.34	22.47	27.66	24.57	26.67	20.58	7.12	4.65	14.05	12.36
EFTA	3.75	2.99	4.01	3.68	2.87	2.07	0.04	0.04	1.09	0.95
Japan	9.09	12.02	7.76	6.80	11.32	9.03	0.21	0.18	0.74	0.55
USA	34.86	25.29	24.96	21.28	16.27	16.70	0.33	0.42	22.46	22.17

Note:

ᵃ Numbers are each region's world share of resource based on a world total for 60 countries.

Source: The authors, based on Bowen (1983a).

example, ranking for each year the US resource shares in Table 1.9 indicates that in 1996 the United States was most abundant in physical capital, followed by arable land, high skilled labor, medium skilled labor and finally unskilled labor. Performing these rankings in each year for the other countries or regions in Table 1.9 reveals a growing similarity over time in the structure of capital and labor resources in the United States, EC-12, EFTA and Japan. Also notable is that Japan, who in 1966 was relatively scarce in capital, became most abundant in capital by 1986 and Asia, who was most abundant in unskilled labor had, by 1986, achieved a factor supply pattern that mirrored Japan's pattern in 1966.

Whereas the pattern of factor abundance of individual countries can change relatively quickly due to substantial differences across countries in rates of factor accumulation, factor supply patterns for broad aggregates of countries change relatively slowly. This is illustrated in Figure 1.5 which shows the factor supply structure of developed and developing countries in 1966 and 1986 with respect to the five resources given in Table 1.9. Figure 1.5 indicates that developed countries are relatively abundant in capital and high skilled labor and relatively scarce in unskilled labor while developing countries are relatively abundant in unskilled labor and arable land and relatively scarce in capital and high skilled labor. These patterns of factor abundance were unchanged between 1966 and 1986.

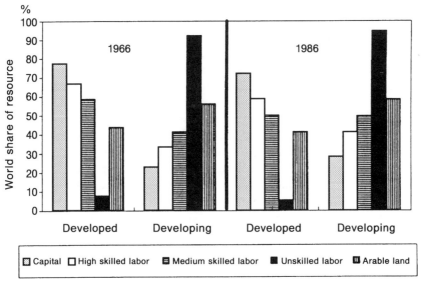

Figure 1.5 *Relative factor supplies in developed and developing countries, 1966 and 1986*

Source: The authors, based on Bowen (1983a).

Trade overlap and intra-industry trade

In Section 1.1 it was noted that intra-industry trade – that is, trade between countries in the same or similar product – can arise when goods are differentiated or markets are imperfectly competitive. Efforts to theoretically model the basis for intra-industry trade started in the late 1970s in response to the observation that actual trade flows evidenced considerable trade overlap. Trade overlap is defined as the value of matching export and import transactions in a given commodity:

$$TO_{ij} = (X_{ij} + M_{ij}) - |X_{ij} - M_{ij}| \tag{1.2}$$

where X_{ij} and M_{ij} are the value of country i's exports and imports, respectively, of commodity j either to the world or on a bilateral basis.[13] A summary measure of the degree of trade overlap is the Grubel–Lloyd (G–L) index:[14]

$$GL_{ij} = 100 \left[\frac{TO_{ij}}{X_{ij} + M_{ij}} \right] \tag{1.3}$$

Values of (1.3) range between 0 (no trade overlap) and 100 (complete trade overlap). Since no level of statistical significance is attached to values of the G–L index, what constitutes a high or low level of trade overlap is largely a matter of personal interpretation.

Trade overlap and categorical aggregation

As discussed in Chapter 9, there are now a number of theoretical models that predict the existence of intra-industry trade (IIT). However, the concordance between the industry based concept of IIT used in these theoretical models and the amount of trade overlap measured in actual trade data is open to question. For example, measured trade overlap may simply reflect 'categorical aggregation' which arises because the system used to classify detailed trade data into a usable number of categories necessarily aggregates dissimilar products into seemingly similar product groups. If trade overlap only reflects categorical aggregation then the theoretical demonstration of intra-industry trade is largely irrelevant for understanding actual trade patterns. A further understanding of this issue is facilitated by considering how actual trade data are collected and categorized.

Countries routinely collect export and import data in order to assemble their national income accounts and as a by-product of collecting taxes levied on their imports and exports. By international agreement, the national agencies responsible for maintaining a country's trade statistics routinely submit these data to supra-national organizations (e.g. the United Nations

Table 1.10 *Example of the Standard International Trade Classification (SITC) system*

Section 7 – Machinery & transport equipment
  Division 79 – Other transport equipment
    Group 792 – Aircraft & associated equipment: spacecraft (including satellites)
            & spacecraft launch vehicles; & parts thereof
      Subgroup 792.8 – Aircraft
        Item 792.81 – Gliders and hang gliders

or the European Statistical Agency) which maintain the data on a consistent basis. To permit international comparisons, the submitted data are classified according to the United Nations' Standard International Trade Classification (SITC) system.[15] The example in Table 1.10 indicates the structure of the SITC system.

As shown, the SITC system consists of five levels of classification. In this case, the 1-digit section 7 is disaggregated into four higher-digit groupings (division, group, etc.). For present purposes it is important to note that the SITC is a product based, not an industry based, classification. Hence, each SITC category necessarily involves some aggregation of products produced by different industries.

How important is the aggregation inherent in the SITC system for the measurement of an industry based concept such as intra-*industry* trade? Table 1.11 considers this question by showing the values of (1.3) computed for the 3-digit SITC group 'Fixed Vegetable Oils' and its 4-digit SITC components using UK trade data for 1977. When measured at the 3-digit

Table 1.11 *Example of the effect of categorical aggregation on measured trade overlap*

SITC	Description	Imports[a]	Exports[a]	G-L index
421	Fixed vegetable oils	27 308	15 888	74.0[b]
421.2	Soya bean oil	6 648	4 220	78.0
421.3	Cotton seed oil	3 355	24	1.0
421.4	Ground nut oil	8 503	224	5.0
421.5	Olive oil	2 012	410	34.0
421.6	Sunflower seed oil	6 440	8	0.2
421.7	Rape, colza and mustard oils	350	11 002	6.0

Notes:
[a] Data are for the UK in 1977. All values in £ millions.
[b] Value is a weighted averge of the index values at the 4-digit SITC level.
Source: Greenaway and Milner (1983).

level[16] the value of the index suggests IIT is substantial in this 'industry'. But measured at the 4-digit level the extent of IIT is often small and there is considerable variation. Since, however, the 4-digit values are not zero, it seems fair to conclude that categorical aggregation is not the only explanation of measured trade overlap.[17]

The extent of trade overlap

Accepting that the theoretical concept of intra-industry trade has an empirical basis, Table 1.12 provides additional evidence on the extent of trade overlap by showing the value of (1.3) for a set of industrialized countries with respect to their bilateral trade with the world and various country groups in 1980. Also shown is the change in the index's value between 1970 and 1980.

Table 1.12 indicates that the degree of trade overlap varies widely among countries, even at similar levels of economic development, and that trade

Table 1.12 *Indexes of total and bilateral IIT in manufactured goods, selected countries, 1970 and 1980*

	All countries		Asian newly industrialized countries		Less developed countries		Developed countries		Centrally planned economies	
Country	*1980 value[a]*	*Change 1970–80*	*1980 value*	*Change 1970–80*	*1980 value*	*Change 1970–80*	*1980 value*	*Change 1970–80*	*1980 value*	*Change 1970–80*
Australia	35.8	5.4	26.9	−8.3	29.2	0.1	22.7	4.2	5.5	−10.6
Belgium	79.9	4.1	29.8	10.7	40.1	16.3	77.6	5.2	29.0	−17.7
Canada	58.5	−3.4	15.7	7.9	33.0	11.6	56.7	−5.4	18.1	−6.5
France	80.4	3.6	29.7	9.2	44.2	19.0	79.2	6.4	40.0	4.0
Germany	65.4	6.6	24.4	7.5	34.6	15.1	74.1	7.4	31.6	−4.2
Italy	65.4	6.6	36.0	1.1	44.3	20.5	59.8	0.3	40.2	8.7
Japan	28.8	−7.3	27.2	10.3	17.6	1.9	33.6	−4.6	11.8	−21.5
Netherlands	74.2	5.5	24.8	11.3	45.5	7.0	70.3	5.7	22.6	−18.8
Sweden	66.5	4.1	15.1	9.0	17.4	4.8	72.5	5.8	30.7	−0.06
UK	79.1	18.3	27.4	−0.8	44.2	12.8	77.5	12.3	30.9	−3.4
USA	60.7	1.4	26.5	2.4	35.0	4.3	66.7	5.8	37.9	6.9

Note:
[a] Value of G–L index averaged (unweighted) across goods at the 4-digit level of the ISIC. Change is the difference in the index's value between 1970 and 1980.
Source: Culem and Lundberg (1986).

Table 1.13 *Indexes of IIT for France's trade with the world, 1850–1938 and 1975[a]*

Product	SITC[a]	G–L index[b]			
		1850–80	1880–1913	1919–38	1975
Agriculture					
Corn	041–045	52	16	19	28
Fish	031	92	85	66	40
Butter/cheese	023, 024	56	68	78	56
Olive oil	421.5	28	49	62	30
Fruit	051	79	79	59	46
Wine	112.1	21	79	63	53
Raw materials					
Hides & skins	211, 212	35	72	83	88
Wool	262	40	61	63	98
Silk	261	54	66	31	10
Wood (rough)	241, 242	34	41	43	39
Textiles					
Leather, manufactured[c]	612	5	25	47	90
Yarn of flax, ramie & true hemp	651.5	70	60	25	58
Cotton fabrics, woven[c]	652.1	52	52	19	80
Woolen fabrics, woven[c]	653.2	27	32	36	82
Silk fabrics, woven[c]	653.1	14	33	16	87
Other					
Clocks	864	38	70	81	84
Iron & steel	67	40	56	31	82

Notes:
[a] SITC Revision 1.
[b] Unweighted averages of G–L index. See Appendix 1 (p. 35) for methods of aggregating the G–L index.
[c] These products do not appear under a specific category from 1850 to 1857.
Source: Messerlin and Becuwe (1986).

overlap has generally risen over time. For example, trade overlap is relatively high for France, Belgium and the United Kingdom but relatively low for Japan and Australia. Trade overlap is generally higher for European countries and, on a bilateral basis, it is generally highest for trade among industrialized countries. That trade overlap has risen over time is not a recent phenomenon. Table 1.13 shows that trade overlap existed in France, and presumably elsewhere, during the late nineteenth century and also between the two world wars.

Table 1.14 *Shares of IIT^a in total trade, by product type, 1980*

Country	All	Consumer (C)	Intermediate (S)	Investment (I)	Developing	Developed
			Type of good			
Australia	35.8	18.6	53.9	32.8	I	S
Belgium	79.9	84.5	76.4	77.0	S	C
Canada	58.8	72.3	43.9	59.0	S	C
France	80.4	70.9	86.2	85.8	S	I
Germany	65.4	62.0	71.4	60.3	S	I
Italy	65.4	51.7	75.5	70.2	S	I
Japan	28.8	18.4	38.0	31.5	S	I
Netherlands	74.2	69.0	74.7	85.8	S	I
Sweden	66.5	67.3	59.2	79.7	S	I
UK	79.1	78.6	78.8	81.0	I	I
USA	60.7	63.1	63.4	54.0	C	S
Number of products	81	36	28	17		

Note:
^{a} Unweighted averages of the G–L index of manufactured goods defined according to the 4-digit ISIC.
Source: Culem and Lundberg (1986).

Another aspect of measured trade overlap is that it varies with the commodity and regional composition of trade. This is revealed in Table 1.14 by the wide differences in trade overlap when manufactured goods are divided into three groups: consumer goods (C), semi-fabricated products (S), and investment goods (I). Regional differences are suggested in the last two columns which report the product group having the highest fraction of trade overlap with respect to each country's trade with developing and developed countries, respectively. For trade with developing countries, trade overlap is greatest in semi-fabricated goods while investment goods contain the highest amount of trade overlap for trade with developed countries.

1.3 International factor movements

Trade between countries involves not only an exchange of goods but also productive factors. In this regard, Chapter 3 considers the theoretical and empirical relevance of international labor flows while Chapter 11, which discusses multinational enterprises and the phenomena of intra-firm trade, considers trade in capital in the form of financial capital movements as measured by direct investment flows. Below we note briefly these international factor flows and consider their relationship to the flow of goods.

Despite facts to the contrary, trade models routinely assume that factors of production are internationally immobile. As explained in Chapters 3 and 4, this assumption is made since, without further assumptions, the pattern of trade in goods would be indeterminate in the sense that there is no way to know if goods, factors, or both would move between countries. The indeterminacy of trade patterns when goods and factors are internationally mobile has interesting implications for the cases in which either goods or factors, but not both, are internationally mobile. For example, in Chapter 4 it is shown that when goods alone are internationally mobile, trade in goods can equalize the returns to factors across countries. Similarly, in Chapter 6 it is shown that when only factors are mobile, international factor movements can equalize the prices of goods across countries. These theoretical relationships suggest that trade in goods and trade in factors are substitutes. Given this, one would expect an increase in the international mobility of goods caused, for example, by a reduction in trade barriers or in transport costs, to reduce the international flow of factors. The following sections consider this predicted relationship between goods flows and factor flows.

Labor flows

Integrated economic areas such as the EC seek to deregulate their commodity and factor markets by removing trade barriers and by removing formal obstacles to the free movement of factors between member countries. If trade and factor flows are substitutes then, in the context of the EC, one would expect an increase in intra-EC trade to decrease factor movements between EC member countries.

Table 1.15 shows summary data on labor migration and trade flows within the EC between 1958 and 1980. These data generally corroborate the hypothesis of substitutability between factor flows and commodity flows. However, these average shares mask the fact that the underlying distribution of the annual shares of intra-EC migration in total EC migration is V-shaped, with a trough at 19.3% in 1969. The distribution of the annual shares of intra-EC trade in total EC trade has a different pattern, first rising from 29.6% in 1958 to 50.1% in 1971 and then fluctuating around this value for the remainder of the sample period. As shown in the last column of Table 1.15, the simple correlation between the annual shares of intra-EC migration and intra-EC trade over the 1958–80 period is −0.553.

Table 1.15 *Labor migration and commodity flows within the EC, 1958–80 (annual averages)*

| Time period | Labor migration as a share of total EC migration | | Trade as a share of total EC trade | | |
	Intra-EC[a] (1)	Extra-EC (2)	Intra-EC (3)	Extra-EC (4)	Correlation of (1) with (3)
1958–73[b]	37.9	62.1	42.1	57.9	−0.902
1973–80	42.4	57.6	49.2	50.8	0.089
1958–80	40.1	59.9	44.1	55.9	−0.553

Notes:
[a] Intra-EC refers to the EC-6 or EC-9 countries; extra-EC refers to non-EC countries.
[b] Figures for 1958–73 are for the EC-6; figures for 1973–80 are for the EC-9.
Source: Straubhaar (1988).

This negative correlation is consistent with the theoretical prediction that commodity flows tend to substitute for labor flows. Note, however, that the period 1973–80 does not support the predicted substitution relationship.

Capital flows

Capital flows, as measured by flows of private investment, are a major part of international exchange. In principle, the determinants of international capital flows can be analyzed in the same framework as the trade in goods since the former represent the exchange of current goods for future goods.

Table 1.16 shows data on the flows of US and Japanese private investment in 1989. Portfolio investment is about 1-third of all US private asset outflows and 2-thirds of all private asset inflows to the United States. Whereas the United States was the major source of direct investment flows after the Second World War, other countries (particularly Western Europe and Japan) now constitute a much greater proportion of world foreign direct investments. These changes in investment flows coincided with the United States becoming a net recipient of direct investment from Western Europe and Japan but a net creditor with respect to Canada and the rest of the world.

Extrapolating from the data in Table 1.16, the bulk of international investment flows takes place between industrialized countries. In particular, almost three-quarters of all direct investment occurs between developed countries, a figure which mirrors the dominant share of industrial countries

Table 1.16 *International private investment, Japan and the United States, 1989[a] (US$million)*

	USA	Japan
Outflows of direct investment	373 436	177 091
to: Western Europe	176 736	30 164
Canada	66 856	3 231
Japan	19 341	—
USA	—	69 699
Latin America/Other Western hemisphere	61 364	31 617[b]
Outflows of portfolio investment	189 625	—
Inflows of direct investment	400 817	—
from: Western Europe	262 011	—
Canada	31 538	—
Japan	69 699	—
USA	—	19 341
Latin America/Other Western hemisphere	20 348	—
Inflows of portfolio investment	624 612	—

Notes:
[a] For Japan, end of fiscal year (31 March 1989).
[b] Latin America only, but includes offshore banking.
Source: US Department of Commerce.

in terms of intra-regional trade (see Table 1.2). This suggests, contrary to the theoretical prediction of substitutability, that international trade in financial capital is complementary with international trade in goods.

Investment overlap

Since the 1970s, countries' inflows and outflows of foreign direct investment have become more similar. By analogy to trade overlap, this phenomenon can be called intra-industry foreign direct investment (IIFDI) and a measure of its importance can be made in the same fashion:

$$IIFDI_{ig} = 100\left[1 - \frac{|O_{ig} - I_{ig}|}{(O_{ig} + I_{ig})}\right] \qquad (1.4)$$

where O_{ig} is the number of foreign subsidiaries established in industry g by the parent firms of country i and I_{ig} is the number of subsidiaries in industry g established by foreign firms in country i. Table 1.17 reports annual values of this index with respect to detailed industries and five countries for the

Table 1.17   *Indexes of intra-industry foreign direct investment, selected countries[a],*
1968–71

Industry	USA	UK	Germany	France	Japan
Meat products	0	92	0	0	0
Dairy products	70	68	0	0	64
Canned products	77	97	0	0	0
Grain mill products	35	92	0	0	0
Beverages	64	68	0	0	0
Tobacco	65	0	0	0	0
Textiles	74	76	54	76	37
Lumber & wood	66	90	0	0	52
Furniture	90	63	0	94	0
Paper products	74	69	91	39	88
Printed matter	30	71	72	52	64
Industrial chemicals	86	93	77	80	11
Plastics & synthetics	77	61	87	39	49
Drugs	73	46	63	79	35
Soap & cosmetics	72	53	49	0	0
Paints	76	56	51	0	17
Refined petroleum	84	75	7	76	11
Other petroleum products	62	68	73	55	0
Tires	23	87	53	74	38
Other rubber products	49	48	61	95	91
Leather products & shoes	89	43	0	0	0
Glass products	69	20	23	13	27
Stone, clay and concrete	24	71	63	52	74
Iron and steel products	45	94	39	97	11
Engines & turbines	70	35	83	25	44
Farm machinery	76	28	0	37	0
Construction machinery	23	39	53	0	83
Special industry machinery	89	44	33	44	77
General industry machinery	89	77	99	42	17
Office machinery & computers	76	21	31	0	27
Other non-electrical machinery	23	39	69	25	77
Electrical transmission equipment	87	96	31	42	74
Electrical lighting and wiring	68	81	41	61	52
Radio, TV & appliances	75	95	65	95	45
Communications equipment	79	73	25	69	97
Electric components	24	45	91	88	97
Other electrical equipment	80	97	86	79	83
Motor vehicles & equipment	18	80	66	76	61
Other transportation	63	35	91	90	0
Overall index	64	64	61	56	46

Note:
[a] Index values corrected for trade imbalance according to Aquino (1978).
Source: Norman and Dunning (1984).

period 1968–71. According to these data, traditional sectors such as food and raw materials generally have lower index values whereas technology-intensive sectors tend to have higher index values. As discussed in Chapter 11, the higher values for technology-intensive sectors are consistent with theories that explain the basis for multinational enterprises.

1.4 Concluding remarks

The past three decades have witnessed an ever-increasing process of globalization and growing interdependence among countries. Over this period, the growth of world trade, fueled by large increases in the trade of manufactured goods, has exceeded the growth in world output. Trade among both old and newly industrialized countries constitutes a significant fraction of the global increase in trade. Intra-regional trade has generally risen faster than inter-regional trade, partly reflecting the implementation of new, and the renewal of existing, regional trade agreements that reduce trade barriers among subsets of countries.

In addition to the changes in regional trade patterns, the composition of trade of individual countries has changed dramatically. For example, the United States once accounted for over four-fifths of the exports of manufactured goods but now accounts for less than 1-third. Japan, once a major exporter of basic textile products, toys, sporting goods and other light manufactures, is now a dominant exporter of automobiles and an importer of its former exports. The trade patterns of many South-East Asian countries now resemble Japan's earlier trade pattern. These changes in the composition of countries' trade have had dramatic effects on standards of living.

Explaining the basis for trade, its pattern within and between countries, and its change over time is one goal of international trade theory. Another is to answer the question: 'does a country gain from trade?' Trade does permit a nation to extend its opportunities for consumption beyond those available to it in isolation, but whether these extended consumption possibilities also imply a national gain must await further analysis.

In considering the basis for trade, trade theory utilizes the important concept of comparative advantage which implies differences in the relative prices of goods across countries. Since relative prices in turn derive from the fundamental determinants of supplies and demands, theories of trade based on comparative advantage look to differences in these fundamentals (e.g. relative factor supplies or technology) across countries as the basis for trade and its composition. Operating in the framework of perfectly competitive markets and homogeneous goods these theories predict the emergence of trade and the goods countries will export and import, that is, the *inter-industry* pattern of trade.

Data on the composition of countries' trade and their revealed comparative advantage suggest that countries with similar economic structures do have similar trade patterns. In addition, data on countries' resource supplies indicate persistent differences between the resource structures of developed and developing countries; developed countries are generally abundant in physical capital and highly skilled labor when compared to developing countries. These differences in relative factor supplies suggest patterns of factor costs that could give rise to comparative advantage and trade. The data also suggest that the resource structures of developed countries are becoming more similar.

Comparative advantage as the basis for trade is compelling, but trade can nonetheless emerge for reasons other than relative price differences. If markets are imperfectly competitive or goods differentiated, countries who are in every respect identical, may still trade. However, the trade that arises under these circumstances is *intra-industry* trade rather than *inter-industry* trade. Data on the extent of intra-industry trade, as measured by the amount of trade overlap in a given statistical industry classification, does appear to be an important feature of actual trade flows, particularly among industrialized countries.

Finally, countries exchange not only goods but also factors of production. The patterns of labor flows within the EC suggest that international movements of goods and factors exhibit a substitute relationship while international movements of goods and capital tend to be complementary. In this context, the majority of direct investment flows are directed at developed countries and, by analogy with trade overlap, investment overlap is becoming increasingly common.

■*Appendix 1*■

Aggregate Indices of Trade Overlap

A.1 Methods of aggregation

A.2 Adjustment for trade imbalances

Studies of trade overlap frequently report values of the Grubel–Lloyd (G–L) index (1.3) at different levels of aggregation. This appendix discusses the measurement of such indexes and issues that arise in this regard.

A.1 **Methods of aggregation**

The literature uses two methods of computing a G–L index at higher levels of aggregation. The first simply sums the trade data at lower levels of aggregation and calculates the G–L index using these values. In this case, trade overlap for 'industry' g is computed as:

$$GL_{ig}^* = 100\left(1 - \frac{|X_{ig}^* - M_{ig}^*|}{X_{ig}^* + M_{ig}^*}\right) \tag{1.5}$$

where $X_{ig}^* = \sum_{j\in g} X_{ij}$ and $M_{ig}^* = \sum_{j\in g} M_{ij}$ are the sum of export and import values, respectively, over products that comprise industry g. The second method takes a weighted average of the index GL_{ij} for each commodity within industry g:

$$GL_{ig}^{**} = \sum_{j\in g}\left(\frac{X_{ij} + M_{ij}}{\sum_{j\in g}(X_{ij} + M_{ij})}\right)GL_{ij}$$

$$= 100\left(1 - \frac{\sum_{j\in g}|X_{ij} - M_{ij}|}{X_{ig}^* + M_{ig}^*}\right) \tag{1.6}$$

where the weights are commodity j's share of total trade in industry g. The key difference between (1.5) and (1.6) is that the former sums any trade imbalances at the commodity level. If these imbalances are of opposite sign they will tend to cancel out. This is not true of the summations in (1.6).

In fact, when computed for the same subset of commodities, (1.6) will tend to be less than (1.5) since

$$\left| \sum_{j \in g} (X_{ij} - M_{ij}) \right| \le \sum_{j \in g} |X_{ij} - M_{ij}|$$

Aggregation of the above industry level indexes to obtain an index for the share of intra-industry trade in country i's total trade similarly takes the form of either the weighted or the unweighted average of either GL_{ig}^{*} or GL_{ig}^{**} over all commodity groups. The weighted averages in each case are:

$$GL_i^* = \sum_g GL_{ig}^* \frac{(X_{ig}^* + M_{ig}^*)}{\sum_g (X_{ig}^* + M_{ig}^*)} \tag{1.7}$$

$$GL_i^{**} = 100 \left(1 - \frac{\sum_j |X_{ij} - M_{ij}|}{(X_i + M_i)} \right) \tag{1.8}$$

The unweighted averages have the simpler form:

$$Z_i^* = \sum_g GL_{ig}^* / G \tag{1.9}$$

$$Z_i^{**} = \sum_g GL_{ig}^{**} / G \tag{1.10}$$

where 'G' is the number of groups. When trade is balanced ($\sum_j X_{ij} = \sum_j M_{ij}$) these aggregate indices range between 0 and 100.

The difference produced by these alternative aggregation methods is illustrated in Table 1.18 which reports values of the unweighted indices Z_i^* and Z_i^{**} for Switzerland and the United Kingdom. As expected, trade overlap is smaller using the unweighted averages of GL_{ig}^{**}. Comparing the two measures, the difference in their values (column (3)) is relatively small at all SITC levels except SITC 4.

Note that regardless of which measure is used, the results in Table 1.18 indicate that higher than average levels of trade overlap occur in SITCs 5–8 (manufactures and consumer goods) than in SITCs 0–4 (foodstuffs and raw or unfinished materials). Moreover, except for SITC 4, trade overlap is higher for the United Kingdom than for Switzerland.

A.2 Adjustment for trade imbalances

Aggregate indices of trade overlap range between 0 and 100 when trade is balanced but are biased downward if the country has an overall trade

Table 1.18 *Values of unweighted G–L indexes at 1-digit SITC level, United Kingdom and Switzerland, 1977[a]*

	UK				Switzerland			
	(1)	*(2)*	*(3)*	*(4)*	*(1)*	*(2)*	*(3)*	*(4)*
SITC	Z_i^*	Z_i^{**}	*(1) – (2)*	*(3) ÷ (1)*	Z_i^*	Z_i^{**}	*(1) – (2)*	*(3) ÷ (1)*
0	35	33	2	0.06	24	18	6	0.25
1	35	22	13	0.37	22	19	3	0.14
2	40	35	5	0.13	33	32	1	0.03
3	58	45	13	0.22	9	9	0	0
4	50	26	24	0.48	65	40	25	0.38
5	69	57	12	0.17	60	56	4	0.07
6	69	63	6	0.09	52	48	4	0.08
7	69	64	5	0.07	53	48	5	0.09
8	80	73	7	0.09	63	57	6	0.10

Note:
[a] Averages computed from G–L indexes computed at the 3-digit SITC level.
Sources: UK figures, Greenaway and Milner (1983); Swiss figures, Greenaway (1983).

imbalance. The greater the trade imbalance the greater will be the share, on average, of net trade in a commodity and hence the smaller the share of intra-industry trade. To correct for this bias Grubel and Lloyd proposed the following modified index:

$$GL_i^B = 100 \frac{\sum_j (X_{ij} + M_{ij}) - \sum_j |X_{ij} - M_{ij}|}{\sum_j (X_{ij} + M_{ij}) - |\sum_j (X_{ij} - M_{ij})|} \qquad (1.11)$$

This can be written in the reduced form:

$$GL_i^B = \frac{GL_i^*}{(1 - b_i)}$$

where GL_i^* is defined in (1.7) and b_i is country i's trade imbalance as a fraction of its total trade:

$$b_i = \frac{|\sum_j (X_{ij} - M_{ij})|}{\sum_j (X_{ij} + M_{ij})} \qquad (1.12)$$

It follows from (1.12) that if all imbalances are 1-sided then GL_i^B will always take the value of unity. This, and the fact that the correction is applied only at the highest level of aggregation, are considered undesirable features that have led others to propose alternative corrections. For example, Aquino

(1978) replaces GL_i^B by

$$Q_i = 100\left[1 - \left(\frac{|\hat{X}_i - \hat{M}_i|}{(\hat{X}_i + \hat{M}_i)}\right)\right]$$

where $\hat{X}_i$ and $\hat{M}_i$ are the hypothetical values of exports and imports under balanced trade, that is,

$$\hat{X}_i = X_i\left[\frac{\sum_j (X_{ij} + M_{ij})}{\sum_j 2X_{ij}}\right]$$

and similarly for $\hat{M}_i$. Other trade imbalance corrections have been proposed and used by Loertscher and Wolter (1980), Bergstrand (1983) and Balassa (1986). However, these alternative procedures introduce still other distortions.

Notes

1. However, economists can model the nature of demand differences as reflected, for example, by differences in income elasticities of demand or a bias toward home produced goods.
2. 'Economies of scale' here refers to economies of scale that are external to firms but internal to an industry. Economies of scale can also be internal to the firm and, if so, imply imperfectly competitive market structures.
3. However, one could take the traditional supply side view and envision this trade as arising from differences in climate and soil between these countries. Hence, in the United States, French soil and climate are relatively scarce (and hence expensive) compared to US soil and climate. France therefore produces French wine relatively more cheaply than does the United States. But if the soil and climate of France could be exactly duplicated in the United States then trade in wine would not take place unless technology or the prices of other factor inputs also differed between these countries. Which country would export 'French wine' would then be determined according to traditional comparative advantage considerations.
4. Note that the measurement concepts for world trade and world production differ. The latter measures world value added whereas trade measures the value of shipments. Hence, the trade data 'double counts' the value of goods.
5. Facilitated by direct sales in foreign markets and, as discussed in Chapter 11, the spread of multinational corporations.
6. These growth rates are computed as $g = \ln(X_{1994}/X_{1992})/(1994-1992)$ where X is the value of trade for a particular region.
7. Trade dependence ratios in excess of 100 may also reflect that trade values, unlike GDP, are not measured in terms of value added.
8. The commodity categories are defined according to the United Nations Standard International Trade Classification (SITC). The particular SITC level of detail shown in Table 1.7 is the 3-digit *group* level. See p. 24 below and the Appendix (p. 597) for further information on the SITC system.

9. Liesner (1958) was the first to utilize an RCA index but it was Balassa (1965) who refined and popularized its use. In fact, (1.1) is commonly referred to as the 'Balassa index' of revealed comparative advantage.
10. Memedovic (1994) critiques many of these RCA indices.
11. See Bowen (1983b) and Hillman (1980).
12. The Appendix (p. 597) discusses the measurement of such resources. Here we note only that capital stocks are measured as discounted investment flows, labor skills are measured by occupational categories and arable land is land area under cultivation.
13. For example, if country i exports \$4 million of commodity j and imports \$6 million, then the amount of trade overlap is \$8 million (\$4 million of exports *plus* \$4 million of 'matching' imports).
14. Grubel and Lloyd (1975). Other measures of trade overlap preceded that of Grubel and Lloyd. See Greenaway and Milner (1986) for a comparative review of these measures.
15. The Appendix (p. 597) further discusses the SITC system.
16. Appendix 1 (p. 35) discusses alternative methods for aggregating values of GL_{ij}.
17. As the example suggests, measured trade overlap rises with the level of commodity aggregation. The literature on intra-industry trade has yet to reach agreement on what constitutes the appropriate level of aggregation for empirical purposes. In principle, the level of aggregation should reflect an 'industry', that is, a collection of goods produced with the same or similar production function. In practice, studies often proceed from the 3-digit SITC level since corresponding data on industry characteristics, which are reported using a different system of classification, are only available at a similar level of disaggregation. See also the Appendix (p. 597).

References and additional reading

World trade and factor flows

GATT (1990), *International Trade, Vols I and II* (Geneva: GATT).

Norman, G. and Dunning, J.M. (1984), 'Intra-industry Foreign Direct Investment', *Weltwirtschaftliches Archiv*, 120, 522–39.

Straubhaar, T. (1988), 'International Labour Migration within a Common Market: Some Aspects of EC Experience', *Journal of Common Market Studies*, 27(1), 45–62.

Summers, R. and Heston, A. (1991), 'The Penn World Table (Mark 5): An Expanded Set of International Comparisons, 1950–1988', *Quarterly Journal of Economics* (May).

US Department of Commerce (various years), *Survey of Current Business* (Washington, DC: US Government Printing Office).

Vaupel, J.W. and Curhan, J.P. (1973), *The World's Multinational Enterprises* (Geneva: Research Unit, Centre d'Etudes Industrielles).

WTO (1995), *International Trade, Trends and Statistics* (Geneva: WTO).

The determinants of trade

Bowen, H.P. (1983a), 'Changes in the International Distribution of Resources and their Impact on US Comparative Advantage'. *Review of Economics and Statistics*, 65(3) (August), 402–17.

Leamer, E.E. (1984), *Sources of International Comparative Advantage: Theory and Evidence* (Cambridge, Mass.: MIT Press).

Ricardo, D. (1817), *The Principles of Political Economy and Taxation*, reprint in Everyman's Library (New York: Dutton), 1950.

Smith, A. (1776), *An Inquiry into the Nature and Causes of Wealth of Nations* (London: W. Straham and T. Cadell).

Indices of revealed comparative advantage

Ballance, R.H., Forstner, H. and Murray, T. (1985), 'On Measuring Comparative Advantage: A Note on Bowen's Indices', *Weltwirtschaftliches Archiv*, 121, 346–50.

Ballance, R.H., Forstner, H. and Murray, T. (1986), 'More on Measuring Comparative Advantage: A Reply', *Weltwirtschaftliches Archiv*, 122, 375–8.

Ballance, R.H., Forstner, H. and Murray, T. (1987), 'Consistency Tests of Alternative Measures of Comparative Advantage', *Review of Economics and Statistics*, 121, 346–50.

Balassa, B. (1965), 'Trade Liberalisation and Revealed Comparative Advantage', *The Manchester School of Economic and Social Studies*, 33, 92–123.

Bowen, H.P. (1983b), 'On the Theoretical Interpretation of Indices of Trade Intensity and Revealed Comparative Advantage', *Weltwirtschaftliches Archiv*, 119(3), 464–72.

Bowen, H.P. (1985), 'On Measuring Comparative Advantage: A Reply and Extensions', *Weltwirtschaftliches Archiv*, 121(2), 351–4.

Bowen, H. P. (1986), 'On Measuring Comparative Advantage: Further Comments', *Weltwirtschaftliches Archiv*, 122(2), 379–81.

Hillman, A.L. (1980), 'Observations on the Relation Beween "Revealed Comparative Advantage" and Comparative Advantage as Indicated by Pre-Trade Relative Prices', *Weltwirtschaftliches Archiv*, 116, 314–21.

Kunimoto, K. (1977), 'Typology of Trade Intensity Indices', *Hitotsubashi Journal of Economics*, 17, 15–32.

Liesner, H.H. (1958), 'The European Common Market and British Industry', *Economic Journal*, 68, 302–16.

Marchese, S. and Nadal De Simone, F. (1989), 'Monotonicity of Indices of "Revealed" Comparative Advantage: Empirical Evidence on Hillman's Condition', *Weltwirtschaftliches Archiv*, 125, 158–67.

Memedovic, O. (1994), 'On the Theory and Measurement of Comparative Advantage', *Tinbergen Institute Research Series*, 65 (Rotterdam).

Intra-industry trade

Aquino, A. (1978), 'Intra-industry Trade and Inter-industry Specialization as Concurrent Sources of International Trade in Manufactures', *Weltwirtschaftliches Archiv*, 114, 275–96.

Balassa, B. (1966), 'Tariff Reductions and Trade in Manufactures among the Industrial Countries', *American Economic Review*, 56, 466–73.

Balassa, B. (1986), 'Intra-industry Trade Among Exporters of Manufactured Goods', in Greenaway, D. and Tharakan, P.K.M. (eds), *Imperfect Competition and International Trade*, 108–28.

Bergstrand, J.H. (1983), 'Measurement and Determinants of Intra-industry International Trade', in Tharakan, P.K.M. (ed.), *Intra-industry Trade: Empirical and Methodological Aspects* (Amsterdam: North-Holland), 201–62.

Chipman, J.S. (1991), 'Intra-Industry Trade in a Loglinear Model', University of Minnesota (mimeo).

Culem, C. and Lundberg, L. (1986), 'The Product Pattern of Intra-industry Trade: Stability among Countries and over Time', *Weltwirtschaftliches Archiv*, 122, 113–30.

Finger, J.M. and Kreinin, M.E. (1979), 'A Measure of "Export Similarity" and its Possible Uses', *Economic Journal*, 89, 905–12.

Glejser, H., Goossens, K. and Vanden Eede, M. (1979), 'Inter-industry and Intra-industry Specialization Do Occur in World Trade', *Economics Letters*, 3, 261–5.

Glejser, H., Goossens, K. and Vanden Eede, M. (1982), 'Inter-industry versus Intra-industry Specialization in Exports and Imports (1959–1970–1973)', *Journal of International Economics*, 12, 363–9.

Greenaway, D. (1983), 'Intra-industry and Inter-industry Trade in Switzerland', *Weltwirtschaftliches Archiv*, 119, 109–21.

Greenaway, D. and Milner, C. (1983), 'On the Measurement of Intra-industry Trade', *Economic Journal*, 93, 900–8.

Greenaway, D. and Milner, C. (1986), *The Economics of Intra-industry Trade* (Oxford: Basil Blackwell).

Greenaway, D. and Milner, C. (1987), 'Intra-industry Trade: Current Perspectives and Unresolved Issues', *Weltwirtschaftliches Archiv*, 123, 39–57.

Greenaway, D. and Tharakan, P.K.M. (eds) (1986), *Imperfect Competition and International Trade: Policy Aspects of Intra-industry Trade* (Brighton: Wheatsheaf).

Grubel, H.G. and Lloyd, P.J. (1975), *Intra-industry Trade* (London: Macmillan).

Kojima, K. (1964), 'The Pattern of International Trade among Advanced Countries', *Hitotsubashi Journal of Economics*, 5, 16–36.

Loertscher, R. and Wolter, F. (1980), 'Determinants of Intra-industry Trade: Among Countries and Across Industries', *Weltwirtschaftliches Archiv*, 116, 280–93.

Messerlin, P.A. and Becuwe, S. (1986), 'Intra-industry Trade in the Long Run: The French Case, 1850–1913', in Greenaway, D. and Tharakan, P.K.M. (eds), *Imperfect Competition and International Trade: Policy Aspects of Intra-Industry Trade* (Brighton: Wheatsheaf), 191–215.

Michaely, M. (1962), *Concentration in International Trade* (Amsterdam: North-Holland).

Tharakan, P.K.M. (ed.) (1983), *Intra-industry Trade: Empirical and Methodological Aspects* (Amsterdam: North-Holland).

■ *Chapter 2* ■

The Instruments and Environment of Trade Policy

A nation's trade policy is defined as the set of taxes, subsidies, quantitative measures, and other impediments or stimulants it undertakes with respect to transactions between domestic and foreign residents. The forms that these policies take are called the instruments of trade policy. Since one nation's trade policies will, by definition, affect the residents of other countries, international laws and institutions have developed to offer a framework for mutually agreeable implementation of trade policies among countries and, when disputes arise, a mechanism for their resolution. These laws and institutions represent the environment of trade policy.

This chapter overviews the main instruments of trade policy and discusses the rules that most countries have agreed will govern the use of these instruments.[1] These rules are, for the most part, contained in three agreements: (1) the General Agreement on Tariffs and Trade (GATT), (2) the General Agreement on Trade in Services (GATS), and (3) the Agreement on Trade-related Aspects of Intellectual Property Rights (TRIPs).[2] These agreements are administered by a newly created institutional body called the World Trade Organization (WTO).[3] The members of the WTO are sovereign states or customs territories; as of June 1994 the WTO had 124 members.

2.1 Instruments of trade policy

Tariffs

A tariff is a tax levied on imports of a good. Its effect is to raise the internal domestic price of the imported good above its external world price. This increase in the domestic price reduces the volume imported and thereby shields a country's domestic industries from foreign competition. A tariff rate can be either *ad valorem* or specific. An *ad valorem* rate is stated as a percentage of the import value of the good while a specific rate is stated as a fixed currency amount per unit of the good.

Ad valorem tariffs are the most widely used instrument for restricting trade. This use is due primarily to the GATT which specifies that *ad valorem* tariffs are the preferred tool for restricting trade. This preference derives from two considerations. First, *ad valorem* tariffs are transparent in the sense that their effect on price is readily calculated. Second, *ad valorem* rates are directly comparable across goods since they are stated in percentage terms. Comparability is important when countries seek to negotiate tariff reductions. Comparing specific rates across products is problematic since they depend on the units in which products are measured. One drawback of an *ad valorem* rate is that it is applied to the *value* of an imported good, and what constitutes the appropriate 'value for duty' is then subject to interpretation and abuse.[4] The GATT therefore contains specific rules on 'customs valuation' in order to limit the discretion of customs officials in setting a value for duty.

Bound versus applied rates

A country's *tariff schedule* lists the tariff rates applicable to imported goods. In this regard, there are two types of tariff rates: the bound rate and the applied rate. The bound (or scheduled) rate is the rate a WTO member country has agreed will be the *maximum* rate that it will levy on a good imported from any other WTO member country. The applied rate is the actual rate a country applies on its imports (from any country). Table 2.1 shows, as of 1994, the number of bound rates on industrial products as a percentage of the total number of tariff rates (tariff lines) for major groupings of WTO members.

Table 2.1   *Bound tariffs on industrial products, 1994*

Country group	Number of tariff lines	Import value (US$ billions)	% of tariff lines bound	% of imports under bound rates
Developed economies	86 968	737.2	99	99
Developing economies	157 805	306.2	72	59
Transition economies	18 962	34.7	98	96

Source: GATT (1994).

Tariff averages

As Table 2.1 suggests, a country's tariff schedule can contain thousands of commodity categories (tariff-line items). Applied analyses involving the use of tariff rate data will therefore require some method of aggregating individual rates.[5] The ideal would be a weighted average with weights equal to the amount of each product a country would import under free trade. However, since free trade import weights are not observable, other approaches are taken. These include: (1) weighting by shares of world imports, (2) weighting by shares in categories corresponding to the end use of goods (e.g. final versus intermediate), (3) weighting by estimates of free trade import levels where the estimates are derived from an econometric model or by adjusting import levels based on estimated import demand elasticities, (4) weighting by a product's share in a country's own imports, and (5) foregoing weights and instead computing the unweighted average of individual rates.[6]

The use of world import share weights has the defect that it fails to recognize the production structure of any particular country. Weighting tariffs by end use assumes that the ratio of imports to consumption would be more or less the same as under free trade which is, *a priori*, a reasonable assumption. However, this method requires comparable disaggregated import data on end use which are not normally available. Using econometric methods to estimate the level of free-trade imports requires a statement of the underlying determinants of trade flows and thus belief in the model's specification. But econometric estimates of tariff averages do have the distinct virtue of providing a measure of the uncertainty associated with the calculated averages. Weighting by a country's own import shares contains a systematic downward bias since goods subject to high tariffs have low weights while goods with low tariffs have relatively higher weights.[7] Despite the bias, many studies have used the last method since the data requirements are easily met, the direction of the bias is known, and the weights approach their theoretical levels as tariffs are progressively lowered. Finally, an unweighted average of tariff rates gives inordinate weight to obscure products and there is a strong upward bias because the product breakdown is usually more detailed for highly protected, import sensitive, industries.

Table 2.2 shows the average *ad valorem applied* tariff rate of developed and developing countries for selected product categories and by source of imports. The group averages are import share weighted averages of individual country average rates, the latter weighted by own-country import shares. Columns (1) and (2) of Table 2.2 indicate that trade among developed countries is relatively unrestricted when judged by tariff rates. The average applied tariff of these countries is low by historical standards and, except for

Table 2.2   *Developed and developing country average[a] applied tariff rates, by sector and import source, 1982 and 1983*

Product category	Average tariff applied by developed countries on imports from[b]		Average tariff applied by developing countries on imports from[c]	
	Developed countries	Developing countries	Developed countries	Developing countries
Food	6.1	6.7	28	27
Agricultural materials	0.9	0.7	19	10
Ores & metals	2.7	1.5	17	16
Fuels	1.2	1.0	7	6
Chemicals	5.7	6.6	17	18
Other manufactured products	6.5	9.3	18	19
All items	5.0	3.8	19	12

Notes:

[a] Own-country import share weighted averages of *ad valorem* tariff rates.

[b] Average for 11 developed countries in 1983.

[c] Average for 23 developing countries in 1982.

Source: Finger and Laird (1987).

'Other manufactured products' and 'Chemicals', there is no sign of geographic discrimination. Columns (3) and (4) of Table 2.2 indicate that tariffs applied by developing countries against developed countries are, on average, four times higher than those applied by the developed countries.[8] These data tend to counter the conventional belief that developed countries levy higher tariffs on imports from developing countries.

The relative height of developing country tariffs shown in Table 2.2 partly reflects the important role of tariff revenue in supporting developing country policy objectives. Equally important is the fact that many developing countries are relatively recent entrants into the WTO, and hence only recently subject to WTO disciplines regarding bound tariff rates. Similarly, the relatively low average tariff rates of developed countries reflect decades of effort by WTO members to reduce tariffs among themselves.

Table 2.3 provides further information on the structure of tariff protection by showing tariff averages for selected countries with respect to their imports from developed and developing countries. For comparison, the table reports unweighted and weighted tariff averages, the latter using own import share weights. Note that the unweighed averages always exceed

Table 2.3 *Average applied tariff rates, selected countries,[a] 1983*

	Tariff applied on imports from			
	Developed countries		Developing countries	
	Trade weighted	Unweighted	Trade weighted	Unweighted
Australia	9.4	12.2	4.8	10.3
Austria	1.5	3.7	5.6	11.8
Canada	4.5	7.2	4.6	5.6
EC[b]	2.8	4.6	2.1	5.3
Finland	0.9	1.8	4.0	8.5
Japan	4.0	6.9	2.4	4.6
New Zealand	13.0	17.2	3.3	16.2
Norway	0.8	1.7	2.8	6.8
Sweden	0.7	1.4	2.5	4.4
Switzerland	0.9	1.6	2.5	3.5
USA	3.4	7.6	4.5	4.7

Notes:
[a] *Ad valorem* equivalents.
[b] Intra-EC trade is excluded.
Source: Finger and Laird (1987).

the weighted averages. Note also that the variation in trade weighted tariff rates across the listed countries is greater for imports from developed countries than for imports from developing countries.

Effective protection and tariff escalation

As detailed in Chapter 5, a tariff raises not only the internal domestic price of an imported good but also the price and production of the domestically produced goods with which it competes. This tariff induced increase in the production of domestic 'import-competing' goods is sometimes called the 'protective effect' of the tariff. However, the rise in domestic production is not an entirely satisfactory measure of protection since what one actually seeks to protect by limiting competition from imports is the income of the factors of production employed in import-competing industries. This income (value added) encompasses payments to primary factor inputs which can include pure economic profit. The amount by which a *nominal* tariff raises an industry's value added above its free trade level is called the Effective Rate of Protection (ERP).

The relationship between the ERP afforded domestic producers of good j and the *nominal* tariff rate applied on good j is given by the following formula:

$$ERP_j = \frac{t_j - \sum_z \phi_{jz} t_z}{1 - \sum_z \phi_{jz}} \qquad (2.1)$$

where t_j = nominal tariff rate on final product j
        t_z = nominal tariff rate on intermediate good z
        ϕ_{jz} = share of intermediate input z in the *value* of one unit (i.e. a dollar's worth) of good j when evaluated at free trade (external) prices.

The term $(1 - \sum_z \phi_{jz})$ is the ratio of valued added to the value of total output computed on the basis of free trade (external or 'world') prices. As (2.1) indicates, the emphasis of the ERP on factor incomes draws attention to the effect of tariffs on imported intermediate inputs. For example, a 10% tariff on rice imports and a 20% tariff on fertilizer imports used in rice production is unlikely to raise value added in domestic rice production.

Problem 2.1:   The ERP formula assumes that intermediate inputs are used in fixed proportions. Discuss the direction of the bias this assumption introduces into the calculation of the ERP if inputs are instead substitutable in production.

Table 2.4 lists the ERP for selected commodities and countries in 1962. In most cases the ERP exceeds the nominal tariff rate but in some cases the

Table 2.4   *Nominal and effective rates of protection, selected countries and industries, 1962 (%)*

	USA		Japan		UK		EC	
Product	*Nominal*	*ERP*	*Nominal*	*ERP*	*Nominal*	*ERP*	*Nominal*	*ERP*
Thread & yarn	11.7	31.8	2.7	1.4	10.5	27.9	2.9	3.6
Textile fabrics	24.1	50.6	29.7	48.8	20.7	42.2	17.6	44.4
Clothing	25.1	35.9	25.2	42.4	25.5	40.5	18.5	25.1
Steel ingots/ primary forms	20.6	106.7	13.0	58.9	11.1	98.9	6.4	28.9
Ships	5.5	2.1	13.1	12.1	2.9	−10.2	0.4	−13.2
Electrical machinery	12.2	18.1	18.1	25.3	19.7	30.0	14.5	21.5
Automobiles	6.8	5.1	35.9	75.7	23.1	41.4	19.5	36.8
Precision instruments	21.4	32.2	23.2	38.5	25.7	44.2	13.5	24.2

Source: Balassa (1965).

Table 2.5 *Tariff escalation, selected products,ᵃ 1984*

Product category	Stage of processing		
	Raw material	Semi-finished	Finished
Textiles & clothing	0.8	11.5	16.7
Leather, footwear, rubber & travel goods	0.0	4.4	10.2
Base metals	0.0	3.2	5.9

Note:
[a] Sector trade weighted tariff averages across developed countries.
Source: Balassa and Balassa (1984).

ERP is negative. Although entirely possible, it is unlikely that an industry would allow its government to impose a tariff rate that reduced its value added. One explanation for persistent negative effective rates is that an industry receives direct or indirect subsidies which are not captured in the calculation of effective rates. Another explanation is that the measurement of the ERP is subject to bias (e.g. Problem 2.1).

From (2.1) it may be seen that the ERP will exceed the nominal rate of protection (t_j) if the nominal rate is above the weighted average of the nominal rates on intermediate goods. The ERP therefore rationalizes a stylized fact of tariff protection: tariff escalation, which refers to the tendency for tariff rates to rise with the stage of fabrication of goods. The phenomenon of tariff escalation was evident in Table 2.2 since the highest tariff rates are those applied on manufactured goods. Table 2.5 makes the relationship more explicit by showing the average tariff rate (across developed countries) applied in each of three product categories by stage of processing.

The ERP is an important concept for understanding the structure of a country's protection and its implications for internal resource allocation (since factors will tend to move to, or remain in, sectors with rising value added). The calculation of effective rates is now less frequent owing to the increasing use of applied general equilibrium (AGE) models (see Chapter 5) which permit one to directly compute the implications of a country's tariff structure for its resource allocation. Nonetheless, the principle underlying the ERP remains valid as does its use for inferring the level of protection, particularly when high levels of commodity or sector detail are required.

Non-tariff barriers

Non-tariff barriers to trade (NTBs) encompass all actions except tariffs that impede transactions between foreign and domestic residents. These can include both trade-related restrictions as well as government intervention in domestic markets via taxes or subsidies and also bureaucratic regulations. NTBs can thus affect trade both directly and indirectly. An example of a direct measure would be a longer delay in certifying that an import versus a domestically produced good meets a country's technical standards. An indirect measure might be an economy-wide wage subsidy.

The use of NTBs – and their importance in restricting trade – increased in the 1970s and 1980s and created a major strain on the world trading system. One problem was that the GATT then in force lacked well defined rules (disciplines) regarding many of the NTBs being adopted. While the growing use of NTBs reflected weaknesses in the existing GATT framework, their use also reflected one of the GATT's major strengths: cumulative and substantial reductions in bound tariff rates. Low bound rates meant that a WTO member wishing to increase protection of its domestic industries had relatively little latitude to achieve this protection by increasing tariffs.[9] Rather, they had to turn to other instruments of protection. As discussed in Section 2.2, recent changes in the GATT and the addition of new agreements have served to bring a number of NTBs within the discipline of the WTO framework. Specifically, the GATT now explicitly prohibits most NTBs. The following discusses some of the more important types of NTBs.

Quantitative restrictions

A major category of NTBs are quantitative restrictions, the most common form being explicit import and export quotas. An import quota sets a limit on the amount of a good that can be imported over a specific period of time. To ensure compliance, the country imposing the quota will establish a system of import licensing. An import licence permits the holder of the license to import a specified amount of the good. Similarly, an export quota sets a limit on the volume of a good that can be exported over a given period of time. Again, to ensure compliance, a system of (export) licensing will be established.

Chapters 5 and 10 examine the economic effects of quantitative NTBs including import and export quotas in detail. A rough summary of these effects is that a quota raises the price of the good whose supply is being restricted and creates rents (pure profit) for the holder of the quota licence[10] due to a difference between the demand and supply price of the restricted good. Who gets the rents generated by a quota is an important issue since these rents determine, in part, the quota's effect on the welfare of the importing and exporting countries.

Recognition that quantitative (and other) restrictions on trade can generate rents leads to the idea of *rent seeking activity* – that is, private agents who attempt to influence the nature of a country's trade policy in order to 'capture' the rents these policies generate. However, since the acquisition of these rents involves only a transfer of income between private agents, *rent seeking activity* is not productive. In fact, such activity imposes a cost on society since the activities involved in seeking to influence trade policies use up real resources (e.g. lobbying law makers or other government officials or hiring lawyers and other professionals in an effort to seek protection for one's industry). As discussed in Chapter 6, the possibility that rent seeking activity may offer an explanation of the observed structure of protection within a country is part of a broader area of inquiry, the political economy of protection.

Voluntary export restraints

One class of NTBs that has received prominent attention is Voluntary Export Restraints (VERs). A VER is 'voluntary' in the sense that an exporting country agrees to limit its exports in some way at the request of the importing country. A VER can involve an explicit export quota or, for example, a price agreement in which the exporting country agrees not to lower its export price (and, in fact, to raise its price to the importing country). Table 2.6 gives an indication of the past use of VERs by showing the number of VERs, by sector, that EC importing countries had negotiated with selected exporting countries as of 1990. It is notable that many of these agreements relate to trade in agricultural products which were not covered by GATT disciplines prior to 1994. As discussed in Section 2.2, the GATT now encompasses *all sectors* including agriculture and it prohibits the use of VERs.

Performance requirements

Various performance requirements are another class of NTBs that grew in importance during the 1970s and 1980s. These typically require foreign firms to meet objectives that may or may not apply to domestic firms. Examples include domestic content and export performance requirements. The former requires that some minimum fraction of a product's value added be derived from domestic factors of production. The stated intent of the policy is to maintain or raise domestic employment and income. A domestic content requirement may also be used to induce foreign firms to locate some or all of

Table 2.6   *EC VERs, per selected sector and exporting country, 1990*

Exporters	Total	Agriculture	Footwear	Textiles	Steel	Machinery	Electronics	Vehicles
Argentina	2	2						
Australia	2	2						
Austria	2	1			1			
Brazil	1				1			
Bulgaria	3	1			1			
Chile	1	1		1				
China	1		1					
CIS^a	1			1				
CSFR^b	3	1	1		1			
Cyprus	1			1				
Egypt	1			1				
Finland	1							
Hungary	2	1			1			
Iceland	1	1			1			
Japan	21	2		1		6	5	2
Korea	6		1	2			2	
Malta	1			1				
Morocco	1				1			
New Zealand	2	2						
Poland	2	1			1			
Romania	3	1	1		1			
Singapore	1							
South Africa	1	1						
Sweden	1				1			
Taiwan	2		1					
Thailand	1							
Tunisia	1			1				
Turkey	1			1				
United States	1				1			
Yugoslavia	2							
Total^c	69	17	6	10	11	6	8	5

Notes:
^{a} Former Soviet Union.
^{b} Former Czechoslovakia.
^{c} Includes exporting countries not listed.
Source: Adapted from Schuknecht (1992, table 6.2) as based on GATT (1991).

their production facilities in the importing country. Developing countries in particular have used such schemes in an effort to transfer knowledge and skills possessed by a foreign firm to the local work force. Chapter 5 examines the economic implications of domestic content requirements.

An export performance requirement requires foreign firms producing in the 'host' country, or host country firms wanting more favorable treatment, to export a certain percentage of their output. Several developing countries use export performance requirements to generate foreign exchange receipts. The GATT now prohibits most types of domestic content and export performance schemes. However, non-WTO member countries may still, as in the past, choose to adopt such policies.

Government procurement

Government procurement and sourcing policies are another important class of NTBs. Governments may prohibit foreign sourcing outright (e.g. US civil servants must fly US air carriers when traveling on official business) or simply make foreign sourcing more difficult. For example, foreign firms may be allowed to bid on government projects but only on special terms or conditions that end up favoring domestic bidders. Such restrictions can be of substantial importance (e.g. procurement by US Government entities was almost 20% of US GDP in 1991). At present, the impact of such activities on trade is unknown. Due partly to this uncertainty over the trade impact, only a subset of WTO member countries have agreed to rules governing government procurement.

Restrictiveness of NTBs

One factor that compounds the friction between countries regarding the use of NTBs is that the restrictiveness of NTBs is often difficult to quantify.[11] Without 'hard' numbers there is considerable scope for countries to disagree about the importance of any given NTB. The difficulty in quantifying NTBs also creates a problem from the viewpoint of an applied analysis of NTBs. As discussed in Chapter 5, one approach to determining the restrictiveness of an NTB is to estimate its *ad valorem* equivalent (AVE) – that is, the *ad valorem* tariff rate that would induce the same level of imports as the NTB in question. The restrictiveness of the NTB can then be determined by considering the effect of a change in this AVE rate on price and trade volume. However, as Chapter 5 discusses, estimating the effects of an NTB using AVE rates requires strong assumptions about the market for the good in question including stable supply and demand curves during the period of estimation.

Another approach to gauging the restrictiveness of NTBs uses data on reported NTBs by country and sector to construct various indices intended to gauge the extent of NTBs.[12] One example is the frequency index (F_g) which measures, for a given country, the frequency of NTBs within a given commodity category g:

$$F_g = \frac{100}{N_g} \sum_{j \in g} D_j \qquad (2.2)$$

where the binary variable D_j equals one when at least one NTB applies to good j and is zero otherwise and N_g is the number of commodities within commodity category g.[13] F_g equals zero when no NTBs are imposed on any of the N_g commodities comprising group g and equals 100 when each of the N commodities faces at least one NTB.

Another index is the coverage ratio (C_g) which weights the incidence of NTBs by import value shares:

$$C_g = 100 \sum_{j \in g} \frac{D_j M_j}{\sum_{j \in g} M_j} \qquad (2.3)$$

where M_j is the value of imports of good j and D_j is as defined for the frequency index. Like the frequency index, the coverage ratio takes values between 0 and 100.

Problem 2.2:   Values of F_g and C_g will normally differ but can be equal under certain circumstances. Determine the conditions under which F_g is greater, less than, or equal to C_g and then use these conditions to offer an interpretation for the differences in these measures as presented in Table 2.7 and Table 2.8.

Table 2.7 and Table 2.8 show values of the frequency and coverage indices for a sample of countries and products in 1966 and 1986. Table 2.7 confirms the increased use of NTBs over this time period. For example, the frequency index indicates that the number of products affected by one or more NTBs rose, on average, 43% in EC countries, by 16% in Japan, and by 30% in the United States. In 1986, France had the highest incidence of NTBs while Norway had the lowest.

Table 2.8 provides an indication of the commodity groups that account for most of the general increase in NTBs evident in Table 2.7. In this regard, NTBs to trade in agriculture and textiles represent a significant fraction of all NTBs. As noted earlier, this partly reflects that GATT rules prior to 1994 did not encompass the trade in such products. Finally, measures of the extent of NTBs applied by developing countries (not shown) show patterns similar to those of developed countries both in terms of the increased incidence of NTBs and products most affected.

Table 2.7 *Prevalence of NTBs, selected countries, 1966 and 1986[a]*

Country	Frequency index		Coverage ratio	
	1966	*1986*	*1966*	*1986*
EC	15	58	21	54
Belgium–Lux.	19	61	31	74
Denmark	11	54	5	37
France	17	66	16	82
Germany	16	60	24	41
Greece	NA	49	NA	26
Ireland	NA	47	2[b]	39
Italy	13	62	27	30
Netherlands	19	59	31	78
UK	10	52	16	38
Finland	NA	41	15[b]	51
Japan	34	50	31	43
Norway	14	30	31	23
Switzerland	12	42	19	50
USA	27	57	36	45

Notes:

[a] Covers imports from all sources in SITC 0–8.

[b] Barriers on food excluded.

Sources: Walter (1972), Laird and Yeats (1990a).

Export promotion

Accompanying the rise in NTB restrictions on imports has also been an increase in measures that instead promote exports. These measures include direct export subsidies and other types of export support programs. Like NTBs, the often opaque nature of export promotion measures results in their becoming a source of trade friction. Export promotion measures in particular raise tensions because they are seen by non-subsidized exporters as devices which constitute 'unfair' trade practices and also result in visible output and employment reductions in non-subsidizing countries. Chapters 5 and 11 consider the pros and cons of export promotion measures in greater detail.

Since its inception, the GATT has explicitly prohibited the use of export subsidies, that is subsidies contingent on export performance. However, not until 1994 was the term 'subsidy' actually defined in the GATT.[14] Pre-1994, the issue of what constituted an export subsidy, apart from overt and direct payments to exporters, was therefore open to interpretation and hence dispute. If a subsidy to exports is deemed to exist, the GATT permits

Table 2.8 *Prevalence of developed country NTBs applied on imports, developed and developing countries, 1984[a]*

	Imports from			
	Developed countries		Developing countries	
Product group	*Frequency*	*Coverage*	*Frequency*	*Coverage*
Agriculture	42	44	35	33
Fuels & ores	13	18	11	10
Industrial	7	14	18	21
Textiles	20	25	58	62
Iron & steel	21	50	21	46
Footwear	14	2	14	4
Electrical machinery	5	10	8	7
Motor vehicles	6	30	10	3
All items	11	17	21	19

Note:
[a] Includes only 'hard core' NTBs (e.g. import quotas, VERs, decreed export prices).
Source: Finger and Olechowski (1987).

member countries to 'countervail' (offset) the price reducing effect of the subsidy by assessing a countervailing duty on imports of the subsidized product. This *administered* (sanctioned) increase in protection, which comes in response to the trade policy of another country, is referred to as *contingent protection*.[15] Prior to 1994, countries routinely charged that other countries were subsidizing exports and, in response, the accusing countries countervailed the perceived subsidies. However, lacking a definition of a subsidy, the method used to determine the appropriate magnitude of the countervailing duty was equally vague and hence also contentious. The GATT now contains specific rules and procedures for determining the subsidy rate and hence also the amount of the countervailing duty, and it also delineates the kinds of subsidies that are actionable (see Section 2.2.).

Four commonly used export support programs are: subsidized export insurance, subsidized supplier credits, subsidized buyer credits, and official development assistance (ODA).[16] The specifics of each program differ, but all share the goal of increasing the net revenue of exporting firms by either lowering the firm's costs or increasing the demand for its output.

Subsidized export insurance involves the home government underwriting all or a part of the cost of insurance that a exporting firm buys. In so doing, it guarantees the exporter's receipts in domestic currency and hence eliminates a source of uncertainty at no cost to the exporting firm. Subsidized seller credits (also called 'soft' loans) are loans a government grants the private sector at terms more favorable than those available in private capital markets. This effectively reduces the exporter's marginal cost. In contrast, subsidized buyer credits provide the foreign importer with more favorable financing than the exporter could provide. This effectively raises the demand facing exporters. Finally, when giving ODA, the donor country can stipulate that the recipient must purchase goods from donor country firms equal in value to the amount of the aid.[17]

Table 2.9 provides an indication of the importance of such export promotion programs by showing the subsidy element (as a percentage of non-EC exports) associated with the export credit programs of Belgium, France and the United Kingdom over the period 1978–84. Whereas France's export promotion is the more substantial, the importance of export credit subsides increased in all three countries over the period.

Table 2.10 provides further information by showing the distribution of export credit subsidies across industry sectors in France and the United Kingdom. These data indicate considerable inter-industry variation in the use of export credits.

Despite the apparent growth in export credit subsidies, export programs in general remain a small fraction of the total subsidies granted to both industry and agriculture.[18] As noted, GATT prohibitions against overt export subsidies have been one factor limiting the size of export promotion schemes. However, various government policies can indirectly affect the costs of exporting firms including soft loans, direct government participation, expenditure on R&D, and the financing of declining industries. One indication of the extent of such overall government aid is provided in Table 2.11.

Table 2.9   *Export credit subsidies,[a] 1978–84*

Year	Belgium	France	United Kingdom
1978	0.2	2.9	0.6
1979	0.3	2.8	0.9
1980	0.2	4.2	1.3
1981	0.3	5.1	1.7
1982	0.4	5.1	1.7
1983	0.4	3.8	1.0
1984	0.5	3.0	1.1

Note:
[a] Subsidies as % of total exports to non-EC countries.
Sources: Melitz and Messerlin (1987); Abraham (1990).

Table 2.10   *Industry export credit subsidies, France and the United Kingdom, 1981–4*

Country	Industry category	Subsidy coverage[a]
France	Non-electrical machinery	11.4
	Metal products	9.9
	Services	9.0
	Electrical equipment	8.1
	Automobiles	5.1
	Aircraft & ships	4.0
	Construction	4.0
	Iron & steel	2.5
	Petroleum products	2.3
	Agro-industry	1.9
	Rubber and plastic	1.5
UK	Transport equipment	4.2
	Construction & services	3.1
	Engineering	2.9
	Electricity & gas	2.7
	Motor vehicles	2.5
	Office machinery	1.5
	Metal products	1.0
	Electrical equipment	0.8

Note:

[a] Subsidies as % of non-OECD exports, except for electrical equipment and aircraft & ships for France, electrical & transport equipment for United Kingdom where exports are non-EC exports. For France, figures are the average over 1981–4; for the United Kingdom figures are the average over 1982–4.

Source: Melitz and Messerlin (1987).

2.2 Administered protection

Reference was made throughout Section 2.1 to the rules (disciplines) of the World Trade Organization (WTO) and the General Agreement on Tariffs and Trade (GATT) regarding the use of trade policy instruments by WTO member countries. Important is that these rules do not prohibit WTO member countries from imposing trade restrictions. Rather, these rules define the scope of such restrictions and a framework for consistent implementation, that is, for the administration of protection – hence the term *administered protection*. This section discusses the WTO and its key agreements in more detail.

Table 2.11 *Overall direct and indirect government support to domestic industries, 1985*

Country	Government support[a] in		Government financed R&D expenditures[c]
	Industry	*Agriculture*	
EC			
Belgium	12.7	7.3	na
Denmark	3.8	8.0	na
France	7.8	12.1	23.8
Germany	6.2	9.8	15.3
Ireland	13.6	13.2	na
Italy	17.4	8.6	16.9
Luxembourg	16.0	12.0	na
Netherlands	4.8	7.2	na
UK	4.6	14.1	23.0
Canada (1985)	2.6[b]	0.8[b]	10.9
USA (1986)	0.5[b]	5.5[b]	33.9
Japan (1985)	1.0[b]	5.1[b]	1.6

Notes:

na = not available.

[a] As % of sector GDP at market prices. For EC countries, support excluding supranational aid, 1981–6.

[b] Measures obtained via the national accounts, substantial underestimates.

[c] As % of total R&D expenditure; covers all industries in 1985.

Sources: Commission of the European Communities (1989); OECD, *Annual National Accounts*; OECD/STIID Data Bank for R&D expenditure.

The World Trade Organization (WTO)

The WTO, established in January 1995, is one of the key outcomes of the 1986–94 Uruguay Round of multilateral trade negotiations. The primary responsibilities of the WTO are: (1) to provide a forum for multilateral trade negotiations and a framework for their implementation; (2) to administer the Trade Policy Review Mechanism (TPRM); (3) to administer the Dispute Settlement Procedures (DSPs).

Prior to the establishment of the WTO, the GATT was the only multilateral framework for administered protection. The latter now represents one of several agreements administered by the WTO (see Figure 2.1). In particular, the Uruguay Round gave rise to two new multilateral agreements: the General Agreement on Trade in Services (GATS) and the Agreement on Trade-related Aspects of Intellectual Property Rights (TRIPs). These

Figure 2.1   *The WTO*

agreements cover forms of trade and also issues previously outside the scope of the GATT. In addition, there are four plurilateral agreements covering government procurement, trade in civil aircraft, trade in bovine meat and trade in dairy products. A plurilateral agreement is binding only on countries that sign the agreement. In contrast, multilateral agreements such as the GATT are binding on all countries who agree to become members of the WTO.

The TPRM is both a function and a set of procedures whereby the WTO monitors the trade policies of member countries. To this end, two reports are prepared; one by the WTO staff and one by the member country being reviewed. The reports detail the country's trade policies and provide an evaluation of these policies from an economic perspective. The stated intent of these reports is to maintain transparency in the formulation and implementation of trade policies by providing a mechanism for multilateral surveillance of member countries' trade practices.[19]

The Dispute Settlement function is a set of procedures that detail how a WTO member can initiate a complaint against the trade practices of another member and how this dispute is to be processed and ultimately resolved. Dispute settlement is discussed below as part of a more general discussion of the GATT.

The General Agreement on Tariffs and Trade (GATT)

The GATT is the cornerstone agreement of the WTO. First signed in October 1947, the GATT was initially intended as an interim measure until a formal institutional body, the International Trade Organization (ITO), could be established. However, by the early 1950s, GATT members had failed to ratify an ITO charter and the GATT became the only formal statement of rules for administered protection. It is important to note that the GATT is only an agreement, not an institution. Prior to the establishment of the WTO, all monitoring and administration of the GATT was the responsibility of a small Secretariat based in Geneva. The WTO supplants this Secretariat and provides the formal institutional foundation for the GATT and other trade agreements. In recognition of this (and other) changes, the pre-WTO GATT is denoted GATT 1947 and the post-WTO GATT is denoted GATT 1994.

One function of the GATT (now WTO) is to provide a forum (i.e. a market) where countries can negotiate (i.e. exchange) reductions in their trade barriers; these fora are called multilateral trade negotiations and each such forum is called a 'round'. When GATT 1947 was first negotiated most of the significant trade barriers were tariffs. The GATT's Articles of Agreement therefore establish procedures for negotiating tariff reductions (*concessions*) among member countries and they delineate the rights and duties of member countries regarding these concessions. Once member countries agree on concessions these concessions become 'bound'. 'Binding' a tariff rate means that no country can unilaterally increase that rate. As noted in Section 2.1, a bound tariff rate is a maximum rate that applies to all WTO members. However, the GATT does permit a country, under prescribed rules, to re-negotiate a previously bound rate. It also permits, under certain conditions (see safeguards on p. 64 below), a country to raise its tariff above the bound rate; but the country must then compensate the exporters harmed by its action.

Key principles

Two key principles underlying the GATT (and all multilateral agreements now forged by the WTO) are that of nondiscrimination (Article I) and national treatment (Article III). The nondiscrimination or 'Most-Favored-Nation' (MFN) principle requires WTO member countries to treat products imported from different trading partners on the same basis.[20] The GATT does permit exceptions to MFN treatment. For example, customs unions are allowed as are certain historically recognized preferential trade relationships. In addition, developing countries may be granted tariff preferences under what is known as the Generalized System of Preferences (GSP).

National treatment requires that foreign goods, once inside the border of a country, be treated the same as domestically produced goods. One implication of national treatment is that trade barriers are only to be applied at the border; domestic policies should not therefore become barriers to trade. National treatment serves to limit the use of domestic policies to restrict trade and permits countries to more easily identify the trade barriers that may need to be overcome.

Tariffication and tariff reductions

An important function of the WTO is to facilitate reductions in trade barriers among its members. To this end, WTO members are required, when specified, to convert any NTB to trade into its *ad valorem* equivalent, a process called *tariffication*. The purpose of tariffication is to make the level of protection afforded by NTBs transparent, and also comparable to tariff rates, for the ultimate purpose of negotiating their reduction. As noted previously, negotiated reductions in trade barriers are conducted during 'rounds' of multilateral trade negotiations.

Since 1947 there have been eight rounds of multilateral tariff negotiations (see Table 2.12). The first five rounds, held between 1947 and 1962, were enormously successful in reducing tariffs. The sixth round (1964–7), known as the *Kennedy Round*, was important for two reasons. First, negotiators addressed both tariff barriers and NTBs and also trade in agriculture goods. Second, bargaining was for across-the-board reductions on all product categories; previous rounds had instead involved only bilateral negotiations on a product by product basis. In the end, little agreement was reached in the areas of agriculture and NTBs (with the EC ultimately strengthening its Common Agricultural Policy or CAP), but tariffs on manufactured goods were cut by an average of one-third. These tariff cuts reduced the average tariff level of most industrialized countries to under 7%.

Table 2.12   *Average tariff reductions under GATT, 1934–94*

GATT rounds	Average tariff reduction	Remaining tariffs as % of 1930 tariffs
Pre-GATT, 1934–47	32.2%	66.8
First Round, 1947	21.1	52.7
Second Round, 1949	1.9	51.7
Third Round, 1950–1	3.0	50.1
Fourth Round, 1955–6	3.5	48.9
Dillion Round, 1961–2	2.4	47.7
Kennedy Round, 1964–7	36.0	30.5
Tokyo Round, 1974–9	29.6	21.2
Uruguay Round, 1986–94	30.0	14.8

Source: Lavergne (1981), augmented to include Uruguay Round.

Failure during the Kennedy Round to mould agreement in the areas of agriculture and NTBs, and the emergence of certain developing countries as significant exporters of manufactured goods resulted in these issues being at the forefront of the subsequent Tokyo Round (1974–9). The Tokyo Round achieved an additional one-third cut in tariffs but failed to successfully address the issues of agricultural trade and the participation of developing countries in GATT disciplines. NTBs received substantial attention, and 'codes of conduct' were adopted covering areas such as subsidies, counter-vailing and anti-dumping duties, health and safety regulations, import licensing procedures, government procurement, customs valuation and safeguards. However, these codes were plurilateral rather than multilateral, and hence binding only on members that signed the code (only about 1-third of the members signed and most were developed countries).

The Uruguay Round, launched in 1986 and concluded on 15 April 1994, dealt seriously with many of the issues addressed but left unfinished in the Tokyo Round. This latest round reached agreements in a number of areas, many of which have already been noted. These included: an additional one-third reduction in tariffs; the extension of GATT disciplines to cover trade in all goods, not just manufactured products, and in particular, agricultural and textile products; the phase-out of the Multi-Fiber Arrangement (MFA) governing trade in textiles;[21] improved rules on the use of temporary import restrictions (see safeguards, p. 64); restraint on the use of subsidies and clearer rules on countervailing duties (see p. 65); tariffication of quantitative restrictions; extension of GATT rules to cover trade in services (the GATS); development of rules to remove adverse trade impacts of investment or 'right-of-establishment' rules,[22] counterfeiting and intellectual property (TRIPs); and finally, institutional reforms, most notably strengthening of the GATT's dispute settlement capabilities and replacement of the GATT Secretariat with the World Trade Organization (WTO). Many of the Uruguay Round agreements were more extensive versions of the Tokyo Round codes. It is important, however, that the Uruguay Round agreements derived from these codes apply to all WTO members – thereby raising them from plurilateral to multilateral status. The Uruguay Round agreements therefore signalled a commitment by WTO members to reverse the trend toward unilateralism and the unequal treatment of trading partners that occurred during the 1970s and 1980s.

Dispute settlement

An important function of the GATT is the administration of a dispute settlement process. The importance of a dispute settlement process is that it makes the commitments of member countries regarding tariffs or other agreements enforceable.

During the turbulent 1970s and 1980s, the dispute settlement process specified in GATT 1947 was found to be both time consuming and weak. Disputes were first addressed by a panel of independent experts whose findings were then submitted to the GATT's governing council (i.e. all GATT members) and a consensus of members was required before the panel's recommendations could be implemented. If the offending country chose not to implement the findings of the panel, the country bringing the complaint could then ask the council for permission to retaliate. Such authorization again required a consensus of all GATT members. The entire process could therefore be blocked at two stages by either one of the parties involved in the dispute. In addition, the process was slow and its outcome highly uncertain. In practice, most disputes were settled before reaching the final stages.

Although cumbersome, the GATT 1947 dispute settlement process was generally successful until the 1970s. Thereafter, globalization and rapid changes in trade exposed a number of weaknesses in the process. One major failure was the inability of the system to deal with trade in politically sensitive sectors such as agriculture which were not covered by GATT 1947. The prolonged nature of the dispute process and the uncertainty of enforcement led to growing impatience with the entire system. Whereas delays did permit issues to settle, many countries simply became unwilling to endure the process and often initiated retaliatory steps before receiving approval by the GATT council. The multilateral system of rules was in danger of collapse.

The Uruguay Round significantly overhauled and strengthened the GATT's dispute settlement process, thereby addressing many of the earlier frustrations. Under GATT 1994 it is now impossible for either party in a dispute to block an inquiry. In addition, the entire process has been streamlined and is subject to standard terms of reference (i.e. consistent and clear rules). An exact timetable for the completion of each procedural step is given. Assisting the repair of the dispute settlement process is that GATT 1994 disciplines cover trade in all goods. Hence, the process can now be used to address disputes arising over the trade in any good, not just manu-factured goods.

Safeguards

Safeguards constitute a safety valve for the world trading system. As trade patterns change, a country may wish to temporarily alter its bound commitments in order to protect domestic sectors threatened by injurious import competition. To this end, the safeguards provisions of the GATT allow a member to withdraw a bound concession under certain circumstances. For example, a country can impose temporary import restrictions to give an industry time to adjust when it is 'seriously injured' by a rapid increase in imports. A country can also restrict all its imports to deal with a serious balance of payments deficit and it can restrict imports that threaten public safety, health, morals, the environment, the general public welfare or national security.

The stated intent of safeguards is to facilitate trade liberalization by allowing countries to impose *temporary* trade barriers, on a non-discriminatory basis, in order to protect producers seriously injured by trade liberalization. GATT 1994 prohibits the use of VERs, orderly marketing arrangements or any other similar measure on the import or export side as a means of implementing protection under a safeguards provision. But despite this prohibition, GATT 1994 does permit an importing country seeking protection via a safeguards action to use a quantitative restriction (QR), and this restriction can take the form of a quota imposed by exporters (i.e. an export quota) if mutually agreed between the importer and all affected exporters. The resolution of this seeming contradiction concerning the legal use of quotas is that, under GATT 1994, any quota must be global, that is, non-discriminatory. Hence, while VERs are prohibited under GATT 1994, VER-like actions are permitted if they are applied on a multilateral basis.[23]

Restrictions imposed under a safeguards provision can last at most eight years; four years initially but then extendible for another four years if injury persists and the domestic industry can demonstrate that it is adjusting. During the first three years the importing country is not required to compensate affected exports for its actions, but if the restriction is continued beyond three years affected exporters can demand compensation.

Anti-dumping and countervailing duties

The safeguards provisions in the GATT also address so-called 'unfair' trade practices, notably dumping and government subsidies. To counter such practices, countries have the right to impose countervailing duties equal to the margin of dumping or the subsidy rate. In principle, these countervailing duties neutralize the effect of the offending practice.

Under GATT 1994, dumping is defined as the sale for export at prices below normal value. 'Normal value' is the comparable price of the like product in the exporting country or, in the absence of such a price, the comparable price for export to any third country or the cost of production in the country of origin *plus* a reasonable addition for selling cost and profit.[24] The difference between the export price and normal value is the margin of dumping. The computed margin of dumping must exceed 2% to be actionable.

An importing country is permitted to levy an anti-dumping duty against the product of an offending exporter(s) if and only if the dumped imports cause, or are likely to cause, injury to the domestic industry or to retard the establishment of a domestic industry.[25] Only injury to producers of like goods is relevant.[26]

Prior to GATT 1994, anti-dumping procedures were often suspended or terminated if the offending exporter satisfied authorities in the importing country that the injurious effect of the dumping was eliminated. Evidence of this could be a commitment to revise export prices upward or to limit export volumes. Such settlements were common under GATT 1947 but, as noted above, GATT 1994 now generally prohibits the use of such discriminatory (e.g. bilateral) export price or export volume restraints to resolve an anti-dumping dispute; a multilateral measure must instead be imposed. GATT 1994 now also clarifies the procedures that national agencies are to follow to determine if dumping has occurred and, if so, the margin of dumping.[27]

Unlike anti-dumping duties, countervailing duties are aimed at the actions of foreign governments rather than of foreign firms. Under GATT 1994, only specific subsidies (i.e. those targeted at specific firms, industries or regions, or to specific activities) can be countervailed. In this context, GATT 1994 distinguishes three classes of subsidies: prohibited, non-actionable and actionable. Prohibited subsidies are those based on export performance (i.e. export subsidies) and those providing incentives to use locally made goods in preference to imports (i.e. local content requirements). Non-actionable subsidies include certain forms of assistance to R&D as well as aid facilitating the adjustment of firms to new environmental standards. 'Actionable subsidies' are subsidies that are permitted but, if they create adverse affects on the trade of a WTO member, can be countervailed at a rate not to exceed the determined subsidy rate. In any case, a countervailing duty can be imposed if and only if the subsidy is determined to cause injury to the domestic industry. Under GATT 1994, countervailing and anti-dumping duties lapse after five years.

It should be noted that the above GATT 1994 rules apply only to subsidies on non-agricultural goods. Agricultural subsidies are instead addressed in the Agreement on Agriculture which requires countries to reduce domestic support to agriculture as measured by the Aggregate Measure of Support (AMS) which includes domestic and border support. The Uruguay Round agreements called for a reduction in the AMS of 20% over its 1986–88 base period. Export subsidies to agriculture are to be reduced by 36% in value terms from a 1986–90 base. The subsidy reductions apply on a product by product basis while the AMS restrictions apply only on an industry-wide basis.

Regional trade agreements (RTAs)

Regional trade agreements (RTAs) such as customs unions and free trade areas are fundamentally at odds with the MFN principle underlying the GATT.[28] However, the GATT does allow such RTAs subject to certain conditions: (1) the trade restrictions against non-RTA members must not rise on average; (2) the agreement must eliminate all duties and other restrictions to trade between RTA members on 'almost all' products that originate from RTA members; (3) the elimination of trade barriers between prospective RTA members must occur within a reasonable length of time (presently less than ten years). If these and other requirements are met then WTO members can, by unanimous agreement, sanction the RTA. In practice, WTO enforcement of the GATT's RTA requirements has been relatively weak. One reason for this was the decision of GATT members during the late 1950s to not closely examine the agreements contained in the Treaty of Rome which established the EC. This precedent has resulted in subsequent RTAs being largely tolerated for political reasons.

Under GATT rules, if prospective RTA members seek to increase bound rates in order to establish a common tariff boundary around RTA members then they must compensate RTA non-members. If agreement cannot be reached regarding compensation the GATT permits RTA non-member countries to retaliate against RTA members.

General Agreement on Trade in Services (GATS)

Since the mid-1980s, trade in services has continued to grow and is, by some measures, becoming a sizable fraction of all trade flows. The growing importance of trade in services has led many (services exporting) countries to consider it their interest to develop rules and procedures regarding such trade. To this end, the GATS sets forth a set of general principles and rules that apply to measures affecting trade in services. The GATS incorporates the MFN and national treatment principles although, as under GATT, exceptions are permitted. The agreement prohibits, in principle, certain market access restrictions, namely, limitations on (1) the number of suppliers, (2) the value of transactions or assets, (3) the total quantity of service output, (4) the number of natural persons that may be employed, (5) the type of legal entity through which a service supplier is permitted to supply a service, (6) the share of equity ownership of a foreign investor or the absolute value of the foreign investment. In addition to these prohibitions, the GATS contains a number of sector specific rules dealing with modes of market conduct and rights of establishment.

General Agreement on Trade-related Intellectual Property Rights (TRIPs)

While tailored to recognize many of the unique characteristics of services, the GATS remains close to its GATT roots in terms of general principles and, in addition, there is no attempt to harmonize trade policies across countries. In contrast, the TRIPs agreement seeks uniformity by establishing minimum standards of intellectual property protection that must be achieved by all member countries. The TRIPs does not state how each government should enforce these minimum standards, but by specifying minimum standards the agreement does require countries to take positive action to protect intellectual property. This requirement for action is in sharp contrast to the GATT and GATS since these do not require governments to undertake a specific policy but instead simply constrain governments regarding the types of policies they can pursue.

Like its sister agreements, the TRIPs adopts the MFN and national treatment principles but also permits exceptions. Regarding the protection of intellectual property, the obligations specify minimum periods of protection in areas such as trademarks, industrial designs, copyright and patents, and that criminal procedures and penalties are to be applied to copyright abuses if these are on a commercial scale. The agreement also contains specific provisions dealing with the application of competition law to intellectual property protection, and it specifies in detail the procedures to be followed for enforcement and dispute settlement.

2.3 Concluding remarks

Countries use a variety of trade policy instruments to restrict or promote their trade. *Ad valorem* tariffs are the preferred, and also the predominant, instrument used to restrict trade. Other trade restricting instruments, called non-tariff barriers (NTBs), are also used and can take a variety of forms, the most common being quantitative restrictions (QRs) in the form of export and import quotas. The promotion of exports is commonly effected through the use of subsidies. However, most countries have agreed to prohibit direct export subsidies and hence indirect subsidies are the most common form of export promotion.

Members of the World Trade Organization (WTO) agree to limit their choice of trade policy instruments and to follow prescribed rules (disciplines) in the application of these instruments. They further agree to reduce trade barriers among themselves. WTO rules are for the most part contained in a set of multilateral agreements, the most important being the

General Agreement on Tariffs and Trade (GATT). First signed in 1947, the GATT underwent a number of transformations during the Uruguay Round of multilateral trade negotiations which concluded in 1994. These changes were significant enough to distinguish the revised GATT from the original GATT. The latter is now called GATT 1947 and the new, revised GATT is called GATT 1994.

By the late 1980s, the multilateral system of rules for the administration of protection was in jeopardy due to widespread and growing use of NTBs and a failure of GATT 1947 to address many of the disputes that arose between countries. In large measure, this failure resulted from the fact that GATT 1947 disciplines applied only to trade in manufactured goods. As an outcome of the Uruguay Round, GATT disciplines now cover trade in all goods. In addition, the system of NTBs, and the unilateral and bilateral protectionist measures built up during the 1970s and 1980s, are being dismantled. WTO members have therefore resolved to continue and strengthen the multilateral framework of administered protection.

Notes

1. Detailed treatment of the economic effects of trade policy instruments appears in Chapters 5 and 10.
2. These are the main multilateral agreements covering trade. See Section 2.2 for further discussion.
3. The WTO was established as part of the Uruguay Round of multilateral trade negotiations which concluded in 1994. The round also significantly revised the GATT. See Section 2.2 for details.
4. Specific rates are therefore easier to administer since customs officials do not need to know the value of a good in order to determine the amount of duty. Also, there is little scope for customs officials to inflate the amount of duty by setting an arbitrary value on the product.
5. Until recently, the product classification system for tariffs was the Brussels Tariff Nomenclature (BTN) and the Customs Cooperation Council Nomenclature (CCCN). The current system is the Harmonized Commodity Description and Coding System (the 'Harmonized System') which provides greater product detail and the flexibility to easily incorporate new products. The design of a product classification is crucial to avoid misclassification and hence inaccurate application of duties by customs officials.
6. The computation of tariff averages is particularly important for the calculation of the welfare effects of tariffs. See Chapter 5 and also the articles by Leamer (1974), Anderson (1994) and Anderson and Neary (1994).
7. For example, a good subject to a prohibitive tariff, that is, one that eliminates all imports of the good, receives zero weight in the average.
8. However, the extent of non-tariff barriers (NTBs) has been found to be roughly similar in developed and developing countries.

9. As discussed in Section 2.2, a WTO member country can raise its bound rate but to do so it must justify the increase and it may also be required to compensate affected exporters.
10. This is not always the case since one also must account for how the license is obtained and at what cost. (See Chapters 5 and 10.)
11. This difficulty can be a virtue for the country adopting the NTB since it may permit the country to achieve a level of protection much higher than that suggested by its applied tariff rate.
12. Basic data for this purpose comes from the United Nations Council on Trade and Development (UNCTAD) which maintains an inventory of NTBs covering most developed economies and about eighty developing countries at the tariff-line level. These data consist of a brief description of the NTB and its coverage.
13. A category can be either a country's total imports or one of the product categories defined according to the SITC system.
14. A subsidy is now deemed to exist when there is a financial contribution by a government and a benefit is thereby conferred.
15. Another form of contingent protection is an anti-dumping duty. An importing country can assess this duty against foreign firms deemed to have 'dumped' their goods in the importing country's market. (See Section 2.2.)
16. Although export promotion measures receive widespread popular attention, they only affect a small number of industries which may, nonetheless, represent a sizable portion of a country's total import value.
17. Poor data has hampered empirical estimation of the effects of various export promotion schemes. Some progress in collecting consistent data has been made by the Commission of the European Communities and the European Free Trade Area (EFTA), but international comparisons remain difficult.
18. Export credit subsidies constitute the bulk of export assistance whereas subsidies on export insurance are of minor importance, at most 1% of total exports. The importance of 'tied' official development aid is more difficult to gauge, but available evidence suggests that it also is of minor importance.
19. Aside from increasing the demand for the services of international economists, these TPRM reports represent a new and important source of data on trade barriers.
20. MFN arose partly for practical reasons related to the method by which negotiations to reduce tariffs were initially conducted. Specifically, bargaining over concessions on individual products was conducted on a bilateral basis between an importing country and its largest supplier. Concessions achieved between these two parties were then made available on an 'unconditional MFN' basis to all other members.
21. The MFA involved a system of bilateral quotas between textile exporting and importing countries.
22. These are the so-called TRIMs – Trade Related Investment Measures.
23. However, the GATT does allow for selectivity in the application of a restriction if imports from some countries are shown to have increased 'disproportionately'. However, such discriminatory measures can be maintained for at most four years.

24. Revealing analyses of the administration of the US anti-dumping law are found in Boltuck and Litan (1991).
25 'Injury' is measured by such variables as the decline in production, market share, profits, capacity utilization.
26. Among the factors taken into account when making a determination of causality are the volume of dumped imports and the extent of price undercutting by exporters. National authorities are not required to balance such injury against the injury that the levying of an anti-dumping duty may cause to other industries or to consumers. A public interest standard, provided for in the law of some jurisdictions, is rarely invoked as a reason for lowering the anti-dumping rate below the margin of dumping.
27. A claim of dumping (or subsidization) against foreign exporters is first made by affected importers or exporters who petition their government to investigate their claim. If the government investigation determines that the claim has merit, the amount of the anti-dumping (or countervailing) duty is then determined and applied. In the case of EC member countries, all such work is undertaken by the European Commission. In Canada and the United States, an agency of the executive branch first establishes whether dumping or subsidization has occurred and also determines the appropriate anti-dumping or countervailing duty. Upon a positive finding, the case is then passed on to another body to resolve the question of whether the foreign action has in fact caused injury.
28. Chapter 12 discusses the theoretical implications of regional trade agreements.

References and additional reading

The WTO and GATT

Baldwin, R.E. (1991), 'The Uruguay Round and Beyond: Problems and Prospects', NBER, *Conference Report*.

Baldwin, R.E. (1995), 'An Economic Evaluation of the Uruguay Round Agreements,' *Annual Trade Review*, Clairmont–McKenna College.

Baldwin, R.E. and Richardson, J.D. (eds) (1988), 'Issues in the Uruguay Round', NBER, *Conference Report*.

Dam, K.W. (1970), *The GATT – Law and International Economic Organization* (Chicago: University of Chicago Press).

Deardorff, A.V. and Stern, R.M. (eds) (1994), *Analytical and Negotiating Issues in the Global Trading System* (Ann Arbor: University of Michigan Press).

GATT (1994), *The Results of the Uruguay Round of Multilateral Trade Negotiations* (November) (Geneva: GATT).

Hoekman, B. (1996), 'Trade Laws and Institutions: Good Practices and the World Trade Organization', *World Bank Discussion Paper*, 282 (Washington, DC: World Bank).

Jackson, J. (1969), *World Trade and the Law of the GATT* (Indianapolis: Bobbs-Merrill).

Jackson, J. (1989), *The World Trading System: Law and Policy of International Economic Relations* (Cambridge, Mass.: MIT Press).

Stern, R.M. (ed.) (1993), *The Multilateral Trading System: Analysis and Options for Change* (Ann Arbor: University of Michigan Press).

Tariff and non-tariff protection

Anderson, J.E. (1994), 'Tariff Index Theory', *Review of International Economics*, 3(2), 156–73.

Anderson, J.E. and Neary, J.P. (1994), 'Measuring the Restrictiveness of Trade Policy', *The World Bank Review*, 8, 151–70.

Balassa, B. (1965), 'Tariff Protection in Industrial Countries: An Evaluation', *Journal of Political Economy*, 73(6) (December), 573–94.

Balassa, B. and Balassa, C. (1984), 'Industrial Protection in the Developed Countries', *World Economy*, 7, 179–96.

Boltuck R. and Litan, R.L. (eds) (1991), *Down in the Dumps: Administration of the Unfair Trade Laws* (Washington, DC: Brookings Institution).

Finger, J.M. and Laird, S. (1987), 'Protection in Developed and Developing Countries: An Overview', *Journal of World Trade Law*, 21, 9–23.

Finger, J.M. and Olechowski, A. (1987), 'Trade Barriers: Who Does What to Whom', in Giersch, H. (ed.), *Free Trade in the World Economy* (Tübingen: J.C.B. Mohr), 37–71.

GATT (1991) *Trade Policy Review Mechanism, European Communities* (March) (Geneva: GATT).

Grossman, G. (1981), 'The Theory of Domestic Content Protection and Content Preference', *Quarterly Journal of Economics*, 96(4) (November) 583–603.

Laird, S. and Yeats, A. (1990a), 'Trends in Nontariff Barriers of Developed Countries, 1966–1986', *Weltwirtschaftliches Archiv*, 299–325.

Laird, S. and Yeats, A. (1990b), *Quantitative Methods for Trade Barrier Analysis* (Basingstoke: Macmillan).

Lavergne, R.P. (1981), 'The Political Economy of US Tariffs', PhD thesis, University of Toronto; partially reproduced in 'US Trade Policy Since World War II' in Baldwin, R.E. and Krueger, A.O. (eds), *The Structure and Evolution of Recent US Trade Policy* (Chicago: University of Chicago Press, 1984).

Leamer, E.E. (1974), 'Nominal Tariff Averages with Estimated Weights,' *Southern Economic Journal*, 41, 34–46.

Melitz, J. and Messerlin, P. (1987), 'Export Credit Subsidies', *Economic Policy*, OECD (April), 149–75.

Mussa, M. (1984), 'The Economics of Content Protection', *NBER Working Paper*, No. 1457.

Munk, B. (1969), 'The Welfare Costs of Content Protection: The Automobile Industry in Latin America', *Journal of Political Economy*, 77(1) (February), 85–98.

Nogués, J.J., Olechowski, A. and Winters, L.A. (1986), 'The Extent of Nontariff Barriers to Industrial Countries' Imports', *World Bank Economic Review*, 1, 181–99.

Schuknecht, L. (1992), *Trade Protection in the European Community* (Chur: Harwood Academic Publishers).

Walter, I. (1972), 'Nontariff Protection among Industrial Countries: Some Preliminary Evidence', *Economic Internazionale*, 25, 335–54.

Safeguards, export subsidies and dumping

Abraham, F. (1990), 'The Effects on IntraCommunity Competition of Export Subsidies to Third Countries: The Case of Export Credits, Export Insurance and Official Development Assistance', report prepared for the Commission of the European Communities.

Abraham, F., Couwenberg, I. and Dewit, G. (1991), 'Towards an EC Policy on Export Financing Subsidies: Lessons from the 1980s and Prospects for Future Reform', *International Economics Research Papers*, 77, Centrum voor Economische Studiën, Katholieke Universiteit Leuven.

Baldwin, R.E. (1992), 'Assessing the Fair Trade and Safeguards Laws in Terms of Modern Trade and Political Economy Analysis', *The World Economy*, 15, 185–202.

Commission of the European Communities (1989), *First Survey on State Aids in the European Community* (Luxembourg: Office for Official Publications of the European Communities).

Finger, J.M. (1993), *Antidumping: How it Works and Who Gets Hurt* (Ann Arbor: University of Michigan Press).

Ford, R. and Suyker, W. (1990), 'Industrial Subsidies in the OECD Economies', (Paris: OECD Department of Economics and Statistics).

Hindley, B. (1994), 'Safeguards, VERs and Antidumping Actions,' in OECD Documents, *The New World Trading System* (Paris: OECD), 91–103.

PART II

Competitive Markets: Trade and Trade Policy

■ *Chapter 3* ■

The Ricardian Framework

The edifice of international trade theory is constructed on the principle of comparative advantage. This basic principle, developed and proved by David Ricardo, is the fundamental explanation of the source of the benefits of specialization.

> Though an awareness of the benefits of specialization must go back to the dim mists of antiquity in all civilizations, it was not until Ricardo that this deepest and most beautiful result in all of economics was obtained. Though the logic applies equally to interpersonal, interfirm and interregional trade, it was in the context of international trade that the principle of comparative advantage was discovered and has been investigated ever since. (Findlay, 1988, p. 514).

Relying on his principle, Ricardo made the argument that trade between two countries of not too different size would be beneficial even if one has an absolute productive advantage (a lower price) in all goods. In the economic philosophical debate of that time, this principle was not only Ricardo's refutation of A. Smith's absolute efficiency as a determinant of trade but also his anti-mercantilist proof that trade could be beneficial for a nation.

This chapter investigates the principle of comparative advantage in various forms and relates it to international trade. In Section 3.1, the concept is first illustrated in a very elementary way, called the Ricardian example. In Section 3.2 the concept is formalized as the Ricardian model. This model is then used to determine the international equilibrium and to discuss the gains from trade. The remainder of the chapter discusses the implications of relaxing the main assumptions of the Ricardian model. In this regard, Section 3.3 focuses on international labor mobility and discusses how it relates to trade. Section 3.4 introduces the various concepts of scale economies and then looks at the pattern of trade and specialization when scale economies are external to the firm. Section 3.5 examines how comparative advantage operates when there is a continuum of goods and discusses the gains from trade in this context. Finally, Section 3.6 summarizes the basic Ricardian propositions and the empirical tests to which they have been subjected.

3.1 The principle of comparative cost advantage

To illustrate the principle of comparative advantage, Ricardo used the example reproduced in panel A of Table 3.1. Each entry in panel A is the constant unit labor requirement for producing either wine or cloth in England and Portugal. In this example, Portugal has an absolute advantage in the production of both goods since it requires only 80 labor years per-unit of wine and 90 labor years per-unit of cloth compared to 120 and 100 labor years in England respectively.

Table 3.1   *The Ricardian example*

A   Labor requirements per-unit of output

	Wine	*Cloth*
England	120	100
Portugal	80	90

B   Trade and efficient labor reallocation (changes in production)

	Wine	*Cloth*
England	−5	+6
Portugal	6.75	−6
	1.75	0

C   Trade and inefficient labor reallocation (changes in production)

	Wine	*Cloth*
England	+5	−6
Portugal	−5	4.44
	0	−1.56

Now consider the effect of allowing international trade on the pattern of production. England could decide to either decrease its production of wine and thereby release labor resources to produce more units of cloth, or conversely increase its production of wine and reduce its production of cloth. Panel B of Table 3.1 outlines the outcome of the former, panel C the latter. If England decreases its production of wine by 5 units, it releases 600 labor years that can be used to produce 6 additional units of cloth. If Portugal then imports these 6 units of cloth, the clothing industry in Portugal can release 540 labor years. Of these, only 400 are needed to compensate for the loss of 5 units of wine in England. Hence, the remaining 140 labor years represent the efficiency gain in world production due to the re-arrangement of production made possible by trade. With 140 labor years Portuguese workers can produce 1.75 additional units of wine (as in panel B), or 1.6 additional units of cloth or various combinations of both commodities (not shown). These gains could in turn be divided up such that Portugal and England could each benefit from trade between the two nations. This gain from trade can be exploited further until one of the following situations is met: the whole labor force in England specializes in cloth production, or the whole labor force in Portugal specializes in wine production or both. Panel C outlines the negative efficiency loss of specialization in the wrong commodities.

The pattern of trade and specialization just described can also be determined by comparing autarky market prices. If labor markets are competitive, the autarky wage rate in each country is unique. If goods markets are competitive, the relative price of cloth (c) and wine (w) in each country is then determined by the relative average cost of production. Using the data provided in panel A of Table 3.1 to compute the average costs of production we obtain the autarky prices: $(p_w/p_c)^P = 8/9$ and $(p_w/p_c)^E = 6/5$. Thus, in autarky, a unit of wine in Portugal exchanges for 8/9 of a unit of cloth, while in England a unit of wine exchanges for 6/5 of a unit of cloth. Since $6/5 > 8/9$, we say that England has a comparative advantage over Portugal in cloth relative to wine and, if trade takes place, England should export cloth and import wine. By inverting the inequality the converse holds as well. We can equivalently state that Portugal has a comparative advantage over England in wine versus cloth. Hence, comparative advantage is an explanation of how international trade can arise and it provides a basis for predicting the direction of such trade.

Nothing has been said so far about absolute costs. To see that these do not matter, refer back to panel A of Table 3.1 and assume that the pre-trade nominal wage in each country equals unity. Then if the exchange rate is also fixed at unity, wine and cloth will be cheaper in Portugal as it has lower labor requirements in both goods. When trade opens, Portuguese firms will be confronted with increased demand for both commodities and will try to hire more workers, thereby bidding up wages and thus costs. In England, international competition will cause English wages to fall as English firms lay off workers. If this process of wage adjustment persists long enough for the Portuguese wage to exceed that in England by more than 100/90, the price of English cloth will become cheaper than in Portugal and England will start producing and exporting cloth. The wage adjustment process will stop when trade balance equilibrium is reached. The resulting equilibrium pattern of trade will be the same as that obtained under the comparative cost analysis.

In contrast to the comparative cost analysis using relative prices, the analysis of nominal cost differences explains the path (in value terms) of adjustment towards the pattern of international specialization. Since the above held the exchange rate fixed, the full weight of the adjustment fell on wages. In practice, both wages and exchange rates contribute to the adjustment toward trade balance.

3.2 **The Ricardian model**

This section formalizes the preceding discussion to an analytical framework known as the Ricardian model. In its barest essentials, the Ricardian model rests on several assumptions.

(1) Two countries, denoted home and foreign (denoted by *).
(2) Two final products, good 1 and good 2.
(3) Each good uses only one input (labor) in production. Labor is homogeneous in quality.
(4) Labor is inelastically supplied in each country.
(5) Labor is perfectly mobile within each country but internationally immobile.
(6) Constant labor requirement per-unit of output. Let a_j and a_j^* be the quantity of home and foreign labor, respectively, required to produce one unit of good j ($j = 1, 2$). These requirements are invariant to the scale of production.
(7) Technologies differ between the two countries: $a_j \neq a_j^*$ ($j = 1, 2$).
(8) No cost of transportation, no trade barriers.
(9) Competition in factor and product markets.

The Ricardian model describes a static equilibrium and therefore assumes that the supply of resources in the economy is inelastic and that tastes and technology do not change.[1]

Production equilibrium

Denote the price of the second commodity in terms of the first by $p = p_2/p_1$. According to the above assumptions, the production function of the jth industry is:

$$q_j = (1/a_j)L_j, \qquad j = 1, 2 \tag{3.1}$$

where $(1/a_j)$ is the productivity of labor in industry j and L_j is the amount of labor employed in industry j. Since labor is assumed uniform in quality and costlessly mobile between sectors, the reward to labor is unique within the country. This, combined with the assumption of a competitive labor market, implies full employment of labor resources:

$$L_1 + L_2 = L \tag{3.2}$$

where L denotes the total labor supply. The substitution of (3.1) into (3.2) gives the economy's production possibility curve $T_1 T_2$ depicted in Figure 3.1:

$$q_1 = \frac{L}{a_1} - \frac{a_2}{a_1} q_2 \tag{3.3}$$

whose slope $(-a_2/a_1)$ is the negative of the ratio of labor requirements, or equivalently the negative of the ratio of labor productivities $(-1/a_1/1/a_2)$.

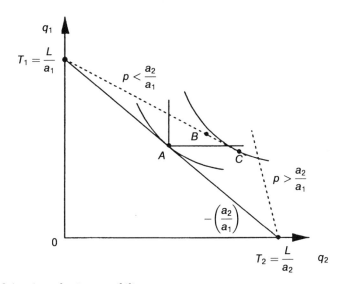

Figure 3.1 *A production possibility curve*

Depending on the relative commodity price there are three possible output configurations:

$$p = a_2/a_1 \quad \text{incomplete specialization on segment } T_1 T_2$$
$$p > a_2/a_1 \quad \text{complete specialization in good 2 at } T_2 \tag{3.4}$$
$$p < a_2/a_1 \quad \text{complete specialization in good 1 at } T_1$$

If the two commodities are produced in positive amounts, competitive forces will equate each commodity price to its average cost, $p_j = a_j w$. Since the wage rate is identical between sectors, the ratio of goods' prices $p = a_2/a_1$ is independent of the wage. Hence, if $p_2/p_1 > a_2 w/a_1 w$, then the relative value of one additional unit of good 2 is greater than the relative cost necessary to make it and firms would increase production of good 2 and reduce production of good 1. This process would continue until all labor is employed in sector 2. A similar reasoning applies if $p < a_2/a_1$.

Demand

Ricardo did not allow for consumer preferences to feature explicitly in the model. However, modern analysis incorporates traditional demand theory in the model in order to determine the world price and hence the trade equilibrium. In this regard, tastes of society are assumed to be represented by a set of social indifference curves, where each indifference curve depicts commodity combinations that yield a constant level of satisfaction to each member of society and society as a whole. The objective of the community is to reach the highest possible indifference curve given the constraint imposed by national income, analogous to the utility maximization problem of a representative consumer. In general, social indifference curves do not have the usual properties of an individual indifference curve. In particular, changing income distributions usually result in intersecting community indifference curves. However, efforts have been undertaken to salvage the concept by stating a set of assumptions which eliminates the problem of changing income distributions and thereby guarantees that a community indifference curve is just an aggregate version of an individual one.[2]

The problem of social preference maximization can be written:

$$\max_{d_1, d_2} U(d_1, d_2) \quad \text{s.t. } d_1 + p d_2 \leq Y \tag{3.5}$$

where d_j is the quantity demanded of the jth commodity ($j = 1, 2$), U represents the social utility function and Y is national income available to consumers. Note that Y is national income expressed in terms of product 1.

The first-order conditions for the above problem are $U_1(d_1, d_2) = \lambda$ and $U_2(d_1, d_2) = \lambda p$, where λ is the Lagrange multiplier and $U_j = \partial U / \partial d_j$ is the marginal utility of the jth commodity. These can be rearranged to give $U_2 / U_1 = p$. Translated into well known geometry, this condition states the tangency condition between the slope of an indifference curve and the budget line. The general solution to this maximization problem is that demand functions depend on prices and income: $d_j = d_j(Y, p)$.

Excess demand functions

In the present framework we are able to calculate the wage rate and consequently national income for the given labor supply and commodity prices. This is made more explicit in (3.12) and (3.13) below. As long as the labor endowment remains unchanged, relative commodity prices comprise all information needed to specify the demand functions and thus we are justified in writing:

$$d_j = d_j(p) \tag{3.6}$$

International equilibrium requires that world supply equals world demand for every commodity. In a 2-country 2-commodity world, this constraint is represented by the following two equations:

$$q_1(p) + q_1^*(p) = d_1(p) + d_1^*(p)$$

$$q_2(p) + q_2^*(p) = d_2(p) + d_2^*(p)$$

where starred variables indicate foreign country values. These equations can be rearranged to give:

$$[q_1(p) - d_1(p)] + [q_1^*(p) - d_1^*(p)] = 0 \tag{3.7}$$

$$[q_2(p) - d_2(p)] + [q_2^*(p) - d_2^*(p)] = 0 \tag{3.8}$$

The brackets in these equations enclose the positive or negative excess demands of the two countries for each of the two commodities. (3.7) and (3.8) contain only one argument, p. The system therefore appears to be overdetermined. However, (3.7) and (3.8) are not independent. Consider the consumer budget constraints:

$$(q_1 - d_1) + p(q_2 - d_2) = 0 \tag{3.9}$$

$$(q_1^* - d_1^*) + p(q_2^* - d_2^*) = 0 \tag{3.10}$$

These equations state that, for each country, the value of production equals the value of consumption or, put differently, that trade must be balanced in each country. Adding (3.9) to (3.10) gives:

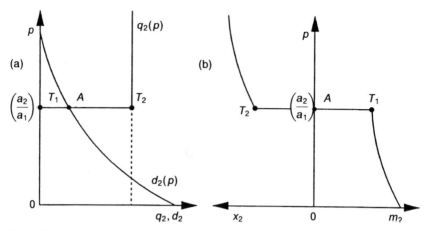

Figure 3.2   *Excess demand for good 2*

$$[(q_1 - d_1) + (q_1^* - d_1^*)] + p[(q_2 - d_2) + (q_2^* - d_2^*)] = 0 \qquad (3.11)$$

(3.11) is Walras' law with only two markets: when one of the markets is in equilibrium then by necessity the other market is also in equilibrium. Hence, it is sufficient to solve either (3.7) or (3.8) alone, since the solution to one equation necessarily implies that the other equation will also be satisfied.

Consider the market for the second commodity illustrated in Figure 3.2. By varying p we can generate the demand function $d_2 = d_2(p)$ and the supply function $q_2 = q_2(p)$ depicted in panel (a). The excess demand function for commodity 2 is derived as the difference between d_2 and q_2 for all values of p. The supply function of good 2, and hence the excess demand function, is not smooth everywhere and has two points of non-differentiability, T_1 and T_2. We know from earlier analysis that T_1 and T_2 correspond to the complete allocation of labor to sector 1 and sector 2, respectively. Autarky price is determined at point A and is therefore given by a_2/a_1. Below a_2/a_1 the home country imports commodity 2 in positive amounts ($m_2 = d_2 - q_2$) while above a_2/a_1 it is a net supplier of good 2 ($d_2 - q_2 < 0$) and will therefore export that good ($x_2 = q_2 - d_2$). The foreign excess demand can be obtained in a similar way.

International equilibrium

Figure 3.3 describes how to obtain the international equilibrium price p_w. From (3.8) equilibrium implies $d_2 - q_2 = q_2^* - d_2^*$. The equilibrium price ratio is therefore determined by the intersection of the excess demand curves of the two countries. Hence, there exists an equilibrium price p_w such that

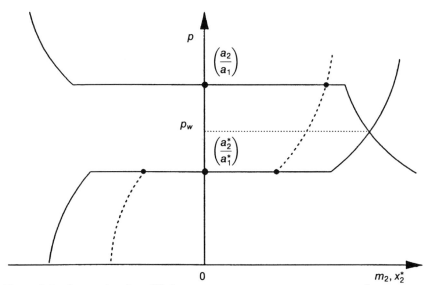

Figure 3.3 *International equilibrium*

the market for good 2 is cleared. At that price the domestic economy imports good 2 in exchange for its exports of good 1.

Implicitly, Figure 3.3 is constructed on the assumption that the home country has a comparative advantage in the first commodity. If one instead assumes that $a_2^*/a_1^* > a_2/a_1$ then the foreign excess demand curve is shifted upward such that the foreign autarky price lies above the domestic one. The international equilibrium is then found in the second quadrant where the second commodity is exported by the domestic economy. We have derived the following results relating to the pattern of trade.

Proposition 3.1 (Ricardo): A country exports that commodity in which it has a comparative labor-productivity advantage.

Proposition 3.2 (Mill): The international price ratio lies in the range spanned by the pre-trade price ratios of the two trading nations, that is $a_2/a_1 \geq p_w \geq a_2^*/a_1^*$ with strict inequality holding if relative country size is not great.

A corollary of the above theorems is that, with free trade, each country specializes completely in the good in which it has a comparative advantage. Mill's conclusion that the world price lies strictly between the pre-trade prices is not possible when the two trading nations are (1) identical in all respects, or (2) grossly unequal in size, The first case is trivial since it leaves no room for international trade. The equilibrium price would then be

$a_2/a_1 = p_w = a_2^*/a_1^*$ and countries would be indifferent between domestic production or trade. The second case is illustrated in Figure 3.3. If the foreign country is comparatively small with an excess demand curve given by the broken curve then the international equilibrium price would be that of the domestic country. As a consequence, the foreign partner realizes the maximum gain in its terms of trade (export price relative to import price). The domestic economy continues, however, to consume the same amount of both goods as before but its production mix changes to accommodate trade with the foreign country. Assuming that the world price lies between the autarky price ratios, trade leads each economy to completely specialize according to its comparative advantage. In the above example, home in good 1 and foreign in good 2.

Gains from trade

Having determined the pattern of international trade, there remains another classic question of trade theory: is international trade beneficial to both countries? Put differently, is it possible to show that the reallocation of labor resources as a result of trade allows each country to consume beyond the boundaries of its autarkic production possibility frontier and thereby reach a higher community indifference curve?

The gains from trade are illustrated in Figure 3.1. An economy benefits potentially from free trade if the relative world price differs from its autarkic level. In Figure 3.1, the equilibrium terms of trade are illustrated by the slope of the dashed line originating from T_1. Every possible autarkic consumption basket such as A is therefore dominated by a free trade consumption point such as B which allows consumption of more of both commodities. However, other free trade consumption patterns such as C could also take place where more of good 2 and less of good 1 than at B is preferred while satisfying the same budget constraint.

It turns out that the gains from trade can be conveniently broken down into gains from exchange and gains from specialization. This decomposition is illustrated in Figure 3.4. Point A represents the autarkic equilibrium and gives rise to the autarkic utility level u_a. Assume that, with free trade, the economy can trade at the international price p_w. Suppose for a moment that the economy cannot change its output. Production therefore remains at A but the decrease in the relative price of good 2 leads to the new consumption point B on a higher utility level u_b. The movement from A to B shows the gains from exchanging the autarky amounts produced. However, as the economy moves to the complete specialization point T_1, consumption takes place at C, showing a higher utility level u_w. The movement from B to C indicates the gains from increased specialization in production.

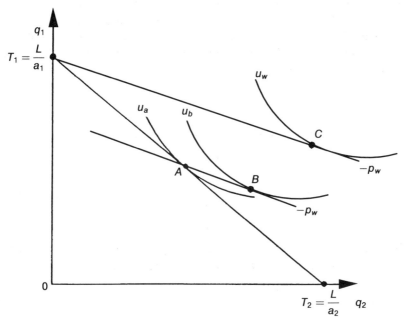

Figure 3.4 *Decomposition of the gains from trade*

Analytically the proof of the gains from trade is more complicated but offers an interesting application of the Ricardian model. A sufficient condition for the gains from trade is to see whether trade is beneficial to every individual in each country. A way to proceed is to look at the domestic and foreign real wages, i.e. the wage rates measured in terms of each good. If wages rise in terms of at least one commodity and do not decrease in terms of any other then one can conclude that both countries are better off by trade.

Consider the autarkic equilibrium of the home country and assume that the country spends a constant share α of its income on the first commodity.[3] Referring to (3.5), this would be the case if $U(\cdot)$ is of the Cobb–Douglas type in d_1 and d_2. On the production side, the domestic production functions are given by (3.1) and the labor resources by (3.2). It is easy to verify that the following is the unique autarky equilibrium if both goods are produced:

$$p_1^a = 1 \qquad p_2^a = \frac{a_2}{a_1} \qquad w^a = \frac{1}{a_1}$$

$$q_1^a = \frac{\alpha L}{a_1} \qquad q_2^a = \frac{(1-\alpha)L}{a_2} \qquad Y^a = \frac{L}{a_1} \qquad (3.12)$$

$$L_1^a = \alpha L \qquad L_2^a = (1-\alpha)L$$

Since the production structure is the same for the foreign country, a similar autarkic equilibrium is achieved with variables denoted by an asterisk.

Assume that tastes are identical for the two countries, $\alpha = \alpha^*$ and consider a trading equilibrium in which the two countries have labor forces L and L^*. Assuming that

$$\frac{a_2}{a_1} > \frac{a_2^*}{a_1^*}$$

we obtain the following solution for the trade equilibrium:

$$p_1 = 1 \qquad p_2 = \frac{a_2^*}{a_1} \frac{(1-\alpha)}{\alpha} \frac{L}{L^*} \qquad w = \frac{1}{a_1}$$

$$w^* = \frac{1}{a_1} \frac{(1-\alpha)}{\alpha} \frac{L}{L^*} \qquad q_1 = \frac{L}{a_1} \qquad q_2 = \frac{L^*}{a_2^*}$$

(3.13)

When trade opens, the equilibrium terms of trade are given by p_2/p_1 and will lie strictly between the cost ratios of the two countries if:

$$\frac{a_2}{a_1} > \frac{a_2^*}{a_1} \frac{(1-\alpha)}{\alpha} \frac{L}{L^*} > \frac{a_2^*}{a_1^*}$$

(3.14)

which simplifies to

$$\frac{a_2}{a_2^*} > \frac{(1-\alpha)}{\alpha} \frac{L}{L^*} > \frac{a_1}{a_1^*}$$

(3.15)

The inequality conditions (3.14) and (3.15) indicate the role of relative work forces (i.e. relative country size) and of consumer preferences in establishing the international equilibrium price ratio. For example, an absolute size effect (a larger L) or a strong preference for good 2 (a lower α) narrows the difference between the domestic autarky price and world price but enlarges the gap between the foreign autarky price and the same world price, and vice versa. As long as (3.15) is satisfied, each economy completely specializes according to its comparative advantage.

To determine if trade is beneficial we can compare the real wages in terms of both goods in autarky and in the trading equilibrium. Using (3.12) and (3.13), one sees that the home wage in terms of good 1 stays constant at $1/a_1$ while in terms of good 2 it is:

$$\frac{w^a}{p_2^a} = \frac{1}{a_2} \qquad \frac{w}{p_2} = \frac{1}{a_2^*} \frac{\alpha}{(1-\alpha)} \frac{L^*}{L}$$

In contrast, the foreign real wage is constant in terms of good 2 (equals $1/a_2^*$) but varies in terms of good 1:

$$\frac{w^{*a}}{p_1^{*a}} = \frac{1}{a_1^*} \qquad \frac{w^*}{p_1} = \frac{1}{a_1} \frac{(1-\alpha)}{\alpha} \frac{L}{L^*}$$

By comparing the real wages in terms of both goods in autarky and in the trading equilibrium, one sees that with trade real wages are not inferior in terms of both goods in the home and foreign country as long as:

$$\frac{1}{a_2^*} \frac{\alpha}{(1-\alpha)} \frac{L^*}{L} > \frac{1}{a_2} \quad \text{and} \quad \frac{1}{a_1} \frac{(1-\alpha)}{\alpha} \frac{L}{L^*} > \frac{1}{a_1^*}$$

which reduces to

$$\frac{a_2}{a_2^*} > \frac{(1-\alpha)}{\alpha} \frac{L}{L^*} > \frac{a_1}{a_1^*}$$

a condition equivalent to inequality (3.15) which determines the requirement for each country to have an improvement in its terms of trade. A difference in relative labor productivities between countries is therefore crucial to the conclusion that both countries gain from trade. Gains are likely to be greatest for trade between economies that are least similar in this regard. In addition, the closer is the world price to the foreign autarky price, the higher are the gains accruing to the domestic country and vice versa. Hence, any improvement in the relative price of home exports (home's terms of trade) increases home's benefits from trade at the expense of the foreign benefits.

Problem 3.1: Find the condition that guarantees that, at the uniquely determined world price ratio, world output of both commodities is greater with trade than its pre-trade level. Relate your answer to inequality (3.14).

Problem 3.2: Show the consequences on individual welfare of a pattern of production and trade where, because of, e.g. government intervention, countries completely specialize in the 'wrong' good.

Problem 3.3: Show that the consumption pattern can be a source of comparative advantage. A way to proceed is to assume $\alpha \neq \alpha^*$, and replace the technology of the Ricardian model described by (3.1) by fixed endowments of each commodity that are similar at home and abroad.

Problem 3.4: Consider the implications on the international equilibrium and country welfare of (1) increasing the foreign country's labor endowment and, (2) decreasing a_1^* and a_2^* in the same proportion (productivity growth). What are the benefits transferred to the other country?

3.3 International labor mobility

The international mobility of labor can be analyzed in the above framework by assuming that labor movement is permitted only after a trade equilibrium is achieved. This sequence of liberalization corresponds to what is generally observed in economic integration processes. Formally, it is interesting to see whether international trade leads to international wage equalization and, if not, to examine the ensuing migration flow that would establish it.

International wage inequality

Suppose a free trade equilibrium is attained at an international price lying strictly between the cost ratios of the two countries and that, as above, the home country completely specializes in good 1. Then the equilibrium wage is such that:

$$p_1 = a_1 w$$

while, in the foreign country,

$$p_2 = a_2^* w^*$$

Dividing these two equations gives:

$$\frac{w^*}{w} = \frac{(1/a_2^*)}{(1/a_1)} \frac{p_2}{p_1}$$

The ratio of foreign to home wage rates now depends on the ratio of foreign to home labor productivities and on the world relative price. The ratio w^*/w must rise if either p_2/p_1 or the ratio of labor productivities increases. Taking the ratio of w^* and w in (3.13) directly provides an alternative expression:

$$\frac{w^*}{w} = \frac{(1-\alpha)}{\alpha} \frac{L}{L^*} \tag{3.16}$$

(3.16) expresses w^*/w in terms of consumer preferences and the relative size of the domestic to foreign labor force: the ratio must rise as either α or L^* decreases as both changes lead to a rise in the world price of p_2. This indicates clearly that the international trade equilibrium achieved in the Ricardian model is not characterized by wage equalization, unless by a fluke. Since this wage difference would be expected to give rise to international labor migration, it explains why Ricardo assumed international labor immobility from the start.

Migration

If international labor mobility is now allowed, how much labor will flow across borders? Denoting labor migration into the foreign country as ΔL, the latter will be such that w^*/w in (3.16) equates to unity:

$$1 = \frac{(1 - \alpha)}{\alpha} \frac{(L - \Delta L)}{(L^* + \Delta L)}$$

A simple manipulation of this last expression using (3.16) gives:

$$\frac{\Delta L}{L} = \alpha \frac{L^*}{L} \frac{(w^* - w)}{w} \tag{3.17}$$

where the wage rates w^* and w are the pre-mobility equilibrium wage rates. By (3.17), migration as a proportion of the domestic labor force is a product of three terms: the wage gap, relative labor forces L^*/L, and α. With $w^* > w$, the ensuing labor movement to the foreign country ($\Delta L > 0$) causes production of good 2 to increase and that of good 1 to decrease, and a decline in the equilibrium price. According to (3.14) and the accompanying reasoning, this decline in p_2 represents a loss in foreign welfare, and a gain in domestic welfare, when compared to the pre-mobility equilibrium.

World production efficiency

Is the trading equilibrium described by (3.13) an efficient pattern of world production? That is, is the trading equilibrium of the preceding section such that it is impossible to increase the production of any good without reducing the output of the other good? The answer is trivially 'no', if one of the two countries enjoys lower absolute labor productivities. To show this, assume international labor mobility, and that $a_1^* < a_1$ and $a_2^* < a_2$, i.e. foreign labor is more productive in all industries. If the domestic country reduces its production of good 1 by 1 unit, it liberates a_1 units of labor. If the latter migrate abroad, they can produce $a_1/a_1^* > 1$ units of good 1. Clearly, this experiment can be repeated until all domestic labor moves abroad. The new equilibrium is one where all production takes place abroad and where labor mobility has substituted for trade. With migration, there is an increase in the world production of good 1 by $L(1/a_1^* - 1/a_1)$ and these gains are all reaped by migrated laborers who now earn the foreign wage $1/a_1^*$ compared to the pre-mobility wage $1/a_1$. Hence, world production with factor mobility (i.e. factors moving from low to high productivity countries) is more efficient than the trading equilibrium.

Empirical results

(3.17) is an often used framework for explaining migration flows. For example, in an attempt to explain migration from the United Kingdom between 1870 and 1913, Hatton (1995) obtained the following results:[4]

$$M_t = -3.49 + 9.85 \, \Delta\ln \left(\frac{w^*}{w}\right)_t + 6.97 \ln \left(\frac{w^*}{w}\right)_{t-1}$$
$$\quad\;\; (0.79) \;\; (1.91) \qquad\qquad (1.92)$$

$$+38.09 \, \Delta\ln L_t^* + 7.35 \, \Delta\ln L_t + 34.40 \ln L_{t-1}^* - 18.28 \ln L_{t-1}$$
$$\quad\; (2.54) \qquad\quad (1.00) \qquad\quad (3.03) \qquad\qquad (3.20)$$

$$+16.77 MST_t + 0.03 \, Time + 0.44 M_{t-1} \qquad\qquad\qquad (3.18)$$
$$\quad\; (0.63) \qquad\quad (0.78) \qquad\; (3.11)$$

$$\bar{R}^2 = 0.81 \qquad RSS = 22.36 \qquad LM(1) = 1.01$$

$$RESET = 6.02 \qquad HETERO = 0.34$$

where

    M_t = net migration rate per 1000 of population (net emigration from the United Kingdom divided through by the UK population)

    w, w^* = wage in the United Kingdom; weighted average of wages in the United States (weight of 1/2), Australia (weight of 1/4) and Canada (weight of 1/4)

    L, L^* = UK employment rate; foreign employment rate (constructed as w^*)

    MST = immigrant stock of United Kingdom born (thousands)

    $Time$ = time trend

It is clear from (3.18) that studies of migration patterns use variables other than wages, mainly to characterize the employment conditions in the country of origin and destination. The main reason for the inclusion of these variables lies in the recognition that, unlike in the Ricardian model, labor markets are imperfect because of, for example, built-in downward nominal wage rigidities. In this spirit, (3.18) includes the employment rates (a proxy for cyclical conditions), the stock of previous emigrants (one aspect of attractiveness of emigration), a time trend (a proxy for the fall in emigration costs) and a lagged dependent variable (the 'friends and relatives' effect).

(3.18) explains more than four-fifths of the variation in net emigration. It gives the expected signs on all variables except for the change in the UK employment rate which turns out positive. However, the lagged level term has the correct sign and is particularly strong. Setting the Δ's to zero and $M_t = M_{t-1}$ we obtain the steady state solution for M. From this, one can read the estimated long-run semi-elasticities for the right-hand side variables on the migration rate: 12.50 for the relative wage, 61.72 for the foreign employment rate, −32.81 for the UK employment rate and 30.08 for the migrant stock. Thus, a permanent 10% increase in the overseas wage relative to the home wage would increase the net emigration rate by 1.25 per thousand. A permanent 10% increase in the overseas employment rate has a more powerful impact, raising the net emigration rate by 6.172 per thousand. The impact of the home employment rate is half this size. Finally, each increase of a thousand existing migrants draws about 30 new migrants overseas.

The regression results (3.18) raise two remarks. The first one is simultaneity. International migration flows are so prominent worldwide (strong migration flows to the United States, migration from Eastern to Western Europe, migration within the Arab world, ...) that they have a significant impact on the international position of these areas. This is illustrated in (3.17) where ΔL is the labor mobility that results in international wage equalization. This shows therefore the need to analyze the causes and consequences of migration in a simultaneous-equations model (Straubhaar, 1988). The second remark is related to the following question: why do some people migrate while others do not? This is not explained by an aggregate relationship such as (3.18), but there are attempts to construct a more general theory which encompasses all aspects of migration, the wage variable being a necessary but not sufficient condition for international labor mobility (Stark, 1992).

3.4 Economies of scale

Increasing returns to scale (IRS) are often presented as a basis for foreign trade even in absence of other causes of trade. In this section we look at the consequences of introducing IRS into the Ricardian model. We start first by defining the general concepts of internal and external scale economies, national and international scale economies. We then illustrate the patterns of trade that arise when economies of scale are national and external to firms. Other ways of introducing IRS in trade models are discussed in Part III.

Concepts and definitions

Internal and external scale economies

Scale economies may be internal or external. These terms were first introduced by Marshall (1890) when analyzing industry production costs as a function of output:

> We may divide the economies arising from an increase in the scale of production of any kind of goods, into two classes – firstly, those

dependent on the general development of the industry; and, secondly, those dependent on the resources of the individual houses of business engaged in it, on their organization and the efficiency of their management. We may call the former *external economies,* and the latter *internal economies.* (Marshall, 1972, p. 221)

In current terminology, scale economies are called internal to the firm if the firm's average costs depend upon, and decrease with, the firm's level of output. This type of scale economies is often attributed to individual firms which are characterized by a high level of fixed costs combined with constant marginal costs. This implies that only a few large plants will satisfy total demand. In contrast, external economies of scale are effects that are external to the firm and only appear at the industry level. The firm's average costs then depend upon, and decrease with, the level of industry output. Some firm activities that would otherwise be undertaken at the firm level are delegated at the industry level as the latter expands. Traditional examples include the construction of a dam for a hydroelectric power plant in a flood-prone rural area and the Swiss watch industry which created specific schooling and infrastructure facilities as the industry expanded. These examples suggest that in order to reap the benefits of external economies production needs to be geographically concentrated.[5]

With external economies, any expansion of a firm's output has no effect on the firm's costs as long as the size of the industry is unchanged. The assumptions of constant returns to scale (CRS) and price taking behavior at the firm level can therefore be maintained. In contrast, internal economies have implications for the market structure. In particular, because of fixed costs, the number of firms cannot be too large for otherwise profit would be negative. Moreover, no firm can be in equilibrium at a level of output on the decreasing segment of its average cost curve, since the firm will always want to increase production if entry is possible. Hence, perfectly competitive price-taking behavior cannot be assumed when scale economies are internal to the firm.[6]

National and international scale economies

Ethier (1979, 1982a) indicated that scale economies can work in other ways and introduced the concepts of national and international scale economies. In analogy to Adam Smith's division of labor in pin production, the idea is that industrial production becomes more efficient if it splits into separate stages. With each firm specialized in undertaking one of the individual steps in the process, a larger market will allow a greater division of production. Scale economies are therefore international if it is easy to ship products from place to place, in which case the various stages of production need not be located in the same country. These international scale economies will depend upon the size of the world market. However, sufficiently high trade barriers and transport costs will make these scale economies national since they force all stages of production to be located in the same country.[7]

External economies of scale

External economies are awkward to examine in a well structured and rigorous analysis since they actually stand for a mixture of static and dynamic factors.[8]

Formally, economies or diseconomies of scale which are external to a firm j ($j = 1, \ldots, n$) are usually represented by a production function of the form $q_j = F_j(\mathbf{e_j}, q)$ where q_j is the output level of the jth firm, $\mathbf{e_j}$ is firm j's vector of factor inputs, q is the size of either the national or the world industry. A property of this production function is that, for a given q, q_j is positively linear homogeneous in $\mathbf{e_j}$.

In the aggregate of all firms, the production structure can be given a useful representation. Consider the autarky equilibrium of the home economy whose resources are still given by (3.2) but replace the production functions (3.1) by:[9]

$$q_1 = \frac{1}{a_1} L_1 \tag{3.19}$$

$$q_2 = \frac{1}{a_2} L_2 q_2^{(\beta-1)/\beta} \tag{3.20}$$

The substitution of production functions (3.19) and (3.20) into the labor supply constraint (3.2) gives the economy's production possibility curve:

$$q_1 = \frac{L}{a_1} - \frac{a_2}{a_1} q_2^{1/\beta}$$

where the marginal rate of transformation is:

$$\frac{\partial q_1}{\partial q_2} = -\frac{a_2}{a_1} \frac{1}{\beta} q_2^{(1-\beta)/\beta} < 0$$

The production function (3.20) conveniently summarizes the situations that could give rise to external and national scale economies. In particular, production of good 2 is homogeneous of degree β so that the value of β determines whether the set of feasible production points is convex or concave. With $\beta > 1$, (3.20) exhibits IRS. The marginal rate of transformation is then increasing in q_2 since each unit of labor transferred from q_1 to q_2 generates a larger increase in q_2 than the previous unit. This gives rise to the

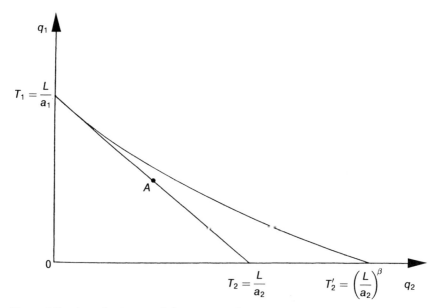

Figure 3.5   *A production possibility curve with increasing returns to scale*

convex production frontier $T_1 T_2'$ depicted in Figure 3.5. With $\beta < 1$, (3.20) exhibits decreasing returns to scale and results in a concave production frontier (not shown) as the marginal rate of transformation is decreasing in q_2. With $\beta = 1$, q_2 is characterized by CRS and the marginal rate of transformation is a constant. This generates the linear production frontier $T_1 A T_2$ in Figure 3.5, similar to that of Figure 3.1.

Problem 3.5:   Show that the convexity of the production possibility curve is reinforced in Figure 3.5 if both sectors have increasing returns.

Autarky with increasing returns to scale

Assume preferences are homothetic so that α is the expenditure share on the first commodity. Assuming $\beta = 2$ in (3.20), it is easy to obtain the autarkic equilibrium with IRS:

$$p_1^a = 1 \qquad p_2^a = a_2^2/a_1(1 - \alpha)L \qquad w^a = 1/a_1$$

$$q_1^a = \alpha L/a_1 \qquad q_2^a = (1 - \alpha)^2 L^2/a_2^2 \qquad Y^a = L/a_1 \tag{3.21}$$

$$L_1^a = \alpha L \qquad L_2^a = (1 - \alpha)L$$

A direct comparison with (3.12) points out a similar distribution of the labor force among sectors. Although the production of good 1 remains the same, the production of good 2 is now the square of that obtained under CRS. Also, the level of welfare under IRS is higher than that achieved in the absence of IRS since the new wage in terms of both goods is not inferior to that under CRS. An additional characteristic of the IRS autarkic equilibrium is that the pre-trade relative price, $(p_2^a/p_1^a) = a_2^2/a_1(1 - \alpha)L$, depends upon consumer preferences and the country's labor endowment. Compared to the pre-trade price in (3.12), the present one falls short of the latter by the factor $a_2/(1 - \alpha)L < 1$.

Free trade equilibrium with no trade

Now consider international trade. Suppose that the two countries have identical relative prices in autarky. By the above reasoning, this would be true if they were identical in all respects, identical tastes and the same amount of labor. No trade is then a possible free trade equilibrium since trade would not take place in a comparative advantage sense. But this outcome would not be Pareto-optimal. Why? The pattern of production would be inefficient in the sense that scale economies have not been exploited. Thus scale economies provide a basis for trade independently of comparative advantage. To focus on these issues, assume the labor forces now differ between countries and assume that each country's labor is measured such that $a_1 = a_1^* = a_2 = a_2^* = 1$. There will be three types of equilibrium. For each type, there can be a mirror image equilibrium in which countries reverse roles, but this will not be illustrated here.

The Ricardian equilibrium (RE)

One possible equilibrium involves complete specialization in each country. A specialization pattern that is consistent with international equilibrium is:

$$p_1 = 1 \qquad p_2 = \frac{(1 - \alpha)L}{\alpha L^{*2}} \qquad w = 1$$

$$w^* = \frac{(1 - \alpha)L}{\alpha L^*} \qquad q_1 = L \qquad q_2^* = L^{*2}$$

(3.22)

It is clear from (3.22) that the foreign wage in terms of both goods is higher than the autarky real wage. For the domestic country, a loss in welfare is not excluded, but it all depends upon the values of α and L/L^*. Hence, the present international equilibrium is undoubtedly preferable to the preceding one for the country that specializes in the IRS commodity. However, there is a mirror image to the equilibrium (3.22) in which the pattern of production and gains from trade are reversed. Hence, if the countries have governments conducting trade policy, each will try to ensure that it becomes the country specialized in producing the IRS commodity.

The wage equalization equilibrium (WE)

Another equilibrium involves one country completely specialized in one commodity with the other country still producing both goods. It makes a great deal of difference which good is produced by both countries. If it is the CRS good 1, labor's value marginal product in good 1, and therefore wages, must be the same internationally which is in sharp contrast to (3.22). The equilibrium is:

$$p_1 = 1 \qquad p_2 = \frac{1}{(1-\alpha)(L+L^*)} \qquad w = w^* = 1$$

$$q_1 = \alpha L + (\alpha - 1)L^* \qquad q_1^* = L^* \qquad q_2 = (1-\alpha)^2(L+L^*)^2 \quad (3.23)$$

$$L_1 = \alpha L + (\alpha - 1)L^* \qquad L_2 = (1-\alpha)(L+L^*)$$

Consequently, both countries will achieve the same welfare level. While the free trade real wage in terms of good 1 equates to the autarky wage, the wage in terms of good 2 is higher. This is a case in which free trade is welfare improving (when compared to autarky).

The Graham equilibrium

The last equilibrium is one in which one country specializes in producing the IRS good while the other country produces both the IRS and CRS goods. International wage equalization is unlikely to take place because the scale of production of the IRS good 2 in the incompletely specialized country is usually insufficient to obtain large gains in labor productivity. Since the price of good 2 is the same in both countries, the wage of the incompletely specialized country needs to be low to compensate for this low labor productivity. Hence, free trade may cause a welfare loss for this country.

Problem 3.6: Give the conditions under which a conflict of interest between the two countries arises, one country gaining and the other losing from trade. This corresponds to Graham's (1923) argument for protection.

Problem 3.7: Give a graphical representation of the three types of equilibria in Figure 3.5. In each of these situations indicate the likely gainers and losers from free trade under IRS.

Multiple Pareto-rankable equilibria

As illustrated above, IRS results in multiple trade equilibria. In some of these equilibria, free trade might lower the welfare of a country relative to autarky. The static model examined here cannot capture the dynamics of transiting from autarky to one of these equilibria. However, the equilibria can be ranked into 'bad' and 'good' according to a welfare measure rule which, in the Ricardian model, is simply the wage rate in terms of both goods. For example, from the discussion in the preceding paragraphs, the following ranking applies to the domestic economy (for $L = L^*$ and $0 < \alpha < 0.50$): $RE <$ autarky $< WE$ where '<' stands for 'is welfare inferior to'. Hence, when there are multiple equilibria, if the economy is in a 'bad' equilibrium (e.g. RE), there exists another equilibrium (e.g. WE), in which everyone would be better off. However, there is no way for this economy to move from this equilibrium to reach a better equilibrium due to what is called a coordination failure.[10] This terminology refers to the inability of agents to coordinate their actions successfully in a many-person decentralized economy. The latter does not provide incentives such that firms could coordinate and jump to a 'good' equilibrium. In contrast, an insightful planner could lead the economy to a Pareto equilibrium. Note that the above ranking of equilibria does not apply to the foreign country and, hence, can potentially lead to a conflict of interest between countries regarding the desired equilibrium.

3.5 **The Ricardian model with a continuum of goods**

Actual trade is characterized by the exchange of a large number of commodities. The SITC nomenclature, for example, has 3118 5-digit entries. The number of goods actually traded is larger, however. Some commodities like textiles are well represented (200 entries) but the trade classification does not fully account for the degree of product differentiation of many other items (e.g. bolts, automobiles,...). This section extends the Ricardian model to the case of many goods using the continuum assumption originally developed by Dornbusch *et al.* (1977). Assuming a continuous rather than discrete number of goods simplifies the analysis and permits questions related to growth, demand shifts and exogenous technological change to be answered with ease.[11] In each case, the focus of the analysis is to determine (1) the dividing line between exported and imported goods, and (2) the position of the relative wage that guarantees trade balance.

The technology

The Ricardian model assumes that each good is produced with a constant unit labor requirement. For good z, let $a(z)$ and $a^*(z)$ be the unit labor requirement in the home and foreign countries, respectively. As usual, an asterisk denotes the foreign country. The ratio $A(z) = a^*(z)/a(z)$ then represents the ratio of domestic to foreign labor productivity. If n commodities are produced, label them so that they are ranked in order of diminishing home comparative advantage:

$$A(1) > A(2) > \cdots > A(i) > \cdots > A(n)$$

Commodity 1, compared to any lower ranked commodity, is characterized by the highest relative domestic productivity and therefore confers the highest comparative advantage to that country. The above inequality could also be read in a different form: commodity n confers the highest comparative advantage to the foreign country.

In working with a continuum of goods, the above relative productivities can be represented by an index constructed on the interval $[0, 1]$ in accordance with diminishing home comparative advantage. Although 'holes' will exist (the number of traded goods is not infinite), these will be ignored by assuming that $A(z)$ is a smooth, continuous and decreasing function of z, $A'(z) < 0$. The function $A(z)$ is graphed in Figure 3.6 as the downward sloping schedule against z varying between 0 and 1.

Multiplying the productivity ratios by the relative foreign wage w^*/w gives an ordered set of relative foreign prices. The domestic country produces therefore the (first) subset of commodities that give a competitive margin with respect to foreign producers (price ratios exceeding one):

$$p(z) = a(z)w < a^*(z)w^* = p^*(z)$$

$$\omega = \frac{w}{w^*} < A(z) \tag{3.24}$$

The other country produces the remaining set of commodities whose price ratios are less than one. Given ω, there exists a borderline commodity $\tilde{z}$ whose production is equally efficient in both countries (price ratio equal to one):

$$\omega = A(\tilde{z}) \quad \text{and} \quad \tilde{z} = A^{-1}(\omega) \tag{3.25}$$

For each ω there is a different borderline commodity $\tilde{z}$. This can be written as $\tilde{z}(\omega)$ with $\tilde{z}'(\omega) < 0$. Given ω, the domestic country will produce efficiently the range of commodities:

$$0 \le z \le \tilde{z}(\omega)$$

while the foreign country will produce all commodities in the range:

$$\tilde{z}(\omega) \le z \le 1$$

Given ω and the state of technology, the above establishes the pattern of international specialization. The equilibrium borderline between these two sets of commodities depends, however, on demand conditions, but the ordering does not.

Demand and equilibrium

On the demand side, we again assume homothetic preferences and in particular that the demand functions derive from a Cobb–Douglas utility function. This specification of demand associates with each commodity a constant expenditure share $b(z)$:

$$b(z) = p(z)d(z)/S > 0$$

$$\int_0^1 b(z)dz = 1$$

where S denotes nominal expenditure, $d(z)$ the demand for, and $p(z)$ the price of commodity z. The fraction of expenditure spent on home goods is equal to:

$$v(\tilde{z}) = \int_0^{\tilde{z}} b(z)dz$$

$$v'(\tilde{z}) = b(\tilde{z}) > 0$$

$$0 \le v(\tilde{z}) \le 1$$

The fraction spent on foreign goods is:

$$1 - v(\tilde{z}) = \int_{\tilde{z}}^1 b(z)dz$$

Identical tastes are assumed for the two countries. Consequently, everyone in the world spends a constant share of his or her income on each good z and this share $v(\tilde{z})$ is common to both countries.

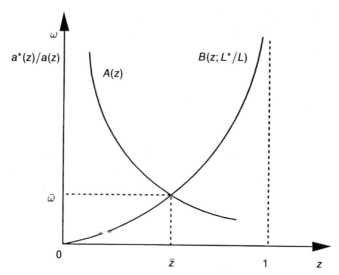

Figure 3.6   *Relative wage and pattern of specialization*

Equilibrium in the market for home goods requires that the total value of spending on home goods equals domestic labor income. The world spending on home goods is $v(\bar{z})$ times world income, the sum of the wages earned at home and abroad. The equilibrium relationship is:

$$wL = v(\bar{z})(wL + w^*L^*) \tag{3.26}$$

An alternative interpretation of the equilibrium can be given by rewriting (3.26) as:

$$(1 - v(\bar{z}))wL = v(\bar{z})w^*L^* \tag{3.27}$$

This is the condition for trade balance: the value of domestic imports equals the value of exports. (3.26) and (3.27) imply a value of w/w^* corresponding to each $\bar{z}$ such that market equilibrium obtains:

$$\omega = \frac{v(\bar{z})}{1 - v(\bar{z})} \frac{L^*}{L} = B(\bar{z};\, L^*/L) \tag{3.28}$$

This schedule is drawn in Figure 3.6. The relative wage ω starts at zero and approaches infinity as $\bar{z}$ approaches unity. In this interval the curve slopes upward since the higher is $\bar{z}$, the higher is the numerator of $B(\cdot)$ and the lower is the denominator of $B(\cdot)$. A characteristic of Figure 3.6 is that, while an economy always stays on its technological curve $A(\bar{z})$, it can temporarily be off its B curve. To the right of the B curve, there is an excess demand for labor and a trade surplus; to the left, the economy has an excess supply of labor and a trade deficit. For example, holding ω fixed, an increase in the range of domestically produced goods could create an excess demand for labor, lower home imports and raise home exports, and thus create a trade surplus. A rise in the domestic relative wage would then be required to restore trade balance and labor market equilibrium.

By combining the demand side of the economy as represented by (3.28) with the condition for efficient specialization (3.25), one obtains the unique relative wage and borderline good $\bar{z}$ combination at which the world is efficiently specialized, trade is balanced, and national labor markets are in equilibrium:

$$\bar{\omega} = A(\bar{z}) = B(\bar{z}; L^*/L) \tag{3.29}$$

Graphically, the solution is given by the intersection of the two schedules. The commodities to the left of $\bar{z}$ are exported by the domestic country, while commodities to the right of $\bar{z}$ are exported by the foreign country. Commodity $\bar{z}$ is either non-traded or gives rise to intra- or inter-industry trade, depending on what is needed for trade balance.

Application: exogenous technical progress

Consider the effect of uniform technical progress in every industry abroad.[12] By the definition of $A(z)$, this implies a reduction in $a^*(z)$ and a proportional downward shift of the $A(z)$ schedule in Figure 3.7. At the initial equilibrium relative wage $\bar{\omega}_1$, this economy-wide productivity increase represents a loss

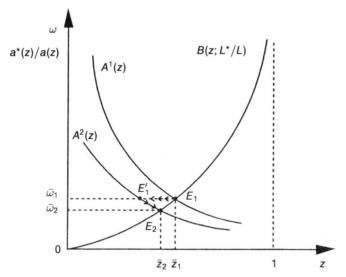

Figure 3.7 *A foreign productivity shock*

Table 3.2   *Domestic welfare and a foreign productivity shock*

Interval	Price	Real wage	Welfare
$(0, \bar{z}_2)$	$p(z) = wa(z)$	$w/p(z) = 1/a(z)$	0
$(\bar{z}_2, \bar{z}_1)$	$p(z) < wa(z)$	$w/p(z) > 1/a(z)$	$+$
$(\bar{z}_1, 1)$	$p(z) = w^*a^*(z)$	$w/p(z) > w/w^*(1/a(z))$	$+$

of domestic industries at the margin in the range $E_1 E_1'$ and a trade deficit. A decrease in the home relative wage is therefore necessary to offset partly the decline in comparative advantage and to restore trade balance. Point E_2 is the new long-run equilibrium where the new range of home produced goods is $(0, \bar{z}_2)$ and the interval of foreign produced goods includes the previous range $(\bar{z}_1, 1)$ and the transitional goods $(\bar{z}_1, \bar{z}_2)$

To remove any ambiguity about the domestic consequences of the foreign productivity improvement, consider the effect on domestic welfare. The latter can be examined by looking at the domestic real wage, i.e. the wage in terms of each good in the continuum. If the domestic real wage either stays the same or rises, then the country is better off. The results are summarized in Table 3.2.

The domestic wage in terms of goods in the interval $(0, \bar{z}_2)$ remains constant because domestic labor productivity is unchanged. For any good z in the transitional interval $(\bar{z}_1, \bar{z}_2)$, the price is now lower than before the productivity shock and, hence, the domestic real wage rises in terms of these goods. In the interval $(\bar{z}_1, 1)$, the price of foreign goods is $p(z) = w^*a^*(z)$. Dividing w by this last expression gives the result in Table 3.2. Knowing that ω falls proportionally less than $a^*(z)$, the domestic real wage increases in this interval. Summing the effects for the three kinds of goods, domestic welfare unambiguously rises as a result of the increase in foreign labor productivity.

Problem 3.8:   Instead of a uniform foreign productivity increase, show the implications for long-run equilibrium and domestic welfare of technical progress in a single foreign industry.

Problem 3.9:   Analyze the full implications of a harmonization of technology across the world caused, e.g. by a transfer of the least cost technology.

3.6 Tests of the Ricardian trade theory

Empirical studies in the Ricardian model implicitly use the rationale of the 2-country, multicommodity framework of the preceding section. There are, however, a number of factors that can modify this purely theoretical approach, e.g. assumptions about the degree of specialization and the wage structure.

Except for the borderline commodity, the sharp implication of the multicommodity Ricardian model concerns the extent of specialization. In practice, the actual commodity classification with which empirical researchers work does not allow goods to be identified unambiguously as either an export or import. Even at sufficiently detailed levels of classification, intra-industry trade exists (see Chapter 1) and hence the Ricardian outcome of complete specialization is rejected in any data set. Looser versions of the Ricardian model are therefore empirically studied.

The assumptions about the wage structure will lead to as many different testing hypotheses about the trade model. The empirical literature makes three types of assumptions about the domestic and foreign wages. The first is that the wage rate in any industry is different both across industries and across countries. Hence, in a competitive economy, the pre-trade price of commodity z will equal its average cost: $p_z = a_z w_z$ where w_z is industry z's wage rate. Using the rationale of the previous section, but assuming a finite number n of traded commodities, this commodity z will be in the subset of domestically exported goods if it has a foreign pre-trade relative price ratio greater than one:

$$\frac{p_z^*}{p_z} = \frac{a_z^* w_z^*}{a_z w_z} > 1 \qquad z = 1, 2, \ldots, m \qquad (3.30)$$

Similarly, the domestic country will import commodity j if

$$\frac{p_j^*}{p_j} = \frac{a_j^* w_j^*}{a_j w_j} < 1 \qquad j = m+1, \ldots, n \qquad (3.31)$$

Hence, combining (3.30) and (3.31),

$$\frac{a_z^* w_z^*}{a_z w_z} > \frac{a_j^* w_j^*}{a_j w_j} \qquad \begin{array}{l} z = 1, 2, \ldots, m \\ j = m+1, \ldots, n \end{array} \qquad (3.32)$$

This is a statement of the Ricardian hypothesis in terms of comparative unit labor costs where the latter, and not labor productivity, is compared. This can be called a Type-I hypothesis.

If instead the inter-industrial pattern of wage rates is identical internationally, then $w_z^*/w_z = w_j^*/w_j$ equals a constant, and we can write:

$$\frac{a_z^*}{a_z} > \frac{a_j^*}{a_j} \qquad \begin{array}{l} z = 1, 2, \ldots, m \\ j = m+1, \ldots, n \end{array} \qquad (3.33)$$

The Ricardian hypothesis is thus restated in its original form, i.e. in terms of labor productivity. Call this a Type-II hypothesis.

Finally, a Type-III hypothesis is obtained if, as in the previous section, the wage is assumed unique in each country but different across countries: $w = w_z = w_j$, $w^* = w_z^* = w_j^*$ where w^*/w is a constant. In this case, the ranking (3.33) of labor productivities is maintained but the relative wage now indicates the borderline that separates exported goods from imported goods:

$$\frac{a_z^*}{a_z} > \frac{w^*}{w} > \frac{a_j^*}{a_j} \qquad \begin{array}{l} z = 1, 2, \ldots, m \\ j = m+1, \ldots, n \end{array} \qquad (3.34)$$

MacDougall's (1951) pioneering study tested this Type-III hypothesis by examining the export performance of the United States relative to the United Kingdom to third markets. His results are reported in Table 3.3. Using 1937 data, MacDougall notes that, at the going rate of exchange £1 = \$4.769, wage rates in the United States were approximately twice those in the United Kingdom. This is important to know since it is expected that the ratio of US exports to UK exports should exceed one whenever the US output per-worker is more than twice the British and vice versa. On the whole, the data provided in Table 3.3 are supportive of the Type-III Ricardian hypothesis.

This study was followed by Balassa (1963), Stern (1962) and MacDougall *et al.* (1962). These studies used alternative estimation techniques, updated data sets, and also examined Type-I and Type-II hypotheses. Balassa (1963) extended the work of MacDougall using 1950 estimates of productivity data and 1951 export data on 28 manufacturing industries. The latter accounted for more than 40% of manufacturing exports in the United States and United Kingdom. Two of his cross-section regression results were:

$$\frac{X_{US}}{X_{UK}} = -53.3 + 0.721 \frac{1/a_{US}}{1/a_{UK}} \qquad R^2 = 0.64$$

$$\frac{X_{US}}{X_{UK}} = -181.2 + \underset{(0.167)}{0.691} \frac{1/a_{US}}{1/a_{UK}} + \underset{(0.102)}{0.14} \frac{w_{US}}{w_{UK}} \qquad R^2 = 0.81$$

where X_{US} and X_{UK} represent American and British exports, set out as index numbers, and standard errors are in parentheses. Balassa's first result corresponds to testing the Type-II hypothesis and seems to substantiate this hypothesis in the sense that an increase in a US industry's productivity ratio leads to an increase in US relative export values. The addition of the wage ratio in the second equation makes it implicitly a test of the Type-I hypothesis. This shows a negligible improvement but, at the same time, the positive sign of the coefficient of the wage ratio is puzzling. Since observed

Table 3.3 *UK relative to US unit labor requirements and exports, 1937*

$a_{z(UK)}/a_{z(US)} > 2$	US exports/UK exports[a]
Wireless sets & valves	8
Pig iron	5
Motor cars	4
Glass containers	$3\frac{1}{2}$
Tin cans	3
Machinery	$1\frac{1}{2}$
Paper	1

$1.4 < a_{z(UK)}/a_{z(US)} < 2$	UK exports/US exports
Cigarettes	2
Linoleum, oilcloth, etc.	3
Hosiery	3
Leather footwear	3
Coke	5
Rayon weaving	5
Cotton goods	9
Rayon making	11
Beer	18

$a_{z(UK)}/a_{z(US)} < 1.4$	UK exports/US exports
Cement	11
Men's & boy's outerclothing of wool	23
Margarine	32
Woollen & worsted	250

Note:

[a] Exceptions: US output per-worker more than twice British output per-worker, but UK exports exceed US exports: electric lamps, rubber tyres, soap, biscuits and matches. (These represent about 3% of the value of trade in the commodities listed).

Source: MacDougall (1951, table 1, p. 698).

wages are inevitably post-trade wages, this suggests causality running from export performance to higher wages rather than from wages to export performance (Leamer, 1992).

Bhagwati (1964) contended that the above statistical analyses have only a remote overlap with the Ricardian hypotheses. Bhagwati's critique is based on the grounds that the behavior of relative export shares or values to third markets is not relevant to the Ricardian hypotheses. In the same article he undertakes a few tests and finds no support for the assumption that labor productivity ratios exhibit the hypothesized relation with price ratios.

McGilvray and Simpson (1973) take up many of Bhagwati's suggestions and therefore examine the Type-III hypothesis which fits closer to the Ricardian theory. The specific trade flows examined were those between the Republic of Ireland and the United Kingdom. As expected, Ireland and the United Kingdom are two actively trading nations with the United Kingdom representing, in 1964, 70% and 50% of Irish merchandise exports and imports, respectively. The authors measure the bilateral trade flows between these two nations, not their relative shares in third country markets, and the scope of their analysis covers the whole of merchandise trade (34 merchandise sectors), not a few selected commodities. First, they rank sectors by their propensity to export (exports divided by GDP) and develop a parallel ranking of sectors by their propensity to import competing goods (imports divided by GDP *plus* imports). Second, they rank the sectorial ratios of Irish labor productivity (in value) relative to those of UK in increasing value. Third, they then compute several Spearman rank correlation[13] analyzes on these pairs of rankings as shown in Table 3.4. If the Type-III hypothesis is to be verified, one should expect

Table 3.4   *Rank correlation coefficients for comparative labor productivities, and export and import propensities, Ireland, 1964 and United Kingdom, 1963*

		Export propensity		Import propensity	
		(1)	*(2)*	*(3)*	*(4)*
	n	*34*	*30*	*34*	*30*
Comparative productivity of	r_s	−0.10	−0.17	0.01	−0.15
direct labor inputs	*t*	−0.54	−0.89	0.04	−0.80
Comparative productivity of direct labor *plus* indirect	r_s	−0.15	−0.24	0.02	−0.14
labor inputs from non-traded goods sectors	*t*	−0.88	−1.32	0.11	−0.77
Comparative productivity of	r_s	−0.22	−0.31	0.21	0.09
direct *plus* all indirect labor inputs	*t*	−1.30	−1.35	1.20	0.48

Notes: n = number of observations (n = 30 with the 4 primary producing sectors excluded); r_s = Spearman rank correlation coefficient; t = Student-t.
Source: McGilvray and Simpson (1973, table 1, p. 452).

to find a positive rank correlation between the labor productivity ranking and the ranking of sectors according to their propensity of export, and a negative rank correlation between the labor productivity ranking and the ranking of sectors according to their propensity to import. In Table 3.4, none of these computed correlation coefficients is significant and all but two are opposite in sign to what would be hypothesized if the Ricardian model were valid.

3.7 Concluding remarks

The academic literature traditionally devotes important coverage to the Ricardian model. One reason is the simplicity of the argument but there is also a widespread tendency to focus on labor productivity, and to consider it as a good approximation of overall productivity (including capital).

It seems useful to summarize the main results of this chapter. First, comparative advantage arises from technological differences between countries. Trade allows for efficiency gains of specialization that can be shared among participating countries. Detailed information on the demand structure is, however, needed to determine the actual world relative price and the actual pattern of production. Second, in absence of technological differences, taste differences can give rise to comparative advantage as well. Third, if countries are similar in all respects, scale economies are a determinant of trade by allowing countries to specialize on fewer tasks. Fourth, under IRS the trade pattern is characterized by the existence of multiple equilibria. These can be ranked according to a welfare measure rule into 'bad' and 'good' equilibria. If an economy is in a 'bad' equilibrium, a decentralized economy may result in a coordination failure that prevents it from moving to a good equilibrium. Fifth, there is so far little empirical support in favor of the Ricardian hypothesis, at least in its traditional formulation. Tests of weaker hypotheses show, however, a significant impact of labor productivity and unit labor costs on trade performance. Tests with scale economies await further research.

Overall, the Ricardian model seems to raise more questions about the sources of comparative advantage than it answers. The Ricardian theory provides no guide as to how labor productivity and comparative advantage can be expected to evolve since it gives no explanation of differences in labor productivities across countries. This sets one of the tasks for subsequent chapters, and in particular the next one, where we consider the Heckscher–Ohlin–Samuelson (H–O–S) model.

Notes

1. Dynamic effects of international trade are therefore not investigated. A series of recent contributions on endogenous growth have developed a set of formal techniques by which the relationship between international trade and long run growth can be explored. See Chapter 14 for the growth and trade links.
2. Readers unfamiliar with the concept of community indifference curves can find a summary of the controversies in Chacholiades (1973, Chap. 5). The few cases where the use of social indifference curves is justified are: (1) a Robinson Crusoe economy, (2) a totalitarian state, (3) a country inhabited by individuals with identical tastes and factor endowments, (4) individuals with identical and homothetic tastes and (5) if income is always reallocated among individuals in such a way as to maximize social welfare. In spite of the questionable validity of these assumptions social indifference curves are used extensively in trade theory and we accordingly follow this tradition here.
3. This assumes homothetic preferences, a common assumption in trade models.
4. The t-statistics are in parentheses; RSS is the residual sum of squares; $LM(1)$ is the Lagrange Multiplier test for first-order serial correlation; $RESET$ is the test for functional form; $HETERO$ is the test for heteroscedasticity. The last three tests are distributed as $\chi^2(1)$ with a critical 5% value of 5.99. Prior to estimating (3.18) the time series properties of the data have been explored. This involves tests for stationarity and cointegration. See Mills (1990) and Hamilton (1994) for a review of time series techniques.
5. An analysis of the long-run trends in US regional specialization and localization over the period 1860–1987 does not, however, support explanations based on external economies (Kim, 1995). The empirical evidence seems more consistent with explanations based on internal scale economies and regional factor endowments (see Chapter 4).
6. See Chapter 9. Some forms of competitive interaction do imply competitive pricing, for example, Bertrand competition as well as contestable markets.
7. Krugman and Venables (1995) examine how increased globalization affects the location of manufacturing as transportation costs are gradually reduced. International scale economies can spontaneously arise in the model and lead to uneven gains from trade between two regions with no inherent comparative advantage.
8. An exception is Okuno-Fujiwara (1988), who identifies the conditions that create Marshallian external economies, introducing interdependence of several industries and oligopolistic competition in at least one of them.
9. For more on the topic of this subsection, see Ethier (1982b, 1987). Ethier (1982b) assumes $a_1 = a_2 = 1$.
10. This literature has been initiated to characterize economies that exhibit underemployment equilibria, but where the results do not derive from the usual Keynesian assumptions of price rigidity (Diamond, 1982; Weitzman, 1982; Heller, 1988; Cooper and John, 1988). This concept is now used to characterize economies in a permanent state of underdevelopment, or certain forms of market structure (Okuno-Fujiwara, 1988).

11. Taylor (1993) extends the continuum Ricardian model of Dornbusch *et al.* (1977) to a dynamic framework. The model incorporates heterogeneity across industries in research and production technologies, and in the technological opportunity for innovation.
12. The material of the rest of this section depends upon Krugman and Obstfeld (1988, pp. 36–8).
13. The Spearman rank correlation coefficient is a non-parametric measure of association when ranks are used instead of actual observations. It measures in Table 3.4 the tendency of labor productivity and trade propensity to relate in a monotone way and, unlike the ordinary sample correlation coefficient, is not restricted to uncovering a linear relation between them. The Spearman coefficient is:

$$r_s = 1 - 6 \sum_{i=1}^{n} d_i^2 / n(n^2 - 1)$$

where n is the number of observations (either 30 or 34 in Table 3.4) and d_i the difference in the rank number between the two variables. Note, that if several observations tie, their score is the sum of their ranks divided by the number of observed ties. Under the null hypothesis of no correlation, the sampling distribution of r_s has mean 0 and the standard deviation $\sigma(r_s) = 1/\sqrt{n-1}$. Since this sampling distribution can be approximated with a normal distribution, we base the test of the null hypothesis on the statistic $t = (r_s - 0)/(1/\sqrt{n-1})$ which has approximately the standard distribution.

References and additional reading

The Ricardian theory

Bhagwati, J.N. and Srinivasan, T.N. (1983), *Lectures on International Trade* (Cambridge, Mass.: MIT Press), Chapters 2–4.

Chacholiades, M. (1973), *The Pure Theory of International Trade* (London: Macmillan).

Findlay, R. (1988), 'Comparative Advantage', in Eatwell, J., Milgate, M. and Newman, P. (eds), *The New Palgrave: A Dictionary of Economics* (London: Macmillan), 514–17.

Ricardo, D. (1821), *The Principles of Political Economy and Taxation* (London: J. Murray).

International labor migration

Hatton, T. (1995), 'A Model of UK Emigration, 1870–1913', *Review of Economics and Statistics*, 77(3), 407–15.

Sapir, A. (1975), 'A Note on Short-Run Greek Labor Emigration to Germany', *Weltwirtschaftliches Archiv*, 111, 356–61.
Stark, O. (1992), *The Migration of Labor* (Oxford: Blackwell).
Straubhaar, T. (1988), *On the Economics of International Labor Migration* (Berne: Verlag Paul Haupt).

The Ricardian model with many goods

Chipman, J.S. (1965), 'A Survey of International Trade: Part I – The Classical Theory', *Econometrica*, 33, 477–519.
Dornbusch, R., Fischer, S. and Samuelson, P.A. (1977), 'Comparative Advantage, Trade, and Payments in a Ricardian Model with a Continuum of Goods', *American Economic Review*, 47(5), 823–39.
Haberler, G. (1936), *The Theory of International Trade* (London: W. Hodge).
Krugman, P.R. and Obstfeld, M. (1988), *International Economics: Theory and Policy* (Glenview: Scott, Foresman), Appendix to Chapter 2, 36–41.
Taylor, M.S. (1993), 'Quality Ladders and Ricardian Trade', *Journal of International Economics*, 34, 225–43.
Viner, J. (1937), *Studies in the Theory of International Trade* (New York: Harper).

Economies of scale, decreasing costs and the pattern of specialization

Ethier, W.J. (1979), 'Internationally Decreasing Costs and World Trade', *Journal of International Economics*, 9, 1–24.
Ethier, W.J. (1982a), 'National and International Returns to Scale in the Modern Theory of International Trade', *American Economic Review*, 72, 388–405.
Ethier, W.J. (1982b), 'Decreasing Costs in International Trade and Frank Graham's Argument for Protection', *Econometrica*, 50(5), 1243–67.
Ethier, W.J. (1987), 'The Theory of International Trade' in Officer, L.M. (ed.), *International Economics* (Boston: Kluwer Academic), 1–57.
Graham, F. (1923), 'Some Aspects of Protection Further Considered', *Quarterly Journal of Economics*, 37, 199–227.
Kim, S. (1995), 'Expansion of Markets and the Geographic Distribution of Economic Activities: The Trends in US Regional Manufacturing Structure, 1860–1987', *Quarterly Journal of Economics*, 110, 881–908.
Krugman, P. R. and Venables, A.J. (1995), 'Globalization and the Inequality of Nations', *Quarterly Journal of Economics*, 110, 857–80.
Marshall, A. (1890), *Principles of Economics* (London: Macmillan; revised edn 1972).
Okuno-Fujiwara, M. (1988), 'Interdependence of Industries, Coordination Failure and Strategic Promotion of an Industry', *Journal of International Economics*, 25, 25–43.

Panagariya, A. (1981), 'Variable Returns to Scale in Production and Patterns of Specialization', *American Economic Review*, 71, 221–30.

Coordination failure

Cooper, R. and John, A. (1988), 'Coordinating Coordination Failures in Keynesian Models', *Quarterly Journal of Economics*, 103, 441–64.

Diamond, P. (1982), 'Aggregate Demand Management in Search Equilibrium', *Journal of Political Economy*, 90, 881–94.

Heller, W.P. (1988), 'Coordination Failure with Complete Markets in a Simple Model of Effective Demand', in Heller,W.P., Starr, R.M. and Starrett, D.A. (eds), *Equilibrium Analysis: Essays in Honor of K.J. Arrow*, Vol. II (Cambridge: Cambridge University Press).

Weitzman, M. (1982), 'Increasing Returns and the Foundations of Unemployment Theory', *Economic Journal*, 787–804.

Ricardian studies

Balassa, B. (1963), 'An Empirical Demonstration of Classical Comparative Cost Theory', *Review of Economics and Statistics*, 45, 231–8.

Bhagwati, J. (1964), 'The Pure Theory of International Trade: A Survey', *Economic Journal*, 74, 1–84.

Leamer, E.E. (1992), 'Testing Trade Theory', *NBER Working Paper*, 3957.

MacDougall, G.D.A. (1951), 'British and American Exports: A Study Suggested by the Theory of Comparative Costs, Part I', *Economic Journal*, 61, 487–521.

MacDougall, G.D.A., Dowley, M., Fox, P. and Pugh, S. (1962), 'British and American Productivity, Prices and Exports: An Addendum', *Oxford Economic Papers*, 14(3), 297–304.

McGilvray, J. and Simpson, D. (1973), 'The Commodity Structure of Anglo–Irish Trade', *Review of Economics and Statistics*, 55, 451–8.

Stern, R.M. (1962), 'British and American Productivity and Comparative Costs in International Trade', *Oxford Economic Papers*, 14(3), 275–96.

Time series techniques

Hamilton, J.D. (1994), *Time Series Analysis* (Princeton: Princeton University Press).

Mills, T.C. (1990), *Time Series Techniques for Economists* (Cambridge: Cambridge University Press).

■ *Chapter 4* ■

The Factor Abundance Model

The predominant explanation of the pattern of comparative advantage is the factor abundance theory. A twentieth-century development, this theory was first enunciated by Eli Heckscher in 1919 and further elaborated by Bertil Ohlin (1933). During the 1950s Paul Samuelson set out a general equilibrium formalization of the insights of Heckscher and Ohlin (H–O) and subsequently derived a set of important theorems. In recognition of Samuelson's contribution, the H–O theory came to be called the Heckscher–Ohlin–Samuelson (H–O–S) theory. More recently, this theory is simply labelled the 'factor abundance' theory in reference to its central tenet: comparative advantage, and hence trade, is the result of differences in the relative supplies of factors between countries.

The analytical foundation of the factor abundance theory is a general equilibrium model of an economy producing J goods using H primary factors of production under conditions of perfect competition in both product and factor markets. The H–O–S model augments this essentially closed economy model by introducing another country and by making additional assumptions about the interaction between countries. These additional assumptions include the international identity of production functions and the international immobility of factors. These additional assumptions serve to eliminate all causes of a difference in autarky relative prices between countries except that of differing relative factor supplies.

This chapter presents the H–O–S model, that is, the analytical model underlying the factor abundance theory. Two methods of presentation are used: a traditional approach which uses production and direct utility functions and a modern approach which uses duality theory to express supply and demand in terms of revenue and expenditure functions. We consider first the supply side of the model and establish two key relationships: that between relative factor prices and an industry's use of factors, and that between relative factor prices and relative output prices.

114

We then demonstrate three important comparative statics results: the Rybczynski theorem, the Stolper–Samuelson theorem, and the reciprocity relations. Next, the demand side of the model is presented and this is then combined with the supply elements to determine the trade equilibrium. Following this we consider the effect of trade upon the domestic allocation of resources and the distribution of income. Finally, we demonstrate the two main predictions of the factor abundance theory, the H–O theorem concerning the pattern of trade, and the Factor Price Equalization theorem concerning the effect of trade on the pattern of factor prices between countries.

4.1 Production equilibrium

This section presents the production relationships which describe the supply side of an economy and develops the conditions for the maximization of the economy's income. The following assumptions are maintained throughout this chapter:

Assumption 1: There is perfect competition in both product and factor markets.

Assumption 2: Factors of production are homogeneous in quality and costlessly mobile between industries.

Assumption 3: The total supply of each factor is independent of its reward, that is, the national supply of each factor is perfectly inelastic.

Additional assumptions needed to derive the basic propositions of the factor abundance theory will be introduced when appropriate.

Traditional analysis

The traditional presentation of the H–O–S model reduces the dimensionality of the underlying general equilibrium model from *J* goods and *H* factors to that of a 'simple' 2-sector model with 2 goods and 2 factors of production, capital and labor. The presentation below adopts this convention. A general version of the model is presented in Chapter 5 when discussing applied modeling in general equilibrium.

The production function

We assume an economy produces 2 commodities, q_1 and q_2, using 2 primary factors, capital K and labor L. The production function for industry j is:

$$q_j = F_j(K_j, L_j) \qquad j = 1, 2 \tag{4.1}$$

where K_j and L_j are the levels of capital and labor employed in industry j, respectively. The production function is assumed to satisfy the following properties:

(1) Some of each factor is required for production:

$$F_j(0, L_j) = F_j(K_j, 0) = 0, \qquad j = 1, 2$$

(2) Linear homogeneity (homogeneity of degree one): for $\gamma > 0$,

$$F_j(\gamma K_j, \gamma L_j) = \gamma F_j(K_j, L_j) = \gamma q_j, \qquad j = 1, 2$$

(3) Factor marginal products are positive but diminishing:

$$\frac{\partial F_j(K_j, L_j)}{\partial K_j} > 0 \qquad \frac{\partial F_j(K_j, L_j)}{\partial L_j} > 0$$

$$\frac{\partial^2 F_j(K_j, L_j)}{\partial K_j^2} < 0 \qquad \frac{\partial^2 F_j(K_j, L_j)}{\partial L_j^2} < 0 \qquad (j = 1, 2)$$

A production function satisfying properties (1)–(3) is called a neoclassical production function.[1] Since linear homogeneity is crucial to establishing the main factor abundance theorems, the remainder of this section discusses some implications of linear homogeneity for the production function.

By linear homogeneity, a proportional change in all inputs will change output in the same proportion, that is, production exhibits constant returns to scale (CRS).[2] Given this, (4.1) can be expressed in several equivalent forms. For example, applying property (2) with $\gamma = 1/q_j$ gives (4.1) as:

$$1 = F_j(a_{jK}, a_{jL}) \tag{4.2}$$

where $a_{jK} = K_j/q_j$ and $a_{jL} = L_j/q_j$ are the *unit factor input requirements*, that is, the amount of each factor required to produce one unit of output. (4.2) implicitly defines the unit isoquant: the combinations of capital and labor required to produce one unit of output.[3]

Another form of the production function is obtained by setting $\gamma = 1/L_j$:

$$q_j = L_j f_j(k_j) \tag{4.3}$$

where $k_j = K_j/L_j$ is industry j's capital–labor ratio. This form illustrates another implication of linear homogeneity: factor average and marginal products only depend on the industry capital–labor ratio.[4] This is directly evident for labor's average product by simply re-arranging (4.3):

$$\frac{q_j}{L_j} = f_j(k_j) \tag{4.4}$$

where

$$\frac{\partial(q_j/L_j)}{\partial k_j} > 0$$

Capital's average product is similarly expressed by setting $\gamma = 1/K_j$ to obtain $q_j/K_j = f_j(1/k_j)$ where

$$\frac{\partial(q_j/K_j)}{\partial k_j} < 0$$

The dependence of factor marginal products on the industry capital–labor ratio is demonstrated by differentiating (4.3) with respect to each factor:

$$\frac{\partial q_j}{\partial K_j} = \frac{\partial(L_j f_j(k_j))}{\partial k_j} \frac{\partial k_j}{\partial K_j} = f'_j(k_j) > 0$$

$$\frac{\partial q_j}{\partial L_j} = \frac{\partial(L_j f_j(k_j))}{\partial k_j} \frac{\partial k_j}{\partial L_j} = f_j(k_j) - k_j f'_j(k_j) > 0$$

where "′" indicates differentiation of the function with respect to its argument. Using these expressions, property (3) can be written compactly as $f'_j(k_j) > 0$ and $f''_j(k_j) < 0$ for all $k_j > 0$, ($j = 1, 2$).[5]

Figure 4.1 illustrates the per-worker production function (4.4). As implied by properties (1)–(3), this function is an increasing, monotonic, and strictly

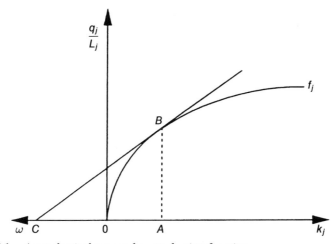

Figure 4.1 *A neoclassical per-worker production function*

concave function of k_j whose slope decreases from infinity at $k_j = 0$ to zero at $k_j = \infty$.

A final implication of linear homogeneity is the 'adding-up' condition, also known as Euler's law:

$$q_j = L_j(f_j - k_j f_j') + K_j f_j' = f_j \qquad j = 1, 2$$

which states that output equals the sum of the contributions made by each factor.

Optimal resource allocation

We now establish the conditions for optimal resource allocation which, for given output prices, imply the maximization of national income. Industry j's profit maximization problem is:[6]

$$\Pi_j(p_j, w_j, r_j) = \max_{L_j, K_j}(p_j q_j - w_j L_j - r_j K_j) \quad \text{subject to } q_j = L_j f_j(k_j) \quad (4.5)$$

where $\Pi_j(p_j, w_j, r_j)$ denotes industry j's maximum profit for the given wage rate (w_j), rental rate (r_j), and output price (p_j), each measured in some arbitrary unit of account. Assuming both commodities are produced in equilibrium, the solution to (4.5) yields the condition that, in each industry, each factor be paid its value marginal product:

$$
\begin{aligned}
w_j &= p_j(f_j - k_j f_j') \\
r_j &= p_j f_j'
\end{aligned}
\qquad j = 1, 2 \qquad (4.6)
$$

Since factors are homogeneous and costlessly mobile between industries, the values of w_j and r_j are common across industries ($w_j = w$ and $r_j = r$, $\forall j$). Given this, (4.6) implies the following condition for optimal factor allocation between industries:

$$
\begin{aligned}
p_1(f_1 - k_1 f_1') &= w = p_2(f_2 - k_2 f_2') \\
p_1 f_1' &= r = p_2 f_2'
\end{aligned}
\qquad (4.7)
$$

Hence, for given output prices, national income is maximized when factors are allocated so as to equate their value marginal product across industries.

Figure 4.2 illustrates the above allocation rule by showing each industry's unit isoquant (4.2) together with an isocost line (AB) whose slope equals (minus) the economy's wage–rental ratio.[7] The point of tangency between the isocost line and each unit isoquant (points e_1 and e_2) determines an allocation of capital and labor satisfying (4.7) in that the ratios of factor marginal products in each industry are equated via the common wage–rental

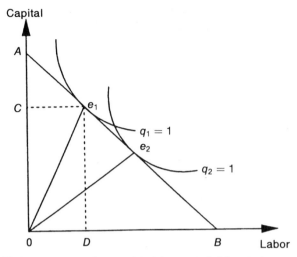

Figure 4.2 *Unit isoquants and cost minimizing capital–labor ratios*

ratio. Note that for given factor prices, points e_1 and e_2 determine a unique cost minimizing capital–labor ratio in each industry as measured by the slope of rays Oe_1 and Oe_2.[8]

Problem 4.1:   Show that at point e_1 in Figure 4.2 the marginal product of capital and labor are $1/OA$ and $1/OB$, respectively. Extend this analysis to show that at point e_1 the marginal rate of substitution of labor for capital (dK_j/dL_j) equals the ratio of labor's marginal product to capital's marginal product.

Whereas the above defines optimal factor allocations between industries, we must also take into account that the economy as a whole is limited by its supply of capital and labor. Since factor markets are perfectly competitive, this factor supply constraint is embodied in the equilibrium condition that resources be fully employed. If K and L denote the economy's total supply of capital and labor, respectively, then the conditions for full employment are:

$$K = K_1 + K_2 \tag{4.8}$$

$$L = L_1 + L_2 \tag{4.9}$$

These constraints can be combined by dividing (4.8) by (4.9) to express the economy's overall capital–labor ratio as a weighted average of industry capital–labor ratios:

$$k = \lambda_1 k_1 + \lambda_2 k_2 \tag{4.10}$$

where $\lambda_j = L_j/L$ is the proportion of the labor force allocated to sector j. Since $\lambda_1 + \lambda_2 = 1$, and assuming $k_1 \neq k_2$, (4.10) can be solved to give the following alternative expressions for λ_1 and λ_2:

$$\lambda_1 = \frac{k - k_2}{k_1 - k_2}$$

$$\lambda_2 = \frac{k_1 - k}{k_1 - k_2}$$

(4.11)

Inserting (4.11) into (4.3), the *per capita* output of each industry can be expressed as a function of both industry and national capital–labor ratios:[9]

$$\frac{q_1}{L} = \lambda_1 f_1(k_1) = \frac{k - k_2}{k_1 - k_2} f_1(k_1)$$

$$\frac{q_2}{L} = \lambda_2 f_2(k_2) = \frac{k_1 - k}{k_1 - k_2} f_2(k_2)$$

(4.12)

We now discuss two key relationships in the H–O–S model: the relationship between factor prices and factor inputs, and the relationship between factor prices and output prices.

Factor prices and factor use

Dividing w by r in (4.6) gives the economy's wage–rental ratio (ω) as a function of an industry's capital–labor ratio:

$$\omega(k_j) = \frac{f_j(k_j)}{f_j'(k_j)} - k_j \qquad j = 1, 2$$

(4.13)

Since

$$\frac{d\omega}{dk_j} = -\frac{f_j f_j''}{(f_j')^2} > 0,$$

(4.13) can be inverted to express each k_j uniquely in terms of the economy's wage–rental ratio, that is, $k_j = k_j(\omega)$ where:

$$\frac{dk_j}{d\omega} = -\frac{(f_j')^2}{f_j f_j''} > 0 \qquad j = 1, 2$$

(4.14)

The positive relationship between k_j and ω derives from the fact that a rise in the wage–rental ratio leads producers in each industry to substitute capital for labor, thus raising the capital–labor ratio.

Problem 4.2: Given (4.13), use Figure 4.1 to show that if $k_j = OA$ then $w = CO$. Also, verify graphically that a rise in w/r raises the cost minimizing capital–labor ratio of each industry.

Problem 4.3: Show that (4.14) is related to the elasticity of substitution of capital for labor and verify that the relationship is positive.

Figure 4.3 illustrates the function $k_j(w)$ for each industry. Consistent with (4.14), each curve is drawn positively sloped. The relative placement of the two curves assumes industry 1 is capital-intensive (equivalently, industry 2 is labor-intensive).[10]
   Whereas the function $k_j(w)$ is defined for all values of w, the full employment constraint (4.10) restricts the range of w. For example, if the economy's overall capital–labor ratio is $K/L = k$, Figure 4.3 indicates that w is restricted to the interval $[w_{min}, w_{max}]$. To see why, note that when $w = w_{min}$ the economy is completely specialized in the production of good 1 since $k_1 = k$ and thus $\lambda_1 = 1$. Inserting these values into (4.13) gives the value of w_{min} as:

$$w_{min} = \frac{f_1(k)}{f'_1(k)} - k$$

Conversely, when $w = w_{max}$ the economy is completely specialized in the production of good 2 since $k_2 = k$ and thus $\lambda_2 = 1$. From (4.13), the value of w_{max} is:

$$w_{max} = \frac{f_2(k)}{f'_2(k)} - k$$

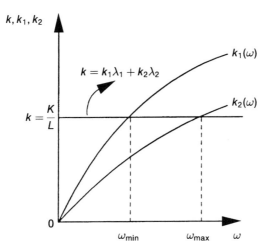

Figure 4.3   *Relationship between industry capital–labor ratios and the wage–rental ratio*

Since ω_{min} and ω_{max} correspond to complete specialization in one good or the other, we must have $\omega_{min} < \omega < \omega_{max}$ if both goods are to be produced in equilibrium.

Problem 4.4:   Verify that if $\omega < \omega_{min}$ or $\omega > \omega_{max}$ some resource must be unemployed.

Factor prices and commodity prices

If both goods are produced in equilibrium, conditions (4.7) imply that we can write:

$$p(\omega) = \frac{f'_1(k_1(\omega))}{f'_2(k_2(\omega))} \tag{4.15}$$

which gives the relative price of good 2 ($p = p_2/p_1$) as a function of ω alone. Totally differentiating (4.15), and making use of (4.13) and (4.14), we obtain:

$$\frac{1}{p}\frac{dp}{d\omega} = \frac{k_1(\omega) - k_2(\omega)}{(\omega + k_2(\omega))(\omega + k_1(\omega))} \gtreqless 0 \quad \text{as } (k_1(\omega) - k_2(\omega)) \gtreqless 0 \tag{4.16}$$

which indicates that the slope of the relationship between relative output prices and relative factor prices depends upon which industry is capital-intensive. Figure 4.4 illustrates (4.15) assuming, as in Figure 4.3, that

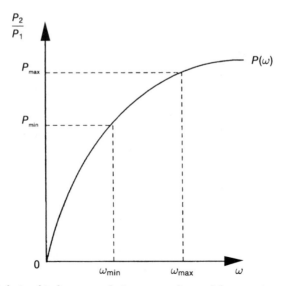

Figure 4.4   *Relationship between relative commodity and factor prices*

industry 1 is capital-intensive at all values of ω (i.e. $(k_1 - k_2) > 0 \; \forall \omega > 0)$.[11] Note that this 'strong factor intensity' assumption ensures a one-to-one relationship between $p(\omega)$ and ω. Since this assumption is important for establishing several key results in the H–O–S model we state it explicitly:

Assumption 4 (no factor intensity reversals): The ordering of industry capital–labor ratios is invariant to changes in ω.

Finally, in Figure 4.4, the function $p(\omega)$ is drawn continuous outside the interval $[p_{min}, p_{max}]$ since nothing restricts the sale of a good at an increasingly favorable price.

Problem 4.5: Let production in each sector be described by the following Cobb–Douglas functions: $q_1 = K_1^\alpha L_1^{1-\alpha}$ and $q_2 = K_2^\beta L_2^{1-\beta}$. (a) Derive relationship (4.15) and its inverse – that is, the relationship between the industry capital–labor ratio and relative factor prices. Does the possibility for factor intensity reversals exist? (b) Assume the following values for the parameters and exogenous variables of the model: $\alpha = 0.5$, $\beta = 0.25$, $p = 0.743$, $K = 0.8$ and $L = 2$. Using the production model described so far, construct a computer program to solve for the level of all endogenous variables $\{q_j, k_j, \lambda_j, w, r\}$.

Changes in factor supplies and output prices

The equations (4.6), (4.11), (4.12), (4.13) and (4.15) comprise a model with ten endogenous variables $\{q_j, k_j, \lambda_j, p_j, w, r\}$. Taking p_j as known, this system can be solved for the remaining eight variables in terms of the economy's factor supplies and commodity prices. Note that this model only covers the supply side of the economy. To also solve for the equilibrium commodity prices we must add demand. This is discussed in Sections 4.2 and 4.3.

Since commodity prices and national factor supplies are given, we can consider how a change in one of these exogenous variables would affect the values of the model's endogenous variables. Two important cases are considered below: the effect of an output price change on factor prices and the effect of a factor supply change on outputs.

With both commodities produced, (4.16) states that a rise in the price of good j will raise (lower) the relative return (ω) to labor if the industry producing good j is labor-intensive (capital-intensive). Given this, we need consider here only the effect of a price change on individual factor rewards.

Consider an increase in p_1, an increase in p_2 being analyzed by analogy. Totally differentiating (4.6) with respect to p_1 yields:

$$\frac{dw}{dp_1} = \frac{k_2 f_1}{k_2 - k_1} \gtreqless 0 \quad \text{as } (k_2 - k_1) \gtreqless 0 \tag{4.17}$$

$$\frac{dr}{dp_1} = \frac{-f_2}{k_2 - k_1} \gtreqless 0 \quad \text{as } (k_2 - k_1) \lesseqgtr 0 \tag{4.18}$$

As indicated, an increase in the price of good 1 will raise the nominal return to the factor used intensively in the production of good 1.

The effect on real factor rewards can be established by comparing the proportional change in nominal factor prices to the proportional change in output price. Writing (4.17) and (4.18) in elasticity form, and making use of (4.13), we can after some manipulation write:

$$\frac{dw}{dp_1} \frac{p_1}{w} = -\frac{k_2(w + k_1)}{w(k_1 - k_2)} \tag{4.19}$$

$$\frac{dr}{dp_1} \frac{p_1}{r} = \frac{w + k_1}{k_1 - k_2} \tag{4.20}$$

If industry 1 is capital-intensive ($k_1 > k_2$) then

$$\frac{dr}{dp_1} \frac{p_1}{r} > 1$$

and

$$\frac{dw}{dp_1} \frac{p_1}{w} < 1 \quad^{12}$$

Hence, if industry 1 is capital-intensive, a rise in the price of good 1 will raise the real return to capital and lower the real return to labor (both returns measured in units of good 1). Since p_2 is held fixed, these changes also apply to the real returns measured in units of good 2.

The preceding effects on factor rewards in response to a change in output price are summarized by the Stolper–Samuelson theorem:

Proposition 4.1 (Stolper–Samuelson): An increase in the price of any good raises the nominal, relative and real return to the factor intensive in the production of that good and lowers the nominal, relative and real return to the other factor.

The effect on production of an exogenous change in national factor supplies is contained in the Rybczynski theorem:

Proposition 4.2 (Rybczynski): If capital–labor ratios differ between industries then, at constant commodity prices, an increase in the supply of one factor alone will cause an expansion of the good intensive in the use of that factor and an absolute decline in the output of the other good.[13]

It suffices to consider an increase in capital since an increase in labor can be analyzed by analogy. By reference to Figures 4.1 and 4.3 (or (4.10) and (4.13)), fixing output prices implies that the values of ω, the k_j, and thus the $f_j(k_j)$, are also fixed. Hence, any change in outputs $q_j = L_j f_j(k_j)$ must come from a change in L_j (equivalently, λ_j, since L is given).[14] Differentiating expressions (4.11) with respect to K gives:

$$\frac{dL_1}{dK} = \frac{1}{k_1 - k_2} \tag{4.21}$$

$$\frac{dL_2}{dK} = -\frac{1}{k_1 - k_2} \tag{4.22}$$

Using these, the effect on production is:

$$\frac{dq_1}{dK} = \frac{f_1}{k_1 - k_2} \gtrless 0 \quad \text{as } (k_1 - k_2) \gtrless 0 \tag{4.23}$$

$$\frac{dq_2}{dK} = \frac{-f_2}{k_1 - k_2} \lessgtr 0 \quad \text{as } (k_1 - k_2) \gtrless 0 \tag{4.24}$$

which establishes the proposition.

Finally, we note three additional results related to this topic. First, the total effect on national income ($Y = p_1 L_1 f_1 + p_2 L_2 f_2$) of an increase in capital is:

$$\frac{dY}{dK} = p_1 f_1 \frac{dL_1}{dK} + p_2 f_2 \frac{dL_2}{dK} = r > 0 \tag{4.25}$$

Hence, at constant output prices, each unit of accumulated capital unambiguously raises national income by an amount equal to its rental price. Second, by manipulating (4.23) and (4.24) we can obtain the following inequality:

$$\hat{q}_1 > \hat{K} > \hat{L} = 0 > \hat{q}_2$$

where the '^' denotes the relative change in a variable (e.g. $\hat{q} = dq/q$). This states that the relative change in capital (labor) must lie between the relative change in outputs. This result is known as a 'magnification effect'.

Finally, by dividing (4.24) by (4.23) we obtain an expression for the relative change in outputs due to the change in capital:

$$\frac{dq_1}{dq_2}\bigg]_{\hat{L}=0} = -\frac{f_1}{f_2} < 0 \tag{4.26}$$

where $\hat{L} = 0$ denotes that labor is held constant. This equation implicitly defines a line in (q_1, q_2) space (with slope given by (4.26)) called a Rybczynski line (R line). Geometrically, an R line connects the production point on the initial production frontier to the production point on the new production frontier resulting from the change in factor supply, with commodity prices held fixed.

Whereas (4.26) relates to an increase in capital, similar reasoning with respect to a change in labor alone leads to the R line for labor:

$$\left. \frac{dq_1}{dq_2} \right]_{\hat{K}=0} = -\frac{f_1 k_2}{f_2 k_1}$$

In general, an R line is negatively sloped with the magnitude of the slope depending on the initial values of $k_1(w)$ and $k_2(w)$, or equivalently, the initial output prices since the capital–labor ratios are functions of w which is in turn a function of relative output prices. The effect on outputs of a combined change in both capital and labor can also be derived by totally differentiating (4.11).

Simulation analysis

The effect of factor supply changes on outputs and factor employment can be illustrated using the computer model of Problem 4.5. Table 4.1 lists these effects under three scenarios: a 10% increase in either K or L alone and a combined 10% increase in both factors. The numbers shown are the

Table 4.1   *Effects of an exogenous change in factor supplies*

| | | % change in variable due to a 10% increase in: | | |
| | Base solution | Capital | Labor | Both |
Variable	(1)	(2)	(3)	(4)
Capital-intensive industry 1				
Output (q_1)	0.958			
Capital employed (K_1)	0.690	17.0	−6.8	10
Labor employed (L_1)	1.330			
Labor-intensive industry 2				
Output (q_2)	0.426			
Capital employed (K_2)	0.110	−33.6	43.5	10
Labor employed (L_2)	0.670			

percentage change in each variable relative to its initial solution value obtained from Problem 4.5 and reproduced in column (1).

As expected, an increase in either factor alone leads to an absolute increase in the output of the industry intensive in the growing factor and an absolute decline in the output of the other industry. The combined 10% increase in labor and capital provides an intermediate outcome. Note that when the supply of both factors is increased the 'magnification effect' on outputs is not obtained. Since goods prices are fixed by assumption, relative price effects are excluded and industries' capital–labor ratios are constant. This together with expressions (4.12) explain why industry j's uses of factors must change at the same rate as industry j's output.

Duality

The preceding section has studied the problem of national income maximization and optimal resource allocation in terms of factor inputs and commodity outputs. In this section, these issues are approached from the dual perspective of cost minimization defined over the space of factor prices and output prices.[15] Since the adjustment within the neoclassical model is based on relative price changes, one can argue that it is preferable to deal with cost functions as they deal directly with prices, rather than production functions which relate to quantities, and are only indirectly affected by prices. A strong advantage of this approach is that we can observe cost functions directly, which is not the case for production functions. Duality allows for a general treatment using the vector method. In what follows we will assume H factor inputs (capital, skilled and unskilled labor, resources,...) and J commodities. But, for some practical applications, the vector dimension will be reduced to two.

The minimum cost function

Consider an economy consisting of J competitive industries. Each industry employs H factor inputs $e_j = (e_{j1}, \ldots, e_{jH})$ to produce an amount q_j of a single good using the production function $q_j = F_j(e_j)$. By the duality between production and cost functions, there exists a minimum cost function:

$$C_j(\mathbf{w}, q_j) = \min_{e_j} \left\{ \mathbf{w} \cdot e = \sum_{h=1}^{H} w_h e_{jh} : F_j(e_j) \geq q_j \right\} \tag{4.27}$$

which serves as a sufficient description of the technology.[16] The set of input requirements comprises all those that can produce at least the output level q_j

according to the production function $F_j(e_j)$. Given an input price vector $\mathbf{w} = (w_1, \ldots, w_H)$, a firm chooses its optimal factor requirements to minimize its total cost (factor payments). Under certain regularity conditions,[17] the minimum cost function $C_j(\mathbf{w}, q_j)$ and the production function $F_j(e_j)$ completely determine each other and are thus equivalent representations of the same underlying technology.

Input demands

If $F_j(e_j)$ is linearly homogeneous then the cost function can be written as $C_j(\mathbf{w}, q_j) = q_j c_j(\mathbf{w})$, where $c_j(\mathbf{w})$ is the unit cost function which represents both average and marginal production cost. An important property of the unit cost function is Shephard's lemma:[18] if $c_j(\mathbf{w})$ is differentiable with respect to $\mathbf{w}$ at the factor price vector $\mathbf{w}'$ then the demand for factor h per-unit of output is given by the partial derivative of the unit cost function with respect to its price:

$$\frac{\partial c_j(\mathbf{w}')}{\partial w_h} = a_{jh} \tag{4.28}$$

where a_{jh} is the demand for factor h per-unit of output j – that is, the optimal unit factor input requirement. Given (4.28), industry j's total demand for factor h is obtained as $e_{jh} = a_{jh} q_j$.

Production equilibrium

We now express the conditions for a competitive equilibrium in the economy in terms of the above unit cost function. The profit maximization problem for industry j is:

$$\Pi_j(p_j, \mathbf{w}) = \max_{q_j} \{q_j[p_j - c_j(\mathbf{w})], q_j \geq 0\} \qquad j = 1, \ldots, J$$

where $\Pi_j(p_j, \mathbf{w})$ denotes industry j's maximum profit for given factor prices $\mathbf{w}$ and output price p_j. The solution to this problem requires that output be chosen so as to equate price and marginal cost. Combining this condition with the long-run equilibrium requirement of zero profits in each industry, a competitive equilibrium requires the following conditions to be satisfied:

$$q_j[p_j - c_j(\mathbf{w})] = 0 \qquad j = 1, \ldots, J \tag{4.29}$$

$$c_j(\mathbf{w}) - p_j \geq 0 \qquad j = 1, \ldots, J \tag{4.30}$$

Together, (4.29) and (4.30) state that any good produced in a long-run equilibrium ($q_j > 0$) must yield zero profit whereas any good with negative profit will not be produced ($q_j = 0$).[19]

To (4.29) and (4.30) we add the factor market equilibrium (full employ-ment) conditions:

$$\sum_{j=1}^{J} a_{jh}q_j \leq e_h \qquad h = 1,\ldots,H \tag{4.31}$$

where e_h is the national supply of factor h and the a_{jh} are as defined in (4.28). If the price of input h is positive ($w_h > 0$) then (4.31) holds with equality, i.e. factor h is fully employed. If $w_h = 0$ then factor h is in excess supply (underemployed).

Finally, multiply (4.29) by q_j and sum over j to state the equality between national income and GDP at market prices:

$$\sum_{j=1}^{J} q_j c_j(\mathbf{w}) = \sum_{j=1}^{J} p_j q_j = \mathbf{pq} \tag{4.32}$$

An equivalent statement in terms of factor payments is obtained by multiplying (4.31) by w_h and summing over h:

$$\sum_{j=1}^{J} q_j \sum_{h=1}^{H} a_{jh}w_h = \sum_{j=1}^{J} q_j c_j(\mathbf{w}) = \sum_{h=1}^{H} w_h e_h = \mathbf{we} \tag{4.33}$$

Hence, in equilibrium, GDP at market prices equals the payments to factors (i.e. $\mathbf{pq} = \mathbf{we}$), the latter being GDP at factor cost.

(4.28), (4.29), (4.30) and (4.31) comprise a J-sector model which can be solved for the input requirements (a_{jh}), input prices (w_h), and outputs q_j in terms of the given national factor supplies (e_h) and commodity prices (p_j). When $H = 2$ and $J = 2$, the production equilibrium described above is identical to that of the traditional analysis of this section.

The revenue function

(4.32) gives the revenue an economy receives for a particular configuration of output prices (**p**) and factor supplies (**e**). Another choice of **p** and **e** would generate another value for the economy's revenue. Hence, there exists a revenue function $G(\mathbf{p}, \mathbf{e})$ that records the highest attainable revenue for a given set of output prices and factor supplies:

$$G(\mathbf{p}, \mathbf{e}) = \mathbf{p} \cdot \mathbf{q}(\mathbf{p}, \mathbf{e}) \tag{4.34}$$

where $\mathbf{q}(\mathbf{p}, \mathbf{e})$ denotes the vector of profit maximizing output choices for given output prices and factor supplies.[20] An important property of the revenue function is Hotelling's lemma: if $G(\mathbf{p}, \mathbf{e})$ is differentiable with respect to **p** at the commodity price vector $\mathbf{p}^0$ then the output supply function of good j is given by the partial derivative of the revenue function with respect to the price of commodity j:

$$\frac{\partial G(\mathbf{p}, \mathbf{e})}{\partial p_j} = q_j \qquad j = 1, \ldots, J \tag{4.35}$$

From (4.33) we can also write this as:

$$\frac{\partial G(\mathbf{p}, \mathbf{e})}{\partial e_h} = w_h \qquad h = 1, \ldots, H \tag{4.36}$$

that is, the equilibrium price of factor h is given as the partial derivative of the revenue function with respect to the supply of factor h.[21]

As an example, consider the maximization of income for an economy producing two goods q_1 and q_2. For given prices p_1 and p_2, national income is then GDP $= p_1 q_1 + p_2 q_2$. Fixing the value of GDP at some level, say $\overline{\text{GDP}}$, this equation can be solved to express the combinations q_1 and q_2 that would yield, at the given prices, the income level $\overline{\text{GDP}}$: $q_1 = \overline{\text{GDP}}/p_1 - (p_2/p_1)q_2$. As shown in Figure 4.5, this equation defines an 'iso-income' line whose intercepts measure real income in units of the good recorded on the particular axis (i.e. $\overline{\text{GDP}}/p_j$, $j = 1, 2$) and whose slope is (minus) the relative price of the other good ($p = p_2/p_1$ in the example).

Given the economy's transformation curve[22] $O_1 A O_2$, the economy's maximal income is obtained by producing the combination of outputs given by point A, where an iso-income line is tangent to the transformation curve. Any other combination of outputs (e.g. point B or C) would lie on a lower iso-income line of the same slope. Finally, we can verify Hotelling's lemma for good 2:

$$\frac{\partial G(\mathbf{p}, \mathbf{e})}{\partial p_2} = q_2 + p_1(\partial q_1/\partial p_2) + p_2(\partial q_2/\partial p_2) = q_2$$

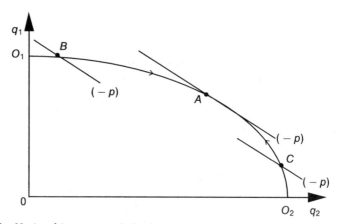

Figure 4.5 *National income maximization*

since

$$\frac{\partial q_1}{\partial q_2} = -p_1/p_2 \quad \text{at point } A.$$

Problem 4.6: The transformation curve in Figure 4.5 is drawn strictly concave with respect to the origin. Show that this is due to the assumption of constant returns to scale, to the difference in industry factor intensities, and to the assumption of competitive markets.

Problem 4.7: Demonstrate that if an economy produces at a point like B or C in Figure 4.5, market clearing via price adjustment would bring the economy back to an equilibrium at point A. How important is the concavity assumption of the transformation curve for this result?

The reciprocity condition

An important implication of the duality between production and cost functions as expressed in (4.35) and (4.36) is the reciprocity condition:

$$\frac{\partial q_j}{\partial e_h} = \frac{\partial w_h}{\partial p_j} \qquad j = 1, \dots, J; \; h = 1, \dots, H \tag{4.37}$$

This is established by differentiating (4.35) with respect to p_j and differentiating (4.36) with respect to e_h and noting that:

$$\frac{\partial^2 G}{\partial e_h \, \partial p_j} = \frac{\partial^2 G}{\partial p_j \, \partial e_h}$$

In words, (4.37) says that the effect of a change in the supply of factor h on the production of good j is equal in magnitude to the effect of a change in the price of good j on the price of factor $h(w_h)$. The left-hand side of (4.37) derives from the Rybczynski theorem whereas the right-hand side derives from the Stolper–Samuelson theorem. The reciprocity condition has important empirical significance since it means that we do not need to separately estimate the effects of factor supply changes and price changes, we can instead infer one from the other.

The factor price frontier

Assume 2 goods and 2 factors (capital and labor) and let the price of good 1 be the numeraire. The zero profit conditions in this case are:

$$p = a_{2L}w + a_{2K}r \tag{4.38}$$

$$1 = a_{1L}w + a_{1K}r \tag{4.39}$$

where a_{jh} is the equilibrium requirement of factor h per-unit of output j and factor prices w and r are measured in units of good 1.[23] Solving (4.38) and (4.39) individually for w, and noting that $a_{jK}/a_{jL} = k_j(\omega)$, we obtain:

$$w = \frac{1}{a_{2L}} p - k_2(\omega)r \tag{4.40}$$

$$w = \frac{1}{a_{1L}} - k_1(\omega)r \tag{4.41}$$

Figure 4.6 depicts (4.40) and (4.41) as the iso-price curves p and 1, respectively. The absolute value of the slope of each curve at a particular combination of w and r equals the industry's capital–labor ratio. By (4.14), each curve is convex to the origin since the capital–labor ratio is an increasing function of the wage–rental ratio. The intersection of the two curves (point A) determines the economy's equilibrium wage $(\bar{w})$ and rental rate $(\bar{r})$ consistent with zero profits in both industries. That the iso-price curves intersect only once is due to the assumption of no factor intensity reversals.

The Stolper–Samuelson theorem again

Using (4.40) and (4.41), it is a simple matter to determine the effect of a change in commodity prices on factor prices. Consider Figure 4.6 and

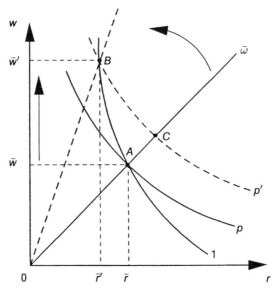

Figure 4.6 *Factor price frontiers*

assume the relative price of good 2 increases from p to p' . This price increase shifts the iso-price curve from p to p' and establishes a new zero profit equilibrium at point B. Hence, $\bar{w}$ rises to $\bar{w}'$ and $\bar{r}$ falls to $\bar{r}'$ The resulting rise in the wage–rental ratio induces both industries to substitute capital for labor as reflected by the steeper slope of each curve at point B relative to point A.

Since good 1 is the numeraire and p has risen, capital's real return has fallen in terms of both goods whereas labor's real return has risen in terms of good 1. To determine labor's return in terms of good 2, note that any point along the line $O\bar{w}$ corresponds to the increase in factor rewards proportional to an increase in p. For example, point C is consistent with a constant ratio of w (or r) to p'. Since point B lies above the ray $O\bar{w}$, the wage has thus also increased relative to the price of good 2.

Finally, Figure 4.6 indicates that there is a 'magnification effect' associated with the relative change in output price and the relative change in factor prices, namely:

$$\hat{w} > \hat{p} > 0 > \hat{r}$$

This relationship can be derived analytically using (4.38) and (4.39) with p replaced by p'.

Simulation analysis

As with factor supply changes, the effect of an output price change can be illustrated using the computer model of Problem 4.5. In this regard, Table 4.2 shows the effect on factor prices, factor employment and outputs due to a 10% increase in the price of good 2. The percentage changes shown are measured relative to the initial solution discussed in Table 4.1.

As expected, a rise in the price of good 2 shifts production from the capital-intensive industry 1 to the labor-intensive industry 2. Consistent with the Stolper–Samuelson theorem, this price increase raises the wage rate and lowers the rental rate, and the resulting rise in the relative wage leads each industry to increase its use of capital relative to labor.

4.2 Specification of demand

Traditional analysis

With identical preferences, utility maximization by consumers results in demand functions which depend on prices and national income: $d_j = d_j(Y, \mathbf{p})$, where national income Y is measured in units of good 1. If

Table 4.2   *General equilibrium effects of a 10% increase in price of good 2*

Variable	Base solution	10% increase in p
Outputs		
Industry 1 (q_1)	0.96	0.52
Industry 2 (q_2)	0.43	1.00
Factor prices		
Rental rate (r)	0.70	0.58
Wage rate (w)	0.36	0.43
Ratio (w/r)	0.51	0.75
Factor inputs		
Capital–Labor ratio		
Industry 1 (k_1)	0.51	0.75
Industry 2 (k_2)	0.17	0.25
Labor employed in		
Industry 1 (L_1)	1.33	0.59
Industry 2 (L_2)	0.67	1.41
Capital employed in		
Industry 1 (K_1)	0.69	0.45
Industry 2 (K_2)	0.11	0.35

these optimal demands are substituted back into the utility function we obtain the indirect utility function, $V(Y, \mathbf{p}) = U(d_1(Y, \mathbf{p}), d_2(Y, \mathbf{p}))$. The indirect utility function records the maximum utility attainable for a particular configuration of prices $\mathbf{p}$ and national income Y. A useful property of the indirect utility function is Roy's identity:

$$d_j(Y, \mathbf{p}) = -\frac{\partial V(Y, \mathbf{p})/\partial p_j}{\partial V(Y, \mathbf{p})/\partial Y} \quad j = 1, \ldots, J \quad (4.42)$$

which establishes that the ordinary demand function for good j can be derived from the indirect utility function as the ratio of partial derivatives with respect to the price of good j and income, respectively.

Duality

Just as duality between output maximization and cost minimization in production gives rise to the GDP or revenue function, duality between utility maximization and expenditure minimization gives rise to the spending (expenditure) function:

$$S(\mathbf{p}, \bar{u}) = \min_{\mathbf{d}} \left\{ \mathbf{p} \cdot \mathbf{d} = \sum_{1}^{J} p_j d_j : u(\mathbf{d}) \geq \bar{u}, \mathbf{d} \geq 0 \right\} \tag{4.43}$$

where $\bar{u}$ denotes a given level of utility and $\mathbf{d}$ is the vector of quantities demanded. The expenditure function records, for given prices $\mathbf{p}$, the minimum expenditure (cost) necessary to obtain utility level $\bar{u}$. By analogy to Shephard's lemma, differentiation of (4.43) with respect to the price of good j yields the compensated (Hicksian) demand functions:

$$\frac{\partial S(\mathbf{p}, \bar{u})}{\partial p_j} = h_j(\mathbf{p}, \bar{u}) \qquad j = 1, \ldots, J \tag{4.44}$$

To relate these compensated demand functions to the ordinary demand functions $(d_j(\mathbf{p}, Y))$ we assume that consumers spend all of their money income in achieving maximum utility so that $Y = S(\mathbf{p}, \bar{u})$. Given this, replace Y in $d_j(\mathbf{p}, Y)$ to express d_j as a function of prices and the utility level $\bar{u}$:

$$h_j(\mathbf{p}, \bar{u}) = d_j(\mathbf{p}, S(\mathbf{p}, \bar{u})) \tag{4.45}$$

Alternatively, solve $Y = S(\mathbf{p}, \bar{u})$ for the level of utility $\bar{u}$ in terms of prices and income, that is, $\bar{u} = V(Y, \mathbf{p})$ where V is the indirect utility function, and then substitute this into $h_j(\cdot)$ to express it as a function of prices and income:

$$h_j(\mathbf{p}, V(\mathbf{p}, Y)) = d_j(\mathbf{p}, Y) \tag{4.46}$$

The effect of a price change on demand can be examined by differentiating (4.45) with respect to p_i:

$$\frac{\partial d_j}{\partial p_i} = \frac{\partial h_j}{\partial p_i} - \frac{\partial d_j}{\partial S} \frac{\partial S}{\partial p_i} \tag{4.47}$$

This states the known result that the effect of a price change on demand is composed of a substitution effect

$$\frac{\partial h_j}{\partial p_i}$$

and a real income effect

$$-\frac{\partial d_j}{\partial S} \frac{\partial S}{\partial p_i}$$

Homothetic preferences

If the utility function is assumed to be homothetic or, more specifically, linear homogeneous[24] the spending function has the simple form

$S(\mathbf{p}, \bar{u}) = \bar{u} \cdot s(\mathbf{p})$ where $s(\mathbf{p}) = S(\mathbf{p}, 1)$ is the 'unit utility' spending function. Since $\bar{u} = V(\mathbf{p}, Y)$, the indirect utility function takes the special form:

$$V(Y, \mathbf{p}) = S(\mathbf{p}, \bar{u})/s(\mathbf{p}) = Y/s(\mathbf{p}) \qquad (4.48)$$

In addition, the compensated demand functions take the form:

$$\frac{\partial S(\mathbf{p}, \bar{u})}{\partial p_j} = \bar{u}\,\frac{\partial s(\mathbf{p})}{\partial p_j} \qquad (4.49)$$

whereas the ordinary demand functions, by Roy's identity, become:

$$d_j(\mathbf{p}, Y) = Y\,\frac{\partial s(\mathbf{p})/\partial p_j}{s(\mathbf{p})} = Y\zeta(\mathbf{p}) \qquad (4.50)$$

where $\zeta(\mathbf{p})$ is some function of relative output prices. A primary implication of homothetic preferences is that the ratio of demands $d_j(\mathbf{p}, Y)/d_i(\mathbf{p}, Y)$ is independent of the level of income or utility. Equivalently, the share of total expenditure spent on any good $(d_j(\mathbf{p}, Y)/Y = \zeta(\mathbf{p}))$ only depends on relative prices.

Problem 4.8:   Assume that the utility function is of the Cobb–Douglas type $U = d_1^\gamma d_2^{1-\gamma}$ with $\gamma = 0.5$. Solve the computable model of Problem 4.5 for the variables of demand, import and export. Add to this the level of social welfare as measured by the value of U.

4.3 Autarky and international equilibria

The preceding sections have presented the supply and demand elements of the competitive general equilibrium model underlying the H–O–S model. This section combines these elements to demonstrate first the determination of a country's autarky prices and then the determination of the post-trade (world) equilibrium prices. We then discuss the stability of the world equilibrium.

Autarky price determination

Figures 4.7 and 4.8 portray the general equilibrium of an economy in autarky, a situation where all commodities are produced and consumed in equilibrium. Figure 4.7 considers the question using the traditional approach, Figure 4.8 using duality.

Figure 4.7 superimposes a social indifference map on the transformation curve O_1AO_2. Autarkic equilibrium is located where the economy attains the highest possible indifference curve given its production possibilities, that

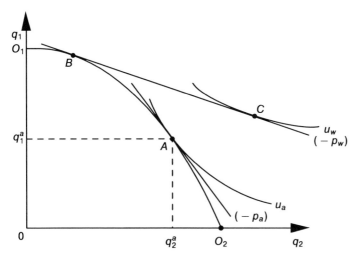

Figure 4.7 *Autarkic equilibrium and community indifference curve*

is point A. At this point, the economy produces and consumes q_1^a units of good 1, q_2^a units of good 2, the equilibrium being achieved at the price p_a. Tangency of O_1AO_2 to the indifference curve u_a implies the equality between the autarkic relative price, the rate of transformation in production and the rate of substitution in consumption.

Figure 4.8 depicts the autarkic equilibrium employing the revenue function (4.34) and the expenditure function (4.43). National revenue and expenditure are measured along the vertical axis. Price p_j is measured along

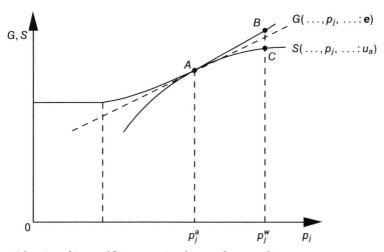

Figure 4.8 *Autarkic equilibrium, national expenditure and income*

the horizontal axis. Given the equilibrium values for all other prices, the expenditure function $S(p_1, \ldots, p_j, \ldots, p_J : u_a)$ gives for each value of p_j the expenditure necessary to obtain the same autarkic utility u_a. The revenue function $G(p_1, \ldots, p_j, \ldots, p_J : e)$ records the increase in national income as the price of good j rises (see n. 21). The slopes of $G(\cdot)$ and $S(\cdot)$ are q_j and h_j respectively, by (4.35) and (4.44). At point A, $h_j = q_j$ so that the autarkic equilibrium price is p_j^a.

After having determined the equilibrium of an isolated economy, the next step is to consider international trade. The opening of international trade implies the introduction of foreign consumers and producers, and therefore a world price ratio that, in general, will be different from the one which prevails under autarky. The next section considers the international equilibrium and, in this regards, extends the concepts first introduced in Section 3.2 (pp. 80–6).

World price determination

Assuming there are only two goods, Figure 4.9 illustrates both the demand and supply functions for good 2 and the associated excess demand function for good 2. The excess demand function is the difference between the demand and supply of good 2 at alternative values of $p = p_2/p_1$.[25] By definition, excess demand is zero at the autarky price p_a. Below p_a, excess demand is positive and corresponds to the country's import demand: $m_2 = d_2(p) - q_2(p)$. Above p_a, there is an excess supply (negative excess

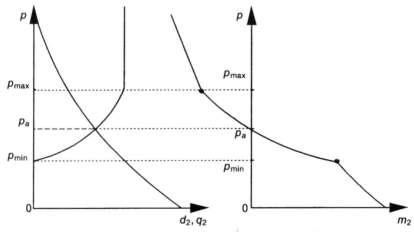

Figure 4.9   *Excess demand function for good 2*

demand) of good 2 and corresponds to the country's export supply $(-m_2 \equiv x_2(p) = q_2(p) - d_2(p))$. Since limited factor supplies constrain the supply of good 2, the excess demand function is not everywhere smooth and there are 2 points of non-differentiability: p_{min} and p_{max}. Assuming good 2 is capital-intensive, the economy produces only good 1 for $p \leq p_{min}$ and produces only good 2 for $p \geq p_{max}$.

In similar fashion, the foreign country's autarky price p_a^* and excess demand function can be derived from its underlying demand and supply functions. Assuming $p_a > p_a^*$, Figure 4.10 combines the excess demand functions of each country in one graph. Given these, trade will result in the equilibrium world price ratio p_w as determined by the point of intersection between home's import demand and foreign's export supply. Note that p_w equates, by definition, the world demand and world supply of good 2 since the equality of excess demands at p_w can also be written $d_2(p_w) + d_2^*(p_w) = q_2(p_w) + q_2^*(p_w)$. By Walras' Law, the price $1/p_w$ also clears the world market for good 1.[26]

The decline in the relative price of good 2 from p_a to p_w is illustrated in Figure 4.7 as a movement of the domestic production point from A to B and of the domestic consumption point from A to C. Point C is better than point A as it lies on a higher indifference curve. This shows the gains from trade. Likewise, gains from trade arise in Figure 4.8 but stem from the curvature of $G(\cdot)$ and $S(\cdot)$. A world price of p_j^w, for example, would provide, *ceteris paribus*, a gain from trade equivalent to the distance BC. This is obtained since $G(\cdot) > S(\cdot)$ for any price greater than p_j^a.

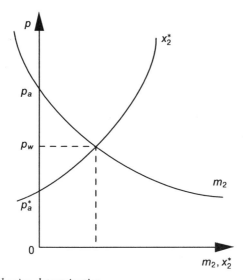

Figure 4.10 *World price determination*

Problem 4.9:   Using the parameter and exogenous values of Problems 4.5 and 4.8: (a) solve the general equilibrium model for the autarkic level of all endogenous variables of the model (including social welfare U); (b) discuss the sensitivity of your results in (a) with respect to changes in the parameters α, β and γ; (c) solve for the international price as a result of trade between two countries similar in all respects except for a higher foreign endowment of labor, namely $L^* = 2.2$. Check that countries are not worse off with the opening of international trade.

Import demand and market stability

A key point to be learned from Figure 4.10 is that the price elasticities of the import demand and export supply functions derive from the properties of the underlying domestic demands and supplies. Since these demand and supply functions have been derived in a general equilibrium setting, the elasticities associated with these functions are also general equilibrium, not partial equilibrium.[27] Below we decompose the import and export price elasticities into their fundamental components and show that the values of these elasticities are crucial for determining the stability of the international equilibrium.

Totally differentiating the expression for the import demand for good 2, i.e. $m_2 = d_2(p, Y) - q_2(p)$, and noting that $S = Y$ gives:

$$dm_2 = \frac{\partial d_2}{\partial p}\, dp + \frac{\partial d_2}{\partial S}\, \frac{\partial Y}{\partial p}\, dp - \frac{\partial q_2}{\partial p}\, dp \tag{4.51}$$

Using (4.47) we can replace

$$\frac{\partial d_2}{\partial p}$$

in (4.51) to get:

$$dm_2 = \left[\frac{\partial h_2}{\partial p} - \frac{\partial q_2}{\partial p}\right] dp - \frac{\partial d_2}{\partial S}\left[\frac{\partial S}{\partial p} - \frac{\partial Y}{\partial p}\right] dp \tag{4.52}$$

Dividing (4.52) by m_2 and noting that

$$\left(\frac{\partial S}{\partial p} - \frac{\partial Y}{\partial p}\right) = (d_2 - q_2) = m_2$$

(4.52) can be written:

$$\hat{m}_2 = \left[\frac{p}{m_2}\frac{\partial h_2}{\partial p} - \frac{p}{m_2}\frac{\partial q_2}{\partial p} - p\frac{\partial d_2}{\partial S}\right]\hat{p} \tag{4.53}$$

where '^' denotes the relative change in a variable (e.g. $\hat{p} = dp/p$). Finally, divide both sides of (4.53) by $\hat{p}$ to obtain the expression for the price elasticity of import demand ($e = -\hat{m}_2/\hat{p}$):

$$e = e_1 + e_2 + e_3 \tag{4.54}$$

where $e_1 = -(p/m_2)(\partial h_2/\partial p)$ is the compensated price elasticity, $e_2 = (p/m_2)(\partial q_2/\partial p)$ is the supply elasticity and $e_3 = p(\partial d_2/\partial S)$ is the marginal propensity to consume good 2 (i.e. the fraction of an increase in expenditure that is spent on importables). Note that $0 < e_3 < 1$ for normal goods, $e_3 > 1$ if good 1 is inferior and $e_3 < 0$ if good 2 is inferior. All elasticities are defined to be positive.[28]

Problem 4.10: Define the price elasticity of home export supply as $f = -\hat{x}_1/\hat{p}$. Show that $f = e - 1$. Define $f^* = \hat{x}_2^*/\hat{p}$ and $e^* = \hat{m}_1^*/\hat{p}$ and show that similar relations hold for the foreign country.

Market stability

Stability of the international equilibrium references the ability of the system to return to its original equilibrium after a disturbance. For example, suppose p were to fall below its equilibrium value. The market for good 2 is then stable if this price decline causes home imports of good 2 to rise relative to foreign exports of good 2, thereby creating a world excess demand for good 2, that is, $(\hat{x}_2^* - \hat{m}_2)/\hat{p} > 0$. From the definition of the trade elasticities (see also Problem 4.10), the world excess demand for good 2 will rise as p falls if $e - (-f^*) = e + f^* > 0$. Since $f^* = e^* - 1$, the condition for a fall (rise) in p to generate a world excess demand (supply) for good 2 becomes:

$$e + e^* > 1 \tag{4.55}$$

This condition, known as the Marshall–Lerner condition, states that the trade equilibrium will be stable if the sum of the price elasticities of domestic and foreign import demand exceeds unity.

Given the importance of market stability, an important empirical question is whether the values of actual price elasticities of import demand satisfy the Marshall–Lerner condition. Table 4.3 reports home and foreign import price elasticity estimates for a number of countries. Where available, estimates of export supply elasticities are also given.

The import price elasticities (e and e^*) are correctly signed and range between 0.44 and 2.73. Where computable (column (3)), the hypothesis that

Table 4.3   *Estimated price elasticities of import demand and export supply*

| | Import demand[a] | | | Export supply[b] |
Country	Home (e) (1)	Foreign (e*) (2)	Sum[c] (e + e*) (3)	(f) (4)
Belgium	—	1.57[b]	—	1.2
Canada	1.02	0.83	1.85 (0.32)	—
France	—	1.33[b]	—	1.9
Germany	0.60	0.66	1.26 (0.20)	—
Italy	—	3.29[b]	—	1.1
Japan	0.93	0.93	1.86 (0.33)	infinite
Netherlands	—	2.73[b]	—	2.5
UK	0.47	0.44	0.91 (0.21)	1.4
USA	0.92	0.99	1.91 (0.42)	6.6
Other industrial	0.49	0.83	1.32 (0.18)	—
Developing countries	0.81	0.63	1.44 (0.32)	—
OPEC	1.14	0.57	1.71 (0.28)	—

Notes

[a] Taken from Marquez (1990), except when indicated, who used single-equation estimation.

[b] Taken from Goldstein and Khan (1978), who used simultaneous equations.

[c] Standard errors in parentheses.

the Marshall–Lerner condition fails to hold can be rejected for all countries except the United Kingdom on the basis of point estimates, Germany and the developing countries on the basis of a 1-tail t-test. The export supply elasticities (f) are positive and range in value from 1.1 for Italy to infinity for Japan. These results corroborate the intuition that a single country is unable to increase its supply of exports at constant prices unless substantial idle resources exist.

4.4 The factor abundance theorems

We now demonstrate the two central theorems of the factor abundance theory: the H–O theorem for the pattern of trade and the Factor Price Equalization (FPE) theorem for the effect of trade on factor prices. These theorems are demonstrated in terms of the 'simple' 2 factor, 2 good H–O–S model. The extension of these theorems to arbitrary numbers of goods and factors is discussed in Chapter 7. The following summarizes the assumptions used to establish these theorems:

(1) Perfect competition prevails in both commodity and factor markets.
(2) Factors of production are homogeneous in quality and costlessly mobile between industries within a country.
(3) The production function for each good is of the neoclassical type and is, in particular, homogeneous of degree one.
(4) Production functions differ between industries.
(5) Consumers have identical and homothetic preferences.
(6) There are no taxes, costs of transport, or other impediments to the domestic movement of goods.
(7) There are 2 countries, 2 goods, and 2 factors of production.
(8) There are no factor intensity reversals.
(9) Factors of production are immobile between countries and inelastically supplied within each country.
(10) The production function for each good is identical across countries.
(11) There are no taxes, costs of transport, or other impediments to the international movement of goods.
(12) Consumer preferences are identical across countries.

In listing these assumptions we have tried to group them into those representing the competitive general equilibrium model (assumptions (1)–(6)) and those representing the H–O–S extensions of the model (assumptions (7)–(12)) to an international context.

Comparative advantage and trade

The factor abundance theorem concerning the basis of comparative advantage and hence the pattern of trade between two countries is the Heckscher–Ohlin (H–O) theorem:

Proposition 4.3 (Heckscher–Ohlin): Given assumptions (1)–(12), a country will have a comparative advantage in, and therefore export, the good that uses its relatively abundant factor intensively in production.

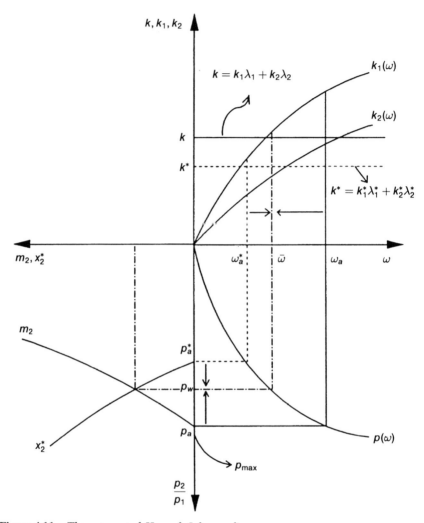

Figure 4.11   *The augmented Harrod–Johnson diagram*

To demonstrate this theorem we must define the concept of factor abundance, the concept of factor intensity having been previously defined. Given 2 factors, capital and labor, the home economy is defined to be abundant in capital compared to labor if either

$$k \equiv \frac{K}{L} > \frac{K^*}{L^*} \equiv k^*$$

or

$$\omega_a > \omega_a^*$$

where an asterisk denotes foreign (rest of world) variables. The first definition is the *physical* definition of abundance since it compares the relative quantities of factors between countries. The second is the *price* definition of abundance since it compares the *autarky* relative factor prices between countries. Like the definition of factor intensity, these definitions of factor abundance involve a relative comparison, that is, what matters is the relative size of K/L and K^*/L^*, of ω_a and ω_a^*, not the numerical value of each ratio.

To illustrate the H–O theorem we use an augmented Harrod–Johnson diagram (Viaene, 1993) as shown in Figure 4.11. This diagram combines Figures 4.3, 4.4 and Figure 4.10, with the latter figure shown in the third quadrant. The first quadrant of Figure 4.11 is drawn assuming industry 1 is capital-intensive and that the home country is capital-abundant on both definitions, that is, $k > k^*$ and $\omega_a > \omega_a^*$.

Closer inspection of Figure 4.11 raises the following question: if $k > k^*$ how can we verify that indeed $\omega_a > \omega_a^*$? Or in Ohlin's words (Ohlin, 1933, p. 13) 'in what way [do] differences in equipment come to be expressed in differences in money costs and prices?'. For example, if consumers in the home country have a strong bias for the capital-intensive good 1 then ω_a may be less than ω_a^*, despite the fact that the home country is physically capital-abundant. The assumption that preferences are identical and homothetic across countries (assumptions (5) and (12)) prevents such demand biases and hence ensures a one-to-one correspondence between the physical and price definitions of factor abundance.

Since industry technologies are identical across countries (assumption (10)), the relationships shown in both the first and fourth quadrants of Figure 4.11 apply to both countries. Moreover, since consumers have everywhere the same tastes, home's relative capital abundance will be reflected in a higher autarky wage–rental ratio: $\omega_a > \omega_a^*$. The one-to-one correspondence between factor prices and output prices in turn implies that the home country's autarky price ratio exceeds that of the foreign country (i.e. $p_a > p_a^*$). Hence, the capital-abundant country has the comparative advantage in the capital-intensive good and, with trade, the home country will export good 1.

Empirical link: the Leontief paradox

The first empirical test of the H–O theorem was conducted by Leontief (1954). Leontief conjectured that if the United States is capital-abundant and the H–O theory is true, then capital per-worker embodied in US exports should exceed the capital per-worker embodied in US imports.[29] Before discussing Leontief's analysis in detail, we must first consider the meaning of 'embodied factor services'.

The 'embodied services' of a factor refer to the amount of a factor's services used up in producing a given amount of some good. For example, the total amount of, say, labor embodied in the production of an economy's entire set of outputs is, with full employment, equal to the economy's total labor supply. Similarly, the services of factor h embodied in, say, a country's exports is computed by multiplying the *total* requirement of factor h needed to produce a unit of good j (z_{hj}) times the amount of good j that is exported (x_j) and then summing the results over all exported goods:

$$\sum_{j=1}^{J} x_j z_{jh} = \text{services of factor } h \text{ embodied in exports}$$

The *total* unit factor input requirements z_{jh} differ from the *direct* unit factor input requirements a_{jh} (defined previously) in that they take into account the fact that an industry uses both primary factors and intermediate goods to produce a unit of output. That is, the total input requirement z_{jh} measures the amount of factor h required both directly (in industry j) and indirectly (via the production of intermediate goods purchased by industry j) to produce a unit of good j.

Total factor input requirements are calculated from the direct unit factor input requirements and an input–output (I–O) matrix which characterizes the interdependence between industries in an economy. The (i,j) entry in an I–O matrix records the amount of sector i's output purchased by sector j for the purpose of producing sector j's output. These purchases by sector j from sector i are expressed per-unit of sector j's gross output. Hence, each entry in the I–O matrix is a 'unit intermediate goods requirement'. If b_{ij} denotes these unit intermediate goods requirements then the equilibrium value added (final demand) in industry j (d_j) can be written:

$$d_j = q_j - \sum_{i=1}^{J} q_i b_{ij} \qquad j = 1, \ldots, J \tag{4.56}$$

Stacking expression (4.56) into one vector yields the vector of final demands as:

$$\mathbf{d} = \mathbf{q} - \mathbf{Bq} \equiv (\mathbf{I} - \mathbf{B})\mathbf{q} \tag{4.57}$$

where $\mathbf{d}$ is the $J \times 1$ vector of final demands, $\mathbf{q}$ is the $J \times 1$ vector of gross outputs, $\mathbf{B}$ is the $J \times J$ input–output matrix of unit intermediate good requirements and $\mathbf{I}$ is the $J \times J$ identity matrix. Since the matrix $(\mathbf{I} - \mathbf{B})$ is square, it can be inverted to solve (4.57) for the levels of gross outputs required to produce the vector of equilibrium final demands:

$$\mathbf{q} = (\mathbf{I} - \mathbf{B})^{-1}\mathbf{d} \tag{4.58}$$

To calculate the amount of each primary factor absorbed in producing the equilibrium final demands **d**, let **A** denote the $H \times J$ matrix of equilibrium (direct) unit factor input requirements (a_{hj}). Pre-multiplying both sides of (4.58) by **A** gives:

$$\mathbf{Aq} = \mathbf{Zd} \tag{4.59}$$

where $\mathbf{Z} = \mathbf{A(I - B)}^{-1}$ is the $H \times J$ matrix of total (direct *plus* indirect) primary input requirements. With full employment, $\mathbf{Aq} = \mathbf{e}$, where **e** is the $H \times 1$ vector of national factor supplies. Hence (4.59) can also be written:

$$\mathbf{e} = \mathbf{Zd} \tag{4.60}$$

which demonstrates that the elements of the matrix **Z** are indeed the *total* factor input requirements per-unit of final demand.

Assuming the total input requirements to be fixed by the conditions of technology, Leontief imagined a scenario in which US exports and imports were reduced by $1 million, with the reduction distributed across industries in proportion to their initial share in total US exports or total US imports.[30] Consequent on these reductions, domestic production would then rise in order to replace the lost imports and it would fall due to the export reduction. By computing the changes in factor employment associated with these changes in domestic production one could then infer the net change in factor employment. Leontief conjectured that, if the United States is capital-abundant and the H–O theory is true, the ratio of capital to labor released due to the export decline will exceed the ratio of capital to labor absorbed in replacing the lost imports with domestic production.

If $\mathbf{S}_x$ and $\mathbf{S}_M$ denote the vectors of commodity export and import shares, respectively, Leontief's calculation of the changes in labor and capital employment due to a $1 million change in exports and imports can be expressed as:

$$\Delta L_X = -\mathbf{z}_L \mathbf{S}_x \Delta x, \quad \Delta L_M = -\mathbf{z}_L \mathbf{S}_M \Delta m \tag{4.61}$$

$$\Delta K_x = -\mathbf{z}_K \mathbf{S}_x \Delta x, \quad \Delta K_m = -\mathbf{z}_K \mathbf{S}_M \Delta m \tag{4.62}$$

where $\mathbf{z}_L$ and $\mathbf{z}_K$ are the $1 \times J$ vectors of total labor and total capital requirements per-unit of final demand and the scalars Δx and Δm are, by assumption, equal to (minus) $1 million. Given (4.61) and (4.62), Leontief's hypothesis was that the following ratio should exceed one:[31]

$$\gamma = \frac{\Delta K_x / \Delta L_x}{\Delta K_m / \Delta L_m} \tag{4.63}$$

Table 4.4 reports Leontief's calculations which used 1947 data on US trade and the US input–output matrix.

These numbers indicate, for example, that the expansion of US production required to replace $1 million of US imports would require an

Table 4.4 *Capital and labor services embodied in 1947 US exports and imports replacements*

	Exports	Imports
Capital ($, 1947 prices)	2 550 780	3 091 339
Labor (man years)	182 313	170 004
Capital–labor ratio	13.99	18.18

additional $3.09 million in capital services (investment) and an additional 170 004 man years of labor. Since total input requirements are assumed fixed, this implies that, on average, the capital–labor ratio across US import-competing industries is about 18.2. In contrast, the average capital–labor ratio in US export industries is around 14. Computing (4.63), the average capital–labor ratio in US import-competing industries is about 30% higher than the average capital–labor ratio in US export industries, a finding contrary to the H–O theorem.

Leontief's 'paradoxical' result generated considerable debate as to its causes, and it is fair to say that for some twenty-five years after Leontief's findings most empirical work directly or indirectly attempted to explain his result. However, one question never addressed by the literature was whether γ accurately reveals a country's abundant factor. That is, if a country is capital-abundant, does the H–O theory imply that γ must exceed unity? Chapter 8 addresses this question in detail and provides a negative answer.

Trade and factor prices

The second factor abundance theorem concerns the effect of trade on factor price difference between countries:

Proposition 4.4 (factor price equalization):   Given assumptions (1)–(12), trade in goods will cause the absolute and relative prices of factors between countries to move toward equality. Complete equalization will be achieved if both countries continue to produce both goods in the trading equilibrium.

Consider first the case of relative factor prices. As Figure 4.11 shows, trade results in the single world price p_w. In moving from autarky to the trade equilibrium, the change in relative output prices causes each country's export industry to expand and its import-competing industry to contract. These shifts in production imply corresponding changes in factor demands and factor prices within each country.

Consider the home country. With the opening of trade, production of good 1 expands, production of good 2 contracts, and capital and labor are released from industry 2 to be re-employed in industry 1. However, since industry 2 is labor-intensive, the amount of labor per-unit of capital released from industry 2 exceeds that which the capital-intensive industry 1 can absorb at the autarky wage and rental rate. Hence, the initial effect of trade on the home country's factor markets is to induce an excess supply of labor or, equivalently, an excess demand for capital, at the home country's autarky factor prices. Restoration of factor market equilibrium therefore requires the wage–rental ratio (ω) to fall. Of course, the same effects are occurring in the foreign country, but in the opposite direction. In particular, an excess supply of capital (excess demand for labor) arises as industry 2 expands and industry 1 contracts. Hence, ω^* must rise in order to restore factor market equilibrium in the foreign country.

The restoration of factor market equilibrium in each country therefore implies that, relative to their autarky values, ω^* will rise and ω will fall until equality is reached at $\bar{\omega}$ (which corresponds to p_w). Note that complete equality can occur only if neither country is completely specialized in production at the equilibrium world price p_w. One rule of thumb for the likelihood of equality is that the difference in countries' relative factor supplies should not be too great.

Problem 4.11: Using Figure 4.6, demonstrate that even with large differences in countries' relative factor supplies, factor prices can still be equalized if capital and labor are highly substitutable within industries and the difference in industries' capital–labor ratios is not too great.

The equalization of absolute factor prices is easily demonstrated using duality relationships. Under free trade both countries face the same prices and hence, given identical production functions, the iso-price curves (denoted $p = p_w$ and 1) in Figure 4.6 are the same for each country. As such, the factor prices given at the point of intersection ($\bar{w}$ and $\bar{r}$) of these isoprice curves are also identical between countries.

Data link

The proposition that trade in goods can equalize the prices of internationally immobile factors is an extremely powerful prediction. Most would agree that, in reality, absolute factor prices are not equalized between countries. However, such interpretation of the data is a great misrepresentation of the power of the FPE proposition. A more useful interpretation is that increased trade can be expected to lower the reward to factors intensive in import competing sectors and to raise the reward to factors intensive in export sectors. That is, the FPE is a statement about a convergence of factor rewards over time. Complete convergence is not expected since the assumptions under which equality is expected are absent in the real world. The prevalent use of trade restrictions and, as will be made clearer in later chapters, institutional constraints also hamper the functioning of the market mechanism. Given the facts of the world, the idea of testing the hypothesis of complete factor price equalization is absurd; this strong form of the FPE theorem can simply be rejected without consulting the data.

Consider, then, what evidence there is in favor of the weaker hypothesis that trade tends to move factor prices toward equality. Table 4.5 reports the average hourly earnings of non-agricultural workers for one subset of EC countries relative to either Germany or the United States in 1967, 1989 and over the entire 1967–89 time period. However, these simple cross-country averages do not account for the possibility of a changing cross-country variation in relative earnings over time. The information about means is therefore complemented by the standard deviations. Mean relative earnings moving closer to unity combined with a decreasing standard deviation therefore reflects a movement toward wage equalization across countries. Complete equalization would imply a mean of unity and a zero standard deviation.

Table 4.5   *Hourly earnings in EC non-agricultural sectors relative to earnings in Germany and the United States, 1967–89*

	Average EC earnings[a] relative to							
	Earnings in Germany[b]				*Earnings in USA[c]*			
	Current prices	*St. dev.*	*1985 prices*	*St. dev.*	*Current prices*	*St. dev.*	*1985 prices*	*St. dev.*
1967	0.77	0.12	1.58	0.39	0.34	0.05	0.42	0.12
1989	0.79	0.08	0.74	0.08	0.83	0.08	0.87	0.14
1967–89	0.81		1.15		0.65		0.73	

Notes:
[a] Average across countries including original EC countries: Belgium–Luxembourg, France, Germany, Italy and the Netherlands. Expressed in SDRs.
[b] Excludes Germany.
[c] Includes Germany.
Source: Compiled by the authors from ILO data.

Table 4.5 indicates some tendency towards an equalization of labor's earnings in that, over time, the mean relative earnings move closer to unity. The standard deviations decline when earnings are measured relative to Germany and are about the same when earnings are measured relative to the United States. Though both statistics (means, standard deviations) have fluctuated over time this provides evidence of a movement toward wage equalization in the course of economic integration and increased trade.

To conclude this section we note that the H–O and FPE theorems are independent of each other in that the validity of one does not determine the validity of the other. For example, trade can still equalize factor prices even if each country exports the good that uses its scarce factor intensively in production. Of course, which good a country exports, or more precisely, which factor is intensive in the export industry, will determine the directional change in factor prices once trade is allowed.

4.5 Concluding remarks

This chapter has presented the elements of the competitive general equilibrium model underlying the factor abundance theory. Denoted as the H–O–S model, this model is used to study the determinants of comparative advantage and the effect of trade upon factor rewards and the distribution of income. This chapter has emphasized relative factor supplies and their role in determining factor prices, production costs and autarky prices. What real-world phenomena does the H–O–S model help us to understand? The following summarizes key conclusions[32] in this regard.

(1) Countries should export those goods whose production makes relatively intensive use of their relatively abundant factors.

(2) Trade (and gains from trade) should be greatest between countries with the greatest differences in economic structure. If the ratios of resources were the same in all countries then there would be no trade.

(3) Trade should cause countries to specialize in production. The production characteristics of the goods a country exports should be distinctly different from those of the goods it imports.

(4) Factor prices between countries should become more equal as trade increases between those countries and also the more similar are the countries' relative factor supplies.

(5) Domestic interest groups lobbying for changes in the terms of trade should be defined on the basis of their function in the production process (laborers, capitalists, land owners, ...) rather than on the basis of the identity of the industries where employed.

Chapters 5–8 will judge the H–O–S model's predictions on the basis of its empirical relevance. As the above implications derive from a set of assumptions of a very close texture, several assumptions will be first relaxed and looked at both theoretically and empirically.

■*Appendix 1*■

The Transformation Curve

The transformation or production possibility curve characterizes an economy's technology and factor supplies. Geometrically, the transformation curve can be derived from the Edgeworth–Bowley box diagram (Figure 4.12) where the dimensions of the box are the total supplies of capital and labor.

Within this box are reproduced the unit isoquants of Figure 4.2. The outputs are measured by reference to the origins, O_1 for good 1 and O_2 for good 2. For example, point A gives one allocation of capital and labor between the two industries which would produce one unit of each good. Point A is not an efficient allocation of the factors between industries since it is possible, as at point C' to produce more of good 2 and no less of good 1. Likewise, at S', it is possible to produce more of good 1 with no less

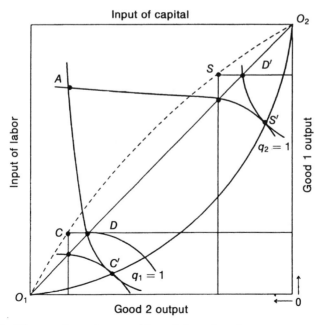

Figure 4.12 *The transformation curve derived from the Edgeworth–Bowley box diagram*

of good 2. Points C' and S' are Pareto-efficient allocations of capital and labor between industries because, at each point, any reallocation of inputs would result in a decrease in the output of at least one commodity (as at D).

The locus of Pareto-efficient factor allocations (the curve $O_1 C' S' O_2$) is the contract curve. Here, the contract curve lies below the diagonal because we assume that industry 1 is capital-intensive. Given this, the transformation curve can be derived by simply recording the isoquant numbers at each point along the contract curve.

A alternative method of deriving the transformation curve is Savosnick's (1958) graphical technique. To demonstrate this technique, we first rescale the axes such that, with respect to the origin labeled O, the output of good 2 is measured along the bottom horizontal axis and the output of good 1 is measured along the right-hand vertical axis. Second, to these axes we project vertical and horizontal lines from the point of intersection between each isoquant and the main diagonal $O_1 O_2$. These projections are then reflected back from the vertical and horizontal axes to determine their point of intersection in the interior of the Edgeworth–Bowley box (e.g. point S or C). Repeating this process of all points of intersection with the main diagonal, the transformation curve is traced out as the locus of all such meeting points. In Figure 4.12 this process results in the curve $O_1 C S O_2$.

Savosnick's technique exploits the 'replication' property of homogeneous functions, that is, the entire isoquant map can be found once one isoquant is specified. This is illustrated in Figure 4.12 for the case of good 1. The unit isoquant q_1 cuts the main diagonal $O_1 O_2$ at point D. The diagonal also cuts an unknown isoquant for good 1 at the point D'. To determine the number of units of good 1 produced on the unknown isoquant, it suffices to measure the ratio of distances,

$$\frac{O_1 D'}{O_1 D} = \lambda$$

that is, the point D' lies on the isoquant corresponding to the output level $\lambda q_1 = \lambda$. Note that since changes in output of good 1 can be measured along the ray $O_1 O_2$, the properties of triangles imply that the same changes in output (ratio of distances) apply along the vertical axis.

Notes

1. See n. 5 for limit conditions on the production function and factor marginal products.
2. Alternatively, CRS means that the level of output (scale) is unimportant for determining the characteristics of the production process. For this reason the H–O–S model focuses on the ratio of variables and not their level.

3. A related concept is the unit *value* isoquant which indicates the combinations of capital and labor that can produce one dollar (or other unit of account) of output. This is obtained from (4.1) by setting $\lambda = 1/p_j q_j$, where p_j is the price of good j.

4. It will be seen in Section 4.4 that property plays a central role in establishing the Factor Price Equalization theorem as well as many of the theory's predictions about the effect of trade on the distribution of income among factor owners.

5. Written in this form, the following limit conditions are appended to property 3:

$$\lim_{k_j \to 0} f_j(k_j) = 0, \quad \lim_{k_j \to \infty} f_j(k_j) = \infty, \quad \lim_{k_j \to \infty} f'_j(k_j) = 0, \quad \lim_{k_j \to 0} f'_j(k_j) = \infty$$

6. Since national income is the sum of income generated by each industry, national income is maximized when each industry achieves its maximum profit.

7. The isocost line is $K_j = \bar{C}_j/r - (w/r)L_j$, where $\bar{C}_j$ is a fixed level of expenditure on inputs K_j and L_j at the given prices r and w, respectively.

8. By linear homogeneity, these cost minimizing capital–labor ratios are invariant to the level of output in each industry.

9. The economy's transformation function $(q_1 = T(q_2))$ can be found by simultaneously solving expressions (4.12) for q_1 as a function of q_2.

10. By definition, industry i is defined to be capital-intensive relative to industry m if $k_i(\bar{\omega}) > k_m(\bar{\omega})$ for some $\bar{\omega} > 0$. Note that the concept of factor intensity is unrelated to the specific value of an industry's capital–labor ratio. For example, industry i can still be capital-intensive even if both k_i and k_m are less than unity.

11. Graphically, this means that the curves in Figure 4.3 never intersect.

12. This is established by subtracting 1 from both sides of (4.19) and (4.20) and verifying the sign of the resulting expressions.

13. This proposition can be interpreted in two ways: either as a comparison of production equilibria within a country after a change in a factor supply or as a cross-country comparison of production equilibria between countries, similar in all respects, except for a difference in K or L.

14. The Rybczynski theorem assumes factor supply changes as purely exogenous and not the result of a change in factor rewards. See Kemp (1969) and Martin (1976) for an analysis of the case of variable factor supplies.

15. The duality between cost and production functions was first established by Shephard (1953) and is surveyed in Diewert (1982). Dixit and Norman (1980) and Woodland (1982) present several applications of duality to international trade. The present treatment follows Woodland (1977) and Mussa (1979).

16. Brackets { } such as those in (4.27) denote a set while the colon means 'such that'. Vectors are printed in **bold face**. No distinction is made between row and column vectors unless warranted.

17. The cost function $C(\mathbf{w}, q)$ must be a non-negative and continuous function defined over $\mathbf{w} > 0$ and $q \geq 0$. Moreover, it is homogeneous of degree one in $\mathbf{w}$, non-decreasing in $\mathbf{w}$, concave in $\mathbf{w}$ and non-decreasing in q. Any minimum cost function with these properties will serve as a suitable description of technology.

18. See Woodland (1982) or Cornes (1992) for proofs of Shephard's and Hotelling's lemmas (see below).

19. The solution $q_j = +\infty$ is also possible but is incompatible with competitive equilibrium since factor prices could no longer be assumed constant if output were to expand without bound.

20. $G(\mathbf{p}, \mathbf{e})$ is a non-negative, non-decreasing, linearly homogeneous function of $\mathbf{p} > 0$ and $\mathbf{e} > 0$ and is concave in $\mathbf{e}$ and convex in $\mathbf{p}$.

21. By (4.35), an increase in the price of good j cannot decrease GDP, and will increase GDP, if good j is produced in equilibrium. Similarly, by (4.36), more of any factor cannot reduce GDP, and will increase GDP if that factor is productive at the margin (a positive shadow price).

22. Appendix 1 discusses the derivation of the transformation function and shows its dependence on the economy's technology and resources supplies.

23. These equations are dual to the unit isoquants (4.2).

24. Since utility functions are unique only up to a monotonic transformation, assuming linear homogeneity makes no sacrifice of generality.

25. In the present framework, we are able to calculate factor prices and consequently the level and distribution of national income as a function of national endowments and commodity prices. As long as endowments remain unchanged, commodity prices comprise all information needed to specify the demand functions that can be written as $d_j = d_j(p)$.

26. For further details see (3.7)–(3.11) (pp. 83–4).

27. See Jones (1969) and Ethier (1983) for further details on partial versus general equilibrium elasticities.

28. Similarly, the price elasticity of foreign imports is $e^* = e_1^* + e_2^* + e_3^*$.

29. McGilvray and Simpson's (1973) analysis of Anglo–Irish trade is an application of Leontief's original test.

30. The levels of non-competitive imports (imported goods not produced domestically) were assumed to remain unchanged.

31. Leontief was specifically interested in capital and labor but γ can be calculated with respect to any two factors.

32. See Ethier (1987).

References and additional reading

The neoclassical model

Bhagwati, J.N. and Srinivasan, T.N. (1983), *Lectures on International Trade* (Cambridge, Mass.: MIT Press), Chapters 5 and 6, 50–81; Appendix B, 384–96.

Chacholiades, M. (1973), *The Pure Theory of International Trade* (London: Macmillan), Chapters 4–6, 81–169.

Dinwiddy, C.L. and Tal, F.J. (1988), *The Two-Sector Equilibrium Model: A New Approach* (Oxford: Philip Allan).

Ethier, W.J. (1983), *Modern International Economics* (New York: Norton), Appendix I, 511–56.

Ethier, W.J. (1987), 'The Theory of International Trade', in Officer, L.M. (ed.), *International Economics* (Boston: Kluwer Academic), 1–57.

Hazari, B.R. (1978), *The Pure Theory of International Trade and Distortions* (London: Croom Helm), Chapter 1, 7–29.

Jones, R.W. (1965), 'The Structure of Simple General Equilibrium Models', *Journal of Political Economy*, 73, 557–72.

Jones, R. W. (1969), 'Tariffs and Trade in General Equilibrium: Comment', *American Economic Review*, 59, 418–24

Kemp, M.C. (1969), *The Pure Theory of International Trade and Investment* (Englewood Cliffs: Prentice-Hall), Chapters 1–4, 5–118.

Metzler, L.A. (1949), 'Tariffs, the Terms of Trade, and the Distribution of National Income', *Journal of Political Economy*, 57, 1–29.

Ohlin, B. (1933), *Interregional and International Trade* (Cambridge, Mass.: Harvard University Press).

Samuelson, P.A. (1953), 'Prices of Factors and Goods in General Equilibrium', *Review of Economic Studies*, 21, 1–20.

Viaene, J.-M. (1993), 'The Harrod–Johnson Diagram and the International Equilibrium', *International Economic Journal*, 7(1), 83–93.

Duality theory

Cornes, R. (1992), *Duality and Modern Economics* (Cambridge: Cambridge University Press).

Diewert, W.E. (1982), 'Duality Approaches to Microeconomic Theory', in Arrow, K.J. and Intrilligator, M.D. (eds), *Handbook of Mathematical Economics* (Amsterdam: North-Holland), 535–99.

Dixit, A. and Norman, V. (1980), *Theory of International Trade* (Cambridge: Cambridge University Press).

Kohli, U. (1991), *Technology, Duality, and Foreign Trade: The GNP Function Approach to Modeling Imports and Exports* (Ann Arbor and London: University of Michigan Press and Harvester Wheatsheaf).

Mussa, M. (1979), 'The Two-Sector Model in Terms of Dual: A Geómetric Exposition', *Journal of International Economics*, 9, 513–26.

Shephard, R.W. (1953), *Cost and Production Functions* (Princeton, NJ: Princeton University Press).

Woodland, A.D. (1977), 'A Dual Approach to Equilibrium in the Production Sector In International Trade Theory', *Canadian Journal of Economics*, 10(1), 50–68.

Woodland, A.D. (1982), *International Trade and Resource Allocation* (Amsterdam: North-Holland).

Production possibility curve

Krauss, M.B., Johnson, H.G. and Skouras, T. (1973), 'On the Shape and Location of the Production Possibility Curve', *Economica*, 40(159), 305–10.

Melvin, J.R. (1971), 'On the Derivation of the Production Possibility Curve', *Economica*, 38(151), 281–94.

Savosnick, K.M. (1958), 'The Box Diagram and the Production Possibility Curve', *Ekonomisk Tidsskrift*, 60(3), 183–97.

The Leontief paradox and the input–output accounting system

Klein, L.R. (1983), *Lectures in Econometrics* (Amsterdam: North-Holland), 21–36.
Leontief, W. (1954), 'Domestic Production and Foreign Trade: the American Position Re-examined', *Economica Internazionale*, 7, 3–32.
McGilvray, J. and Simpson, D. (1973), 'The Commodity Structure of Anglo–Irish Trade', *Review of Economics and Statistics*, 55, 451–58.

Variable factor supply

Kemp, M.C. (1969), *The Pure Theory of International Trade and Investment* (Englewood Cliffs: Prentice-Hall), Chapter 5, 119–33.
Martin, J.P. (1976), 'Variable Factor Supplies and the HOS Model', *Economic Journal*, 820–31.

Price elasticities

Goldstein, M. and Khan, M.S. (1978), 'The Supply and Demand for Exports: A Simultaneous Approach', *Review of Economics and Statistics*, 60, 275–86.
Goldstein, M. and Khan, M.S. (1985), 'Income and Price Effects in Foreign Trade', in Jones, R.W. and Kenen, P.B. (eds), *Handbook of International Economics*, Vol. II (Amsterdam: North-Holland), Chapter 20, 1041–1105.
Khan, M.S. and Ross, Z. (1977), 'The Functional Form of the Aggregate Demand Equation', *Journal of International Economics*, 7, 149–60.
Leamer, E.E. (1981), 'Is it a Demand Curve or is it a Supply Curve? Partial Identification through Inequality Constraints', *Review of Economics and Statistics*, 63, 319–27.
Marquez, J. (1990), 'Bilateral Trade Elasticities', *Review of Economics and Statistics*, 72, 75–86.
Thursby, J. and Thursby, M. (1984), 'How Reliable are Simple, Single Equation Specifications of Import Demand?', *Review of Economics and Statistics*, 66, 120–8.

■ *Chapter 5* ■

Trade Policy

5.1 Tariffs   5.3 Applied methods
5.2 Quantitative restrictions

This chapter examines the resource allocation and welfare implications of trade restrictions in competitive markets. We first examine the theoretical implications of price based trade policy instruments such as tariffs and export subsidies. We then consider the broad class of non-price restrictions by examining three specific forms of quantitative restrictions (QRs): import quotas, export quotas and domestic content requirements. Having considered the theoretical implications of alternative trade restrictions, we then discuss methods for estimating the welfare effects of such restrictions. Finally, we discuss the use of applied general equilibrium (AGE) models which are an increasingly popular tool for evaluating the effects of trade policies. The material presented in this chapter is an important foundation for the analyses of Chapter 10 which considers many of the same issues in a world of increasing returns to scale and imperfect competition.

5.1 Tariffs

A tariff is a tax levied on imports. The tariff rate can be stated as either an *ad valorem* or specific rate. An *ad valorem* tariff states the tax as a percentage of the value of imports. A specific tariff states the tax as a fixed currency amount per unit of the good imported. These two forms of a tariff are not equivalent, but it is common when analyzing the effects of a tariff to assume it is *ad valorem*.

To examine the effects of a tariff we adopt the 2-good model developed in Chapter 4. In this context, we now assume that the home country imposes an *ad valorem* tariff τ on its imports of good 2 (good 1 is therefore exported). This tariff will 'drive a wedge' between the world price and the domestic internal price of the imported good:[1]

$$p_d = (1 + \tau)p_w \tag{5.1}$$

where p_w and p_d are, respectively, the world and (tariff inclusive) domestic relative price of the imported good 2.[2] Because the tariff will change the domestic, and possibly the international, price of the imported good, it will alter patterns of consumption, production and trade. Moreover, since the tariff creates a distortion between the domestic and world price it will also alter national and world welfare. We now turn to a detailed examination of these economic effects.

Small country

Figure 5.1 illustrates a trading equilibrium for a small country – that is, one unable to affect the prices of goods on world markets. Under free trade the country achieves the welfare level u_0 by producing at point A, consuming at point B and thus exporting aA units of good 1 in exchange for aB units of good 2. Since the world price p_w is fixed, the imposition of a tariff on good 2 raises the domestic relative price of imports according to (5.1). Producers respond to this increase in the domestic relative price by shifting production to point A'. The tariff therefore raises domestic production of good 2 and lowers production of the exported good 1. This shift in production reduces the economy's GDP valued at world prices by the amount ef when measured in terms of good 1 (EF when measured in terms of good 2). Since international equilibrium requires the value of exports to equal the value of imports at international prices, the economy's new consumption point must lie along the international budget line eE. Since this budget line lies

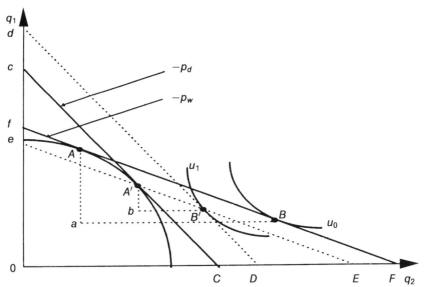

Figure 5.1   *General equilibrium effects of a tariff – small country*

everywhere below the pre-tariff international budget line fF, the country must be worse off as the result of the tariff.

The exact welfare level achieved under the tariff is determined by locating the country's new consumption point. To do so, note first that the tariff generates revenue for the government and one must consider how this revenue is spent. A common assumption is that the government redistributes this revenue back to consumers via a lump-sum transfer. Consumers will therefore spend the country's entire income according to their preferences. Given this, the new consumption point is found as follows. First, as noted above, international equilibrium requires consumption to take place along the international budget line eE. Second, consumers will equate their marginal rate of substitution between goods 1 and 2 to the domestic, tariff inclusive, price p_d. These two requirements imply that consumption must occur at point B', which is the only point on the budget line eE where a social indifference curve exhibits a slope equal to the tariff inclusive domestic price ratio p_d. The tariff revenue, expressed in terms of good 1, equals cd. The tariff therefore reduces national welfare from u_0 to u_1 and, in the new equilibrium, the country exports $A'b$ of good 1 in exchange for bB' units of good 2. Hence, the tariff also reduces the volume of trade.

Problem 5.1: Demonstrate that the distance cd in Figure 5.1 equals the tariff revenue $\tau p_w m_t$ where m_t is the post-tariff level of imports (i.e. the distance bB' in Figure 5.1).

Problem 5.2: Work out the computer program of the small open economy of Chapter 4.1 to incorporate the effects of a tariff along the lines discussed so far. Assume $\tau_2 = 0.1$ and compare your results with the free trade solution of the previous chapter.

Distributional effects

The economy-wide welfare reduction illustrated in Figure 5.1 masks changes in the welfare of different agents within the economy (e.g. consumers, producers and the government). Understanding how, and in what direction, tariff protection alters the welfare of different domestic agents is important for grasping the motives for different groups to favor or oppose such protection. To examine the distributional effects that arise from a tariff we take a partial equilibrium approach[3] which focuses on the domestic market for the imported good. Panel (a) of Figure 5.2 illustrates this market.

In Figure 5.2 the foreign export supply (x_2^*) is drawn infinitely elastic at the world price p_w to reflect the assumption of a small country. The free trade equilibrium occurs at the intersection of the domestic demand (d_2) and

162

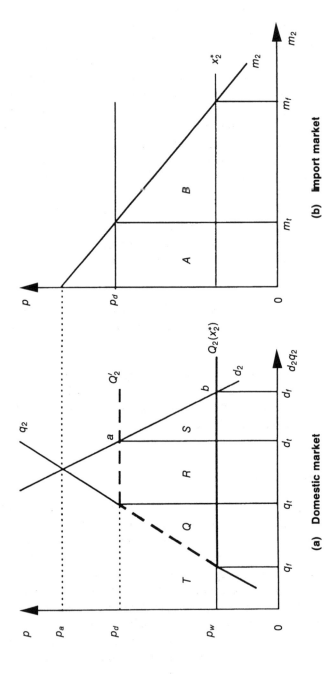

Figure 5.2 *Partial equilibrium analysis of a tariff – small country*

(a) **Domestic market**

(b) **Import market**

the market supply curve Q_2, the latter derived as the sum of the domestic (q_2) and foreign export supply curves. Hence, under free trade, the domestic price of good 2 equals the world price p_w. At this price, consumers purchase d_f units of which q_f are supplied by domestic producers and $d_f - q_f$ units are imported.

Imposition of a tariff raises the market supply curve to Q_2' and the domestic equilibrium price therefore rises from p_w to p_d. This price increase lowers consumption from d_f to d_t, raises domestic production from q_f to q_t, and hence lowers imports to $d_t - q_t$ units.

The increase in the domestic price of good 2 clearly harms consumers. A measure of their loss is the decrease in consumer surplus given by the trapezoidal area $p_d abp_w$. This loss to consumers can be decomposed into income transfer and efficiency cost components. The income transfer has two subcomponents: a transfer from consumers to producers measured by area T and a transfer from consumers to the government measured by area R (which equals tariff revenue). The tariff therefore benefits domestic producers and the government at the expense of domestic consumers of good 2.

The efficiency cost also has two subcomponents: a production cost measured by area Q and a consumption cost measured by area S. The production cost is the additional cost to the importing country of obtaining ($q_t - q_f$) units of good 2 from domestic producers rather than on world markets at the lower cost $p_w(q_t - q_f)$.[4] The consumption cost measures the loss that arises as consumers substitute away from good 2 and into good 1 (more generally, into other goods) as the price of good 2 rises above its true resource cost. Since the income transfer components are a redistribution of income among domestic agents, the net change in welfare for the country as a whole is the sum of the production and consumption efficiency costs.

Panel (b) gives an equivalent illustration of the effects of the tariff but now in terms of the market for imports alone. The import demand curve (m_2) is derived as the horizontal difference between the domestic demand (d_2) and domestic supply (q_2) in panel (a) for each price below the autarky price p_a. This construction assumes that good 2 is homogeneous across countries and hence that the domestic and imported good are perfect substitutes. The initial free trade equilibrium occurs at the intersection of the home country's import demand and the foreign export supply (x_2^*). A tariff raises the foreign export supply and implies a rise in the domestic price of imports and a fall in the volume of imports. The price increase implies that consumers of the import good experience a welfare loss equal to the loss in consumer surplus as measured by areas A and B in panel (b). By construction, area A equals area R in panel (a) and area B equals the sum of areas Q and S in panel (a). Area B therefore measures the country's net welfare loss from the tariff. Note that the change in consumer surplus in panel (b) excludes the income transfer from consumers to domestic producers (i.e. area T in panel (a)).

Problem 5.3: Demonstrate that a subsidy to domestic producers that raises their production from q_f to q_t in panel (a) of Figure 5.2 would involve a lower net welfare cost to the country than if the same increase in production were obtained via a tariff. List some reasons why a country might use a tariff rather than a direct production subsidy if the intent was to increase domestic production.

Problem 5.4: Preferential government procurement is a policy that favors domestic firms in the granting of government contracts. Show that this policy is equivalent to a production subsidy. Does the relative size of government contracts with respect to the industry matter? Explain.

Large country

We now assume that the country is large and hence able to influence the prices of goods on world markets. This assumption is illustrated in Figure 5.3 by the positively sloped foreign export supply function (x_2^*). As drawn, foreign export supply is assumed elastic at the initial free trade equilibrium denoted as point a. Since a tariff raises the domestic price of the imported good, domestic residents will import less of commodity 2 at any given world

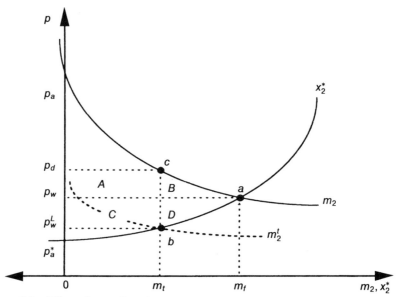

Figure 5.3   *Effect of a tariff on domestic and world prices when foreign export supply is elastic*

price. Hence, as shown in Figure 5.3, the tariff displaces the import demand curve downward from m_2 to m'_2 so that the new 'tariff ridden' international equilibrium occurs at point b. The tariff inclusive domestic price is then p_d with cb/bm_t being the *ad valorem* tariff rate τ. Since supply is upward sloping, the new equilibrium involves a lower world price and lower imports, and hence a lower value of imports at world prices relative to the free trade equilibrium. The magnitude of the change in world price and volume of imports depends importantly on the elasticity of foreign export supply; the less elastic is foreign export supply the larger will be the fall in world price and the smaller the fall in the quantity of imports.

Welfare

Taking a partial equilibrium perspective, the net welfare change of the tariff imposing country is represented in Figure 5.3 as area C *minus* area B. This is demonstrated as follows. Relative to free trade, the tariff reduces the welfare of domestic consumers by the loss in consumer surplus which equals areas A and B in Figure 5.3. Tariff revenue to the government equals areas A and C. Areas C and D equal the loss in the surplus of foreign exporters due to a deterioration in their terms of trade. Note that area C, which accrues to the importing country as tariff revenue, measures the gain to the importing country arising from the improvement in its terms of trade. The net change in the importing country's welfare is therefore area C *minus* area B which, for some values of τ, could be positive. Since areas A and C are transfers of income, respectively, within and between countries, areas B and D measure the reduction in world welfare arising from the tariff. Finally, since the importing country's terms of trade gain is a terms of trade loss for the foreign country, the latter may retaliate by imposing a restriction on its imports from the home country. Such retaliation would eliminate some or all of the importing country's terms of trade gain and, since it must reduce further the volume of trade, would increase the efficiency costs, and hence the welfare loss, at the world level.

A formal statement of the general equilibrium welfare changes suggested by Figure 5.3 can be made by assuming that welfare is measured by the following indirect utility function:

$$V(p, S) \equiv U(d_1(p, S), d_2(p, S)) \tag{5.2}$$

where $d_j(p, S)$ is the demand for commodity j ($j = 1, 2$) and S is expenditure at domestic prices as given by the economy's budget constraint:

$$S(p_d, u_1) \equiv q_1 + p_d q_2 + (p_d - p_w)m_2 = Y + \tau p_w m_2 \tag{5.3}$$

where u_1 is the post-tariff level of utility. Expression (5.3) states the equality, at domestic prices, between total expenditure and income from all sources (i.e. production *plus* tariff revenue). Totally differentiating (5.2) and applying Roy's identity (i.e. $d_2(p, S) = -(\partial V/\partial p)/(\partial V/\partial S)$), the welfare change due to the tariff can be expressed as a function of the change in domestic prices:

$$dW = dS - d_2 dp_d \qquad (5.4)$$

where $dW = (\partial V/\partial S)^{-1} dV$ (with $\partial V/\partial S > 0$) measures the change in real income (in units of the numeraire) that is equivalent to the change in utility (dV).[5] The welfare change in (5.4) can also be expressed as a function of the world price and volume of imports. To do so, we first obtain expressions for dp_d and dS by totally differentiating (5.1) and (5.3) and then substitute these expressions into (5.4) to obtain:

$$dW = -m_2 dp_w + \tau p_w dm_2 \qquad (5.5)$$

Expression (5.5) states the net change in the welfare of the tariff imposing country as the sum of two components.[6] The first relates to the change in the country's terms of trade (dp_w) while the second to the change in import volume (dm_2). Since $\tau p_w = p_d - p_w$, the second component measures the efficiency cost of the tariff arising from the distortion between the domestic and world price of imports. As shown in Figure 5.3, the tariff reduces both the world price and the volume of imports, that is, $dp_w < 0$ and $dm_2 < 0$.[7] By (5.5), the terms of trade improvement raises welfare while the fall in import volume reduces welfare. Since these two effects are of opposite sign, the change in welfare could be positive, that is, a tariff could raise the welfare of a large country. By definition, the terms of trade effect is zero for a small country and hence (5.5) reconfirms the analysis in Figure 5.1, namely, that a tariff must reduce the welfare of a small country.

Problem 5.5: Suppose the domestic economy introduces an export subsidy. Give the domestic and global welfare consequences of this policy.

Metzler paradox

Figure 5.3 assumes that foreign export supply is elastic at the free trade equilibrium. In contrast, Figure 5.4 illustrates the extreme case in which the foreign export supply curve bends backward. In this case the tariff reduces not only the world price but also the domestic price of good 2 and hence the quantity imported increases. Figures 5.3 and 5.4 suggest that a tariff could raise, lower or leave unchanged the domestic price of the imported good. These possibilities then raise a question concerning the expected effect of a tariff on domestic resource allocation. In particular, if a tariff lowers the

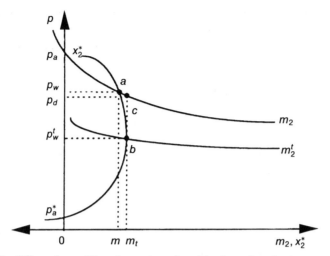

Figure 5.4 *Effect of a tariff on domestic and world prices when foreign export supply is backward bending*

domestic price of imports then domestic production of good 2 will fall, not rise. This decline in domestic production may be contrary to what policy makers had intended by imposing the tariff.

The possibility that a tariff could lower the domestic price of the imported good was first pointed out by Metzler (1949) and is hence known as Metzler's paradox. The conditions under which this paradoxical outcome does not occur are stated below.

Metzler condition The imposition of a tariff increases the domestic price of the imported good if and only if the price elasticity of foreign import demand exceeds the domestic marginal propensity to spend on the export good.

To derive the Metzler condition, write (5.1) in relative change form:

$$\hat{p}_d = \hat{p}_w + \frac{d\tau}{(1 + \tau)} \tag{5.6}$$

International equilibrium requires that the trade balances at home and abroad be zero. In turn, this implies that the value of imports in each country be equal: $m_2 p_w = m_1$. Writing this relationship in relative change form gives:

$$\hat{p}_w = \hat{m}_1 - \hat{m}_2 \tag{5.7}$$

Expressions (5.6) and (5.7) indicate that we need to find expressions for $\hat{m}_1$ and $\hat{m}_2$ in terms of the world price and tariff rate. Consider first $\hat{m}_2$ and assume that the tariff revenue is returned to domestic consumers via a lump-sum transfer.[8] Noting that import demand is $m_2 = d_2(p_d, S(p_d, u_1)) - q_2(p_d)$, where expenditure (S) is given by (5.3), we can repeat the steps taken to derive (4.53) to obtain:

$$\hat{m}_2 = -e\hat{p}_w - (e_1 + e_2)d\tau \tag{5.8}$$

Recall from Chapter 4 that e and e_1 are, respectively, the uncompensated and compensated price elasticities of import demand while e_2 is the elasticity of domestic supply of good 2. Derivation of (5.8) assumes the country was initially in free trade, that is, $\tau = 0$ and $p_d = p_w$. Note that for any given level of imports (i.e. $\hat{m}_2 = 0$), the term $(e_1 + e_2)d\tau$ in (5.8) indicates the size of the downward displacement of the import demand curve illustrated in Figure 5.3 or Figure 5.4.

Turning now to $\hat{m}_1$, foreign import demand will react normally to the change in world price so the expression for $\hat{m}_1$ takes the simpler form:

$$\hat{m}_1 = \hat{p}_w e^* \tag{5.9}$$

where e^* is the price elasticity of foreign import demand. Substitution of (5.8) and (5.9) into (5.7) gives:

$$\hat{p}_w = -\frac{e_1 + e_2}{e^* + e - 1} d\tau \tag{5.10}$$

Expression (5.10) is negative since $e_1 > 0$, $e_2 > 0$ and trade balance stability requires $(e^* + e - 1) > 0$.[9] The tariff therefore improves the home country's terms of trade unless the country is small (i.e. $e^* = \infty$). The effect of this terms of trade improvement on the domestic price of the imported good is found by substituting (5.10) into (5.6) to obtain (with $\tau = 0$)

$$\hat{p}_d = \frac{e^* - (1 - e_3)}{e^* + e - 1} d\tau \gtreqless 0 \quad \text{as } e^* \gtreqless (1 - e_3) \tag{5.11}$$

where use has been made of (4.54). Expression (5.11) states the Metzler condition: a tariff will raise the domestic price of the imported good if the foreign import price elasticity e^* exceeds the domestic marginal propensity to spend on the export good $(1 - e_3)$. A tariff which lowers the domestic price of the imported good relative to its free trade level will lower domestic production of the import competing good and hence make the domestic industry worse off compared to free trade. A fall in the domestic price also implies a fall in the relative and real return to the factor used intensively in the import competing industry. This change in factor rewards is opposite to that predicted by the Stolper–Samuelson theorem (which assumes a small country). While theoretically possible, no case of Metzler's paradox has been empirically demonstrated.[10]

The optimum tariff

Expression (5.5) indicates that a tariff can raise the welfare of a large country through an improvement in its terms of trade. However, (5.5) also indicates that the welfare gain from an improved terms of trade is set against a loss arising from the distortion between domestic and world prices introduced by the tariff. These offsetting effects on welfare suggest that there exists a tariff rate that would just balance these gains and losses at the margin, and hence maximize the welfare of the tariff imposing country. This welfare maximizing tariff rate is called the optimum tariff. Its value is found by setting dW to zero in (5.5) and solving for τ:

$$\tau^* = \frac{1}{\hat{m}_2/\hat{p}_w} = \frac{1}{f^*} \tag{5.12}$$

The second equality in (5.12) follows from (5.7) and (5.9) and the equality $f^* = e^* - 1$. As (5.12) indicates, the size of the optimum tariff is inversely related to the elasticity of foreign export supply. Note that (5.12) further confirms that a small country maximizes its welfare under free trade since $\tau^* = 0$ when $f^* = \infty$.

Tariffs and export subsidies

Tariffs favor domestic import competing producers relative to foreign producers in the home market. In contrast, export subsidies give domestic exporters an advantage over foreign producers in foreign markets. Since a subsidy is a negative tax, the preceding analyses of a tariff are easily adapted to examine the welfare and resource allocation implications of an export subsidy. Specifically, the welfare implications of an export subsidy can be inferred from (5.5) by assuming that good 2 is instead exported so that $-m_2 = x_2$ and p_w is now the country's terms of trade. Then, by (5.5), an export subsidy unambiguously decreases the welfare of the subsidizing country. The subsidy deteriorates the country's terms of trade ($dp_w < 0$) and the trade volume effect, which in this case measures the increase in domestically financed subsidy payments consequent to the increase in exports, adds to this welfare loss.[11]

Taking an export subsidy as representative of policies that stimulate trade and a tariff as representative of policies that restrict trade, the above analyses imply the following proposition regarding a country's optimal choice of trade policy instrument:

Trade policy prescription When markets are perfectly competitive, trade policy should take the form of restrictions rather than stimulants to trade.

Symmetry of import and export taxes

A tariff changes the pattern of domestic production and consumption because it changes the domestic *relative* price of imports. We now show that this relative price change, and hence the effects of a tariff, can be duplicated if the country instead imposes a tax on its exports. Consider first the case of a tariff. The domestic nominal price of imports is $p_{2d} = (1 + \tau)p_{2w}$ while the domestic nominal price of the export good equals the world price ($p_{1d} = p_{1w}$). The domestic relative price of imports is therefore $p_{2d}/p_{1d} = (1 + \tau)p_{2w}/p_{1w}$. Now let the country instead impose an *ad valorem* tax τ on its exports of good 1. By assumption, the domestic price of imports now equals the world price ($p_{2d} = p_{2w}$) but the domestic nominal price of exports (net of the tax) is now below the world price since $p_{1d}(1 + \tau) = p_{1w}$ or $p_{1d} = p_{1w}/(1 + \tau)$. The domestic relative price of imports is therefore $p_{2d}/p_{1d} = (1 + \tau)p_{2w}/p_{1w}$ which is the same as the case of a tariff. Hence, a tax on imports and a tax on exports result in the same change in domestic relative prices and in this sense are equivalent. This result is known as the Lerner Symmetry Theorem:

Lerner symmetry theorem   A tax on exports has the same effect on domestic relative prices as an equal tariff on imports.

Since a uniform tariff on all imports has exactly the same effect as a uniform tax on all exports, all the preceding conclusions about the resource allocation effects of a tariff apply without change to the case of an export tax. In particular, this symmetry implies the existence of an optimum export tax equivalent to the optimum tariff.

5.2 Quantitative restrictions

Tariffs and other 'price' measures distort relative prices and reduce trade volumes. Under perfect competition, the same results in terms of prices and trade volumes can be attained by policies that target quantities rather than prices. Quantitative restrictions (QRs) can be explicit, as when they take the form of export and import quotas or implicit, as when they take the form of a domestic content requirement (DCR). Below we examine the effects of such restrictions in a partial equilibrium framework. Although the price and volume effect of a quantitative restriction can often be duplicated by an appropriate tariff, these policies generally differ in their welfare effects. In particular, tariffs generate revenue for the home government while quantitative restrictions generate pure economic profit (rent) for those who hold the right to import or export the restricted good. If the holders of these 'quota rights' are not domestic agents then the quota rent is a transfer of domestic income to foreigners which is then added to the efficiency costs that a country experiences when restricting its trade.

Import quotas

Figure 5.5 illustrates the case of a large country. The initial free trade equilibrium is at point *a* with the domestic price of the imported good equal to the world price p_w. An import quota that limits imports to $\bar{m}$ units implies that import demand becomes vertical (downward) at point *c* and a new international equilibrium is established at point *b*. The import quota therefore lowers the world price from p_w to p'_w. However, the price that clears the domestic market for imports is p_d. Since the same world and domestic prices, and therefore quantity imported, would result if a tariff $\tau = (p_d - p'_w)/p'_w$ had instead been imposed,[12] the quota imposes the same welfare cost to consumers, namely, the decrease in consumer surplus equal to areas *A* and *B*. However, under the quota, areas *A* and *C* are not tariff revenue but rather pure economic profit (rent). Assuming this rent accrues to domestic importers, the *net* change in the quota imposing country's welfare is the same as under a tariff, namely area *C minus* area *B* while the loss to the foreign country again equals areas *C* and *D*. However, this is not the only possible outcome. Any part of the quota rents that fails to accrue to domestic agents would entail an uncompensated loss of income for the importing country. In the extreme, all rents could go to foreign agents.[13] But regardless of who captures the quota rents, world welfare falls by an amount equal to areas *B* and *D*.

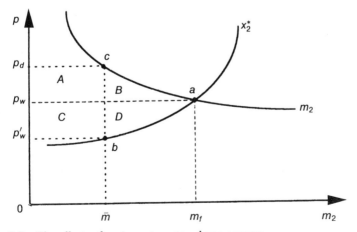

Figure 5.5 *The effects of an import quota – large country*

Who earns the rents generated by a quota depends on how, and by whom, the quota is administered. Import quotas are always administered by the importing country, which sets a limit on the volume of imports that can be admitted over a given period of time. A global import quota limits imports from all suppliers while a country-specific quota limits imports from only certain countries, normally just the largest suppliers.

Administration of an import quota usually takes one of two forms: imports enter on a first-come, first-served basis until the total volume of imports reaches the prescribed limit, or the importing country issues licences which identify the importer and the volume of imports covered by the licence. Under the first scheme, importers who are first to import goods up to the limit set by the quota get the quota rents. Under the second scheme, the government can either issue licences on a first-come, first-served basis, allocate licences across importers based on predetermined criteria,[14] or sell the licences at an auction. If licenses are simply issued (essentially for free) then importers who receive licences get the quota rents.[15] If licences are sold at auction, the revenue earned by the government equals, in theory, the quota rents.[16] If so, then an 'auctioned import quota' is equivalent in both its revenue and welfare effect to that of a tariff.[17]

Problem 5.6: We have stated that the price and quantity effects of a quota can be duplicated by a tariff. Examine therefore whether the Metzler paradox is also possible under an import quota, that is, is it possible for an import quota to lower the domestic price of the import good relative to its initial free trade level?

Export quotas

Export quotas are administered by the exporting country, which sets a limit on the volume of exports that can be shipped over a specified period of time. The methods for administering an export quota are the same as those for an import quota: the country can allow exports to be shipped on a first-come, first-served basis or export licences can be issued or sold at auction. Whoever acquires the right to export will capture the rents generated by the quota (except if the licences are auctioned). Before considering the economic effects of an export quota we note that just as there exists a tariff that can duplicate the price and volume effects of an import quota, there also exists an export tax that can duplicate the price and volume effects to an export quota. Given this, the Lerner Symmetry Theorem between export and import taxes implies a similar symmetry between export and import quotas, that is, there exists an export quota that has the same price and volume effects as an import quota.

Voluntary export restraint

Countries sometimes use export quotas to limit sales of 'strategic' goods such as natural resources or 'sensitive' technology. More prevalent, however, are export quotas that arise from a voluntary restraint agreement (VRA). A VRA is negotiated between an importing country and one or more of its supplier countries with the intent of limiting its imports. Since the importing country 'requests' exporters to limit their supply, the resulting export quota is called a Voluntary Export Restraint (VER).[18]

The effect of a VER on the importing country can be illustrated using Figure 5.5. Starting from the free trade equilibrium (point *a*), a quota that limits exports to $\overline{m}$ units implies that the foreign export supply becomes vertical at point *b* and hence the new international equilibrium is established at point *c*. The world price of exports therefore rises from p_w to p_d which is also the new domestic price in the importing country. The rise in the world price under the VER contrasts with the fall in world price (from p_w to p'_w) that arises in the case of an import quota that limits imports to $\overline{m}$ units. That is, a VER deteriorates, while an import quota improves, the importing country's terms of trade. The terms of trade deterioration implies the loss in consumer surplus equal to areas *A* and *B*. Since foreign exporters receive the price p_d but supply $\overline{m}$ units at a marginal cost of p'_w they receive a rent of $(p_d - p'_w)$ per-unit exported. Total rents therefore equal to areas *A* and *C* in Figure 5.5. The importing country's net welfare loss is then areas *A* and *B*.[19] Since this loss exceeds that arising under an equal import quota where the rents accrue to domestic importers we can conclude that, for the importing country, a VER is welfare inferior to an import quota as a policy for reducing its imports.[20]

In the exporting country, the quota reduces producer surplus by areas *C* and *D* but generates rent equal to areas *A* and *C*. The net benefit to the exporting country is therefore area *A* *minus* area *D*. If the foreign government auctioned export licences it could capture the quota rents (areas *A* and *C*) which, by assumption, would be redistributed to (foreign) consumers. In this case the distributional effects of the quota within the foreign country would be identical to an *ad valorem* export tax $t = (p_d - p'_w)/p'_w$ (assuming the tax proceeds are redistributed to consumers). Finally, like an import quota, the VER leads to a net decline in world welfare equal to areas *B* and *D*.

Domestic content requirement

A domestic content requirement (DCR) requires firms that sell in the domestic market to purchase a specified minimum proportion of their intermediate inputs from domestic suppliers.[21] If firms comply with the requirement, import duties are waived on imported intermediate goods or some other benefit is granted. If firms fail to meet the requirement then a penalty can be imposed or the firm may be prohibited from selling its final product in the domestic market.[22] A DCR is therefore a quantitative restriction that involves a minimum purchase requirement.

A DCR can be specified in physical terms or in terms of value added. The physical base is usually applied when the imported and domestic inputs are homogeneous while the value added base is applied if the inputs are heterogeneous. When defined as a required share of value added, several refinements are possible. For example, capital costs may be excluded from the definition of value added.

The essential aspects of a DCR can be understood using a simple partial equilibrium model in which a final good is produced using one intermediate 'component' good.[23] It is assumed that production of one unit of the final good requires one unit of the component and that domestic and imported components are perfectly substitutable in producing the final good. The importing country is assumed to be small so the supply of imported components (x^*) is infinitely elastic at the fixed world price p_w. The supply of domestic components (q) is given by the (inverse) supply function $p_d = p_d(q)$ where p_d is the price of domestic components and $\partial p_d / \partial q > 0$. The assumption of a fixed input–output relation between the component and final good implies that total domestic demand for components (D) is just the amount produced of the final good (z):

$$D = q + x^* = z \tag{5.13}$$

where x^* is the quantity of the imported component. Now assume that the government imposes a DCR which specifies that the fraction λ ($0 \leq \lambda \leq 1$) of all components purchased must be purchased from domestic suppliers. This restriction implies that the demand for domestically produced components (d) is:

$$d = \lambda(q + x^*) = \lambda z \tag{5.14}$$

The minimum purchase requirement also implies that final good producers now pay an average price ($\bar{p}$) for components equal to:

$$\bar{p} = \lambda p_d + (1 - \lambda) p_w \tag{5.15}$$

Figure 5.6 illustrates the domestic market for components. Under free trade, equilibrium occurs at point e with the domestic price of components equaling the world price p_w. At this price, final good producers purchase D_0 components of which q_0 units are purchased from domestic suppliers while $D_0 - q_0$ units are imported. The imposition of the DCR implies that final good producers face a 'composite' supply function ($\bar{q}$) for components which, assuming $\lambda \neq 1$ or 0, lies between the domestic and import supply functions.[24] Therefore, under the DCR, final good producers demand a

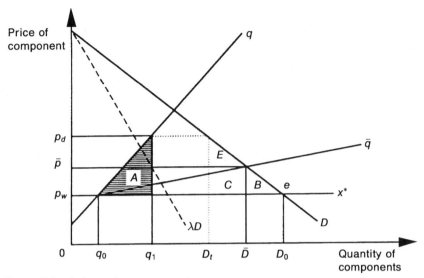

Figure 5.6 *A domestic content requirement*

total of $\overline{D}$ components at the average price $\bar{p}$ given by (5.15). Of this total, $q_1 = \lambda \overline{D}$ components must be purchased from domestic suppliers. To supply these q_1 units domestic component producers must receive the price p_d. In summary, the price of domestic components rises from p_w to p_d, domestic production of components rises from q_0 to q_1 units, and imports of components fall to $\overline{D} - q_1$ units.

Comparing the welfare effects of the DCR to a tariff $(\tau = (p_d - p_w)/p_w)$ that would also raise the production of domestic components to q_1 we note that, from Figure 5.6, the tariff brings about the same deadweight loss (area A) on the production side. However, the consumption deadweight loss (area B) is smaller under the DCR than under the tariff (areas B, C and E) since, under the tariff, final good producers will demand a total of D_t components. Intuitively, a DCR involves a lower welfare cost than a tariff since the former allows imported components to be purchased at the world price whereas the tariff raises the price of both domestic and imported components. A DCR is therefore superior to a tariff if the intent is to raise production of domestic components.

5.3 Applied methods

Estimating welfare effects

This section presents partial and general equilibrium methods that are used to estimate the distributional and net welfare effects of trade policies. The calculation of these effects is an important area of applied work in international trade. Quantifying the welfare costs and benefits of trade policies provides important input into the policy making process; the decision by government officials to grant or remove protection is often influenced by the magnitude of the calculated effects. The calculated welfare effects can also serve as data for empirical investigations of the motives for protection and other areas of research.

The calculation of welfare effects arising from trade policy changes has traditionally been made using formulas derived from partial equilibrium analysis. In the first half of this section we derive and discuss the use of several of these formulas. Although these formulas have been used to measure welfare changes arising from large scale changes in trade policy, such as multilateral tariff reductions, their use in such cases is now overshadowed by the use of applied general equilibrium (AGE) models (see p. 196). AGE models simplify the measurement of net welfare changes since they assume an explicit form for the utility function. The second half of this section discusses the measures of welfare changes that are used in this context. Although now widely used, the data and computational require-ments of an AGE model are orders of magnitude greater than those of a partial equilibrium analysis. The traditional partial equilibrium methods therefore remain preferred when only a few products are to be examined and such methods are often the only feasible way to proceed when welfare effects are to be computed at a detailed commodity level.

Partial equilibrium methods

Partial equilibrium methods for calculating the welfare effects of trade policies ignore the price and quantity changes for all but a few commodities. Moreover, these methods use demand functions which treat income as exogenous and therefore ignore the income effects that arise from a trade policy change. Our analysis of partial equilibrium methods assumes that there are two goods, one imported and the other domestically produced. We begin with the case of a small country and consider estimating the welfare effects that arise from complete removal of an existing tariff. This analysis makes the simplifying assumption that the imported and domestically produced goods are perfect substitutes and that the relevant demand and supply functions are linear. We then extend the analysis by dropping the assumption of linear demands and supplies and by considering a partial reduction in an existing tariff. In this framework we discuss the cases of a small and large country and then consider the case in which the imported and domestically produced goods are imperfect substitutes. With this foundation, the section concludes by considering the estimation of welfare effects associated with partial changes in nontariff barriers (NTBs), as illustrated by the cases of a reduction in an import quota and an export quota.

Tariffs

Small country

To illustrate as simply as possible the methods used to estimate the welfare effects of trade policies consider first the case of a small country who has in place an *ad valorem* tariff τ on its imports of a homogeneous good. This case is depicted by panels A and B of Figure 5.2. Looking first at panel A, elimination of the tariff implies four effects to be estimated: the two transfer effects (areas T and R) and the two efficiency effects (areas Q and S). If the demand and supply functions are linear then these effects are easily calculated for given values of the tariff and the elasticities of demand and supply. Since we are interested in the effects of complete tariff elimination, the effect on tariff revenue (area R) does not require estimation since the government will lose the existing tariff revenue and the latter is directly observable. Given this, let $\Delta p = (p_w - p_d) < 0$, $\Delta d = (d_f - d_t) > 0$ and $\Delta q = (q_f - q_t) < 0$ denote, respectively, the changes in domestic price, domestic demand and domestic production that will arise from tariff elimination. Noting that $\Delta p / p_d = -\tau/(1 + \tau)$, the reader can verify the following formulas for the three remaining areas shown in panel A:

$$\text{Area } T: \qquad -\Delta p(q_t + \Delta q/2) = \frac{\tau V_q}{2(1 + \tau)}\left(2 - \frac{\tau \varepsilon_d}{(1 + \tau)}\right) \qquad (5.16)$$

$$\text{Area } Q: \qquad \Delta p \Delta q/2 = \left(\frac{\varepsilon_d V_q}{2}\right)\left(\frac{\tau^2}{(1 + \tau)^2}\right) \qquad (5.17)$$

$$\text{Area } S: \qquad -\Delta p \Delta d/2 = \left(\frac{\eta_d V_d}{2}\right)\left(\frac{\tau^2}{(1 + \tau)^2}\right) \qquad (5.18)$$

In these formulas, $\eta_d > 0$ and $\varepsilon_d > 0$ are, respectively, the price elasticities of domestic demand and domestic supply and $V_q = p_d q_t$ and $V_d = p_d d_t$ are, respectively, the values of domestic production and domestic consumption at the tariff inclusive domestic price. Except for the elasticity values, these formulas involve variables that are readily available from national statistics on trade and production.

The sum of (5.16)–(5.18) *plus* the tariff revenue (i.e. $-\Delta p(d_t - q_t)$) equals the change in the surplus of domestic consumer (ΔCS):

$$\Delta CS = \frac{\tau V_d}{2(1 + \tau)}\left(2 + \frac{\eta_d \tau}{(1 + \tau)}\right) \qquad (5.19)$$

Finally, the economy-wide net change in welfare (ΔW) is the sum of (5.17) and (5.18):

$$\Delta W = \left(\frac{\varepsilon_d V_q + \eta_d V_d}{2}\right)\left(\frac{\tau^2}{(1+\tau)^2}\right) \tag{5.20}$$

Multiplying (5.20) by V_m/V_m where $V_m = p_d m_t$ is the initial (tariff inclusive) value of imports, and using $\eta_m = (V_q/V_m)\varepsilon_d + (V_d/V_m)\eta_d$, where $\eta_m > 0$ is the elasticity of import demand, (5.20) can also be written

$$\Delta W = \frac{V_m \eta_m \tau^2}{2(1+\tau)^2} \tag{5.21}$$

As expected, (5.21) is the value of area B in panel (b) of Figure 5.2.

The above formulas have been widely used to calculate the distributional and net welfare effects of tariff elimination. By reversing the logic, the estimated effects can be interpreted as the transfer and efficiency costs incurred by maintaining the existing tariff. Hence, these formulas collectively provide for the measurement of the various aspects of the 'cost of protection'.

A major attraction of these formulas are their simplicity in terms of data requirements. But whereas tariff rates and import values are readily obtained from published statistics, values of the demand and supply elasticities are more difficult to obtain. Values of these elasticities must either be estimated by the analyst or culled from the literature. In the latter case, several estimates are often available and these may refer to 'commodities' at higher or lower levels of aggregation than the commodity being examined. When several estimates are available, a 'best guess' value (usually the average of available estimates) is often used. Regardless of their source, the elasticity values are only an estimate of the 'true' elasticity. To some, the uncertainty about the 'true' value of an elasticity represents a weakness of these formulas since it implies that the 'true' size of the effects cannot be known. However, this view is too strong. Rather, although rarely done, such uncertainty can be incorporated by using the upper and lower values of, say, a 95% confidence interval for the relevant elasticity estimate.[25] The estimated transfer and welfare effects would then be presented as interval estimates with an associated level of confidence. Finally, because of the difficulties in obtaining elasticity values, the net change in welfare is usually calculated using (5.21) rather than (5.20) since the latter formula only requires one elasticity value.

Partial tariff reduction

We now assume that the initial tariff τ_1 is to be reduced to a new level $\tau_2 \neq 0$ and henceforth drop the assumption of linear demand and supply functions.

In this context, our analysis focuses on determining the formula for estimating the net welfare change arising from the tariff reduction. Given this, Figure 5.7 illustrates the market for the imported good for the case of a small country. Given the initial tariff τ_1, the equilibrium domestic price of imports (p_1) is given by the intersection of import demand (m) and the tariff inclusive import (foreign export) supply (x_1^*). Reducing the tariff from τ_1 to τ_2 lowers the tariff inclusive import supply from x_1^* to x_2^* and implies a fall in the domestic price of imports from p_1 to p_2 and an increase in imports from m_1 to m_2 units.

The tariff reduction benefits consumers of the imported good by the change in consumer surplus (ΔCS) equal to areas A and B in Figure 5.7.[26] Formally, this area can be measured as:

$$\Delta CS = \int_{\tau_2}^{\tau_1} m(p_m) \frac{dp_m}{d\tau} d\tau \tag{5.22}$$

where p_m denotes the domestic price of imports. For what follows it is convenient to work with the following equivalent form of (5.22):

$$\Delta CS = \int_{p_2}^{p_1} m(p_m) dp_m \tag{5.23}$$

Absent a functional form for import demand ($m(p_m)$), the value of (5.23) has traditionally been approximated using the trapezoid rule:[27]

$$\Delta CS = -\Delta p_m (m_1 + m_2)/2 = -\hat{p}_m V_1 (\hat{m} + 2)/2 \tag{5.24}$$

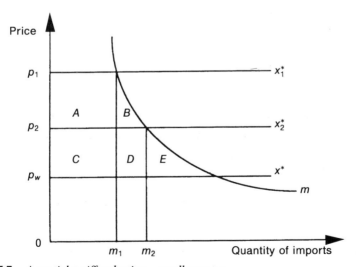

Figure 5.7 *A partial tariff reduction – small country*

where $V_1 = p_1 m_1$ is the initial (tariff inclusive) value of imports and $\hat{m} = (m_2/m_1 - 1)$ and $\hat{p}_m = (p_2/p_1 - 1) = (\tau_2 - \tau_1)/(1 + \tau_1)$ are, respectively, the relative changes in the volume and domestic price of imports. Since $\hat{p}_m$ is known, calculation of (5.24) requires only an estimate of the relative change in imports, the natural choice being $\hat{m} = -\eta_m \hat{p}_m$, where $\eta_m > 0$ is the price elasticity of import demand. Substituting for $\hat{m}$ and $\hat{p}_m$ in (5.24) gives

$$\Delta CS = V_1 \frac{(\tau_2 - \tau_1)}{2(1 + \tau_1)} \left(\frac{\eta_m(\tau_2 - \tau_1)}{(1 - \tau_1)} - 2 \right) \tag{5.25}$$

Since the tariff reduction is partial and not complete, the change in tariff revenue (ΔR) is not the pre-existing amount of revenue but instead $\Delta R = (p_2 - p_w)dm - m_1 dp_m$ which equals area D *minus* area A in Figure 5.7. This revenue change is equivalently measured as areas B and D *minus* areas A and B. While cumbersome, the latter formulation allows us to express the revenue change in terms of integrals associated with the direct and inverse import demand functions:

$$\Delta R = \int_{m_1}^{m_2} \{ p_m(m) - p_w \} dm - \int_{p_2}^{p_1} m(p_m) dp_m \tag{5.26}$$

The net change in domestic welfare (ΔW) is the sum of the changes in consumer surplus (5.23) and tariff revenue (5.26):[28]

$$\Delta W = \int_{m_1}^{m_2} \{ p_m(m) - p_w \} dm \tag{5.27}$$

which equals areas B and D in Figure 5.7.[29] Approximating (5.27) by the trapezoid rule gives:

$$\Delta W \cong \Delta m \{ p_2 + p_1 - 2p_w \}/2 \tag{5.28}$$

where $\Delta m = (m_2 - m_1) > 0$. Multiplying the right-hand side of (5.28) by m_1/m_2 and substituting $p_i = (1 + \tau_i)p_w$ gives

$$\Delta W \cong V_1 \frac{(\tau_1 + \tau_2)}{2(1 + \tau_1)} \hat{m} \tag{5.29}$$

Finally, substituting $\hat{m} = -\eta_m \hat{p}_m = -\eta_m(\tau_2 - \tau_1)/(1 + \tau_1)$ in (5.29), an estimate of the net welfare change due to the tariff change is[30]

$$\Delta W \cong V_1 \eta_m \frac{(\tau_1^2 - \tau_2^2)}{2(1 + \tau_1)^2} \tag{5.30}$$

From (5.30), the formula for the net welfare change from complete tariff elimination $(\tau_2 = 0)$ is $\Delta W \cong V_1 \eta_m (\tau_1^2/2(1 + \tau_1)^2)$ which equals the sum of areas A, B, C, D and E in Figure 5.7. Not unexpectedly, this expression equals that in (5.21) since we have used trapezoid approximations to the integrals of interest.

Apart from the assumptions imposed by a partial equilibrium analysis (e.g. consumer income and the prices of all other goods are assumed constant) and the issue of uncertainty associated with using an estimate of η_m, there are two additional issues concerning the accuracy of the net welfare change computed using (5.30). One is that (5.30) is derived using a trapezoid approximation. The other is that η_m is a point elasticity and hence its use in (5.30) assumes that the tariff change is 'small'. A 'large' tariff change will then necessarily introduce some error in the calculation.[31] Both of these issues can be addressed by specifying a functional form for import demand. To see this, write (5.27) in its complete form:[32]

$$\Delta W = -\int_{t_2}^{t_1} (p_m[m(\tau, p_w)] - p_w) \frac{dm(\tau, p_w)}{d\tau} \, d\tau \tag{5.31}$$

where $m(\tau, p_w)$ denotes import demand as a function of the tariff and world price. Since the tariff rate is *ad valorem* and p_w is fixed (small country) we have $p_m[m(\tau, p_w)] = p_w(1 + \tau)$. Substituting this in (5.31) gives:

$$\Delta W = -\int_{t_2}^{t_1} \tau p_w \frac{dm(\tau, p_w)}{d\tau} \, d\tau \tag{5.32}$$

Hence, given a functional form for the import demand function one can compute $dm(\tau, p_w)/d\tau$ and directly calculate (5.32).

A common approach is to assume that import demand has the constant elasticity form $m = kp_m^{-\eta_m}$ (or $p_m = (m/k)^{-1/\eta_m}$), where k is a constant representing all other variables in the demand equation, and to then use this functional form when computing price and quantity changes. For example, using this demand specification to compute price changes implies that (5.29) would be written:

$$\Delta W \cong V_1 \frac{(\tau_1 + \tau_2)}{2(1 + \tau_1)} ((p_2/p_1)^{-\eta_m} - 1)$$

$$\cong V_1 \frac{(\tau_1 + \tau_2)}{2(1 + \tau_1)} \left(\left(\frac{(1 + \tau_1)}{(1 + \tau_2)} \right)^{\eta_m} - 1 \right) \tag{5.33}$$

Of course, (5.33) is still a trapezoid approximation to (5.32). But this is unnecessary if one assumes a form for the demand function since (5.32) can instead be computed. For example, if demand is $m(\tau, p_m) = k(p_w(1 + \tau))^{-\eta_m}$ then $dm(\tau, p_w)/d\tau = -\eta_m k p_w^{-\eta_m}(1 + \tau)^{-(\eta_m + 1)}$. Inserting the latter into (5.32) one obtains:

$$\Delta W = \eta_m k(p_w)^{1 - \eta_m} \int_{t_2}^{t_1} \tau(1 + \tau)^{-(\eta_m + 1)} \, d\tau \tag{5.34}$$

Assuming $\eta_m \neq 1$, (5.34) evaluates to

$$\Delta W = \frac{V_1}{\gamma_1(\eta_m - 1)} \left((1 + \eta_m \tau_2)\left(\frac{\gamma_1}{\gamma_2}\right)^{\eta_m} - (1 + \eta_m \tau_1) \right) \qquad (5.35)$$

where $\gamma_i = (1 + \tau_i)$, $i = 1, 2$.[33] What difference do these alternative formulas make for the calculated change in welfare? Assume that the 'true' demand function has the constant elasticity form and let $\eta_m = 2$, $\tau_1 = 0.2$ and $\tau_2 = 0$ (i.e. complete tariff removal). Then calculating the net welfare change as a percentage of the initial value of imports (i.e. $\Delta W/V_1$) using (5.30), (5.33) and (5.35) yields, respectively, 2.78%, 3.67% and 3.33%.[34] Hence, using the trapezoid approximation but not imposing the constant elasticity assumption (when true) underestimates the 'true' welfare change (3.33%) while making this assumption, but still using a trapezoid approximation, overstates the 'true' welfare change. The moral is that if one is willing to specify the form of the import demand function then one can calculate the value of the integral rather than use an approximation.

Large country

Figure 5.8 illustrates the case when import supply (x^*) is positively sloped. In the initial tariff-ridden equilibrium, consumers import m_1 units at the tariff inclusive domestic price p_1. The world price is p_w^1 so that tariff revenue equals areas A, C and E. A reduction in the tariff from τ_1 to τ_2 shifts the tariff inclusive import supply from x_1^* to x_2^* and lowers the domestic price of

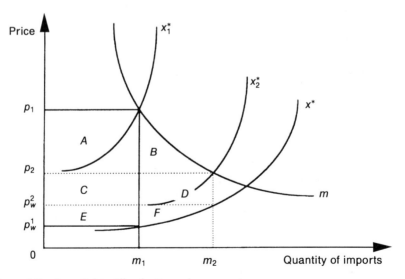

Figure 5.8   *A partial tariff reduction – large country*

imports to p_2. Since import supply is positively sloped, the world price rises to p_w^2 (a terms of trade deterioration).

The tariff reduction benefits consumers of the imported good by the change in consumer surplus (areas A and B):

$$\Delta CS = \int_{p_2}^{p_1} m(p_m)\, dp_m \tag{5.36}$$

The change in tariff revenue is $\Delta R = (p_2 - p_w^2)\, dm - (dp_w - dp)m_1$ which equals area D *minus* areas A and E in Figure 5.8. This change can also be measured as areas B, D, and F *minus* areas A, B, E, *and* F:

$$\Delta R = \int_{m_1}^{m_2} (p_m(m) - p_w(m))\, dm \quad \text{(areas } B + D + F) \tag{5.37}$$

$$- \int_{p_2}^{p_1} m(p_m)\, dp_m \qquad \text{(areas } A + B)$$

$$- \int_{p_w^1}^{p_w^2} x^*(p_w)\, dp_w \qquad \text{(areas } E + F)$$

where $p_w = p_w(m)$ and $m = x^*(p_w)$ are, respectively, the inverse and direct import supply functions. Adding expressions (5.36) and (5.37), the net change in welfare is

$$\Delta W = \int_{m_1}^{m_2} (p_m(m) - p_w(m))\, dm - \int_{p_w^1}^{p_w^2} x^*(p_w)\, dp_w \tag{5.38}$$

which equals areas B and D minus area E in Figure 5.8. Approximating (5.38) using the trapezoid rule gives:

$$\Delta W \cong \tfrac{1}{2}(\Delta m[p_1(1 + p_2/p_1) - p_{w1}(1 + p_w^2/p_w^1)] - \Delta p_w x_1^*(1 + x_2^*/x_1^*)) \tag{5.39}$$

where $\Delta p_w = (p_{w2} - p_{w1}) > 0$. We now want to express the price and quantity changes in (5.39) in terms of the underlying elasticities of import demand and supply. To do so, first define the 'pass-through' coefficients

$$\rho_m = \hat{p}_m = (p_2/p_1) - 1$$

$$\rho_w = \hat{p}_w = (p_w^2/p_w^1) - 1 \tag{5.40}$$

which measure, respectively, the percentage change in the domestic and world price of the import good. Using (5.40), and setting $x_2^*/x_1^* = \hat{x}^* + 1$, (5.39) can be written:

$$\Delta W \cong \tfrac{1}{2}(\Delta m((\rho_m + 2)p_1 - p_w^1(\rho_w + 2)) - \Delta p_w x_1^*(\hat{x}^* + 2))$$

Multiplying the first bracketed expression by m_1/m_2 and using $m_1 = x_1^*$ as well as $p_w^1 = p_1/\gamma_1$, where $\gamma_1 = (1 + \tau_1)$, gives

$$\Delta W \cong \frac{V_1}{2\gamma_1} \left(\hat{m}(\gamma_1(\rho_m + 2) - (\rho_w + 2)) - \rho_w(\hat{x}^* + 2)\right) \tag{5.41}$$

Using $\hat{m} = -\eta_m \rho_m$ and $\hat{x}^* = \varepsilon_m \rho_w$, where ε_m denotes the elasticity of import supply, the preceding expression can be written:

$$\Delta W \cong \frac{V_1}{2\gamma_1} \left(-\eta_m \rho_m(\gamma_1(\rho_m + 2) - (\rho_w + 2)) - \rho_w(\varepsilon_m \rho_w + 2)\right) \tag{5.42}$$

Values for the pass-through coefficients are obtained by solving the equilibrium condition $-\eta_m \rho_m = \varepsilon_m \rho_w$ (i.e. $\hat{m} = \hat{x}^*$) with the equation for the change in the domestic price of imports: $\rho_m = \hat{\gamma} + \rho_w$, where $\hat{\gamma} = d\gamma/\gamma = d(1 + \tau)/(1 + \tau)$.

$$\rho_m = \frac{\hat{\gamma}}{(\varepsilon_m + \eta_m)} \tag{5.43}$$

$$\rho_w = \frac{-\eta_m \hat{\gamma}}{(\varepsilon_m + \eta_m)}$$

Inserting these values into (5.42), one can, after considerable manipulation, write (5.42) as

$$\Delta W \cong \frac{-V_1 \eta_m}{2\gamma_1} \left(\mu\left(\left(\frac{\hat{\gamma}\varepsilon_m}{(\varepsilon_m + \eta_m)} + 1\right)^2 - 1\right) + 2\hat{\gamma}\eta_m\right) \tag{5.44}$$

where $\mu = (1 + \eta_m + \gamma_1 \varepsilon_m)$. The reader can verify that (5.44) reduces to (5.30) when $\varepsilon_m = \infty$. Comparing (5.44) to (5.30), the major complication introduced by assuming a large country is that an estimate of the import supply elasticity is now needed.[35] However, the literature contains relatively few estimates of import supply elasticities for individual commodities. For this reason, welfare estimates using (5.44) are often presented for a range of assumed values for the supply elasticity (e.g. $\varepsilon_m = 1$ and $\varepsilon_m = 10$).

Imperfect substitutes

We now assume that the imported and domestic good are imperfect, rather than perfect, substitutes. Modeling imported and domestic goods as imperfect substitutes is important since the assumption of perfect substitutes is inconsistent with empirically estimated values of price elasticities of demand. Note that the assumption of imperfect substitutes implies that import demand is no longer derivable as the difference between the domestic demand and domestic supply of a good, and that one must now account for any cross-price effects that arise between the imported and domestic good when the tariff is changed. To incorporate such effects we now write import demand as $m = m(p_m, p_d)$ and the demand for the domestic good as $d = d(p_d, p_m)$, where p_m and p_d denote, respectively, the domestic prices of the imported and domestic good. With these changes, panel (a) of Figure 5.9 illustrates the market for the imported good while panel (b) illustrates the market for its domestic substitute. For expositional purposes we assume a small country so that, in panel (a), the supply of imports is perfectly elastic at the world price p_w. Given the initial tariff τ_1, consumers purchase m_1 units of imports at the tariff inclusive domestic price p_m^1. In panel (b), demand for the domestic good is then $d(p_d, p_m^1)$ so that, given the domestic

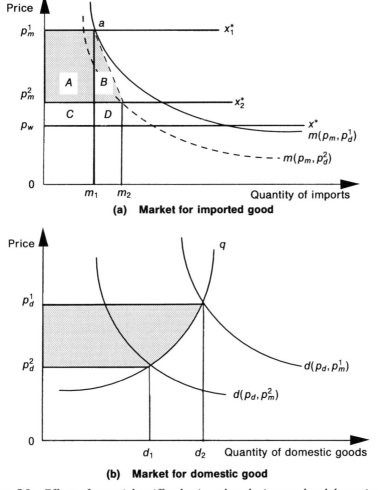

(a) Market for imported good

(b) Market for domestic good

Figure 5.9 *Effects of a partial tariff reduction when the imported and domestic good are imperfect substitutes*

supply q, consumers purchase d_1 units of the domestic good at the initial equilibrium price p_d^1.

As shown in panel (a), reducing the tariff from τ_1 to τ_2 lowers import supply from x_1^* to x_2^* and the domestic price of imports falls from p_m^1 to p_m^2. In panel (b), this decline in the price of imports lowers demand for the domestic good from $d(p_d, p_m^1)$ to $d(p_d, p_m^2)$ and the price of the domestic good therefore falls from p_d^1 to p_d^2. This fall in the price of the domestic good then lowers import demand from $m(p_m, p_d^1)$ to $m(p_m, p_d^2)$ in panel (a). Since import supply is infinitely elastic, the fall in import demand has no subsequent feedback on the market for the domestic substitute. Hence, panels (a) and (b) show the final equilibrium position in each market after the tariff reduction.[36] In the new equilibria, consumers purchase m_2 units of imports at the domestic price p_m^2 (panel (a)) and d_2 units of the domestic good at the price p_d^2 (panel (b)).

Despite a somewhat different graphical representation, the net welfare effect when cross-price effects are allowed differs little from when these effects are ignored. In particular, the benefit to consumers of the tariff reduction is again a change in consumer surplus. However, this change is now the sum of that arising in the two markets:[37]

$$\Delta CS = \int_{p_m^2}^{p_m^1} m(p_m, p_d)\, dp_m + \int_{p_d^2}^{p_d^1} d(p_m, p_d)\, dp_d \tag{5.45}$$

The first integral in (5.45) is the change in consumer surplus arising in the import market while the second integral is the change in consumer surplus arising in the domestic market. The graphical illustration of the change in consumer surplus in the market for imports makes the simplifying assumption that the changes in price and quantity take place along the cord connecting the initial and final equilibria. This hypothetical 'path' of price and quantity changes is indicated by line segment aa in panel (a). The gain in consumer surplus in panel (a) is then (approximately) equal to areas A and B. The gain in consumer surplus in the domestic market is given by the shaded area in panel (b). This area is effectively the amount that consumers of the domestic good would be willing pay to have the price of imports reduced from p_m^1 to p_m^2. Note that the shaded area in panel (b) also equals the loss in the surplus of domestic producers.[38] The changes in consumer and producer surplus in the domestic market therefore cancel when the net change in the economy's welfare is computed.

Since the change in tariff revenue equals area D *minus* area A in panel (a), the net change in welfare when cross-price effects are allowed is computed exactly the same as when they are ignored,[39] namely,

$$\Delta W = \int_{m_1}^{m_2} \{ p_m(m) - p_w \}\, dm \tag{5.46}$$

Writing this welfare change in terms of the underlying tariff change gives:

$$\Delta W = \int_{\tau_2}^{\tau_1} (p_m(m) - p_w) \times \left[\frac{\partial m(p_m, p_d)}{\partial p_m} \frac{dp_m}{d\tau} + \frac{\partial m(p_m, p_d)}{\partial p_d} \frac{dp_d}{dp_m} \frac{dp_m}{d\tau} \right] d\tau$$

(5.47)

which makes explicit that the change in imports derives from a change in the prices of both the imported and domestic good. The trapezoid approximation to (5.46) is the same as (5.29):

$$\Delta W \cong V_1 \frac{(\tau_1 + \tau_2)}{2(1 + \tau_1)} \hat{m}$$

(5.48)

However, in this case the relative change in imports $\hat{m}$ is no longer a price elasticity times the change in import price. Instead, as is clear from (5.47), what is needed is an expression for the change in imports that also takes into account the change in the price of the domestic substitute. A common approach is to specify a system of equations for each market and to then solve these for the comparative static changes in price and quantity in terms of the tariff change. Below we illustrate this approach for the more general case of a large country. The solution for $\hat{m}$ applicable to the small country case illustrated above can then be inferred from the solution to this more general model.

Holding income and the prices of all other goods constant, the following equations will hold for any tariff change:

$$\hat{m} = -\eta_{mm}\hat{p}_m + \eta_{md}\hat{p}_d$$

(5.49)

$$\hat{x} = \varepsilon_m(\hat{p}_m - \hat{\tau})$$

(5.50)

$$\hat{d} = \eta_{dm}\hat{p}_m - \eta_{dd}\hat{p}_d$$

(5.51)

$$\hat{q} = \varepsilon_d\hat{p}_d$$

(5.52)

$$\hat{m} = \hat{x}$$

(5.53)

$$\hat{d} = \hat{q}$$

(5.54)

where $\hat{\tau} = d\tau/(1 + \tau)$, and η_{ij} is the elasticity of demand for good i ($i = m, d$) with respect to a change in the price of good j, and ε_i is the elasticity of supply of good i. Equations (5.49) and (5.50) describe, respectively, the changes in import demand and import supply, (5.51) and (5.52) describe, respectively, the changes in the demand and supply of the domestic substitute, and equations (5.53) and (5.54) are the equilibrium conditions for each market. The assumption of a large country is embodied in (5.50) since the supply of imports varies with the world price (i.e. $\hat{p}_w = (\hat{p}_m - \hat{\tau})$). The above system comprises four independent equations which can be solved for the price and quantity changes in each market. It is easily verified that the solutions are

$$\hat{p}_m = \frac{\varepsilon_m(\eta_{dd} + \varepsilon_d)}{\Omega} \hat{\tau} \tag{5.55}$$

$$\hat{p}_d = \frac{\varepsilon_m \eta_{dm}}{\Omega} \hat{\tau} \tag{5.56}$$

$$\hat{m} = \varepsilon_m \left(\frac{\varepsilon_m(\eta_{dd} + \varepsilon_d)}{\Omega} - 1 \right) \hat{\tau} \tag{5.57}$$

$$\hat{d} = \frac{\eta_{dm} \varepsilon_d \varepsilon_m}{\Omega} \hat{\tau} \tag{5.58}$$

where $\Omega = (\eta_{dd} + \varepsilon_d)(\eta_{mm} + \varepsilon_m) - \eta_{dm}\eta_{md} > 0$. It is also easily verified[40] from (5.57) that the solution for $\hat{m}$ when import supply is perfectly elastic ($\varepsilon_m = \infty$) is:

$$\hat{m} = \left(\frac{\eta_{md}\eta_{dm} - \eta_{mm}}{(\eta_{dd} + \varepsilon_d)} \right) \hat{\tau}$$

where $(\eta_{md}\eta_{dm} - \eta_{mm}) < 0$. Substituting the above expression for $\hat{m}$ in (5.48) gives the welfare change for a small country as:

$$\Delta W \cong V_1 \frac{(\tau_1^2 - \tau_2^2)}{2(1 + \tau_1)^2} \left(\frac{\eta_{mm} - \eta_{md}\eta_{dm}}{\eta_{dd} + \varepsilon_d} \right) \tag{5.59}$$

As (5.59) indicates, an estimate of the welfare change requires values for the cross-price elasticity, the domestic supply elasticity, and the import demand elasticity.[41] For countries such as the United States, estimates of domestic supply elasticities do appear in the literature. More difficult to obtain are values for the cross-price elasticities. In particular, econometric estimation of cross-price elasticities is hampered by collinearity among the price data and, for this reason, analysts often resort to indirect methods to obtain values for these elasticities (see Appendix 2 in this chapter).

Problem 5.7: Derive the expression analogous to (5.59) for the case where the supplies of imports and of the domestic good are infinitely elastic.

Table 5.1 shows the income transfer and efficiency costs associated with removing tariffs on selected US commodities. These estimates assume that the imported and domestically produced good are imperfect substitutes. One feature to note is the size of the income transfers relative to the net welfare effect, the former are typically much larger than the latter.[42] Also of interest is column (2), 'In import market', which lists the fraction of the total change in consumer surplus that arises in the import market. Finally, column (6)

Table 5.1 *Partial equilibrium estimates of welfare changes from removing selected US tariffs,[a] 1988 (Values in US$ million unless noted)*

Product	Consumer surplus (gain) Total (1)	In import market[b] (2)	Tariff revenue (loss) (3)	Producer surplus (loss) (4)	Net welfare[c] (gain) (5)	Cost per job protected[d] (6)
Footwear	290.8	75.2%	−190.1	−72.1	28.5	145.4
Ceramic tiles	96.5	82.7%	−77.6	−16.7	2.3	24.1
Luggage	205.5	71.0%	−139.8	−59.6	6.1	137.0
Leather gloves	33.8	48.2%	−15.0	−17.5	1.3	67.6
Women's handbags	145.5	72.8%	−103.4	−39.6	2.5	132.3
Glassware	238.6	44.5%	−99.0	−132.5	7.2	91.8
Electronic capacitors	94.1	47.6%	−42.3	−49.3	2.5	62.7
Bicycles	42.1	64.4%	−26.4	−15.0	0.8	105.2
Optical instruments	18.6	62.4%	−11.2	−7.0	0.4	46.5
Canned tuna	88.8	30.0%	−21.4	−62.2	5.2	126.9

Notes:
[a] Estimates assume that the elasticity of domestic supply is unity.
[b] Figure is percentage of total consumer surplus change arising in the import market. This is computed by adding the (negative) change in producer surplus to the change in total consumer surplus and then dividing by the total change in consumer surplus.
[c] Sum of reduction in production and consumption efficiency costs.
[d] Total change in consumer surplus divided by change in industry employment estimated to arise from tariff removal, in US$ thousand.
Source: Adapted from United States International Trade Commission (1989).

lists the ratio of the change in consumer surplus to the change in industry employment estimated to result from tariff removal. This ratio is an estimate of the cost to domestic consumers of maintaining employment in the industry via the tariff. For example, the first row shows that US consumers paid the equivalent of $145,400 per year to maintain the average job in the US footwear industry. Since this amount is substantially in excess of the annual wage of a worker in the footwear industry, consumers would be better off if the tariff were removed and consumers simply paid each subsequently unemployed footwear worker his or her wage.

This section has shown that obtaining an estimate of the welfare changes arising from a tariff change is relatively simple. However, a number of practical and theoretical considerations arise when implementing the formulas used to estimate these changes. First, each layer of complexity added to the underlying model increases the number of elasticities whose values need to be known. Unfortunately, estimates of the elasticities needed to implement a full supply and demand model are rarely available. One approach to this problem is to assume that certain elasticities take a range of values and to then present the corresponding range of welfare estimates. Alternatively, one can make assumptions that reduce the number of required elasticity values. A common assumption in this regard is that import supply is infinitely elastic (small country).[43]

Second, when a welfare formula involves only one elasticity value the uncertainty associated with the estimated elasticity can be incorporated by presenting the welfare calculation as an interval estimate. However, when a formula involves several elasticities there is no simple way to summarize the joint uncertainty associated with the elasticity estimates. One way around this problem is to forgo formulas stated in terms of underlying supply and demand elasticities and instead directly estimate the change in imports arising from a tariff change. This alternative approach requires the estimation of an econometric model that links import volumes to prices and tariffs.[44] Having estimated such a model, the import change arising from a tariff change can then be forecast and used to calculate the welfare change (e.g. using (5.48)). Since the standard error of the forecast will incorporate the joint uncertainty of the estimated parameters, a confidence interval can easily be constructed for the estimated welfare change. One caution in using this approach is that tariff rates may be endogenous since protection may have been obtained at the request of industries undergoing significant import competition. Hence, high tariffs may be associated with industries with high imports. If so, this relationship between tariff rates and import volumes would imply a 'simultaneity bias' that would be expected to bias downward estimates of the effects of tariffs (or other trade barriers) on import volumes. Hence, any calculated welfare change would also be biased downward.[45]

Export market effects

The analysis of cross-price effects given above assumed that the domestic good is not traded. However, if this good were also exported[46] then the following welfare effect must be added to the welfare change given in (5.46):

$$\Delta W_x = \int_{\tau_2}^{\tau_1} (q - d) \frac{dp_d}{d\tau} \, d\tau$$

where $(q - d)$ is the volume of exports of the domestic good. This additional welfare effect measures the change in the surplus of foreign consumers which is captured by domestic exporters. This arises because a tariff reduction decreases demand for the domestic good and hence also increases the supply of exports of the domestic good. This shift in export supply implies a fall in the price of the export good and a reduction in producer surplus (gain in foreign consumer surplus) that subtracts from the welfare gain achieved in the import market. Hence, the net change in welfare could be negative.[47]

Multiple tariff changes

Estimation of the total change in welfare arising from a change in several tariff rates can be made by summing the individual partial equilibrium estimate for each good. However, since each estimate ignores the income effect associated with a tariff change the summation of these estimates only compounds the error of omitting income effects. Since the accuracy of the estimated total welfare change is likely to fall as the scope of the tariff changes increases, welfare changes arising from large scale tariff changes (e.g. multilateral tariff reductions) are now estimated using applied general equilibrium (AGE) models. However, when the analysis covers commodities at a detailed level of disaggregation an AGE model may be impractical due to data requirements. In such cases, summation of the individual partial equilibrium estimates may be the only practical method for presenting the 'total' effect of multiple tariff changes.

Non-tariff barriers

We now examine methods for estimating the welfare effects of non-tariff restrictions to trade by considering quantitative restrictions in the form of import and export quotas. Since the price and quantity effects of quotas can, under perfect competition, be duplicated by taxes on trade, the results of the preceding section are directly applicable to estimating the welfare effects of quotas. All that is required in most cases is to estimate the change in the domestic price of the traded good implied by the quantitative restriction and to then plug this change into the appropriate formula. The methods used to estimate the welfare effects of quotas apply equally well to other forms of non-tariff barriers as long as the price (or quantity) effects of the restriction can be determined. However, since quotas and other non-tariff restrictions often create economic rents, a careful assessment of the distribution of these rents is needed when determining the correct formula for calculating welfare changes.

Import quotas

Figure 5.10 illustrates the case of a partial reduction in an import quota. The supply of imports is assumed infinitely elastic at the world price p_w (small country) and we ignore any cross-price effects between the imported and domestic good. Assuming an initial import quota of $\bar{m}_1$ units, import supply is given by x_1^* and the domestic price of imports is therefore p_1. An expansion of the quota to $\bar{m}_2$ units raises import supply to x_2^* and the domestic price falls from p_1 to p_2.

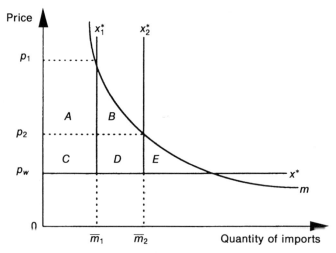

Figure 5.10   *Partial reduction in an import quota – small country*

Areas A and B in Figure 5.10 measure the gain to consumers of the imported good arising from the quota expansion. Since this change in consumer surplus is the same as that arising from a tariff reduction expression (5.23) is applicable. In the present case the trapezoid approximation to this change in consumer surplus is:

$$\Delta CS \cong -\Delta p(\overline{m}_2 + \overline{m}_1)/2$$

where $\Delta p = (p_2 - p_1) < 0$. Since the change in import quantity is known[48] we must now infer the price change Δp. The simplest method is to use the elasticity formula: $\Delta p = -p_1 \hat{m}/\eta_m$. Substituting this into the above expression, the formula for the change in consumer surplus is:

$$\Delta CS \cong \frac{V_1}{2\eta_m} \hat{m}(\hat{m} + 2)$$

Now consider the change in quota rents (ΔQR) which equals area D *minus* area A in Figure 5.10. Since these rents are assumed to accrue to domestic agents the change in quota rents is equivalent to a change in tariff revenue which implies that the expression for the net welfare change is given by (5.27). To calculate (5.27) we can either make the required substitutions for the price changes implicit in (5.28) or replace the tariff rates in (5.30) with their *ad valorem* equivalents (AVE). The latter are defined as $\tau_1^* = (p_1/p_w - 1)$ and $\tau_2^* = (p_2/p_w - 1)$.[49] Since $p_1 = V_1/\overline{m}_1$ and $p_w = V_w/\overline{m}_1$ are observable, where V_w is the value of imports at world prices, only an estimate of p_2, and hence τ_2^*, is required.[50] By definition, $p_2 = (1 - \eta_m/\hat{m})p_1$.

Hence, using the preceding definitions of p_1 and p_w, the value of p_2/p_w can be estimated as

$$p_2/p_w = (1 - \eta_m/\hat{m}) \frac{V_1}{V_w}$$

Given this, the AVE tariff rates corresponding to quota levels $\bar{m}_1$ and $\bar{m}_2$ are computed as, respectively,

$$\tau_1^* = \frac{V_1}{V_w} - 1 \tag{5.60}$$

and

$$\tau_2^* = \frac{(1 - \eta_m/\hat{m})V_1 - V_w}{V_w} \tag{5.61}$$

The above discussion implies that calculation of welfare effects in the case of a large country and when the imported and domestic good are imperfect substitutes only requires an estimate of the AVE tariff rates applicable to each case. These rates can then be inserted into the appropriate formula derived for a tariff change. Since the initial AVE tariff rate is always that given by (5.60), only an expression for $\tau_2^* = (p_2/p_w - 1)$ is needed. If the country is large and goods are perfect substitutes it is easily verified that an estimate of the AVE tariff rate is:[51]

$$\tau_2^* = (p_2/p_w^2 - 1) = \frac{\varepsilon_m V_1(\eta_m - \hat{m})}{\eta_m V_w(\varepsilon_m + \hat{m})}$$

If the country is large and goods are imperfect substitutes then the supply equation in (5.50) can be replaced with $\hat{x}^* = (\bar{m}_2 - \bar{m}_1)/\bar{m}_1$ and the resulting system of equations solved for the relative price changes. The estimated AVE tariff rate in this case is:

$$\tau_2^* = (p_2/p_w^2 - 1) = \frac{\varepsilon_m V_1(\Omega - \hat{m})}{\Omega V_w(\varepsilon_m + \hat{m})} - 1$$

where $\Omega = \eta_{mm}(\varepsilon_d + \eta_{dd}) - \eta_{dm}\eta_{md}$. Hence, if quota rents accrue to domestic agents and the import quota is binding at $\bar{m}_2$ units then the calculation of welfare effects requires only minor modification to the formulas derived for a tariff change.

Export quotas

The methods for calculating the welfare effects of an export quota are the same as those of an import quota. In particular, AVE tariff rates can be calculated and inserted into the appropriate welfare formula. One practical difficulty is that computation of the AVE tariff rates requires data on producer prices in the exporting country which are often difficult to obtain.

In addition, the accuracy of the AVE tariff rates is likely to be less than in the case of an import quota since differences between domestic and world prices may arise for any number of reasons, including costs of transport within a country.[52]

Our analysis of an export quota considers a partial reduction in a VER. In this case, interest normally focuses on the welfare changes in the importing country rather than the exporting country. Figure 5.11 illustrates this case for a large country. With an initial quota of $\bar{x}_1$ units, the world price is p_w^1 and exporters receive rent of $p_w^1 - p_1$ on each unit exported. Expansion of the quota from $\bar{x}_1$ to $\bar{x}_2$ reduces the world price from p_w^1 to p_w^2 and raises the producer price from p_1 to p_2. Per-unit rent therefore falls to $p_w^2 - p_2$.

The benefit of the quota expansion to the importing country is the gain in consumer surplus given by areas A and B in Figure 5.11. The exporting country loses quota rents equal to areas A and E but gains rent equal to area D. In addition, exporter surplus rises by areas E and F. The net change in foreign welfare is therefore areas F and D *minus* area A. We leave to the reader the task of writing down the expressions for these welfare changes in terms of AVE tariff rates and underlying supply and demand elasticities.

Table 5.2 lists estimated welfare gains and losses from removing VERs on selected products imported into the United States. Since foreigners receive the quota rents generated by these VERs, the net welfare gain to the United States from removing these restrictions is substantially larger than in the case of tariffs.

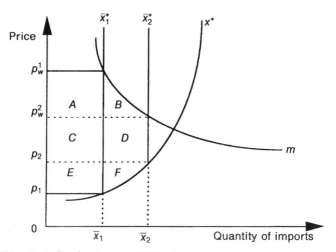

Figure 5.11   *Partial reduction in a VER – large country*

Table 5.2 *Partial equilibrium estimates of welfare changes arising from removal of VERs on selected products imported by the United States (all values in US$ million unless noted)*

	Change in				
Product	Consumer surplus	Tariff revenue[a]	Foreign quota rents	Domestic producer surplus	Net welfare[b]
Carbon and specialty steel	895.5	−486.0	−22.6	−343.0	66.6
Machine tools	56.0	−29.0	−5.5	−19.1	7.9

Notes:
[a] Estimates also include the effects of removing pre-quota tariffs. Estimates are for 1988 and assume that the elasticity of domestic supply is 1.38.
[b] Sum of reduction in production and consumption deadweight losses *plus* repatriation of quota rents earned by foreign entities.
Source: Adapted from United States International Trade Commission (1989).

Quota removal

The methods discussed above have assumed a partial expansion of a quota rather than complete removal. A partial change in a quota simplifies estimation of the price change (or the AVE tariff rate) arising from the quota expansion since the amount traded after the expansion is simply the new level set by the quota. However, if the quota were instead eliminated, or the new quota level could not be assumed to be binding, then the new volume of trade, and hence the change in trade, must be estimated. Estimation of the hypothetical quantity change is often done using an econometric model of the market being examined.[53] The estimated quantity change is then used to calculate the hypothetical price change or AVE tariff rate which is then used to calculate welfare changes using the formulas developed in this section.

Price changes and unit values

Estimates of the welfare effects arising from a quota require data on the domestic and world price of the restricted good. However, these price data are rarely available. Instead, prices are calculated by dividing the export or import value of a good by its quantity. This would be valid if the good were homogeneous. However, in practice the 'good' is often an aggregate category (e.g. footwear) consisting of several varieties. Since price varies across varieties, dividing the value of the aggregate by its quantity gives an average price. This average price is called a unit value. Since it is a weighted average, the value of a unit value depends on both the prices of the individual items and the composition of items within the aggregate category. Hence, the actual change in a unit value will reflect changes in both these components. But when changes in unit values are used to estimate price changes, and hence AVE tariff rates, the composition of items is implicitly held fixed. The failure to account for changes in the composition of items leads to an underestimate of the actual price change that will result when a quota (or tariff) is changed. For example, tightening a quota raises the prices of all items covered by the quota but the proportionate increase in the prices of low price items will exceed the proportionate increase in the prices of high price items. Consumers respond to these relative price changes by increasing their demand for high price relative to low price items. Similarly, expanding a quota lowers the prices of all items but the proportionate fall in the prices of low price items will exceed the proportionate fall in the prices of high price items. Consumers respond by increasing their demand for low price relative to high price items. Since the estimated price change does not account of these changes in consumer spending it understates the size of the actual price change. Hence, calculated welfare gains and losses will also be understated.[54]

General equilibrium methods[55]

This section considers the measurement of the net welfare change arising from a change in trade polices in a general equilibrium framework. This analysis extends the welfare decomposition analysis presented on pp. 165–6 to the case of many goods and when imported and domestically produced goods are imperfect substitutes.

Assume there are N goods, each good is produced domestically and also imported.[56] Denote the vector of world prices of imported goods as $\mathbf{p}_w = (p_{w1}, \ldots, p_{wN})$ and the vectors of domestic prices of domestic and imported goods as $\mathbf{p}_d = (p_{d1}, \ldots, p_{dN})$ and $\mathbf{p}_m = (p_{m1}, \ldots, p_{mN})$, respectively. The utility level (u_0) a country achieves under its current set of trade policy instruments (e.g. tariff or quotas) can be found by equating its expenditure (S) to its current income from all sources:

$$S(\mathbf{p}_d, \mathbf{p}_m, \mathbf{p}_w, u_0) = G(\mathbf{p}_d) + \sum_{i=1}^{N} (p_{mi} - p_{wi})m_i \qquad (5.62)$$

Expression (5.62) is the N-good analogue of (5.3). The right-hand side of (5.62) states that income derives from two sources: production, as given by the economy's GDP function $G(\mathbf{p}_d)$, and tariff revenue or quota rents, as reflected by the difference between the domestic and world prices of imports.[57] By definition of the expenditure function, this income level (just) allows the economy to achieve utility level u_0.

We now desire a measure of the welfare change a country would experience if it adopted a different set of trade policies. In this regard, a widely used measure of welfare change is the equivalent variation (EV).[58] In the present context, the EV measures the amount of income that consumers would need to receive (give up), at the prices existing under the initial trade polices, to obtain the utility level that will arise under the new set of trade policies. The expression for this amount of income is:

$$EV = S(\mathbf{p}_d, \mathbf{p}_m, \mathbf{p}_w, u_1) - S(\mathbf{p}_d, \mathbf{p}_m, \mathbf{p}_w, u_0) \tag{5.63}$$

where u_1 denotes the utility level that would obtain under the new set of trade policies. If the income change (5.63) is positive (negative) then the new set of trade policies would represent a welfare gain (loss) compared to the existing trade policies. If the form of the expenditure function (S) is known, (5.63) can be used to calculate the welfare change due to any change in trade policies. Computable general equilibrium models perform exactly this calculation since they normally assume an explicit form of the utility function and can therefore derive the associated expenditure function.

If the form of the expenditure function is unknown then one can calculate a local approximation to the welfare change given in (5.63). To see how, substitute (5.62) into (5.63) to get:[59]

$$EV = \left(G(\mathbf{p}_d) + \sum_{i=1}^{N} (p_{mi} - p_{wi})m_i \right) - S(\mathbf{p}_d, \mathbf{p}_m, \mathbf{p}_w u_0) = 0 \tag{5.64}$$

Holding utility constant at the level u_0, total differentiation of (5.64) gives

$$dEV = \sum_{i=1}^{N} \left[\frac{\partial G}{\partial p_{di}} dp_{di} + (dp_{mi} - dp_{wi})m_i + (p_{mi} - p_{wi})dm_i \right.$$
$$\left. - \left(\frac{\partial S}{\partial p_{di}} dp_{di} + \frac{\partial S}{\partial p_{mi}} dp_{mi} \right) \right] \tag{5.65}$$

By the properties of the income and expenditure functions we have $\partial G/\partial p_{di} = q_i$, $\partial S/\partial p_{di} = d_i$ and $\partial S/\partial p_{mi} = m_i$, where q_i and d_i are the production and consumption of domestic good i. Substituting these expressions in (5.65) gives:

$$dEV = \sum_i [((q_i - d_i) dp_{di} - m_i dp_{wi}) + (p_{mi} - p_{wi}) dm_i] \tag{5.66}$$

This expression is the N-good analogue of (5.5) and holds for a small change in trade policies. As in (5.5), the net change in welfare derives from two sources. First is the change in the terms of trade which now encompasses both exports ($q_i - d_i$) and imports. Second is the price distortion or trade volume effect which measures the change in tariff revenue or quota rents as the volume of imports changes. The value of (5.66) can be computed if the price and quantity changes are known. However, the price and quantity changes in (5.66) are general equilibrium changes which take into account all interactions between markets. The computation of these changes therefore requires a fully specified general equilibrium model. In the absence of such a model, the price and quantity changes in (5.66), and hence the net welfare change, can be approximated using partial equilibrium changes.

Applied general equilibrium modeling

In the early 1970s analysts began to develop and use applied general equilibrium (AGE) models to evaluate the welfare and resource allocation effects of trade and domestic tax policies. AGE models are also called computable general equilibrium (CGE) models. These models are 'computable' because they posit explicit forms for demand and supply functions[60] which make it possible to numerically solve for the equilibrium values of prices and quantities once the model is fitted to a set of data. AGE models capture the interactions that take place between markets and provide the policy maker with considerable detail on production and consumption effects, as well as the welfare changes, arising from trade policy changes.

The focus of all AGE models is the computation of changes in the equilibrium values of a model's endogenous variables arising from changes in exogenously given policy variables (e.g. tariffs). These changes in endogenous variables are obtained using one of two methods. The first derives the global changes in the model's endogenous variables while the second method derives the local, comparative static, changes. The calculation of welfare effects arising from policy changes is then made using the expenditure function implied by the assumed form of the utility function or by summing the welfare change in each market as in (5.66).

Implementing an AGE model can involve considerable time and effort in terms of data collection and model specification. Since the details of each model vary with the interests of the modeler and the set of policy questions to be examined, no one account of an 'AGE model' is possible. Therefore, in this section we provide an outline of the main elements of AGE modeling and leave the specific details of the many alternative models to the references listed at the end of this chapter.

Theoretical foundation
The theoretical foundation for all AGE models is the competitive general equilibrium model. Hence, it is appropriate to begin our discussion of AGE modeling with a review of this model in the case of many goods and many factors.[61] Most AGE models introduce modifications to the assumptions of

this standard model. In particular, unlike here, goods are assumed to be imperfectly substitutable and the production sector uses intermediate goods as well as primary factor inputs. To these extensions are often added assumptions concerning factor mobility, unemployment, imperfectly competitive pricing or economies of scale. However, regardless of the assumptions, each model ultimately reduces to a system of demand and supply equations and a set of income–expenditure identities.[62]

Consider first the supply side relationships which will determine factor prices and therefore national income. Assume an economy in which there are J competitive industries. Each industry is assumed to employ H factor inputs to produce an amount q_j of a single homogeneous good using the production function $q_j = F_j(e_j)$, where $e_j = (e_{j1}, \ldots, e_{jH})$ is the vector of factor inputs employed in industry j. The production function for industry j is assumed to be linear homogeneous and it can therefore also be expressed as

$$1 = F_j(a_{j1}, \ldots, a_{jH}) \tag{5.67}$$

where $a_{jh} = e_{jh}/q_j$ is the demand for factor h per unit of output j. Since factors of production are assumed homogeneous and perfectly mobile between industries, equilibrium requires that a factor's value marginal product equal its market price. Denote the vector of factor prices as $\mathbf{w} = (w_1, \ldots, w_H)$ and the vector of commodity prices as $\mathbf{p} = (p_1, \ldots, p_J)$. Then the conditions for equilibrium are:

$$p_j(\partial F_j/\partial e_h) \leq w_h \qquad j = 1, \ldots, J; \quad h = 1, \ldots, H \tag{5.68}$$

These equations hold with equality of every factor actually used in production.

Let $\mathbf{e} = (e_1, \ldots, e_H)$ denote the vector of total factor supplies within the country. The supply of each factor is assumed to be perfectly inelastic so that $\mathbf{e}$ can be regarded as a vector of constants. The requirement that all factors be fully employed is then:

$$e_h = \sum_j e_{jh} = a_{1h}q_1 + \cdots + a_{Jh}q_J \qquad h = 1, \ldots, H \tag{5.69}$$

The set of equations in (5.67) to (5.69) are sufficient to determine the supply side of the model. Together, there are $J + JH + H$ independent equations to determine JH optimal unit factor requirements, H factor prices and J output supplies. It is therefore possible to solve for an equilibrium in terms of the given values of the factor supplies and commodity prices.

Now consider demand. As long as factor supplies are fixed, relative commodity prices contain all the information needed to specify the demand functions:

$$d_j = d_j(p_1, \ldots, p_j, \ldots, p_J) \qquad j = 1, \ldots, J \tag{5.70}$$

These functions are homogeneous of degree zero in prices. We now consider the market clearing and income–expenditure identities that must hold in general equilibrium.

First, in the absence of trade, domestic supply must equal domestic demand for each good:

$$q_j = d_j \quad j = 1, \ldots, J \tag{5.71}$$

These market clearing identities are not independent by virtue of the income–expenditure identity:

$$\sum_{j=1}^{J} p_j q_j \equiv \sum_{h=1}^{H} w_h e_h = \sum_{j=1}^{J} p_j d_j \tag{5.72}$$

Thus, we can drop any one equation in (5.71). Counting the number of equations we find $J + JH + H + J - 1$ independent relations to determine the J outputs, JH factor demands, H factor prices and J commodity prices. Hence, the number of endogenous variables exceeds by one the number of independent relations. To resolve this, prices are expressed in terms of any one good (i.e. the numeraire) whose price is then set equal to unity. Given this, the autarky equilibrium is then determinate – that is, the model can be solved for the outputs, factor demands, factor prices and $J - 1$ relative prices in terms of the given factor supplies.

Now assume there are N separate trading countries where each is described by the above technology and tastes. A superscript is used to denote each country $n = 1, \ldots, N$. With trade it is no longer true that production and consumption of each good are equal within a country. Instead, production must equal consumption for the world as a whole:

$$\sum_{n=1}^{N} d_j^n = \sum_{n=1}^{N} q_j^n \quad j = 1, \ldots, J \tag{5.73}$$

Assuming balanced trade in each country implies that the total value of production equals the total value of consumption for each country, that is,

$$0 = p_1^n (q_1^n - d_1^n) + \cdots + p_j^n (q_j^n - d_j^n) + \cdots$$
$$+ p_J^n (q_J^n - d_J^n) \quad n = 1, \ldots, N \tag{5.74}$$

Summing (5.74) over countries, and noting that free trade equates commodity prices across countries, we obtain:

$$0 = p_1 \sum_{n=1}^{N} (q_1^n - d_1^n) + \cdots + p_j \sum_{n=1}^{N} (q_j^n - d_j^n) + \cdots$$
$$+ p_J \sum_{n=1}^{N} (q_J^n - d_J^n) \tag{5.75}$$

This is Walras' Law with J markets: when $J - 1$ markets are in equilibrium then by necessity the remaining market is also in equilibrium. Hence, it is sufficient to solve $(J - 1)$ of the equations in (5.73) for the $(J - 1)$ world relative prices.

Given the world prices, the J equations in (5.67), the JH equations in (5.68), the H equations in (5.69) and the J equations in (5.70) in each of the N countries solve for the $(JH + 2J + H)$ country unknowns, namely, the a_{ij}, q_j, d_j and w_h. The equilibrium is therefore determined for a given distribution of world factor endowments among countries.

Implementation

Implementing an AGE model typically involves five steps:

(1) Model selection
(2) Specification;
(3) Data collection;
(4) Calibration and verification;
(5) Counterfactual policy simulations.

The following summarizes each of these steps.

Model selection

The selection of an AGE model refers to the question of whether the model is to be country specific or multilateral. The answer to this question depends on the intent of the analysis and data availability. The majority of AGE models are single country models since the narrower focus permits greater detail regarding industry structure and consumer behavior. In addition, the analyst can often incorporate specific institutional detail such as wage rigidities or specific domestic policies. In addition, limiting the analysis to a single country avoids problems of data availability and comparability.

Multicountry models incorporate interactions between countries as reflected in the world markets for their goods. Such models can in turn be either global or regional. Regional models typically specify sector detail for a subset of countries while treating the remaining countries as a 'rest of world' residual. An example of a regional model is that developed to examine the effects of forming the free trade area between Canada, the United States and Mexico (i.e. NAFTA; see Chapter 12). Global models allow for interactions among all countries but typically sacrifice industry detail due to data limitations.

To give orders of magnitude, a typical single country model might specify supplies and demands for some 80 sectors while a regional model might reduce this to 30 or 40 sectors. A global model might contain only 10 to 15 sectors. The principal limitations when constructing regional and global models are obtaining detailed and comparable input–output tables for the different countries and in reconciling the different national systems of data classification.

Specification
Specification of an AGE model involves choosing both the underlying behavioral structure of the model and explicit functional forms for the supply and demand equations. The question of behavioral structure concerns the choice of, for example, whether markets will be assumed perfectly competitive or which, if any, factors will be mobile between countries. As for the choice of functional forms, AGE models typically use Cobb–Douglas and CES (Constant Elasticity of Substitution) functions to represent underlying utility and production functions and from these derive the implied form of the supply and demand functions. Table 5.3 lists functional forms commonly used in AGE models. Which functional form is chosen depends

Table 5.3   *Common functional forms used in AGE models*

	Cobb–Douglas	Constant elasticity of substitution (CES)	Linear expenditure system (Cobb–Douglas variety)
Utility or production function	$\prod_i x_i^{\alpha_i}$	$\left(\sum_i \alpha_i^{1/\sigma} x_i^{(\sigma-1)/\sigma} \right)^{\sigma/(\sigma-1)}$	$\prod_i (x_i - c_i)^{\alpha_i}$
Demand equation	$x_i = \alpha_i Z / p_i$	$x_i = \alpha_i Z \left/ \left(p_i^{\sigma} \sum_{j \neq i} \alpha_j p_j^{(1-\sigma)} \right) \right.$	$x_i = c_i + \left(\dfrac{\alpha_i}{p_i} \right) \left(I - \sum_j p_j c_j \right)$
Expenditure or cost function	$\prod_i (p_i/\alpha_i)^{\alpha_i}$	$\left(\sum_i \alpha_i p_i^{(1-\sigma)} \right)^{(1-\sigma)}$	$\prod_i (p_i/\alpha_i)^{\alpha_i}$
Side conditions	$\sum_i \alpha_i = 1$	$\sum_i \alpha_i^{1/\sigma} = 1$	$\sum_i \alpha_i = 1$

Notes:
x_i is the quantity of good or factor i; p_i is the price of x_i; σ is the elasticity of substitution between any pair x_i and x_j, Z is either income (commodity equation) or output (input demand); α_i is an expenditure (or cost) share depending on the definition of x_i. In the LES specification, c_i is the minimum demand requirement of good i.

on the interests of the modeler and the availability of data on the elasticity parameters that characterize these functions. Since elasticity values are crucial to AGE models (they cannot be solved without them) modelers maintain inventories of elasticity estimates culled from the literature or estimate elasticities as needed.

AGE models commonly assume that the pattern of demand is determined by a multistage budgeting process. In the first stage expenditure is allocated among goods. Preferences at this stage are modelled either as Cobb–Douglas or as a Linear Expenditure System (see Table 5.3). In the second stage, expenditure on each good is then allocated between imports and a domestically produced variety. The specification of second stage preferences varies across models although most adopt some form of the Armington (1969) specification that goods are differentiated by their country of production (see below). Some models forgo the assumption of a constant elasticity of substitution and instead utilize a 'flexible' functional form which permits the elasticity of substitution to vary over pairs of goods. Finally, some models forgo the assumption of product differentiation entirely and instead assume that imports and domestic goods are perfect substitutes. These different assumptions are not without importance. In particular, output responses will be larger when perfect substitutes are assumed.

Armington assumption

Most AGE models adopt the Armington (1969) assumption of national product differentiation when modeling the demand for goods. Under this assumption imports are differentiated by country of origin and thus, symmetrically, each country is the sole producer of its export good. Consumers within a country then use a two-stage budgeting procedure to determine their demand for imports. In the first stage, they choose the total amount to be spent on imports without regard to country of origin. In the second stage they determine the allocation of their aggregate spending on imports across supplier countries. This process leads to conditional import demand functions[63] which are implemented by modeling them as CES functions of domestic and imported varieties of goods.

A central attraction of the Armington specification is that it serves to model, without explaining, the observed phenomena of intra-industry trade. It thus allows goods to be modeled as imperfect substitutes (and hence, differentiated). While convenient, the Armington specification is restrictive since it assumes that while all varieties of a domestically produced good are perfect substitutes, these varieties are imperfect substitutes for the varieties produced in other countries.[64] In addition, the specification implies that a country, no matter how small, enjoys market power with respect to its export good. Another troubling aspect of the Armington specification are the implied cross-price effects that arise between imported goods and their domestically produced, and exported, substitutes. These cross-price effects imply export market price changes whose effect on welfare is opposite from that arising in the domestic markets for imported goods. Sufficiently strong cross-price effects can therefore result in net welfare changes opposite those expected when import restrictions are reduced. In fact, these cross-price induced welfare changes have generally been found to dominate the import market efficiency gains associated with import liberalization with the result that the calculated net welfare change from tariff reductions is often found to be negative.[65]

The Armington specification is one example of a specification that gives rise to the nesting of functions that is common in AGE models. Figure 5.12 gives a schematic of the type of nesting that might be used to model the output of a given sector. In Figure 5.12, gross output of the sector is modelled as a Leontief function of both value added and an intermediate input. This function would be represented as $q_j = \min(V_j/a_{V_j}, H_j/a_{H_j})$ where V_j is sector j's value added, H_j is the composite intermediate input, and a_{V_j} and a_{H_j} are the unit input requirements of, respectively, value added and the composite intermediate. The value added (net output) function is then modelled as a CES function of capital (K_j) and labor input (L_j) which can be written as $V_j = \gamma_j(\alpha_{jL}L_j^{(\sigma_j-1)/\sigma_j} + \alpha_{jK}K_j^{(\sigma_j-1)/\sigma_j})^{\sigma_j/(\sigma_j-1)}$. In this function, γ_j is a scale parameter whose value is determined during the calibration stage (see below). The composite intermediate H_j is then modelled as a Leontief function of M composite intermediates (i.e. $H_j = \min(Z_{ji}/a_{ji}; i = 1,\ldots,M)$).

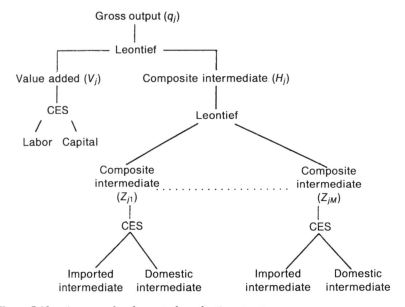

Figure 5.12   *An example of a nested production structure*

Each of these M composite intermediates is itself a CES function of a domestically produced and imported variety. If the imported intermediate were further disaggregated by country of export then the CES composite function would be an implementation of the Armington assumption. The structure shown in Figure 5.12 allows substitution between domestic and imported varieties of each primary intermediate, but no substitution occurs between the composites of these intermediates nor between the intermediate and value added.

Data

The data used to implement an AGE model are the flows of income and expenditure between agents within an economy and with the rest of the world. Modelers often represent these flows in the form of a Social Accounting Matrix (SAM). The rows and columns of the SAM denote groupings of economic agents while the entries in the matrix are the expenditure–income flows among agents.

Table 5.4 shows a simplified SAM for an economy consisting of five agents or institutional groupings: suppliers, households, government, rest of world and a capital account reflecting savings and investment. The entries in each column record the transaction flow from group j to group i while the entries in a given row record the income received by group i from group j. The sum of the elements in column j is the total expenditures by group j while the sum of the elements in row i is the total income received by group i. If the income–expenditure identities are to be satisfied then the sum of the elements in row i equals the sum of the elements in column i.

Table 5.4 *A simplified social accounting matrix (SAM)*

Receipts by	Suppliers *(1)*	Households *(2)*	Government *(3)*	Rest of world *(4)*	Capital account *(5)*	Total
			Expenditures by			
(1) Suppliers		Purchases	Purchases	Exports	Investment	**Aggregate Demand**
(2) Households	Income					**Income**
(3) Government			Taxes			**Taxes**
(4) Rest of world	Imports					**Imports**
(5) Capital Account		Savings	Savings	Savings		**Aggregate Savings**
Total	**Aggregate supply**	**Expenditure**	**Expenditure**	**Foreign exchange**	**Investment**	

The primary purpose of constructing a SAM is to check the consistency of the data and thus ensure that the accounting identities are satisfied. This consistency check is crucial since the data are often collected from several different sources. In addition, one usually needs to reconcile differences in the units in which income and expenditure are measured (e.g. the value of sales measured at producer prices versus household expenditure measured at market prices). A SAM is also the format which many computer programmes[66] developed to solve AGE models expect the data to be provided.

The level of disaggregation within a SAM will reflect the degree of detail desired by the modeler. Generally, the supplier group is divided into 'activities' and 'commodities'. Activities are the basic production units of the economy in that they purchase intermediate inputs and hire factor services to produce commodities. The 'commodities' combine domestic supply with imports and distribute these goods for intermediate use and final demand. The activities and commodities can then be further disaggregated into individual product categories to provide sector detail. Additional disaggregation of agents would identify 'factors' (which receive value added) and 'enterprises' (which receive profits).

Calibration

Calibration involves 'fitting' an AGE model to a given set of data. There are two aspects to calibration. First is the selection of elasticity values and the use of observed data to compute values of function parameters such as factor shares, consumption expenditure shares, etc., all of which are parameters that appear in the demand and supply equations. Second is calculating the value of parameters that represent the units of measurement of the variables. This latter step is required only if a global solution to the model is sought. If the effects of policy changes are instead calculated using local, comparative static, approximations then the process of calibration ends with the selection of elasticity values and the computation of the various function parameters.

Computing a global solution requires that the model first be adjusted to account for differences in the units of measurement of the variables. This adjustment involves estimating the value of scale parameters, one of each equation, so that the model fits the observed data in levels. This process can be envisioned by thinking of a single linear equation $y = a + bx$ in which the value of coefficient b is known. Given data on y and x, calibration to the level of y then amounts to finding the value of parameter a (i.e. $a = y - bx$).

In practice, the scale parameters are estimated by arbitrarily setting all prices in the model to unity. Since prices and the values of all other endogenous variables are then known, the equations can be solved to determine the unknown scale parameters. The solution value of each scale parameter is then appended to its corresponding equation as a known parameter and the full model is then solved, this time for the vector of equilibrium prices. By construction, the solution values of the prices should be unity. However, computational accuracy often results in prices slightly different from unity (e.g. 0.999998). These solution values for the prices and the model's other endogenous variables then become the *benchmark* or initial solution data set against which all subsequent counterfactual solutions are compared.

The process of solving for the equilibrium prices and the benchmark data set is referred to as model verification. Once the model is solved, not only does it fit the adjusted data (and vice versa), but if the prices are found to differ greatly from unity then the modeler knows that either incorrect values of the scale parameter have been entered or there is some other data inconsistency. Hence, model verification serves to check for data entry errors in either parameter values or equations as well as generating the benchmark equilibrium data set.

Counterfactuals
Two methods are used to obtain the effects of counterfactual changes in policy variables: the global solution method and the Johansen method.[67] The global solution method involves resolving the model for each alternative value of the policy variable(s) and then comparing each new set of equilibrium values to those of the benchmark equilibrium.

The Johansen method uses the comparative static derivatives implied by the model to determine the effect of changes in exogenous policy variables rather than solving for the levels of the variables each time a new policy experiment is considered. The main difference between the global solution and Johansen methods is that the effects of policy changes computed using the latter are local approximations to the global changes obtained using the global solution method. The comparative static derivatives are found by first totally differentiating the (usually log-linear) system of supply and demand equations and then expressing these derivatives as relative changes.[68] The result of this differentiation is a system of linear equations which, by construction, has as many unknowns (the relative changes in the endogenous variables) as equations. Since the equation system is linear, solutions for the unknown comparative static derivatives can be found by matrix inversion. Once the solution matrix of comparative static changes is found, post-multiplying this matrix by a vector of relative changes in the policy variables then gives the corresponding changes in the endogenous variables of the model. The Johansen method is often used to compute the effects of policy changes[69] despite the fact that algorithms for computing a global solution are now widely available and relatively simple to implement.

To indicate the type of results obtained from an AGE model, Tables 5.5 and 5.6 show the results of a global solution simulation of the Uruguay Round of GATT negotiations. The model used to generate these simulations

Table 5.5 *Estimates of % changes in real and relative wages due to trade barrier reductions under Uruguay Round agreements (% change relative to 1992 base values)*

Country/region	Real wage (%)		Wage–rental ratio (%)	
	CRS/PC[a]	IRS/IP	CRS/PC	IRS/IP
Australia/New Zealand	0.71	0.04	−0.12	−0.35
Japan	0.13	0.13	−0.01	−0.19
Canada	0.67	0.61	−0.04	0.03
USA	0.30	0.32	−0.04	−0.17
EU	0.29	0.33	−0.00	−0.01
EFTA	0.33	0.29	0.05	0.12
Africa	0.41	0.71	0.21	0.36
China	1.89	1.69	0.46	1.67
East Asia	1.93	1.49	0.39	1.35
South Asia	2.13	2.84	0.59	4.15
Latin America	0.65	0.63	−0.12	−0.20
Transition economies	0.17	0.25	−0.03	−0.05
Rest of world[b]	3.10	3.39	0.13	0.27

Notes:
[a] CRS = constant returns to scale, PC = perfect competition; IP = imperfect competition.
[b] Mostly Turkey and South Africa.
Source: Adapted from Francois *et al.* (1995), tables 15 and 16.

contained 19 sectors and 13 country/regions. The model also used 2 alternative specifications for production and market conduct: constant returns to scale and perfect competition (CRS/PC) and increasing returns to scale and imperfect (monopolistic) competition (IRS/IP).

Table 5.5 shows the changes in the real wage and relative price of labor that the model projects to occur if the trade liberalizations agreed to in the Uruguay Round are fully implemented. Table 5.6 shows the projected welfare changes for each country/region as a percentage of its GDP in 1992 (the benchmark equilibrium year). For each country/region, the welfare change is broken down into four product groups which indicate the sources of the income change. The measure of welfare change is the equivalent variation (see (5.63)). Hence, the welfare changes measure the increase in national income that would be necessary at base year (1992) prices to achieve the welfare gain (or loss) that would arise from the Uruguay Round liberalizations.

Table 5.6 *Estimates of welfare changes[a] due to trade barrier reductions under Uruguay Round agreements (% 1992 GDP)*

Country/region	Total[b]		Industrial products		Agricultural products		Non-agricultural primary products	
	CRS/PC	IRS/IP	CRS/PC	IRS/IP	CRS/PC	IRS/IP	CRS/PC	IRS/IP
Australia & New Zealand	0.09	0.03	−0.11	−0.17	0.18	0.18	0.02	0.01
Japan	0.04	0.16	0.05	0.17	0.01	−0.01	−0.00	−0.00
Canada	0.13	0.12	−0.01	0.03	0.13	0.07	0.01	0.02
USA	0.17	0.28	0.16	0.29	0.00	−0.01	0.00	0.00
EU	0.22	0.26	0.14	0.25	0.07	0.01	0.01	0.01
EFTA	0.03	0.04	0.10	0.03	−0.07	0.00	−0.00	−0.00
Africa	0.24	0.81	0.23	0.51	−0.05	0.16	0.07	0.13
China	0.84	2.79	0.79	2.69	0.03	0.06	0.01	0.03
East Asia	0.35	2.00	0.38	1.95	0.00	0.04	−0.01	0.00
South Asia	0.37	2.77	0.43	2.89	−0.07	−0.06	−0.00	−0.06
Latin America	0.01	0.33	0.01	0.25	0.02	0.09	0.00	−0.00
Transition economies	−0.04	0.21	0.05	0.17	−0.09	0.03	0.01	0.01
Rest of world[c]	0.98	2.28	0.51	2.40	0.20	0.03	−0.10	−0.14
Total	0.17	0.44	0.07	0.42	0.02	0.02	0.00	0.01

Notes:
[a] Equivalent variation measured as a % of 1992 base GDP.
[b] CRS = constant returns to scale, PC = perfect competition; IP = imperfect competition.
[c] Mostly Turkey and South Africa.
Source: Adapted from Francois *et al.* (1995), tables 17 and 19.

The results in Table 5.5 indicate that the agreed liberalizations are projected to raise the real wage in all countries/regions while the wage–rental ratio generally falls in the industrial countries. These across-the-board real wage increases can occur because the model assumes that labor also derives income from the ownership of capital. The real wage gains appear to be largest in the Asia regions. Increasing returns to scale and imperfect competition tend to give more or less the same real wage changes while changes in the wage–rental ratio are larger under the IRS/IP specification that under the CRS/PC specification.

As shown in Table 5.6, welfare gains arise mostly from the liberalization of Industrial Products and Other Primary Products and so indicate the importance of the agreed liberalization of tariffs and NTBs in these sectors.

With the exception of Latin America, the gains from liberalization tend to favor developing regions. The relatively large gains for China and the Asian regions reflect the projected liberalization of trade in textiles and apparel.

Caveats

AGE models make it possible to calculate sectoral output and employment consequences of alternative trade policies as well as net welfare effects. While many praise the efforts of AGE modelers to quantify the detailed workings of a trading world, AGE modeling has its critics. One substantive criticism is that the values calculated from such models have no statistical foundation since the estimates derived have no associated standard error. Hence, there is no way to assess the reliability of the estimates. In principle, the remedy would be to estimate the parameters of the model's equations using times series observations on all relevant variables. However, the data to do this are simply not available at the level of detail required.

A second criticism is that AGE models lack transparency, that is, the detailed interrelationships and nesting of functions make it extremely difficult to determine what drives the results of any particular model. In response, AGE modelers often conduct sensitivity analyses by varying the values of one or more elasticity parameters and reporting the difference this makes for key results. Although helpful, this type of sensitivity analysis does not fully reveal the dependence of the results on particular linkages within the model nor on the functional forms chosen to represent the equations of the model.

■*Appendix 1*■

Measures of Welfare Change

A.1 Compensating and equivalent variation	*A.2* Consumer surplus

This appendix reviews three commonly used measures of welfare change, the Hicksian compensating and equivalent variation and the Marshallian consumer surplus.[70]

A.1 Compensating and equivalent variation

Hicks (1939) proposed the compensating variation (CV) and equivalent variation (EV) as concepts for empirically measuring the change in welfare that arises from price changes. Each concept measures a change in real income (measured in units of the numeraire) that is equivalent to a change in utility. The concepts differ only with respect to the reference set of prices used to evaluate the consumer's consumption decision. In this regard, the CV uses the new set of prices while the EV uses the initial set of prices. Assume there are N goods and let $\mathbf{p}_0 = (p_2^0, \ldots, p_N^0)$ and $\mathbf{p}_1 = (p_2^1, \ldots, p_N^1)$ denote two alternative vectors of relative goods prices (good 1 is the numeraire). Using the expenditure function, the compensating and equivalent variations can be defined as:

$$CV = S(\mathbf{p}_1, u_1) - S(\mathbf{p}_1, u_0) \tag{5.76}$$

$$EV = S(\mathbf{p}_0, u_1) - S(\mathbf{p}_0, u_0) \tag{5.77}$$

where u_0 and u_1 are, respectively, the utility levels achieved at prices $\mathbf{p}_0$ and $\mathbf{p}_1$. By definition, the CV is the amount of income (in units of the numeraire) that at prices $\mathbf{p}_1$ would just restore the consumer's utility to the level u_0 (i.e. $S(\mathbf{p}_1, u_0) = S(\mathbf{p}_1, u_1) - CV$). Hence, if the CV is negative it implies a loss to the consumer since he or she would need to be given (compensated) the CV amount of income to be as well off after the price change as before the price change. Alternatively, if the CV is positive then the price change from $\mathbf{p}_0$ to $\mathbf{p}_1$ represents a gain to the consumer since he or she could give up income equal to the CV and be just as well off after the price change as before the price change.

The EV measures the income change that, at the initial prices p_0, would allow the consumer to achieve the welfare level u_1 in the absence of the price change. In this sense, the EV is the income change that is 'equivalent' to the welfare change arising from the price change from p_0 to p_1. Again, a positive (negative) EV represents a gain (loss) due to the price change.

Figure 5.13 illustrates the measurement of the CV and EV concepts for the case of 2 goods. In Figure 5.13, the price change is assumed to result from a tariff imposed on imports of good 2 (in this sense Figure 5.13 is comparable to Figure 5.1). Under free trade consumers face prices $p_0 = p_w$ and achieve utility level u_0 by consuming at point A'. Under the tariff consumers face domestic prices $p_1 = p_d$ and achieve utility level u_1 by consuming at point B'. By definition, $CV = S(p_d, u_1) - S(p_d, u_0)$ and $EV = S(p_w, u_1) - S(p_w, u_0)$. Since the CV and EV are negative the price change (i.e. the tariff) results in a welfare loss. We note that if measured in units of good 2, the CV equals (the negative of) distance de while EV equals (the negative of) distance fh in Figure 5.13. Note also that the EV can be decomposed into two parts: a consumption loss (fg) and a production cost (gh), where the latter measures the welfare change at prices p_w associated with the increase in the production of good 2 (and decline in the production of good 1) arising from the tariff.

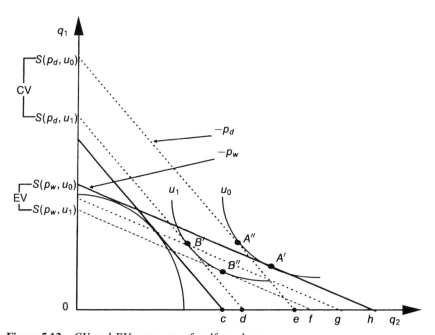

Figure 5.13   *CV and EV measures of welfare change*

Calculation of the compensating variation or equivalent variation is possible if the form of the expenditure function is known.[71] As discussed on p. 202, applied general equilibrium models typically assume a specific form for the utility function and can therefore derive the form of the associated expenditure function.

A.2 **Consumer surplus**

Closely related to the above Hicksian measures is the Marshallian concept of consumer surplus.[72] Under this concept, the effect of a price change on a consumer's welfare is measured by the area to the left of the demand curve and between the new and old price. This measure is shown in Figure 5.14 as the area $p_d B' A' p_w$ associated with the ordinary (money income constant) demand curve $d_2(p, Y)$.

Figure 5.14 also shows the Hicksian (compensated) demand functions $h_2(p, u_0)$ and $h_2(p, u_1)$ for good 2. These give the change in demand resulting from a price change while maintaining utility constant at either u_0 or u_1, respectively. For comparison, the price–quantity points in Figure 5.14 correspond to the similarly labelled points in Figure 5.13. At the price p_w, $d_2(p, Y)$ and $h_2(p, u_0)$ yield the same quantity demanded. This is a direct application of (4.45) and (4.46) which state the equality of these demands when income Y equates to the minimum expenditure (i.e. $S(p, u_0)$) necessary to attain utility level u_0. The compensated demand function $h_2(p, u_0)$ is

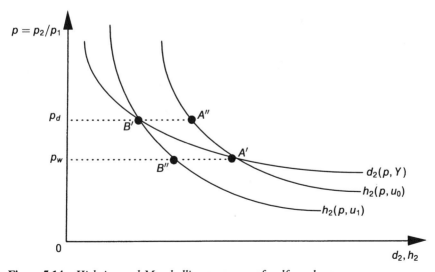

Figure 5.14 *Hicksian and Marshallian measures of welfare change*

steeper than $d_2(p, Y)$ at A' if good 2 is normal and flatter than $d_2(p, Y)$ if good 2 is inferior (see (4.47)). The two curves coincide if demands are unresponsive to income.

It can be shown that the CV measured in units of good 2, the distance *de* in Figure 5.13, equals area $p_d B' B'' p_w$ in Figure 5.14 and that EV, the distance *fh* in Figure 5.13, corresponds to the area $p_d A'' A' p_w$ in Figure 5.14.[73] As suggested by Figure 5.14, the Marshallian consumer surplus will lie between the EV and the CV measures unless demands are unresponsive to income.

∎*Appendix 2*∎

Deriving Cross-price Elasticities of Demand

| *A.1* Using demand theory | *A.2* The elasticity of substitution |

Estimates of welfare changes in the partial equilibrium imperfect substitutes model discussed in this chapter require values for the cross-price elasticities between the imported and domestic good. However, since colinearity among the price data often makes econometric estimation of these elasticities difficult, analysts often resort to indirect methods to derive values of cross-price elasticities. This appendix discusses two of these methods.

A.1 **Using demand theory**

The first method derives values of the cross-price elasticities using relationships implied by the theory of demand. Assume there are N goods. Since demand functions are homogeneous of degree zero in prices, the sum of the own and cross-price elasticities of demand for good i with respect to a change in prices sum to the negative of the income elasticity:

$$\sum_{j=1}^{N} \eta_{ij} = -\varepsilon_i \qquad (i = 1, \ldots, N) \tag{5.78}$$

where $\eta_{ij} = (\partial X_i/\partial P_j)(P_j/X_i)$ is the (uncompensated) elasticity of demand for good i given a change in the price of good j and $\varepsilon_i = (\partial X_i/\partial y)(y/X_i)$ is the income elasticity of demand for good i. Without loss of generality, assume that the domestic and imported good are goods 1 and 2, and for clarity, denote these goods by the subscripts d and m, respectively. Then, from (5.78), the equations corresponding to the domestic and imported good can be used to obtain the following expressions for the cross-price elasticities of interest:

$$\eta_{dm} = -\varepsilon_d - \eta_{dd} - \sum_{j=3}^{N} \eta_{dj} \tag{5.79}$$

$$\eta_{md} = -\varepsilon_m - \eta_{mm} - \sum_{j=3}^{N} \eta_{mj} \tag{5.80}$$

These expressions show that each cross-price elasticity (i.e. η_{dm} and η_{md}) can be computed for given values of the income and own price elasticities, as well as the remaining $N-2$ cross-price elasticities. Since obtaining values for the latter are problematic, an obvious step is to assume these latter cross-price elasticities are zero. However, this assumption is too strong. To see why, write each uncompensated cross-price elasticity in its Slutsky form $\eta_{ij} = \phi_{ij} - \lambda_j \varepsilon_i$, where ϕ_{ij} is the compensated cross-price elasticity and λ_j is the share of expenditure on good j. Assuming that $\eta_{ij} = \phi_{ij} - \lambda_j \varepsilon_j = 0 \; \forall \, j \neq d$ or m then amounts to imposing the restriction that the substitution and income effects are equal (i.e. $\phi_{ij} = \lambda_j \varepsilon_i$). A more sensible assumption is that the compensated cross-price elasticities $\phi_{ij} \; \forall \, j \neq d$ or m are instead zero. This assumption is sometimes called 'want independence', and it implies that the indifference curves between, say, the domestic good and each of the other $N-2$ goods are L shaped. Therefore, assuming want independence, and noting that the symmetry of the substitution effects implies $\lambda_m \phi_{md} = \lambda_d \phi_{dm}$ or $\phi_{md} = \phi_{dm}(\lambda_d/\lambda_m)$, (5.79) and (5.80) can be written

$$\phi_{dm} = -\varepsilon_d + \lambda_m \varepsilon_d - \eta_{dd} + \sum_{j=3}^{N} \lambda_j \varepsilon_d \tag{5.81}$$

$$\phi_{dm}(\lambda_d/\lambda_m) = -\varepsilon_m + \lambda_d \varepsilon_m - \eta_{mm} + \sum_{j=3}^{N} \lambda_j \varepsilon_m \tag{5.82}$$

Subtracting (5.82) from (5.81) and using

$$\sum_{j=3}^{N} \lambda_j = 1 - (\lambda_d + \lambda_m)$$

gives:

$$\phi_{dm} = \frac{\lambda_m}{(\lambda_m - \lambda_d)} \left((\eta_{mm} - \eta_{dd}) + (\lambda_m \varepsilon_m - \lambda_d \varepsilon_d) \right) \tag{5.83}$$

Since, by definition, $\eta_{dm} = \phi_{dm} - \lambda_m \varepsilon_d$ we can add $-\lambda_m \varepsilon_d$ to both sides of (5.83) and obtain

$$\eta_{dm} = \frac{\lambda_m}{(\lambda_m - \lambda_d)} \left((\eta_{mm} - \eta_{dd}) + (\lambda_m \varepsilon_m - \lambda_d \varepsilon_d) \right) - \lambda_m \varepsilon_d \tag{5.84}$$

The analogous expression for η_{md} is[74]

$$\eta_{md} = \frac{\lambda_d}{(\lambda_m - \lambda_d)} \left((\eta_{mm} - \eta_{dd}) + (\lambda_m \varepsilon_m - \lambda_d \varepsilon_d) \right) - \lambda_d \varepsilon_m \tag{5.85}$$

Hence, assuming want independence, the cross-price elasticities can be estimated using data on the expenditure shares and the income and own price elasticities of domestic and import demand.

Finally, a further simplification is to assume equal income elasticities of demand (i.e. $\varepsilon_d = \varepsilon_m = \varepsilon$). Under this assumption expressions (5.84) and (5.85) simplify to

$$\eta_{dm} = \frac{V_m}{(V_m - V_d)} (\eta_{mm} - \eta_{dd}) \tag{5.86}$$

$$\eta_{md} = \frac{V_d}{(V_m - V_d)} (\eta_{mm} - \eta_{dd}) \tag{5.87}$$

where V_i is total spending on good i, $i = d, m$. Note that, under the assumptions used to derive (5.86) and (5.87), the cross-price elasticities are undefined if the same amount is spent on the domestic and imported good.

A.2 The elasticity of substitution

A second method for imputing cross-price elasticities is based on the concept of an 'elasticity of substitution' between the domestic and imported good. This elasticity (σ_{dm}) is defined as

$$\sigma_{dm} = \frac{d(d/m)}{d(p_d/p_m)} \frac{(p_d/p_m)}{(d/m)} = \frac{d\ln(d) - d\ln(m)}{d\ln(p_d) - d\ln(p_m)}$$

where d and m are the quantities consumed, and p_d and p_m are the prices, of the domestic and imported good, respectively. Since a change in the relative price p_d/p_m can arise from two sources (i.e. dp_d and dp_m) we can write:

$$\sigma_{dm} = \frac{d\ln(d) - d\ln(m)}{d\ln(p_d)} = \eta_{dd} - \eta_{md}$$

$$\sigma_{dm} = \frac{d\ln(d) - d\ln(m)}{d\ln(p_m)} = \eta_{dm} - \eta_{mm}$$

Hence, the desired cross-price elasticities can be estimated from

$$\eta_{md} = \eta_{dd} - \sigma_{dm}$$

$$\eta_{dm} = \sigma_{dm} + \eta_{mm}$$

Estimates of σ_{dm} are obtained from a regression of the form $\ln(d/m) = \alpha + \beta \ln(p_d/p_m)$ computed using either time series or pooled time series, cross-section data. Note that the very concept of an elasticity of substitution assumes $\eta_{dd} - \eta_{md} = \eta_{dm} - \eta_{mm}$ (or $\eta_{dd} + \eta_{dm} = \eta_{mm} + \eta_{md}$). Since this restriction on the elasticities has no apparent theoretical justification, Leamer and Stern (1970) concluded that the elasticity of substitution concept has dubious value in applied trade analysis. However, with just 2 goods, this elasticity restriction amounts to assuming equal income elasticities of demand since degree zero homogeneity of the demand functions implies

$\eta_{jd} + \eta_{jm} = -\varepsilon_j$ $(j = d, m)$. Hence, the restriction on demand elasticities implied by the elasticity of substitution concept appears no worse than other assumptions one might use in order to compute values of cross-price elasticities from data on income and own price elasticities of demand.

Notes

1. In practical applications the world price p_w is taken to be the c.i.f. (cost, insurance and freight) price of imports, that is, the price at the boundary of the importing country. The domestic or internal price is then the c.i.f. price *plus* the applicable tariff. The price received by exporters is measured by the f.o.b. (free on board) price. The difference between the c.i.f. and the f.o.b. price of a good is often used to measure the cost of transport. For simplicity, the analysis of this chapter ignores transport and related costs.

2. For a specific tariff (τ^*) the relationship is $p_d = p_w + \tau^*$. If the world price p_w is constant, a specific tariff of $\tau^* = \tau p_w$ has exactly the same effect on p_d as an *ad valorem* tariff of τ. The equivalence breaks down if p_w changes. For example, a fall in p_w would reduce p_d by a less than equal proportion under a specific tariff but would reduce p_d by an equal proportion under an *ad valorem* tariff.

3. The demand functions therefore treat income and the prices of all other goods as exogeneous, unlike the general equilibrium demand functions in Chapter 4.

4. Recall that the height of the domestic supply curve measures the opportunity cost (in terms of forgone output of good 1) of producing an additional unit of good 2.

5. This income measure of the change in utility is the Hicksian equivalent variation. See Appendix 1 of this chapter.

6. The decomposition of the welfare change due to a small change in trade policy appears in a variety of contexts. Examples include Lloyd's (1982) analysis of a customs union and Viaene's (1987) analysis of land reclamation. Applications to the case of imperfectly competitive markets include Rodrik (1988), Helpman and Krugman (1989) and Feenstra (1995). A later section extends the decomposition of the welfare change to the case of many goods and when imported and domestic goods are imperfect substitutes.

7. See, however, the following section on Metzler's paradox.

8. Metzler (1949) also considers the extreme cases in which the government spends the tariff revenue either entirely on the export good or entirely on the import good.

9. This is the Marshall–Lerner condition. See (4.55) in Chapter 4.

10. However, column (2) of Table 4.3 shows that some estimated values of e^* are less than 1. Hence Metzler's paradox is empirically possible.

11. Note that a foreign export subsidy only affects the welfare of the home country through a terms of trade effect. Hence, while a foreign export subsidy creates a distortion between the world and domestic price of exports in the foreign country, no such distortion exists in the importing country. The latter therefore benefits from the lower import price and its welfare increases. As such,

countering the foreign export subsidy with say, a countervailing tariff, would only serve to offset the importing country's welfare gain and may even turn it into a net loss.

12. This tariff rate is known as an 'implicit' or '*ad valorem* equivalent' tariff rate. Implicit tariff rates are often used to estimate the welfare effects of NTBs to trade (see p. 191).

13. The next section discusses an example of this outcome.

14. For example, licenses might be 'proportionally distributed', that is, distributed to importers in proportion to their share of pre-quota imports or some other measure of pre-quota market presence.

15. Note that an 'importer' can be either a domestic or foreign entity. Hence, the allocation of quota rights by the importing country does not guarantee that the quota rents accrue only to domestic entities. If the domestic importer is a foreign owned entity then quota rents may be transferred abroad either by the direct repatriation of profits or indirectly by setting higher transfer prices between the parent 'exporter' and its subsidiary 'importer.' Taxation of repatriated profits by the importing country could recapture some of these quota rents. Note that the issue of domestic versus foreign 'importers' is mute if the government instead auctions the quota licences.

16. Since the (maximum) price each importer is willing to pay to import one unit of the good equals the difference between the post-quota domestic and world price.

17. This may not be the case when markets are imperfectly competitive. (See Chapter 10.)

18. One widely studied VER is that between the United States and Japan in which Japan agreed to limit its exports of certain motor vehicles to the United States. Another important example is the MFA (Multi-Fiber Arrangement) which specified a system of quotas on textile exports *vis-à-vis* industrial country importers (as noted in Chapter 2, the MFA is being abolished under the Uruguay Round Agreements). These are but some of the many VRAs that have been negotiated. For example, by the mid-1990s the European Community had negotiated some fifty VRAs (GATT 1991).

19. To see this, consider the equivalent case of an import tariff where the tariff imposing country transfers all tariff revenue to the foreign country. In this case, home consumers lose areas *A* and *B*, the home government collects revenue equal to areas *A* and *C* which is then paid to the foreign government. The net loss to the home country is therefore areas *A* and *B*.

20. This raises the question of why an importing country would negotiate a VER rather than impose an import quota. One reason is that GATT rules prohibit countries from undertaking unilateral import restrictions unless 'justified'. Even if deemed justified, GATT rules require the importing country to compensate affected exporters by reducing trade barriers on other products it imports from the affected countries. During the 1980s, many importing countries found these rules cumbersome and the GATT's process of obtaining approval for 'justified' import restrictions too slow. Negotiating with an 'offending' exporter to limit exports was much faster, and also provided compensation to the exporter in the

form of a potential welfare gain equal to area *A minus* area *D*. Moreover, prior to the GATT's Uruguay Round negotiations which concluded in 1994, bilateral agreements that limited exports were not covered under GATT rules and hence explicit compensation was not required. Exporting countries often agreed to VERs for fear that not doing so would bring even greater limits on their trade should the importing country instead adopt import restrictions. Agreements reached under the Uruguay round are intended to phase out the use of bilateral VER agreements.

21. Johnson (1971) and Corden (1971) contain some of the earliest work on this subject.

22. In some cases firms can offset a portion of a DCR by exporting rather than using domestically produced components. For example, in order to satisfy a Mexican DCR, US auto firms in Mexico exported Mexican made components to the US even though these components were cheaper to produce in the United States.

23. This model follows the analysis of Vousden (1987).

24. The composite inverse supply function (5.15) can be written: $\bar{p}(z, p_w, \lambda) = \lambda p_d(\lambda z) + (1 - \lambda)p_w$ since under the DCR $q = \lambda z$. With λ and p_w fixed, $d\bar{p}/dz = \lambda^2(\partial p_d/\partial z)$ so that, for example, if $\lambda = 0.5$ then the slope of the composite inverse supply curve ($\bar{q}$) in Figure 5.6 is one quarter that of the domestic inverse supply curve (q).

25. Applied general equilibrium models also ignore the uncertainty associated with elasticity values (and other model parameters) when making welfare calculations.

26. Unless production of the domestic good is zero, this change in consumer surplus is not the change for *all* domestic consumers since it ignores the effect of the tariff change on the price of the domestic good, and hence the surplus of consumers (and producers) of the domestic good. However, since these domestic market effects are merely an income transfer between domestic producers and consumers their omission does not affect the measurement of the change in the economy's net welfare.

27. The trapezoid rule states that an integral of the form $\int_a^b f(x)\,dx$ can be approximated as $(b - a)((f(a) + f(b))/2$ and that the error associated with this approximation is no greater than $(b - a)^3(Z/12)$. The number Z is chosen so as to satisfy $|\partial^2 f(x)/\partial x^2| \leq Z$ for $a \leq x \leq b$. The approximation error is therefore zero when $f(x)$ is affine.

28. This ignores the change in the surplus of domestic producers (a loss) and consumers of the domestic good (a gain). Ignoring these changes does not affect measurement of the net change in welfare since they are simply offsetting transfers between domestic producers and domestic consumers. These components of the welfare change will be considered when we allow for cross-price effects between the imported and domestic good.

29. Since tariff revenue is assumed to be returned to consumers, area *D* is properly part of the welfare gain to consumers. Note that the net gain in tariff revenue restores a portion of the consumer surplus lost as the result of the initial tariff τ_1. Hence, the welfare gain to consumers of the imported good from a complete removal of the tariff $\tau_2 = 0$ would just be the change in consumer surplus given as areas *A*, *B*, *C*, *D* and *E*.

30. Since the trapezoid approximation is exact when the underlying function is linear, the preceding formulas can also be derived from Figure 5.7 assuming that the demand and supply functions are linear and then using appropriate formulas for computing the areas of triangles and rectangles.

31. For example, application of the formula $\hat{m} = -\eta_m \hat{p}_m$ could yield an estimate of the new level of imports that is negative, implying that the estimated change in imports is too large.

32. The minus sign preceding the integral in (5.31) reflects that, in the limits of integration, as imports vary from m_1 to m_2 in (5.27) the tariff rate varies from τ_1 to τ_2. However, since $\tau_1 > \tau_2$, we follow the convention of putting the smaller value (t_2) as the lower limit. Alternatively, the minus sign accounts for the fact that $dm(\tau, p_w)/d\tau < 0$.

33. Derivation of (5.35) uses

$$p_w^{(1-\eta_m)} = \left(\frac{p_1}{1+\tau_1}\right)^{(1-\eta_m)} = \frac{V_1}{k}(1+\tau_1)^{(\eta_m-1)}$$

where the latter equality follows from $V_1 = p_1 m_1 = k p_1^{(1-\eta_m)}$.

34. Hence, if the initial value of imports were \$100 million, the welfare change could be estimated to be as low as \$2.78 million and as high as \$3.67 million.

35. As previously discussed, the constant elasticity restrictions $m = k_0 p_d^{-\eta_m}$ and $x^* = k_1 p_w^{\varepsilon_m}$ could be imposed when deriving (5.44). Alternatively, these could be used to directly compute (5.38) which in this case is

$$\Delta W = \int_{\tau_2}^{\tau_1} t p_w(m(\tau)) \left|\frac{\partial m(\tau)}{\partial \tau}\right| \partial \tau - \int_{\tau_2}^{\tau_1} x^*[p_w(\tau)] \left|\frac{\partial p_w(\tau)}{\partial \tau}\right| \partial \tau$$

where $p_w(\tau) = (1 + tau)^{-\eta_m/(\eta_m + \varepsilon_m)}$, $m(\tau) = (1 + \tau)^{-(2\eta_m^2 + \eta_m \varepsilon_m)/(\eta_m + \varepsilon_m)}$ and $x^*(p_w(\tau)) = (1 + \tau)^{-\eta\varepsilon/(\eta + \varepsilon)}$

36. If import supply is not perfectly elastic then the reduction in import demand would further reduce the price of imports and thus further reduce the demand and price of the domestic good. Assuming this process converges, the final equilibrium will be like that depicted in panels A and B of Figure 5.9.

37. This assumes that the domestic substitute is not traded. This assumption is relaxed below.

38. It may help to compare this area to area T in Figure 5.2. Alternatively, you can convince yourself that the shaded area in panel B is the change in consumer surplus by considering (5.66) which gives the expression for the economy's net welfare change assuming that the domestic good is exported. The first term in (5.66) is the net welfare change arising in the market for the domestic good and is zero if the domestic good is not exported (as presently assumed). Hence, when the domestic good is not traded, the changes in producer and consumer surplus arising in the domestic market must be of equal magnitude but opposite in sign.

39. Of course, the changes differ in magnitude.

40. Note that

$$\varepsilon_m \left(\frac{\varepsilon_m(\eta_{dd} + \varepsilon_{dd})}{\Omega} - 1 \right) = \varepsilon_m \left(\frac{\eta_{dm}\eta_{md} - \eta_{mm}(\eta_{dd} + \varepsilon_d)}{(\eta_{dd} + \varepsilon_d)(\eta_{mm} + \varepsilon_m) - \eta_{dm}\eta_{md}} \right)$$

in (5.57).

41. The formula for the net welfare change in the case of a large country can be obtained from (5.41) by setting $\rho_w = (\rho_m - \hat{r})$ and then replacing ρ_m with (5.55) and $\hat{m}$ and x^* with (5.57). In this case, calculation of the welfare change will also require an estimate of the import supply elasticity.

42. The finding that the net welfare change is small is common in studies of the costs of protection.

43. Also, that the domestic good is not traded. See the following section.

44. Examples include Grossman (1986) and Leamer (1988).

45. Trefler (1993) found that treating tariff rates as endogenous resulted in an estimate of the restrictiveness of US tariffs ten times larger than when tariffs were taken to be exogenous.

46. This can be modelled by adding the foreign demand equation $\hat{m}^* = -\eta_{dm} \cdot \hat{p}_d$, where $m^* = m^*(p_d)$ is the foreign demand for home exports, to the system of equations (5.55)–(5.58) and modifying the equilibrium condition for the domestic market to $\hat{q} = \lambda_d \hat{d} + \lambda_{m} \cdot \hat{m}^*$, where λ_d and λ_{m} are, respectively, the value shares of domestic and foreign consumption (i.e. exports) of the domestic good. Alternatively, one can simply re-interpret (5.51) to be the total demand (domestic plus foreign) for the domestic good and note that the demand elasticity η_{dd} in (5.51) would be replaced with $\theta_{dd} = \lambda_d \eta_{dd} + \lambda_{m} \cdot \eta_{dm}$ where θ_{dd} is now the price elasticity of demand for the domestic good and η_{dd} and η_{dm} are, respectively, the price elasticities of the domestic demand and the foreign demand for the domestic good.

47. The welfare effect that arises when the domestic substitute is also exported is an example of the effect that arises when the 'Armington specification' of national product differentiation is used in applied general equilibrium models (see p. 203).

48. This assumes the import quota is binding at the new level $\bar{m}_2$, that is, $\bar{m}_2$ is below the level of imports that would obtain under free trade.

49. These are also called 'implicit tariffs'. The ratio of the domestic to world price is sometimes called a nominal protection coefficient.

50. Of course, p_1 and p_w are themselves estimates in the sense that they are computed by dividing a total value by a measure of quantity. See the discussion of unit values later in this section.

51. This is derived using $p_w = V_w/\bar{m}_1$, $p_1 = V_1/\bar{m}_1$, $p_2 = p_1(1 - \hat{m}/\eta_m)$ and $p_w^2 = p_w^1(1 + \hat{m}/\varepsilon_m)$, where p_w^1 and p_w^2 are the world prices when imports are respectively, $\bar{m}_1$ and $\bar{m}_2$.

52. See Baldwin (1989) for a critique of AVEs and other methods for measuring the price impact of NTBs.

53. See Pelzman (1988) for an example of this approach.

54. The shift toward high priced varieties when a quota is tightened is referred to as 'quality upgrading'. While this terminology suggests a gain to consumers, 'upgrading' is actually a loss since consumer choice is being restricted to higher price items. Expanding an import quota (or VER) implies 'quality downgrading'

and more choice, and hence a welfare gain. Boorstein and Feenstra (1991) find that the welfare gain associated with quality downgrading is equal in size to the traditional welfare gain calculated from price changes alone. Hence, by ignoring compositional changes, the traditional welfare calculation may understate by as much as one-half the actual welfare gain from reducing a trade restriction.

55. This section is based on Feenstra (1995).

56. It may be helpful to think of there being N classes of goods, where each class of good consists of a domestic and imported variety.

57. This assumes that all quota rents accrue to domestic agents.

58. Appendix 1 reviews this and other measures of welfare change.

59. Alternatively, (5.64) is just the difference between the left- and right-hand sides of (5.62).

60. If you worked Problems 4.5 and 4.9 in Chapter 4 then you have already developed an AGE model without calibration.

61. The classic treatment of this model is Samuelson (1953).

62. This is not strictly true since under imperfect competition supply functions do not exist. Instead, equations that specify pricing rules assume this role.

63. Conditional on total expenditure allocated to imports. See any advanced text on microeconomics (e.g. Varian, 1992) for a discussion of conditional demand functions.

64. For example, all varieties of German automobiles are perfect substitutes as are all varieties of Japanese automobiles, but German and Japanese automobiles are imperfect substitutes.

65. Such results have led many AGE modelers to question the Armington specification as a method for modeling product differentiation. In particular, Brown (1987) shows that the substitution possibilities implied by the Armington specification imply excessive terms of trade changes. Hence AGE models that use this specification are biased toward finding negative welfare changes from trade liberalization. Brown's findings have led some to suggest that product differentiation should be modeled at the level of the firm rather than the level of a country.

66. See, for example, Brooke *et al.* (1988).

67. Named for Johansen (1960) who is usually credited as conducting the first AGE exercise.

68. This is the approach used by Jones (1965) in presenting his analysis of the 2-sector general equilibrium model.

69. Examples include Deardorff and Stern (1986) and Dixon *et. al.* (1982).

70. Other measures include the equivalent and compensating surpluses (Hicks, 1939) and the money metric approach. These concepts are, however, methodologically related to the equivalent and compensating variations. See Deaton and Muellbauer (1980) and Boadway and Bruce (1984) for reviews of alternative measures.

71. More generally, computation of the CV or EV requires that u_0 and u_1 be known. Willig (1976), Seade (1978), Vartia (1983) and others have developed techniques that overcome this estimation problem and also allow a direct comparison with the Marshallian measure discussed below.

72. This concept is originally due to Dupuit but Marshall (1890) popularized the concept as an important tool in applied welfare economics.

73. An algebraic demonstration of this is given in Burns (1973).
74. This is derived from (5.83) using $\phi_{md} = \phi_{dm}(\lambda_d/\lambda_m)$, and noting that $\eta_{md} = \phi_{md} - \lambda_d \varepsilon_m$.

References and additional reading

Impediments to trade

General Agreement on Tariffs and Trade (1991), *European Communities. Report by the Secretariat* (Geneva: Trade Policy Review Mechanism).

Helpman, E. and Krugman, P.R. (1989), *Trade Policy and Market Structure* (Cambridge, Mass.: The MIT Press).

Lerner, A. (1936), 'The Symmetry between Import and Export Taxes', *Economica*, 3, 306–13.

Metzler, L.A. (1949), 'Tariffs, the Terms of Trade, and the Distribution of National Income', *Journal of Political Economy*, 57, 1–29.

Schuknecht, L. (1992), *Trade Protection in the European Community* (Chur: Harwood Academic).

Vousden, N. (1990), *The Economics of Trade Protection* (Cambridge: Cambridge University Press).

Decomposition of welfare changes

Helpman, E. and Krugman, P.R. (1989), *Trade Policy and Market Structure* (Cambridge, Mass: The MIT Press), Section 2.7, 22–5.

Lloyd, P.J. (1982), '3 × 3 Theory of Customs Unions', *Journal of International Economics*, 12, 41–63.

Rodrik, Dani (1988), 'Imperfect Competition, Scale Economies, and Trade Policy in Developing Countries,' in Baldwin, R.E (ed.), *Trade Policy Issues and Empirical Analysis* (Chicago: University of Chicago Press).

Varian, H.R. (1992) *Microeconomic Analysis* (New York: W.W. Norton), 3rd edn.

Viaene, J.-M. (1987), 'Factor Accumulation in a Minimum-Wage Economy', *European Economic Review*, 31, 1313–28.

Welfare measures

Boadway, R.W. and Bruce, N. (1984), *The Pure Theory of Welfare Economics* (Oxford: Basil Blackwell).

Burns, M.E. (1973), 'A Note on the Concept and Measure of Consumer's Surplus', *American Economic Review*, 63, 335–44.

Deaton, A. and Muellbauer, J. (1980), *Economics and Consumer Behavior* (Cambridge: Cambridge University Press).

Hicks, J. (1939), 'Foundations of Welfare Economics', *Economic Journal* 49, 696–712.

Marshall, A. (1890), *Principles of Economics* (London: Macmillan; revised edn. 1972).

Seade, J. (1978), 'Consumer's Surplus and Linearity of Engel Curves', *Economic Journal*, 88, 511–23.

Vartia, Y. (1983), 'Efficient Methods of Measuring Welfare Change and Compensated Income in Terms of Ordinary Demand Functions', *Econometrica*, 51, 79–98.

Willig, R.D. (1976), 'Consumer's Surplus without Apology', *American Economic Review*, 66, 589–97.

Domestic content protection

Beghin, J.C. and Knox Lovell, C.A. (1993), 'Trade and Efficiency Effects of Domestic Content Protection: The Australian Tobacco and Cigarette Industries', *Review of Economics and Statistics*, 75, 623–69.

Bourgeois, J., Vermulst, E. and Waer, F. (1994) (eds), *Rules of Origin in International Trade: A Comparative Study* (Ann Arbor: University of Michigan Press).

Corden, W.M. (1971), *The Theory of Protection* (London: Allen & Unwin).

Grossman, G.M. (1981), 'The Theory of Domestic Content Protection and Content Preference', *Quarterly Journal of Economics*, 9, 583–603.

Hollander, A. (1987), 'Content Protection and Transnational Monopoly', *Journal of International Economics*, 23, 283–97.

Johnson, H.G. (1971), *Aspects of the Theory of Tariffs* (London: Allen & Unwin).

Krishna, K. and Itoh, M. (1988), 'Content Protection and Oligopolistic Interactions', *Review of Economic Studies*, 55, 107–25.

Krishna, K. and Krueger, A.O. (1994), 'Implementing Free Trade Areas: Rules of Origin and Hidden Protection', in Deardorff, A., Levinhson, J. and Stern, R. (eds), *New Directions in Trade Theory* (Ann Arbor: University of Michigan Press).

Richardson, M. (1991), 'The Effects of a Content Requirement on a Foreign Duopsonist', *Journal of International Economics*, 31, 143–55.

Vousden, N. (1987), 'Content Protection and Tariffs under Monopoly and Competition', *Journal of International Economics*, 23, 263–82.

Trade policy modeling

Armington, P.A. (1969), 'A Theory of Demand for Products Distinguished by Place of Production,' *International Monetary Fund Staff Papers*, 16, 159–76.

Baldwin, R.E. (1989) 'Measuring Nontariff Trade Policies,' *NBER Working Paper*, 2978 (May).

Baldwin, R.E. (ed.) (1988), *Trade Policy Issues and Empirical Analysis* (Chicago: University of Chicago Press and National Bureau of Economic Research).

Boorstein, R. and Feenstra, F.C. (1991), 'Quality Upgrading and its Welfare Cost in US Steel Import, 1969–74', in Helpman, E. and Razin, A. (eds), *International Trade and Trade Policy* (Cambridge, Mass.: MIT Press), 167–86.

Brooke, A., Kendrick, D. and Meeraus, A. (1988), *GAMS, A User's Guide* (California: Scientific Press).

Brown, D.K. (1987) 'Tariffs, the Terms of Trade, and National Product Differentiation', *Journal of Policy Modeling*, 9(4), 503–26.

de Melo, J. and Tarr, D. (1992), *A General Equilibrium Analysis of US Foreign Trade Policy* (Cambridge, Mass: MIT Press).

Deardorff, A.V. and Stern, R.M. (1986), *The Michigan Model of World Production and Trade* (Cambridge, Mass.: MIT Press).

Deardorff, A.V. and Stern, R.M. (1990), *Computation Analysis of Global Trading Arrangements* (Ann Arbor: University of Michigan Press).

Dixon, P., Parmenter, B., Sutton, J. and Vincent, D. (1982), *ORANI: A MultiSector Model of the Australian Economy* (Amsterdam: North-Holland).

Feenstra, R. (1989), *Trade Policies for International Competitiveness* (Chicago: University of Chicago Press and National Bureau of Economic Research).

Feenstra, R. (1995), 'Estimating the Effects of Trade Policy', Chapter 30 in Grossman, G. and Rogoff, D. (eds), *Handbook of International Economics, Vol. III* (Amsterdam: North-Holland).

Feenstra, R. (ed.) (1988), *Empirical Methods for International Trade* (Cambridge, Mass.: MIT Press).

Francois, J.F., McDonald, B. and Nordström, H. (1995), 'Assessing the Uruguay Round', paper presented at the World Bank Conference, *The Uruguay Round and the Developing Economies* (January).

Grossman, G. (1986), 'Imports as a Cause of Injury: The Case of the US Steel Industry', *Journal of International Economics*, 20, 201–23.

Hufbauer, G.C., Berliner, D.T. and Elliott, K.A. (1986), *Trade Protection in the United States: 31 Case Studies* (Washington, D.C.: Institute for International Economics).

Johansen, L. (1960), *A Multi-Sectoral Study of Economic Growth* (Amsterdam: North-Holland).

Jones, R.W. (1965), 'The Structure of Simple General Equilibrium Models', *Journal of Political Economy*, 73, 557–72.

Laird, S. and Yeats, A. (1990), *Quantitative Methods for Trade-Barrier Analysis* (New York: New York University Press).

Leamer, E.E. (1988), 'Measures of Openness', in Baldwin R.E. (ed.), *Trade Policy Issues and Empirical Analysis* (Chicago: University of Chicago Press and National Bureau of Economic Research), 147–200.

Leamer, E.E. and Stern, R.M. (1970), *Quantitative International Economics* (Boston: Allyn and Bacon).

Pelzman, J. (1988), 'The Tariff Equivalents of the Existing Quotas under the Multi-fiber Arrangement', US Department of Labor, Bureau of International Labor Affairs, Washington, DC.

Roussland, D.J. and Soumela, J.W. (1985), 'Calculating the Consumer and Net Welfare Costs of Import Relief', *Staff Research Study*, 15, United States International Trade Commission.

Samuelson, P.A. (1953), 'The Prices of Factors and Goods in General Equilibrium', *The Review of Economics Studies*, 21, 1–20.

Saxonhouse, G.R. (1989), 'Differentiated Products, Economies of Scale and Access to the Japanese Market', in Feenstra, R.C. (ed.), *Trade Policies for International Competitiveness* (Chicago: University of Chicago Press and National Bureau of Economic Research).

Shoven, J.H. and Whalley, J. (1992), *Applying General Equilibrium* (Cambridge: Cambridge University Press).

Trefler, D. (1993) 'Trade Liberalization and the Theory of Endogenous Protection: An Econometric Study of US Import Policy', *Journal of Political Economy*, 101, 138–60.

■ *Chapter 6* ■

Factor Specificity, Mobility and Unemployment

6.1 The specific factors model	*6.3* Minimum wage unemployment
6.2 The international mobility of factors	*6.4* Concluding remarks

Faced with weak empirical support[1] for the 2-factor H–O–S model, many analysts sought to resolve the apparent inconsistency between theory and data by modifying the assumptions of the 2-factor H–O–S model one by one to see what phenomena might be explained. This chapter considers three such modifications and examines their influence both theoretically and empirically: (1) the specific factors model, which weakens the assumption of domestic factor mobility, (2) international mobility of factors, and (3) resource unemployment due to a binding minimum wage floor.

6.1 The specific factors model

Since it characterizes the long run equilibrium of an economy, the H–O–S theory assumes that factors of production are costlessly mobile within a country. However, recent empirical evidence on the dispersion of wages and capital returns across industries questions this assumption. For example, even after correcting for differences in worker ability, persistent wage differences across industries and over time have been found for both the United States and Germany (Krueger and Summers, 1988; Katz and Summers, 1989; Fels and Grundlach, 1990). Evidence for the returns to capital also suggests persistent, long run, differences across industries (Grossman and Levinsohn, 1989). These findings suggest that both capital and labor may be relatively immobile between industries, even in the long run.

The specific factors (SF) model modifies the H–O–S assumption of long run factor mobility by allowing some or all factors to be immobile between industries. In particular, the SF model characterizes the extent of domestic factor immobility in terms of three periods: the short run, the medium run and the long run. In the short run all factors are completely immobile between industries. In the long run, there is complete factor mobility as in

228

the H–O–S model. Between these extremes is the medium run, in which some factors are mobile while others are immobile. A key feature of the SF model is that the extent of factor mobility influences how factor prices, and hence factor incomes, respond to shocks, such as an exogenous change in output prices.

Below we first describe production equilibrium, and hence optimal factor allocations, in the SF model (Neary, 1978). We then trace the effect of an output price change on production, factor employment and income distribution in moving from the short run to the long run. Interpreting the output price change to be the result of a tariff, it is then shown how the changes in factor incomes imply transitional coalitions of factor owners that either favor or oppose the tariff. This analysis of coalition formation serves as an introduction to the political economy of protection; that part of trade theory that deals with the endogenous determination of trade policy.

Optimal factor allocation

The implications of the SF model can be brought out with the aid of panels (a) and (b) in Figure 6.1. Each panel presents an alternate view of the allocation of an economy's labor and capital between two industries. Panel (a) depicts the optimal allocation of labor, holding fixed the allocation of capital. Panel (b) shows an Edgeworth–Bowley production box which depicts the allocation of both factors simultaneously.[2] Together, panels (a) and (b) permit us to trace the transition of factor allocation, production, and factor incomes from the short run to the long run.

In panel (a), the economy's total labor force is measured by the distance O^1O^2 along the horizontal axis. The left and right vertical axes measure labor's nominal wage in industry 1 and industry 2, respectively. Since the length of the horizontal axis measures the economy's total labor force, any point on the axis denotes an allocation of labor between the two industries. Curves V_1^a and V_2^a, drawn with reference to origins O^1 and O^2, respectively, are labor's value marginal product in each industry. Each curve is a decreasing function of industry employment owing to diminishing marginal returns. By definition, the curve for each sector is drawn holding fixed the price of its output and the amount of capital employed.

In panel (b), the horizontal axes measure the economy's total labor force and the vertical axes measure the economy's total supply of capital. The optimal long run allocations of capital and labor between industries occur along the contract curve O_1O_2.

Given these figures, the optimal allocation of factors is determined as follows. In the absence of complete specialization, competition and perfect

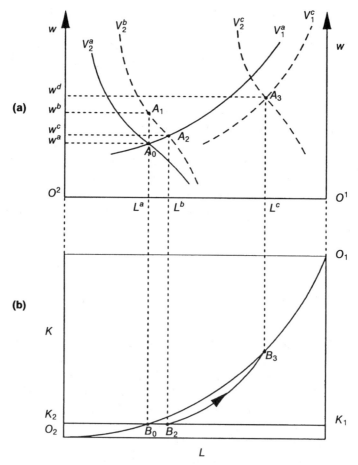

Figure 6.1   *Factor allocation in the SF model*

factor mobility imply equality between factor value marginal products and nominal factor rewards:

$$p_1 F_1^L(K_1, L_1) = w = p_2 F_2^L(K_2, L_2) \tag{6.1}$$

$$p_1 F_1^K(K_1, L_1) = r = p_2 F_2^K(K_2, L_2) \tag{6.2}$$

where superscripts denote marginal products, w is the nominal wage, r is nominal rental on capital, and p_j is the nominal price of good j ($j = 1, 2$). These conditions imply, in panel (a), the equilibrium wage and labor allocation given at the intersection point A_0. At the wage w^a, the quantity of labor employed in sector 1 is $L^a O^1$ and the quantity of labor in sector 2 is $O^2 L^a$. At any other wage, the implied allocation of labor between industries would leave some of the economy's labor unemployed (holding fixed the levels of capital employed). In panel (b), the optimal allocation of capital and labor between sectors is at point B_0. The levels of capital employed in each industry are given by the distances O_1K_1 and O_2K_2. These levels of capital are implicit in the positions of curves V_1^a and V_2^a in panel (a).

Adjustment to changes in output price

We now suppose there is an exogenous increase in the price of good 2 alone. In panel (a), this price increase leaves V_1^a unaffected but shifts V_2^a upward (to V_2^b) in proportion to the price increase. Assuming both factors are immobile, a new short run equilibrium occurs at A_1 in panel (a) and at B_0 in panel (b). With neither factor mobile, re-establishing the equality between value marginal products and factor rewards in each sector now requires factor rewards to differ between sectors. In particular, nominal wages and rentals in sector 2 must rise in proportion to the price increase while wages and rentals in sector 1 remain unchanged. These changes in nominal factor rewards imply that, if one excludes the extreme case that each individual spends exclusively on his own produced commodity, the real income of the owners of the factors employed in sector 2 increases while the real income of the owners of the factors employed in sector 1 falls. The following inequality summarizes these short-term changes in nominal factor returns:

$$\hat{w}_2 = \hat{r}_2 = \hat{p}_2 > \hat{w}_1 = \hat{r}_1 = \hat{p}_1 = 0 \tag{6.3}$$

where a 'hat' ($\hat{\ }$) over a variable denotes its percentage change with respect to the initial long run equilibrium.

Moving to the medium run, we assume labor becomes mobile while capital remains immobile. Given the short run wage differential, labor will now flow from sector 1 to sector 2 until nominal wages are again equalized. This implies a new equilibrium at point A_2 in panel (a) and B_2 in panel (b). Since capital employment remains fixed, this reallocation of labor raises the output of good 2 and reduces the output of good 1.

We now inquire further into the changes in factor returns. Note that we can measure these changes relative to either the initial long-run values or the short-run values determined above. Measured relative to the initial long-run values, labor's nominal wage has risen (from w^a to w^c in panel (a)). Since the proportional rise in the nominal wage is less than the proportional increase in p_2 ($= w^b/w^a$), labor's real return has fallen in terms of good 2 ($\hat{w} < \hat{p}_2$) and risen in terms of good 1 ($\hat{w} > \hat{p}_1$) These conflicting movements in real returns mean that the change in labor's welfare is ambiguous, that is, it depends on labor's preferences for good 2 versus good 1.[3] Finally, when measured relative to their preceding short run values, labor's nominal and real return fell in sector 2 but increased in sector 1.

Turning to capital's return, the flow of labor from sector 1 to sector 2 raises capital's marginal product in sector 2 but lowers it in sector 1.[4] Since p_2 increased but p_1 did not change, these changes in capital's marginal product imply that its nominal return fell in sector 1 but rose in sector 2. These changes in nominal returns, coupled with the change in p_2, imply that the real income of the owners of capital employed in sector 1 declined in terms of either good (both r_1/p_1 and r_1/p_2 fell) while the real income of the owners of capital employed in sector 2 increased (both r_2/p_1 and r_2/p_2 rose). These same changes in capital's nominal and real return occur if the changes are measured relative to their short run values. The following summarizes the medium run changes in factor rewards when measured relative to the initial equilibrium:

$$\hat{r}_2 > \hat{p}_2 > \hat{w} > \hat{p}_1 = 0 > \hat{r}_1 \qquad (6.4)$$

Moving to the long run, we assume that both capital and labor are mobile. In view of the medium run differential in capital's return across sectors, capital will now move from sector 1 to sector 2 until its return is equalized. The final equilibrium is shown at A_3 in panel (a) and at B_3 in panel (b). The curve $B_2 B_3$ in panel (b) depicts a possible path for this reallocation of capital. In panel (a), the reallocation of capital shifts V_1 and V_2 to the right since an increase (decrease) in the quantity of capital employed raises (decreases) labor's marginal product at all levels of employment. To determine the changes in returns relative to their initial long run values, we can employ the Stolper–Samuelson theorem to conclude that, if sector 2 is labor-intensive, nominal and real wages must rise whereas nominal and real rentals must fall:

$$\hat{w} > \hat{p}_2 > \hat{p}_1 = 0 > \hat{r} \qquad (6.5)$$

Note that the medium run ambiguity over the change in labor's real income is resolved in the long run (i.e. compare (6.5) with (6.4)).[5]

Winners and losers from protection

The above changes in factor incomes imply 'winners' and 'losers' from protection. To see this, we need only interpret the increase in the price of good 2 to be the result of a tariff imposed on imports of good 2. Given this, Figure 6.2 summarizes the evolution of nominal factor returns from which real returns can be derived by comparison to the relative price movements (Ethier, 1987). Initially, the nominal prices of goods and factors are assumed to be normalized to unity by an appropriate choice of units. Therefore, imposition of a tariff at time SR raises both the domestic relative price of good 2 ($p_d = p_2/p_1$), and the nominal return to each factor in sector 2, from unity to $(1 + \hat{p}_d)$.[6] Looking now at capital's return, the transition from SR

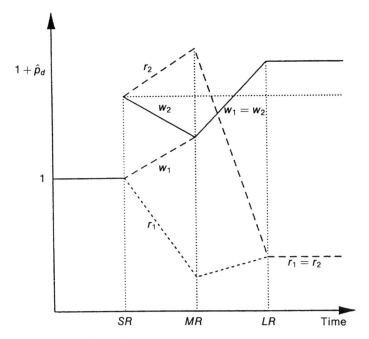

Figure 6.2 *Protection of good 2 and nominal factor rewards*

to *MR* involves a further rise in the nominal and real return to capital in sector 2 and a fall in the returns to capital in the unprotected sector. Proceeding from *MR* to *LR*, the return to capital in sector 2 declines until, at time *LR*, the nominal and real returns to capital are below their pre-tariff value of unity. The path of labor returns shows that labor in the protected sector gains in the short run while labor (overall) gains even more in the long run. Note that, in moving from *SR* to *MR*, nominal and real wages rise in sector 1 but fall in sector 2; this corresponds to the above noted ambiguity over the change in labor's welfare at this stage.

The political economy of tariffs

The political economy of protection deals with the endogenous determination of commercial policy. It asks, among other questions, why different countries have different structures of protection and what gives rise to any particular structure. A conventional assumption is that self-interest motives govern the behavior of economic agents who then join coalitions according

Table 6.1 *Factor owner coalitions (capital immobile except in long run)*

Periods	Favor free trade	Favor protection	Ambiguous
SR	K_1, L_1	K_2, L_2	–
MR	K_1	K_2	L_1, L_2
LR	K_1, K_2	L_1, L_2	–

to whether they are potential gainers or losers from a policy. These coalitions then attempt to achieve their preferred policy through the political system by lobbying lawmakers or supporting political candidates (Hillman, 1989).

For example, what coalitions of domestic factor owners might we expect to form if a country's residents were offered the choice of free trade or protection? Assuming capital is immobile except in the long run, Table 6.1 indicates coalitions that would be predicted to form in different 'runs'. If factor owners consider only their long run interests, the Stolper–Samuelson theorem would predict that capital owners and labor owners would form separate and opposing coalitions. However, if both short and medium run interests are considered, the SF model is applicable. Note that the short run and long run interests of some factor owners can differ (e.g. labor in sector 1 (L_1) and capital in sector 2 (K_2)). Note also that, in contrast to the Stolper–Samuelson case, workers and capital owners within the same industry might, at some stage, jointly demand either free trade or protection.

Problem 6.1: Suppose instead that labor is the immobile factor except in the long run. Capital is therefore mobile except in the short run where both factors are immobile. Fill in the cells of Table 6.1 corresponding to that particular case. Make statements over the consequences of a tariff on good 2 for the reward of the immobile factor in general.

Empirical analysis

As discussed above, the SF and H–O–S models offer alternative predictions about the way a society's lobbying activities might be organized. With imperfect factor mobility, the SF model predicts coalitions based largely on industry affiliation whereas the H–O–S model, in assuming perfect factor mobility, predicts coalitions based solely on factor ownership (i.e. the Stolper–Samuelson case).

Magee (1980) examined the empirical merits of these predictions about lobbying activity by considering three hypotheses, each of which corresponds to the prediction of the Stolper–Samuelson theorem:

- *Marxian hypothesis*: capitalists and workers will oppose each other on the issue of free trade or protection in an industry, capital favoring free trade and labor favoring protection if the country is capital abundant and labor scarce (underlying assumptions of Table 6.1).
- *Unanimity hypothesis*: each factor will favor either free trade (capital) or protection (labor) but not both (see third row of Table 6.1).
- *Independence hypothesis*: a factor's position does not depend on whether it works in the export sector or in the import-competing sector.

To test each proposition, Magee used data on the position taken by labor unions and industry trade associations on the issue of either increasing or reducing protection during US Congressional hearings on the US Trade Reform Act of 1973.

With respect to the first proposition, Table 6.2 shows the pairing of interests in 21 of the 33 US industries where both labor and capital (i.e. the industry association) expressed an unambiguous preference. These results are contrary to the H–O–S model since the two interest groups adopted a common position on trade policy in all but two industries (tobacco and petroleum).

If the country in question were capital abundant, the unanimity hypothesis would imply that, in all industries, capital would favor free trade while labor

Table 6.2 *Lobbying on the 1973 Trade Reform Act: industry agreement (disagreement) of labor and capital*

		Position of the industry's labor	
		Protection	*Freer trade*
Position of the industry's capital owners	Protection	Distilling, Shoes, Chemicals, Textiles, Stone products, Apparel, Iron & steel, Cutlery, Plastics, Hardware, Rubber shoes, Bearings, Leather, Watches	Tobacco
	Freer trade	Petroleum	Paper, Machinery Trucks, Aviation, Tractors

Source: Magee (1980).

Table 6.3   *Free trade or protection: labor's and capital's position, by industry*

	Industry	Protection	Free trade	Odds ratio
Capital (obs. = 24)	Import-competing	10 ($p_{11} = 0.42$)	3 ($p_{12} = 0.12$)	4.0
	Export	5 ($p_{21} = 0.21$)	6 ($p_{22} = 0.25$)	
Labor (obs. = 21)	Import-competing	11 ($p_{11} = 0.52$)	1 ($p_{12} = 0.05$)	8.8
	Export	5 ($p_{21} = 0.24$)	4 ($p_{22} = 0.19$)	

Source: Magee (1980).

would favor protection. Table 6.2 reveals no such unanimity for the (capital-abundant) United States. This finding is corroborated in an even larger sample of industries than that reported here.[7] Again, these findings are consistent with the theoretical predictions of the SF model (see the first and second row of Table 6.1) and do not support Stolper–Samuelson's factor mobility assumption.

The third hypothesis states that a factor's preferred policy is independent of the industry in which it works. Table 6.3 shows, for each factor, its policy preference versus its industry affiliation. Each cell measures responses as both an absolute count and as a proportion of the total number of observations. For example, 10 of the 24 (42%) capitalists associated with the import-competing sector preferred protection.

The odds ratio shown in Table 6.3 is defined as $(p_{11}/p_{12})/(p_{21}/p_{22})$, where p_{ij} is the proportion of responses in cell (i, j) relative to the number of observations. The numerator of this ratio measures the preference for protection versus free trade for a factor working in the import-competing sector; the denominator measures this relative preference for a factor working in an export sector. A value of unity therefore implies independence between industry affiliation and a factor's preferences whereas values above unity favor the SF model since this implies low values for p_{12} and p_{21}.

Table 6.3 indicates that the odds of capital in the import-competing sector favoring protection are four times those of capital in the export sector; for labor the odds ratio is 8.8. Statistically, the hypothesis of independence can be rejected at the 5% level of significance for capital and at the 10% level of significance for labor.[8]

6.2 The international mobility of factors

In this section we relax the H–O–S assumption of international factor immobility and examine the coexistence of international trade in goods and factors. One issue in this context is whether goods flows and factor flows are substitutes or complements. Another issue is the possibility of 2-way movements of factors, particularly capital. This section can be regarded as an extension of the analysis of international factor mobility in Section 3.3 to the case of 2 factors. Chapter 1 provides a factual basis for this analysis.

Substitutability of goods and factors

Mundell (1957) is credited with the first formal analysis of the interaction between the international flow of goods and factors. Adopting the H–O–S model, but relaxing the assumption of international factor immobility, Mundell derived the following result:

Proposition 6.1 (Mundell): An increase in trade impediments stimulates factor movements and an increase in restrictions to factor movements stimulates trade.

In extreme form, this result implies that if factors are internationally mobile then trade in goods will cease. More generally, the result states that goods trade and factor flows are substitutes. Below we examine the analysis that establishes the first part of this proposition.[9]

Consider a trading equilibrium for a small economy such as that depicted in Figure 6.3. Production occurs at point Q, consumption is at point D, and good 2 is imported at the free trade price p_w. The country's post-trade level of income, measured in terms of numeraire good 1, is OY. This equilibrium assumes trade has equalized factor prices between countries and that factors are internationally immobile. If factors were now allowed to move internationally, no flows would in fact take place since factor prices have already equalized between countries. Therefore, to generate an international flow of factors we must introduce a difference in factor returns.

Assume the country depicted in Figure 6.3 now imposes a prohibitive tariff on the labor-intensive good 2. By definition, this will cause trade to cease as production moves to the autarky point Q_a. Since good 2 is labor-intensive, the resulting increase in the production of good 2 will, by the Stolper–Samuelson theorem, raise labor's marginal product and lower capital's marginal product. If we now allow labor to be internationally mobile, the rise in labor's marginal product will induce an inflow of labor from the rest of the world. By assumption, output prices and factor

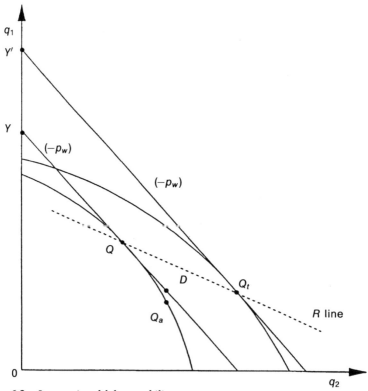

Figure 6.3   *International labor mobility*

marginal products are constant in the rest of the world. Consequently, the inflow of labor will continue until factor rewards in the tariff imposing country return to their pre-tariff level. Hence, with marginal products unchanged, so also is the real income accruing to domestic factors. This means that the post-tariff consumption point must lie along the pre-tariff income line YQ in Figure 6.3, that is, consumption will remain at point D.

Whereas the income of domestic factors is unchanged, some production now takes place using foreign labor and thus a part of the economy's income must be paid to these foreign workers. This implies that the new production equilibrium must generate income greater than OY so that, once the wage payments are remitted abroad, the country will retain its original, pre-tariff, income level OY. The production equilibrium satisfying this requirement is Q_t in Figure 6.3. Production at Q_t is feasible since the inflow of labor expands the country's transformation curve. That Q_t is the new equilibrium production point is confirmed by noting that at any production point to the left of Q_t, and along the Rybczynski line, the country would need to import good 2 (since consumption must take place at D). However, imports are not possible due to the prohibitive tariff. At Q_t, income from production (GDP) is OY'. Of this income, OY (GNP) is retained by domestic factors, YY' is remitted abroad as payment to the 'imported' labor and is financed by an equal amount of exports of good 1.

Given this new equilibrium, the tariff could be completely removed without affecting production, consumption, or trade. That is, by prohibiting trade in goods but allowing international factor mobility, the resulting equalization of factor rewards has resulted in the equalization of goods prices. This is just the factor price equalization theorem 'turned on its head' to become a commodity price equalization theorem.

As Mundell shows, the above result does not depend on the tariff rate – any positive tariff will eliminate the trade in goods. The assumption that the country is small (i.e. faces constant terms of trade) is also unimportant. Rather, the important assumptions are those which ensure factor price equalization, including incomplete specialization. It is also important that only one country imposes the restriction on trade. If both countries impose restrictions then trade need not vanish since both factor prices and commodity prices need not be equalized.

Problem 6.2: Show graphically the second part of the Mundell proposition – that is, an increase in restrictions to factor movements stimulates trade.

A simulation analysis: labor migration

The Mundell theorem establishes a substitutability between commodity and factor movements. If empirically valid, the theorem has an important policy implication: as international labor movements are sensitive to wage differentials (see (3.17)) countries can, by liberalizing their trade, reduce the wage differentials and thereby moderate the flux of foreign immigrants. Recent examples of such trade liberalization are the 1991 reunification of the Germanies and the 1993 Free Trade Agreement between Mexico and the United States. This section focuses on the labor flows between Mexico and the United States.

Hill and Méndez (1984) have simulated the impact of liberalized commodity trade on Mexican migration to the United States. This is accomplished by applying the H–O–S general equilibrium model of Chapter 4 to two economies, the United States and Mexico, both producing manufactures (M) and primary goods (P) by means of capital and labor. Both countries are assumed to be small in world markets and to use a constant elasticity of substitution (CES) technology in each sector i ($i = M, P$) with σ_i

being the elasticity of factor substitution. In the case of Mexico, Hill and Méndez amend the H–O–S model by specifying a dual labor market according to Harris and Todaro's (1970) specification:

$$w_M = \overline{w}_M \tag{6.6}$$

$$w_p = w_M(L_M/(\overline{L} - L_p)) \tag{6.7}$$

where $\overline{L}$ is labor supply and L_i is i's sectoral employment ($i = M, P$). By (6.6), the nominal wage rate in the manufacturing sector is set by institutions. By (6.7), the intersectorally mobile labor equates the wage rate in the P sector to the expected wage rate in the M sector. The ratio $L_M/(\overline{L} - L_p)$ proxies the probability of finding employment in the M sector. (6.6) and (6.7) solve for w_p and the equilibrium level of unemployment.[10]

Table 6.4 contains the simulated effects of eliminating all Mexican and all US trade restrictions on the Mexican real wage, on the US real wage and on the net supply of Mexican immigrants to the United States. Prior to obtaining these results, country estimates of the parameters of the model were extracted from the empirical literature and country data were used to solve, first for the initial equilibrium with trade barriers, and then for the equilibrium of free trade.

Table 6.4 is divided into four rows, each corresponding to a different set of elasticities of factor substitution in the M and P sectors. This table is also divided into four columns, the first two giving the percentage change in the real wage in Mexico and the United States respectively, the last two giving

Table 6.4　*The effect of Mexican and US trade liberalization on Mexican migration[a]*

Assumed elasticities of substitution	US real wage[b] (1)	Mexican real wage[b] (2)	Immigrant supply $\varepsilon = 0.5$[c] (3)	Immigrant supply $\varepsilon = 2.0$[c] (4)
$\sigma_M = \sigma_p = 0.5$	−6.0	7.6	−6.8	−27.2
$\sigma_M = \sigma_p = 1.0$	−5.3	6.7	−6.1	−24.0
$\sigma_M = 0.5, \quad \sigma_p = 1.0$	−7.1	10.6	−8.9	−35.6
$\sigma_M = 1.0, \quad \sigma_p = 0.5$	−4.7	0.8	−2.8	−11.0

Notes:
[a] % changes with respect to the initial trade-distorted equilibrium.
[b] The real wage is the weighted average of nominal wages divided by the weighted average of goods prices.
[c] ε = wage elasticity of Mexican immigrant supply.
Sources: Hill and Méndez (1984), tables 2 and 3.

the response of the net supply of Mexican immigrants according to a wage elasticity of immigrant supply (ε) of 0.5 and 2.0 (column (3) and (4), respectively).

The simulation results of Table 6.4 indicate that a bilateral free trade policy between Mexico and the United States would increase the Mexican real wage somewhere between 0.8 and 10.6%. Unlike in Mexico, a free trade policy in the United States would lead to a decrease in the US real wage ranging from 5.3 to 7.1%. The subtraction of column (2) from column (1) gives an approximation of the change in the ratio of real United States–Mexican wages, that falls by 5.5 to 17.7%. The latter numbers multiplied by either 0.5 or 2.0 gives the approximated percentage change in Mexican migration to the United States. A striking feature of the results is their large dispersion and their low absolute values. The largest reduction occurs when $\varepsilon = 2.0$ and σ_p exceeds σ_m but, even then, the maximum reduction of 35.4% is a very modest outcome.

Problem 6.3: Work out the computer program of the small open economy of Problem 5.1 to allow for international labor movements. Assume the wage elasticity of the latter is 2.0 ($\varepsilon = 2.0$), maintain $\tau_2 = 0.1$ and compare the results of the tariff with and without international labor movements. Interpret the results.

Case for complementarity

Correlations between the international flow of goods and factors offer mixed evidence on the above proposition of substitutability. Analysis of international labor flows to the EC corroborates substitutability (see Chapter 1) but casual observation suggests complementarity between long term capital flows and goods trade. This has led some to search for an explanation of such complementarity within the context of received trade models.

The theory

Markusen's (1983) analysis offers one such attempt. The model assumes a world of 2 identical countries (including identical factor endowments) and all H–O–S assumptions satisfied. As such, the initial equilibrium is one of no trade. Given this, it is then asked which assumption, when relaxed, would lead to (1) trade; (2) an inequality in factor rewards across countries; and (3) a relatively high price for the factor used intensively in the production of a country's export good. The latter condition ensures that once factor mobility is allowed, there will be an inflow of the country's abundant factor. The motives for trade examined by Markusen include a foreign production tax, monopoly, returns to scale, factor taxes and differences in production technology. We only take up the case of a foreign production tax.

Assume two identical countries and let point *A* in Figure 6.4 denote each country's autarky equilibrium along its production possibilities curve $T_1 T_2$. Now suppose the foreign country imposes an *ad valorem* tax on the production of labor-intensive good 2. Since the tax lowers the price to producers and raises the price to consumers, the foreign country's autarky equilibrium will move to a point such as *B*. Since autarky prices are now different across countries, allowing trade gives rise to home country exporting good 2. Why? Assuming internationally immobile factors, trade will cause the relative price facing consumers in each country to converge to the world price p_w. At this price, the home country produces at point *H* and consumes at point *C* whereas the foreign country produces at point *F* and consumes at point *D*. Balanced trade is implied by the equality of the distances *CH* and *DF*.

Whereas home country producers receive the world price p_w, foreign country producers receive the net price $p_d^* = p_w / (1 + \tau^*)$, where τ^* is the *ad valorem* rate of tax. This gap in producer prices implies a cross-country difference in factor rewards. Since $p_d^* < p_w$, it must be that labor earns more, and capital earns less, in the home than in the foreign country. Hence, if factors are allowed to flow across borders, the home country will attract foreign labor and generate an outflow of capital. As such, the home (foreign) country's supply of capital relative to labor falls (rises). As

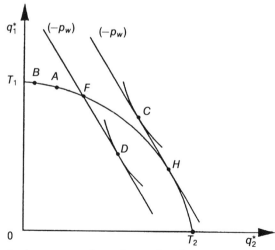

Figure 6.4 *Production tax as a determinant of trade*

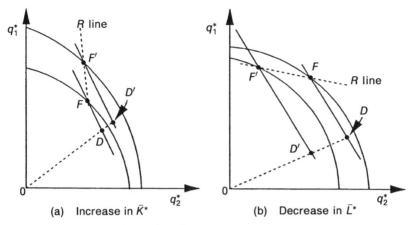

Figure 6.5 *Factor mobility and trade*

established below, these factor movements imply that the volume of trade between the two countries will increase. Hence we have the result that factor movements lead to an increased willingness of countries to trade and, in this sense, factor movements and trade in goods are complementary.[11]

We now establish that trade will increase as each country receives more (less) of the factor used intensively in the production of its export (import) good. Consider the foreign country which experiences an increase in its capital stock and a decrease in its labor force. As shown in panel (a) of Figure 6.5, the increase in capital shifts the production point from F to F' along the Rybczynski line (R line). Moreover, the inflow of capital raises aggregate income and, since preferences are assumed homothetic, consumption moves from D to D'. Consequently, the new trade vector becomes $F'D'$, which exceeds the initial trade vector FD.

Panel (b) of Figure 6.5 shows the separate effect of the shrinking of the labor endowment. In this case, the labor outflow shrinks production from F to F' along the Rybczynski line while consumption moves from D to D'. Again, the new trade vector $F'D'$ exceeds the initial trade vector FD. Repeating this analysis for all possible terms of trade confirms the proposition that trade will rise if factor movements raise the relative supply of the factor used intensively in the export industry.

A final remark concerns the equalization of factor rewards across countries. Because the production tax creates a wedge between the world price and the price received by foreign producers, the equilibria explained thus far do not involve an equality of factor rewards between countries. Hence, factors will continue to flow between countries which will push them toward complete specialization in production. Only when one country reaches specialization can factor rewards be equalized.

Empirical analysis: complementarity or substitution?

Having presented alternative theoretical models that predict opposite results concerning the relationship between the international trade in goods and in factors, it is a matter of empirical research to characterize this relationship. The main reference of this section is Wong (1988), who estimated the effects of the movements of capital and labor on the volume of trade and factor prices of the United States over the period 1948–83.

Consider the problem of a competitive economy that produces and exports two goods, durables (d), non-durables and services (n), and imports non-domestically produced goods and services (m). There are three primary factors, land (a), labor (l) and capital (k), available in the fixed quantity $e = (e_a, e_l, e_k)$. This economy trades freely with the rest of the world at the vector of fixed prices $p = (p_d, p_n, p_m)$ and gives a transfer of b abroad.

The production technology is represented by the revenue function $G(p, e)$.[12] The preferences of the consumers are represented by the indirect trade utility (ITU) function $T(p, e, b)$. This function, first introduced by Woodland (1980), gives the maximum level of utility $V(p, G(p, e) - b)$ that this economy achieves at the fixed prices p and the national expenditure $G(p, e) - b$. The usefulness of using the ITU function follows from the following derivatives:

$$\frac{\partial T(p, e, b)}{\partial p} = \lambda(q - d) \equiv \lambda x(p, e, b) \tag{6.8}$$

$$\frac{\partial T(p, e, b)}{\partial e} = \lambda w(p, e, b) \tag{6.9}$$

$$\frac{\partial T(p, e, b)}{\partial b} = -\lambda \tag{6.10}$$

where λ is the marginal utility of income, w is the vector of factor prices, q, d and x, are the vectors of commodity supply, commodity demand and net exports respectively.

The functional form that has been chosen for T and G for the purpose of econometric estimation is the transcendental logarithmic (translog). A first advantage of a translog function is that it takes explicit account of the constraints imposed by homogeneity and symmetry. A second advantage of the function is that, by making use of (6.8)–(6.10) combined with (4.35) and (4.36), the shares of net exports in the domestic expenditure, $p_j x_j / (G - b)$, and the shares of factor payments in the domestic product, $w_h e_h / G$, are dependent upon all domestic endowments, all commodity prices and the

Table 6.5 *Elasticities of exports and imports with respect to factor supply*[a]

Year	ε_{dk}	ε_{dl}	ε_{nk}	ε_{nl}	ε_{mk}	ε_{ml}
1948	0.4041	0.2044	−0.0492	0.8158	0.2237	0.8494
1953	0.6678	0.7846	0.0325	1.7120	0.3038	1.2146
1958	0.6277	0.7005	0.0137	1.4305	0.2880	1.1170
1963	0.6539	0.7932	0.0489	1.4579	0.3448	1.2884
1968	0.6513	1.0108	0.1229	1.7957	0.3517	1.3466
1973	0.6211	1.3890	0.1681	1.7248	0.3679	1.5378
1978	0.6661	1.5688	0.3589	2.0711	0.4282	1.5624
1983	0.7028	1.4878	0.4249	2.1900	0.4496	1.5295
Standard error[b]	0.1283	0.1794	0.1173	0.1659	0.0041	0.0170

Notes:
[a] ε_{jh} = Elasticity of exports ($j = d, n$) and of imports ($j = m$) with respect to factor endowments ($h = l, k$).
[b] Standard errors are calculated using the values of variables for 1972.
Source: Wong (1988).

transfer b ($j = d, n, m; h = a, l, k$). Our particular interest lies in the estimated response of the vector of net exports with respect to the vector of endowments.

Table 6.5 shows the elasticities ε_{jh} ($j = d, n, m; h = l, k$) of exports and imports with respect to labor and capital endowments. There are two main conclusions that can be made from Table 6.5. First, all elasticities in the table are significantly different from zero. Second, and more importantly, all elasticities are positive except in one year for ε_{nk} suggesting, for the United States, a strong complementarity result between factor supplies and international trade. This implies that any increase in US factor endowments causes an increase in the volume of US trade (exports and imports) with the rest of the world.

Problem 6.4: A comparison of the columns of Table 6.5 suggests that $\varepsilon_{dk} > \varepsilon_{mk} > \varepsilon_{nk}$ and that, except for some years, $\varepsilon_{nl} > \varepsilon_{ml} > \varepsilon_{dl}$. Given this, which of the goods is capital-intensive and labor-intensive? What are the assumptions about demand that allow such characterization? Explain.

2-way capital flows

Chapter 1 has shown that capital flows predominantly between industrialized countries and that it flows in both directions for the same country pair. The first characteristic relates to the complementarity of trade and factor flows discussed above. The second relates to the 'cross-hauling' of foreign direct investment (FDI), or 2-way capital flows. As the latter observation cannot be explained by the Markusen model, we now expand on a model by Jones *et al.* (1983) to explain 2-way capital flows in the context of a competitive trade model.

The model is a specific-factors model of a small country producing a traded (T) good and a non-traded (N) good.[13] Labor is assumed to be mobile across sectors but internationally immobile. Capital, by contrast, is assumed to be sector-specific but internationally mobile. Also the supply of capital is perfectly elastic at a fixed rental rate determined on the world market. Below we first determine the equilibrium wage rate and output prices. We then establish the equilibrium allocation of capital and labor in each sector. Finally, we use comparative statics to derive conditions under which capital flows between countries.

Whereas the price of traded goods $\bar{p}_T$ is fixed on world markets, the price of non-traded goods p_N is determined domestically through a market clearing condition: $d_N = q_N$. Given this, Figure 6.6 illustrates the equilibrium in this model. Since the rentals $\bar{r}_N$, $\bar{r}_T$, and price of traded goods ($\bar{p}_T$), are given on world markets, the only variables left to determine would appear to be the wage rate and the price of non-traded goods. However, even the wage rate cannot be freely determined in this model. To see this, note that since $\bar{p}_T$ is fixed, so too is the position of its iso-price curve. Given this, the exogeneity of $\bar{r}_t$ means that the wage rate must be w_0 if the traded goods sector is to cover its costs. With w_0 thus completely determined, p_N must adjust endogenously so as to cover costs as well.

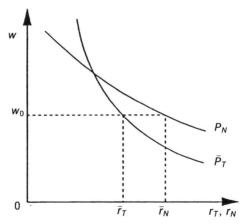

Figure 6.6 *Determination of capital rentals and the wage rate*

We now determine the equilibrium allocations of capital and labor. The demand for labor and capital in each sector ($j = N, T$) is given by:

$$L_j = a_{jl}q_j \tag{6.11}$$

$$K_j = a_{jk}q_j \tag{6.12}$$

where a_{jh} is the input requirement of factor h ($h = l, k$) per-unit of output j. Substituting these expressions into the domestic labor constraint $L_N + L_T = L$ and after some manipulation we obtain:

$$K_N/k_N(\bar{\omega}_N) + K_T/k_T(\bar{\omega}_T) = L \tag{6.13}$$

here $k_j(\cdot) = a_{jk}/a_{jl}$ and $\bar{\omega}_j = w_0/\bar{r}_j$ are sector j's capital–labor and wage–rental ratio, respectively. Hence, for fixed world prices ($\bar{p}_T, \bar{r}_N, \bar{r}_T$), $\bar{\omega}_j$ and thus $k_j(\cdot)$ are fixed. (6.13) thus gives the combinations of capital in each sector that are consistent with the domestic supply of labor and the sectoral capital–labor ratios. In Figure 6.7, (6.13) is graphed as the line KK with ordinate $K_T = k_T(\cdot)L$, abscissa $K_N = k_N(\cdot)L$ and slope $-[k_T(\cdot)/k_N(\cdot)]$.

As long as world prices are unchanged, the domestic commodity and factor prices remain unchanged and, with given national supplies of labor (L) and capital (unspecified in this model), the economy has constant aggregate income. Hence, the demands for the traded and non-traded goods are determined. Since $d_N = q_N$, the total capital requirement in sector N is:

$$K_N = a_{Nk}d_N \tag{6.14}$$

The corresponding equilibrium is point A in Figure 6.7 where, after deriving K_N from (6.14), K_T is determined from the KK line. Using Figure 6.7, we can

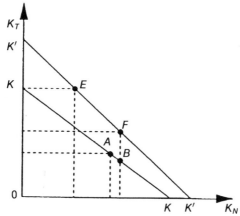

Figure 6.7 *Sectoral demand for capital*

generate conditions under which 'cross-hauling' of capital may occur following exogenous shocks. Consider a shift in consumer preferences in favor of the non-traded good, that is, with the same income and relative commodity prices, more N goods are consumed. In Figure 6.7, this shift in preferences moves the equilibrium from A to B, which requires an inflow of capital into the N sector and an outflow from the T sector, implying cross-hauling.

Another shock of this type would be an exogenous increase in the labor supply. This would cause the KK locus to shift outwards to $K'K'$. Several points on this locus can be hypothesized as the new equilibrium, depending upon how consumers use the marginal increase in income (marginal product of labor times the increase in the labor supply). At a point like F, implying an inflow of capital in both sectors, more of both goods is consumed. Alternatively, at a point such as E, which implies cross-hauling, there has been a shift in demand toward traded goods. The general result that seems to come from this model is that 2-way capital flows are more likely to result from a disturbance that is sector-specific than one which is economywide.

Problem 6.5:   Indicate how an increase in the world price of traded goods ($\bar{p}_T$) and in the capital rentals ($\bar{r}_N, \bar{r}_T$) affects the graphical solutions of Figure 6.6 and Figure 6.7. Are 2-way capital flows likely to result from these increases?

6.3 **Minimum wage unemployment**

Most economies in Northern America and Western Europe subject their entire labor market to a minimum wage floor. Specifics of the minimum wage regulation, though, vary across countries. Five EC member states (France, Luxembourg, the Netherlands, Portugal and Spain) set a statutory national minimum wage. In Belgium and Greece by contrast, the general minimum wage is laid down by national collective agreement. Other members set minimum rates of pay by industry level collective agreement (Denmark, Germany and Italy) or for certain industries only through special bodies (Wages Councils in the United Kingdom and Joint Labour Committees in Ireland).[14]

This section modifies the H–O–S model to include a minimum wage restriction, thereby introducing the possibility of unemployment. The central reference is Brecher (1974) who showed how this modification invalidates a number of the standard trade theory results, including the desirability of free trade relative to no trade. Since minimum wage regulation is increasingly under attack, how removing such regulation would affect trade and production is also addressed.

Production and employment

Proceeding from the 2-commodity, 2-factor model of Section 4.1, we assume that the entire economy is subjected to an exogenously specified real wage floor.[15] The real wage floor, defined in terms of good 2, is specified as the level $\bar{F}_2^L$.[16] Hence, the conditions for labor market equilibrium are modified to reflect that the equality of marginal products is now possible only for real wages greater than or equal to the wage floor:

$$\frac{1}{p} F_1^L(K_1, L_1) = F_2^L(K_2, L_2) \geq \bar{F}_2^L \tag{6.15}$$

where $p = p_2/p_1$ and, F_j^L is labor's marginal product in industry j $(j = 1, 2)$.[17] In addition, since the wage floor may exceed the wage required for full employment, the full employment constraint must be modified to allow for unemployment:

$$L_1 + L_2 = L < \bar{L} \tag{6.16}$$

where $\bar{L}$ denotes the economy's total labor supply and L denotes actual employment. The full employment of capital is assured by assuming that capital's reward remains perfectly flexible. We now examine how the wage constraint modifies an economy's production possibilities.

Unlike the standard model, changes in output prices in a minimum wage economy may not result in variations in the wage–rental ratio but result instead in changes in employment. To demonstrate this, we need to see how a minimum wage modifies the traditional full employment production possibility frontier (PPF).

In Figure 6.8, $T_2 R_2 T_1$ is the traditional PPF whereas $T_2 R_2 R_1 T_1$ is the PPF derived under the wage constraint. Frontier $T_2 R_2 R_1 T_1$ is derived by first assuming that constraint (6.15) holds with equality at a tangency point such as R_2 (with associated prices p^0). Given this, we can now derive the three segments $T_2 R_2$, $R_2 R_1$ and $R_1 T_1$.

Suppose the price of good 2 (the labor-intensive commodity) rises from p^0 to p^{00}. Appealing to Figure 4.6, the profit maximizing wage at prices p^{00} will lie above the wage floor (assuming incomplete specialization). That is, the wage constraint is not binding at p^{00}, nor at any price above p^0. Given this, the production equilibrium associated with any price above p^0 will lie along a segment such as $T_2 R_2$, corresponding to a portion of the conventional PPF. The distance $T_2 R_2$ will fall if the level of the minimum wage is increased since, as shown in Figure 4.6, the output price at which the wage constraint is just binding will now be above p^0.

The segment $R_1 R_2$ is a Rybczynski line which shows, at prices p^0, the output combinations that result from successive reductions in the economy's total labor supply. At prices p^0, R_2 is a possible tangency point between the

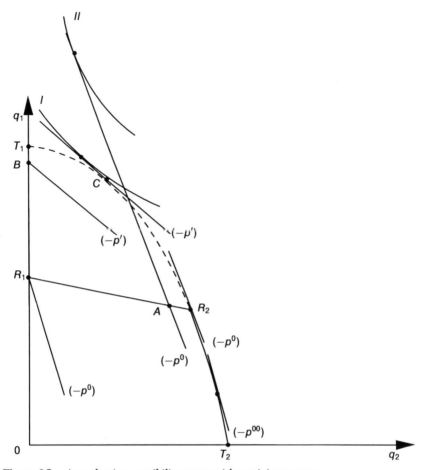

Figure 6.8   *A production possibility curve with a minimum wage*

price line and the transformation curve, but point A on an intermediate transformation curve with lower employment (not shown) is equally feasible. Hence, when $p = p^0$, there exist an infinite number of production equilibria consistent with the minimum wage floor, each equilibria reflecting a different level of unemployment. This production indeterminacy will be resolved once demand and international trade are introduced.

Now suppose the price ratio falls from p^0 to p'. This induces resources to shift from industry 2 to industry 1 and the tangency point moves down. Appealing once more to Figure 4.6, the profit maximizing, full employment, wage is now below the wage floor, hence the wage constraint is binding at prices below p^0. As such, the new production equilibrium cannot be located on the conventional segment R_2T_1. Instead, given the wage floor, the labor-intensive commodity 2 is now unprofitable at prices p', and therefore all resources will shift to industry 1. However, at the minimum wage, the capital-intensive industry 1 is unwilling to hire all the available labor and unemployment arises. The new production equilibrium will thus fall to B (the bottom of the R line through point C). At point B, the economy is completely specialized in producing good 1.

Note that the level of employment at B is higher than at R_1. To see this, note that $F_1^L(\cdot) = p^0 \overline{F}_2^L$ at R_1 and $F_1^L(\cdot) = p' \overline{F}_2^L$ at B. Since $p' < p^0$, labor's marginal product at R_1 ($F_1^L(\cdot)$) must therefore be higher than at B, and employment at B thus exceeds employment at R_1. Sufficiently small values of p are capable of achieving full employment at T_1.

International equilibrium

Figure 6.9 contrasts the excess demand curve for good 2 derived under a minimum wage assumption to that of the excess demand curve derived from the standard model (dotted line). At prices below p_{min}, the economy is fully employed and completely specialized in good 1. For prices in the interval $p_{min} \le p < p^0$, the economy specializes in good 1 but there is unemployment (which decreases demand for all commodities). When price equals p^0, production is indeterminate and good 2 could be either exported or imported. For price in the interval $p^0 < p \le p_{max}$, the economy is fully employed and both goods are produced. Conversely, for prices $p > p_{max}$, the economy is fully employed and completely specialized in good 2.[18] World

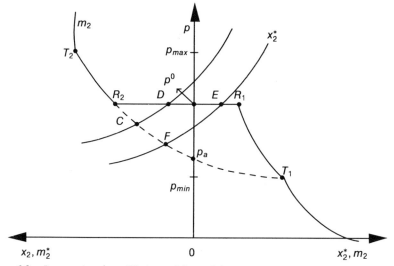

Figure 6.9 *International equilibrium with a minimum wage*

equilibrium occurs at a point such as *D*, where the domestic excess demand curve for good 2 intersects the foreign excess supply. At this price, domestic and foreign markets are in equilibrium and, by the underlying equilibrium relationship between the product–price ratio and the level of employment discussed above, the level of domestic unemployment is determined.

Is free trade optimal?

We now ask if free trade remains desirable in the presence of a minimum wage. If we assume the economy exports good 1, the opening of trade will involve a fall in p (a terms of trade improvement). As such, a movement to free trade is equivalent to the change in price from p^{00} to p' in Figure 6.8. As seen above, this would result in unemployment and lower welfare as the economy moves to production point *B*. Hence, free trade may be inferior to no trade. Using the same logic one can also establish that (1) an increase in foreign demand for home exports may be detrimental to the home country and (2) for given terms of trade, a country's optimal trade policy is not necessarily free trade.

Removing the wage floor

Minimum pay regulations have come under increasing attack in a number of countries as certain employer organizations claim that these regulations hinder recruitment. It is also argued that removing a wage floor will restore full employment.[19] The preceding analysis appears to support such claims since, as the minimum wage is decreased, the excess demand curve for commodity 2 approaches that of the standard model with full employment. However, while removing the wage floor completely restores full employment, this policy may have undesired effects. Figure 6.9 illustrates two possibilities.

Let the initial international equilibrium be at point *D* so that good 1 is imported, good 2 exported and the world price is p^0. Removal of the minimum wage would cause the relative price of commodity 2 to decline as the international equilibrium moves from *D* to *C*. This constitutes an unambiguous worsening of the terms of trade and thus lower welfare.

Now suppose the initial equilibrium is at point *E* with commodity 2 now imported. Removing the minimum wage again implies a decline in the relative price of commodity 2, but this price decline may or may not imply a worsening of the terms of trade. If the foreign excess supply curve is sufficiently elastic, the new equilibrium could occur at a point like *F*. If so, commodity 2 is now exported and the decline in relative price would again be detrimental for the home country. On the other hand, if the excess supply curve were sufficiently inelastic, the new equilibrium point (not drawn) could lie in the same quadrant as E which preserves the direction of trade. In this case the price decline would represent an improvement in the terms of trade. Lastly, if good 2 is labor-intensive, the decline in its relative price may reduce welfare. Such a case is shown in Figure 6.8 by comparing the welfare level before (II) removing the wage floor to the welfare level (I) after removal.[20]

Problem 6.6: Using the logic of Section 6.3 (pp. 251–2), show that (1) an increase in foreign demand for home exports may be detrimental to the home country and (2) for given terms of trade, a country's optimal trade policy is not necessarily free trade.

6.4 **Concluding remarks**

The seeming lack of empirical support for the predictions of the factor endowments theory led to a systematic search for alternative trade models. This chapter considered three such attempts, each relaxing one of the assumptions of the H–O–S model. The specific factors model was considered first. It assumes some factors are domestically immobile. In this model, a price shock leads to transitional changes in the real income of factor owners which differ from the income changes predicted by the H–O–S model. Also, the specific factors model explains the phenomenon that coalitions for or against trade policy issues would form on the basis of industry affiliation rather than factor ownership (laborers, capitalists, land owners, . . .), as predicted by the H–O–S model.

If the international mobility of factors is allowed, trade in goods and international factor movements are substitutes in the standard H–O–S model. However, if trade in commodities is not based on the difference in factor endowments, then trade and factor flows can be complementary. More specifically, trade in factors causes trade in commodities. Other types of models that explain 2-way capital flows put forward the conclusion that interindustry capital flows are more likely to result from a disturbance that is sector-specific rather than economywide.

The introduction in the H–O–S model of a binding minimum wage floor implies that part of the labor force becomes unemployed. With minimum wage unemployment, a country's welfare may fall upon the opening of trade and free trade is not necessarily the optimal trade policy. In addition, removing the wage floor can cause a country's pattern of trade to reverse.

Notes

1. See the Leontief paradox and the measurement of intra-industry trade.
2. See Appendix 1 (p. 153).
3. Real income in terms of good 1 (w/p_1) and good 2 (w/p_2) corresponds to the intercepts of a worker's budget constraint. If w/p_1 and w/p_2 change in opposite directions then a knowledge of a worker's preferences is needed to determine his/ her change in real income (level of utility). Ruffin and Jones (1977) call this the 'neoclassical ambiguity'.
4. These changes in capital's marginal product as labor alone is changed derive from the technological complementarity between capital and labor inherent in the two factor, neoclassical, production function.
5. The comparison of (6.4) and (6.5) suggests two other remarks. First, equalization of commodity prices through free trade will in general not lead to the equalization of factor rewards in the short and medium run. Second, one appealing element of the SF model is that (6.4) holds regardless of the assumption over the relative factor supply while the Stolper–Samuelson result (6.5) depends critically on it.
6. In sector 2, w rises to $w_2 = (1 + \hat{p}_d)w_0$ and r rises to $r_2 = (1 + \hat{p}_d)r_0$, where $r_0 = w_0 = 1$.
7. In the overall sample, Magee found that 37% of the capital owners, and 24% of the labor unions, supported freer trade.
8. See Magee (1980) for more details on these significance tests.
9. We consider only the first part of the proposition since the second part follows by reversing the steps of the analysis.
10. Unemployment in a 2-sector model is also discussed in Section 6.3. There, a binding minimum wage floor for the whole economy will create an excess supply of labor.
11. It is important to note that in the H–O–S model, the difference in factor endowment is the cause of trade in commodities. In Markusen's model, trade in commodities is the result of other determinants of comparative advantage and of differences in factor endowments that emerge endogenously in response to these determinants of comparative advantage.
12. The properties of the revenue function are given by (4.35) and (4.36) and further explored on pp. 129–31.
13. It is Caves' (1971) analysis of FDI which initiated this strand of literature.
14. For an overview of the minimum wage regulation in the United States, see Card and Krueger (1995).
15. The exogeneity of the restriction is taken to reflect the existence of an institutional body which sets and enforces the regulation.
16. One could also express the real minimum wage in terms of good 1 or in terms of a constant utility combination of goods 1 and 2.
17. This type of economy wide constraint (6.15) adequately represents wage floor regulation in all EC member states except Denmark, Germany, Ireland, Italy and the United Kingdom. In the latter countries, the wage floor can be imposed in only one sector. In such cases, labor mobility between sectors can still equalize value marginal products as in (6.15). Alternatively, the minimum wage could be

rigid in money terms. But as Johnson (1969) noted, the last two methods of expressing a wage floor need not lead to unemployment.

18. In Figure 6.9, the section from T_1 to the horizontal axis is the demand function for good 2 with full employment. The segment $T_1 R_1$ is the demand function for good 2 with unemployment. The segments $R_1 R_2$, $R_2 T_2$, and above T_2 are the excess demand for (difference between demand for and supply of) good 2 since positive production of good 2 occurs only at prices greater than or equal to p^0.

19. Some argue this to be a highly persistent misconception. Card and Krueger (1995), for example, have empirically demonstrated that a rise in the minimum wage increases employment in some sectors.

20. Applications of the minimum wage model are mainly theoretical and include Brecher (1980) and Viaene (1987) among others. Brecher examines factor accumulation and finds that for a small country (fixed terms of trade), foreign investment might worsen, rather than improve, employment and welfare. In a similar vein, Viaene found that the existence of a minimum wage reduced the possibility of favorable welfare and employment effects from the Netherlands' policy of land reclamation.

References and additional reading

Specific factors model

Ethier, W.J. (1987), 'The Theory of International Trade', in Officer, L.M. (ed.), *International Economics* (Boston: Kluwer Academic), 1–57.

Fels, J. and Gundlach, E. (1990), 'More Evidence on the Puzzle of Interindustry Wage Differentials: The Case of West Germany', *Weltwirtschaftliches Archiv*, 3, 544–60.

Grossman, G.M. and Levinsohn, J.A. (1989), 'Import Competition and the Stock Market Return to Capital', *American Economic Review*, 79(5), 1065–87.

Hillman, A.L. (1989), *The Political Economy of Protection* (Chur: Harwood Academic).

Katz, L.F. and Summers, L.H. (1989), 'Industry Rents: Evidence and Implications', in Baily, M.N. and Winston, C. (eds), *Brookings Papers on Economic Activity: Microeconomics* (Washington, DC: Brookings Institution), 208–75.

Kohli, U. (1993), 'US Technology and the Specific-Factors Model', *Journal of International Economics*, 34, 115–36.

Krueger, A.B. and Summers, L.H. (1988), 'Efficiency Wages and the Inter-industry Wage Structure', *Econometrica*, 56, 259–93.

Magee, S.P. (1980), 'Three Simple Tests of the Stolper–Samuelson Theorem', in Oppenheimer, P. (ed.), *Issues in International Economics* (London: Oriel Press), 138–53.

Neary, J.P. (1978), 'Short-Run Capital Specificity and the Pure Theory of International Trade', *Economic Journal*, 88, 488–510.

Ruffin, R. and Jones, R. (1977), 'Protection and Real Wages: The Neo-Classical Ambiguity', *Journal of Economic Theory*, 14, 337–48.

International factor mobility

Burgess, D.F. (1978), 'On the Distributional Effects of Direct Foreign Investment', *International Economic Review*, 19, 647–64.

Caves, R.E. (1971), 'International Corporations: The Industrial Economics of Foreign Investment', *Economica*, 38, 1–27.

Hill, J.K. and Méndez, J.A. (1984), 'The Effect of Commercial Policy on International Migration Flows: The Case of the United States and Mexico', *Journal of International Economics*, 17, 41–53.

Jones, R.W., Neary, J.P. and Ruane, F.P. (1983), 'Two-Way Capital Flows', *Journal of International Economics*, 14, 357–66.

Markusen, J.R. (1983), 'Factor Movements and Commodity Trade as Complements', *Journal of International Economics*, 14, 341–56.

Melvin, J.R. (1970), 'Commodity Taxation as a Determinant of Trade', *Canadian Journal of Economics*, 3, 62–78.

Mundell, R. (1957), 'International Trade and Factor Mobility', *American Economic Review*, 47, 321–35.

Wong, K.-Y. (1988), 'International Factor Mobility and the Volume of Trade: An Empirical Study', in Feenstra, R.C. (ed.), *Empirical Methods for International Trade* (Cambridge, Mass.: MIT Press), 231–50.

Wong, K.-Y. (1995), *International Trade in Goods and Factor Mobility* (Cambridge, Mass.: MIT Press).

Woodland, A.D. (1980), 'Direct and Indirect Trade Utility Functions', *Review of Economic Studies*, 47, 907–26.

Unemployment and minimum wage

Brecher, R.A. (1974), 'Minimum Wage Rates and the Pure Theory of International Trade', *Quarterly Journal of Economics*, 98–116.

Brecher, R.A. (1980), 'Increased Unemployment from Capital Accumulation in a Minimum-Wage Model of an Open Economy', *Canadian Journal of Economics*, 13, 152–8.

Card, D. and Krueger, A.B. (1995), *Myth and Measurement: the New Economics of the Minimum Wage* (Princeton: Princeton University Press).

Harris, J.R. and Todaro, M.P. (1970), 'Migration, Unemployment and Development: A Two-Sector Analysis', *American Economic Review*, 54, 961–74.

Johnson, H.G. (1969), 'Minimum Wage Laws: A General Equilibrium Analysis', *Canadian Journal of Economics*, 2, 599–604.

Viaene, J.-M. (1987), 'Factor Accumulation in a Minimum-Wage Economy', *European Economic Review*, 31, 1313–28.

■ *Chapter 7* ■

Higher Dimensional Issues

This chapter discusses extensions of the basic propositions of modern trade theory to arbitrary numbers of goods and factors. Following a review of the equilibrium conditions for a closed economy with N goods and H factors, we first consider a generalization of the concept of comparative advantage. We then focus on the factor abundance model and consider extensions of the Heckscher–Ohlin theorem, the Stolper–Samuelson and Rybczynski propositions, and finally the factor price equalization (FPE) theorem. Except for FPE, extension of these propositions normally involves a comparison of pre- and post-trade equilibrium conditions expressed in terms of an economy's domestic income and expenditure functions under the assumption that firms minimize costs and consumers maximize utility. The properties of the income and spending functions are then used to derive inequalities that are interpreted as *average* relationships that must hold between prices, outputs and inputs. For empirical purposes, these average relationships are interpreted as *correlations* that should exist between prices, outputs and inputs.

7.1 Autarky equilibrium with many goods and factors

Let $\mathbf{p} = (p_1, p_2, \ldots, p_N)$ be a vector of N product prices, $\mathbf{e} = (e_1, e_2, \ldots, e_H)$ a vector of H national factor supplies and $\mathbf{q} = (q_1, q_2, \ldots, q_N)$ a vector of national outputs. As discussed in Chapter 4, a country's GDP (gross domestic product) function $G(\mathbf{p}, \mathbf{e})$ gives the maximum income that the country can achieve when facing prices $\mathbf{p}$ and endowed with resource supplies $\mathbf{e}$. The GDP function is derived from the maximization of national income with respect to outputs for a given set of prices and subject to the constraint imposed by the economy's transformation function. Thus, $G(\mathbf{p}, \mathbf{e})$ depends upon technology as well as factor supplies. By definition,[1]

$$G(\mathbf{p}, \mathbf{e}) = \mathbf{pq} \tag{7.1}$$

where the outputs are those which maximize national income at prices $\mathbf{p}$ and are feasible – that is, can be produced from the given factor supplies and technology. By Hotelling's Lemma, differentiation of (7.1) with respect to the price of good i yields the output supply function of good i:

$$\frac{\partial G(\mathbf{p}, \mathbf{e})}{\partial p_i} = q_i(\mathbf{p}) \tag{7.2}$$

In Chapter 4 it was also shown that total income from production must equal the total payments to the factors of production:

$$G(\mathbf{p}, \mathbf{e}) = \mathbf{pq} = \mathbf{we} \tag{7.3}$$

where $\mathbf{w} = (w_1, w_2, \ldots, w_H)$ is the vector of equilibrium factor prices. This income identity implies a dual interpretation of $G(\mathbf{p}, \mathbf{e})$: it is the minimum amount that can be paid to an economy's factors and have the average cost of production no less than price in each industry (that is, industry profits are at most zero).[2] Thus, in (7.3), $\mathbf{w}$ is the vector of factor prices that minimize expenditure on factors subject to the constraint that profits in each industry be nonpositive.

Whereas the GDP function summarizes the supply side of an economy, the domestic expenditure or spending function $S(\mathbf{p}, u)$ summarizes the demand side. The expenditure function gives the minimum expenditure at prices $\mathbf{p}$ that would enable a country to purchase a mix of commodities that provide a level of welfare no less than u.[3] By definition,

$$S(\mathbf{p}, u_0) = \mathbf{ph} \tag{7.4}$$

where the commodity demands $\mathbf{h}$ have been chosen so as to minimize expenditure subject to the constraint that the utility level is u_0. By Shephard's Lemma, differentiation of (7.4) with respect to the price of good i gives the (compensated) demand function for good i:

$$\frac{\partial S(\mathbf{p}, u_0)}{\partial p_i} = h_i(\mathbf{p}, u_0). \tag{7.5}$$

The GDP and expenditure functions permit one to determine an economy's equilibrium price vector and equilibrium level of utility. In particular, the equilibrium conditions are

$$\frac{\partial G(\mathbf{p}, \mathbf{e})}{\partial p_j} = \frac{\partial S(\mathbf{p}, u)}{\partial p_j} \qquad j = 1, \ldots, N \tag{7.6}$$

$$G(\mathbf{p}, \mathbf{e}) = S(\mathbf{p}, u) \tag{7.7}$$

The equalities in (7.6) state the equality of demand and supply for each good while (7.7) is the economy's overall budget constraint. However, (7.7) is redundant since it can be derived by multiplying both sides of (7.6) by p_j and summing over j. Thus, of the $(N + 1)$ equations in (7.6) and (7.7), only N are independent. These N equations enable the determination of $(N - 1)$ relative prices and u, the level of utility achieved in equilibrium. Since the above economy does not, by assumption, engage in trade, the equilibrium price vector $\mathbf{p}$ is the economy's autarky price vector and the equilibrium level of utility is the level of utility obtainable in autarky.

7.2 Generalized law of comparative advantage

The law of comparative advantage states that trade results from, and can thus be predicted by, differences in autarky relative product prices between countries. In Chapter 3 the law of comparative advantage was generalized to many goods and a single (or single composite) factor in the form of the Ricardian chain proposition. Here we extend the law of comparative advantage to an arbitrary number of goods and factors.

We first state some very general relationships between price changes and quantity changes which derive from properties of the income and expenditure functions in competitive equilibrium. These relationships are then used to demonstrate that differences in autarky prices between countries will be correlated with countries' net exports. The relationships we will derive are very general in that they hold irrespective of the exact form of a country's technology and preferences. The only restrictions are the convexity requirements needed to ensure solutions to the underlying producer (profit maximization) and consumer (utility) optimizations implicit in the definitions of the GDP and expenditure functions.

Let $\mathbf{q}_0$ be the output vector produced at equilibrium prices $\mathbf{p}_0$ and let $\mathbf{q}_1$ be the output vector produced at equilibrium prices $\mathbf{p}_1$. From the definition of the GDP function, the optimum output bundles at their respective prices yield maximum income. As such, we can write the following inequalities:

$$\mathbf{p}_0\mathbf{q}_0 \geq \mathbf{p}_0\mathbf{q}_1 \Rightarrow \mathbf{p}_0(\mathbf{q}_0 - \mathbf{q}_1) \geq 0 \tag{7.8}$$

$$\mathbf{p}_1\mathbf{q}_1 \geq \mathbf{p}_1\mathbf{q}_0 \Rightarrow -\mathbf{p}_1(\mathbf{q}_0 - \mathbf{q}_1) \geq 0 \tag{7.9}$$

Adding these inequalities gives:

$$(\mathbf{p}_0 - \mathbf{p}_1)(\mathbf{q}_0 - \mathbf{q}_1) \geq 0 \tag{7.10}$$

This states that price changes and output changes are, on average, positively correlated and, in this sense, price changes can be said to predict output changes.

A similar set of inequalities derives from the expenditure function. Specifically, if h_0 and h_1 are demanded at prices p_0 and p_1 when utility is held constant then we can write:

$$\mathbf{p}_0\mathbf{h}_0 \leq \mathbf{p}_0\mathbf{h}_1 \Rightarrow \mathbf{p}_0(\mathbf{h}_0 - \mathbf{h}_1) \leq 0 \qquad (7.11)$$

$$\mathbf{p}_1\mathbf{h}_1 \leq \mathbf{p}_1\mathbf{h}_0 \Rightarrow -\mathbf{p}_1(\mathbf{h}_0 - \mathbf{h}_1) \leq 0 \qquad (7.12)$$

Combining these inequalities gives:

$$(\mathbf{p}_0 - \mathbf{p}_1)(\mathbf{h}_0 - \mathbf{h}_1) \leq 0 \qquad (7.13)$$

This states that price changes and demand changes are, on average, negatively correlated and, in this sense, price changes predict demand changes.

Combining inequalities (7.11) and (7.13) permits us to derive a statement about the change in prices when moving from autarky to trade and the accompanying changes in outputs and demands. It may be guessed that since domestic outputs respond, on average, positively to price changes while domestic demands respond, on average, negatively to price changes, the difference between supply and demand (net exports) should respond, on average, positively to price changes. That is, in moving from autarky to trade, goods whose prices were lower in autarky will, on average, be associated with rising domestic supply and falling domestic demand, that is, positive net exports. Conversely, goods whose prices were higher in autarky will, on average, be associated with falling domestic supply and rising domestic demand, that is, negative net exports ($=$ net imports).

Let $\mathbf{p}_T$ be the vector of prices under free trade and let $\mathbf{p}_A$ denote a country's autarky price vector. Using (7.10) we may write the relationship between autarky and free trade incomes as:

$$(\mathbf{p}_A - \mathbf{p}_T)(\mathbf{q}_A - \mathbf{q}_T) \geq 0 \qquad (7.14)$$

where it is assumed that the production mix that exists under trade ($\mathbf{q}_T$) is feasible, that is, producible from the country's resources and technology. Likewise, we can express (7.13) in terms of autarky and free trade expenditure:

$$(\mathbf{p}_A - \mathbf{p}_T)(\mathbf{h}_A - \mathbf{h}_T) \leq 0 \qquad (7.15)$$

Combining inequalities (7.14) and (7.15) yields:

$$(\mathbf{p}_A - \mathbf{p}_T)(\mathbf{h}_A - \mathbf{h}_T) \leq (\mathbf{p}_A - \mathbf{p}_T)(\mathbf{q}_A - \mathbf{q}_T) \qquad (7.16)$$

$$(\mathbf{p}_A - \mathbf{p}_T)(\mathbf{h}_A - \mathbf{q}_A) - (\mathbf{p}_A - \mathbf{p}_T)(\mathbf{h}_T - \mathbf{q}_T) \leq 0 \qquad (7.17)$$

$$-(\mathbf{p}_A - \mathbf{p}_T)(\mathbf{h}_T - \mathbf{q}_T) \leq 0 \qquad (7.18)$$

since $(\mathbf{h}_A - \mathbf{q}_A) = 0$ by definition of autarky. Finally, if $\mathbf{t} = -(\mathbf{h}_T - \mathbf{q}_T) = (\mathbf{q}_T - \mathbf{h}_T)$ denotes the vector of commodity net exports (excess supplies) then (7.18) becomes:

$$(\mathbf{p}_A - \mathbf{p}_T)\mathbf{t} \leq 0 \qquad (7.19)$$

Proposition 7.1: In moving from autarky to free trade, the difference between a country's autarky prices and the prices existing under free trade will, on average, be negatively correlated with changes in the country's excess supplies of goods. Goods with higher prices in autarky relative to free trade will, on average, have negative excess supplies (be imported) whereas goods whose prices were lower in autarky will have positive excess supplies (be exported).

It is important to note that Proposition 7.1 does not say that each good whose price was lower in autarky will be exported, that is, we cannot predict the precise *commodity composition* of trade.

Repeating the above analysis with respect to the foreign country (rest of the world) yields:

$$(\mathbf{p}_A^* - \mathbf{p}_T)\mathbf{t}^* \leq 0 \qquad (7.20)$$

where asterisks denote foreign country magnitudes. We can now state a relationship between the difference in autarky prices between countries and the pattern of trade. With balanced world trade (i.e. $\mathbf{p}_T\mathbf{t}^* = -\mathbf{p}_T\mathbf{t}$), and noting that $\mathbf{t}^* = -\mathbf{t}$, conditions (7.19) and (7.20) imply:

$$(\mathbf{p}_A - \mathbf{p}_A^*)\mathbf{t} \leq 0 \qquad (7.21)$$

Proposition 7.2 (Generalized Law of Comparative Advantage): Assuming that, in each country, firms minimize costs and consumers maximize utility, the difference in countries' autarky prices will be negatively correlated with the pattern of net exports that exists under free trade.

Proposition 2 is completely general in that it does not rely on any specific assumption about the nature of technology or preferences. However, this generality comes at a price: we are unable to predict the exact commodity composition of trade between countries.

7.3 Factor abundance and trade

We now recast the above generalized law of comparative advantage in terms of factor input requirements and factor abundances in order to generalize the factor abundance (Heckscher–Ohlin) model. As usual, we will want to consider factor abundance measured either by autarky factor prices (the price version) or autarky factor supplies (the quantity version).

We begin by stating the set of equations that must be satisfied by an economy in a competitive general equilibrium:

$$(\mathbf{p} - \mathbf{w}\mathbf{A}(\mathbf{w}))\mathbf{q} = 0 \tag{7.22}$$

$$\mathbf{w}\mathbf{A}(\mathbf{w}) \leq \mathbf{p} \tag{7.23}$$

$$\mathbf{A}(\mathbf{w})\mathbf{q} = \mathbf{e} \tag{7.24}$$

In these equations, $\mathbf{A}(\mathbf{w})$ denotes the $H \times N$ matrix of equilibrium input requirements per unit of output which are a function of factor prices; $\mathbf{w}\mathbf{A}(\mathbf{w})$ is thus the vector of unit cost functions. Equation (7.22) states the condition for zero profits in each industry whereas (7.23) states the requirement that for any good, average cost must equal or exceed its price. Together, (7.22) and (7.23) ensure that positive production of any good ($q_j > 0$) must yield zero profits. Finally, (7.24) states the requirement for factor market equilibrium, that is, full employment of all resources.

We now consider a change in goods prices under the assumption that the set of goods produced is the same both before and after the price change. Given this assumption, we can characterize the change in goods prices by the total differential of the zero profit condition (7.23):

$$d\mathbf{p} = d\mathbf{w}\mathbf{A}(\mathbf{w}) + \mathbf{w}d\mathbf{A}(\mathbf{w}) \tag{7.25}$$

which reduces to

$$d\mathbf{p} = d\mathbf{w}\mathbf{A}(\mathbf{w}) \tag{7.26}$$

since $\mathbf{w}d\mathbf{A}(\mathbf{w}) = 0$ as a condition of cost minimization. Post-multiplying both sides of (7.26) by the vector of price changes yields:

$$d\mathbf{p}d\mathbf{p} = d\mathbf{w}\mathbf{A}(\mathbf{w})d\mathbf{p} \tag{7.27}$$

The left-hand side of (7.27) is a strictly positive scalar since it is just the sum of squared price changes. Hence,

$$d\mathbf{w}\mathbf{A}(\mathbf{w})d\mathbf{p} > 0 \tag{7.28}$$

which states that small changes in goods prices must be positively correlated with $d\mathbf{w}\mathbf{A}(\mathbf{w})$ or, equivalently, that small changes in factor prices ($d\mathbf{w}$) must be positively correlated with changes in $A(\mathbf{w})d\mathbf{p}$. In either case, (7.28) suggests the following:

Proposition 7.3: Small changes in goods prices will, on average, be associated with increases in the prices of those factors employed most intensively in producing those goods whose prices have risen the most, and associated with decreases in the prices of factors employed less intensively in producing those goods whose prices have fallen.

We note that this result follows from the assumption of cost minimization in competitive markets and does not depend on special characteristics of technology or even the number of goods and factors. Again, however, there is a price for this generality: we cannot say anything about the relationship between the price of a specific factor and the price of a specific good; we can only speak of an average relationship between changes in factor prices and changes in goods prices.

Factor prices and trade

We now link the results contained in Proposition 7.3 to trade and the factor abundance model. Post-multiplying (7.26) by the vector of commodity excess supplies (**t**) gives:

$$d\mathbf{pt} = d\mathbf{w}\mathbf{A}(\mathbf{w})\mathbf{t} \tag{7.29}$$

Since $d\mathbf{pt} \le 0$ (see (7.20)), we can write:

$$d\mathbf{w}\mathbf{A}(\mathbf{w})\mathbf{t} \le 0 \tag{7.30}$$

Equation (7.30) provides one statement of the link between factor abundance, factor inputs, and trade. First, we can interpret the vector of factor price changes ($d\mathbf{w}$) as the difference between home and foreign autarky factor prices. Thus, negative elements of $d\mathbf{w}$ indicate factors whose autarky prices are lower in the home country than in the foreign country and, in this sense, are abundant in the home country. Given that each element of the matrix $\mathbf{A}(\mathbf{w})$ is positive, (7.30) implies the following:

Proposition 7.4: A country will tend, on average, to be a net exporter of goods whose production is intensive in those factors that are relatively inexpensive (abundant) in autarky and a net importer of goods whose production is intensive in those factors that are relatively expensive (scarce) in autarky.

Proposition 7.4 relates factor prices, factor use, and goods trade on the average and thus it need not hold with respect to any particular factor and good. In this sense, Proposition 7.4 is a *weak* form of the Heckscher–Ohlin theorem.

We note that (7.30) can also be interpreted as a statement about the relationship between factor abundance and a country's trade in factor services:

$$d\mathbf{wf} \leq 0 \qquad (7.31)$$

where $\mathbf{f} = \mathbf{A(w)t}$ is the factor content of (net) trade.[4] Hence, Proposition 7.4 can be stated in the equivalent form:

Proposition 7.5:   A country will tend, on average, to be a net exporter of the services of its less expensive (abundant) factors and a net importer of the services of its expensive (scarce) factors.

A caveat concerning both (7.30) and (7.31) is that they hold strictly only for small price changes since $\mathbf{A(w)}$ is the home country's autarky factor requirements, that is, the factor requirements associated with the home country's (initial) autarky factor prices. Since we would expect a movement from autarky to free trade to change factor prices and thus factor input requirements both within and between countries, we need to restate (7.28) in a way that holds for arbitrary (i.e. large) price changes.

Consider two alternative equilibria characterized by output price vectors $\mathbf{p_0}$ and $\mathbf{p_1}$ and associated factor price vectors $\mathbf{w_0}$ and $\mathbf{w_1}$ (which we can interpret as the autarky prices in the home and foreign country, respectively). We continue to assume that the same goods are produced in each equilibrium. Given this, define the scalar valued function $z(\mathbf{w}) = \mathbf{wA(w)(p_1 - p_0)}$ and consider the change in this function between the two equilibria. Using the mean-value theorem[5] this change can be expressed as

$$z(\mathbf{w_1}) - z(\mathbf{w_0}) = (\mathbf{w_1} - \mathbf{w_0})dz(\mathbf{\bar{w}}) \qquad (7.32)$$

where $\mathbf{\bar{w}}$ is some factor price vector that lies 'between' $\mathbf{w_0}$ and $\mathbf{w_1}$. The differential $dz(\mathbf{\bar{w}})$ equals $[\mathbf{A(\bar{w})} + \mathbf{\bar{w}}d\mathbf{A(\bar{w})}](\mathbf{p_1 - p_0})$ which can be simplified by noting (as in deriving (7.26)) that the term $\mathbf{\bar{w}}d\mathbf{A(w)}$ vanishes by virtue of cost minimization. Hence, (7.32) can be written

$$z(\mathbf{w_1}) - z(\mathbf{w_0}) = (\mathbf{w_1} - \mathbf{w_0})\mathbf{A(\bar{w})(p_1 - p_0)} \qquad (7.33)$$

or, since $z(\mathbf{w_1}) - z(\mathbf{w_0}) = (\mathbf{p_1} - \mathbf{p_0})(\mathbf{p_1} - \mathbf{p_0})$,[6]

$$(\mathbf{p_1 - p_0})(\mathbf{p_1 - p_0}) = (\mathbf{w_1} - \mathbf{w_0})\mathbf{A(\bar{w})(p_1 - p_0)} \qquad (7.34)$$

Since the left-hand side of (7.34) is strictly positive we can write:

$$(\mathbf{w_1} - \mathbf{w_0})\mathbf{A(\bar{w})(p_1 - p_0)} > 0 \qquad (7.35)$$

This result is similar to (7.29) but differs in that there is some freedom in the choice of a factor price vector and thus the factor input requirements matrix.[7]

As with (7.30), (7.34) can be used to link autarky factor prices and trade flows. Specifically, eliminate the term $(\mathbf{p}_1 - \mathbf{p}_0)$ from both sides of (7.34) and then post-multiply both sides of the resulting equation by $\mathbf{t}$ to obtain:

$$(\mathbf{p}_1 - \mathbf{p}_0)\mathbf{t} = (\mathbf{w}_1 - \mathbf{w}_0)\mathbf{A}(\bar{\mathbf{w}})\mathbf{t} \tag{7.36}$$

Since $(\mathbf{p}_1 - \mathbf{p}_0)\mathbf{t} \geq 0$ (see (7.19)), we can write:

$$(\mathbf{w}_1 - \mathbf{w}_0)\mathbf{A}(\bar{\mathbf{w}})\mathbf{t} \geq 0 \tag{7.37}$$

Alternatively, we can express (7.37) in terms of a country's trade in factor services:

$$(\mathbf{w}_1 - \mathbf{w}_0)\bar{\mathbf{f}} \geq 0 \tag{7.38}$$

where $\bar{\mathbf{f}} = \mathbf{A}(\bar{\mathbf{w}})\mathbf{t}$ is the vector of factor contents. Expressions (7.37) and (7.38) have the same interpretation as (7.30) and (7.31), respectively, with respect to the average relationship between abundant factors (in the price sense) and net trade or net factor service flows. The primary difference is that (7.37) and (7.38) relate to large price changes and in this sense are more general.

Factor intensity reversals

Whereas (7.37) and (7.38) are more general than (7.30) and (7.31), this additional generality is not without some difficulty since (7.37) and (7.38) assume that countries use the same factor input requirements (i.e. $\mathbf{A}(\bar{\mathbf{w}})$), as would be the case if trade equalized factor prices between countries. The generality of (7.37) and (7.38) is thus limited by the fact that factor prices may not be equalized by trade and also that higher dimensional analogs to factor intensity reversals might exist.[8] To resolve this issue we need to find a factor input matrix such that (7.37) or (7.38) holds even if factor prices are not equalized or when high order 'factor intensity reversals' are present.

To understand the difficulty, consider the 2×2 example of a factor intensity reversal in which the trading equilibrium is such that countries' post-trade factor prices lie on either side of this reversal. Given this, suppose that the home country exports good X and imports good Y and that good X is capital-intensive in the home country. The foreign country exports good Y but, due to the factor intensity reversal, Y is capital-intensive in the foreign country. If we were to calculate, for each country, the factor content of its trade using its domestic techniques of production we would observe that both the home country and the foreign country were net exporters of the services of capital. However, based on autarky factor price differences, only one country can be capital abundant. Thus, it is impossible that each country is a net exporter of the services of its *abundant* factor.

A solution to this problem can be seen by considering the calculation of factor contents in the above 2×2 case. Let the home country's unit capital and labor requirements be a_{Kx} and a_{Lx} in industry x and a_{Ky} and a_{Ly} in industry y and let $t_x > 0$ denote the net exports of good x and let $t_y < 0$ denote the home country's net imports of good y. By choice of units we can normalize goods prices to unity so that the condition for balanced trade can be written $-t_x = t_y$. Given this, the factor content of Home's trade vector can be written:

$$\begin{pmatrix} a_{Kx} & a_{Ky} \\ a_{Lx} & a_{Ly} \end{pmatrix} \begin{pmatrix} t_x \\ t_y \end{pmatrix} = \begin{pmatrix} a_{Kx} & a_{Ky} \\ a_{Lx} & a_{Ly} \end{pmatrix} \begin{pmatrix} t_x \\ -t_x \end{pmatrix} = \begin{pmatrix} (a_{Kx} - a_{Ky})t_x \\ (a_{Lx} - a_{Ly})t_x \end{pmatrix} \quad (7.39)$$

Since $t_x > 0$ by assumption and industry x is capital-intensive $((a_{Kx} - a_{Ky}) > 0)$ the country exports the services of capital $((a_{Kx} - a_{Ky})t_x > 0)$ and imports the services of labor $((a_{Lx} - a_{Ly})t_x < 0)$ via its imports of the labor intensive good y. Letting an asterisk denote foreign input requirements, and remembering that industry y is capital-intensive in the foreign country (i.e. $(a_{Ky}^* - a_{Kx}^*) > 0$), the factor contents of Foreign's trade is:

$$\begin{pmatrix} a_{Kx}^* & a_{Ky}^* \\ a_{Lx}^* & a_{Ly}^* \end{pmatrix} \begin{pmatrix} t_x^* \\ t_y^* \end{pmatrix} = \begin{pmatrix} a_{Kx}^* & a_{Ky}^* \\ a_{Lx}^* & a_{Ly}^* \end{pmatrix} \begin{pmatrix} -t_x \\ t_x \end{pmatrix} = \begin{pmatrix} (a_{Ky}^* - a_{Kx}^*)t_x \\ (a_{Ly}^* - a_{Lx}^*)t_x \end{pmatrix} \quad (7.40)$$

since $-t_i^* = t_i$ $(i = x, y)$. As expected, Foreign exports the services of capital $((a_{Ky}^* - a_{Kx}^*)t_x > 0)$ and imports the services of labor $((a_{Ly}^* - a_{Lx}^*)t_x < 0)$.

A solution to this problem is to note that, if the home country is capital-abundant (capital is cheaper relative to labor in the home country compared to the foreign country), it must be the case that each industry in the home country employs more capital per unit of labor than does the corresponding industry in the foreign country. This follows from the property that, within any industry, the higher is the price of labor compared to the price of capital, the higher will be the amount of capital employed per unit of labor. This property implies the following inequalities:

$$(a_{Kx} - a_{Kx}^*) > 0 \quad \text{and} \quad (a_{Ky} - a_{Ky}^*) > 0 \quad (7.41)$$

$$(a_{Lx} - a_{Lx}^*) < 0 \quad \text{and} \quad (a_{Ly} - a_{Ly}^*) < 0 \quad (7.42)$$

Since $a_{Kx} > a_{Ky}$ and $a_{Lx} < a_{Ly}$, inequalities (7.41) and (7.42) imply, respectively, the following:

$$(a_{Kx} - a_{Ky}^*) > 0$$
$$(a_{Lx} - a_{Ly}^*) < 0 \quad (7.43)$$

This monotonicity of factor input requirements with respect to factor prices in any given industry suggests that we should calculate the factor content of a country's trade using the factor requirements of the country of origin of a good (i.e. the exporting country). That is, we should use Home's factor requirements for good x and Foreign's factor requirements for good y. Adopting this procedure, the factor content of Home's trade becomes

$$\begin{pmatrix} a_{Kx} & a^*_{Ky} \\ a_{Lx} & a^*_{Ly} \end{pmatrix} \begin{pmatrix} t_x \\ -t_x \end{pmatrix} = \begin{pmatrix} (a_{Kx} - a^*_{Ky})t_x \\ (a_{Lx} - a^*_{Ly})t_x \end{pmatrix} \tag{7.44}$$

Given (7.43) we have $(a_{Kx} - a^*_{Ky})t_x > 0$ and $(a_{Lx} - a^*_{Ly})t_x < 0$, that is, the home country exports the services of capital and imports the services of labor. Applying this procedure to Foreign's trade vector gives:

$$\begin{pmatrix} a_{Kx} & a^*_{Ky} \\ a_{Lx} & a^*_{Ly} \end{pmatrix} \begin{pmatrix} t^*_x \\ -t^*_x \end{pmatrix} = \begin{pmatrix} (a_{Kx} - a^*_{Ky})t^*_x \\ (a_{Lx} - a^*_{Ly})t^*_x \end{pmatrix} \tag{7.45}$$

Since $t^*_x < 0$, (7.43) implies $(a_{Kx} - a^*_{Ky})t^*_x < 0$ and $(a_{Lx} - a^*_{Ly})t^*_x > 0$, that is, Foreign imports the services of capital and exports the services of labor.

We now extend this procedure to an arbitrary number of goods and factors. Let $\bar{\mathbf{A}}$ be the factor input requirements matrix whose ith column represents the input requirements of the country exporting good i. If $\mathbf{t}$ denotes a country's net export vector, the factor content of that country's trade is then $\bar{\mathbf{f}} = \bar{\mathbf{A}}\mathbf{t}$.

Now consider a trading equilibrium between two countries and let $\mathbf{h}_T$ denote a country's free trade consumption vector. Since countries share the same technologies (production functions), it would be possible for a country to produce for itself the vector $\mathbf{h}_T$ by using factors $\mathbf{e} + \bar{\mathbf{f}}$. One way to imagine this is that the factors $\bar{\mathbf{f}}$ are made available to the country not through goods trade, but rather by the direct movement of the factors. Alternatively, the country could simply cease producing exports and instead produce its bundle of imports using the same techniques used in the exporting country. In any event, this alternate production plan is unlikely to be profitable when valued at the country's autarky prices $\mathbf{w}_A$ and $\mathbf{p}_A$:

$$\mathbf{w}_A(\mathbf{e} + \bar{\mathbf{f}}) \geq \mathbf{p}_A\mathbf{h}_T \tag{7.46}$$

where $\mathbf{w}_A(\mathbf{e} + \bar{\mathbf{f}})$ is the total cost of employing factors $(\mathbf{e} + \bar{\mathbf{f}})$ at their prices $\mathbf{w}_A$ and $\mathbf{p}_A\mathbf{h}_T$ is the expenditure that would be required to purchase the post-trade consumption bundle valued at autarky prices. Since the country chose the consumption bundle $\mathbf{h}_T$, it must be the case that this bundle costs at least as much as bundle $\mathbf{h}_A$ at prices $\mathbf{p}_A$, since otherwise the country would have chosen $\mathbf{h}_T$ since it involves higher utility, that is, $\mathbf{p}_A\mathbf{h}_T \geq \mathbf{p}_A\mathbf{h}_A$. Combining this inequality with that in (7.46) gives:

$$\mathbf{w}_A(\mathbf{e} + \bar{\mathbf{f}}) \geq \mathbf{p}_A\mathbf{h}_A \tag{7.47}$$

which after rearrangement yields:

$$\mathbf{w}_A\bar{\mathbf{f}} \geq (\mathbf{p}_A\mathbf{h}_A - \mathbf{w}_A\mathbf{e}) = 0 \tag{7.48}$$

For the rest of the world we may derive a similar expression, namely $\mathbf{w}_A^* \bar{\mathbf{f}}^* \geq 0$. Since $\bar{\mathbf{f}} = -\bar{\mathbf{f}}^*$, we may combine these inequalities to get:

$$(\mathbf{w}_A - \mathbf{w}_A^*)\bar{\mathbf{f}} \geq 0 \tag{7.49}$$

Proposition 7.6:   Using as the factor input requirements for good i the factor input requirements of the country exporting good i, a country will, on average, be a net exporter of the services of its abundant factors and a net importer of the services of its scarce factors, where abundance is defined in terms of autarky factor prices.

Lastly, substitute $\bar{\mathbf{f}} = \bar{\mathbf{A}}\mathbf{t}$ into (7.49) to relate factor price differences to factor use and commodity trade:

$$(\mathbf{w}_A - \mathbf{w}_A^*)\bar{\mathbf{A}}\mathbf{t} \geq 0 \tag{7.50}$$

The interpretation of this inequality is now familiar: countries will, on average, export goods which make relatively intensive use of their abundant (relatively inexpensive) factors.

In this section we have related differences in autarky factor prices to a country's use of factors and its trade in goods, and also to the country's trade in factor services. Despite the validity of each set of relationships, it can be argued that the relationship between factor prices, factor use, and trade in goods is perhaps less 'precise' than that between factor prices and factor services trade since the former depends on a somewhat ad hoc definition of factor intensity (i.e. the elements of the factor input requirements matrix).

Factor supplies and trade

We now consider the relationship between trade flows and factor abundance where the latter are measured by factor supplies rather than autarky factor prices. The first step is to place restrictions on demand so as to rule out the possibility of 'demand biases' which could reverse the normally expected negative relationship between relative factor supplies and relative factor prices. As in the 2×2 model, such 'demand reversals' are precluded by assuming countries have identical and homothetic preferences. Given this, we now establish the multifactor, multicommodity relationship between physical factor abundance and factor prices between countries.

As shown in Chapter 4 (pp. 135–6), the assumption of homothetic preferences permits us to write the expenditure function in the separable form:[9]

$$S(\mathbf{p}_A; u_A) = u_A \bar{s}(\mathbf{p}_A) \tag{7.51}$$

where u_A is the utility level reached under autarky at prices $\mathbf{p}_A$. Using this, equilibrium condition (7.7) becomes

$$u_A \bar{s}(\mathbf{p}_A) = G(\mathbf{p}_A; \mathbf{e}) = \mathbf{we} \qquad (7.52)$$

where $\mathbf{w}$ is the vector of factor prices that minimize expenditure on factors subject to the constraint of nonpositive profits in all industries.

Suppose an autarky equilibrium is characterized by output prices $\mathbf{p}_A$ and factor prices $\mathbf{w}_A$. Then by (7.52) we can write $G(\mathbf{p}_A; \mathbf{e}) = \mathbf{w}_A \mathbf{e}$. By definition, any other price vectors $\mathbf{p}$ and $\mathbf{w}$ would yield either lower income or greater expenditure on factors. Thus, given the equilibrium $G(\mathbf{p}_A; \mathbf{e}) = \mathbf{w}_A \mathbf{e}$, it must be true that $\mathbf{w}_A^* \mathbf{e} \geq \mathbf{w}_A \mathbf{e}$ and $G(\mathbf{p}_A; \mathbf{e}) \geq G(\mathbf{p}_A^*; \mathbf{e})$ where the asterisk denotes foreign country prices. These inequalities imply

$$\mathbf{w}_A^* \mathbf{e} \geq G(\mathbf{p}_A^*; \mathbf{e}) \qquad (7.53)$$

Now, if u_0 is the utility level achievable at foreign prices $(G(\mathbf{p}_A^*; \mathbf{e}) = u_0 \bar{s}(\mathbf{p}_A^*))$ then $u_0 \geq u_A$ since the possibility to exchange at prices other than one's autarky prices $(\mathbf{p}_A)$ must involve higher utility. Given this, and (7.53), we can write

$$\mathbf{w}_A^* \mathbf{e} \geq G(\mathbf{p}_A^*; \mathbf{e}) = u_0 \bar{s}(\mathbf{p}_A^*) = \frac{u_0 \bar{s}(p_A^*)}{u_0 \bar{s}(p_A)} u_0 \cdot \bar{s}(\mathbf{p}_A)$$

$$= \lambda G(\mathbf{p}_A; \mathbf{e}) = \lambda \mathbf{w}_A \mathbf{e} \qquad (7.54)$$

or

$$(\mathbf{w}_A^* - \lambda \mathbf{w}_A) \mathbf{e} \geq 0 \qquad (7.55)$$

where

$$\lambda = \bar{s}(p_A^*)/\bar{s}(p_A).$$

Letting u_1 be the level of utility obtainable by the foreign country when facing prices $\mathbf{p}_A$ (home country autarky prices), the above logic when applied to the foreign country implies:

$$\mathbf{w}_A \mathbf{e}^* \geq G(\mathbf{p}_A; \mathbf{e}^*) = u_1 \bar{s}(\mathbf{p}_A) = \frac{u_1 \bar{s}(p_A)}{u_1 \bar{s}(p_A^*)} u_1 \cdot \bar{s}(\mathbf{p}_A^*)$$

$$= \lambda^* G(\mathbf{p}_A^*; \mathbf{e}^*) = \lambda^* \mathbf{w}_A^* \mathbf{e}^* \qquad (7.56)$$

or

$$(\mathbf{w}_A - \lambda^* \mathbf{w}_A^*) \mathbf{e}^* \geq 0 \qquad (7.57)$$

where

$$\lambda^* = \bar{s}(p_A)/\bar{s}(p_A^*).$$

Since $\lambda = 1/\lambda^*$, this can be written

$$(\lambda\mathbf{w}_A - \mathbf{w}_A^*)\mathbf{e}^* \geq 0 \tag{7.58}$$

The scalar λ is a measure of foreign relative to domestic price levels. By choice of a numeraire, we can normalize the price levels in each country so that $\lambda = 1$. Given this, subtract (7.58) from (7.55) to obtain:

$$(\mathbf{w}_A - \mathbf{w}_A^*)(\mathbf{e} - \mathbf{e}^*) \leq 0 \tag{7.59}$$

where we have used $(\mathbf{w}_A^* - \lambda\mathbf{w}_A) = -(\lambda\mathbf{w}_A - \mathbf{w}_A^*)$ to reverse the inequality. Since positive (negative) elements of the vector $(\mathbf{e} - \mathbf{e}^*)$ indicate factors in greater (lesser) supply in home compared to foreign while negative (positive) elements of $(\lambda\mathbf{w}_A - \mathbf{w}_A^*)$ indicate factors which are cheaper (dearer) in home compared to foreign, (7.59) states that countries will tend, on average, to have lower prices of those factors which are in relatively greater supply.

We now wish to relate factor supply differences to differences in autarky goods prices. A direct way to do this would be to replace the autarky factor price differences in (7.59) by the relationship between factor prices and output prices. The link between output prices and input prices is given by the zero profit conditions in each country:

$$\mathbf{p}_A = \mathbf{c}(\mathbf{w}_A)$$
$$\mathbf{p}_A^* = \mathbf{c}(\mathbf{w}_A^*) \tag{7.60}$$

where the elements of $\mathbf{c}(\cdot)$ are industry unit cost functions. If we could solve these zero profit equations for factor prices in terms of output prices, we could place these solutions into (7.59) to arrive at a relationship between autarky output prices and factor supplies. That is, if the functions $\mathbf{c}(\mathbf{w}_A)$ and $\mathbf{c}(\mathbf{w}_A^*)$ are invertible, then we could write $\mathbf{w}_A = \mathbf{w}(\mathbf{p}_A)$ and $\mathbf{w}_A^* = \mathbf{w}(\mathbf{p}_A^*)$ and write (7.59) as

$$(\mathbf{w}(\mathbf{p}_A) - \mathbf{w}(\mathbf{p}_A^*))(\mathbf{e} - \mathbf{e}^*) \leq 0 \tag{7.61}$$

The problem, of course, is the conditions under which the unit cost functions are invertible. This issue, known as the univalence problem, is related to the 2×2 problem of factor intensity reversals. Essentially, what we require is that the mapping from factor prices to output prices be one-to-one. Suffice it to say that invertibility requires severe restrictions on the cost functions.[10]

In order to complete our discussion we assume the cost functions are invertible and we adopt the explicit form of the zero profit equations involving the unit input requirements, namely, $\mathbf{p} = \mathbf{w}\mathbf{A}(\mathbf{w})$. Solving this set of equations for $\mathbf{w}$ then yields $\mathbf{w} = \mathbf{p}\mathbf{A}(\mathbf{w})^{-1}$. Note that $\mathbf{A}^{-1}$ is square so we are assuming that the number of goods equals or exceeds the number of factors.

We can now apply the same logic used to derive equation (7.37). First expand (7.60):

$$w(\mathbf{p}_A)(\mathbf{e} - \mathbf{e}^*) - w(\mathbf{p}_A^*)(\mathbf{e} - \mathbf{e}^*) \leq 0 \tag{7.62}$$

and replace $w(\mathbf{p})$ by $\mathbf{p}A(\mathbf{w})^{-1}$ to get

$$[\mathbf{p}_A A(\mathbf{w}_A)^{-1}(\mathbf{e} - \mathbf{e}^*)] - [\mathbf{p}_A^* A(\mathbf{w}_A^*)^{-1}(\mathbf{e} - \mathbf{e}^*)] \leq 0 \tag{7.63}$$

This difference can be characterized as the difference between a scalar valued function $z(\mathbf{p}, \mathbf{e}) = \mathbf{p}A(\bar{\mathbf{w}})^{-1}(\mathbf{e} - \mathbf{e}^*)$ evaluated at the two points $\mathbf{p}_A$ and $\mathbf{p}_A^*$, that is,

$$z(\mathbf{p}_A, \mathbf{e}) - z(\mathbf{p}_A^*, \mathbf{e}^*) \leq 0 \tag{7.64}$$

As with (7.32), we can specify this difference using the mean-value theorem applied to the function $z(\mathbf{p}, \mathbf{e})$. Thus, for some vector of prices $\bar{\mathbf{p}}$ between $\mathbf{p}_A$ and $\mathbf{p}_A^*$[11] we can express (7.64) as:

$$z(\mathbf{p}_A) - z(\mathbf{p}_A^*) = (\mathbf{p}_A - \mathbf{p}_A^*)\frac{\partial z(\bar{\mathbf{p}})}{\partial \mathbf{p}} \tag{7.65}$$

By definition, the matrix of partial derivatives[12] $\partial z(\bar{\mathbf{p}})/\partial \mathbf{p}$ equals $A(\bar{\mathbf{w}})^{-1}(\mathbf{e} - \mathbf{e}^*)$ so we can write:

$$z(\mathbf{p}_A) - z(\mathbf{p}_A^*) = (\mathbf{p}_A - \mathbf{p}_A^*)A(\bar{\mathbf{w}})^{-1}(\mathbf{e} - \mathbf{e}^*) \tag{7.66}$$

Finally, by (7.63), we can write

$$(\mathbf{p}_A - \mathbf{p}_A^*)A(\bar{\mathbf{w}})^{-1}(\mathbf{e} - \mathbf{e}^*) \leq 0 \tag{7.67}$$

If the elements of $A(\bar{\mathbf{w}})^{-1}$ are taken as a measure of factor intensity then (7.67) implies:

Proposition 7.7: Countries will tend, on average, to have lower autarky prices (i.e. a comparative advantage) for those goods that make intensive use of factors that are relatively abundant in the physical sense.

Finally, since trade flows are inversely related to the difference in autarky prices (see (7.21)), the following may be inferred from (7.67):

Proposition 7.8: Countries will, on average, export those goods that make intensive use of the factors that are relatively abundant in the physical sense.

In contrast to the price version (7.37), the above quantity version involves the inverse of the factor requirements matrix. Since inversion of the factor input matrix is only possible if the number of goods is as least as large as the number of factors, we may conclude that the above quantity version will not hold in the case of more factors than goods.

Finally, greater structure can be obtained if we not only assume that goods at least outnumber factors but also that free trade results in factor price equalization. In this case, the input matrix $A(\bar{w})^{-1}$ is not only the same for every country, it is also observable since $\bar{w}$ is now the vector of observable factor prices in the trading equilibrium. Denoting these factor prices as w, we can write a country's trade in factor services as:

$$A(w)t = A(w)q - A(w)h \qquad (7.68)$$

With full employment, $A(w)q = e$ so we can write the above as:

$$A(w)t = e - A(w)h \qquad (7.69)$$

If preferences are assumed identical and homothetic, the factor content of consumption $A(w)h$ can be written $\alpha A(w)(h + h^*)$ where α is the country's share of world GDP. In addition, since world consumption equals world production $(h + h^*) = (q + q^*)$, we can write $\alpha A(w)(h + h^*) = \alpha A(w)(q + q^*) = \alpha(e + e^*)$, where $(e + e^*)$ is the vector of world factor supplies. Given this, we can write (7.69) as

$$A(w)t = e - \alpha(e + e^*) \qquad (7.70)$$

Pre-multiplying both sides of (7.70) by the vector $(e - \alpha(e + e^*))$ we have

$$(e - \alpha(e + e^*))A(w)t = (e - \alpha(e + e^*))(e^* - \alpha(e + e^*)) \qquad (7.71)$$

Since the right-hand side is a nonnegative scalar we may write:

$$(e - \alpha(e + e^*))A(w)t \geq 0 \qquad (7.72)$$

which can also be written in terms of the trade in factor services as

$$(e - \alpha(e + e^*))f \geq 0 \qquad (7.73)$$

If a country is defined to be abundant in factor k if $(e_k - \alpha(e_k + e_k^*)) > 0$ and likewise scarce in factor k if $(e_k - \alpha(e_k + e_k^*)) < 0$ then (7.72) implies

Proposition 7.9: If free trade equalizes factor prices between countries and countries have identical and homothetic preferences then each country will, on average, be a net exporter of those goods that make relatively intensive use of the country's physically abundant factors.

Similarly, (7.73) implies:

Proposition 7.10: If free trade equalizes factor prices across country and countries have identical and homothetic preferences then each country will, on average, be a net exporter of the services of its physically abundant factors and a net importer of its physically scarce factors.

Expression (7.73), and hence Proposition 7.10, is the foundation for the Heckscher–Ohlin–Vanek (H–O–V) rank and sign propositions which relate physical factor abundance to trade in factor services when factor prices are equalized. Chapter 8 considers the H–O–V propositions in detail and in particular their role in formulating empirical tests of the factor abundance theory in an *N*-good, *H*-factor setting.

7.4 The Stolper–Samuelson proposition

Extension of the Stolper–Samuelson theorem involves considering the effect of output price changes on nominal and real factor returns. The effect on nominal factor rewards is already contained in (7.35), which is reproduced below:

$$(\mathbf{w}_1 - \mathbf{w}_0)\mathbf{A}(\bar{\mathbf{w}})(\mathbf{p}_1 - \mathbf{p}_0) > 0 \qquad (7.74)$$

This states that, on average, factor rewards will tend to increase the most for those factors that are used most intensively in the production of goods whose relative prices have risen the most and, conversely, factor rewards will tend to decrease the most for those factors used least intensively in industries whose relative prices have fallen the most.[13]

To deduce the effect of price changes on real rewards we first consider a rise in the price of only one good, say good *i*. Assuming this good was produced in the initial equilibrium then its price initially equalled its average cost of production:

$$p_i = w_k a_{ik} \qquad (7.75)$$

Subsequent to a rise in p_i, competition will serve to constrain any rise in the cost of production of good *i* to be greater than or equal to the rise in price. Hence, we can write

$$\hat{p}_i \leq \sum_k \hat{w}_k \theta_{ik} \qquad (7.76)$$

where $\theta_{ik} > 0$ is the share of factor *k* in the total cost of producing good *i* and $\sum_k \theta_{ik} = 1$. Since the prices of all other goods are held constant ($\hat{p}_j = 0$, $\forall j \neq i$), (7.76) implies that for some factor, say the first,

$$\hat{w}_1 \geq \hat{p}_i > \hat{p}_j = 0, \quad \forall j \neq i \qquad (7.77)$$

This states that the return to some factor, here factor 1, will rise in terms of all goods and fall in terms of no good.

We now establish that the real return to some other factor must fall consequent to the rise in the price of good i. By assumption, the price of good m $(m \neq i)$ did not change $(\hat{p}_m = 0)$. Hence, if good m is produced in the new equilibrium, then it must be the case that the proportional rise in its price exceeded the rise in its average costs, that is,

$$0 = \hat{p}_m \geq \sum_k \hat{w}_k \theta_{mk} \tag{7.78}$$

By assumption, factor 1 is employed in producing good m so that $\theta_{m1} > 0$. In addition, it was established above that $\hat{w}_1 > 0$. Hence, since $\sum_k m\theta_{mk} = 1$, it must be the case that for some factor, say factor 2, $\hat{w}_2 < 0$ and thus

$$\hat{w}_2 < \hat{p}_m = 0 < \hat{p}_i, \quad \forall m \neq i \tag{7.79}$$

This states that the return to factor 2 rose in terms of no good and fell strictly in terms of good i. Hence, every good is a 'friend' to some factor and an 'enemy' to some other factor.[14]

Proposition 7.11: A rise in the price of one good alone will raise the real reward of some factor in terms of all other goods and lower it in terms of no good, and it will lower the real return to some other factor in terms of all goods.[15]

Proposition 7.11 is a generalization of the 2×2 model's *magnification effect* of an output price change on factor prices. Note that this proposition is very general in that no restrictions have been imposed on the number of goods relative to the number of factors. Finally, we note that Proposition 7.11 applies to arbitrary changes in relative goods prices.[16]

7.5 The Rybczynski proposition

The effect of factor supply changes on outputs is extended by considering initial and terminal equilibria characterized by endowment vectors $\mathbf{e}_1$ and $\mathbf{e}_2$, respectively. Assuming factor prices are initially equalized across countries, full employment in each equilibrium gives, $\mathbf{e}_1 = \mathbf{A}(\mathbf{w})\mathbf{q}_1$ and $\mathbf{e}_2 = \mathbf{A}(\mathbf{w})\mathbf{q}_2$. Note that factor prices, and hence factor input requirements, are the same in each equilibrium. This is a consequence of the fact that, with factor prices initially equalized, a sufficiently small change in factor supplies will leave factor prices unchanged (i.e. only outputs need change). Given this we have:

$$\mathbf{e}_2 - \mathbf{e}_1 = \mathbf{A}(\mathbf{w})(\mathbf{q}_2 - \mathbf{q}_1) \tag{7.80}$$

Pre-multiplying both sides by $e_2 - e_1$ gives:

$$(e_2 - e_1)A(w)(q_2 - q_1) > 0 \tag{7.81}$$

which is analogous to the Stolper–Samuelson correlation (7.74).

Proposition 7.12: Factor supply changes will raise, on average, the output of goods relatively intensive in those factors whose supply has increased the most and will reduce, on average, the output of goods which make relatively little use of those factors whose supply has increased the most.

Since Proposition 7.12 requires factor price equalization it applies only when the number of goods equals or exceeds the number of factors.

To obtain a more general statement of the effect of factor supply changes we can mimic the preceding Stolper–Samuelson analysis. Specifically, suppose the supply of one factor alone increases, say the first (i.e. $\hat{e}_1 > 0$, $\hat{e}_k = 0$, $\forall k \neq 1$). With factor prices unchanged, it must be the case that the subsequent rise in the demand for the growing factor must, if factor prices are unchanged, equal or exceed the growth in the supply of that factor:

$$\hat{e}_1 \leq \sum_i \lambda_{i1}\hat{q}_i \tag{7.82}$$

where $\lambda_{i1} > 0$ is the fraction of factor 1 employed in sector i and $\sum_i \lambda_{i1} = 1$. Given this, (7.82) implies that there must be one good, say good j, for which $\hat{q}_j \geq \hat{e}_1 > 0 = \hat{e}_k$, $\forall k \neq 1$. Moreover, if good j also uses another factor, say factor 2, which is initially fully employed then

$$0 = \hat{e}_2 \geq \sum_i \lambda_{i2}\hat{q}_i \tag{7.83}$$

where $\lambda_{i2} > 0$ is the fraction of factor 2 employed in sector i and $\sum_i \lambda_{i2} = 1$. Since $\hat{q}_j > 0$ and by assumption $\lambda_{j2} > 0$, (7.83) requires that for some good, say good m, $\hat{q}_m < 0$. Hence, we have $\hat{q}_j \geq \hat{e}_1 > 0 > \hat{q}_m$.

Proposition 7.13: A rise in the supply of any one factor will, at unchanged factor prices, raise the output of at least one good and lower the output of some other good, provided that the growing factor is subsequently fully employed and that every industry which uses the factor also uses another factor that is fully employed.

Whereas Proposition 7.13 is very general, it does require factor prices to remain fixed as factor supplies are changed. Whether this condition is satisfied depends on the relative numbers of goods and factors. When the number of goods equals or exceeds the number of factors, Proposition 7.13 holds.[17] However, if factors outnumber goods then Proposition 7.13 will fail since factor prices then also depend on factor supplies and hence cannot remain constant when the latter change. This issue of dimensionality was not important for the Stolper–Samuelson Proposition 7.11.

7.6 Factor price equalization

Whether free trade in goods equalizes factor prices between countries has been the subject of considerable study since the mid-1950s. From an empirical perspective, factor price equalization (FPE) is perhaps less interesting than weaker hypotheses concerning the effects of trade on factor prices (e.g. that trade in goods tends to reduce differences in factor prices, with no presumption that they will become equal). However, for completeness, this section considers the theoretical issues concerning the likelihood of factor price equalization in the context of many goods and factors. A key concept to emerge from this analysis is that of an integrated equilibrium.

Initial inquiry into factor price equalization focused on the question of the global univalence of the mapping between goods prices and factor prices. Assuming equal numbers of goods and factors, and that all countries produce the same set of goods, the question of global univalence centers on the issue of finding technological restrictions such that the zero profit conditions

$$\mathbf{p} = \mathbf{w}\mathbf{A}(\mathbf{w}) \qquad\qquad (7.84)$$

yield a one-to-one mapping between $\mathbf{w}$ and $\mathbf{p}$. In two dimensions the requirement is that of no factor intensity reversals. In higher dimensions, the non-singularity of $\mathbf{A}$ guarantees local univalence between $\mathbf{p}$ and $\mathbf{w}$ but not global univalence. A sufficient condition for the latter was provided by Gale and Nikaido (1965) who established that (7.84) is globally univalent if the principle minors of $\mathbf{A}$ are all positive (in which case $\mathbf{A}$ is called a P-matrix). Unfortunately, the conditions for the global univalence of (7.84) embody little economic intuition and while these conditions are of theoretical importance, their relevance for empirical applications has yet to become evident.

A more intuitive approach to the likelihood of factor price equalization involves the concept of an integrated equilibrium. The essential idea is as follows. Consider a world economy without 'countries' and assume that all factors and goods are mobile. An equilibrium in this world economy will then entail one set of goods prices and one set of factor prices. Now partition this world into arbitrary 'countries' by assigning to each country some amount of the world's supply of each factor. This division of world resources then implies a pattern of production and consumption across countries. We then ask whether this partition of factor supplies supports a pattern of production such that each country can fully employ its share of factors using the integrated economy's production techniques. If the answer is 'yes', then there exists a trade equilibrium in which all countries have the same factor prices as in the integrated equilibrium (i.e. factor prices are equalized). If the answer is no, then the post-partition equilibrium will involve a different set of factor and goods prices, with the former differing between countries. The discussion below formalizes this idea.

Integrated equilibrium[18]

Let there be H factors, and N goods and, for simplicity, 2 countries. We assume countries share the same CRS production function for each good and that product and factor markets are perfectly competitive. Letting asterisks denote foreign variables and functions, where different from that of the home country, the following gives the equilibrium conditions for each country.

For production equilibrium:

$$\mathbf{wA(w)} \geq \mathbf{pq} \geq 0 \tag{7.85}$$

$$\mathbf{w^*A(w^*)} \geq \mathbf{pq^*} \geq 0 \tag{7.86}$$

where $\mathbf{wA(w)}$ are the unit cost functions and $\mathbf{A(w)}$ is the $H \times N$ matrix of factor input requirements.

For factor market equilibrium:

$$\mathbf{A(w)q} = \mathbf{e} \tag{7.87}$$

$$\mathbf{A(w^*)q^*} = \mathbf{e^*} \tag{7.88}$$

For world output market equilibrium:

$$\mathbf{q} + \mathbf{q^*} = \mathbf{d(p, w, e)} + \mathbf{d^*(p, w^*, e^*)}.^{[19]} \tag{7.89}$$

Equations (7.85)–(7.89) comprise a system of $2N + 3H$ equations in as many unknowns (the elements of $\mathbf{p}$, $\mathbf{w}$, $\mathbf{e}$, $\mathbf{q}$, $\mathbf{w^*}$, $\mathbf{e^*}$, $\mathbf{q^*}$). Deducting one unknown by choice of normalization for prices and one equation by Walras' law, this system is determinate and we will assume that it has a unique solution.

We now seek the conditions under which the solution to the above system will have the property that $\mathbf{w} = \mathbf{w^*}$. Suppose such a common solution $\bar{\mathbf{w}}(= \mathbf{w} = \mathbf{w^*})$ exists. Then, with all goods produced somewhere, appropriate selection from among the equations in (7.85) implies that equilibrium goods prices will be given as $\bar{\mathbf{p}} = \bar{\mathbf{w}}\mathbf{A}(\bar{\mathbf{w}})$. Substituting this into the demand functions permits world demand to be expressed as a function of the common factor prices, say $\mathbf{d}(\bar{\mathbf{w}})$.[20] If $\bar{\mathbf{q}}$ represents the world output vector then the above system can be written:

$$\bar{\mathbf{w}}A(\bar{\mathbf{w}}) = \bar{\mathbf{p}} \tag{7.90}$$

$$A(\bar{\mathbf{w}})\bar{\mathbf{q}} = \bar{\mathbf{e}} \tag{7.91}$$

$$\bar{\mathbf{q}} = \mathbf{d}(\bar{\mathbf{w}}) \tag{7.92}$$

where $\bar{\mathbf{q}} = \mathbf{q} + \mathbf{q}^*$ and $\bar{\mathbf{e}} = \mathbf{e} + \mathbf{e}^*$. Comparing this system of equations to those in (7.85)–(7.89) it may be seen that equations (7.90)–(7.92) describe an equilibrium in an integrated world economy in which both factors and goods are mobile. Note that (7.91) is just the addition of (7.87) and (7.88) when $\mathbf{w} = \mathbf{w}^*$. Hence, system (7.90)–(7.92) demonstrates that any trade equilibrium in which factor prices are equal but factors are immobile must also be an equilibrium in which goods and factors are mobile. Given this, the likelihood of factor prices being equalized by trade can be judged by considering the conditions under which a division of world production (via a division of world factor supplies) between countries will replicate the integrated equilibrium. Hence, we seek the conditions under which a partition of world output $\bar{\mathbf{q}} = \mathbf{q} + \mathbf{q}^*$ into non-negative components is also a solution to (7.85)–(7.89).

Given a solution $\bar{\mathbf{q}}$, $\bar{\mathbf{w}}$, $\bar{\mathbf{p}}$, any division of $\bar{\mathbf{q}}$ between countries will satisfy conditions (7.85), (7.86) and (7.89). Hence, the issue reduces to whether a given partition of $\bar{\mathbf{q}}$ will also satisfy the factor market conditions (7.87) and (7.88). This will be possible if and only if equations

$$A(\bar{\mathbf{w}})\mathbf{q} = \mathbf{e} \tag{7.93}$$

have a solution in $\mathbf{q}$ such that $0 \le \mathbf{q} \le \bar{\mathbf{q}}$. If so, then foreign production $\mathbf{q}^*$ is easily determined as $\mathbf{q}^* = \bar{\mathbf{q}} - \mathbf{q}$. Hence, the possibility of factor price equalization reduces to the condition that the system (7.93) have a non-negative solution in $\mathbf{q} \le \bar{\mathbf{q}}$.

If is useful to consolidate these ideas in terms of a geometric representation of the set of all factor supply allocations that would replicate the integrated equilibrium. Consider first the set of all 2-country worlds defined by different allocations of world resources. This set can be represented as an H-dimensional rectilinear box with the lengths of its sides given by the amounts of world resources. Any point in this box then denotes a division of world resources such that amounts $\mathbf{e}$ are located in the home country and amounts $\mathbf{e}^* = \bar{\mathbf{e}} - \mathbf{e}$ are located in the foreign country. Given this, suppose there exists an integrated world equilibrium with solution $\bar{\mathbf{q}}$, $\bar{\mathbf{w}}$ and $\bar{\mathbf{p}}$. Then the set of factor allocations that will replicate the integrated equilibrium can be defined as:

$$\Omega = \{\mathbf{e} | A(\bar{\mathbf{w}})\mathbf{q} = \mathbf{e}, 0 \le \mathbf{q} \le \bar{\mathbf{q}}\} \tag{7.94}$$

For all values of **e** (i.e. partitions of **ē** between **e** and **e***) that lie within this set there will be an equilibrium with the same factor prices even when only goods are mobile. Partitions of **ē** that lie outside this set will entail different factor prices across countries.

What are the properties of this set of factor allocations? First, note that since $\mathbf{A}(\bar{\mathbf{w}})\mathbf{q} = \bar{\mathbf{e}}$ in the integrated equilibrium, $\mathbf{A}(\bar{\mathbf{w}})(\lambda\mathbf{q}) = \lambda\mathbf{A}(\bar{\mathbf{w}})\mathbf{q} = \lambda\bar{\mathbf{e}}$, $0 \leq \lambda \leq 1$ is also an element of Ω. This means that as λ is varied between zero and one we trace out the diagonal of the box of factor allocations. Hence, if countries have the same factor proportions there will be factor price equalization. Further details of the set Ω can be deduced by denoting $\mathbf{a}_j(\bar{\mathbf{w}})$ as the jth column of $\mathbf{A}(\bar{\mathbf{w}})$. This H-dimensional vector gives the unit factor requirements for good j in the integrated equilibrium. Using this, we can write

$$\mathbf{e} = \mathbf{A}(\bar{\mathbf{w}})\mathbf{q} = \sum_{j=1}^{N} \begin{bmatrix} \mathbf{a}_{1j} \\ \vdots \\ \mathbf{a}_{Hj} \end{bmatrix} q_j = \sum_{j=1}^{N} \mathbf{a}_j(\bar{\mathbf{w}})q_j \tag{7.95}$$

Using (7.95) we can express Ω in an alternative form that facilitates geometric interpretation. Specifically, let $\lambda_j = q_j/\bar{q}_j$ be the home country's share of the integrated equilibrium's production of good j. Given this, we can substitute $q_j = \lambda_j\bar{q}_j$ on the right-hand side of (7.95) to get

$$\mathbf{e} = \sum_{j=1}^{N} \lambda_j\mathbf{a}_j(\bar{\mathbf{w}})\bar{q}_j = \sum_{j=1}^{N} \lambda_j\mathbf{a}_j(\bar{\mathbf{w}})\bar{q}_j \tag{7.96}$$

which expresses the factor allocation **e** as a convex combination of the integrated equilibrium sectoral employment vectors $\mathbf{a}_j(\bar{\mathbf{w}})\bar{q}_j$. Given this, the set A can be written in the equivalent form

$$\Omega = \left\{ \mathbf{e} \mid \exists\lambda_j, 0 \leq \lambda_j \leq 1 \;\forall j \text{ s.t. } \mathbf{e} = \sum_j \lambda_j\mathbf{a}_j(\bar{\mathbf{w}})\bar{q}_j \right\}^{21} \tag{7.97}$$

As the λ_j are varied between zero and unity the vector sum $\sum_j \lambda_j\mathbf{a}_j(\bar{\mathbf{w}}_j)\bar{q}_j$ yields convex combinations of the sectoral employment vectors $\mathbf{a}_j(\bar{\mathbf{w}}_j)\bar{q}_j$. Hence, if the number of goods equals or exceeds the number of factors $(N \geq H)$ these linear combinations will span at most a subset of H-dimensional real space. However, if factors outnumber goods $(H > N)$ then it will in general not be possible to construct the set Ω since we have only N factor employment vectors. Hence, when $H > N$, FPE is unlikely.

Consider, for simplicity, the even $(N = H)$ case of 2 goods and 2 factors. Figure 7.1 shows the box of world factor allocations between 2 countries. The length of the box is the world supply of labor and the height is the world supply of capital. A point in the box divides these resources between the 2 countries. Assuming goods and factors are mobile, we can derive unique

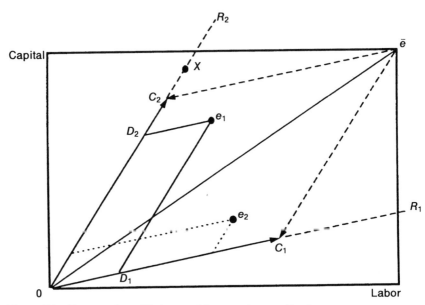

Figure 7.1   *Integrated equilibrium and factor price equalization*

integrated equilibrium solution $\bar{q}$, $\bar{w}$, and $\bar{p}$ which then defines the equilibrium factor input requirements vectors $[\mathbf{a}_1(\bar{w}), \mathbf{a}_2(\bar{w})] \equiv \mathbf{A}(\bar{w})$. These vectors correspond to rays OR_1 and OR_2 in Figure 7.1. The lengths $C_1 = \mathbf{a}_1(\bar{w})\bar{q}_1$ and $C_2 = \mathbf{a}_2(\bar{w})\bar{q}_2$ along rays OR_1 and OR_2, respectively, are the sectoral factor employment levels in the integrated equilibrium. That is, full employment in the integrated equilibrium requires the allocation C_1 of capital and labor to the production of good 1 and the allocation C_2 of capital and labor to the production of good 2. The vector sum of OC_1 and OC_2 is thus the world supply vector ($\bar{e}$) which defines the parallelogram $OC_1\bar{e}C_2$.

Now suppose Home receives the allocation e_1 (foreign receives $e_2 = \bar{e} - e_1$) of world capital and labor. This allocation can be decomposed into components parallel to OC_1 and OC_2 to yield points D_1 and D_2 which are the allocations of capital and labor across sectors that yield full employment in Home. Hence, $\lambda_1 = OD_1/OC_1$ and $\lambda_2 = OD_2/OC_2$. As shown, a similar decomposition can be performed for Foreign's allocation e_2. The allocation e_1 permits each country to produce less than the total amount of each good produced in the integrated equilibrium, that is, allocation e_1 permits positive levels of production with full employment in each country. Hence, this division of world factor supplies (production) between countries replicates the integrated equilibrium and hence is also a trade equilibrium with equal factor prices.

It can be verified that any allocation of world factor supplies outside the parallelogram $OC_1\bar{e}C_2$ would require negative production of some good, or equivalently unemployed resources, in order to replicate production in the integrated equilibrium. For example, suppose Home receives the allocation denoted X in Figure 7.1. In this case, full employment would require Home to employ all its capital and labor in sector 2 and thus Home would specialize in producing good 2. However, Home's employment levels in sector 2 exceed those at C_2 (i.e. $X/C_2 > 1$) which means Home's production of good 2 exceeds that in the integrated equilibrium ($\lambda_2 > 1$). Hence, to achieve the integrated equilibrium production levels Foreign must produce a negative amount of good 2. Since it is not possible, using the integrated equilibrium factor input requirements, to replicate the integrated equilibrium with weakly positive outputs, factor allocation X cannot be a trade equilibrium with equal factor prices.

Figure 7.1 suggests that the 'likelihood' of FPE can be measured by the size of Ω (the parallelogram) relative to the size of the box. If so, then FPE is unlikely when factors (H) outnumber goods (N) since, as noted earlier, the N factor input vectors can span, at most, an N-dimensional factor space. If goods outnumber factors then there are more factor input vectors than needed to span H-dimensional factor space. This implies that while a trade equilibrium with FPE is possible when $N > H$, production and trade patterns will be indeterminate since, with equal factor prices, there are many

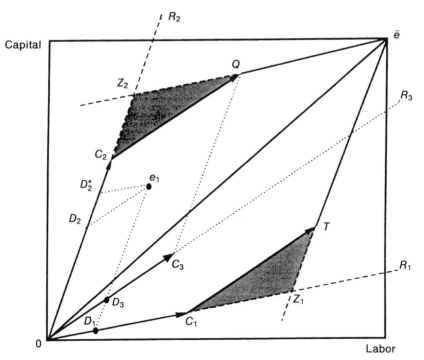

Figure 7.2 *Factor price equalization with 3 goods and 2 factors*

production patterns that can fully employ a given set of factors in each country. Figure 7.2 illustrates the case of 3 goods and 2 factors.

In Figure 7.2 we have added a third factor input requirement vector OR_3 corresponding to sector 3. To construct the set Ω, we determine the integrated equilibrium which determines rays OR_j and lengths $OC_j = \mathbf{a}_j(\bar{\mathbf{w}})\bar{q}_j$ along these rays. The vector sum of the OC_js equals the world supplies of capital and labor ($\bar{\mathbf{e}}$) reflecting factor market clearing (full employment) in the integrated equilibrium. Given this, the set of factor allocations compatible with FPE (i.e. the set Ω) is given by the parallel-sided hexagon $OC_2 Q\bar{e}TC_1$. Comparing this region to that of the case of 2 goods and 2 factors (the parallelogram $OZ_1\bar{e}Z_2$ in Figure 7.2), the addition of good 3 reduces the size of Ω by an amount equal to the 2 shaded regions.

Now consider the factor allocation $\mathbf{e}_1$. Home could fully employ these factors by employing OD_2 in sector 2, OD_3 in sector 3 and none in sector 1. Alternatively, it could employ OD_2^* in sector 2 and OD_1 in sector 1 and thus not produce good 3. Several other full employment production patterns are possible.[22] Hence, whereas the integrated equilibrium solution may be unique when goods outnumber factors, the country patterns of production and trade when factor prices are equalized is indeterminate.

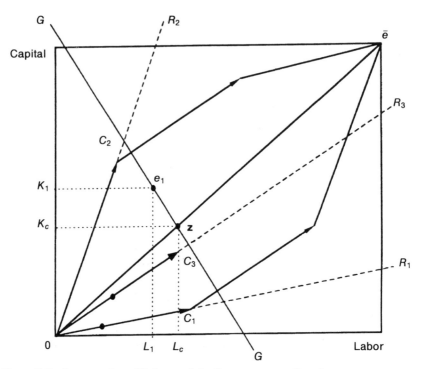

Figure 7.3 *Integrated equilibrium and the factor content of trade*

Finally, note that while the pattern of trade in goods is indeterminate when goods outnumber factors, the factor content of trade is determinant. This is shown in Figure 7.3 which adds to Figure 7.2 the iso-income line GG passing through e_1. The slope of GG equals (minus) the wage–rental ratio in the integrated equilibrium.[23] With identical homothetic preferences across countries (as assumed here), the intersection of line GG with the diagonal of the box (point z) gives the factor content of Home's consumption vector, that is, the capital and labor services consumed by Home (denoted K_c and L_c).[24] Subtracting Home's factor supply (e_1) from its desired consumption of factors (z) defines Home's trade in factor services, that is, the factor content of its net trade. In the present case, Home exports the services of capital ($K_1 - K_c > 0$) and imports the services of labor ($K_1 - K_c < 0$).

In summary, if countries' factor supply vectors lie within the 'cone' defined by the integrated equilibrium factor input requirement vectors then a trade equilibrium with immobile factors will replicate the integrated equilibrium and hence factor prices will be equalized. In general, this requires the number of goods to equal or exceed the number of factors and that countries' factor supply vectors not differ 'too greatly'.

7.7 Concluding remarks

The concept of comparative advantage, the price and quantity versions of the H–O theorem, the Stolper–Samuelson and Rybczynski propositions, and the factor price equalization remain largely intact when considered in the context of a general N-good, H-factor perfectly competitive model. Where dimensionality is important, the critical requirement is that the number of goods exceed the number of factors.[25] This requirement on the relative numbers of goods and factors applies most stringently to strong forms of the Rybczynski proposition, the quantity version of the H–O theorem and the likelihood of FPE. However, assuming only that firms minimize costs and that consumers maximize utility, without regard to the exact form of technology or preferences, or the relative numbers of goods and factors, these propositions (except FPE) do hold in the weaker form of correlations between (variously) factor prices, goods prices, factor use and trade.

Whereas general results in the form of correlations can be derived, nothing can be said about individual components. For example, one is unable to predict the commodity composition of trade in goods in the case of the weakened H–O theorem. In these cases the concept of a country's trade in factor services, that is, the factor content of trade, proves particularly useful as a parallel generalization of the H–O theorems. The factor content formulations also permits one to resolve cases in which the pattern of production, and hence trade in goods, is indeterminate. The usefulness of the factor content formulation is further highlighted in Chapter 8 when empirical tests of trade theory involving N goods and H factors are discussed.

Lastly, the proposition that free trade in goods will equalize factor prices between countries leads to consideration of an integrated world equilibrium in which goods and factors are mobile. In this context, if country factor supplies do now differ too greatly then it is possible for factor prices to be equalized when the number of goods equals or exceeds the number of factors.

Notes

1. For notational simplicity we omit the transpose symbol ''' and instead assume that the vectors and matrices are conformable for the indicated multiplication.
2. Formally $G(\mathbf{p}, \mathbf{e}) = \min_{\mathbf{w}} \{ \mathbf{we} | c_j(\mathbf{w}) \geq p_j, \forall j \}$ where $c_j(\mathbf{w})$ is industry j's unit cost function (see Chapter 4).
3. As in other chapters, this chapter maintains the assumption that there exists a collective utility function which depends upon the aggregate consumption of each good.
4. The factor content of net trade measures a country's net exchange of factor services that is implicit in its exchange of goods through trade. See Chapter 8 for further discussion.
5. If the function $y = f(x)$ is continuous and differentiable on the interval $[x_1, x_0]$ then the mean-value theorem states that there exists some $\bar{x}$ between points x_1 and x_0 such that

$$y(x_1) - y(x_0) = \frac{\partial f(\bar{x})}{\partial x} (x_1 - x_0).$$

6. By definition, $z(\mathbf{w}_0) = \mathbf{w}_0 A(\mathbf{w}_0)(\mathbf{p}_1 - \mathbf{p}_0)$ and $z(\mathbf{w}_1) = \mathbf{w}_1 A(\mathbf{w}_1)(\mathbf{p}_1 - \mathbf{p}_0)$. Hence $z(\mathbf{w}_1) - z(\mathbf{w}_0) = \mathbf{w}_1 A(\mathbf{w}_1)(\mathbf{p}_1 - \mathbf{p}_0) - \mathbf{w}_0 A(\mathbf{w}_0)(\mathbf{p}_1 - \mathbf{p}_0)$. Using the zero profit condition $\mathbf{p} = \mathbf{w}A(\mathbf{w}), z(\mathbf{w}_1) - z(\mathbf{w}_0) = \mathbf{p}_1(\mathbf{p}_1 - \mathbf{p}_0) - \mathbf{p}_0(\mathbf{p}_1 - \mathbf{p}_0) = (\mathbf{p}_1 - \mathbf{p}_0)(\mathbf{p}_1 - \mathbf{p}_0)$.
7. Note that (7.36) can be considered a generalized form of the Stolper–Samuelson proposition. Section 7.5 contains further details.
8. In addition, the factor price vector $\bar{\mathbf{w}}$ may not correspond to the factor price vector that exists under free trade. That is, the mean-value theorem states only that (7.33) holds for *some* $\bar{\mathbf{w}}$ between $\mathbf{w}_0$ and $\mathbf{w}_1$. But no guidance is given as to how $\bar{\mathbf{w}}$ should be selected.
9. See also Varian (1992, p. 147) or Dixit and Norman (1980, pp. 325–6).
10. See Section 7.4.
11. Alternatively, a vector of factor prices $\bar{w}$ between $\mathbf{w}_A$ and $\mathbf{w}_A^*$ since output prices uniquely determine input prices when factor supplies $\mathbf{e}$ are given.

12. Note that factor supplies **e** and **e*** are being held fixed.

13. Recall that $A(\bar{w})$ defines factor input requirements at some inter-mediate wage $\bar{w}$ between the w_0 and w_1. Hence, there is the possibility, due to 'factor intensity reversals', that the change in **w** may change factor requirements to such an extent that (7.75) may no longer be valid.

14. See Jones and Scheinkman (1977).

15. As Ethier (1984) notes, this requires $\theta_{mk} > 0$ for all m in both the initial and new equilibria. This means that every factor employed by the industry whose price has risen must be re-employed somewhere else in the economy in the new equilibrium.

16. See Ethier (1984).

17. In fact, even more general statements are possible in this case. See Ethier (1984).

18. This section based on Dixit and Norman (1980).

19. This assumes identical tastes among consumers in each country.

20. This also assumes that the distribution of factor ownership across countries is fixed so that demands are independent of where factor incomes are generated. See Dixit and Norman (1980, p. 107) for further discussion.

21. In the case of N countries the set of factor allocations that will replicate the integrated equilibrium is:

$$\Omega = \left\{ \mathbf{e}_1, \ldots, \mathbf{e}_N \mid \exists \lambda_{ij}, 0 \leq \lambda_{ij} \leq 1 \; \forall j \; \text{s.t.} \; \mathbf{e}_i = \sum_j \lambda_{ij} \mathbf{a}_i(\bar{w}) \bar{q}_j \right\}$$

where j indexes goods, i indexes countries and each $\mathbf{e}_i$ is an H element vector of factor supplies allocated to country i. The trade equilibrium output of good j in country i when all resources are fully employed is $q_{ij} = \lambda_{ij} \bar{q}_j$.

22. In general, if $N > H$ the equations $\bar{\mathbf{e}} = A(\bar{w})\mathbf{q}$ have potentially many solutions since at most H of the N columns of A can be linearly independent. This means that (at most) $N - H$ outputs can be expressed in terms of the remaining H outputs.

23. For country i, this line is derived from $GDP_i = \bar{r}K_i + \bar{w}L_i$.

24. With identical homothetic preferences, country i will consume the fraction $\alpha_i = GDP_i / \sum_i GDP_i$ of every good, $0 < \alpha_i < 1$. It then follows that country i's consumption vector ($\mathbf{d}_i$) is proportional to the integrated world's output (= consumption) vector ($\mathbf{q}$) : $\mathbf{d}_i = \alpha_i \bar{\mathbf{q}}$. To see this, pre-multiply the latter equation by the factor requirements matrix to derive country i's implicit consumption of factors as $A(\bar{w})\mathbf{d}_i = \alpha_i A(\bar{w})\bar{\mathbf{q}}$. Since $A(\bar{w})\bar{\mathbf{q}} = \bar{\mathbf{e}}$ we have $A(\bar{w})\bar{\mathbf{d}}_i = \alpha_i\bar{\mathbf{e}}$.

25. Ethier (1984) suggests that the relevant requirement is that the number of international markets should exceed the number of factors. This derives from the fact that the dimensionality issue concerns the number of linearly independent columns (rows) in the $H \times N$ factor input matrix $A(\mathbf{w})$. For example, in the case of FPE let H_T factors be traded internationally and H_N be immobile. In this case the prices of the traded factors will be determined in international markets so that the dimensionality requirement in terms of $A(\mathbf{w})$ becomes $N \geq H_N$. Since $H_T + H_N = H$, the latter can also be written as $N + H_T \geq H$ which states that the number of international markets (in goods and factors) should exceed the number of factors.

References and additional reading

Chang, W. (1979), 'Some Theorems of Trade and General Equilibrium with Many Goods and Factors', *Econometrica*, 47(3), 709–26.

Chang, W., Ethier, W. and Kemp, M. (1980), 'The Theorems of International Trade with Joint Production', *Journal of International Economics*, 10 (August), 377–94.

Deardorff, A.V. (1979), 'Weak Links in the Chain of Comparative Advantage', *Journal of International Economics*, 9(2), 197–209.

Deardorff, A.V. (1980), 'The General Validity of the Law of Comparative Advantage', *Journal of Political Economy*, 88(5), 941–57.

Deardorff, A.V. (1982), 'The General Validity of the Heckscher–Ohlin Theorem', *American Economic Review*, 72, 683–94.

Dixit, A. and Norman, V. (1980), *Theory of International Trade* (London: Cambridge University Press).

Ethier, W. (1984), 'Higher Dimensional Issues in Trade Theory', Chapter 3 in Jones, R. and Kenen, P. (eds), *Handbook of International Economics, Vol. I* (Amsterdam: North Holland), 131–84.

Gale, D. and Nikaido H. (1965), 'The Jacobian Matrix and the Global Univalence of Mappings,' *Mathematische Annalen*, 159, 81–93.

Jones R. and Scheinkman J. (1977), 'The Relevance of the Two-Sector Production Model in Trade Theory', *Journal of Political Economy*, 85, 909–35.

Varian, H.R. (1992), *Microeconomic Analysis* (New York: W.W. Norton and Company), 3rd edn.

Woodland, A.D. (1982), *International Trade and Resource Allocation* (New York: North Holland).

■ *Chapter 8* ■

Empirical Tests of the Factor Abundance Model

8.1 Trade in factor services
8.2 Regression analyses of trade
    in goods

8.3 Concluding remarks

The Heckscher–Ohlin–Samuelson (H–O–S) factor abundance model predicts that a country will export the good that uses its abundant factor intensively in production. This chapter discusses the translation of this theoretical statement into one or more empirically verifiable hypotheses and considers alternative empirical methods for testing these hypotheses. The translation from theory to empirical specification is not trivial, and is one reason why efforts to determine the empirical validity of the H–O–S model have occupied the interest of trade economists for over 40 years. Among the issues to be confronted are the problem of extending the model to a world of many countries, many goods and many factors as well as the ambiguity of concepts such as factor intensity and factor abundance in higher dimensions. Perhaps more important is that the H–O–S model does not predict, except in some average sense, the composition of trade in *goods* in a multifactor, multicommodity framework. As seen below, many of these issues are dealt with by considering the trade in factor services rather than the trade in goods.

The predictions of the H–O–S model derive from a complex interaction between three sets of variables (trade, factor use and factor supplies) and any empirical investigation of the model should therefore employ measures of all three sets of variables. Only recently have empirical tests of the H–O–S model met this requirement. Since many earlier tests of the H–O–S model, beginning with that of Leontief (1953),[1] have been incomplete either in terms of data or model specification, the results of much of this work have been been considered inconclusive with respect to the validity of the H–O–S model.

8.1 Trade in factor services

The H–O–V model

The trade in factor services is a useful framework for translating the predictions of the H–O–S model into a set of testable hypotheses. The standard model of such trade in a multifactor, multicommodity, multi-country setting is the Heckscher-Ohlin-Vanek (H–O–V) model. To develop this model, assume there are J commodities, H productive factors and N countries. Let $\mathbf{Q}_i$ and $\mathbf{C}_i$ denote, respectively, the $J \times 1$ vectors of net outputs and final demand for country i.[2] By definition, the $J \times 1$ vector of net trades for country i is then $\mathbf{T}_i \equiv \mathbf{Q}_i - \mathbf{C}_i$. Let $\mathbf{A}_i$ denote the $H \times J$ matrix of equilibrium total factor input requirements. An element of $\mathbf{A}_i$, a_{hj}, is the amount of factor h used to produce one unit of net output of good j given the equilibrium factor prices and state of technology.[3] Pre-multiplying the vector of net trades $(\mathbf{T}_i)$ by $\mathbf{A}_i$ yields country i's net trade in factor services $(\mathbf{F}_i)$

$$\mathbf{F}_i \equiv \mathbf{A}_i \mathbf{T}_i = \mathbf{A}_i \mathbf{Q}_i - \mathbf{A}_i \mathbf{C}_i \tag{8.1}$$

The net trade in factor services is also called the factor content of trade. Let $\mathbf{E}_i$ denote the $H \times 1$ vector of country i's factor supplies. Then, assuming full employment of all resources implies $\mathbf{E}_i = \mathbf{A}_i \mathbf{Q}_i$. If preferences are identical and homothetic across countries then the final demand vector of country i is proportional to the world final demand vector $(\mathbf{C}_w)$: $\mathbf{C}_i = \mu_i \mathbf{C}_w$ where μ_i is country i's share of world expenditure. Since world final demand equals world net output[4] for each good we can also write $\mathbf{C}_i = \mu_i \mathbf{Q}_w$ where $\mathbf{Q}_w$ is the $J \times 1$ vector of world net outputs. Substituting these full employment and final demand relationships in (8.1) gives:

$$\mathbf{F}_i \equiv \mathbf{A}_i \mathbf{T}_i = \mathbf{E}_i - \mu_i \mathbf{A}_i \mathbf{Q}_w \tag{8.2}$$

We assume that free trade in goods equalizes factor prices across countries which implies that all countries use the same factor input requirements, that is, $\mathbf{A}_i = \mathbf{A} \, \forall \, i$. Given this, $\mathbf{A}_i \mathbf{Q}_w$ in (8.2) equals the vector of world factor supplies $\mathbf{E}_w$ since $\mathbf{A}_i \mathbf{Q}_w = \mathbf{A}_i \sum_{z=1}^{N} \mathbf{Q}_z = \sum_{z=1}^{N} \mathbf{A} \mathbf{Q}_z = \sum_{z=1}^{N} \mathbf{E}_z = \mathbf{E}_w$. Finally, the expenditure share can be written $\mu_i = \alpha_i - \lambda_i$ where $\alpha_i = Y_i / Y_w$ is the ratio of country i's income (GDP) to world income (expenditure) and $\lambda_i = b_i / Y_w$, is the ratio of country i's trade imbalance to world income.[5] Substituting these expressions in (8.2) gives:

$$\mathbf{F}_i = \mathbf{E}_i - (\alpha_i - \lambda_i)\mathbf{E}_w \tag{8.3}$$

The equations in (8.3) are referred to as the H–O–V equations. Each equation links country i's net trade in the services of a factor to the country's excess supply of that factor.

Definitions of factor abundance

The derivation of H–O–S-type propositions in the H–O–V model requires a definition of factor abundance. Two commonly used definitions are given below.

Relative factor abundance Factor h is abundant relative to factor z in country i if country i's world share of factor h exceeds its world share of factor z, that is, if $e_{ih}/e_{wh} > e_{iz}/e_{wz}$, where $e_{i.}$ and $e_{w.}$ are the factor supplies in country i and the world, respectively.

The definition of relative abundance implies that the ranking of all H factor shares for one country defines that country's 'structure of factor abundance'.

Absolute factor abundance Factor h is absolutely abundant in country i if country i's share of the world supply of factor h exceeds country i's share of world income, that is, if $e_{ih}/e_{wh} > Y_i/Y_w = \alpha_i$.[6]

Absolute factor abundance is also a measure of relative abundance, but with abundance being measured relative to an average of all resources. This follows since the income share α_i is an average of the resource shares:

$$Y_i/Y_w = \sum_z \left(\frac{w_z e_{iz}}{\sum_z w_z e_{wz}} \right) = \sum_z \left(\frac{w_z e_{wz}(e_{iz}/e_{wz})}{\sum_z w_z e_{wz}} \right) = \sum_z \omega_{wz} \frac{e_{iz}}{e_{wz}}$$

where w_z is the world price of factor z and ω_{wz} is factor z's share of world income (expenditure). Finally, note that an *absolutely* abundant factor can be *relatively* scarce compared to some other factor. In addition, all *absolutely* abundant factors are also *relatively* abundant compared to all *absolutely* scarce factors.

Given these factor abundance definitions, the H–O–V model (8.3) implies two propositions about the relationship between factor services trade and factor abundance.

Proposition S (sign proposition): If trade is balanced, a country exports (net) the services of its *absolutely* abundant factors and imports (net) the services of its *absolutely* scarce factors.

Proposition R (rank proposition): If country i is abundant in factor h *relative* to factor z, then country i's *proportionate* net trade in the services of factor h exceeds its *proportionate* net trade in the services of factor z.

The *proportionate* net trade is the net trade in the services of a factor divided by either the country's total supply of that factor or the world supply of that factor. A third proposition that is similar to proposition R is:

Proposition L (Leontief proposition): If country i is abundant in factor h *relative* to factor z, then the ratio of its exports of factor h to its exports of factor z exceeds the ratio of its imports of factor h to its imports of factor z.

Propositions *R* and *L* differ in their concept of net trade, the latter measuring it as the ratio of exports to imports. Proposition *L* was initially investigated by Leontief (1953). Whether this proposition is valid is considered below.

Problem 8.1:   Use the following data for a 3-factor, 3-good model to calculate the factor supply vectors E_i and E_w; the expenditure share $(\alpha_i - \lambda_i)$; the excess factor supply vector and the factor content of trade. Does the pattern of factor contents conform to absolute factor abundance? To relative factor abundance?

$$
A = \begin{bmatrix} 3 & 2 & 3 \\ 4 & 1 & 4 \\ 2 & 1 & 1 \end{bmatrix}, \, Q_i = \begin{bmatrix} 1 \\ 2 \\ 6 \end{bmatrix}, \, Q_w = \begin{bmatrix} 12 \\ 4 \\ 12 \end{bmatrix}, \, P = \begin{bmatrix} 2 \\ 1 \\ 1 \end{bmatrix}, \, T_i = \begin{bmatrix} -2 \\ 1 \\ 3 \end{bmatrix}
$$

Propositions *S*, *R* and *L* may hold even if (8.3) is not exact (i.e. holds as an equality) and are therefore considered 'weakened' forms of the exact H–O–V hypothesis of strict equality between the net trade in factor services and the excess supply of factors. A test of the exact H–O–V hypothesis would involve measuring the trade vector T_i, the factor input matrix A, and the vector of excess factor supplies $(E_i - (\alpha_i - \lambda_i)E_w)$ and then computing the extent to which these data violate the equalities in (8.3). In contrast, tests of propositions *S*, *R*, and *L* only require conformity between the right and left-hand sides of (8.3) in terms of sign or rank.

   In addition to being weaker forms of the exact H–O–V hypothesis, propositions *S*, *R*, and *L* share the idea that the trade in factor services 'reveals' factor abundance (i.e. the left-hand side of (8.3) 'reveals' the right-hand side of (8.3)). Because of these similarities, and the fact that proposition *L* was the first to be subjected to empirical verification (by Leontief), these propositions, and their corresponding tests, are referred to as 'Leontief-type'.

   Like the H–O–S model, the H–O–V model involves a relationship between trade, factor use and factor supplies. The H–O–V model also contains a prediction about the pattern of trade in *goods*, albeit weaker than that of the H–O–S model. Specifically, the content of factor *h* in net trade is a weighted average of country *i*'s net trade in goods where the weights are equal to the requirements of factor *h* in each industry: $f_{ih} = \sum_j a_{ijh} t_{ij}$. A positive factor content therefore implies that the composition of net trade is biased, on average, toward goods that use relatively more, *per unit of output*, of a factor in which the country is abundant (i.e. $f_{ih} > 0$ when factor *h* is absolutely abundant). Such statements about the average relationship between trade, factor inputs and factor supplies will arise later when alternative methods for testing the H–O–S/H–O–V model are considered.

Problem 8.2: The H–O–V model (8.3) is stated in terms of the quantities of goods and factors. Let *diag*($\mathbf{Z}$) denote the diagonal matrix whose elements are the elements of the vector $\mathbf{Z}$. Use the fact that $diag(\mathbf{P}_i)^{-1}\mathbf{A}_i\, diag(\mathbf{W}_i) = \mathbf{W}_i'\mathbf{E}_i$, where $\mathbf{P}_i$ is the J element vector of goods prices in country i and $\mathbf{W}_i$ is the $H \times 1$ vector of factor prices in country i, to reformulate the H–O–V equations (8.3) in terms of the values of trade and factor supplies. Then formulate definitions of factor abundance such that propositions similar to propositions S and R can be stated.

Leontief-type tests

The Leontief proposition

For more than twenty-five years after Leontief's classic paper (1953) proposition L was at the core of any test of the H–O–S theory. Testing proposition L is no longer desirable since, as shown below, it may not hold even when the H–O–V model is valid. However, the historical significance of this proposition warrants its discussion.

Consider two factors, capital (K) and labor (L). Proposition L states that if capital is abundant relative to labor in country i, ($K_i/K_w > L_i/L_w$), country i's exports of capital per-worker will exceed its imports of capital per-worker, $K_x^i/L_x^i > K_m^i/L_m^i$, where K^i and L^i are the capital and labor, respectively, embodied in country i's exports (x) or imports (m). The tradition since Leontief is to express the latter inequality as a ratio (the 'Leontief ratio'):

$$\psi_{KL}^i = (K_x^i/L_x^i)/(K_m^i/L_m^i) \tag{8.4}$$

Similarly, the factor abundance inequality can be expressed as a ratio:

$$\pi_{KL}^i = (K_i/L_i)/(K_w/L_w) \tag{8.5}$$

where $\pi_{KL}^i > 1$ when capital is abundant. Let $sign(z)$ denote the sign of z. Then proposition L can be expressed as:

$$sign(\pi_{KL}^i - 1) = sign(\psi_{KL}^i - 1) \tag{8.6}$$

A test of proposition L therefore involves computing (8.4) and (8.5) and then comparing signs according to (8.6). However, most tests of proposition L do not compute $sign(\pi_{KL}^i - 1)$ but instead assert it. For example, Leontief assumed that capital was abundant relative to labor in the United States, he did not measure it. But not computing $sign(\pi_{KL}^i - 1)$ means that a test of proposition L is incomplete,[7] and any conclusion about the validity of proposition L is problematic. For example, if $sign(\psi_{KL}^i - 1)$ is found to be opposite from that expected, should one reject the H–O–V model or one's conjecture about factor abundance?

Even if $sign(\pi^i_{KL} - 1)$ is computed a difficulty remains. Suppose capital is abundant relative to labor in country i. A test of proposition L can then be thought to involve testing the null hypothesis $H0: (\psi^i_{KL} - 1) \geq 0$ against the alternative $H1: (\psi^i_{KL} - 1) < 0$. But hypothesis $H1$ is unsatisfactory in that no alternative model (or assumption) is clearly stated. Thus, if $H0$ is rejected in favor of $H1$, one can only speculate about the alternative model that is being accepted. A further difficulty is that statements as to the statistical significance associated with such tests are often difficult to formulate.

Whereas the problems of incomplete data and an unclear alternative hypothesis are important, tests of proposition L face a more serious objection: proposition L may not hold even when the H–O–V model is valid. To see this, consider the H–O–V equations for capital and labor:

$$f_{iK} = (K^i_x - K^i_m) = K_i - (\alpha_i - \lambda_i)K_w \tag{8.7}$$

$$f_{iL} = (L^i_x - L^i_m) = L_i - (\alpha_i - \lambda_i)L_w \tag{8.8}$$

where subscripts x and m again refer to the amount of a factor embodied in exports and imports, respectively. Dividing (8.7) by K^i_m and (8.8) by L^i_m and then subtracting the latter from the former we can write:

$$(\psi^i_{KL} - 1) = [(K_i - \alpha_i K_w)/K^i_m - (L_i - \alpha_i L_w)/L^i_m$$

$$+ \lambda_i(K_w/K^i_m - L_w/L^i_m)](L^i_m/L^i_x) \tag{8.9}$$

This indicates that $sign(\psi^i_{KL} - 1)$ depends upon the sign of three elements: the two excess factor supplies $(K_i - \alpha_i K_w)/K^i_m$ and $(L_i - \alpha_i L_w)/L^i_m$ and a term reflecting trade imbalance $\lambda_i(K_w/K^i_m - L_w/L^i_m)$.

If trade is balanced ($\lambda_i = 0$) then (8.9) reduces to

$$(\psi^i_{KL} - 1) = [(K_i - \alpha_i K_w)/K^i_m - (L_i - \alpha_i L_w)/L^i_m](L^i_m/L^i_x) \tag{8.10}$$

and hence $sign(\psi^i_{KL} - 1)$ now depends only on the signs of the excess factor supply terms. In a world of only 2 factors, trade balance implies that the excess factor supplies $(K_i - \alpha_i K_w)$ and $(L_i - \alpha_i L_w)$ are of opposite sign.[8] Thus, if capital is abundant[9] then the bracketed term in (8.10) is positive and implies $(\psi^i_{KL} - 1) > 0$. Thus, in a world of only 2 factors, trade balance is sufficient for $sign(\psi^i_{KL} - 1)$ to correctly indicate the relatively abundant factor.

If trade in not balanced then $sign(\psi^i_{KL} - 1)$ may fail to indicate the relatively abundant factor since the sign of the bracketed term in (8.9) also depends on the sign of $\lambda_i(K_w/K^i_m - L_w/L^i_m)$. Whereas λ_i takes the sign of the trade imbalance, the sign of the term $(K_w/K^i_m - L_w/L^i_m)$ is problematic. Consequently, $(\psi^i_{KL} - 1) > 0$ could be consistent with either capital abundance or capital scarcity.[10]

When there are more than 2 factors a Leontief ratio (ψ^i) can be computed with respect to any pair of factors and an equation analogous to (8.9) holds for that pair of factors. Given any 2 factors h and z, two sufficient conditions for $sign(\psi_{hz}^i - 1)$ to correctly reveal the relatively abundant factor are:

Condition L1: Balanced trade.

Condition L2: One factor is *absolutely* abundant and one factor is *absolutely* scarce.

Condition $L1$ ensures that $sign(\psi_{hz}^i - 1)$ depends only on the sign of the sum of the excess factor supply terms in (8.9). Condition $L2$ ensures that the sign of the sum of the 2 excess factor supplies is the same as $sign(e_{ih}/e_{wh} - e_{iz}/e_{wz})$. Finally, if trade is balanced, the following condition is equivalent to condition $L2$:

Condition L3: One factor is exported (net) and one factor is imported (net).

That proposition L may fail to hold is convincingly demonstrated by Leamer's (1980) examination of Leontief's original data for the United States. In the year examined by Leontief the United States had a trade surplus and, on the basis of this alone, one might not expect $sign(\psi_{KL}^{US} - 1)$ to correctly reveal the relatively abundant factor. Using proposition R, Leamer ranked the US *proportionate* net trade in capital and labor services (see Table 8.1). This ranking revealed capital to be abundant relative to labor (contrary to Leontief's finding). One can only speculate on the direction that empirical and theoretical research in international trade would have taken had Leontief used proposition R instead of proposition L to reveal US factor abundance!

To summarize, if conditions $L1$ and $L2$ (or $L3$) are satisfied then $sign(\psi_{hz}^i - 1)$ correctly reveals the relatively abundant factor. A test of the H–O–V model is then to compare this 'revelation' with the measurement of relative factor abundance given by $sign(\pi_{hz}^i - 1)$. In practice, condition $L1$ is unlikely to hold. However, one can attempt to adjust the trade data to force

Table 8.1 *Factor content of 1947 US trade and production*

Factor services embodied in:	Capital ($ million)	Labor (million man years)
Net trade	23 450	1.99
Production	328 519	47.273
Ratio of net trade to production	0.0714	0.0424

Source: Leamer (1980).

trade balance[11] and, if so, condition $L3$ can then be checked by computing the net trade in each factor (using the trade imbalance adjusted data) to see if they are opposite in sign. But note that when checking if condition $L3$ is satisfied, one is *already* revealing the relatively abundant factor. Thus, subsequent computation of $sign(\psi^i_{hz} - 1)$ would be redundant. Since determining if the conditions needed for proposition L to hold are satisfied is, by itself, sufficient to determine the relatively abundant factor, actually testing proposition L is unnecessary.

Sign proposition

Unlike proposition L, propositions S and R are direct implications of the H–O–V model. However, tests of these propositions still require careful formulation and, in particular, attention should be given to the influence of any trade imbalance.

Consider first proposition S. The H–O–V equation for factor h is

$$f_{ih} = e_{ih} - \alpha_i e_{wh} + \lambda_i e_{wh} \qquad (8.11)$$

The possibility of trade imbalance is taken into account by defining the *adjusted* net trade in factor h (f^A_{ih}):

$$f^A_{ih} \equiv f_{ih} - \lambda_i e_{wh} = e_{ih} - \alpha_i e_{wh} \qquad (8.12)$$

The adjusted factor content f^A_{ih} is the net trade in factor h that would be observed if trade were balanced.[12] From (8.12), $sign(f^A_{ih}) = sign(e_{ih} - \alpha_i e_{wh})$ and proposition S follows immediately from the definition of absolute factor abundance.[13]

Given data on the adjusted net trade in a factor and the excess supply of that factor, proposition S can be tested by examining if the sign of the former matches the sign of the latter. Tests of proposition S are subject to some of the same criticisms that were discussed in the context of testing proposition L. Namely, the alternative hypothesis associated with testing proposition S is unclear regarding the alternative model against which the H–O–V model is being tested. Tests of proposition S also face the problem of specifying the appropriate level of significance.

Rank proposition

Proposition R states that the ranking of country i's *proportionate* net trade (adjusted for any trade imbalance) in the services of each of H factors duplicates its structure of factor abundance, that is, the ranking

$$\frac{f^A_{i1}}{z_1} > \cdots > \frac{f^A_{ih}}{z_h} > \cdots > \frac{f^A_{iH}}{z_H} \qquad (8.13)$$

duplicates the ranking of world resource shares

$$\frac{e_{i1}}{e_{w1}} > \cdots > \frac{e_{ih}}{e_{wh}} > \cdots > \frac{e_{iH}}{e_{wH}}$$

The variable z_h in (8.13) can be either the supply of factor h in the world or in country i.

Given data on the *proportionate* adjusted factor contents and world resource shares, proposition R can be tested by comparing the ranking of the former to the ranking of the latter. Methods for gauging the conformity of these rankings have included computing the coefficient of rank correlation and the number of correct pairwise rankings among factors (or countries)[14] out of all possible pairwise rankings.

Like tests of propositions L and S, tests of proposition R face the problem that the alternative hypothesis is unclear as to the alternative model. But tests of proposition R face an additional problem. In practice, the H–O–V equations are not equalities and thus the form in which the factor contents and factor supplies are expressed can led to alternative results. For example, the following are equivalent ways of expressing proposition R:

$R1:$ $rank(f_{ih}^A) = rank(e_{ih} - \alpha_i e_{wh})$

$R2:$ $rank(f_{ih}^A/e_{wh}) = rank(e_{ih}/e_{wh} - \alpha_i)$

$R3:$ $rank(f_{ih}^A/e_{ih}) = rank(1 - \alpha_i e_{wh}/e_{ih})$

$R4:$ $rank(f_{ih}^A/\alpha_i e_{wh}) = rank(e_{ih}/\alpha_i e_{wh} - 1)$

$R5:$ $rank(f_{ih}^A/\alpha_i) = rank(e_{ih}/\alpha_i - e_{wh})$

These alternative expressions for proposition R can be thought to be generated by a linear transformation of the factor contents and excess factor supplies. For example, $R2$ can be obtained by multiplying both sides of $R1$ by $1/e_{wh}$ whereas $R3$ is obtained by multiplying $R1$ by $1/e_{ih}$. Such transformations can be represented by an equation of the form $\nu_h + \gamma_h z_{ih}$. Thus, $R2$ can be derived from $R1$ by letting $\nu_h = 0$ and $\gamma_h = 1/e_{wh}$ and then setting z_{ih} equal to f_{ih}^A or $(e_{ih} - \alpha_i e_{wh})$.

To see that rankings can be reversed when the H–O–V equations are not equalities, let $x_{ih} = f_{ih}^A$ and $y_{ih} = (e_{ih} - \alpha_i e_{wh})$ and suppose initially that proposition R holds for country i with respect to 2 values of x_{ih} and y_{ih} ($h = 1, 2$), that is, suppose $x_{i1} > x_{i2}$ and $y_{i1} > y_{i2}$. Now suppose that a linear transformation of each x_{ih} and y_{ih} reverses the rankings of the y_{ih} values, that is, $(\nu_1 + \gamma_1 x_{i1}) > (\nu_2 + \gamma_2 x_{i2})$ but now $(\nu_1 + \gamma_1 y_{i1}) < (\nu_2 + \gamma_2 y_{i2})$. This particular reversal will occur if

$$1 < \frac{x_{i1}}{x_{i2}} < \frac{\nu_1 - \nu_2 + \gamma_1}{\gamma_2} < \frac{y_{i1}}{y_{i2}} \tag{8.14}$$

More generally, a linear transformation can reverse the ranking of one set of values while preserving the ranking of the other set of values if $(\gamma_1 + (\nu_1 - \nu_2))/\gamma_2$ lies in the interval $[\min(x_{i1}/x_{i2}, y_{i1}/y_{i2}), \max(x_{i1}/x_{i2}, y_{i1}/y_{i2})]$.

Setting $x_{ih} = f_{ih}^A$ and $y_{ih} = (e_{ih} - \alpha_i e_{wh})$, this interval with respect to any two factors h and z is:

$$\left[\min\left(\frac{f_{ih}^A}{f_{iz}^A}, \frac{(e_{ih} - \alpha_i e_{wh})}{(e_{iz} - \alpha_i e_{wz})} \right), \max\left(\frac{f_{ih}^A}{f_{iz}^A}, \frac{(e_{ih} - \alpha_i e_{wh})}{(e_{iz} - \alpha_i e_{wz})} \right) \right] \qquad (8.15)$$

If the H–O–V equations are exact then this interval is empty (i.e. $\min(\cdot) = \max(\cdot)$) and a reversal of rankings is then impossible. Conversely, if the H–O–V equations are not exact then reversals are possible and are more likely the greater the H–O–V equations deviate from equality. In practice, the H–O–V equations are unlikely to be exact so that all forms of proposition R should be computed and analyzed.

Table 8.2   *Tests of the H–O–V sign proposition (country by country)*

Country	Proportion of sign matches (%)
Argentina	33
Australia	33
Austria	67
Belgium–Lux.	50
Brazil	17
Canada	75
Denmark	42
Finland	67
France	25
Germany	67
Greece	92
Hong Kong	100
Ireland	92
Italy	58
Japan	67
Rep. of Korea	75
Mexico	92
Netherlands	58
Norway	25
Philippines	50
Portugal	67
Spain	67
Sweden	42
Switzerland	67
UK	92
USA	58
Yugoslavia	83

Source: Bowen *et al.* (1987).

Tables 8.2–8.5 indicate of the kind of results obtained when propositions *S* and *R* are tested. Table 8.2 and Table 8.3 report the proportion of correct matches when the sign of the adjusted net trade in the services of a factor is compared to the sign of the excess supply of that factor according to (8.12). Overall, proposition *S* holds for 61% of these pairwise comparisons. When the comparisons are made country by country (Table 8.2), proposition *S* holds more convincingly for some countries than others (e.g. Hong Kong versus Argentina). When the comparisons are made factor by factor (Table 8.3), proposition *S* holds less frequently.

Whereas the results in Table 8.2 and Table 8.3 indicate that proposition *S* fails to hold in a number of instances, do such results permit one to reject proposition *S* and by implication the H–O–V model? This question raises the issue of choosing a level of significance. For example, whereas a lower bound of 50% on the proportion of correct sign matches seems reasonable, the choice of a higher (critical) value for the proportion is problematic. At best, such results only indicate that the H–O–V equations are not exact, but the source of the inexactness cannot be determined.

Tables 8.4 and 8.5 show the corresponding tests of proposition *R* (form *R*4). Two sets of results are presented in each table. First is the rank correlation between the factor contents and factor abundances. Second is the proportion of correct rankings when the ordering of factor contents and factor abundances are compared two at a time. Both the correlations

Table 8.3 *Tests of the H–O–V sign proposition (factor by factor)*

Factor	Proportion of sign matches (%)
Capital	52
Labor (total)	67
Professional/Technical	78
Managerial	22
Clerical	59
Sales	67
Service	67
Agricultural	63
Production	70
Land	
Arable	70
Pasture	52
Forest	70

Source: Bowen *et al.* (1987).

Table 8.4   *Tests of the H–O–V rank proposition (country by country)*

Country	Rank correlation	Proportion of correct pairwise rankings (%)
Argentina	0.164	58
Australia	−0.127	44
Austria	0.091	56
Belgium–Lux.	0.273	64
Brazil	0.673	86
Canada	0.236	64
Denmark	−0.418	29
Finland	0.164	60
France	0.418	71
Germany	0.527	76
Greece	0.564	80
Hong Kong	0.745	89
Ireland	0.491	76
Italy	0.345	69
Japan	0.382	71
Rep. of Korea	0.345	69
Mexico	0.673	86
Netherlands	−0.236	38
Norway	−0.236	38
Philippines	0.527	78
Portugal	0.091	56
Spain	0.200	62
Sweden	0.200	62
Switzerland	0.381	69
UK	0.527	78
USA	0.309	67
Yugoslavia	−0.055	49

Source: Bowen *et al.* (1987)

and the proportion of correct pairwise rankings suggest that proposition R holds more often than does proposition S. Yet, the rankings are not exact, and since the choice of a critical value for the proportion of correct rankings is largely subjective, the extent to which proposition R is to be considered validated is also subjective.

The results for proposition R in Table 8.4 and Table 8.5 use form $R4$. Are these results changed when alternative forms of proposition R are used? Table 8.6 reports a sample of Kohler's (1991) results of examining alternative forms of proposition R using the same data set underlying the results in Table 8.4 and Table 8.5. The numbers in Table 8.6 are the percentage of turnovers in pairwise rankings when alternative forms of

Table 8.5 *Tests of the H–O–V rank proposition (factor by factor)*

Factor	Rank correlation	Proportion of correct pairwise rankings (%)
Capital	0.140	45
Labor (total)	0.185	46
Professional/Technical	0.123	33
Managerial	−0.254	34
Clerical	0.134	48
Sales	0.225	47
Service	0.282	44
Agricultural	0.202	47
Production	0.345	48
Land		
Arable	0.561	73
Pasture	0.197	61
Forest	0.356	65

Source: Bowen *et al.* (1987).

proposition *R* are used. For example, the value 42.09 indicates that when the form of proposition *R* is changed from *R*3 to *R*1, 42.09% of the pairwise comparisons among factors across the sample of 27 countries switched from being correct to being incorrect. These results underscore the importance of computing each form of proposition *R* and, perhaps more importantly, further reveal that the H–O–V equations are not equalities when actual data are used.

In summary, tests of proposition *S* or *R* do permit a test of the H–O–V model. Alternatively, if the H–O–V model (8.3) is assumed to be valid, then

Table 8.6 *Number of reversals (%) when testing proposition R using alternative forms of the H–O–V equations*

		Form of H–O–V equation	
		R1	*R4*
*R*1	Across factors	–	43.76
	Across countries	–	24.13
*R*3	Across factors	42.09	43.76
	Across countries	27.27	8.64

Source: Kohler (1988).

appeal to these propositions allows one to use the factor content of trade to 'reveal' the structure of a country's factor abundance. In general, the alternative hypotheses associated with tests of propositions S and R (as presently formulated) are unclear regarding the model against which the H–O–V model is being tested. Consequently, the reasons for rejecting the H–O–V model, if rejected, are also unclear. These difficulties lead one to consider alternative methods for testing the H–O–V model.

Regression analyses of the H–O–V equations

The H–O–V equations (8.3) specify an exact relationship between the factor content of trade and excess factor supplies. A test of this relationship is therefore to compute the extent to which the factor content vector deviates from the vector of excess factor supplies. But such an analysis requires some sensible way of measuring the distance between the two vectors,[15] that is, measuring the extent to which the equations are not exact. Leontief-type tests provide one indication of the inexactness of the H–O–V equations but are inadequate since the alternative hypotheses associated with these tests are unclear. An alternative is to study the H–O–V equations using regression analysis. This approach, properly formulated, permits one to test the hypotheses embodied in (8.3) against unambiguous alternative hypotheses.

In general, regression analysis of the H–O–V equations requires one to first specify the relationship between factor contents and factor supplies, and thus a set of parameters to estimate, under one set of assumptions. Changing one or more of these initial assumptions then implies an alternative specification and a corresponding set of parameters. In some cases, changing an assumption may simply correspond to restricting the value of certain parameters in the original specification. If so, conventional procedures for testing the significance of parameter restrictions can be employed. Such analyses permit one to identify those assumptions that may account for any failure of the H–O–V equations to be exact.

Relaxing the assumptions underlying the H–O–V model is likely to impose costs in terms of increasing the complexity of the relationship between factor contents and factor supplies. For example, incorporating economies of scale may lead to non-linearities which can complicate, or even preclude, estimation. In practice, some compromise will need to be made between the generality of the specification and the tractability of estimation.

The procedure outlined above for testing the H–O–V model will normally involve testing one or more of the *assumptions* of this model rather than an alternative theory, *per se*. This reflects that models which attempt to explain the composition of trade are built upon the principle of comparative costs.

Thus, testing one model against another is really an attempt to discover which of the many potential determinants of relative cost is the more important. For example, if relaxing the assumption of identical technologies improves our ability to predict the pattern of trade, then both technological differences and factor supply differences must be considered as important determinants of the difference in relative costs. Determining which influence is the relatively more important may prove difficult, but should nonetheless represent one goal of the analysis.

To illustrate the methods for testing the H–O–V model in a regression framework, consider testing the H–O–V assumption of identical technologies against the alternative assumption that technologies instead differ across countries. Maintaining all other assumptions of the H–O–V model, including that of identical and homothetic preferences across countries, the vector of country i's net trades in factor services can be written:

$$\mathbf{F}_i \equiv \mathbf{A}_i\mathbf{T}_i = \mathbf{E}_i - \mathbf{A}_i\mu_i\mathbf{Q}_w \tag{8.16}$$

Equations (8.16) are simply the H–O–V equations (8.3) except that the technology matrix now includes a country subscript. To model technological differences we assume that these differences are neutral across countries. This assumption implies that input matrices are proportional between countries and therefore that the input matrix of country i can be expressed in terms of the input matrix of some 'reference' country, that is, $\delta_i\mathbf{A}_i = \mathbf{A}_R$ where the subscript 'R' denotes the reference country and δ_i is a positive scalar. By definition, $\delta_R = 1$ so that values of δ_i below (above) unity imply that country i is less (more) productive than the reference country. Multiplying (8.16) through by δ_i and using $\delta_i\mathbf{A}_i = \mathbf{A}_R$ gives:

$$\mathbf{F}_i^R = \delta_i\mathbf{E}_i - \mu_i\sum_j \delta_j\mathbf{E}_j \tag{8.17}$$

where we have also used $\mathbf{Q}_w = \sum_j \mathbf{A}_j^{-1}\mathbf{E}_j = \mathbf{A}_R^{-1}\sum_j \delta_j\mathbf{E}_j$. In (8.17), $\mathbf{F}_i^R$ denotes that country i's trade in factor services has been computed using the input requirements matrix of the reference country. With this parameterization, imposing the H–O–V assumption of identical technologies corresponds to restricting $\delta_i = 1$ for all i.[16] Finally, note that the assumption of neutral differences in technology preserves the linearity of the model, an important consideration for estimation purposes.

The specification in (8.17) can be used to test if the pattern of trade in factor services is better explained when neutral differences in technology are allowed. In particular, given data across countries on the factor contents ($\mathbf{F}_i^R$), factor supplies ($\mathbf{E}_i$) and the expenditure shares (μ_i) in a particular year, estimation of (8.17) will yield parameter estimates $\hat{\delta}_i$. Re-estimating (8.17) with the values of the δ_i restricted to the theoretical value of unity then allows one to test the null hypothesis of neutral technological differences against the alternative of identical technologies. The significance of the parameter restrictions can be determined using a standard *F*-test.

Pioneering work by Bowen *et al.* (1987) investigated a number of alternatives to the assumptions underlying the H–O–V model using specifications more general than (8.17). These alternative assumptions included neutral technological differences and also non-proportional consumption.[17] Using 1966 data and defining the United States as the reference country, Bowen *et al.* found that they could reject the H–O–V assumption of identical technologies in favor of neutral technological differences but could not reject the H–O–V assumption of proportional consumption (i.e. identical and homothetic preferences) across countries. Trefler (1993) extended the Bowen *et al.* analysis of technological differences and alternative preference assumptions and also examined data for 1983. Like Bowen *et al.*, Trefler (1993) found that the data favored the assumption of neutral technological differences[18] and the H–O–V assumption of homothetic preferences. However, Trefler also found support for the assumption that consumption is biased toward home goods.[19]

Table 8.7 lists estimates of the neutral technological differences parameters (i.e. the δ_i in (8.17)) obtained by Trefler for 1966 and 1983. Also shown is the value of each country's real GDP *per capita* relative to that of the United States (see columns (1) and (4)). Since we would expect a country whose productivity is half that of the United States to also have a *per capita* income half that of the US, these relative GDP *per capita* numbers should be highly correlated with the estimates of relative productivity (i.e. the δ_i). In fact, the correlation is 0.89 for 1983 and 0.71 for 1966.

Regression analysis of the H–O–V equations has proved an extremely useful method for testing the assumptions of the H–O–V model against a number of sensible alternative assumptions (models). As noted, the evidence from such studies is that the H–O–V assumption of identical technologies is not supported by the data and, while homothetic preferences cannot be rejected, there is evidence of a bias toward home produced goods.[20] More work is needed to further delineate the nature of technological differences and to examine alternative assumptions about preferences. An important task for this research will be to determine the importance of technological differences and alternative preference structures relative to factor supplies (factor costs) in determining the trade in factor services.

Problem 8.3: The alternative assumption of neutral technological differences introduced above can be extended by assuming that subsets of industries exhibit neutral technological differences, but that these neutral differences are different between subsets of industries. How would this assumption be stated in terms of differences in the factor requirements matrices between countries? Derive a specification for the H–O–V equations

Table 8.7 *H–O–V regression estimates of technological differences, 1983 and 1966*

	1983			1966[b]		
Country	GDP per capita[a] (1)	Productivity (2)	t-statistic (3)	GDP per capita (4)	Productivity (5)	t-statistic (6)
Argentina	na	na	na	0.32	0.34	13.01
Australia	na	na	na	0.73	0.13	29.72
Austria	0.65	0.65	2.73	0.49	0.48	4.49
Bangladesh	0.04	0.03	47.71	na	na	na
Belgium	0.67	0.72	2.66	0.58	0.65	3.07
Brazil	na	na	na	0.17	0.22	19.68
Canada	0.95	0.48	2.11	0.77	0.59	7.44
Colombia	0.21	0.28	3.24	na	na	na
Denmark	0.72	0.57	4.09	0.70	0.68	2.16
Finland	0.70	0.65	2.17	0.52	0.55	3.51
France	0.73	0.69	1.80	0.61	0.61	8.33
Greece	0.35	0.42	9.40	0.24	0.41	4.58
Hong Kong	0.61	0.45	4.63	0.28	0.17	5.02
Indonesia	0.11	0.10	39.51	na	na	na
Ireland	0.39	0.58	8.04	0.35	0.54	1.92
Israel	0.60	0.60	3.03	na	na	na
Italy	0.66	0.47	1.25	0.48	0.67	5.56
Japan	0.66	0.74	4.84	0.41	0.41	17.95
Rep. of Korea	na	na	na	0.10	0.07	15.11
Mexico	na	na	na	0.30	0.33	11.95
Netherlands	0.69	0.78	3.80	0.61	0.54	4.93
New Zealand	0.62	0.40	4.12	na	na	na
Norway	0.82	0.73	1.92	0.59	0.48	3.48
Pakistan	0.08	0.09	32.10	na	na	na
Panama	0.23	0.29	11.35	na	na	na
Philippines	na	na	na	0.11	0.11	17.70
Portugal	0.30	0.16	18.41	0.19	0.22	5.75
Singapore	0.66	0.38	7.89	na	na	na
Spain	0.41	0.55	2.91	0.40	0.43	8.14
Sri Lanka	0.12	0.17	23.80	na	na	na
Sweden	0.75	0.60	7.16	0.72	0.65	3.65
Switzerland	0.91	0.55	9.82	0.93	0.52	4.41
Thailand	0.16	0.14	9.63	na	na	na
Trinidad	0.69	0.49	2.91	na	na	na
UK	0.66	0.70	7.15	0.59	0.57	8.67
USA	1.00	1.00	—	1.00	1.00	—
Uruguay	0.31	0.09	14.85	na	na	na
West Germany	0.73	0.79	1.41	0.63	0.57	10.95
Yugoslavia	0.30	0.11	19.46	0.20	0.21	12.04

Notes:
na = Not available.

[a] GDP *per capita* and productivity are measured relative to that of the United States; *t*-statistic is the asymptotic *t*-statistic for testing the null hypothesis that a country's relative productivity parameter equals unity (i.e. $\delta_i = 1$).

[b] Uses 1967 trade data and 1966 factor supply data.

Source: Trefler (1993), table 2 (columns (1), (2) and (3)) and table 4 (columns (1), (2) and (3)).

assuming such neutral differences with respect to two industry groups (e.g. manufacturing and agriculture). How would one attempt to estimate such an equation?

8.2 Regression analyses of trade in goods

The prediction of the H–O–S model regarding the pattern of trade in goods has traditionally been examined using cross-section regression analysis. These analyses can be classified into one of three types: interindustry, cross-country and pooled. These approaches are easily understood by representing the pattern of world trade at a point in time by a matrix of trade flows (see Figure 8.1). In this matrix the rows index countries and the columns index commodities (industries).

An *interindustry* analysis/regression focuses on one country (a row of the matrix) and attempts to explain the variation in the pattern of that country's trade across commodities (the columns of the matrix). This approach forces one to select industry characteristics (e.g. factor input requirements) as explanatory variables. Since only trade and industry characteristics are observed, the estimation can be thought to be inferring the unobserved characteristics of the selected country. Interindustry regression has been the most common type of analysis.

A *cross-country* analysis/regression focuses on one industry (a column) and attempts to explain variations in the pattern of trade in that commodity or industry across countries. This approach forces one to select country characteristics (e.g. factor supplies) as the explanatory variables. Since only trade and country characteristics are observed, the estimation can be thought to be inferring the unobserved characteristics of the selected industry.

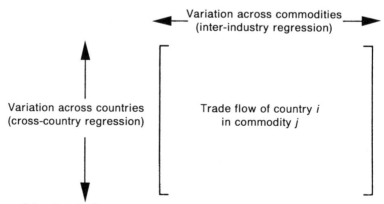

Figure 8.1   *A trade flow matrix*

A *pooled* analysis/regression considers the variation across both industries and countries and thus uses both industry and country characteristics as explanatory variables.

As we will soon discover, none of these regression approaches are legitimate methods for testing the H–O–S model. A deficiency of the interindustry and cross-country analyses is that they use only two of the three variables (trade, factor supplies and factor inputs) needed for a proper test of the H–O–S model whereas the pooled analysis lacks a precise theoretical foundation. Although each approach is deficient as a method for testing the H–O–S theory, they can nonetheless be useful for extracting other information about the pattern of trade. For example, the interindustry approach can be used to infer differences in relative factor prices between countries.[21] Since the focus here is on the narrower issue of using each approach to rigorously test the H–O–S model, the appropriateness of each empirical specification can only be judged relative to that implied by the underlying theoretical model. For the H–O–S model, the relevant empirical specification is the H–O–V model. Hence, in what follows the H–O–V model is taken as the basis for judging the merits of each empirical approach.

Interindustry regression

An interindustry regression hypothesizes the existence of a stable relationship between trade and factor input requirements across industries. For convenience, the relationship is usually assumed to be linear:

$$\mathbf{T}_i = \beta_0 \mathbf{1} + \mathbf{A}_i' \boldsymbol{\beta}_i + \boldsymbol{\varepsilon}_i \tag{8.18}$$

where $\mathbf{T}_i$ is the $J \times 1$ vector of net trades, $\mathbf{1}$ is a $J \times 1$ vector of ones, β_0 is a scalar constant, $\boldsymbol{\beta}_i$ is the $H \times 1$ vector of 'slope' coefficients and $\boldsymbol{\varepsilon}_i$ is a $J \times 1$ vector of random errors. Common practice is to interpret the sign of each slope coefficient as indicating whether the corresponding factor is a 'source' of country i's comparative cost advantage. Since the relative abundance of factors determines comparative costs in the H–O–S model, a positive (negative) slope coefficient is taken to imply that the corresponding factor is abundant (scarce) within the country being examined.

The estimation of an equation such as (8.18) has a long tradition in empirical studies of the H–O–S model. The popularity of this approach can be attributed to three factors, each of which refers to the fact that an interindustry analysis focuses on the trade of a single country:

- Intense efforts to resolve the Leontief paradox with respect to the United States.
- Limited availability of internationally comparable data on countries' factor supplies.

- Theoretical statements of the H–O–S model invariably focus on the trade of a single country and thereby foster the intuition that a country's trade pattern should be correlated with its pattern of factor use (factor intensity) across industries.

Does theory imply a relationship between trade and factor inputs? The answer is yes, but not exactly the form expressed in (8.18). Specifically, if one assumes that there are equal numbers of goods and factors then the input requirements matrix $\mathbf{A}_i$ is square and can be inverted. Consequently, the H–O–V equations (8.3) can be solved for the trade vector:

$$\mathbf{T}_i = \mathbf{A}_i^{-1}(\mathbf{E}_i - (\alpha_i - \lambda_i)\mathbf{E}_w) \tag{8.19}$$

This expresses trade as a linear function of the *inverse* of the factor requirements matrix. Hence, in theory, a regression of trade on $\mathbf{A}_i^{-1}$ would yield estimates of the excess factor supplies $(\mathbf{E}_i - (\alpha_i - \lambda_i)\mathbf{E}_w)$. But this is not the regression specified in (8.18).

Although theory does not imply specification (8.18), theory does support the intuition of such specifications, namely, that a country's trade should be correlated with the use of factors across industries. However, the theoretically correct correlation is the simple correlation, not the partial correlation implicit when estimating specifications such as (8.18). To see this, recall that the H–O–V model contains a prediction about the average composition of a country's trade in goods. This prediction can be restated as the simple correlation between country i's trade vector and its vector of input requirements with respect to factor h ($\mathbf{A}_{ih}$):

$$\rho(\mathbf{A}_{ih}, \mathbf{T}_i) = \frac{\sum_j (a_{ihj} - \bar{a}_{ih})(t_{ij} - \bar{t}_i)}{\sqrt{\sum_j (a_{ihj} - \bar{a}_{ih})^2 \sum_j (t_{ij} - \bar{t}_i)^2}} \tag{8.20}$$

where $\bar{t}_i$ and $\bar{a}_{ih}$ are the average net trade and average input requirement of factor h across J industries. If trade is balanced then $\bar{t}_i = 0$ and (8.20) reduces to

$$\rho(\mathbf{A}_{ih}, \mathbf{T}_i) = \frac{\sum_j (a_{ihj} - \bar{a}_{ih})t_{ij}}{\sqrt{\sum_j (a_{ihj} - \bar{a}_{ih})^2 \sum_j (t_{ij})^2}} = \frac{(e_{ih} - \alpha_i e_{wh})}{\sqrt{\sum_j (a_{ihj} - \bar{a}_{ih})^2 \sum_j (t_{ij})^2}}$$

Since $sign(\rho(\mathbf{A}_{ih}, \mathbf{T}_i)) = sign(e_{ih} - \alpha_i e_{wh})$, the sign of the correlation indicates the absolute abundance or scarcity of factor h. Moreover, factoring out the world supply of factor h (e_{wh}) gives

$$\rho(\mathbf{A}_{ih}, \mathbf{T}_i) = \frac{(e_{ih}/e_{wh} - \alpha_i)}{\sqrt{\frac{1}{e_{wh}^2} \sum_j (a_{ihj} - \bar{a}_{ih})^2 \sum_j t_{ij}^2}} \tag{8.21}$$

This shows that the relative size of $\rho(\mathbf{A}_{ih}, \mathbf{T}_i)$ depends on the magnitude of both $(e_{ih}/e_{wh} - \alpha_i)$ and the variance $\sum_j (a_{ihj} - \bar{a}_{ih})^2/e_{wh}^2$. The jth element of this variance is the amount of commodity j that would be produced in the world if commodity j only used resource h. This variance is thus a scale free measure of the variability of use of factor h across industries and can be interpreted as a measure of factor intensity. Thus, theory does imply that the abundance of a factor can be inferred from the sign of the *simple* correlation between trade and the input requirements of a factor across industries.

Although theory does not imply the direct regression of trade on factor inputs as given in (8.18), one can still ask if the sign of a coefficient estimated using specification (8.18) might nonetheless indicate the abundance or scarcity of a factor. To address this question, consider an interindustry regression of the form

$$\mathbf{T}_i = \mathbf{A}_i'\boldsymbol{\beta}_i + \varepsilon_i \tag{8.22}$$

where $\boldsymbol{\beta}_i$ is a $H \times 1$ vector of regression coefficients (excluding a constant term) and ε_i is a $J \times 1$ vector of random errors. The estimates of the coefficients in (8.22) are computed as:

$$\hat{\boldsymbol{\beta}} = (\mathbf{A}_i\mathbf{A}_i')^{-1}\mathbf{A}_i\mathbf{T}_i \tag{8.23}$$

Assuming trade balance, the H–O–V equations are $\mathbf{A}_i\mathbf{T}_i = (\mathbf{E}_i - \alpha_i\mathbf{E}_w)$ and can be inserted into (8.23) to give

$$\hat{\boldsymbol{\beta}} = (\mathbf{A}_i\mathbf{A}_i')^{-1}(\mathbf{E}_i - \alpha_i\mathbf{E}_w) \tag{8.24}$$

If $sign(\hat{\boldsymbol{\beta}})$ is to equal $sign(\mathbf{E}_i - \alpha_i\mathbf{E}_w)$ then the transformation matrix $(\mathbf{A}_i\mathbf{A}_i')^{-1}$ must leave the signs of the elements of the excess factor supply vector unchanged. Aw (1983) derived a sufficient condition for such a 'sign preserving' transformation: the matrix $(\mathbf{A}_i\mathbf{A}_i')^{-1}$ should be diagonal with strictly positive elements. To satisfy Aw's condition we would thus need to assume that each industry employs one, and only one, factor.

Problem 8.4: Verify that Aw's condition (i.e. $(\mathbf{A}_i\mathbf{A}_i')^{-1}$ is diagonal with strictly positive elements) ensures that the sign of a regression coefficient (i.e. sign of the partial correlation) estimated in a multiple regression is the same as the sign of the simple correlation between trade and the input requirements of a given factor.

Since industries actually employ several inputs, $(\mathbf{A}_i\mathbf{A}_i')^{-1}$ will contain several non-zero, off-diagonal elements or 'factor complementarities'. Given this, there is no reason to expect that, in practice, the sign of an estimated coefficient would equal the sign of the corresponding element of either the vector of factor contents or the vector of excess factor supplies.

Whereas the theoretical importance of factor complementarities is evident, one can question their empirical importance. In particular, if actual factor complementarities are 'small,' then the above theoretical statements may be empirically unimportant and inferences about factor abundances based on coefficient signs might be reliable.

Bowen and Sveikauskas (1992) examined this issue by comparing the signs of estimated coefficients with those of the factor content vector $A_i T_i$ for each of twenty-seven countries. When factor inputs were measured as broad aggregates such as capital, skilled and unskilled labor and land, they found that the sign of a regression coefficient (when significant) matched the sign of the corresponding factor content in over 90% of the comparisons.[22] Thus, for aggregate definitions of factor inputs, coefficient signs appear to be reliable indicators of the net trade in factor services. But even if coefficient signs are more reliable than theory would suggest, directly computing the factor contents, rather than inferring their signs from regression coefficients, is a much simpler and more direct way to infer factor abundances.

How can the results from an interindustry regression be used to test the H–O–S/H–O–V model? As suggested by the above, if factor complementarities are assumed to be 'small', one can simply compare the signs of estimated coefficients (if significant) with the signs of the corresponding excess factor supplies. In principle, one could also compare the ranking of the estimated coefficients with the ranking of world factor shares.[23] However, these analyses are simply indirect tests of propositions S and R and must rely on the absence of damaging factor complementarities for reliability. Again, direct computation and comparison of the factor contents with the excess factor supplies is preferred.[24]

Given the above, column (1) of Table 8.8 reports a sample of the results of Baldwin's (1971) classic interindustry regression study of 1962 US trade. Note that the list of explanatory variables includes non-factor input characteristics such as the degree of unionization and that the factor inputs have been divided by an industry's total employment. Below we consider the appropriateness of such scalings of the factor input data. For now we assume that the sign of the factor's coefficient indicates its abundance or scarcity. From these results one would conclude that, given the H–O–S/H–O–V model, the United States was *absolutely* scarce in capital, laborers and service workers and *absolutely* abundant in scientists and engineers in 1962. Except for the scarcity of capital, these inferences appear plausible.

Can factor complementarities explain the implied scarcity of capital in the United States? Column (2) of Table 8.8 shows the sign of the net trade in each factor (uncorrected for any trade imbalance). Since these match the coefficient signs, factor complementarities do not appear to explain the negative sign for capital.

Table 8.8 *Inter-industry regression estimates and US factor abundance, 1962*

Explanatory variable	Estimated coefficient (1)	Sign of net trade in factor (2)
Capital–labor ratio[a]	−1.37	−
% of industry employment classified as:		
Scientists & engineers[a]	7011.00	+
Other professional/Technical	−1473.00	na
Clerical & sales	71.00	
Craftsman & foremen	1578.00	+
Operatives	−248.00	
Nonfarm laborers & service	−761.00	
Farmers and farm laborers[b]	845.00	+
Index of scale economies	−421.00	+
Index of unionization	343.00	+
$R^2 = 0.44$		

Notes:
[a] Coefficient significant at 95% level.
[b] Coefficient significant at 90% level.
Source: Baldwin (1971), table 3, p. 137.

Does the implied scarcity of capital in the US mean that the H–O–S/H–O–V model should be rejected? Formally, the answer is 'no'. Without corresponding data on US excess factor supplies in 1962 there is no way of knowing if the implied scarcity (or abundance) of any factor is consistent with its actual abundance. Moreover, the factor contents, and by implication the regression coefficients, have not been adjusted for a possible trade imbalance.[25] Finally, although the US is a net importer of the services of capital *per worker*, this does not necessarily imply that the US is also a net importer of capital services alone.

Another example of the interindustry approach is the study of US trade conducted by Stern and Maskus (1981). In each year between 1958 and 1976, they regressed US trade on three factor inputs (capital, human capital and total industry employment).[26] In addition, for two of the years they were able to compute the net trade in the services of each factor (uncorrected for trade imbalance). Table 8.9 shows a sample of their results.

In both 1958 and 1972 (and all other years considered), the signs of the regression coefficients imply that the US is *absolutely* scarce in capital and labor and *absolutely* abundant in human capital. However, in neither year

Table 8.9   *Inter-industry regression estimates and US factor abundance, 1958 and 1972*

Explanatory variable	Coefficient estimates (1)		Sign of net trade in factor (2)	
	1958	*1972*	*1958*	*1972*
Capital[a]	−0.03	−0.05	+	−
Human capital[b]	0.04	0.05	+	−
Labor	−0.43	−1.76	+	−
R^2	0.25[b]	0.08[b]		

Notes:
[a] Significant at 90% level.
[b] Significant at 95% level.
Source: Stern and Markus (1981), tables 1 and 6.

do the factor contents conform to this pattern of abundance. Specifically, the factor contents imply that all factors were *absolutely* abundant in 1958 and that all factors were *absolutely* scarce in 1972. These results probably reflect the US trade surplus in 1958 and the US trade deficit in 1972 since no correction for a trade imbalance was made. More important is the fact that the results for both years suggest that factor complementarities were a problem. Specifically, in 1958, the coefficient signs for labor and capital are opposite those of the factor contents, whereas in 1972 the signs for human capital do not conform. These results highlight the potential for invalid inferences about the sign of the factor contents and, by implication, the excess factor supplies, using the signs of regression coefficients.

Should the H–O–S/H–O–V model be rejected on the basis of these results? Again, a formal test of the model requires that the implied factor abundances be compared to measurements of the excess factor supplies. Moreover, since no correction for trade imbalance has been made, the signs of the factor contents in this case contain no information about *absolute* abundance.

Finally, Stern and Maskus were able to compute and rank the *proportionate* net trade in each factor using total US employment of each factor as a measure the total US supply of each factor. In 1958, human capital ranked first followed by labor and then capital. In 1972, the ranking was human capital, capital and then labor. These rankings imply that capital is scarce relative to human capital. Unfortunately, Stern and Maskus did not have data on the corresponding world factor shares and were thus unable to test proposition *R*.

In summary, an interindustry regression of trade on factor input requirements is ill-suited for testing the traditional H–O–S/H–O–V theory. In particular, it requires that factor complementarities be 'small' if coefficient signs
are to conform to the signs of either a country's net trade in factor services or
its excess factor supplies. There is evidence that factor complementarities may
often be small, particularly for highly aggregated classifications of inputs. But
even in the absence of factor complementarities, the interindustry regression
approach is not cost-effective compared to simply computing the net trade in
factor services.

Problem 8.5: Use the data in Problem 8.1 to derive the regression
coefficients $\hat{\beta} = (\mathbf{AA'})^{-1}\mathbf{AT}$. Do the signs of the coefficients equal the signs
of the country's net trade in factors? Do the sign and rank of these
coefficients conform to the country's absolute and relative factor abundance? Are factor complementarities important in this example?

Specification issues

Until recently, the use of an interindustry specification to test the factor
abundance theory was based more on the intuition that trade and factor inputs
ought to be correlated rather than on any formal theoretical derivation. The
absence of an explicit theoretical statement for the specification meant that
there was considerable scope for disagreement about the proper measure of
the trade variable, the choice of explanatory variables, etc. The following
discusses the central issues that have arisen and, where possible, evaluates
them in terms of the H–O–V model.

Choice of sample (industries)

Interindustry regression studies often limit the sample of industries to
manufacturing and thus exclude agricultural and natural resource industries. This is clearly inappropriate if the sign or rank of the estimated
coefficients are to be compared to direct measures of factor abundance in
order to test (indirectly) propositions S and R. One reason natural resource
industries are often excluded is that suitable measures of land or mineral
resource inputs are unavailable. Of course, the solution to this problem is to
collect the needed data. Failing that, it should be recognized that the
regression estimates will be biased in the sense that the factor contents are

understated. Thus, even if factor complementarities are absent, inferences about the actual factor contents may be incorrect.

Choice of trade variable

A variety of variables have been used to measure a country's trade 'performance' including net exports, the ratio of exports to imports, the level of exports or imports, indices of 'revealed comparative advantage'[27] and discrete classifications indicating if a good is exported, imported or not traded. However, the H–O–S/H–O–V model specifies that net exports should be the dependent variable. Therefore, while the use of exports or imports alone as the dependent variable may be appropriate when analysing intra-industry trade or, more generally, models that incorporate imperfect competition and production differentiation, analyses of the H–O–S/H–O–V model should use some measure of net exports as the dependent variable.

Choice of explanatory variables

Two questions concerning the explanatory variables are: (1) what inputs should be included in the list of explanatory variables, and (2) should input requirements be measured on a direct or total (direct plus indirect) basis.

The answer to the first question is simple: all primary factors of production should be included as explanatory variables. At a minimum, these would be measures of capital, labor and land. Although most interindustry studies typically include measures of capital and labor, they rarely include measures of land input. To the extent that any omitted factor input is correlated with those included, the estimated coefficients will be subject to a specification error bias.

The question of direct versus total (direct *plus* indirect) factor intensities arises when an industry's output is produced by combining intermediate goods together with primary factors. In such cases, the industry uses both direct factor inputs and indirect factor inputs, the latter being embodied in its intermediate inputs. Concern arises because a ranking of industries on the basis of direct factor intensities could be opposite the ranking based on total factor intensity, for example, in a model that includes a 'pure' intermediate good. If true, the estimated relationship (i.e. the regression coefficients) between trade and factor inputs using direct factor input requirements could differ from that derived using total factor input requirements.

If the regression estimates are to be used to test the H–O–V model then total requirements must be used since the excess factor supplies equal the factor contents only when the latter are computed using the total factor requirements. More generally, since one is ultimately concerned with the underlying relative costs of production, the real question is whether direct or total input requirements determine these relative costs (autarky prices). The answer is the total factor input requirements.[28]

Scaling the trade variable[29]

A common practice in interindustry regression studies has been to scale the trade variable by some measure of commodity size. In part, this practice reflects concern over possible heteroscedasticity that might be associated with industry size. Variables commonly chosen to scale the trade data are national outputs, world outputs or world exports in each industry.

Is such scaling appropriate? Is there a 'correct' scaling variable? A sensible answer to these questions can only be given on the basis of a theoretical model. In the context of the H–O–V model, a scaling of the data is generally inappropriate since it breaks the link between the sign of a regression coefficient and the sign of the corresponding excess factor supply which indicates the abundance of a factor. To demonstrate this, assume that preferences are identical and homothetic across countries and that trade is balanced. The net trade identity for country i can then be written

$$T_i = Q_i - \alpha_i Q_w \tag{8.25}$$

Let $diag(\mathbf{Z})$ denote the $J \times J$ diagonal matrix whose diagonal entries are the elements of the vector $\mathbf{Z}$. In the present context, the elements of $\mathbf{Z}$ could be national outputs, world outputs, etc. A scaling of (8.25) by the elements of $\mathbf{Z}$ can be written

$$diag(\mathbf{Z})^{-1}\mathbf{T}_i = diag(\mathbf{Z})^{-1}(\mathbf{Q}_i - \alpha_i\mathbf{Q}_w) \tag{8.26}$$

Pre-multiplying both sides of (8.26) by the factor input matrix gives

$$\mathbf{A}_i\, diag(\mathbf{Z})^{-1}\mathbf{T}_i = \mathbf{A}_i\, diag(\mathbf{Z})^{-1}(\mathbf{Q}_i - \alpha_i\mathbf{Q}_w) \tag{8.27}$$

Given this general formulation, consider first the case of scaling only trade data. The interindustry regression equation is

$$diag(\mathbf{Z})^{-1}\mathbf{T}_i = \mathbf{A}_i'\beta_i \tag{8.28}$$

and the estimates of the parameters are

$$\hat{\beta}_i = (\mathbf{A}_i\mathbf{A}_i')^{-1}\mathbf{A}_i\, diag(\mathbf{Z})^{-1}\mathbf{T}_i \tag{8.29}$$

In the absence of factor complementarities, the sign of each regression coefficient equals the sign of its corresponding élement in the vector $\mathbf{A}_i\, diag(\mathbf{Z})^{-1}\mathbf{T}_i$ or, given (8.25), its corresponding element in $\mathbf{A}_i\, diag(\mathbf{Z})^{-1}(\mathbf{Q}_i - \alpha_i\mathbf{Q}_w)$.

To make sense, the sign of an element in the latter vector should indicate factor abundance according to the H–O–V definitions. The hth element of $\mathbf{A}_i \, diag(\mathbf{Z})^{-1}(\mathbf{Q}_i - \alpha_i\mathbf{Q}_w)$ is

$$\mathbf{A}_{ih} \, diag(\mathbf{Z})^{-1}(\mathbf{Q}_i - \alpha_i\mathbf{Q}_w) = \sum_j a_{hj}(q_{ij} - \alpha_i q_{wj})/z_j$$

$$= \sum_j (e_{ihj} - \alpha_i e_{whj})/z_j \qquad (8.30)$$

where $\mathbf{A}_{ih}$ is the hth row of $\mathbf{A}$ and $e_{\cdot hj}$ is the amount of factor h employed in the production of commodity j in either country i or the world. The sign of (8.30) depends on the values of the z_j (e.g. the output mix in country i if the z_j are industry outputs) which differ across industries. Thus, the sign of (8.30) need not conform to the abundance of factor h as given by $sign(e_{ih} - \alpha_i e_{wh})$. Only if the z_j are constant across industries ($z_j = z\,\forall j$) could we be certain that the sign of an estimated regression coefficient correctly indicates the absolute abundance of a factor.

Problem 8.6: Show that scaling the trade data by industry outputs (i.e. $diag(\mathbf{Z})^{-1} = diag(\mathbf{Q}_i)^{-1}$) is appropriate when the initial equation involves a regression of the *levels* of net trade on the *levels* of factors employed in each industry (i.e. $\mathbf{T}_i = \mathbf{M}'_i\beta_i$, where $\mathbf{M}_i$ is the $H \times J$ matrix of factor employment levels in country i) and no intermediate inputs are used in production (i.e. the direct and total factor requirements are identical). Does your conclusion remain valid if intermediate inputs are also used in production?

Scaling the explanatory variables

Many interindustry regression studies express the input requirements as a ratio (e.g. the capital–labor ratio). How does this scaling affect the interpretation of the sign of a coefficient? Consider scaling the factor requirements in each industry by the requirement of factor z. The regression equation is

$$\mathbf{T}_i = diag(\mathbf{A}_{iz})^{-1}\mathbf{A}'_i\beta_i \qquad (8.31)$$

where $\mathbf{A}_{iz}$ is the J element vector of input requirements of factor z. The parameter estimates are

$$\hat{\beta}_i = (\mathbf{A}_i \, diag(\mathbf{A}_{iz})^{-2}\mathbf{A}'_i)^{-1}\mathbf{A}_i \, diag(\mathbf{A}_{iz})^{-1}\mathbf{T}_i. \qquad (8.32)$$

In the absence of factor complementarities, the sign of an estimated coefficient equals the sign of its corresponding element in the vector $\mathbf{A}_i \, diag(\mathbf{A}_{iz})^{-1}\mathbf{T}_i$. Does the sign of this element conform to the definition of factor abundance? The hth element of $\mathbf{A}_i \operatorname{diag}(\mathbf{A}_{iz})^{-1}\mathbf{T}_i$ is

$$\sum_j a_{ihj} t_{ij}/a_{izj} = \sum_j (e_{ihj} - \alpha_i e_{whj})/a_{izj} \tag{8.33}$$

where a_{izj} is amount of factor z required to produce a unit of commodity j. Since the sign of (8.33) depends on the distribution of the requirements of factor z across industries it need not equal $\operatorname{sign}(e_{ih} - \alpha_i e_{wh})$. Note that (8.33) is simply a weighted average of the net trades, that is, $\sum_j \omega_{ij} t_{ij}$ where the weights α_{ij} are the ratio of factor h to factor z employed in industry j.

The preceding discussion shows that scaling either the trade or the factor input data will in general break the connection between the sign of a regression coefficient and the H–O–V definition of factor abundance. The one exception is when the regression equation is initially specified in terms of the levels of net trade and the levels of factor inputs (see Problem 8.6). In this case alone, theory dictates that the trade data should be scaled by the national output in each industry. Hence, regardless of the statistical justification for scaling the data (e.g. heteroscedasticity), such scaling invariably precludes direct inferences about factor abundance on the basis of the sign of an interindustry regression coefficient.

Linearity

The relationship between trade and factor input requirements is usually assumed to be linear. The is no special reason for this other than simplicity. One might argue that linearity is justified on the grounds that the H–O–V equations (8.3) imply that trade is a linear function of the (inverse of) the factor requirements matrix.

A rarely discussed issue is whether a constant term should be included in the regression. Whereas the H–O–V model (8.3) does not suggest the inclusion of a constant term, most studies nonetheless include one, largely for econometric reasons. A literal interpretation of the constant term is that it is the value of the dependent variable when all the explanatory variables are zero. The interpretation of the constant therefore depends on the nature of the dependent variable (the regressand). For example, if the regressand is exports then the constant term is *a priori* expected to be zero and should therefore be excluded. If the regressand is instead net exports, the constant term is the level of *imports* of each commodity (with the sign of the constant term *a priori* expected to be negative). In any case, an interindustry regression implicitly assumes a common value of the constant term across industries; and this assumption seems difficult to justify. More about the constant term will be said below when we consider its implications with respect to the treatment of a trade imbalance.

Heteroscedasticity

The issue of whether heteroscedasticity exists in the context of an interindustry regression is both general and complex. One argument might be that heteroscedasticity could arise from omitting some factor inputs from the list of explanatory variables. Another argument might be that consumption is not properly accounted for in the equation. Concern about these and other possible sources of heteroscedasticity has motivated, in part, a practice of scaling the dependent variable by some measure of commodity size or importance. More generally, weighted least squares with the weights equal to some function (e.g. square root) of industry outputs is commonly employed. Although the H–O–V model does not imply such procedures, some form of adjustment for heteroscedasticity may nonetheless be warranted. However, it is incumbent on the analyst to characterize as explicitly as possible the source of the presumed heteroscedasticity so that an appropriate form of adjustment can be determined.

Trade imbalance

Given the importance of accounting for a trade imbalance when conducting Leontief-type tests, one should also expect the need for a trade imbalance correction when estimating an interindustry regression.

Correcting for a trade imbalance in the context of interindustry regression corresponds to requiring that the signs of the regression coefficients conform to the signs of the *adjusted* factor contents $(\mathbf{A}_i\mathbf{T}_i - \lambda_i\mathbf{E}_w)$ and not the unadjusted factor contents $(\mathbf{A}_i\mathbf{T}_i)$. This ensures that the signs of the regression coefficients conform to the definitions of factor abundance based on the excess factor supplies $\mathbf{E}_i - \alpha_i\mathbf{E}_w$.

An implicit correction for trade imbalance arises when an interindustry regression equation is estimated with a constant term. Specifically, inclusion of a constant term has the effect of measuring all variables as deviations from their means. If $\mathbf{Z} = \mathbf{I} - \mathbf{1}(\mathbf{1}'\mathbf{1})^{-1}\mathbf{1}'$ is the $J \times J$ idempotent matrix (i.e. $\mathbf{Z}'\mathbf{Z} = \mathbf{Z}$), where $\mathbf{I}$ is a $J \times J$ identity matrix and $\mathbf{1}$ is a $J \times 1$ vector of unit elements, then inclusion of a constant term implies that the estimates of the 'slope' coefficients can be written:

$$\hat{\beta}_i = (\mathbf{A}_i\mathbf{Z}\mathbf{A}_i')^{-1}\mathbf{A}_i\mathbf{Z}\mathbf{T}_i \qquad (8.34)$$

Since $\mathbf{Z}\mathbf{T}_i = \mathbf{T}_i - b_i\mathbf{1}/J$, where b_i is country i's trade imbalance, the correction for trade imbalance implied by including a constant term is to subtract from each industry's net trade the fraction $1/J$ of the country's trade imbalance. This correction, stated in terms of the factor content of trade, is

$$\hat{\beta}_i = (\mathbf{A}_i\mathbf{Z}\mathbf{A}_i')^{-1}(\mathbf{A}_i\mathbf{T}_i - \bar{\mathbf{A}}_ib_i) \qquad (8.35)$$

where $\bar{\mathbf{A}}_i$ is a $H \times 1$ vector whose hth element is the average requirement of input h (across J industries). Ignoring factor complementarities, (8.35) indicates that unless trade is balanced, including a constant term implies that the coefficient signs equal the signs of the elements of the vector $(\mathbf{A}_i\mathbf{T}_i - \bar{\mathbf{A}}_ib_i)$ and not the signs of the elements of the vector of adjusted factor contents $(\mathbf{A}_i\mathbf{T}_i - \lambda_i\mathbf{E}_w)$. Thus, if trade is not balanced, including a constant term implies that the coefficient signs may not conform to either the adjusted factor contents or the factor abundances (as measured by the signs of the elements of the excess factor supply vector $(\mathbf{E}_i - \alpha_i\mathbf{E}_w)$). Thus, even in the absence of factor complementarities, inferences about actual factor abundances based on coefficient signs might be incorrect.

Proper correction for trade imbalance in a regression context follows simply from the correction applied in the case of the trade in factor services (i.e. $\lambda_i\mathbf{E}_w$). In particular, since $\lambda_i = b_i/Y_w$ and $\mathbf{E}_w = \mathbf{A}\mathbf{Q}_w$, the vector of *adjusted* factor contents can be written

$$\mathbf{A}_i(\mathbf{T}_i - b_i\mathbf{S}_i) \tag{8.36}$$

where $\mathbf{S}_i$ is the $J \times 1$ vector of world output shares ($s_j = q_{wj}/Y_w$). Thus, the proper correction for a trade imbalance is to subtract from industry j's net trade the fraction s_j of the country's trade imbalance prior to estimation.

In practice, the measurement of $\mathbf{S}_i$ would require detailed data on world outputs which are usually not available. One solution to this problem of insufficient data is derived from the H–O–V assumption of identical and homothetic preferences. Specifically, homotheticity implies that a country's share of expenditure devoted to commodity j equals the share of the world's expenditure on commodity j

$$N_{ij}/N_i = N_{wj}/Y_w \tag{8.37}$$

But since world expenditure equals world production, (8.37) can also be written

$$N_{ij}/N_i = q_{wj}/Y_w = s_j \tag{8.38}$$

Thus, given the assumption of identical and homothetic preferences, the expenditure shares of only one country can be used in place of the world output shares s_j in (8.36).

Finally, since the trade imbalance correction involves the world output of each commodity, estimating an interindustry regression without the correction involves a left-out variable (i.e. the world outputs). Since the values of this left-out variable (i.e. b_iq_{wj}/Y_w) are absorbed into the regression error term, this specification error will introduce heteroscedasticity into the regression equation. This specification error may help explain the common finding in interindustry studies of a positive correlation between the regression residuals and national outputs.[30] If so, then it suggests that if the trade data are not corrected for trade imbalance prior to estimation, one could justify estimation using weighted least squares with weights equal to the inverse of the world output in each industry.

Cross-country regression

A traditional use of cross-country regressions has been the study of development processes, the analysis often taking the form of a regression of some economywide variable such as total exports on aggregate country characteristics such as GNP *per capita* and population. Only recently has the cross-country approach been adopted to study the pattern of trade with respect to individual commodities across countries.

In the context of the H–O–S/H–O–V model, the theoretical basis for the cross-country specification is firmer than the interindustry approach. In particular, given the assumptions of the H–O–V model, and assuming equal numbers of commodities and factors, trade is a linear function of the excess factor supplies. Hence, from (8.19), the equation for country i's trade in commodity j is

$$t_{ij} = (\mathbf{A}'_{ij})^{-1}(\mathbf{E}_i - (\alpha_i - \lambda_i)\mathbf{E}_w) \tag{8.39}$$

where $(\mathbf{A}'_{ij})^{-1}$ is a $1 \times J (= H)$ vector whose elements a_{ijh}^{-1} are the elements (row) of the inverse of the factor requirements matrix corresponding to industry j.

An equivalent expression of this relationship between trade and factor supplies is obtained by noting that, with balanced trade ($\lambda_i = 0$) and full employment ($\mathbf{A}_i\mathbf{Q}_i = \mathbf{E}_i$), the expenditure share $\alpha_i = N_i/N_w$ can be written

$$\alpha_i = \frac{\mathbf{P}'\mathbf{Q}_i}{N_w} = \frac{\mathbf{P}'(\mathbf{A}_i^{-1}\mathbf{E}_i)}{N_w} = \frac{\mathbf{W}'\mathbf{E}_i}{N_w} \tag{8.40}$$

where $\mathbf{P}$ is the $J \times 1$ vector of world output prices and $\mathbf{W}$ is the $H \times 1$ vector of world factor prices. The term $\mathbf{W}'\mathbf{E}_i$ is national expenditure at *factor cost*, and follows from the long-run zero profit condition: $\mathbf{W}' = \mathbf{P}'\mathbf{A}_i^{-1}$. Using (8.40) together with (8.39) gives

$$t_{ij} = (\mathbf{A}'_{ij})^{-1}\left[\mathbf{E}_i - \frac{(\mathbf{W}'\mathbf{E}_i)\mathbf{E}_w}{N_w}\right]$$

$$t_{ij} = (\mathbf{A}'_{ij})^{-1}\mathbf{E}_i - (\mathbf{A}'_{ij})^{-1}\frac{\mathbf{E}_w(\mathbf{W}'\mathbf{E}_i)}{N_w}$$

$$t_{ij} = \left[(\mathbf{A}'_{ij})^{-1} - \frac{(\mathbf{A}'_{ij})^{-1}\mathbf{E}_w\mathbf{W}'}{N_w}\right]\mathbf{E}_i \tag{8.41}$$

Using the condition for world full employment $(A'_{ij})^{-1}E_w = q_{wj}$, where q_{wj} is the world output of commodity j, (8.41) can be further simplified

$$t_{ij} = \left[(A'_{ij})^{-1} \frac{q_{wj}W'}{N_w} \right] E_i$$

(8.42)

$$t_{ij} = R'_{ij}E_i$$

where R'_{ij} is a $1 \times H(=J)$ vector with elements $r_{ijh} = (a_{ijh}^{-1} - q_{wj}w_h/N_w)$. These elements are the net effect (production *minus* consumption) of a change in the supply of resource h on country i's net trade in good j. In this regard, the term a_{ijh}^{-1} is the Rybczynski effect, that is, it is the amount by which the production of good j changes when the supply of factor h changes by one unit (i.e. $a_{ijh}^{-1} = \partial q_{ij}/\partial e_{ih}$). Unlike (8.39), (8.42) expresses trade as a function of country i's total factor supplies. The convenience of this specification is that it does not require one to measure world factor supplies or world expenditure in order to perform the estimation.

Problem 8.7: State the H–O–V equations (8.3) for the case of 2 goods and 2 factors assuming trade balance. Next, invert the matrix A to derive (8.39). Show that for this case the signs of the elements of A^{-1} ensure that a country is always an exporter of its absolutely abundant factors.

Equation (8.39) indicates that a regression of the trade in good j on the vector of excess factor supplies across countries would, in theory, yield estimates of the vector $(A'_{ij})^{-1}$. In principle, the H–O–S/H–O–V model could be tested by comparing these estimates to independent measurements of the elements of $(A'_{ij})^{-1}$. Alternatively, one could regress trade on factor supplies according to (8.42) and compare the coefficient estimates with direct measures of R_{ij}.

Although specifications (8.39) and (8.42) are direct implications of the H–O–V model, the use of these specifications for testing the H–O–S/H–O–V model requires the assumption of equal numbers of commodities and factors. If the number of commodities exceeds the number of factors there are multiple solutions to the H–O–V equations (8.3) (i.e. multiple values of the $(A'_{ij})^{-1}$). In this case, comparing actual values of $(A'_{ij})^{-1}$ with regression estimates is futile. If the number of factors instead exceeds the number of goods, then the solution to the H–O–V equations (8.3) is non-linear so that specification becomes difficult, if not impossible.

These problems indicate that a cross-country regression of trade on factor supplies is limited as an approach for directly testing the H–O–S/H–O–V model with respect to the trade in goods. However, since the cross-country approach can be directly derived from the H–O–V equations, it may be better suited than the interindustry approach when the focus is on weaker hypotheses about the relationship between trade and factor supplies.

Pooled regression

Pooled regression combines features of the interindustry and cross-country regression approaches. Specifically, it proposes that trade is explained by the combined interaction of countries' factor input requirements and factor supplies. This leads one to specify an equation in which trade is a function of both factor input requirements *and* factor supplies. One specification that has been employed[31] has the form

$$t_{ij} = \sum_h (\phi_{ih} \, ln(v_{jh}) + \gamma_{ih} \, ln(e_{ih}) + \beta_{ih} \, ln(v_{jh}) \, ln(e_{ih})) \qquad (8.43)$$

where v_{jh} is the amount of factor h employed in industry j, e_{ih} is the supply of factor h in country i and ϕ_{ih}, γ_{ih} and β_{ih} are parameters to be estimated. Regression estimation of this relationship would be made using a data set pooled across countries (i) and industries (j). This type of hybrid specification cannot be directly derived from the strict H–O–V model. Rather, the specification embodies the intuition noted earlier about the average relationship between trade, factor inputs and factor supplies implied by the H–O–V model. Recall that the H–O–V model predicts that a country's trade will be biased toward industries that employ more per unit of output of the country's abundant factors. An extension of this correlation result is obtained by pre-multiplying both sides of (8.3) by the vector of excess factor supplies:

$$(\mathbf{E}_i - (\alpha_i - \lambda_i)\mathbf{E}_w)'(\mathbf{A}_i\mathbf{T}_i)$$

$$= (\mathbf{E}_i - (\alpha_i - \lambda_i)\mathbf{E}_w)'(\mathbf{E}_i - (\alpha_i - \lambda_i)\mathbf{E}_w) > 0 \qquad (8.44)$$

Since $(\mathbf{E}_i - (\alpha_i - \lambda_i)\mathbf{E}_w)'\mathbf{A}_i\mathbf{T}_i > 0$, this can be interpreted to mean that a country will, on average, be an exporter of the services of its (absolutely) abundant factors. Re-grouping the elements of this vector multiplication we can write

$$((\mathbf{E}_i - (\alpha_i - \lambda_i)\mathbf{E}_w)'\mathbf{A}_i)\mathbf{T}_i > 0 \qquad (8.45)$$

The interpretation of this vector product is that the composition of a country's trade in goods ($\mathbf{T}_i$) will be positively associated with 'something', the something being an interaction between the country's factor supplies and factor input requirements $(\mathbf{E}_i - (\alpha_i - \lambda_i)\mathbf{E}_w)'\mathbf{A}_i$. Given this, one might consider the following specification:

$$\mathbf{T}_i = \phi_i(\mathbf{A}_i'(\mathbf{E}_i - (\alpha_i - \lambda_i)\mathbf{E}_w)) \qquad (8.46)$$

where ϕ_i is a positive scalar. If ϕ_i is assumed to be the same for all countries, then estimates of ϕ ($= \phi_i \forall i$) could be obtained by pooling data on countries' trade, factor supplies and factor inputs. However, this seems a rather indirect way to compute the implied correlation between the trade in the services of a factor and the excess supply of that factor across countries. Moreover, there is no reason to believe that the ϕ_i would be the same across countries.

The interaction hypothesis specified by equations such as (8.46) is difficult to interpret in terms of the H–O–V model and therefore appears to have little use as an approach for testing the specific hypotheses implied by the H–O–S/H–O–V model. Again, however, this type of analysis may have greater value when addressing weaker hypotheses about the relationship between trade, factor inputs and factor supplies.

8.3 **Concluding remarks**

This chapter has examined several of the empirical methodologies used to test the Heckscher–Ohlin–Samuelson (factor abundance) theory of trade. When there are many goods and factors, the empirically testable statement of the factor abundance theory is the Heckscher–Ohlin–Vanek (H–O–V) model. The latter links a country's net trade in factor services to its relative abundance of factors.

Leontief's pioneering test of the factor abundance theory with respect to US trade indicated rejection of the theory. However, this finding is unreliable since it is now understood that the test methodology adopted by Leontief is incorrect in the context of the H–O–V model. Specifically, the 'Leontief ratio', which compares ratios of factors exported to factors imported, may fail to correctly identify a country's abundant factors. Instead, the proper measure of a country's exchange of factor services is its net trade in factor services.

Examination of the signs of estimated coefficients derived from a regression of commodity trade on factor inputs across industries, or a regression of commodity trade on factor supplies across countries, is also an unreliable methodology for testing the factor abundance model. Instead, theoretically valid tests of the factor abundance model must involve a direct analysis of the H–O–V equations which relate the net trade in factor services to factor supplies. Importantly, this analysis must also make use of data on three independent sets of variables: factor supplies, commodity trade and factor inputs.

Recent tests of the factor abundance theory that directly examine the H–O–V equations also indicate rejection of the theory. However, unlike earlier tests of the theory, these analyses test the H–O–V model against clear alternative hypotheses (i.e. models). In this regard, differences in technology across countries appear significant for explaining the rejection of the 'pure' H–O–V model which assumes identical, constant returns to scale, production functions across countries. In addition, there is evidence that demand differences, as reflected by a bias for home produced goods,[32] may also be significant for explaining the pattern of trade in factor services. Does the evidence rejecting the 'pure' H–O–V model, and by implication the H–O–S model, mean that relative factor supply differences across countries should be rejected as an explanation of trade patterns? The answer is 'no'. What has been found is that factor supply differences *alone* are not sufficient to explain trade patterns. Demand differences and technological differences also appear important. Further work is needed to understand the nature of these demand and technological differences and their importance relative to factor supplies in determining trade patterns.

Notes

1. See Chapter 4 (pp. 145–8).
2. By definition, the vector of net outputs is $Q_i = (I - B)G$ where I is a $J \times J$ identity matrix, B is the $J \times J$ matrix of intermediate goods requirements and G is the $J \times 1$ vector of gross outputs.
3. Let D_i denote the $H \times J$ matrix of equilibrium direct factor input requirements. Then, with reference to fn. 2, the matrix of total (direct plus indirect) factor input requirements is $A_i = D_i(I - B)^{-1}$.
4. That is, $C_w = \sum_{z=1}^{N} C_z = \sum_{z=1}^{N} Q_z = Q_w$.
5. Let P be the $J \times 1$ vector of world prices of goods. Pre-multiply the net trade identity $T_i = Q_i - \mu_i C_w$ by this price vector and solve for the expenditure share to get $\mu_i = (P'Q_i - P'T_i)/P'C_w = (Y_i - b_i)/Y_w$.
6. An equivalent statement of absolute factor abundance is: factor h is absolutely abundant in country i if income per unit of factor h in country i is less than income per unit of factor h in the world, that is, if $(Y_w/e_{wh}) > (Y_i/e_{ih})$.
7. Analyses which compute only ψ^i are said to be 'revealing' factor abundance.
8. If w and r are the returns to labor and capital, respectively, then trade balance expressed in terms of the trade in factor services is: $rf_{iK} + wf_{iL} \equiv r(K_i - \alpha_i K_w) + w(L_i - \alpha_i L_w) = 0$. Since both r and w are positive, $(K_i - \alpha_i K_w)$ and $(L_i - \alpha_i L_w)$, must be of opposite sign.
9. With 2 factors and balanced trade, absolute and relative abundance are equivalent. Trade balance implies $r(K_i - \alpha_i K_w) = -w(L_i - \alpha_i L_w)$ so if capital is absolutely abundant then $(K_i/K_w - \alpha_i) > 0$ and $(L_i/L_w - \alpha_i) < 0$. These inequalities imply $K_i/K_w > \alpha_i > L_i/L_w$ or $K_i/K_w > L_i/L_w$, i.e., capital is relatively abundant.
10. Knowing only the sign of the *sum* of the excess factor supply terms in (8.10) is not sufficient to determine the relatively abundant factor. The crucial condition is that the excess factor supplies are of opposite sign.
11. One such adjustment is presented below.
12. The form of the adjustment will depend on what is assumed about preferences. Here the adjustment assumes preferences are identical and homothetic across countries.

13. Proposition S led Brecher and Choudhri (1983) (BC) to declare that Leamer's resolution of the Leontief paradox raised another paradox. Specifically, in Leamer's data the US exported labor services. By proposition S, BC argued that the US should then also have an excess supply of labor. However, BC then noted that the difference between US *per capita* GDP and world *per capita* GDP implied an *absolute* scarcity of labor in the US. BC's paradox is then that proposition S did not hold. Casas and Choi (1985) (CC) later argued that BC did not account for trade imbalance. With balanced trade, they showed that the US *imported* labor ($f_{iL}^A < 0$). Thus, proposition S does hold and there is no paradox. Note that this debate mixes the definitions of *absolute* and *relative* factor abundance. For example, Leamer infers *relative* abundance while BC and CC infer *absolute* abundance. Leamer's inference of US abundance in capital relative to labor would therefore remain valid even if CC had not validated proposition S.

14. The traditional statements of propositions S and R refer to a given country so the comparison of signs or ranks is made across factors. The reader should verify that similar statements of these propositions can also be made for a given factor and that in this case the comparison of signs or ranks would be made across countries.

15. More generally, between two matrices, one with columns equal to the factor contents of trade for each country, and the other matrix with columns equal to the excess factor supplies for each country.

16. The terms $\delta_i E_i$ in (8.17) indicate that assuming neutral differences in technology is equivalent to assuming neutral differences in the efficiency ('quality') of factors across countries.

17. Specifically, that consumption depends upon *per capita* income.

18. Importantly, Trefler also found evidence of non-neutral differences in productivity across factors so that, for example, capital rich countries use relatively capital-intensive techniques while labor rich countries use relatively labor intensive techniques. This implies that capital rich and capital poor countries lie in different 'cones of diversification' and suggests the absence of relative factor price equalization between capital rich and capital poor countries but relative factor price equalization within each group of countries.

19. This is modelled by modifying the H–O–V consumption equation $C_i = \mu_i Q_w$ to be $C_i = \mu_i(\lambda_i Q_i + (1 - \lambda_i)(Q_w - Q_i))$ where Q_i is home goods, $Q_w - Q_i$ is foreign goods and $0 < \lambda_i \leq 1$ measures consumption bias toward home goods.

20. For additional evidence on technological differences in the context of the H–O–V model see Trefler (1993). On preferences as a determinant of trade see Hunter and Markusen (1988) and Roy and Viaene (1998).

21. See Baldwin and Hilton (1983).

22. However, this degree of reliability holds only if the trade data are first corrected for any trade imbalance. See the section on specification issues below.

23. Suitably scaled to remove the units in which each factor is measured.

24. Using the regression method to test propositions S and R may be preferred to the factor contents if the trade vector alone is subject to additive errors of measurement. In this case the estimated regression coefficients are consistent estimates of the 'true' factor contents whereas the computed factor contents would contain the error and are thus biased.

25. In 1962 the US had a trade surplus. Correcting the factor contents for a trade surplus will, in general, increase the measured net imports of a factor. However, one cannot conclude from Baldwin's data that US imports of capital would have been greater after correcting for the trade surplus since Baldwin calculated factor contents using as data the net trade in each industry measured as the difference between its export share and its import share. Moreover, if net trade levels had been used to calculate factor contents it is unclear if capital would still have been imported.

26. Human capital is measured as the discounted differential between the annual average wage bill in an industry and the median annual wage bill for all US workers with eight or less years of education. This assumes that higher wages reflect higher levels of human capital.

27. See Chapter 1.

28. See Hamilton and Svensson (1983).

29. This and the following section based on Bowen (1992).

30. If the only source of this correlation was a failure to correct for a trade imbalance, then the sign of the correlation would be the same as the sign of the trade imbalance of the country being analyzed and the correlation would be zero if trade were balanced.

31. Balassa (1986).

32. As Leamer and Levinsohn (1995) note, this may reflect the (often ignored) importance of distance in determining trade patterns.

References and additional reading

General surveys

Deardorff, A. (1984), 'Testing Trade Theories and Predicting Trade Flows', in Jones, R.W. and Kenen, P.B. (eds), *Handbook of International Economics, Vol. I* (Amsterdam: North-Holland), 467–517.

Leamer, E.E. and Levinsohn, J. (1995), 'International Trade Theory: The Evidence', Chapter 26 in Grossman, G. and Rogoff, K. (eds), *Handbook of International Economics, Vol. III* (Amsterdam: North-Holland), chapter 26, 1339–94.

Stern, R.M. (1975), 'Testing Trade Theories', in Kenen, P.B. (ed.) *International Trade and Finance: Frontiers for Research* (New York: Cambridge University Press), 3–49.

Factor content

Bowen, H.P., Leamer, E.E. and Sveikauskas, L. (1987), 'Multicountry, Multifactor Tests of the Factor Abundance Theory', *American Economic Review*, 77(5), 791–809.

Brecher, R. and Choudhri, E. (1982), 'The Leontief Paradox, Continued', *Journal of Political Economy*, 90, 820–3.

Brecher, R. and Choudhri, E. (1988), 'The Factor Content of Consumption in Canada and the United States: A Two Country Test of the Heckscher–Ohlin–Vanek Model', in Feenstra, R.C. (ed.), *Empirical Methods for International Trade*, (Cambridge, Mass.: MIT Press) 5–17.

Casas, F.R. and Choi, E.K. (1985), 'The Leontief Paradox, Continued or Resolved?', *Journal of Political Economy*, 93, 610–15.

Hamilton, C. and Svensson, L.E.O. (1983), 'Should Direct or Total Factor Intensities be Used in Tests of the Factor Proportions Hypothesis?', *Weltwirtschaftliches Archiv*, 119(3), 453–63.

Kohler, W. (1991), 'How Robust Are Sign and Rank Order Tests of the Heckscher–Ohlin–Vanek Theorem?', *Oxford Economic Papers*, 43(1), 158–71.

Leamer, E.E. (1980), 'The Leontief Paradox Reconsidered', *Journal of Political Economy*, 88(3), 495–503.

Leontief, W. (1953), 'Domestic Production and Foreign Trade: The American Capital Position Re-Examined', *Proceeding of the American Philosophical Society*, 97, 332–49.

Maskus, K.V. (1985), 'A Test of the Heckscher–Ohlin–Vanek Theorem: The Leontief Commonplace', *Journal of International Economics*, 9, 201–12.

Trefler, D. (1993), 'International Factor Price Differences: Leontief was Right!', *Journal of Political Economy*, 101(6), 961–87.

Trefler, D. (1995), 'The Case of the Missing Trade and Other Mysteries', *American Economic Review*, 85(5), 1029–46.

Interindustry regression

Aw, B.-Y. (1983), 'The Interpretation of Cross-Section Regression Tests of the Heckscher–Ohlin Theorem with Many Goods and Factors', *Journal of International Economics*, 14(1–2), 163–67.

Baldwin, R.E. (1971), 'Determinants of the Commodity Structure of US Trade', *American Economic Review*, 61, 126–46.

Baldwin, R.E. and Hilton, S. (1983), 'A Technique for Indicating Comparative Costs and Predicting Changes in Trade Ratios', *Review of Economics and Statistics*, 105–10.

Bowen, H.P. (1992), 'Data Transformations in Interindustry Regression Tests of Trade Theory', mimeo, Graduate School of Management, University of California at Irvine.

Bowen, H.P. and Sveikauskas, L. (1992), 'Judging Factor Abundance', *Quarterly Journal of Economics,* 107(2), 599–620.

Branson, W. and Monoyios, N. (1977), 'Factor Inputs in US Trade', *Journal of International Economics*, 7, 111–31.

Harkness, J. (1978), 'Factor Abundance and Comparative Advantage', *American Economic Review,* 68, 784–800.

Kohler, W. (1988), 'Modeling Heckscher–Ohlin Comparative Advantage in Regression Equations: A Critical Survey', *Empirica*, 15(2), 263–93.

Leamer, E.E. and Bowen, H.P. (1981), 'Cross-Section Tests of the Heckscher–Ohlin Theorem: Comment', *American Economic Review*, 71(4), 1040–3.

Stern, R.M. and Maskus, K.V. (1981), 'Determinants of US Foreign Trade, 1958–76', *Journal of International Economics*, 11(2), 207–24.

Cross-country regression

Bowen, H.P. (1983), 'Changes in the International Distribution of Resources and Their Impact on US Comparative Advantage', *Review of Economics and Statistics*, 65, (August), 402–17.

Hunter, L. and Markusen, J. (1988), 'Per-Capita Income as a Determinant of Trade', in Feenstra, R.C. (ed.) *Empirical Methods for International Trade* (Cambridge, Mass.: MIT Press).

Leamer, E.E. (1984), *Sources of International Comparative Advantage: Theory and Evidence* (Cambridge, Mass.: MIT Press).

Roy, S. and Viaene, J.-M. (1998), 'Preferences, Country Bias and International Trade,' *Review of International Economics* (forthcoming).

Pooled regression

Balassa, B. (1986), 'Comparative Advantage in Manufactured Goods: A Reappraisal', *Review of Economics and Statistics*, 68(2), 315–19.

PART III

Imperfectly Competitive Markets: Trade and Trade Policy

■ *Chapter 9* ■

Imperfect Competition

The theories of trade presented in earlier chapters established a link between cross-country differences in either efficiency or endowments and the direction and composition of trade. They did not, however, explain two striking features of the data presented in Chapter 1. First was the disproportionately large volume of trade between industrialized countries. Presuming these countries to be similarly endowed, conventional theory would suggest that trade among them as a proportion of their GDPs would be rather smaller. Second was the extent of intra-industry trade. The standard theory, since it assumes homogeneous goods, has little to say about intra-industry trade or its possible causes.

This chapter relaxes the assumptions of the conventional theory regarding market structure and conditions of production. It focuses on the roles of imperfect competition and scale economies. The recognition that these factors could serve as independent explanations of trade is not new, but it is only since the early 1980s that these influences have been integrated into general equilibrium models.

Imperfect competition modifies some fundamental relationships encountered in earlier chapters, and the partial equilibrium analysis of oligopolistic markets conducted in the first part (section 9.1) of this chapter clarifies in what ways it does so. The remaining sections embed the oligopolistic and monopolistically competitive interactions in a general equilibrium structure. In this framework the direction of interindustry trade is still influenced by cross-country differences in relative endowments, while differentiation and relative country size determine the volume and the composition of trade.

When the number of competitors is small, the equilibrium depends on the type of oligopolistic interaction. This chapter considers the implications of the basic 1-period Cournot and Bertrand approaches. While not exhaustive of all the possibilities, these approaches provide the basic insights.

Section 9.1 explores the effects of country size and industry structure in determining the direction of trade. It also investigates the role of transport cost. The analysis then turns to general equilibrium. It shows that when competition is imperfect trade does not necessarily increase welfare for all countries. It then develops sufficiency conditions for trade to be welfare improving. The effects of trade liberalization on industry performance are then examined empirically. The chapter concludes with a model of monopolistic competition and an empirical evaluation of that model.

9.1 Partial equilibrium analysis with homogeneous goods

In this section we examine first how the direction of trade is determined by country size and by market structure. We consider an industry which consists of n home firms and n^* foreign firms all selling the same homogeneous good. We let q stand for the quantity produced by an individual firm, with q_l denoting sales in its local market, and q_x denoting its export sales. Similarly, we let Q_l and Q_x denote local sales and export sales by the industry as a whole.[1] Variables pertaining to foreign firms are starred and the subscripts a and f are used when warranted to signify autarky and free trade values.

Inverse demands in the home and foreign markets are written, respectively,

$$p = p(Q) \quad \text{and} \quad p^* = p^*(Q^*)$$

where   (9.1)

$$Q = Q_l + Q_x^* \quad \text{and} \quad Q^* = Q_x + Q_l^*$$

We always start our analysis assuming that the number of firms in a country is exogenous so that it remains the same when the country moves from autarky to free trade. We then relax this assumption, letting the number of firms change when countries switch from one regime to the other.

Cournot rivalry[2]

We assume that at any price foreign consumers demand a quantity equal to λ times the quantity demanded by home consumers, i.e. $p^*(Q^*) = p(Q^*/\lambda)$ for any $\lambda > 0$ and $Q^* > 0$. This ensures that demand elasticities are the same in each country when prices are the same.[3] We also assume that cost functions have the form $C(q) = F + cq$ and $C^*(q^*) = F^* + c^*q^*$. The fixed and variable cost components may vary across countries but are assumed not to differ across firms within the same country. This latter assumption will imply symmetric equilibria in which all firms within a country produce the same quantity (hence, when describing such equilibria, there is no need to index firms within the same country).

The equilibrium of the closed economy is now established as a benchmark.

Autarky equilibrium

Each home firm's profit function is $\pi = p(Q)q - cq - F$. Differentiating this function gives

$$\frac{\partial \pi}{\partial q} = p(\overline{Q} + q) + q \frac{dp(\overline{Q} + q)}{d(\overline{Q} + q)} \frac{\partial(\overline{Q} + q)}{\partial q} - c$$

where $\overline{Q} = Q - q$ is the output produced by rival firms. Under Cournot rivalry we have

$$\frac{\partial \overline{Q}}{\partial q} = 0$$

since firms choose quantity *as though* the production of rivals were fixed. Under autarky, the first-order condition therefore reads

$$p(Q_a) + q_a \frac{dp(Q_a)}{dQ_a} = c \tag{9.2}$$

(9.2) implicitly defines the reaction function since it determines the firm's profit maximizing quantity as a function of the quantity produced by all other firms.[4] With identical marginal costs, one has $Q_a = nq_a$ and inserting this into (9.2) gives:

$$p(Q_a) + \frac{Q_a}{n} \frac{dp(Q_a)}{dQ_a} = c \tag{9.3}$$

When the number of producers is given exogenously, (9.3) determines total output and substituting that output into the inverse demand yields the equilibrium price.

The left-hand side of (9.3) is called the individual firm's *perceived marginal revenue* (*mr*). It measures the change in revenue of a particular firm as it alone moves away from the symmetric equilibrium by changing its production. This contrasts with industry marginal revenue defined by

$$MR \equiv p(Q_a) + Q_a \frac{dp(Q_a)}{dQ_a}$$

Since an increase in the quantity produced by one firm lowers the revenue of its rival producers by an amount

$$\frac{(n-1)Q_a}{n}\frac{dp(Q_a)}{dQ_a}$$

industry marginal revenue is strictly lower than perceived marginal revenue when $n > 1$.

Figure 9.1 displays the 2 reaction functions for the case where demand is linear and $n = 2$. Firm 1's reaction function (r_1) intersects firm 2's reaction function (r_2) at point H.

Since each firm's reaction function represents the firm's 'best response' to the other firm's quantity, it must be the locus of maxima of iso-profit curves. Two of firm 1's iso-profit curves, denoted π_0^1 and π_1^1 are depicted in Figure 9.1. Since for any q_1 firm 1's profits are lower when q_2 is larger, it must be true that π_1^1 represents higher profits than π_0^1. Curves closer to the horizontal axis are the locus of higher profits by firm 1. A similar set of iso-profit curves exists for firm 2. They are vertical at their point of intersection with r_2 and represent higher profits when closer to the vertical axis. The Cournot equilibrium is given by the coordinates of H, the point at which the

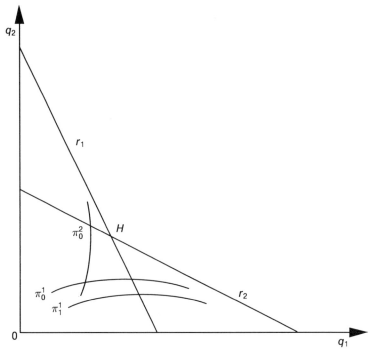

Figure 9.1   *Reaction functions and Cournot equilibrium*

quantity chosen by each firm is optimal given the quantity chosen by the other firm.

It can be shown that $p'(Q) + qp''(Q) < 0$, where single and double primes denote, respectively, first and second derivatives, ensures that r_1 has a slope steeper than -1 and r_2 has a slope bounded by 0 and -1. This ensures stability of the equilibrium. The condition $p'(Q) + qp''(Q) < 0$ is equivalent to $2p'(Q) + qp''(Q) < p'(Q)$, that is, the slope of the perceived marginal revenue function exceeds the slope of the demand function.[5]

It is useful at this point to spell out the autarky equilibrium conditions for the home and foreign firms, respectively, as

$$p(Q_a)\left[1 + \frac{1}{n\xi(p_a)}\right] = c \tag{9.4a}$$

$$p^*(Q_a^*)\left[1 + \frac{1}{n^*\xi^*(p_a^*)}\right] = c^* \tag{9.4b}$$

The terms $\xi = (dQ_a/dp_a)(p_a/Q_a)$ and $\xi^* = (dQ_a^*/dp_a^*)(p_a^*/Q_a^*)$ are, respectively, the home and foreign market elasticities of demand while $n\xi$ and $n^*\xi^*$ represent the demand elasticities perceived by each individual home and foreign producer.

We now show that allowing trade perturbs the autarky equilibria even when autarky prices are the same in both countries.

Trade equilibrium

We consider first the case where $c = c^*$ and $n = n^*$, and we note that by virtue of (9.4) autarky prices in both countries are the same even if country sizes are different. In the absence of transportation cost, the possibility to trade implies that there is only a single integrated market with inverse demand $\bar{p} = \bar{p}[(Q + Q^*)/(1 + \lambda)]$, i.e. with the same elasticity as the individual country demands when price is the same.[6] Since demand in the integrated market is the sum of individual country demands, it also follows that if each firm produces the very same quantity as under autarky, the price under trade must equal the common autarky price of both countries, i.e.

$$\bar{p}(Q_a + Q_a^*) = p\left(\frac{Q_a + Q_a^*}{1 + \lambda}\right) = p(Q_a) = p^*(Q_a^*) \tag{9.5}$$

However, with $n + n^*$ Cournot competitors now active in the integrated market, the first-order condition for each firm is

$$p\left(\frac{(n + n^*)q_f}{1 + \lambda}\right)\left[1 + \frac{1}{(n + n^*)\xi(p_f)}\right] = c \tag{9.6}$$

where q_f [$q_f = (Q_f + Q_f^*)(n + n^*)$] denotes the equilibrium output for each home and foreign firm under free trade.

Since at the autarky production levels the price in the integrated market equals the autarky prices, and since this ensures that the elasticity of the integrated market demand equals the elasticity of individual country demands, it must follow from (9.4) and (9.5) that

$$
p\left(\frac{Q_a + Q_a^*}{1 + \lambda}\right)\left[1 + \frac{1}{(n + n^*)\xi(p_a)}\right] > c
$$

This carries the implication that the free trade equilibrium quantity determined by (9.6) is larger than the sum of autarky quantities.

Consumers in both countries are better off in the trade equilibrium, since the free trade price p_f is lower than the autarky price p_a. Also, since the number of firms is constant (by assumption), total fixed cost $nF + n^*F^*$ is unchanged. Therefore, world welfare must be higher under trade than under autarky.

To examine the effects of trade on individual country welfare, it is useful to start with the simplest case where $\lambda = 1$. Except for a possible difference in fixed cost, the two countries are now mirror images of each other. Therefore, half of the world's gain in welfare must accrue to each country. Since $\lambda = 1$ ensures that individual firms in each country produce the same output in autarky as well, the change in regime must bring about an equiproportionate increase in output by firms in both countries. Hence, the decrease in profits is the same in both countries.[7]

Our symmetry assumptions ensure that both countries produce and consume exactly the same amount of output. Hence, no trade is actually taking place, even though there are no impediments to trade. Still, there is a gain in welfare which flows from the possibility to trade. The pro-competitive effect of trade operates through the increase in the elasticity of demand preceived by individual firms.

Consider now the case where $\lambda > 1$ while keeping $n = n^*$. Autarky prices are still the same, but output per firm is now higher in the foreign country than in the home country. Since total output is larger in the trade equilibrium than under autarky, and since all firms in the world produce the same output when they trade freely, it must follow that the move from autarky to trade increases the output of home firms proportionately more than it increases total output. A first implication is that the home country exports in the trading equilibrium.

The fact that $\lambda > 1$ also allows two outcomes that are impossible in the perfectly symmetric case : (a) the home industry *may* gain by moving from autarky to trade; (b) the losses incurred by firms in the large foreign country *may* exceed the gains of local consumers, resulting in a net loss in welfare for the country as a whole. The first of these possibilities arises when the increase in home industry output is proportionately larger than the reduction in the mark-up over marginal cost; the second is attributable to a severe decline in the share of foreign demand supplied by foreign firms. The dependence of such outcomes on demand and market structure parameters is made more precise in the problem below.

Problem 9.1: Let the home and foreign demands be $Q = a - p$ and $Q^* = (a - p^*)\lambda$ and assume $n = n^* = 2$ as well as $c = c^* = 0$. Determine the range of λs for which welfare increases in both countries as a result of a move from autarky to free trade, as well as the values of λ for which one country gains and the other loses. Define welfare as the sum of consumer surplus and industry profits.

Finally, consider the case where $c = c^*$ and $n \neq n^*$. The home industry's share of world output in the trade equilibrium is now $n/(n + n^*)$. Since consumers in both countries face the same price, the home country demands a fraction $1/(1 + \lambda)$ of world output. Hence, the home country imports (exports) if λ is larger (smaller) than n/n^*. When $n < n^*$ the autarky price is higher in the home country than in the foreign country. Thus consumers in the home country benefit more from being able to trade than consumers in the foreign country.

Problem 9.2: Assume that $c \neq c^*$ and show for the general case where $n \neq n^*$ and $\lambda \neq 1$ that differences in autarky prices can no longer predict the direction of trade.

Free entry and exit

In this section, we let the number of active producers be determined by free entry and exit. Under Cournot competition freedom of entry and exit means that all n active producers must earn non-negative profits and that given total industry output no additional firm can earn non-negative profits by joining the industry. Formally,

$$[p(Q) - c]q_j - F \geq 0 \text{ and } [p(Q + q_{n+1}) - c]q_{n+1} - F < 0 \text{ for } q_{n+1} > 0$$

where q_{n+1} is the output of a candidate entrant, q_j is determined by first conditions (9.2) and $Q = \sum_{j=1}^{n} q_j$.

Where there is freedom of entry and exit, the number of firms in the industry depends on the magnitude of scale economies relative to market size. To clarify the relationship between scale economies and the number of active firms, assume an initial equilibrium in which profits are zero. Now choose $\tilde{F} > F$ and $\tilde{c} < c$ such that $C(q) = F + cq = \tilde{C}(q) = \tilde{F} + \tilde{c}q$ for the value of q which solves (9.2). Clearly, the degree of scale economies is larger with $\tilde{C}$ than with C. Since we have $mr(q) > \tilde{c}$ an expansion of output is called for. However, as Cournot output is never less than monopoly output, the expansion must bring about a fall in profits and, since these profits were zero to start with, they must become negative if quantity increases. Exit restores an equilibrium in which profits are non-negative, through 2 channels. First, average cost falls since industry output is shared (equally) among fewer firms. Second, firms' perceived marginal revenue is brought closer to industry marginal revenue, inducing firms to curtail output.

If profits had been strictly positive at the initial equilibrium, there would have existed a range of $\tilde{F}$s larger than F and a corresponding range of $\tilde{c}$'s smaller than c for which the industy profits, although lower than initially, would have remained non-negative as the total industry output expanded to satisfy (9.2). For changes in F and c limited to that range, the number of firms in the industry would have remained unchanged.

To endogenize the number of producers, we have to add the following zero profit condition to the model

$$[p(nq) - c]q - F = 0$$

Strictly speaking, freedom of entry and exit only implies that the profits of active firms are non-negative, not that they are zero. However, profits are approximately zero when the degree of economies of scale is small relative to market size.[8]

Assuming that demands are of the form $p(Q) = a - b(Q/L)$ and $p^*(Q^*) = a - b(Q^*/L^*)$, where Q/L and Q^*/L^* denote, respectively, *per capita* consumption in the home and foreign country, one easily shows that for $c = c^*$ and $F = F^*$, freedom of entry and exit yields the following autarky quantities $q_a = \sqrt{FL/b}$ and $q_a^* = \sqrt{FL^*/b}$ for home and foreign firms as well as $n_a = (a - c)\sqrt{L/Fb} - 1$ and $n_a^* = (a - c)\sqrt{L^*/Fb} - 1$. Under trade $q_f = q_f^* = \sqrt{F(L + L^*)/b}$ and $(n_f + n_f^*) = (a - c)\sqrt{(L + L^*)/Fb} - 1$. Hence, with free entry and exit, output per firm in each country is larger under trade than under autarky.[9]

Welfare results follow. Since average cost is lower under free trade and since price equals average cost, home as well as foreign consumers must gain from a move to free trade. As profits are zero, the increase in total welfare equals the increase in consumer surplus.

Problem 9.3:   Assume that demands in the home and foreign country are $p = a - by$ and $p^* = a - by$ where y and y^* are the *per capita* quantities consumed and that there are L and L^* consumers in each country. Explore how moving from autarky to free trade affects the total number of active firms.

Transport costs

We now assume that firms incur a transport cost $\tau > 0$ per-unit exported but that the transport cost on local sales is zero.[10] We already know that under perfect competition trade arises only if the gap in autarky prices exceeds the cost of transport, that is, if $|p_a - p_a^*| > \tau$. This necessary condition no longer applies when markets are served by a finite number of Cournot firms. To see why, consider an autarky equilibrium in which $p_a = p_a^*$. Since in autarky each firm sells only in its own market, and since autarky prices are equal, it must be true that when trade becomes possible, the perceived marginal revenue derived from exporting a first unit exceeds the perceived marginal revenue from selling that unit in the local market. This follows from the fact that the firm can initially sell at the same price in both markets, but without incurring a drop in revenue on inframarginal units if it sells in the export market. Allowing trade must therefore precipitate some export sales if transport costs are not too high.[11]

To explore the role of transport costs, we assume that there are arbitrageurs who buy in one market and resell in the other, incurring the cost τ as they transport one unit from one country to the other. Then, one of the following conditions must hold:

$$|p_f - p_f^*| < \tau \tag{9.7a}$$

$$|p_f - p_f^*| = \tau \tag{9.7b}$$

When (9.7a) holds, markets are said to be *segmented*. Markets are often called integrated when (9.7b) holds. However, to avoid confusion with the case of integrated economies studied in later sections, the (9.7b) case will be labelled *markets connected by arbitrage* or simply *connected markets*.

When markets are segmented, the quantity in one market may change without this having any effect on the price in the other market. This, however, applies only for changes that take place within certain bounds. Crossing a bound means a switch from a condition where markets are segmented to one where they are connected by arbitrage. We now consider each of the two possibilities.

Segmented markets

We now assume that firms not only set total output but also the quantities in each individual market. The profit function of a home firm is then:

$$\pi = p(Q + Q_x^*)q_l + p^*(Q_x + Q_l^*)q_x - c(q_l + q_x) - \tau q_x - F$$

Similarly, the profit function of a foreign firm is

$$\pi^* = p(Q_l + Q_x^*)q_x^* + p^*(Q_x + Q_l^*)q_l^* - c^*(q_l^* + q_x^*) - \tau q_x^* - F^*$$

First-order conditions as they apply to the home market are now:

$$p(Q_l + Q_x^*) + q_l p'(Q_l + Q_x^*) = c \qquad \text{(for a home firm)} \qquad (9.8a)$$

$$p(Q_l + Q_x^*) + q_x^* p'(Q_l + Q_x^*) = c^* + \tau \quad \text{(for a foreign firm)} \qquad (9.8b)$$

where $Q_l = nq_l$ and $Q_x^* = n^* q_x^*$. Since the first-order conditions in one market are mirror images of those in the other market, we need only consider the equilibrium in one of them. We note that the first-order conditions (9.8a) and (9.8b) are independent of the parameters of foreign demand. This is due to constant marginal costs. Technically, this is equivalent to assuming that foreign firms produce for the home country market in a local plant where they incur the marginal cost $c^* + \tau$.[17] Thus, moving from autarky to trade is equivalent to an addition of n^* firms with marginal cost $c^* + \tau$ to the home market and an addition of n firms with unit cost $c + \tau$ to the foreign market and brings about an increase in output and a fall in price in both countries.

As shown in Figure 9.2, equilibrium in the home country is given by the intersection of the home and foreign *industry* reaction functions. The home (foreign) industry reaction function describes the output of the home (foreign) industry as a function of the output of the foreign (home) industry, given that all home (foreign) firms act as Cournot rivals.

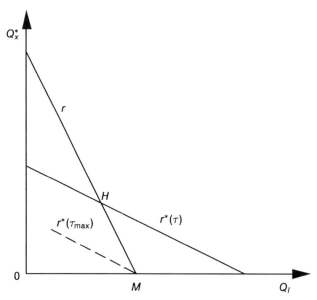

Figure 9.2 *Industry reaction functions*

Problem 9.4: Derive the explicit form of the home industry reaction function using the first-order conditions that apply to the home firms.

Using (9.8b), we find

$$\left[\frac{n^* + 1}{n^*} p' + q_x^* p''\right] dQ_x^* - d\tau = 0 \quad \text{for } dQ_l = 0^{13}$$

Given stability, this condition implies that the industry reaction function r^* will shift downward as τ increases until it intersects r at the point M (shown in Figure 9.2).[14] Let the critical value of the transport cost at which the letter occurs be called τ_{max}. Then, for all $\tau < \tau_{max}$ foreign firms do export to the home market.

Since the analysis is identical for the foreign market, we have in fact shown that under segmentation Cournot competition may bring about 2-way trade in the same homogeneous good. This is an outcome that cannot arise in a perfectly competitive environment.

Brander and Krugman (1983) have pointed out that such trade may give rise to an equilibrium in which firms located in one market dump into the other market.[15] They have labelled this outcome 'reciprocal dumping'. To illustrate, consider the particular case of perfect symmetry where $n = n^*$ and $c = c^*$ so that prices in the trading equilibrium are the same in both countries in spite of market segmentation. Given this, it must be true that, once freight is subtracted, the price a firm receives on export sales will be lower than the price it receives on home sales.[16]

Welfare analysis
To examine how transport costs affect the gains from trade, we assume that demand originates from a utility function of the form $u = U(Q) + M$, where M is expenditure on a competitively supplied 'numeraire' good. Such utility is practical for welfare analysis since marginal utility of the numeraire good is constant which implies that welfare changes are exactly measured by the surplus method. Using W^w to denote the contribution to world welfare made by the the market under investigation, we have

$$W^w = [U(Q_l + Q_x^*) - cQ_l - (c + \tau)Q_x - nF]$$

$$+ [U^*(Q_x + Q_l^*) - c^*Q_l^* - (c^* + \tau)Q_x^* - n^*F^*]$$

The first bracketed term represents the sum of gains accruing to home consumers and the home industry, while the second term represents the same for foreign consumers and foreign firms. Differentiating this expression and using $p = U'(Q)$ (which is true by virtue of utility maximization) we obtain:

$$\frac{dW^w}{d\tau} = - \left[\frac{d\tau(Q_x + Q_x^*)}{d\tau} \right]$$
$$+ \left[(p - c) \frac{d(Q_l + Q_x^*)}{d\tau} + (p^* - c^*) \frac{d(Q_x + Q_l^*)}{d\tau} \right]$$
$$- (c^* - c) \frac{d(Q_x^* - Q_x)}{d\tau}$$

This condition states that a change in transport cost affects welfare through three distinct channels. The first is the actual change in resources consumed in conveying the goods from their point of origin to their point of destination. A change in τ affects this cost through the change in the resources consumed per-unit transported and through its effects on the quantity exported. The middle term is the competitive effect. Since price is higher than marginal cost, the sign of the middle term is negative if an increase in transportation cost lowers the total quantity sold in each market. Finally, the third term measures the welfare consequence that flows from the change in production cost due to a reshuffling of output between high and low cost firms.

We now show that the middle term is indeed negative. Differentiation of (9.8) implies $-1 < dQ_l/dQ_x^* < 0$ when the stability condition $p' + qp'' < 0$ holds. Since $dQ_x^*/d\tau < 0$, it must be true that

$$d(Q_l + Q_x^*)/d\tau = [(\partial Q_l/\partial Q_x^*) + 1](dQ_x^*/d\tau) < 0$$

and, in the same way, one shows that $d(Q_x + Q_l^*)/d\tau < 0$. Since price exceeds marginal cost in both countries, it follows that a fall in transport costs has a pro-competitive effect in both countries.

The change in total welfare though remains ambiguous. We show this for the case where $n = n^*$ and $c = c^*$ (the latter allowing one to disregard the third term). First, we note that

$$\left. \frac{d\tau(Q_x + Q_x^*)}{d\tau} \right|_{\tau=0} = Q_x + Q_x^*$$

which implies

$$\left. \frac{d\overline{W}^w}{d\tau} \right|_{\tau=0} < 0$$

We then note that

$$\left. \frac{d\tau(Q_x + Q_x^*)}{d\tau} \right|_{\tau=\tau_{\max}} = \tau_{\max} \frac{d(Q_x + Q_x^*)}{d\tau} < 0$$

which by virtue of $p - c - \tau_{\max} = p^* - c^* - \tau_{\max} = 0$ and $dQ_l/d\tau = dQ_x/d\tau > 0$ implies $dW^w/d\tau|_{\tau=\tau_{\max}} > 0$.

Since welfare is decreasing in τ when the transportation cost is zero but increasing in τ when it is just prohibitive, and since welfare is continuous in τ within this interval, its shape is likely of a form shown by Figure 9.3. This means in particular that when the transport cost is close to prohibitive, a move from autarky to free trade must be welfare decreasing. The negative effect of trade on world welfare when transportation costs are high can be attributed to the waste of resources consumed in the cross-hauling of identical commodities.[17]

Problem 9.5:   Assume $c = c^*$ and $n = n^*$ and examine how the distribution of gains from trade across countries varies with the disparity in market sizes when $\tau > 0$. Compare your result to the case where $\tau = 0$.

Finally we note that what we found here is true only when the number of firms is fixed. Under freedom of entry and $p^*(Q^*) = p(Q^*/\lambda)$ an increase in transportation cost always lowers welfare.[18]

Markets connected by arbitrage
When markets are connected, one of the following conditions holds

$$p = p^* + \tau \tag{9.9a}$$

$$p^* = p + \tau \tag{9.9b}$$

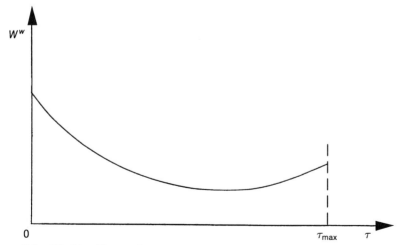

Figure 9.3   *World welfare and transport cost*

Imposing either (9.9a) or (9.9b) means that an additional unit of output sold in one market will be redistributed by arbitrageurs such that the proportion $p^{*'}/(p^{*'} + p')$ goes to home consumers and the proportion $p'/(p^{*'} + p')$ goes to foreign consumers.

Expressions (9.9a) and (9.9b) are mirror images of each other and hence we can limit our discussion to case (9.9a). When (9.9a) holds, the foreign firm is indifferent between the following options: (a) selling all its output in the local market at the price p^* and letting arbitrageurs re-export some of that output to the home market; (b) shipping directly to both markets and hence incurring a transport cost on export sales but getting the higher home country price for exports.

A home country firm by contrast sells only in its local market. To see why, note that from (9.9a) we have

$$(p^* + \tau) + qp'p^{*'}/(p^{*'} + p') > p^* + qp'p^{*'}/(p^{*'} + p')$$

that is, the marginal revenue a home firm derives from local sales is higher than its marginal revenue from export sales. This by itself is sufficient to discourage export sales. The fact that export sales require costly transportation whereas local sales do not, increases the gap between the profitability of home sales and export sales even further.

Since home firms only sell locally when (9.9a) holds (similarly, foreign firms do not export when (9.9b) holds), intra-industry trade in the homogeneous good will not occur when markets are connected by arbitrage. Conditions (9.9) also imply that dumping is inconsistent with markets being connected.

Problem 9.6: Assume that demands in both countries are of the form $p = 1 - Q$; that $n = n^* = 1$ and $c > ac^*(a > 1)$. Explore the relationship between the margin of dumping and τ as well as α. In this context, indicate the range of parameter values for which markets are segmented and determine the equilibrium price when markets are connected by arbitrage.

Bertrand rivalry

Under Bertrand competition, the firm's decision variable is price rather than quantity. Every firm chooses its price as if the prices of its rivals remain fixed and then supplies the quantity that consumers demand from it at that price. As with Cournot competition, we study only the case in which all firms act once and simultaneously (i.e. a static, 1-period, game), but now we assume $F = F^* = 0$.

When average costs are constant but not equal across firms, Bertrand competition yields an equilibrium in which the firm with the lowest unit cost is the only one to produce positive output. The equilibrium price depends on the difference between the unit cost of the firms with lowest and second lowest unit cost. When the cost of the firm ranked second lowest exceeds the price the least cost firm would set if it were alone in the market, then the monopoly price associated with the cost of the most efficient firm will be the equilibrium price. By contrast, when the monopoly price is higher than the unit cost of the second most efficient firm, the Bertrand price is equal (or, more precisely, slightly below) the unit cost of the second most efficient firm. In either case, the most efficient firm is the sole active producer in equilibrium.

Consider the case of two countries and two firms, one in each country. Assume transport costs are zero and that $c < c^*$ and $p_m(c) \geq c^*$, that is, the foreign firm's unit cost is below the price a domestic monopolist would set. Then, when $n = n^* = 1$, the autarky prices are the monopoly prices $p_m(c)$ and $p_m^*(c^*)$. When trade is allowed, the two markets become one and, since $p_m(c) \geq c^*$, price falls to c^* in both countries (or, more precisely, to $c^* - \varepsilon$). The home country firm is then the sole supplier to each market. Welfare increases in each country since consumer gains are larger than producer losses.

When there are at least two firms in each country, autarky prices will equal the local unit cost (c or c^*). With $c < c^*$, allowing trade lowers the price in the foreign country to c. The foreign country gains from trade since foreign consumers will receive a larger surplus whereas foreign producers, whose profits were zero in autarky, neither gain nor lose. The home country's welfare is unaffected since consumer and producer surplus are unchanged.

Transport costs

Allowing positive transport costs increases the number of possible outcomes. In particular, firms could set price independently in each country. When such discrimination is possible, there are two cases to consider: $c < c + \tau < c^*$ and $c < c^* < c + \tau$. Denote the former as case (a) and the latter as case (b).

Let $n = n^* = 1$ and assume that $p_m(c) > c^* + \tau$ and $p_m^*(c^*) > c + \tau$. In this case, trade will cause the price in the home country to drop to $c^* + \tau$, which is the cost at which the foreign firm can supply domestic consumers. This outcome holds for both case (a) and case (b) above. The foreign price will fall to c^* for case (a) and $c + \tau$ for case (b). However, in case (a) the home firm supplies both home and foreign consumers whereas in case (b) foreign producers survive and supply foreign consumers. Thus, in case (b) trade does not take place. In both cases, though, the possibility to trade raises world welfare. Under case (b) the welfare gain is due only to increased competition while under case (a) there is the additional gain from a fall in the cost of production.

When n and n^* exceed unity, the autarky equilibrium in each country is already the competitive equilibrium. Hence, trade can yield a welfare benefit only if it lowers the cost of production. We already know that this will happen when $c < c + \tau < c^*$.

When discrimination across markets is not possible, the home firm must determine whether its profits are larger by (1) setting a price low enough to evict its foreign rivals and hence supply both markets or (2) abandoning the foreign market to the foreign firm and setting a higher price in its home market. It is left to the reader to explore the equilibria that result from such rivalry as well as the welfare consequences of trade.

Whereas Bertrand competition has intuitive appeal, the modelling of homogeneous markets typically assumes that firms 'play' Cournot – that is, that they are are quantity setters. The reason is that Cournot competition, unlike Bertrand competition, generates equilibria which approach the competitive equilibrium continuously as the number of firms increases. This property appeals to many economists.[19] Although popular, the Bertrand and Cournot models are not the only approaches to modelling imperfect competition. Other approaches, e.g. those in which a firm sets price but the quantity it can supply is constrained, are also found in the literature. Some attempts have been made to reconcile Bertrand and Cournot models, most notably by Kreps and Scheinkman (1983).

9.2 General equilibrium with homogeneous goods

The above partial equilibrium analysis treats incomes and factor prices as given and hence ignores how changes in these variables alter demand and cost functions as one moves from autarky to trade. To incorporate these effects, this section calls on the 2-factor, 2-sector general equilibrium model developed in Chapter 4. To account for the effects of imperfect competition, it assumes that there is only 1 firm in industry 2. Industry 1 remains perfectly competitive. As in Chapter 4, each sector is assumed to produce a homogeneous good using the services of 2 factors, capital and labor. Factor markets are perfectly competitive, factors are perfectly mobile across industries, and firms are price takers in their input markets. Industry 2 is more capital-intensive than industry 1. All consumers have identical and homothetic preferences.

To individualize the effects of market power alone from the combined effect of market power and scale economies, it is assumed at first that the technology in each sector exhibits constant returns to scale. The combined effect of market power and scale economies is examined subsequently.

Constant returns to scale[20]

Autarky equilibrium

Given the preceding assumptions, the economy's production possibility frontier (PPF) has all the properties detailed in Chapter 4, including strict concavity. Efficient resource allocation requires the ratio of factor marginal productivities to be equal across industries. This condition is met since all firms are price takers in factor markets. Hence, production takes place on the boundary of the PPF. Industry structure in the product market determines the precise point on the PPF.

Note first that profit maximization requires $p_1 = c_1$ for industry 1 and $p_2[1 + (1/\xi)] = c_2$ for industry 2, where c_i denotes marginal cost in industry i and ξ is the elasticity of demand for good 2. Letting $p = p_2/p_1$ denote the relative price of good 2, and observing that the slope of the PPF equals the ratio of marginal costs (i.e. $-dQ_1/dQ_2 = c_2/c_1$), implies that the following condition must hold at the profit maximizing production point:

$$-\frac{dQ_1}{dQ_2} = p\left[1 + \frac{1}{\xi(p)}\right] \equiv MR$$

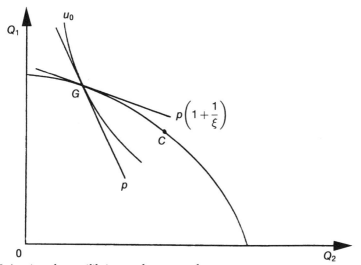

Figure 9.4 *Autarky equilibrium under monopoly*

Since in equilibrium the marginal rate of substitution in consumption equals p, the economy's autarky equilibrium must occur at a point such as G in Figure 9.4, where a social indifference u_0 curve intersects the PPF.

Markusen (1981) shows that when the social indifference curves can be represented by a CES function of the form $u = (aQ_1^{-\beta} + bQ_2^{-\beta})^{-1/\beta}$, values of ξ smaller than 1 in absolue value exist for $\beta < 0$ and that $1/\xi$ decreases monotonically as Q_2 increases relative to Q_1. An increase in the elasticity of demand facing the monopolist would reduce the gap between MR and p and move the equilibrium point G clockwise along the PPF. For the reasons given in Chapter 4 (see (4.13)), this movement would be accompanied by a fall in the price of labor relative to capital and hence a fall in the capital–labor ratio in each industry.

Trade equilibrium

We now introduce a foreign country, identical to the home country described above except that it is λ times larger ($\lambda > 1$). Since the foreign PPF is simply a radial expansion of the home PPF, the autarky price p and *per capita* consumption of each good are the same in both countries. When free trade becomes possible, each monopolist becomes a duopolist. If rivalry among them is Cournot then both duopolists' perceived marginal revenue will, for the reasons given in the previous section, exceed their marginal cost at their autarky production levels.

In previous sections, we have examined the adjustments which follow under the assumption that marginal cost remained constant. We now investigate the effects of a move from autarky to trade, when factor prices, and hence marginal cost, respond to output adjustments.

In the trading equilibrium, the first-order conditions in industry 2 are $p_{2f}[1 + \zeta/\xi] = c_2$ and $p_{2f}[1 + \zeta^*/\xi] = c_2^*$ for the home and foreign producer, respectively, with p_{2f} denoting the common free trade price and ζ and ζ^* denoting market shares. Since the slope of each country's PPF equals the ratio of marginal costs in the two industries,[21] and since by virtue of concavity the slope of the PPF is steeper when the ouput of industry 2 is larger relative to industry 1, we can conclude from the first-order conditions that

$$\zeta^* > \zeta \Leftrightarrow Q_2^*/Q_1^* < Q_2/Q_1 \tag{9.10}$$

We use (9.10) to show that in the trading equilibrium the output of industry 2 in the foreign country will be less than λ times the output of industry 2 in the home country.

The points $Q = (Q_1, Q_2)$ and $Q^* = (Q_1^*, Q_2^*)$ shown in Figure 9.5 denote the free trade quantities produced in the home and foreign country, respectively. We note that $Q_2^* > \lambda Q_2$ cannot be true since it entails $\zeta^* > \zeta$ and $Q_2^*/Q_1^* > Q_2/Q_1$ which violates (9.10). We note next that it cannot be true either that $Q_2^* < Q_2$ since it implies $\zeta^* < \zeta$ and $Q_2^*/Q_1^* < Q_2/Q_1$ which again violates (9.10). Hence, Q^* must lie somewhere on the segment RF shown in Figure 9.5. We therefore conclude that if trade increases the output of good 2 in both countries, it must do so proportionately less in the larger country; that is, in the trading equilibrium, we have $Q_2^* < \lambda Q_2$.

Since all consumers have the same homothetic preferences, and since trade equalizes the prices of both goods, we can also conclude that the smaller (home) country must export good 2.[22] We also note that, since in the trade equilibrium Q and Q^* do not lie on the same ray through the origin, factor intensities in production must differ between countries. Thus, trade produces a divergence in factor prices between countries with the same relative endowments.

We do not know yet how the absolute quantities produced in the trading equilibrium compare to autarky quantities. These quantities, as well as the world output of good 2, can be determined with the aid of Figure 9.6. The horizontal axis measures the amount of good 2 produced by the large (foreign) country and the vertical axis measures the quantities of good 2 produced by the smaller (home) country. The coordinates of A denote the autarky amounts of good 2 in each country. The line gg with slope -1 is the locus of cross-country production allocations that yield the world output under autarky. Figure 9.6 also displays the reaction functions of home (r)

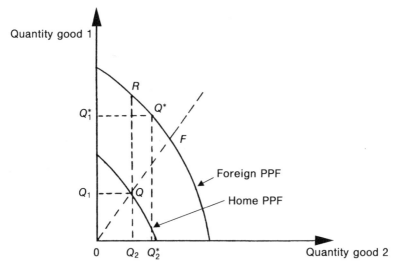

Figure 9.5 *Home and foreign production*

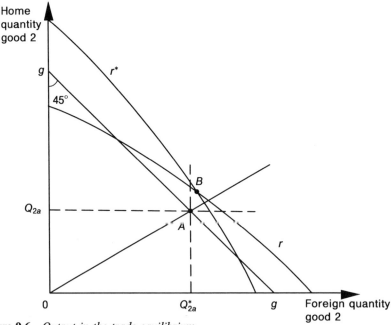

Figure 9.6   *Output in the trade equilibrium*

and foreign (r^*) duopolists. The slopes of the reaction functions are obtained from the first-order conditions. Diminishing marginal revenue and concavity of the production frontier (which connotes that the marginal cost of one good in terms of the other is increasing) imply that r^* has a slope steeper than -1 and that the slope of r is bounded by 0 and -1.[23] We now show that both reaction functions must pass-through the area located northeast of point A.

Suppose that free trade production levels were also located at point A. Since production of both goods would then be the same as under autarky, marginal costs would also be the same. Since preferences are homothetic and identical across countries, the elasticity of demand under trade would be equal to the autarky elasticities of demand in each country. However, under free trade, each producer would have a market share less than 1 and would therefore face a higher perceived marginal revenue than in autarky. The best response by the foreign producer to the quantity set by the home firm (Q_{2a}) would then be to set a quantity larger than Q^*_{2a}. Similarly, if the foreign firm sets Q^*_{2a}, the home firm's profit maximizing quantity would be larger than Q_{2a}. Both reaction functions must therefore pass-through the area located to the northeast of point A.

This, and the fact that r is flatter than gg while r^* is steeper than gg, ensure that both reaction functions do not intersect more than once, and do so at a point above gg.

As shown in Figure 9.6, the trade equilibrium occurs at a point B. Since under free trade the home country's share of world output of good 2 is larger than λ (which is the share under autarky), B must lie above the ray passing through points O and A. Since at point B each country produces more of good 2 than in autarky, trade raises world output by the imperfectly competitive industry.

The equilibrium depicted by point B in Figure 9.6 is not the only possible outcome. The reaction functions may also intersect at a point above gg but to the left of point A. If so, the large country produces less of good 2 under free trade than in autarky. However, regardless of whether r intersects r^* to the northeast or the northwest of A, world output of industry 2 as well as industry 2 output by the small country are larger in the trading equilibrium than under autarky.

The gains from trade

In Section 9.1, we made a distinction between gains from trade that derive from bringing prices closer to marginal costs and classical gains that flow from a shift of production towards low cost producers. We now explore the gains from trade in the context of our general equilibrium model. First, we present a sufficient condition for trade to generate welfare gains. This condition is valid for economies with 2 or more industries of which several may be imperfectly competitive. Second, we show that, even though trade reduces the disparity between price and marginal cost, a country harboring an imperfectly competitive industry may actually experience a loss in welfare as it moves from autarky to free trade.

A sufficiency condition
Trade benefits an economy if its consumers can purchase their autarky consumption bundle at free trade prices. Formally, this condition reads:

$$\sum_j p_{jf} Q_{ja} \leq \sum_j p_{jf} Q_{jf} \tag{9.11}$$

where p_{jf} denotes the free trade output price of industry j while Q_{jf} and Q_{ja} are, respectively, the free trade and autarky outputs of industry j. Following Helpman and Krugman (1985), we write

$$\sum_j p_{jf}(Q_{jf} - Q_{ja}) = \sum_j (p_{jf} - mr_{jf})(Q_{jf} - Q_{ja})$$

$$+ \sum_j mr_{jf}(Q_{jf} - Q_{ja}) \tag{9.12}$$

where mr_{jf}s are the marginal revenues faced by producers under free trade. Since profit maximization requires these marginal revenues to equal marginal costs, and since the marginal rate of transformation between any pair of goods equals the ratio of their marginal costs, the marginal rate of transformation between any pair of goods equals the corresponding ratio of marginal revenues.

Figure 9.7 illustrates these relationships for a 2-sector economy. As shown, the trade equilibrium is the same as would arise if the value of national output were maximized with marginal revenues acting as (shadow) prices. Since the PPF is strictly concave and its slope equals the ratio of marginal revenues, it must be true that $\sum_j mr_{jf}Q_{jf} > \sum_j mr_{jf}Q_j$ for any combination of Q_js on the frontier but different from the free trade outputs, in particular, for $Q_j s = Q_{ja} s$. This implies that the second term of the right-hand side of (9.12) is positive. Hence, a sufficient condition for a country to gain from trade is

$$\sum_j (p_{jf} - mr_{jf})(Q_{jf} - Q_{ja}) \geq 0 \qquad (9.13)$$

Expression (9.13) holds trivially when all industries are competitive and will also hold for imperfectly competitive industries if these industries expand as a result of trade. If some of these industries expand while others contract, then (9.13) will hold only if, in some average sense, the expanding industries are those with the largest deviation between price and marginal cost.

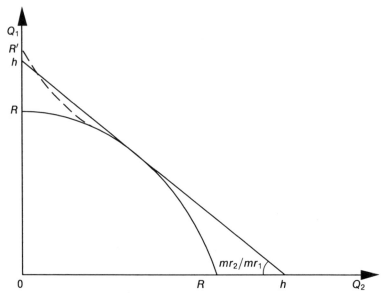

Figure 9.7   *Maximization of value with marginal revenues as shadow prices*

Returning to the model of the preceding section, we can now ask if both countries gain from a move from autarky to trade. Since industry 1 is competitive, condition (9.13) implies that each country gains if trade expands its output in the non-competitive industry 2. We know that the output of industry 2 expands in the smaller country and this allows us to conclude that the small country gains from trade. The large country, however, may gain or lose from trade since trade may increase or decrease its production in industry 2.

This possibility is illustrated in Figure 9.8 with Q_a, Q_f and C_f denoting, respectively, pre-trade production, post-trade production and post-trade consumption in the home country, while Q_a^*, Q_f^* and C_f^* similarly denote these amounts in the foreign country. Since consumers face identical prices under free trade, the slopes of the indifference curves passing through C_f and C_f^* are the same. In contrast, the slope of the PPFs at Q_f and Q_f^* differ since the marginal revenue of the home country duopolist does not equal that of the foreign duopolist.

To see that world welfare increases with trade even when welfare in the large country falls, write (9.11) for the world as a whole as

$$\sum_j p_{if}(Q_{ja} + Q_{ja}^*) \le \sum_j p_{if}(Q_{if} + Q_{if}^*)$$

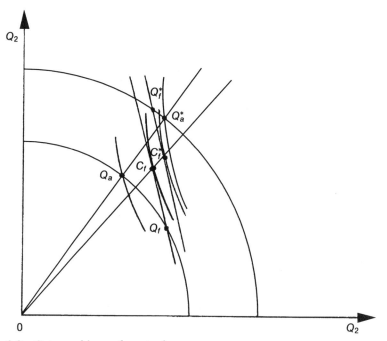

Figure 9.8 *Gains and losses from trade*

By applying the same reasoning as above, we can obtain a similar sufficiency condition. The only difference is that world outputs replace individual country outputs. Since we already know that world output of industry 2 expands, we can conclude that trade increases world welfare.

In summary, the conventional result that trade raises world welfare remains valid when one of the industries is a monopoly under autarky. However, unlike the perfectly competitive case, it is no longer true that no country can lose. Only the small country, which under our symmetry assumptions exports the non-competitive good, is assured of gains from trade. The large country may gain or lose.

Internal economies of scale

We now assume that industry 2's technology exhibits global economies of scale (EOS).[24] In Chapter 3, it was shown that economies of scale (EOS) external to the firm (but internal to the industry) cause *some or all* portions of an economy's PPF to become convex.[25] This is also true when scale economies are internal to firms. For our purposes, it is important to note that EOS (internal or external) imply that a proportional increase in the supply of all factors within a country need not cause an equiproportional increase in its capacity to produce all goods. Hence, the PPFs of countries that differ in size only (i.e. are scalar replicas of one another) are no longer radial expansions of the PPF of the smallest country. An implication of this is that EOS *may* reverse the pattern of trade that would arise from market power alone.[26]

The relationship between EOS, the PPF, and the trade pattern of a large and small country is considered in Figures 9.9(a) and 9.9(b).[27] Since, by assumption, production of good 1 exhibits constant returns to scale, a proportional increase in factor supplies would be expected to expand the capacity to produce good 2 by more than it expands the capacity to produce good 1. This implies that, with good 2 on the horizontal axis, the frontier of the country with proportionately more resources is flatter than the frontier of the smaller country along the same ray from the origin.

This relationship between the slopes of large and small country PPFs in the presence of EOS is quite general.[28] It implies that, for any output pair Q and Q^* which satisfies $Q_2/Q_1 \leq Q_2^*/Q_1^*$, the slope of the larger country's PPF at its production point Q^* is flatter than the slope of the small country's PPF at its production point Q. However, in contrast to the constant returns to scale case, a flatter slope of the large country's PPF at its production point Q^* than the slope of the small country PPF at its production point Q, does *not* entail $Q_2/Q_1 \leq Q_2^*/Q_1^*$. Therefore, (9.10) must be modified to read $\zeta^* > \zeta \Leftarrow Q_2^*/Q_1^* \geq Q_2/Q_1$.

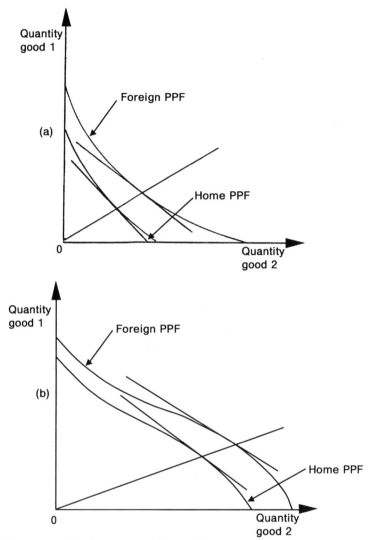

Figure 9.9 *PPFs under (a) large and (b) small economies of scale*

Since $\zeta^* > \zeta$ is consistent with $Q_2/Q_1 < Q_2^*/Q_1^*$ we cannot, as on p. 347, rule out $Q_2^* > \lambda Q_2$ in the trading equilibrium. We conclude that, with increasing returns to scale in industry 2, the large country may (but need not) export good 2 in Cournot equilibrium.[29]

When EOS are weak, in the sense that they have very little effect on the concavity of the PPF, the locations and slopes of the reaction functions will remain as shown in Figure 9.7 since the marginal cost of one good in terms of the other is still increasing. In this case, trade would lead to an increase in world output and, by virtue of (9.13), an increase in world welfare.[30]

However, if EOS are strong and differences in factor intensities small, convexity of the PPF implies several possible outcomes. For example, both countries may continue to produce good 2 in the trading equilibrium and world production of good 2 would be higher under trade than in autarky. Also, the equilibrium with both countries diversified may be unstable.

The gains from trade revisited

Since the PPF may be convex in the presence of EOS, condition (9.13) no longer assures the existence of gains from trade. Recall that the proof of (9.13) required that no point on the frontier be located above the revenue line tangent to the PPF. Clearly, this requirement may be violated if the PPF is not globally concave, e.g. when the frontier is RR' rather than RR in Figure 9.7.

The gains from trade in the presence of scale economies have been extensively studied by a number of authors and several sufficiency conditions for gains from trade have been proposed.[31] One of the conditions is due to Grinols (1991). It has the advantage of being very general since it applies equally to convex and concave PPFs and does not require that factor supplies remain fixed across equilibria.

While the condition applies to any number of goods and factors, the idea which underlies it can be explained diagrammatically for an economy which produces 2 goods. Let Q_a and Q_f in Figure 9.10 denote the production points under autarky and free trade and let u_a and u_f be the social utility levels associated with the autarky consumption $C_a = Q_a$ and free trade consumption C_f. Free trade prices are given by the slopes of the lines through points Q_f and Q_a.[32] The welfare gain can be measured as the increase in expenditures needed to move from u_a to u_f, given free trade prices. This increase is shown in Figure 9.10 by a shift of the (budget) line from b_1 to b_3. As shown in Figure 9.10, this shift decomposes into a shift from b_1 to b_2 and then an increase from b_2 to b_3. The first of these shifts corresponds to consumption gains and is always positive since b_1 minimizes the expenditure that achieves the utility level u_a at free trade prices. The shift from b_2 to b_3 is the production gain.[33]

Turning to the multidimensional case, the change in welfare can be written

$$\Delta W = \Lambda + \sum_j [(p_{jf}Q_{jf} - \mathbf{w}_f \cdot \mathbf{e}_{jf}) - (p_{jf}Q_{ja} - \mathbf{w}_f \cdot \mathbf{e}_{ja})] \qquad (9.14)$$

where the first term Λ denotes gains on the consumption side and the second term captures the welfare effect of the change in production. The terms p_{jf} and p_{ja} are free trade and autarky prices of good j, and Q_{jf} and Q_{ja} are the corresponding quantities. The factors employed by industry j under autarky and under trade are given by the elements of the vectors $\mathbf{e}_{jf}$ and $\mathbf{e}_{ja}$ respectively. The vector $\mathbf{w}_f$ denotes free trade factor prices. Since the output of one

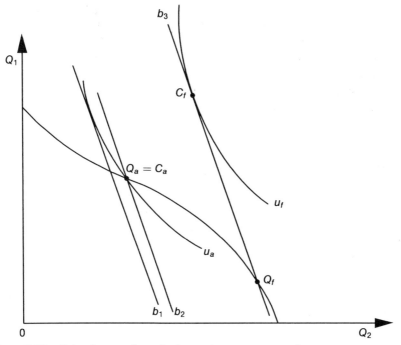

Figure 9.10   *Gains from trade under increasing returns to scale*

production process may be an input into another production process, components of the **e** vector relate to the same goods as the components of Q. Correspondingly, their **w** s will be the same as the ps of these other goods. For goods not used as inputs in the production of j, the corresponding element of $\mathbf{e}_{jf}$ or $\mathbf{e}_{ja}$ is zero. Hence, the second term of (9.14) represents the change in value of net output at free trade prices. Since $\mathbf{w}_f \cdot \mathbf{e}_j$ represents total cost incurred by industry j, one can also write

$$\Delta W = \Lambda + \sum_j \{[p_{jf}Q_{jf} - C_j(\mathbf{w}_f, Q_{jf})] - [p_{jf}Q_{ja} - C_j(\mathbf{w}_f, Q_{ja})]\}$$

$$= \Lambda + \sum_j \left\{ Q_{jf}\left[p_{jf} - \frac{C_{jf}(Q_{jf})}{Q_{jf}}\right] - Q_{ja}\left[p_{jf} - \frac{C_{jf}(Q_{ja})}{Q_{ja}}\right] \right\}$$

where C_{jf} and C_{ja} are shorthand for the cost functions under free trade and autarky factor prices.

Since $\Lambda > 0$, a sufficient condition for welfare gains is that the second term be non-negative. In this regard, note first that for competitive industries profit maximization entails $p_{jf} - C_{jf}(Q_{jf})/Q_{jf} = 0$ and $p_{jf} - C_{jf}(Q_{ja})/Q_{ja} < 0$ for $Q_{jf} \neq Q_{ja}$. Hence, competitive industries contribute non-negatively to welfare.

In the case of increasing returns-to scale industries, $Q_{jf} > (<) Q_{ja}$ implies $C_{jf}(Q_{jf})/Q_{jf} < (>) C_{jf}(Q_{ja})/Q_a$. Hence, increasing returns to scale industries that earn non-negative profits contribute positively (negatively) to welfare when their output increases (decreases).[34] For a given quantity change, the impact on welfare is larger, the higher the degree of EOS in the industry.

If all industries displaying constant or decreasing returns to scale are competitive, gains from trade are more likely to occur the larger the increase in the output of non-competitive industries that exhibit the greatest degree of EOS.

The role of factor supplies

We now relax the assumption that countries differ only in absolute size and examine the relationship between trade and differences in factor supplies across countries. As discussed in Chapter 4, trade in goods alone may equalize factor prices across countries when all sectors are perfectly competitive. Helpman and Krugman (1985) show that factor price equalization remains a possibility when the economy is not fully competitive. We also determine that, if factor prices are equalized, relative factor supplies are a predictor of the factor content of trade.

A 2-factor, 3-sector model

We assume a 3-sector economy in which sectors 1 and 2 are perfectly competitive while sector 3 is oligopolistic. Production in all three sectors uses only capital and labor. Technology is constant returns to scale in the competitive industries and increasing returns to scale in the oligopolistic industry. The oligopolistic industry consists of n Cournot firms, each producing with exactly the same technology. If K and L denote the economy's fixed supplies of capital and labor, the factor market clearing conditions can be written:

$$\sum_{j=1}^{2} a_{Lj}(w,r)Q_j + a_{L3}(w,r,q_3)nq_3 = L \qquad (9.15a)$$

$$\sum_{j=1}^{2} a_{Kj}(w,r)Q_j + a_{K3}(w,r,q_3)nq_3 = K \qquad (9.15b)$$

where a_{L3} and a_{K3} are the equilibrium unit factor input requirements in industry 3, Q_j is industry output in the competitive sector j and q_3 is output per firm in the oligopolistic sector. Note that unit factor input requirements in the oligopolistic industry are functions of output as well as of factor prices since the technology is not homogeneous of degree one.

Assuming identical and homothetic preferences, consumers' expenditure shares on individual commodities depend only on relative prices. Hence, aggregate consumption is given by $Q_j = \zeta_j(p_2/p_1, p_3/p_1)Y$ where Y is the country's income.

The goods market clearing conditions therefore take the form:

$$\zeta_j\left(\frac{p_2}{p_1}, \frac{p_3}{p_1}\right) = \frac{p_j Q_j}{\sum_{j=1}^{3} p_j Q_j} \quad \text{for } j = 1, 2, \text{ and } 3 \tag{9.16}$$

All firms in the 2 competitive industries earn zero profits so that

$$p_j = c_j(w, r) \quad (j = 1, 2) \tag{9.17}$$

where

$$c_j = \frac{\partial C_j(w, r, q_j)}{\partial q_j} = \frac{C_j(w, r, q_j)}{q_j}$$

The first-order conditions for an oligopolistic firm were derived in Section 9.1. Here, we write these conditions for the more general case where marginal cost in the oligopolistic industry is not independent of firm output:

$$p_3\left[1 + \frac{1}{n\xi(p_1, p_2, p_3)}\right] = \frac{\partial C_3(w, r, q_3)}{\partial q_3} \tag{9.18}$$

Finally, we note that the unit factor input requirements in (9.15) relate to the cost functions in (9.17) and (9.18) in the following way:

$$a_{Lj} = \frac{\partial c_j(w, r)}{\partial w} \qquad a_{Kj} = \frac{\partial c_j(w, r)}{\partial r} \qquad (j = 1, 2) \tag{9.19a}$$

$$a_{L3} = \frac{1}{q_3}\frac{\partial C_3(w, r, q_3)}{\partial w} \qquad a_{K3} = \frac{1}{q_3}\frac{\partial C_3(w, r, q_3)}{\partial r} \tag{9.19b}$$

Conditions (9.15)–(9.19) describe the autarky equilibrium in the home country. They determine Q_1, Q_2, q_3, r, w, as well as the relative prices p_2/p_1 and p_3/p_1. Note that we did not specify a zero profit condition for industry 3 since we assumed that the number of firms in the industry is a given. The equilibrium values determined by (9.15)–(9.19) also establish the profits of the oligopolistic industry denoted Π and national income $Y = wL + rK + \Pi$.

Factor price equalization and the integrated economy

We now assume a foreign country that differs from the home country in terms of its supplies of capital and labor as well as in terms of the number of industry 3 firms. In addition, we assume that free trade between these countries equalizes the prices of goods and factors. Since cost functions are assumed identical across countries, factor price equalization implies that marginal costs in industry 3 are the same in 2 countries when outputs per firm are the same. Furthermore, since preferences are identical and homothetic, demands have the same elasticity when prices are the same. Thus, condition (9.18) and the corresponding condition in the foreign country are simultaneously satisfied when $q_3 = q_3^*$. This implies that each country's share of world production of good 3 equals the share of industry 3 firms located within its boundaries.

As in Chapter 7, we can construct the set of country factor endowments that is consistent with factor price equalization. Consider Figure 9.11 in which O and O^* are the origins of the home and foreign country, and labor and capital endowments are measured on the horizontal and vertical axes, respectively. By assumption, industry 1 is the most capital-intensive, industry 2 the most labor-intensive, and industry 3 intermediate. Factor utilization for the integrated economy is shown by the vectors OQ_1^w and OQ_2^w for industries 1 and 2 and by $Q_1^w Q_3^w$ for the non-competitive sector.

If all technologies were constant returns to scale and if each industry were mobile internationally, the hexagon $OQ_1^w Q_3^w O^* GQ_2^w$ would be the factor price equalization set. However, by assumption, firms in the oligopolistic sector do not move from one country to another. Since they also use increasing returns to scale technologies, the equilibrium of the integrated

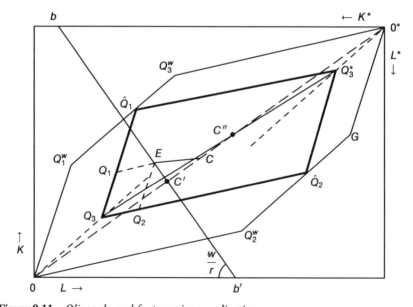

Figure 9.11   *Oligopoly and factor price equalization*

economy cannot be reproduced unless each country's share of world output of good 3 equals its proportion of industry 3 firms. This means that the factor price equalization set must be smaller than $OQ_1^w Q_3^w O^* GQ_2^w$

The factor price equalization set is constructed as follows. First, use as new origins the points Q_3 and Q_3^* with OQ_3 and $O^* Q_3^*$ parallel to $Q_1^w Q_3^w$ and

$$OQ_3 = \frac{n}{n + n^*} \, Q_1^w Q_3^w \quad O^* Q_3^* = \frac{n^*}{n + n^*} \, Q_1^w Q_3^w$$

where n and n^* are the numbers of home and foreign industry 3 firms. Through these new origins draw lines parallel to OQ_1^w and OQ_2^w. The resulting parallelogram $Q_3 \hat{Q}_1 Q_3^* \hat{Q}_2$ is the factor price equalization set. By construction, the position of the set within the box depends on the cross-country allocation of industry 3 firms. Keeping the total number of oligopolistic firms constant while increasing the proportion of firms located in the home country slides the parallelogram $Q_3 \hat{Q}_1 Q_3^* \hat{Q}_2$ upward.[35]

For any factor endowment point within the parallelogram, the allocation of production across countries is determined exactly as for the competitive economy studied in Chapter 7. Specifically, with endowment E, and proper normalization of units, the home country produces $Q_3 Q_1$ units of product 1 and $Q_3 Q_2$ units of product 2. If the endowment point E is located above the diagonal OO^* then the home country is capital-abundant. Since preferences are assumed homothetic, the consumption point must lie on the diagonal OO^*.

In contrast to the fully competitive case, the amount of each factor absorbed in consumption is not necessarily given by the coordinates of C', which is the point at which the factor income line bb' intersects the diagonal OO^*. The reason is that Cournot oligopolists make pure profits, and these must count as part of the domestic income of the country in which the firms are located. A country's share of world income may therefore be higher or lower than its share of factor income. Since each country's share of world profits under factor price equalization is the same as its share of industry 3 firms, profit shares are found at the intersection of the diagonal OO^* with the line that connects the points Q_3 and Q_3^*. These shares are OC''/OO^* for the home country and $O^* C''/OO^*$ for the foreign country.[36] Since domestic income contains factor income as well as profits, the ratio of national incomes must correspond to something like $OC/O^* C$, with C lying between C' and C''. The larger profits relative to factor income, the closer C is to C''.

Trade in factor services is shown by the vector EC. However, the presence of profits means that the value of factor services exported need not equal the value of factor services imported. Indeed, if the share of profits in domestic income is substantial, a country with a large fraction of oligopolistic firms may be a net importer of the services of every factor. When the home country is capital-abundant, it is either a net exporter of capital services and a net importer of labor services or a net importer of the services of both factors. In the latter case its net imports of labor services exceed its net imports of capital services. Note that these outcomes are identical to the Heckscher–Ohlin–Vanek (H–O–V) relationship between the trade in factor services and the notions of absolute and relative factor abundance derived in Chapter 8. In particular, the role of profits relative to factor incomes in determining the consumption share, and hence the measured trade in factor services, plays a role identical to that of a trade imbalance in the H–O–V model.[37]

9.3 Empirical analysis of trade and market power

The finding that trade improves welfare by bringing price closer to marginal cost lends itself to empirical verification. Analysis of determinants of the margin between price and marginal cost has long been a staple of the industrial organization literature.[38] While this literature has been mainly concerned with the effects of domestic concentration and entry barriers on the ability of firms to set price above cost, it has not overlooked the effects of foreign trade.

Typically, this literature has estimated equations inspired by the conditions which describe the maximizing behavior of a quantity setting oligopoly, but not necessarily a Cournot oligopoly. First-order conditions which admit, but do not presume, Cournot behavior can be written

$$p(Q) + q_i \frac{dp(Q)}{dQ} \psi_j - \frac{dC_j(q_j)}{dq_j} = 0 \quad \text{for } i = 1, 2, \ldots, n \tag{9.20}$$

The term $\psi_j \equiv \partial Q / \partial q_j$ is called firm j's conjectural variation or conjectural variation parameter. Since $\psi_j = n$ for all j yields the monopoly outcome, $\psi_j = 1$ for all j implies Cournot rivalry and $\psi_j = 0$ yields the competitive equilibrium, lower conjectural variations are regarded as indicative of a more competitive environment. An old interpretation of the conjectural variations is that they represent firms' beliefs about the effect their quantity changes have on rivals' production decisions, and hence on total industry output. This interpretation has been criticized as nonsensical in a static model, since the very idea of having an effect on someone else is inherently dynamic. Nonetheless, the conjectural variations approach remains in use in empirical work where estimates of ψ_j derived from a static model are regarded as a measure of the intensity of rivalry in an underlying – but unspecified – dynamic game.

Condition (9.20) can be rewritten :

$$\frac{p - c_j}{p} = -\frac{\zeta_j \psi_j}{\xi} \tag{9.21}$$

where $\zeta_j = q_j/Q$ denotes the market share of firm j, c_j denotes its marginal cost and ξ is the elasticity of demand faced by the industry. Multiplying both sides by q_j/Q and summing over all firms gives

$$\frac{pQ - \sum_{j=1}^{n} c_j q_j}{pQ} = -\frac{1}{\xi} \sum_{j=1}^{n} \zeta_j^2 \psi_j \tag{9.22}$$

When Cournot behavior is assumed, as many studies have done, the right-hand side of (9.22) reduces to

$$-\left[\sum_{j=1}^{n} \zeta_j^2 \right] \Big/ \xi$$

The numerator of this ratio is called the Herfindahl index of concentration. It can be shown that, for a given number of firms, the Herfindahl index increases in the variance of the size distribution of market shares.

The cross-industry method

This method assesses the link between market structure and the price mark-up over marginal cost, using cross-industry data. The mark-up in question is often measured by the price–cost margin (PCM) obtained by dividing the difference between total revenue and total variable cost by total revenue (i.e. $PCM = (pQ - C(Q))/pQ$). PCM equals the left-hand side of (9.22) only if marginal cost equals average cost. According to (9.22), the explanatory variables should be concentration and the elasticity of demand faced by the industry. However, since the elasticity is rarely if ever known on an industry-by-industry basis, most studies use proxies, in particular, variables that capture barriers to entry, e.g. scale economies, capital intensity and product differentiation.[39] Also, since variables such as concentration and imports can be presumed not to be exogenous, simultaneous equations methods are frequently applied.

A representative study is Jacquemin *et al.* (1980). It focuses on domestic concentration and openness to trade as determinants of the PCM in a cross-section of Belgian manufacturing industries and finds

$$PCM = 0.245 - 0.005^{**}(H^* t_m) - 0.002^* t_m + 0.039 t_x$$

$$- 0.349^* DIV + 0.180^* GVA$$

$$R^2 = 0.48 \qquad F = 4.78^*$$

where * and ** denote significance at the 1% and 5% levels (1-tail test). The variable definitions are PCM = (value added − payroll)/total sales; H = Herfindahl index of domestic concentration where the market shares are calculated after subtracting export sales; t_m = the ratio of imports to domestic shipments; t_x = the ratio of exports to total sales; DIV = the percentage of firms which engage in a second activity in another industry; GVA = the growth of industry value added.

Since imports can reduce domestic PCMs only if these margins would exist in the absence of imports, the import-to-sales ratio is entered interactively with the concentration variable. The GVA variable is common in structure–performance studies and it accounts for the fact that fast growing industries are more profitable. Jacquemin *et al.* associate a high value of DIV with a lower likelihood of collusion and hence a lower price-cost margin.

The negative and significant estimated coefficients for t_m and the multiplicative term Ht_m are consistent with the expectation that trade reduces PCMs and that this effect is stronger the higher the degree of concentration.[40] The negative coefficient for the import-penetration ratio agrees with the findings of many studies regarding this variable and its relationship to the PCM. In contrast to imports, exports do not appear to have a significant effect on the PCM.[41]

Numerous studies have used similar specifications to explore the effect of imports on market power and to distinguish the effect of actual imports from that of potential imports. For example, Jacquemin and Sapir (1991) find that PCMs for France, Germany, Italy and the United Kingdom are unrelated to intra-EC imports but are significantly and negatively related to imports from outside the EC. This accords with their expectation that horizontal and vertical agreements within the EC reduce competition. They also find that potential imports, captured by dummy variables that proxy for trade barriers, correlate positively with the price–cost margins.

Cross-sectional studies have been criticized on the ground that they fail to capture important factors idiosyncratic to industries, for example, variations in the elasticity of demand and differences in conduct as parametrized by the conjectural variation. Shifting the analysis from an inter-industry to a within-industry time series analysis does mitigate some of these problems since one can more legitimately assume that such unobservables are more stable over time within an industry rather than across industries.

The within-industry approach

The within-industry approach has received more emphasis in recent work which has also favored an approach in which the distance between price and marginal cost is estimated rather than calculated using ad hoc assumptions about the shape of the cost function.[42]

An example of this new approach is Levinsohn's (1993) study on the effect of Turkey's trade liberalization on the price–cost margins of Turkish firms. Levinsohn assumes that the production function of each firm in industry j at time t takes the form $q_{jt} = \phi_{jt} f(e_{jt})$ where e_{jt} is an H-dimensional vector of input quantities and ϕ_{jt} is a productivity shock. Taking a linear approximation to the production function around q_{jt} yields:[43]

$$\Delta q_{jt} = \phi_{jt} \left[\sum_{i=1}^{H} \frac{\Delta f_{jt}}{\Delta e_{ijt}} \Delta e_{ijt} \right] + f_{jt} \Delta \phi_{jt} \tag{9.23}$$

where Δ is the first-difference operator, that is, $\Delta x_t = x_t - x_{t-1}$. The productivity shock is assumed to follow a random walk such that $\Delta \phi_{jt} = \gamma_t + v_{jt}$ with $E(\gamma_t) = E(v_{it}) = 0$, while $E(\gamma_t \gamma_s) = \sigma_\gamma^2$ and $E(v_{it} v_{is}) = \sigma_v^2$ for $t = s$. Thus, all producers within an industry are assumed to be subject to a common productivity shock in any given year, as well as to a firm-specific shock. A useful feature of (9.23) is that it requires data only on changes in input use rather than on input stocks which are often difficult to obtain.

Since $\phi_{jt}(\Delta f_{jt}/\Delta e_{ijt}) = w_{ijt}/[dC(q_{jt})/dq_{jt}]$, where w_{ijt} is the price paid by firm j for factor i at time t, (9.21) can be used – properly indexed – to rewrite (9.23) as:[44]

$$\Delta q_{jt} = \beta_{jt} \left[\sum_{i=1}^{H} \frac{w_{ijt}}{p_t} \Delta e_{ijt} \right] + f_{jt}(\gamma_t + v_{jt}) \tag{9.24}$$

where

$$\beta_{jt} \equiv \frac{p_t}{c_{jt}} = \left[1 + \frac{\zeta_{jt} \psi_{jt}}{\xi_t} \right]^{-1}$$

Levinsohn estimates the following modified version of (9.24) using annual firm level data:

$$\Delta q_{jt} = \beta_1 \left[\sum_{i=1}^{H} \frac{w_{ijt}}{p_t} \Delta e_{ijt} \right] D_1$$

$$+ \beta_2 \left[\sum_{i=1}^{H} \frac{w_{ijt}}{p_t} \Delta e_{ijt} \right] D_2 + f_{jt}(\gamma_t + v_{jt}) \tag{9.25}$$

In (9.25), D_1 and D_2 are dummy variables that capture the timing of Turkey's trade liberalization which occurred in 1984. The data cover the 4-year period 1983–7, but since the estimated equation is on first differences, there are observations for three periods only. We have $D_1 = 1$ for $t = 1984$ and $D_1 = 0$ for $t > 1984$, and $D_2 = 0$ for $t = 1984$ and $D_2 = 1$ for $t > 1984$. Note that (9.25) assumes that all firms within an industry have the same ratio of price to marginal cost (i.e. β_1 and β_2 lack firm subscripts). This assumption is not theoretically justified. Levinsohn adopts (9.25) after experiments with alternative specifications produce nonsensical results.

Estimating (9.25) for each of 10 different industries, Levinsohn finds only 3 industries whose βs > 1 (95% level of confidence) during the pre-liberalization. This number falls to 1 in the post-liberalization period. Levinsohn then partitions the 10 industries into three groups: (1) imperfectly competitive industries for which trade was liberalized. Theory implies that liberalization should lower mark-ups in these industries,[45] (2) industries in which protection increased and (3) remaining industries.

All industries in the first group experienced a decline in the mark-up following liberalization; the decline was significant (90% level) for two of these industries. For the second group, the data supported the hypothesis that the price to marginal cost ratio should have increased or remained at 1. Theory does not yield any prediction about the effect of liberalization for the third group and this is evidenced in the results. In particular, the PCM for some industries in the third group declines while for others it remains constant or increases.

9.4 Differentiated goods and monopolistic competition

This section introduces product differentiation as a means of explaining both the observed high volume of trade between 'similar countries' and also the higher volumes of intra-industry exchanges evident in their trade.[46] When there is product differentiation, trade occurs because the residents will want to consume both foreign and domestically produced varieties of a product. A model of monopolistic competition among firms producing with increasing returns to scale engendered intra-industry trade, originated with Krugman (1979) who later extended the analysis to inter- as well as intra-industry trade. This and other models were developed further in Helpman and Krugman (1985). The material in this section is based on the work of Helpman and Krugman. Their model of differentiated product–monopolistic competition (DPMC) integrates the main approaches to product differentiation found in the industrial organization literature with the general equilibrium framework of traditional trade theory. It lets one disentangle the effects of factor supply differences and product differentiation on the volume and composition of trade.

The demand for variety

A key component of the DPMC model is the hypothesis that consumers have a demand for variety. Two approaches to defining the origin of this demand dominate the literature: 'love-of-variety' and 'most preferred variety'. The first approach postulates that the consumer has a taste for variety *per se*. This signifies that, if given a choice between two equally priced baskets containing the same quantity of a differentiated good, the consumer would prefer the basket with the largest number of varieties. This assumption is implemented by adopting a specific form of the utility function. The 'most preferred variety' approach posits that the consumer derives the highest utility by consuming a single variety (the 'most preferred') of a differentiated good and that this is true regardless of the quantity of the differentiated good being consumed. A demand for variety then arises at the market level because the most preferred variety differs across consumers. Each of these approaches is discussed below.

Love-of-variety

Following Spence (1976) and Dixit and Stiglitz (1977), love of variety is modelled by letting the total quantity consumed of each variety of a product enter symmetrically a subutility function of the form

$$V_i = \left[\sum_{j=1}^{n} v_{ij}^{(\varepsilon-1)/\varepsilon} \right]^{\varepsilon/(\varepsilon-1)} \tag{9.26}$$

where v_{ij} denotes consumption of variety j by consumer i and n is the number of varieties.[47] The subutility function (9.26) assumes a constant elasticity of substitution ε between any pair of varieties. If $\varepsilon > 1$, the varieties are imperfect substitutes and V_i increases as the number of varieties increases. The aggregate consumption of all varieties by consumer i is denoted

$$Q_{2i} = \sum_{j=1}^{n} v_{ij} {}^{48}$$

The subutility (9.26) is then embedded in a homothetic utility function $U = U(Q_{1i}, V_i)$ assumed identical across consumers, where Q_{1i} denotes consumption by consumer i of a single (or aggregate group of) homogeneous product(s) produced by industry 1. The function $U(Q_{1i}, V_i)$ is increasing and concave in each of its arguments.

With preferences as described, utility maximization involves a 2-step process. First, the consumer decides on the allocation of total income Y_i

between expenditure on the differentiated good, denoted Y_{Vi} and expenditure on the homogeneous good. Then, the amount Y_{Vi} is divided across individual varieties of the differentiated good.[49]

The allocation of Y_{Vi} across individual varieties is obtained by maximizing V_i subject to

$$\sum_{j=1}^{n} p_j v_{ij} = Y_{Vi}$$

and yields the following demands:

$$v_{ij} = \frac{p_j^{-\varepsilon}}{\sum_{j=1}^{n} p_j^{1-\varepsilon}} Y_{Vi} \tag{9.27}$$

It is apparent from (9.27) that the amount spent on variety j depends on the price of variety j relative to the price of all varieties. Raising both sides of (9.27) to the power $(\varepsilon - 1/\varepsilon)$ and summing over individual varieties gives:

$$Y_{Vi} = \left[\sum_{j=1}^{n} v_{ij}^{(\varepsilon-1)/\varepsilon} \right]^{\varepsilon/(\varepsilon-1)} \left[\sum_{j=1}^{n} p_j^{1-\varepsilon} \right]^{1/(1-\varepsilon)} \tag{9.28}$$

Since Y_{Vi} is total spending on the differentiated good by consumer i, the first term in (9.28) can be interpreted as a quantity index and the second term as a price index. Denoting the latter as P, the demands in (9.27) can be written:

$$v_{ij} = \left[\frac{p_j}{P} \right]^{-\varepsilon} Y_{Vi}$$

The value of Y_{Vi} is found by maximizing the upper-tier utility $U(Q_{1i}, V_i)$ subject to $Q_{1i} + PV_i = Y_i$. Note that in this maximization V_i and P play a role formally equivalent to the usual quantity and price of a product. Since $U(Q_{1i}, V_i)$ is homothetic, individual demands for 'product' V_i have the form $V_i = \zeta(P)Y_i$.[50] Finally, since preferences are also assumed identical across consumers, market demand has the same form as individual demands except that incomes are summed across all consumers.

In the case where all individual varieties are equally priced – which is the case that will be examined below – their common price will be denoted p. Then, the amount consumed of each variety will be the same, that is, $v_{ij} = v_i$ for all i. The latter implies $v_i = n^{\varepsilon/(1-\varepsilon)} V_i$ and $p = n^{1/(1-\varepsilon)} P$.

Hence, the quantity of each variety demanded by consumer i is $v_i = \varphi(p, n)Y_i$ and the total number of units of the differentiated product consumed by consumer i is $Q_{1i} = nv_i$. This implies a market demand for a single variety of the form:

$$v = \varphi(p, M)Y \tag{9.29}$$

where

$$Y = \sum_i Y_i$$

Finally, the total number of units of the differentiated product consumed in the economy is $Q_2 = \sum_{i \in I} Q_{2i} = nv$ and the share of income allocated to the differentiated good is

$$\zeta(p,n) \equiv \frac{pnv}{Y} = pn\varphi(p,n) \tag{9.30}$$

Most preferred variety[51]

The preferred variety specification originates with Lancaster (1979), who has adapted the Hotelling (1929) model of spatial competition to study product differentiation. In Lancaster's model, a particular location in space corresponds to a product specification. The distance between locations then conveys a measure of the disparity in the characteristics of product types. However, the precise nature of these characteristics is not specified. Since a higher degree of disparity means less substitutability between varieties, substitutability and distance are negatively related.

To illustrate this approach, assume that the configuration of varieties is represented as points on a circle of unit circumference as shown in Figure 9.12. Points R and S represent two separate varieties. Each consumer is assumed to have an ideal product type which also corresponds to a point on the circle, e.g. point B in Figure 9.12. The consumer is assumed to be indifferent between any quantity v of a variety located at B and the quantity $vh(\delta)$ of a variety positioned at a distance δ from B. The function h captures the compensation in terms of quantity which makes up for a less-preferred specification. It is assumed that $h'(\delta)$ and $h''(\delta)$ are positive for all $\delta > 0$ and that $h(0) = 1$.

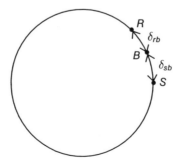

Figure 9.12 *The variety specification circle*

Consumer i's upper-tier preferences are assumed to be represented by a homothetic and concave utility function

$$U_i(Q_{1i}, V_i) = U_i\left(Q_{1i}, \sum_{j=1}^{n} \frac{v_{ij}}{h(\delta_{ij})}\right)$$

where Q_{1i}, V_i and v_{ij} have the same interpretations as above. The variable δ_{ij} denotes the shortest arc distance between the location of the ideal variety for consumer i and (the location of) variety j.

Again, the maximization process breaks down into two stages. In the second stage, consumer i maximizes the subutility $\sum_{j=1}^{n} v_{ij}/h(\delta_{ij})$ subject to $\sum_{j=1}^{n} p_j v_{ij} = Y_{Vi}$. This involves choosing the one variety with the lowest effective price $h(\delta_{ij})p_i$ – a choice that does not depend on the amount spent on the differentiated product. When b is the variety with the lowest effective price, the quantity purchased by consumer i is given by $v_{ib} = Y_{Vi}/p_b$ and the subutility is $V_i = v_{ib}/h(\delta_{ib})$. When all varieties are equally priced, the consumer chooses the variety closest to his ideal specification.

The first-stage maximization for consumer i, which involves the allocation of the consumer's income between the homogeneous and the differentiated goods, proceeds exactly as in the pure love of variety model. Since $U(\cdot)$ is homothetic, one has $V_i = \phi[p_b h(\delta_{ib})]Y_i$ and hence the demand for the variety b selected by consumer i is given by $v_{bi} = \phi[p_b h(\delta_{ib})]h(\delta_{ib})Y_i$.

The transition from individual demands to market demands is not as simple as in the love of variety model. The reason is that not all consumers have the same preferred variety. As a result, a change in the price of a variety affects the market demand for that variety in two distinct ways: some consumers who purchased the variety in question prior to the change in price continue to do so but in different quantities, others switch to or from that variety.

To make the determination of market demand more tractable and to eliminate differences in preferences as a source of trade, it is assumed that all consumers have the same income ($Y_i = Y$) as well as the same homothetic utility function ($U_i = U$). In addition, preferences for the ideal variety are assumed to be distributed uniformly on the circle.

When the varieties are equally spaced on the circle as well as equally priced, these assumptions ensure that the set of consumers purchasing a particular variety will consist of those individuals whose ideal specification lies on both sides of that variety's location within an arc-distance $1/2n$.[52] Thus, the width of the market area is $1/n$, declining in the number of varieties. The quantity demanded by each individual consumer belonging to the variety's market area depends on the price as well as on the distance between the location of his ideal specification and the location of the variety.

The market demand for a particular variety is derived by summing the individual demands for all consumers that belong to that variety's market area. When consumers are distributed uniformly on the circle, and varieties are equally spaced and priced, the quantities demanded of every variety are the same. The general form is the same as (9.29).[53] Hence, the conclusions to be drawn about the effects of trade on market quantities and prices are the same regardless of the underlying source of the demand for variety.

Production in the differentiated sector

We now develop the supply side of the economy. As stated above, we assume that a firm produces only a single variety. It chooses a variety as well as a price as though taking as given the specification and price choices of all other firms. We also assume that the cost of producing a given quantity of the differentiated product is the same regardless of the variety chosen. This assumption is needed to allow for an equilibrium where all varieties are equally priced and, in the case of the most preferred variety model, also equally spaced.

As the love of variety model accounts only for the number of varieties, product specification is limited to the decision whether to select a variety produced or not produced by another firm. Since every variety competes equally with all other varieties, a firm is always better off by selecting a variety that has not been chosen by others. By so doing it avoids having to share the demand for its variety with another firm. In the most preferred variety model, the choice of product specification is a 2-stage decision process: first, the selection of the two neighboring varieties – one on each side – then the determination of a location on the segment of the circle bounded by the two neigboring firms. When the firm shifts its location on that segment, it increases the quantity demanded by consumers with ideal specifications on one side of its market area and decreases the quantity demanded by consumers with ideal specifications on the other side. The specification is optimal when a slight shift in either direction leaves the quantity demanded unchanged.

With each firm producing one variety and no variety being produced by more than one firm, the output of firm j denoted q_j is equal to the total quantity of variety j, i.e. $q_j = \sum_{i \in I} v_{ij}$.[54] Let $\pi_j = [p_j q_j - C_2(w, r, q_j)]$ denote the profit function for the firm that produces variety j where the cost function $C_2(w, r, q_j)$ is assumed identical across all varieties.[55] Profit maximization by firm j with respect to *price*, yields the first-order condition:

$$p_i(1 + 1/\rho_j) = \partial C_2(w, r, q_j)/\partial q_j \tag{9.31}$$

where ρ_j is now the elasticity of demand perceived by the producer of variety j.

Assuming free entry and exit, firms earn zero profits and thus price equals average cost. Hence,

$$p_j = C_2(w, r, q_j)/q_j \tag{9.32}$$

Since demands and cost functions are assumed identical for all varieties, (9.31) and (9.32) imply that $q_j = q$, $p_j = p$ and $\rho_j = \rho$ for all j. Conditions (9.31), (9.32) and the demand jointly determine the price for each variety, the number of firms and the output per firm in the differentiated industry as functions of the two factor prices and the income spent on the differentiated good.

The number of varieties affects the elasticity of demand ρ faced by the individual producers. In the love of variety model, ρ converges to ε when the number of varieties increases. To see this, note that a change in the price of an individual variety affects the quantity demanded in three ways: a direct effect captured by the partial derivative of (9.27) with respect to p_i and two indirect effects: the first operates through P which is a function of p_j while the second operates through Y_{Vi} which is influenced by p_j through its effect on P. The larger is n, the smaller are these indirect effects. Hence, as the number of producers becomes sufficiently large the value of the elasticity of demand approaches the value it would take if only the direct effect were present.[56]

In the most preferred variety case the elasticity of aggregate demand for a variety, depends on prices as well as on the number of varieties. It converges to infinity as the number of firms becomes large.[57]

Autarky equilibrium

To determine the factor prices and the income allocated to each sector, the model is closed using additional conditions: first, a zero profit condition for the industry which supplies the undifferentiated good. Since the competitive sector uses a constant returns to scale technology, taking the competitively supplied good as the numeraire yields

$$c_1(w, r) = 1 \tag{9.33}$$

where $c_1(w, r)$ is the average and marginal cost for a competitive firm.

The next conditions state that the demand for factors equals the supply.

$$a_{L1}(w, r)Q_1 + a_{L2}(w, r, q)nq = L \tag{9.34a}$$

$$a_{K1}(w, r)Q_1 + a_{K2}(w, r, q)nq = K \tag{9.34b}$$

Where L and K are the economy's total supply of labor and capital, Q_1 is the total production of the homogeneous commodity and the as denote factor requirements per unit of output. They are given as $a_{L1} = \partial c_1(w,r)/\partial w$, $a_{K1} = \partial c_1(w,r)/\partial r$, $a_{L2} = \partial[C_2(w,r,q)/q]\,\partial w$ and $a_{K2} = \partial[C_2(w,r,q)/q]\,\partial r$.

Finally, by virtue of Walras' law, goods market clearing in the final output market can be limited to a single condition in the market for differentiated goods

$$\zeta(p,n) = pnq/(Q_1 + pnq) \tag{9.35}$$

Condition (9.35) states that the share of income spent on the differentiated products equals its share in production. Conditions (9.31) to (9.35) jointly determine the equilibrium values of product price (p), factor rewards (w, r), the number of firms and output per firm in the differentiated industry (n, q) and output of the homogeneous commodity (Q_1). The total number of units of the differentiated good is $Q_2 = nq$. Finally, since there are no pure profits, income is given by $Y = wL + rK$.

Trade with factor price equalization

To examine trade, we assume that the home and foreign countries share the same technology and consumer preferences, but that they differ in terms of their relative supplies of capital and labor. We let the equilibrium of the integrated world economy be described by conditions (9.31)–(9.35) with endowment values properly reinterpreted and we explore how the pattern of trade depends on the division of the world endowment of factors across countries.

The direction of trade

Consider Figure 9.13 where the coordinates of points Q_1^w and Q_2^w with origin O, denote the input requirements used by the integrated economy to produce the homogeneous and the differentiated products. Now, choose units such that OQ_1^w and OQ_2^w measure output quantities. Since the differentiated products sector is assumed capital-intensive, the slope of ray OQ_2^w exceeds that of ray OQ_1^w.[58]

With the endowment allocation at E, trade alone equalizes factor prices and both countries use the factor proportions of the integrated economy. Hence, the home country produces OQ_2 of the differentiated good and OQ_1 of the homogeneous commodity.

Since preferences are identical and homothetic, each country's consumption will embody the same ratio of capital to labor which equals the world

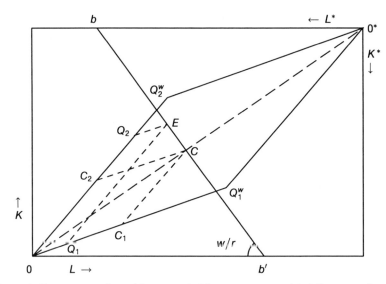

Figure 9.13   *Integrated equilibrium with 1 homogeneous and 1 differentiated product*

endowment ratio (i.e. the diagonal of the box). Factors embodied in home consumption are given by the coordinates of C (with origin O) with OC_2, the amounts embodied in the differentiated good and OC_1, the amounts embodied in the homogeneous good.

However, unlike the equilibria shown in Figures 7.1 of Chapter 7 and Figure 9.11 in this chapter, the equilibrium depicted in Figure 9.13 involves the home country exporting *and* importing products of the differentiated good sector. There is 2-way trade in the differentiated industry, driven by consumers' taste for variety. Each country consumes every variety produced in the world: the home country consumes the share OC/OO^* of each variety. The number of varieties produced in the world is given by OQ_2^w/q with q determined by the equilibrium conditions (9.31)–(9.35). Also, output per firm in the differentiated industry is the same in both countries since cost functions are the same and factor prices are equalized. The proportion of varieties produced in the home country is OQ_2/OQ_2^w. Note that, while the model determines the number of varieties produced in each country, it does not establish where any particular variety is produced.

The net exports of the differentiated home industry are given by C_2Q_2. Thus, relative factor endowments determine the direction of interindustry trade as in the traditional, homogeneous goods model. Specifically, the factor content of trade is given by the vector EC in Figure 9.13. In contrast to a H–O–S world, though, trade does not disappear when E lies on the diagonal OO^*. It is only the interindustry component of trade that vanishes and this means that each country produces the same quantity of both goods that it consumes. However, given that each country consumes all varieties of the differentiated good, there remains intra-industry trade. This trade does not show up in the form of a vector EC because there is no net factor trade.

The volume of trade

We now ask whether it is possible to go one step further and associate country characteristics and the volume of trade. Letting z and z^* respectively express the home and foreign country's share of world income, the value of total trade VT can be written:

$$VT = z^* p Q_2 + \{z p Q_2^* + [z(Q_1 + Q_1^*) - Q_1]\}$$

where the first term represents the home country's exports and the second its imports. Equilibrium requires balanced bilateral trade. Hence,

$$VT = 2z^* p Q_2$$

Totally differentiating this expression and noting that p is constant as long as we remain in the factor price equalization set gives

$$dVT/VT = dz^*/z^* + dQ_2/Q_2 \tag{9.36}$$

(9.36) can be used to explore how trade is affected by shifts of the endowment point E within the parallelogram $OQ_2^w O^* Q_1^w$.[59]

Consider first an equiproportionate change in all home country factor supplies along the ray passing through O and E', as shown in Figure 9.14. Since such displacement leaves the home country's capital–labor ratio unchanged, and since factor prices do not change, the home country's output of both goods changes equiproportionally. Thus, as one moves from O towards E', it must be true that $dz/z = dGDP/GDP = dQ_2/Q_2 > 0$. Since $z^* = 1 - z$, we obtain $-d(z^*/z^*)/(z/z^*) = dQ_2/Q_2$. Finally, combining the latter expression with (9.36) implies (9.37) shown below for equiproportionate changes in factor supplies within the factor price equalization set

$$dVT/VT = [1 - (z/z^*)]\, dQ_2/Q_2 \tag{9.37}$$

The sign of (9.37) depends on whether z/z^* is smaller or larger than 1 and the latter depends on whether the budget line passing through the endowment point cuts the diagonal below or above its mid-point M. Hence, as the home country's endowment point moves along the ray from O to E', total trade increases until both countries are of equal size. It declines with further increases in home country size.

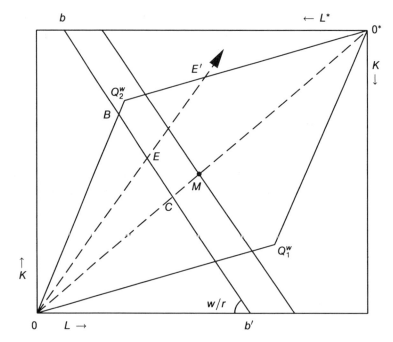

Figure 9.14   *Endowment changes and the volume of trade*

Consider now movements of the endowment point along the line bb' in Figure 9.14. As such movements leave income and thus country size unchanged, it follows from (9.36) that

$$dVT/VT = dQ_2/Q_2 \qquad (9.38)$$

Since an upward movement along the segment CB makes the home country more capital-abundant, it increases the home country's production of the differentiated good. As shown by (9.38) this movement also increases total trade.

We can conclude that any reallocation of factor endowments that increases the disparity in countries' capital–labor ratios, while keeping relative country sizes unchanged, increases total trade. This same result was encountered in the traditional H–O–S model.

Note that movements of E along the iso-revenue line bb' involve a change in endowments which maintains country sizes constant, whereas a change along OE' does not. Also, with world endowments fixed, equiproportional increases in factor supplies in the capital-abundant country must lower the capital–labor ratio in the other country.

By decomposing a movement of E into an equiproportional change and a displacement along an iso-revenue line one can show that the loci of all endowments which generate a given amount of total trade are curves such as those displayed in Figure 9.15. The further a curve from the diagonal the larger the volume of total trade associated with it.

The analysis of the link between relative country size and volume of trade can be extended to the case where industry 1 also produces differentiated goods. Total trade is then given by

$$VT = z(Q_1^* + pQ_2^*) + z^*(Q_1 + pQ_2)$$

where $Q_1^* + pQ_2^* = GDP^*$ and $Q_1 + pQ_2 = GDP$ denote, respectively, foreign and home gross domestic product. Letting $GDP^w \equiv (GNP + GNP^*)$ yields $GDP = zGDP^w$ and $GDP^* = z^*GDP^w$. In addition, trade balance requires $zGDP^* = z^*GDP$. Hence, we can write

$$VT = 2zz^*GDP^w = (1 - z^2 - z^{*2})GDP^w \tag{9.39}$$

Since GDP^W is constant for all divisions of the world endowment within the factor price equalization set, it must follow from (9.39) that movements of E within the FPE set influence VT only through their effect on country size (this is true when both goods are differentiated). The volume of trade attains a maximum when the two countries are of equal size.

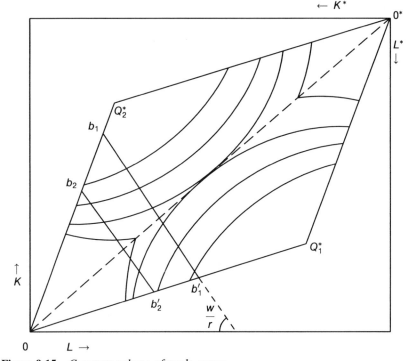

Figure 9.15 *Constant volume of trade curves*

Since both countries' income is constant along line segments such as bb' in Figure 9.15, these segments are also the loci of endowment allocations which yield constant VT when both goods are differentiated. As the disparity in country sizes is smaller under b_1b_1' than under b_2b_2' the volume of trade is also larger under b_1b_1'. Finally, note that, when both sectors produce differentiated goods, the direction of net exports continues to be determined by relative endowments.

The composition of trade

Intra-industry trade (IIT) represents the sum of 2-way flows which, if somehow eliminated, would leave the trade balance in equilibrium. In a 2-sector economy with one industry differentiated and one homogeneous, the share of intra-industry trade is:

$$IIT = \min[z^*pQ_2, zpQ_2^*]/(z^*pQ_2) \tag{9.40}$$

Recall that any movement of E along a line bb' (See Figure 9.14) which keeps the endowment point in the factor price equalization set leaves p, z and z^* unchanged but affects the quantity of good 2 produced in each country. Beginning on the diagonal and then moving E upward increases the denominator in (9.40) and decreases the numerator. This shows that the share of IIT falls if the capital-abundant country becomes more capital-rich.[60]

Multidimensional extensions

The preceding results concerning the determinants of the volume and composition of trade would appear to lend themselves to empirical testing. However, before considering empirical work, one must explore the form in which these results extend to a multicommodity, multicountry setting.

The direction of trade

As demonstrated in Chapter 7 and discussed further in Chapter 8, when there are more goods than factors, the pattern of trade in goods cannot be predicted but the factor content of trade is uniquely determined. This same result carries over to the case where goods are differentiated. Although a country which produces varieties of a differentiated good will export them to all other countries, the factor content of trade will be uniquely determined by factor abundance when factor prices are equalized.

The volume of trade

As seen above, when there are 2 industries, 1 producing a differentiated good and 1 a homogeneous commodity, the volume of trade depends in a complex way on both capital–labor ratios and relative country sizes. We now consider this linkage for the cases where (1) there are many differentiated and homogeneous goods and (2) all goods are differentiated.

Consider first the case where homogeneous and differentiated goods are produced. In this context, note first that (9.40) is a valid measure of the share of IIT because each variety of the differentiated good is produced in 1, and only 1, country. For (9.40) to remain a valid measure of IIT when there are many homogeneous goods, it must be assumed that each homogeneous good is produced in only 1 country. This assumption, together with the assumption that preferences are homothetic and that goods prices are equalized by trade, implies that the value of country i's exports of a good or a variety j of a differentiated product equals $p_j Q_j^i (1 - z^i)$ and that aggregate world exports are

$$VT^w = \sum_{i \in I} \sum_{j \in J} p_j Q_j^i (1 - z^i) = \sum_{i \in I} GDP^i (1 - z^i)$$

$$= \sum_{i \in I} GDP^w (1 - z^i) z^i = GDP^w \left[1 - \sum_{i \in I} (z^i)^2 \right] \qquad (9.41)$$

where

$$\sum_{i \in I} (z^i)^2 = N\sigma^2 + \frac{1}{N}$$

and σ^2 denotes the variance of the distribution of income shares while N is the number of countries. Thus, given the number of countries and world income, VT is decreasing in the dispersion of country sizes.[61]

Consider now the volume of trade among a subset of countries referred to as group A. Since country i imports the fraction GDP^i / GDP^w of every homogeneous product and variety of the differentiated good produced in the rest of the world, the value of country i's imports from country h is given by $GDP^i GDP^h / GDP^w$. Total trade *among* the members of the group A having gross domestic product GDP^A is therefore:

$$VT^A = \sum_{\substack{i \in A}} \sum_{\substack{h \in A \\ i \neq h}} GDP^i \, GDP^h / GDP^w$$

$$= \sum_{\substack{i \in A}} \sum_{\substack{h \in A \\ i \neq h}} \left(\frac{GDP^i}{GDP^A} \right) \left(\frac{GDP^h}{GDP^A} \right) \left(\frac{GDP^A}{GDP^w} \right) GDP^A$$

$$= z^A GDP^A \sum_{\substack{i \in A}} \sum_{\substack{h \in A \\ h \neq i}} (z^{iA} z^{hA}) = z^A GDP^A \left[1 - \sum_{i \in A} (z^{iA})^2 \right] \qquad (9.42)$$

where z^A is the group share in world output, and $z^{kA} = GDP^{kA}/GDP^A$ for $k = \{i, h\}$. (9.42) indicates that the volume of total intra-group trade is proportional to the group's share of world GDP. This relationship is used in empirical work discussed in the next section.

It must be stressed that the derivations of (9.41) and (9.42) do not require factor prices to be equalized as long as each variety of a differentiated good and each homogeneous good is produced in no more than 1 country. When this condition holds, the homotheticity of preferences and the equalization of goods prices through trade are sufficient to yield (9.41) and (9.42).

Monopolistic competition and scale economies enter the picture indirectly. The more common are these features the less likely that a particular good will be produced in more than 1 country, which is precisely the condition under which (9.41) and (9.42) apply.

The composition of trade

Let there be J commodities in the economy and denote X_j^{ih} the value of exports of good j by country i to country h. With homothetic preferences and final good prices equalized across countries, intra-industry trade between countries i and h is:

$$2 \sum_{j \in J} \min(X_j^{ih}, X_j^{hi}) = 2 \sum_{j \in J} p_j \min(z^i Q_j^h, z^h Q_j^i)$$

The share of intra-industry trade between countries i and h is therefore:

$$IIT_{ih} = \frac{2 \sum_{j \in J} p_j \min\lfloor z^i Q_j^h, z^h Q_j^i \rfloor}{\sum_{j \in J} p_j [z^i Q_j^h + z^h Q_j^i]} \tag{9.43}$$

The relation between intra-industry trade and relative factor endowments is not easily generalized to a multidimensional setting since the reasoning used in the $2 \times 2 \times 2$ case applied only to the case of factor price equalization. However, some insight can be derived from the Lerner diagram displayed in Figure 9.16. This diagram depicts the unit value isoquants for each of four goods. Each isoquant indicates the labor and capital requirements needed to produce one dollar's worth of output. Good 1 is the most capital-intensive while good 4 is the least capital-intensive. The capital–labor endowment ratio for country i is represented by the ray from the origin labelled $k_i = K_i/L_i$. Given its endowment ratio, full employment requires country 1 to specialize in goods 1 and 2 and hence the wage–rental ratio in country 1 is given by the slope of the common tangent to the unit isovalue curves [1] and [2]. In contrast, country 2's endowment calls for production of a

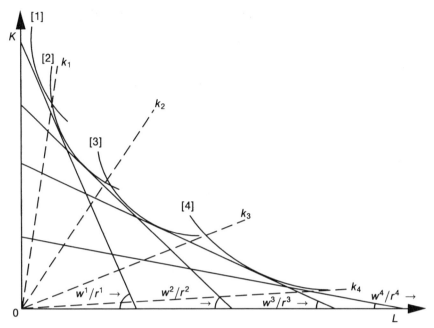

Figure 9.16 *A Lerner diagram*

combination of goods 2 and 3 and it has a wage–rental ratio given by the common tangent to the isovalue curves [2] and [3]. Country 3 produces goods 3 and 4 whereas country 4 specializes in good 4 alone and its wage–rental ratio is given by the slope of [4] at the point where it intersects the ray k_4.

A capital-rich country produces one or two of the more capital-intensive goods; a capital-poor country produces one or two of the more labor-intensive goods; an intermediate country produces a good ranked in the middle of factor intensities.

If industries can be ranked by factor intensity – which requires that the ranking not depend on the scale of output – a model of specialization and hence a pattern of trade emerges from the diagram. *If* the goods are differentiated, then this figure 'suggests' intra-industry trade between country pairs with similar relative factor supplies, e.g. between countries 1 and 2, 2 and 3 as well as 3 and 4, but no intra-industry trade between country 1 and either 3 or 4 or between countries 2 and 4.

Finally, note that Figure 9.16 assumes that factor prices are not equal across countries, which contrasts with our previous analysis of monopolistic competition in which factor price equalization was assumed.[62]

9.5 Trade with differentiated products: empirical analysis

Empirical examination of the determinants of the volume and the composition of international exchange has predated the development of the monopolistic competition model of trade. Gravity models – which go back to the 1950s – have related bilateral trade to countries' incomes, populations and distance from each other, and have had many successes in 'accounting for' a significant share of the variance of aggregate bilateral trade flows.[63] They have, in particular, displayed a consistent strong negative correlation between aggregate trade flows among country pairs and the distance between them. Early empirical work has typically not been solidy grounded in theory, but in later work the gravity equation has been given theoretical underpinnings.[64]

Econometric studies have also found correlations between the extent of intra-industry trade among country pairs and *per capita* income as well as measures of cross-country differences in *per capita* income. Data analysis was spurred by the work of Grubel and Lloyd (1971, 1975)[65] and the Burenstam Linder (1961) hypothesis was invoked to explain the positive correlation between the share of intra-industry trade and similarity in *per capita* incomes.[66] The hypothesis states that much trade arises from similarities in tastes among consumers across different countries. Manufactured goods are produced in countries where there is a strong demand for them, and are then exported from those countries to other countries with similar demand. Countries with similar tastes do therefore import and export similar goods. If similarity in tastes relates positively to similarity in *per capita* incomes, one should expect a positive correlation between the latter and the intensity of intra-industry trade.[67]

An empirical study that flows directly from the model developed in this chapter and which focuses on the determinants of the value of total trade and its division between inter- and intra-industry components is Helpman (1987).

Using a data set that covers a group of 14 OECD countries over the period 1956–81, Helpman investigates first whether intra-group trade as a proportion of group GDP is negatively related to the disparity in country sizes as implied by (9.42). A graph with VT^{OECD}/GDP^{OECD} plotted against an index of size similarity (i.e. $1 - \sum_{i \in oecd} (z^i)^2$ where z^i is country i's share of OECD GDP) suggests that these variables were indeed positively correlated.[68] Although this finding is consistent with the monopolistic competition model, one should remember that for VT^{OECD}/GPD^{OECD} to depend on the distribution of country sizes alone each product variety must be assumed to be produced in no more than one country. Helpman does not report the extent to which this requirement was evidenced in the data.[69]

Helpman then examined two hypotheses that relate to intra-industry trade. The first was that the share of intra-industry trade as a share of total trade within the group was larger during periods in which the dispersion of *per capita* income was smaller. The second was that intra-industry trade as a share of bilateral flows was larger for country-pairs more similar in *per capita* incomes.[70] He examined the first additional hypothesis by graphing annual values of the IIT indices for the group as a whole against the Herfindahl measure of the dispersion of *per capita* incomes within the OECD group. This graph indicated a negative relationship. No formal test of this correlation was conducted due to the small sample size. To examine the second hypothesis, Helpman regressed indices of bilateral intra-industry trade against variables indicative of country size and income similarity. A typical equation (for the year 1976) is given below:

$$IIT_{ih} = a - 0.04^*\log(GDP_i/POP_i - GDP_h/POP_h)$$

$$+ 0.035^*\min[\log(GDP_i), \log(GDP_h)]$$

$$- 0.021\max[\log(GDP_i), \log(GDP_h)] \qquad (R^2 = 0.141)$$

where i and h are country indices, *POP* denotes population, and an asterisk denotes significance of a coefficient at the 5% level. The difference in *per capita* GDPs proxies for differences in relative factor endowments while the third and fourth terms are intended to capture the effect of country size.

The negative partial correlation between the share of intra-industry trade and the dissimilarity in *per capita* incomes accords with the preceding model as does the finding that the size of the small country is positively related, and the size of the large country negatively related to intra-industry trade. However, the latter coefficient is not statistically significant. However, joint size of a country pair, as measured by the sum of the size coefficients, is positively related to the share of intra-industry trade between them. This finding is consistent with (9.42). Estimates for other sample years show the same pattern of coefficients, but in latter sample years the R^2 falls and the correlation between IIT and the difference in *per capita* incomes ceases to be significant.

Hummels and Levinsohn (1995) have made the point that the hypo-thesized positive correlation between the trade to income ratio and size similarity holds for country groups of any size. In their follow-up to the Helpman paper, they treat individual country pairs in the OECD group as individual observations (unlike Helpman who used the entire OECD as an observation) when fitting the trade to-income ratios to the Herfindahl measure of size similarity.[71] Their estimation of an equation derived from (9.45) accord with Helpman's finding.

Interestingly, Hummels and Levinsohn find that when the model is re-estimated for a set of mostly low income non-OECD countries it also 'predicts' much of the variation in the volume of trade. The fit is good and the coefficients are correctly signed. Since the monopolistic competition model does *a priori* appear inappropriate as an explanation of the pattern of trade of these countries, Hummels and Levinsohn conclude that something different lies at the basis of the observed correlations.[72]

Turning their attention to intra-industry trade, Hummels and Levinsohn first reproduce Helpman's results. They then pool 22 years of data into a single panel and use panel data estimation techniques to sweep away cross-sectional as well as time series variations in the IIT index. Idiosyncratic country factors may include distance, seasonal trade, language and cultural ties, and trade barriers. They find that the estimation results derived from the pooled sample are dramatically different. While the 'explanatory' power of the regressions increases substantially when country-pair effects are introduced, the coefficients of variables that proxy for endowment differences become either positive or insignificant. Country pair-specific effects explain most of the variance in intra-industry trade, and an analysis of residuals suggest that they are largely related to distance.

These findings considerably weaken the earlier conclusion that the model of monopolistic competition and international trade is supported empirically. Hummels and Levinsohn suggest that distance and possibly tax policy toward multinationals – variables not included in the models tested – could be important factors excluded from the empirical model.

9.6 Concluding remarks

In an imperfectly competitive setting, potential gains from trade may flow from the elimination or reduction of distortions that result from market power and from an increase in the size of firms that produce by means of increasing returns to scale technologies. Also, gains may flow from the mere possibility to trade even if actual trade does not take place. However, there is no guarantee that the gains will in fact be realized. The sufficiency conditions we have presented link the gains to an expansion of the sectors where monopoly power causes the greatest distortion and those which display the highest scale economies. Trade, however, does not necessarily lead to an expansion of these sectors. Transportation costs introduce an additional difficulty. When transportation costs are high, 2-way exports by Cournot firms may drive world welfare below its autarky level.

The direction of trade depends in a complex way on the size of countries relative to the structure of their imperfectly competitive industries as well as on traditional comparative advantage. Factor endowments remain a predictor of the direction of trade and factor flows under factor price equalization. However, since oligopolistic industries may generate pure profits which are part of national income, a country may be a net importer of the services of all factors.

The monopolistic competition model provides a rationale for intra-industry trade and gives insights into the determinants of trade volumes. The model also offers an explanation as to why the share of trade that is intra-industry would be positively related to factor endowment similarity across countries. The more alike are countries in terms of relative factor endowments the larger the share of their trade that is intra-industry. Similarity of size between countries is also positively related to the volume of trade among them.

Empirically, the effect of trade on market power can be assessed and, in this regard, the effects predicted by theory are supported by the data. There are as of yet few analyses of the relationships between the volume of total trade or intra-industry trade and country characteristics inspired by the monopolistic competition model. Existing analyses raise a number of puzzling questions. We need empirical specifications that nest alternative models in the same equation for 'rival' theories to be tested within the same framework.

Notes

1. Since the firms encountered in this chapter will be selling into each other's markets, the term 'domestic sales' could connote either sales in the home market or sales by home firms. To avoid confusion, the term 'home sales' is reserved for sales by firms based in the home country and the term 'foreign sales' stands for total sales by foreign-based firms.
2. The main sources of this section are Brander and Krugman (1983) and Helpman and Krugman (1985).
3. To illustrate, assume that individual consumers in each country have identical demands of the form $d = a - bp$ and $d^* = a - bp^*$. Let L and L^* denote, respectively, the number consumers in the home and foreign country. Aggregate demands under autarky are then $Q = (a - bp)L$ and $Q^* = (a - bp^*)L^*$. Using $L^* = \lambda L$ yields the following inverse demands: $p = (a - Q/L)/b$ and $p^* = (a - Q^*/L^*)/b = (a - Q^*/\lambda L)/b = p(Q^*/\lambda) = p^*(Q^*)$.
4. The term 'reaction function' is a misnomer since it suggests that firms react to each other. Since reacting requires that one observes what one is reacting to, a firm cannot in fact react to a move by another firm which occurs simultaneously as is the case in the Cournot model.

5. See Seade (1980). The condition also states that the perceived marginal revenue of one firm is declining in the output of another firm. For a more general cost function the stability condition is $p' + qp'' - C''(q) < 0$. For some specifications of demand and cost functions, the reaction curve slopes upward (see Bulow et al., 1985).

6. This is easily checked for the case where country demands are those given in n. 2. The inverse demand of the integrated market is then $p = [a - (Q + Q^*/ L + L^*)]/b = [a - (Q + Q^*)/L(1 + \lambda)]/b$.

7. Profits decline since total output, which was at least as large as monopoly output under autarky, increases through trade.

8. To see this intuitively, note that, when fixed costs are high, entry must occur at a large scale to allow the entrant to cover his fixed cost. This, however, means that entry results in an important drop in price. Hence, price can remain significantly in excess of average cost without engendering entry. The lower the scale of entry, the closer are the post-entry and pre-entry prices, and therefore the closer price must be to average cost if entry is not to take place. In the limiting case where $F = 0$, no further entry requires that price equal average cost.

9. Horstmann and Markusen (1986) generalize this result to a wider class of demands.

10. To save on notation, we use the same symbol as for a tariff. We do this because firms respond to a transportation cost in the same way as to a tariff. Hence, the analysis can proceed in the same way except for welfare assessments.

11. If output per firm were artificially maintained at the autarky level, export sales would occur at the expense of domestic sales until the marginal revenue on domestic sales were equal to marginal revenue on export sales *less* transportation cost. But, we already know that output per firm expands when trade is allowed and hence domestic sales do not necessarily contract as export sales expand.

12. In reality conditions, (9.8) apply only if the difference between c and c^* is not too large. It is left to the reader to determine how large the gap in marginal costs can become before (9.8) ceases to describe an equilibrium.

13. To see this, replace Q_x^* in (9.8b) by $n^* q_x^*$ and differentiate.

14. Hence, under the symmetry assumption $c = c^*$ and $n = n^*$, one can conclude that the domestic industry sells more in the home market than the foreign industry. The latter is certainly also true when $n > n^*$ but may not be verified $n < n^*$.

15. Roughly speaking, dumping occurs when a firm sells in a foreign market at a price below the price it charges in its home market. A more precise definition of dumping is given in Chapter 10.

16. Dumping can also arise with less than perfect symmetry and it need not be reciprocal. Weinstein (1989) has shown that a Cournot model can generate unilateral dumping by firms in a country endowed with many firms into a market with fewer firms.

17. It must be stressed that Figure 9.3 has been drawn under the assumption that the markets remain segmented, regardless of the value of τ. This need not be the case as one may switch from a segmented regime to a connected regime for $\tau > 0$.

18. This result is derived in Venables (1985). The model is presented in Chapter 10.

19. The Bertrand model will be revisited later in this chapter as well as in Chapter 10 and will be used to explore the workings of a market in which goods are differentiated. With product heterogeneity the Bertrand model provides a link between market performance and industry structure that more closely resembles that of a Cournot model.

20. This section is based on Markusen (1981).

21. $-dQ_1/dQ_2 = c_2/c_1$ for the home country and $-dQ_1^*/dQ_2^* = c_2^*/c_1^*$ for the foreign country.

22. Compare this with the partial equilibrium of Section 9.1 which relates country size and the number of firms to the direction of trade.

23. See Markusen (1981) for the formal derivation of the slopes of these reaction functions.

24. Let **e** denote any vector of factor inputs. A production function $q = F(\mathbf{e})$ is said to exhibit globally increasing returns to scale (GIRS) if, for any **e**, $F(\lambda \mathbf{e}) > \lambda F(\mathbf{e})$ for λ larger than one. Letting **w** denote the vector of input prices, an equivalent definition of GIRS in terms of the cost function is $C(\mathbf{w}, \lambda q)/\lambda q < C(\mathbf{w}, q)/q$ for all **w**. GIRS imply that the firm's average cost is everywhere below its marginal cost. GIRS is therefore incompatible with perfect competition. See Scherer and Ross (1990) for a discussion of the various sources of economies of scale.

25. The intuition for convexity is simple. Let Q_1 and Q_2 denote the maximal amounts of good 1 and good 2 an economy could produce if its entire endowment L of a single factor were allocated to one industry. Now consider the resources required to produce the output combination $(Q_1/2, Q_2/2)$. If industry 1 exhibits EOS, then more than half of the endowment is required to produce $Q_1/2$. The same applies to industry 2 if it also exhibits EOS. Hence, the production combination $(Q_1/2, Q_2/2)$ requires an amount of resources that exceeds the available endowment. This is true for any production point on the line connecting Q_1 and Q_2, i.e. $vQ_1 + (1 - v)Q_2 = 0$ where $0 < v < 1$ which implies that the PPF must pass below such a line. But this is just the definition of convexity. Things are more complicated when there are more factors since the shape of the PPF will in general be determined by the relative strength of two opposing effects: differences in factor intensities which tend to make the PPF concave and EOS which tends to make the PPF convex. The PPF may therefore be globally convex, or it may be characterized by alternating regions of convexity and concavity (see Herberg and Kemp, 1969; Melvin, 1969; Markusen and Melvin, 1984).

26. In this context, a persistently popular argument is that since large countries have large (internal) markets they will have an advantage over small countries in goods whose production exhibits EOS. As Deardoff (1984) notes, this argument ignores that the distinction between large and small markets is irrelevant once free trade is allowed since, with trade, the relevant market is the world market. This implies that country size alone is not sufficient to determine the direction of trade unless transport costs are introduced or post-trade production is assumed to somehow reflect autarky production.

27. The production frontier must be convex in the neighborhood of $Q_2 = 0$ (see Herberg and Kemp, 1969; Markusen and Melvin, 1984).

28. See Markusen and Melvin (1984). It applies to PPFs that are globally con-cave- as in Figure 9.9(a) as well as to PPFs with an inflection point as shown in Figure 9.9(b).

29. Markusen (1981) points out that this outcome becomes more likely the higher the degree of economies of scale.

30. If the PPF is concave everywhere, except in the small neighborhood where $Q_2 = 0$, then it can be expected to lie below the revenue line except at the tangency point.

31. Important articles include Kemp and Negishi (1970), Eaton and Panagariya (1979), Markusen and Melvin (1984), Helpman (1984) and Helpman and Krugman (1985).

32. That the free trade price of good 2 is higher than the marginal cost of production of good 2 in terms of good 1 may reflect the fact that good 2 is supplied under imperfectly competitive conditions.

33. If firms maximized value at free trade prices, positive production gains would be guaranteed if free trade prices were different from autarky prices.

34. Similarly, welfare is increased by a contraction of decreasing returns-to-scale industries that earn non-positive profits.

35. Note though that when output per firm industry 3 is large relative to total industry output – perhaps as a result of scale economies – a reallocation of firms from one country to the other will result in a discrete jump of the factor price equalization parallelogram.

36. Note that OC''/OO^* goes from zero to unity as $n/n + n^*$ goes from zero to unity.

37. Finally, we can now also explain why trade causes factor rewards to diverge in the $2 \times 2 \times 2$ world of Section 9.2. To construct the factor price equaliza-tion set as we just did, we would start by setting the new origins equidistant from O and O^* since each country has only one firm in its non-competitive industry. The factor price equilization would be limited to the line linking these new origins and this line must intersect the diagonal OO^* at its midpoint. Therefore any endowment point on the diagonal but not at its mid-point – which is the case for countries that differ in size only – lies outside the factor price equalization set.

38. A recent review of the literature can be found in Martin (1993).

39. The variables may also serve to control for the effect of variable cost components which because of a lack of data are not included in the calculation of the price–cost margin.

40. When H is entered separately in the equation, its coefficient is not significant.

41. See also Caves (1985) on the effect of exports on profitability. Significant posi-tive as well as negative signs for the export intensity variable appear in the literature.

42. A clear presentation of the new approach is found in Bresnahan (1989). The old and the new approaches are contrasted in Schmalensee (1989) and Martin (1993).

43. This approximation is acceptable if the technology is nearly constant returns to scale.

44. Note that the derivation of (9.24) assumes that factor prices, but not goods prices, can differ across firms.

45. These industries are identified as those with a significant positive mark-up during the pre-liberalization period, not on the basis of concentration ratios.

46. One explanation for 'pure' 2-way trade has already been encountered in this chapter. However, the assumptions necessary for this earlier result are simply too restrictive to regard it as a serious explanation of much intra-industry trade.

47. Since we will assume below that each firm produces a single variety, the number of varieties has already been set equal to n which is the number of active firms.

48. Note that (9.26) in no way accounts for the characteristics of the varieties being consumed.

49. This specification is equivalent to the Armington model which specifies products as differentiated by country of production (see Chapter 5).

50. See Chapter 4 (pp. 135–6).

51. This section is based on Helpman (1981), and Helpman and Krugman (1985).

52. One-half of the consumers (i.e. $1/2n$) have ideal specifications on one side of the location of the variety in question, the other half on the other side.

53. The formal derivation of this demand is given in Helpman (1981).

54. The issue whether a firm optimally produces one or more varieties is not discussed. A useful reference on this question is Judd (1985).

55. Note that industry factor proportions are no longer independent of output since returns to scale are variable.

56. See Yang and Heijdra (1993) and Wong (1995) for further discussion of the elasticity.

57. See Helpman (1981).

58. Since the technology is nonhomothetic, this statement means the differentiated sector is capital-intensive at all factor prices *and* all output levels.

59. Since prices do not change for movements of E within the factor price equalization set, it does not matter whether one refers to the volume or the value of trade.

60. Figure 8.7 in Chapter 8 of Helpman and Krugman (1985) depicts the combinations of endowments for which IIT is constant and suggests that IIT increases as the difference in factor composition falls. The figure also suggests a slight negative relationship between IIT and the relative size of the country that is the net exporter of the differentiated good.

61. Note that VT is proportional to 1 *minus* the Herfindahl concentration index of world production.

62. Since, under FPE, the pattern of production and net trade is indeterminate when the number of goods is larger than the number of factors, the pattern of intra-industry trade is indeterminate as well. Graphically, this indeterminacy arises when one unit cost line is tangent to more than two isoquants.

63. Early models are Tinbergen (1962) and Linnemann (1966).

64. Important contributions to this literature have been Anderson (1979), Bergstrand (1985, 1988, 1990) and Harrigan (1994, 1995).

65. An earlier study is Balassa (1966), who found that the formation of the EEC was followed by a rapid increase in intra-industry trade in Europe.

66. For example, Loertscher and Wolter (1980), and Balassa and Bauwens (1987).
67. Various other 'explanatory' variables – in particular, aggregate measures of trade restrictions – have been included in estimated equations, e.g. Caves (1981) and Balassa and Bauwens (1987).
68. Due to a small sample size no formal statistical test of the significance of this correlation was conducted.
69. Such specialization is more prevalent the greater the extent of product differentiation and increasing returns to scale technologies. The stronger the degree of scale economies the greater should be the amount of intra-industry trade since scale economies make it less attractive to produce in a country varieties already produced in other countries.
70. In order for differences in *per capita* income to be a good proxy for differences in K/L ratios, it is necessary that there be no more than 2 factors.
71. This provided 2002 observations as opposed to 26 observations in Helpman's study.
72. While intra-industry trade is 25.3% of total trade for the OECD group, it amounts to only 0.5% for the non-OECD group.

References and additional reading

General

Caves, R.E. (1985), 'International Trade and Industrial Organization: Problems, Solved and Unsolved', *European Economic Review*, 28, 377–95.
Dixit, A.K. and Norman, V. (1980), *Theory of International Trade* (Cambridge: Cambridge University Press).
Helpman, E. and Krugman, P.R. (1985), *Market Structure and Foreign Trade, Increasing Returns, Imperfect Competition, and the International Economy* (Cambridge, Mass. and London: MIT Press).
Scherer, F.M. and Ross, D. (1990), *Industrial Market Structure and Economic Performance* (Boston: Houghton Mifflin), 3rd edn.
Wong, K. (1995), *International Trade in Goods and Factor Mobility* (Cambridge, Mass. and London: MIT Press).

Oligopoly and scale economies

Brander, J.A. and Krugman, P.R. (1983), 'A "Reciprocal Dumping" Model in International Trade', *Journal of International Economics*, 15, 313–23.
Bulow, J., Geanakoplos, J. and Klemperer, P. (1985), 'Multimarket Oligopoly: Strategic Substitutes and Complements', *Journal of Political Economy*, 93, 488–511.

Eaton, J. and Panagariya, A. (1979), 'Gains from Trade under Variable Returns to Scale, Commodity Taxation, Tariffs and Factor Market Distortions', *Journal of International Economics*, 9, 481–501.

Grinols, E.L. (1991), 'Increasing Returns and the Gains from Trade', *International Economic Review*, 32(4), 973–84.

Helpman, E. (1984), 'Increasing Returns, Imperfect Markets and Trade Theory', in Jones, R. and Kenen, P. (eds), *Handbook of International Economics*, Vol. 1 (Amsterdam: North-Holland), 325–65.

Herberg, H. and Kemp, M.C. (1969), 'Some Implications of Variables Returns to Scale', *Canadian Journal of Economics*, 3, 403–15.

Horstmann, I.J. and Markusen, J.R. (1986), 'Up the Average Cost Curve: Inefficient Entry and the New Protectionism', *Journal of International Economics*, 20, 225–47.

Kemp, M.C. and Negishi, T. (1970), 'Variable Returns to Scale, Commodity Taxes, Factor Market Distortions and Their Implication for Trade Gains', *Swedish Journal of Economics*, 72(1), 1–11.

Kreps, D.A. and Scheinkman, J.A. (1983), 'Quantity Precommitment and Bertrand Competition Yield Cournot Outcomes', *Bell Journal of Economics*, 4, 326–37.

Markusen, J.R. (1981), 'Trade and Gains from Trade with Imperfect Competition', *Journal of International Economics*, 11, 531–51.

Markusen, J.R. and Melvin, J. (1984), 'Trade, Factor Prices, and the Gains from Trade with Increasing Returns to Scale', *Canadian Journal of Economics*, 14, 450–69.

Martin, S. (1993), *Advanced Industrial Economics* (Cambridge, Mass. and Oxford: Blackwell).

Melvin, J.R. (1969), 'Increasing Returns to Scale as a Determinant of Trade', *Canadian Journal of Economics* 3, 389–402.

Seade, J. (1980), 'On the Effects of Entry', *Econometrica*, 48, 479–89.

Tirole, J. (1988), *The Theory of Industrial Organization* (Cambridge, Mass.: MIT Press).

Venables, A.J. (1985), 'Trade and Trade Policy with Imperfect Competition: The Case of Identical Products and Free Entry', *Journal of International Economics*, 19, 1–19.

Weinstein, D. (1989), 'Competition, Unilateral Dumping and Firm Profitability', *Seminar Discussion Paper*, 249, Research Seminar in International Economics, University of Michigan.

Trade and product differentiation

Anderson, S.P., de Palma, A. and Thisse, J.F. (1990), 'Demand for Differentiated Products, Discrete Choice Models, and the Characteristics Approach', *Review of Economic Studies*, 56, 21–35.

Dixit, A. and Stiglitz, J.E. (1977), 'Monopolistic Competition and Optimum Product Diversity', *American Economic Review*, 67, 297–303.

Helpman, E. (1981), 'International Trade in the Presence of Product Differentiation, Economies of Scale, and Monopolistic Competition: A Chamberlin–Heckscher–Ohlin Approach', *Journal of International Economics*, 11, 305–40.

Hotelling, H. (1929), 'Stability in Competition', *Economic Journal*, 39, 41–57; reprinted in Stigler, G.J. and Boulding, K.E. (eds), *AEA Readings in Price Theory* (Chicago: Richard D. Irwin, 1952), 467–84.

Judd, K.L. (1985), 'Credible Spatial Preemption', *Rand Journal of Economics*, 16(2), 153–66.

Krugman, P.R. (1979), 'Increasing Returns, Monopolistic Competition, and International Trade', *Journal of International Economics*, 9, 469–79.

Krugman, P.R. (1981), 'Intra-Industry Specialization and the Gains from Trade', *Journal of Political Economy*, 89, 959–73.

Lancaster, K. (1979), *Variety, Equity and Efficiency* (New York: Columbia University Press).

Spence, A.M. (1976), 'Product Differentiation and Welfare', *American Economic Review*, 66(2), 407–14.

Yang, X. and Heijdra, B.J. (1993), 'Monopolistic Competition and Optimum Product Diversity: Comment', *American Economic Review*, 83, 295–301.

Empirical and related studies

Anderson, J.E. (1979), 'A Theoretical Foundation for the Gravity Equation', *American Economic Review*, 69(1), 106–16.

Balassa, B. (1966), 'Tariff Reductions and Trade in Manufactures among the Industrial Countries', *American Economic Review*, 56, 466–73.

Balassa, B. and Bauwens, L. (1987), 'Intra-Industry Specialization in a Multi-Industry Framework', *Economic Journal*, 97, 923–39.

Bergstrand, J.H. (1985), 'The Gravity Equation in International Trade: Some Microeconomic Foundations and Empirical Evidence', *Review of Economics and Statistics*, 67, 474–81.

Bergstrand, J.H. (1989), 'The Generalized Gravity Equation, Monopolistic Competition, and the Factor-Proportions Theory in International Trade', *Review of Economics and Statistics*, 71(1), 143–53.

Bergstrand, J.H., (1990), 'The Heckscher–Ohlin–Samuelson Model, the Linder Hypothesis, and the Determinants of Bilateral Intra-Industry Trade', *Economic Journal*, 100, 1216–29.

Bresnahan, T.F. (1989), 'Empirical Studies of Industries with Market Power', Chapter 8 in Schmalensee, R. and Willig, R.D. (eds), *Handbook of Industrial Organization*, Vol. II (Amsterdam: North-Holland).

Burenstam Linder, S. (1961), *An Essay on Trade and Transformation* (New York: Wiley).

Caves, R.E. (1981), 'Intra-Industry Trade and Market Structure in the Industrial Countries', *Oxford Economic Papers*, 33, 203–23.

Deardorff, A.V. (1984), 'Testing Trade Theories and Predicting Trade Flows', in Jones, R.W. and Kenen, P.B. (eds), *Handbook of International Economics* (New York: Elsevier), 467–517.

Greenaway, D., Hine, R. and Milner, C. (1995), 'Vertical and Horizontal Intra-Industry Trade: A Cross Industry Analysis for the United Kingdom', *Economic Journal*, 105, 1505–18.

Grubel, H.G. and Lloyd, P.J. (1971), 'The Empirical Measurement of Intra-Industry Trade', *The Economic Record* 47, 494–517.

Grubel, H.G. and Lloyd, P.J. (1975), *Intra-Industry Trade, the Theory and Measurement of International Trade in Differentiated Products* (London: Macmillan).

Harrigan, J. (1994), 'Scale Economies and the Volume of Trade', *The Review of Economics and Statistics*, 76(2), 321–8.

Harrigan, J. (1995), 'Factor Endowments and the International Location of Production', *Journal of International Economics*, 39, 123–41.

Helpman, E. (1987), 'Imperfect Competition and International Trade: Evidence from Fourteen Industrial Countries', *Journal of the Japanese and International Economies*, 1, 62–81.

Hummels, D.L. and Levinsohn, J. (1995), 'Monopolistic Competition and International Trade: Reconsidering the Evidence', *Quarterly Journal of Economics*, 799–835.

Jacquemin, A., De Ghellinck, E. and Huveneers, C. (1980), 'Concentration and Profitability in a Small Open Economy', *Journal of Industrial Economics*, 29(2), 131–44.

Jacquemin, A. and Sapir, A. (1991), 'The Discipline of Imports in the European Market', in de Melo, J. and Sapir, A. (eds), *Trade Theory and Economic Reform: North, South, and East, Essays in Honor of Bela Balassa* (Cambridge, Mass. and Oxford: Blackwell).

Leamer, E.E. and Levinsohn, J. (1995), 'International Trade Theory: the Evidence', in Grossman, G. and Rogoff, K. (eds), *Handbook of International Economics*, Vol. III (New York: Elsevier) 1339–94.

Levinsohn, J. (1993), 'Testing the Imports as Market Disciple Hypothesis', *Journal of International Economics*, 35, 1–22.

Linnemann, H. (1966), *An Econometric Study of International Trade Flows* (Amsterdam: North-Holland).

Loertscher, R. and Wolter, F. (1980), 'Determinants of Intra-Industry Trade: Among Countries and Across Countries', *Weltwirtschafliches Archiv*, 116, 280–93.

de Melo, J. and Urata, S. (1986), 'The Influence of Increased Foreign Competition on Industrial Concentration and Profitability', *International Journal of Industrial Organization*, 4, 287–304.

Neumann, M., Bobel, I. and Haid, A. (1985), 'Domestic Concentration, Foreign Trade and Economic Performance', *International Journal of Industrial Organization*, 3, 1–19.

Pugel, T.A. (1980), 'Foreign Trade and US Market Performance', *Journal of Industrial Economics*, 29(2), 119–29.

Schmalensee, R. (1989), 'Inter-Industry Studies of Structure and Performance', Chapter 2 in Schmalensee, R. and Willig, D. (eds), *Handbook of Industrial Organization* (Amsterdam: North-Holland).

Stalhammar, N.O. (1991), 'Domestic Market Power and Foreign Trade: The Case of Sweden', *International Journal of Industrial Organization*, 9(3), 407–29.

Tinbergen, J. (1962), *Shaping the World Economy: Suggestions for an International Economic Policy* (New York: Twentieth Century Fund).

■ Chapter 10 ■

Trade Policy in Imperfectly Competitive Markets

10.1 Rivalry in a single market	*10.5* Contingent protection
10.2 Rivalry across markets	*10.6* Quantification: computable
10.3 Extensions	partial equilibrium modelling
10.4 Quantitative restrictions	*10.7* Implications for trade policy

This chapter examines the effects of trade policies in a world where international trade is dominated by oligopolistic rivals. In such a world the response of firms to trade policy, and the effect of such policy on domestic welfare, can differ markedly from that under perfect competition.

Systematic analysis of trade policy in non-competitive environments first appeared in the late 1970s. Early work focused on monopoly. It examined how a movement to free trade limited monopoly power and how tariffs could be used to extract rents accruing to a foreign monopolist.[1] In the early 1980s work appeared on trade policy under oligopoly. A key result was the demonstration that, contrary to the competitive model, an export subsidy could raise the welfare of the subsidy imposing country by shifting the terms of rivalry in favor of its producers. This early work on the effects of trade policies in the presence of oligopolistic rivalry inspired a now large body of literature on what has come to be labelled 'strategic trade policy'.[2]

The focus of this chapter is very much on oligopoly and, since its primary objective is to underscore the trade policy issues that originate specifically from market power, asymmetries between countries and among firms within countries are largely disregarded. The entire analysis is conducted in a partial equilibrium framework. As in Chapter 9, the focus is on static models and simple forms of oligopolistic interaction, namely, Cournot and Bertrand competition. In addition, the analysis considers only pure trade instruments, that is, whether a particular trade policy improves or worsens welfare compared to the free trade equilibrium. Interactions between trade instruments and other policies such as antitrust or employment incentives are not examined.

The chapter builds from the simple to the more complicated. It starts with an exploration of import tariffs and export subsidies. Basic results are

393

derived first for special cases where the determination of optimal trade policies does not involve a trade off between consumer and producer interests. The early findings serve as building blocks in the ensuing work, where the analysis turns to empirically more relevant settings.

Section 10.4 investigates quotas and VERs and contrasts their effects with those of tariffs. It also examines the consequences of quantitative restrictions (QRs) on the quality of imports. Contingent protection in the form of antidumping and countervailing duties is considered in Section 10.5. Section 10.6 illustrates the computable partial equilibrium techniques commonly used to quantify the effects of trade policy under oligopoly. The chapter concludes with an examination of the implications of imperfect competition for trade policy.

10.1 Rivalry in a single market[3]

This section assumes that when home and foreign oligopolists compete they do so in one market only. This simplification makes it possible to examine basic effects of trade policy in the absence of interactions between markets. First, tariff policy is investigated in a setting in which a foreign oligopoly supplies the home market. Next, the policies that bear upon exports by a home oligopoly are explored, starting with the case where the home oligopoly faces no foreign oligopoly, and then turning to the case where it does. The section concludes with a comparison of the effects of trade policy undertaken by a single country, the other country remaining a free trader, with the consequences of policy when all countries adopt an activist stance.

A tariff against a foreign oligopoly

In this section we consider a framework in which n^* foreign oligopolists export to the home market and do so without encountering any competition from home country firms.[4] Each foreign firm has a cost function of the form $C^*(q^*) = F^* + c^* q^*$ and the number of exporters is fixed. The home and foreign markets are assumed to be segmented. This assumption, and the constancy of marginal cost, imply that the foreign oligopolists set their quantities in the home country market as if it were the only market in which they operated. Hence, the influence of sales by the foreign oligopolists to other markets can be ignored. Finally, with identical cost functions across firms, all foreign firms will export the same quantity to the home market. This, and the preceding assumptions, imply that we can equate sales in the home market (i.e. exports) to total output of each firm, that is $q_x^* = q^*$ and hence $Q_x^* = Q^*$, where uppercase Q denotes total sales, and lowercase q denotes sales per firm.

The home country is assumed to have set an *ad valorem* tariff τ on its imports. Foreign firms therefore receive the net of duty price $p/(1 + \tau)$ and earn profits $\pi^* = \{p(Q^*)/(1 + \tau) - c^*\}q^* - F^*$. Assuming Cournot rivalry, profit maximization then implies the following first-order condition for each firm:

$$\left\{ p(Q^*) + q^* \frac{dp(Q^*)}{dQ^*} \right\} - (1 + \tau)c^*$$

$$= \left\{ p(Q^*) + \frac{Q^*}{n} \frac{dp(Q^*)}{dQ^*} \right\} - (1 + \tau)c^* = 0 \tag{10.1}$$

The term in accolades is the firm's perceived marginal revenue [mr] which can be written as a weighted average of average revenue [i.e. $p(Q^*)$] and industry marginal revenue [$MR(Q^*)$]:

$$mr(Q^*, n^*) = \frac{1}{n^*} MR(Q^*) + \left[1 - \frac{1}{n^*} \right] p(Q^*) \tag{10.2}$$

Since perceived marginal revenue approaches average revenue as n^* increases, the equilibrium solution derived from (10.1) monotonically approaches the competitive outcome as the number of exporters increases.

Problem 10.1: As written, the profit function posits that profits from exporting are realized in the foreign country. An alternative would be to assume that c^* is the value to which the duty is applied, in which case the profit function would read $\pi^* = [p - c^*(1 + \tau)]q^*$. Examine the consequences of having marginal cost as the value for holding the rate τ fixed.

Price and quantity effects

We now determine the effects of tariff changes on the volume of exports and on the price received by foreign firms. The first is found by differentiating (10.1) with respect to the tariff. Holding the number of foreign firms fixed (i.e. $dn^* = 0$) differentiation yields:

$$\frac{dQ^*}{d\tau} = c^* \left[\left(1 + \frac{1}{n^*} \right) p'(Q^*) + \frac{1}{n^*} Q^* p''(Q^*) \right]^{-1}$$

$$= c^* \left[\left(1 - \frac{1}{n^*} \right) p'(Q^*) + \frac{1}{n^*} MR'(Q^*) \right]^{-1} < 0 \tag{10.3}$$

where the negativity follows from the second-order condition $\partial^2\pi^*/\partial q^{*2} = (1 + 1/n)p'(Q^*) + q^*p''(Q^*) < 0$. Hence, increasing the tariff lowers total exports and, since the number of firms is assumed fixed, exports per firm as well.

Since it reduces the total quantity, the increase in the tariff raises the price paid by home consumers. It also widens the gap between the price paid by home consumers and the price received by foreign exporters, which we will also refer to as the producer price. The net effect of a small tariff change on the producer price, again holding the number of firms fixed, is:

$$\frac{d(p/(1 + \tau))}{d\tau} = \frac{1}{1 + \tau}\left\{p'\frac{dQ^*}{d\tau} - \frac{p}{1 + \tau}\right\}$$

$$- c^*\left\{-\frac{MR' - p'}{MR' + (n^* - 1)p'} - \frac{(p - c^*)}{c^*}\right\} \qquad (10.4)$$

where the second equality follows from (10.1) and (10.3). (10.4) states that $MR' - p' < 0$ i.e. industry marginal revenue more negatively sloped than demand is a sufficient condition to have an increase in the tariff lower the price received by exporting firms. This condition holds for all concave and linear demands but will not hold for very convex demands (e.g. constant elasticity demands).

Welfare

In our partial equilibrium framework home welfare (W) derived from the market under examination equals the sum of consumer surplus and of tariff revenue:[5]

$$W(\tau) = \left[\int_0^{Q^*} p(v)dv - p(Q^*)Q^*\right] + pQ^*\tau/(1 + \tau)$$

Differentiation of this expression gives:

$$\frac{dW(\tau)}{d\tau} = -Q^*p'(Q^*)\frac{dQ^*}{d\tau}$$

$$+ \frac{1}{1 + \tau}\left[\frac{pQ^*}{1 + \tau} + \tau Q^*\frac{dp}{d\tau} + \tau p\frac{dQ^*}{d\tau}\right] \qquad (10.5)$$

The first term indicates that consumer surplus is decreasing in the tariff, but the sign of the second term is ambiguous for arbitrary τ. This second term shows that a tariff increase affects revenue through the following channels: It raises revenue by increasing the amount of duty collected per-unit imported at a *given* price, it jacks up the value to which the rate is applied and, it lowers the volume of imports. The latter effect contributes negatively to revenue, the first two contribute positively.

If we consider imposing a small tariff starting from free trade (i.e. for $\tau = 0$) then expression (10.5) reduces to:

$$\left.\frac{dW(\tau)}{d\tau}\right|_{\tau=0} = -Q_x^* \frac{d(p/1+\tau)}{d\tau} > 0 \tag{10.6}$$

Hence, the imposition of a small tariff raises home welfare and does so by lowering the price paid to exporters, i.e. by generating a terms of trade effect favorable to the importing country.

Figure 10.1 illustrates the effects of the tariff. The free trade demand and associated perceived marginal revenue are denoted p and mr. With marginal cost equal to c^*, free trade imports by the home country are Q_1^*. Under a tariff, the demand faced by the exporting oligopoly is $p/1 + \tau$ and perceived marginal revenue is $mr/1 + \tau$. The tariff reduces exports to Q_2^* and, as a result, consumer surplus falls by an amount represented by the sum of the areas marked A and B. Since the gain in tariff revenue is shown by the sum of areas A and C, the net change in welfare is given by area C *minus* area B. The source of gain for the home country resides in the capture of foreign exporters' surplus. However, this gain has to be set against a loss brought about by a widening wedge between price paid by home consumers and the cost of imports to the home economy.

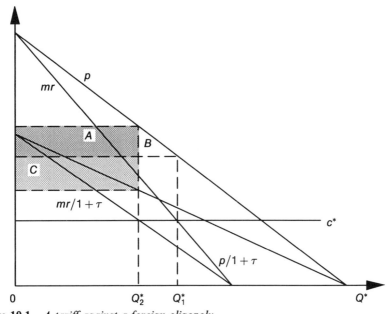

Figure 10.1   *A tariff against a foreign oligopoly*

An increase in the tariff always increases the size area of B but may increase or decrease the size of area C. However, as shown by (10.6) a small tariff is assured to generate an area C larger than the associated area B. This is due to the fact that the size of area C is proportional to τ whereas that of area B is proportional to τ^2.

The source of gain to the home economy is partial absorption of the tariff by the foreign industry. The extent to which such absorption takes place depends on the number of exporters. For larger n^*, the perceived marginal revenue is closer to demand and the producer price is nearer marginal cost. In terms of Figure 10.1 this means that area B is larger relative to area C. With n^* tending towards infinity the price paid by consumers would increase by the amount of the tariff and the price received by exporters would not vary in response to tariff changes. This, as we already know, is precisely the effect of a tariff levied by a small country on a competitively supplied import.

As in Chapter 5, we can determine the tariff rate that would maximize the home country's welfare. In terms of Figure 10.1, the tariff rate is optimal when a small increase would add to area B as much as it adds to area C. Formally, the optimal tariff rate is found by setting (10.5) to zero and solving for τ. As in the case of the fully competitive large economy, we find that the welfare maximizing tariff rate is lower than the revenue maximizing tariff. The reason again is that home welfare includes consumer surplus in addition to tariff revenue, and the former is decreasing in the tariff.

Finally, we note that although the optimal tariff is positive notwithstanding the fact that the importing country is small, it is not a first best instrument. The importing country would be better off by imposing a price ceiling, and the optimal ceiling would be the lowest consistent with positive exports.

Problem 10.2:   Examine the effect of a tariff on home country welfare assuming that foreign oligopolistic exporters face a competitive fringe of domestic producers. (*Note*: the demand faced by the foreign oligopoly is now equal to consumer demand *less* the supply of the fringe.)

An export tax on domestic oligopoly

Now consider the case polar to that above, namely, n domestic firms that export to a foreign country in which there are no local rivals.[6] In this framework consider the effect of a tax on the exports of home firms. As before, assume that all firms have the same cost function $C(q) = F + cq$ and that competition is Cournot. Also assume that there is no home consumption of the good exported by the home industry.[7] Since the entire production of home firms is consumed in the foreign country, we equate foreign sales by home firms to their output i.e. $q_x = q$ and, for the industry, $Q_x = Q$.

The home country is assumed to have in place an *ad valorem* tax θ on exports so that the net price received by each firm is $p^*(Q)/(1 + \theta)$, where $p^*(Q)$ denotes inverse demand in the foreign country. Profits are then $\pi = [p^*(Q)/(1 + \theta) - c]q - F$ and they attain a maximum when

$$p^*(Q) + q \frac{dp^*(Q)}{dQ} - (1 - \theta)c = p^*(Q) + \frac{Q}{n} \frac{dp^*(Q)}{dQ} - (1 + \theta)c = 0 \quad (10.7)$$

(10.7) has the same form as (10.1) and hence the effect of a change in θ on quantities and prices is also the same. In particular, $dQ/d\theta < 0$ and, for $MR^{*\prime} - p^{*\prime} < 0$, one has $d[p^*/(1 + \theta)]d\theta < 0$.

The home welfare from exporting equals the sum of after-tax profits and tax receipts, or equivalently, industry profits before export taxes,[8] i.e.

$$W(\theta) = \left[\frac{1}{1 + \theta} p^*(Q) - c \right] Q - nF$$

$$+ \frac{\theta}{1 + \theta} p^*(Q)Q = [p^*(Q) - c]Q - nF \quad (10.8)$$

Holding the number of home firms fixed (i.e. $dn = 0$), total differentiation of (10.8) implies a welfare change due to the export tax given by

$$\frac{dW(\theta)}{d\theta} = [p^* + Qp^{*\prime} - c] \frac{dQ}{d\theta} = [MR^* - c] \frac{dQ}{d\theta} \quad (10.9)$$

(10.7) implies that under free trade (i.e. when $\theta = 0$), one has $[MR^* - c] < 0$ when $n > 1$. Since $dQ/d\theta < 0$, it follows from (10.9) that home welfare must be higher under some positive export tax than under free trade. The optimal tax (θ^0) obtained by setting (10.9) to zero is

$$\theta^0 = -\frac{1}{c} \left(1 - \frac{1}{n} \right) Q^0 p^{*\prime}(Q^0) \quad (10.10)$$

where Q^0 is the quantity that solves $dW(\theta)/d\theta = 0$.[9] (10.10) shows that the optimal tax rate induces the home industry to produce the same quantity as a monopoly in the absence of the tax. The economic intuition for this result is as follows: Since domestic welfare is maximized when total industry profits are highest, the optimal industry quantity is the monopoly quantity. Since Cournot firms do not internalize the effect of their output decision on the profits of other firms, industry quantity is too large from the standpoint of domestic welfare. An export tax, equal to the loss in revenue that other industry members suffer as a result of one firm's increase in output, induces each of them to act as if they internalized the effects of their quantity decisions on the profits of other industry members. The result is monopoly profits for the industry.

The determination of the optimal export tax is illustrated in Figure 10.2. The free trade demand faced by the home industry is denoted p^* and the associated perceived marginal revenue is mr^*. The average and perceived marginal revenues facing the home industry when its exports are taxed are $p^*/(1 + \theta)$ and $mr^*/(1 + \theta)$. Industry marginal revenue is given by MR^*. The export tax reduces exports from Q_1 to Q_2. Since $MR^* = c$ at Q_2 the export

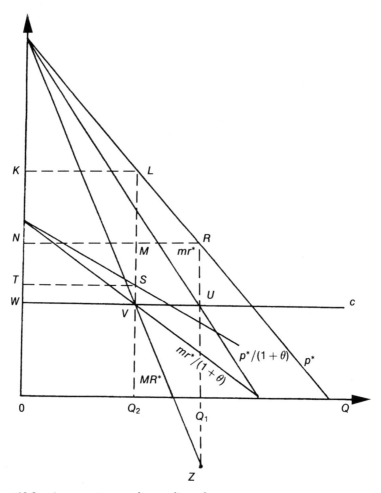

Figure 10.2   *An export tax on home oligopoly*

tax is optimally chosen. It has the effect of reducing exporters' net of tax profits by an amount equal to the difference in the size of the areas *NRUW* and *TSVW*. Tax collections by the home government are given by the area *KLST* and the portion *KLMN* of this area is a transfer of surplus from foreign consumers to the home treasury. By taxing exports optimally the home country gains an amount represented by the area *VUZ*.

Multicountry oligopoly

We now allow home oligopolists to compete with foreign oligopolists. In this context, we explore first how trade taxes and subsidies are set when one country pursues a trade policy and the other remains passive. We then turn to the case where both countries engage in trade policy. Each of these cases is examined under the Cournot and Bertrand forms of rivalry. To facilitate a comparison with the results obtained in the previous section, the next two sections assume that firms in each country export their entire production to a third country. This assumption ensures that trade policy determines each country's welfare only through profits and government revenue or expenditures. This assumption is relaxed in Section 10.2.

Rivalry in a third market: 1 country adopts free trade

Cournot competition
Consider a framework in which the home and foreign industries sell in a third market. We showed above that when home oligopolists have no foreign rivals, an export tax reduces the volume of exports and increases home welfare. However, when there are foreign rivals, a reduction in home exports will bring about an expansion of exports by the foreign oligopolists which will lower price in the export market. Since the latter will affect home profits adversely, an export tax may no longer be optimal.

To investigate this issue, let inverse demand in the third country be denoted $\tilde{p} = \tilde{p}(Q + Q^*)$ and assume that the cost functions of home and foreign firms are those given in the previous sections. To capture the possible policy outcomes specify a profit function which admits both an export tax and an export subsidy. In this regard, define $\varphi = [(1 + \theta)/(1 + \sigma)]$ where $\theta \geq 0$ is the export tax rate and $\sigma \geq 0$ is the export subsidy rate. Only one instrument can be used at a time (i.e. $\sigma = 0$ when $\theta > 0$ and $\theta = 0$ when $\sigma > 0$). By definition, $\varphi = 1$ when there is free trade and $\varphi > 1$ (< 1)

when there is an export tax (subsidy). Using this specification, the profit functions can be written

$$\pi = \left[\frac{1}{\varphi}\tilde{p}(Q+Q^*) - c\right]q - F \qquad \text{(for a home firm)}$$

$$\pi^* = [\tilde{p}(Q+Q^*) - c^*]q^* - F^* \qquad \text{(for a foreign firm)}$$

Under Cournot rivalry the first-order conditions are

$$\tilde{p}(Q+Q^*) + \frac{Q}{n}\,\tilde{p}'(Q+Q^*) - \varphi c = 0 \quad \text{(for a home firm)} \qquad (10.11a)$$

$$\tilde{p}(Q+Q^*) + \frac{Q^*}{n^*}\,\tilde{p}'(Q+Q^*) - c^* = 0 \quad \text{(for a foreign firm)} \qquad (10.11b)$$

Since an export tax is formally equivalent to a transport cost we know from Chapter 9 (p 338) that it causes a downward shift of the home industry's reaction function. Likewise the home reaction function is shifted upward by a home export subsidy. This implies, that under an export tax (subsidy) the optimally chosen level of home exports is smaller (larger) for any given volume of foreign exports than under free trade.

Since there is no home consumption, home country welfare W equals the sum of net profits by home firms and government receipts (under a tax) or expenditures (under a subsidy):

$$W[Q(\varphi), Q^*(\varphi)] = \left[\frac{1}{\varphi}\,\tilde{p}(Q+Q^*) - c\right]Q$$

$$+ \left(1 - \frac{1}{\varphi}\right)\tilde{p}(Q+Q^*)Q = [\tilde{p}(Q+Q^*) - c]Q$$

Assuming the number of firms in each country fixed, the change in home welfare due to a small change in φ is then given by

$$\frac{dW}{d\varphi} = \frac{\partial W}{\partial Q}\frac{dQ}{d\varphi} + \frac{\partial W}{\partial Q^*}\frac{dQ^*}{d\varphi}$$

$$= [\widetilde{MR}(Q+Q^*) - c]\frac{dQ}{d\varphi} + Q\tilde{p}'(Q+Q^*)\frac{dQ^*}{d\varphi} \qquad (10.12)$$

The term in square brackets has the same form as in (10.9), and has the same interpretation. The second term measures the effect of the home country's trade policy on the output of foreign exporters. Called the 'strategic effect', this term is negative for all values of φ since $dQ/d\varphi < 0$, $\partial Q^*/\partial Q < 0$ and $\tilde{p}' < 0$. It captures the welfare consequence that flow from the impact of home trade policy on the foreign firms' quantity decisions.

We already know that under free trade $\widetilde{MR} - c < 0$ and, since $dQ/d\varphi < 0$, the first term in (10.12) is positive. However, this alone does not entail the optimality of an export tax since the second term, which is negative, calls for a subsidy.

The optimal trade policy

Setting (10.12) to zero we can solve for the tax or subsidy which maximizes home welfare:

$$\varphi^0 = 1 - \frac{1}{c}\left[\left(1 - \frac{1}{n}\right) + \frac{\partial Q^*}{\partial Q}\right]Q\tilde{p}'(Q^0 + Q^{*0}) \tag{10.13}$$

where Q^0 and Q^{*0} maximize W and the slope of the reaction function is evaluated at that same point. The optimal policy is obtained by rewriting (10.11a) as

$$\left[\widetilde{MR}(Q + Q^*) - c + Q\tilde{p}'(Q + Q^*)\frac{\partial Q^*}{\partial Q}\right]$$

$$- \left[\left(1 - \frac{1}{n} + \frac{\partial Q^*}{\partial Q}\right)Q\tilde{p}'(Q + Q^*) - (1 - \varphi)c\right] = 0$$

setting the second term equal to zero.

Since

$$\text{sign}(\varphi^0 - 1) = \text{sign}\left(1 - \frac{1}{n} + \frac{\partial Q^*}{\partial Q}\right)$$

we find, in contrast to the result obtained on p. 399, that maximization of home country welfare may call for an export subsidy rather than an export tax.

To make the possibility of a subsidy explicit, consider the simple case of a duopoly involving one home and one foreign firm (i.e. $n = n^* = 1$). In this case

$$\text{sign}(\varphi^0 - 1) = \text{sign}(\partial Q^*/\partial Q) < 0$$

that is, an increase in home welfare requires a subsidy rather than a tax.

The duopoly case is illustrated in Figure 10.3 which shows the free trade home and foreign reaction functions – r_f and r_f^*, respectively.[10] Point R is the free trade equilibrium.

Since the foreign firm, acting as a Cournot duopolist, always chooses a quantity on its own reaction function, home country profit is maximized when the home government applies an export subsidy – formally equivalent to a decrease in marginal cost – which shifts the home reaction function to r so that it intersects r_f^* at the point where the latter is tangent to the home iso-profit curve. In Figure 10.3, this occurs at point S.[11] Point S is the Stackelberg equilibrium, i.e. the equilibrium that would arise in the absence of a subsidy if the home firm could commit to a quantity before the foreign firm made its quantity choice. Here it is the home government which makes the commitment to the subsidy before firms engage in quantity competition. In doing so it confers a first-mover advantage to the home firm and this in spite of the fact that all producers do in fact choose quantity simultaneously.

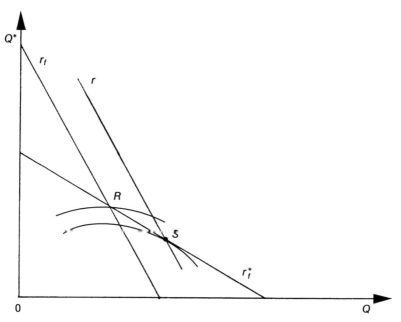

Figure 10.3   *Export subsidy under Cournot competition*

The total quantity sold in the third country is larger at S than at R. This follows from the fact that the slope of r_f^* is flatter than a 45° line.[12] Hence, the equilibrium price in the importing country is lower at S than at R. Since the price, as well as the foreign export volume are lower when the equilibrium is at S than when it is at R, foreign profits must also be lower.

The subsidy increases home profits net of subsidy at the expense of foreign profits. The literature refers to this effect as 'profit shifting'. Note though, that the decline in foreign profits is not matched by a commensurate increase in home profits. Also, home welfare increases in spite of an adverse terms of trade effect.

Bertrand competition
If firms engage in Bertrand competition then the above conclusion regarding the optimality of an export subsidy is radically changed. To see what is involved, assume that $n = n^* = 1$, $c = c^*$ and let the third country's demand for each good be $Q = \tilde{d}(p, p^*)$ and $Q^* = \tilde{d}^*(p, p^*)$ where $dQ/dp < 0$, $dQ/dp^* > 0$, $dQ^*/dp > 0$, $dQ^*/dp^* < 0$.[13] Defining φ as before, the profit functions are:

$$\pi = \left[\frac{p}{\varphi} - c \right] \tilde{d}(p, p^*) - F \qquad \text{(for the home firm)}$$

$$\pi^* = [p^* - c] \tilde{d}^*(p, p^*) - F^* \qquad \text{(for the foreign firm)}$$

With each firm choosing its price as if taking the price of the other firm as given, the first-order conditions are:

$$\tilde{d} + p \frac{\partial \tilde{d}}{\partial p} - \varphi c \frac{\partial \tilde{d}}{\partial p} = 0 \qquad \text{(for the home firm)} \qquad (10.14\text{a})$$

$$\tilde{d}^* + p^* \frac{\partial \tilde{d}^*}{\partial p^*} - c \frac{\partial \tilde{d}^*}{\partial p^*} = 0 \qquad \text{(for the foreign firm)} \qquad (10.14\text{b})$$

(10.14) implicitly defines 2 reaction functions in price space which, given our assumptions about demand, are now upward sloping.[14] The second-order condition for the home firm is $2(\partial \tilde{d}/\partial p) + (p - c)(\partial^2 \tilde{d}/\partial p^2) < 0$.

Figure 10.4 displays the home and foreign reaction functions for the case when demands are linear. Also shown are iso-profit curves of the home firm. Unlike Figure 10.3, higher home firm profits are now represented by curves

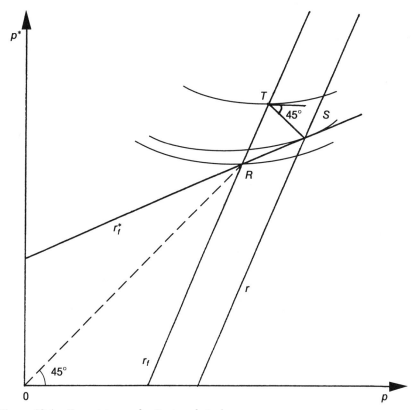

Figure 10.4 *Export tax under Bertrand rivalry*

that lie farther from the horizontal axis since, when p^* is higher, the home firm can sell a larger quantity at any price p. This means, in particular, that the home firm's profits at point S are higher than its profits at the free trade Bertrand equilibrium R.[15]

As before, the home welfare maximizing equilibrium lies at the point of tangency of a home iso-profit curve with the foreign reaction function (i.e. point S in Figure 10.4). This equilibrium is attained if the home government shifts the home firm's reaction function from r_f to r. We now show that the desired shift calls for an export tax rather than a subsidy.

Differentiating the home firm's first-order condition in (10.14a) for $dp^* = 0$ yields:

$$\frac{dp}{d\varphi} = \frac{c}{2(\partial \tilde{d}/\partial p) + (p - c)(\partial^2 \tilde{d}/\partial p^2)} \frac{\partial \tilde{d}}{\partial p} > 0 \qquad (10.15)$$

The positive sign follows from the second-order condition and the assumption that $\partial \tilde{d}/\partial p < 0$. Positivity of (10.15) implies in turn that for higher φ, the best response by the home firm to any price p^* set by the foreign firm is a higher price p. Since an increase in φ starting from free trade means that the country taxes its exports, (10.15) shows that the government must tax rather than subsidize exports in order to shift the home reaction function so that it intersects r_f^* at S. It is now the tax which confers upon the home firm the role of first-mover.

The optimality of an export tax when $n = n^* = 1$ is not the only result that differs from the Cournot case. In particular, under Bertrand competition the foreign firm gains from the home country's trade policy since the equilibrium price of the home firm is higher when exports are taxed. The symmetry assumptions which underlie Figure 10.4 imply that point T is the mirror image of S and hence foreign profits at S equal home profits at T. But, home firm profits at T are larger than at S. Thus, the move from R to S provides larger gains for the foreign country than for the home country.

Turning now to the case where there are several home firms, we note that when firms choose prices taking the prices of others as given, there arises an added incentive to tax exports. Again this is due to an absence of internalization. Every increase in price by one firm increases the profits of all other firms. However, since individually firms do not take this effect into account, equilibrium prices are too low from a home welfare point of view. As in the Cournot case, this can be corrected with a tax.

We conclude that, unlike Cournot competition which may call for a tax or subsidy depending on the number of home firms, price competition always calls for an export tax.

Rivalry in a third market: neither country adopts free trade

Although the national welfare maximizing policy under Bertrand and Cournot rivalry can differ, the analysis thus far has shown that some form of interference with free trade is welfare increasing when the other country remains passive. But does this conclusion also hold if both countries pursue an activist policy?[16] To examine this issue we analyze such '2-sided' government policy by means of a 2-stage game. In the first stage each government commits to a policy variable (i.e. either an export subsidy or tax). In the second stage firms engage in Cournot or Bertrand competition taking the choices of the governments as given. The two governments are assumed to set their policy variables simultaneously – that is, each acts as if the policy choice of the other government were given. In choosing policy, governments take into account the response of firms in the subsequent period.[17] As in the previous section, we will examine the duopoly case of a single home firm and a single foreign firm who each sell only into a third country market.

Cournot competition
We have found that under Cournot competition, a unilateral export subsidy maximizes national welfare when $n = n^* = 1$. Since both countries are now assumed to engage in trade policy, the home and foreign reaction curves, are implicitly defined by

$$\bar{p}[Q + Q^*] + Q\bar{p}'[Q + Q^*] - \frac{c}{1 + \sigma} = 0 \qquad \text{(for a home firm)}$$

$$\bar{p}[Q + Q^*] + Q^*\bar{p}'[Q + Q^*] - \frac{c^*}{1 + \sigma^*} = 0 \qquad \text{(for a foreign firm)}$$

The intersection of the reaction functions for $\sigma = \sigma^* = 0$ – i.e. for the case of free trade – is shown as point R in Figure (10.5a). In response to a home subsidy, the home reaction function will shift upward while the foreign reaction function will move upward as the foreign subsidy increases. Therefore, in equilibrium the quantities will depend on both subsidies. Hence, the home country's welfare (W) which in the absence of home consumption is equal to profits *less* subsidy payments, can be written in the general form $W[Q(\sigma, \sigma^*), Q^*(\sigma, \sigma^*)]$; similarly foreign welfare is $W^*[Q(\sigma, \sigma^*), Q^*(\sigma, \sigma^*)]$. In the first stage game each government will set its subsidy taking into account the effect of the subsidy on the quantities set by both firms. Formally, the subsidies are determined by the conditions

$$\frac{dW}{d\sigma} = \left[\frac{\partial \pi}{\partial \sigma} + \frac{\partial \pi}{\partial Q}\frac{\partial Q}{\partial \sigma} + \frac{\partial \pi}{\partial Q^*}\frac{\partial Q^*}{\partial \sigma}\right] - \frac{d\sigma \tilde{p}Q}{d\sigma}$$

$$= \left[\tilde{p}Q + (1+\sigma)\tilde{p}'Q\frac{\partial Q^*}{\partial \sigma}\right]$$

$$- \tilde{p}Q - \sigma\tilde{p}\frac{\partial Q}{\partial \sigma} - \sigma\tilde{p}'Q\frac{\partial(Q+Q^*)}{\partial \sigma}$$

$$= -\sigma[\tilde{p} + \tilde{p}'Q]\frac{\partial Q}{\partial \sigma} + \tilde{p}'Q\frac{\partial Q^*}{\partial \sigma} = 0 \qquad (10.16)$$

(for the home government)

$$\frac{dW^*}{d\sigma^*} = \left[\frac{\partial \pi^*}{\partial \sigma^*} + \frac{\partial \pi^*}{\partial Q}\frac{\partial Q}{\partial \sigma^*} + \frac{\partial \pi^*}{\partial Q^*}\frac{\partial Q^*}{\partial \sigma^*}\right] - \frac{d\sigma^*\tilde{p}Q^*}{d\sigma}$$

$$= -\sigma^*(\tilde{p} + \tilde{p}'Q^*)\frac{\partial Q^*}{\partial \sigma^*} + \tilde{p}'Q^*\frac{\partial Q}{\partial \sigma^*} = 0$$

(for the foreign government)

Let the subsidy pair which solves these first-order conditions be denoted (σ_N, σ_N^*). Since $\partial Q/\partial\sigma > 0$ and $\partial Q^*/\partial\sigma^* > 0$ whereas $\partial Q/\partial\sigma^* < 0$ and $\partial Q^*/\partial\sigma < 0$ both σ_N and σ_N^* must be positive if $\tilde{p} + \tilde{p}'Q < 0$, the latter condition, stating that perceived marginal revenue in the third country is steeper than demand.[18]

In can be shown that the pair (σ_N, σ_N^*) does not maximize world welfare. This is again due to an absence of internalization but, in this case, attributable to governments. Indeed, when choosing the rate of subsidy each government only takes into account the effect of the subsidy on the profits of the domestic industry. Since an increase in the rate of subsidy by one country lowers profits in the other country, world welfare would increase if starting from (σ_N, σ_N^*) either country would slightly reduce its subsidy. Formally,

$$\frac{d(W+W^*)}{d\sigma}\bigg|_{(\sigma_N,\sigma_N^*)} = \frac{dW^*}{d\sigma}\bigg|_{(\sigma_N,\sigma_N^*)} < 0$$

and

$$\frac{d(W+W^*)}{d\sigma^*}\bigg|_{(\sigma_N,\sigma_N^*)} = \frac{dW^*}{d\sigma^*}\bigg|_{(\sigma_N,\sigma_N^*)} < 0$$

The properties of the (perfect Nash) equilibrium in subsidies appear very clearly when considering Figure (10.5a). The reaction functions which intersect at R (drawn for linear demand and symmetric costs) correspond to zero subsidies by both countries.

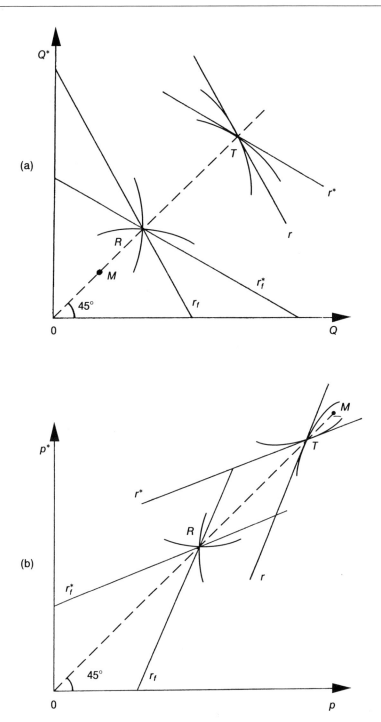

Figure 10.5 *Nash equilibria in* (a) *subsidies and* (b) *taxes*

Since each government views the reaction function of the firm based in the other country as given, and since it (optimally) subsidizes the exports of the domestic industry, both reaction functions are shifted to the right. At the equilibrium T associated with σ_N and σ_N^* the reaction function of each firm is tangent to an isoprofit curve of the other firm. The assumed symmetry ensures that point T lies on the 45° line that passes through O and R.

As total exports by the home and foreign firm are larger at T than at R, and since the total quantity at R is already larger than the monopoly quantity (shown as M in Figure 10.5a), profits at T must be lower than at R. Since each firm's profits are equal to one half of total profits, both countries lose if they cannot agree to refrain from subsidizing their exports.

The 2 countries would be better off if they could agree to tax their exports.[19] In the absence of an agreement, both governments are faced with a prisoner's dilemma. Each finds that the domestic industry benefits from a unilateral export subsidy, but when the two governments subsidize exports, welfare in both countries is lower than under free trade.[20]

Bertrand competition

Things are again different under Bertrand rivalry. The reason is that a tax imposed by one government raises the consumer price of both varieties. When the two countries tax their exports, the equilibrium prices are given by the coordinates of T in Figure 10.5b. At T, prices exceed the free trade prices given by the coordinates of R. Remarkably, both firms have higher profits at T than under a unilateral export tax. This is due to the fact that a price increase by one firm increases the profit of the other firm. Hence, both are better off when the two governments tax exports than when a single government does. Even so, joint profits are not maximized at T. The sum of profits is highest when the isoprofit loci of the two firms are tangent to each other. This cannot be the case at point T since, at this point, the isoprofit curves are tangent to reaction lines at the very point where these lines intersect.

Unsurprisingly the failure to maximize joint profits must again be attributed to an absence of internalization. Neither of the two governments takes into account the favorable effects of its export tax on the profits of the industry based in the other country. Hence, tax rates are set below the level that maximizes joint profits. To achieve the latter governments would have to cooperate and set taxes which shift the two reaction functions further out, until they intersect at M, the point chosen by a firm which is the only seller of both varieties.

In summary, we see that under Bertrand competition, the equilibrium is better in terms of total profits when both countries determine trade policy non-cooperatively than when only one government adopts an activist stance. This finding is in stark contrast to the Cournot case where joint profits are highest under free trade and lowest when the two governments subsidize exports.

Extension: cost differences across firms

The preceding sections assumed that all firms within a country have the same costs. Therefore, the quantity of resources consumed in the production of a *given* volume of output could change as a result of a reallocation of output across countries, but not within countries. When there is cost heterogeneity within a country, trade policy also affects welfare through a channel not yet encountered; the reallocation of output among firms located in the same country. This is illustrated below for the case of a tax levied on exports of a Cournot home industry which sells into a foreign market where it faces no competitors.

Absent local consumption of the export good, the industry's contribution to home welfare is

$$W(\theta) = p^*(Q)Q - \sum_{j=1}^{n} c_j q_j - \sum_{j=1}^{n} F_j = [p^*(Q) - \phi]Q - \sum_{j=1}^{n} F_j$$

where c_j and F_j are marginal and fixed costs of firm j, q_j is firm j's output, ζ_j its market share and

$$\phi = \sum_{j=1}^{n} c_j \frac{q_j}{Q} = \sum_{j=1}^{n} c_j \zeta_j$$

Hence,

$$\frac{dW(\theta)}{d\theta} = [p^*(Q) + Qp^{*\prime}(Q) - \phi]\frac{\partial Q}{\partial \theta} + Q\sum_{j=1}^{N} \frac{\partial \phi}{\partial \zeta_j}\frac{\partial \zeta_j}{\partial \theta}$$

We show first that when $MR^{*\prime} - p^{*\prime} < 0$, an equal increase in the marginal cost of all firms, for n fixed, lowers the market share of the firms with below average shares.

Under Cournot competition the first-order conditions are now $p + \zeta_j Q p^{*\prime} - c_j = 0$, hence implying

$$[(1 - \zeta_j)p^{*\prime} + \zeta_j MR^{*\prime}]dQ + Qp^{*\prime}d\zeta_j = dc_j \qquad (10.17)$$

Summing these equalities over all firms and dividing the sum by n yields $[(1 - 1/n)p^{*\prime} + MR^{*\prime}/n]dQ = (1/n)d\sum_{j=1}^{n} c_j$. The latter equation can be solved for dQ and upon insertion into (10.17) yields

$$dc_j = ([(1 - \zeta_j)p^{*\prime} + \zeta_j MR^{*\prime}]/[(1 - 1/n)p^{*\prime} + MR^{*\prime}/n])(1/n)d\sum_{j=1}^{n} c_j + Qp^{*\prime}d\zeta_j.$$

An equal change in the marginal cost of all firms (i.e. $(1/n) \sum_{j=1}^{n} c_j = dc_j = dc$) must therefore imply

$$d\zeta_j/dc = [(1/n - \zeta_j)(MR^{*\prime} - p^{*\prime})]/[(1 - 1/n)p^{*\prime} + MR^{*\prime}/n]Qp^{*\prime}.$$

For $MR^{*\prime} - p^{*\prime} < 0$ it must then be true that

$$\text{sign}(d\zeta_j/dc) = \text{sign}(\zeta_j - 1/n)$$

We have shown that an *equal* increase in the marginal costs of all firms increases the market share of the firms with above average shares (the low cost producers) and lowers the shares of firms whose shares are below average (the high cost producers). We know from (10.7) that an *ad valorem* export tax has the same effect on the equilibrium quantities as an *equiproportional* increase in marginal costs. Hence it must tilt market shares in favor of the low cost producers even more than an equal increase in marginal cost. The upshot is that the tax will lower the resource cost of a given quantity of exports. This is an additional source of welfare gain.

Problem 10.3:   There are 2 firms in the home country and 1 firm in the foreign country producing the same homogeneous good and exporting it to a third country which is the only one consuming the good in question. The foreign firm produces at the marginal cost c^*. The first home firm produces at the same marginal cost as the foreign firm, i.e. $c_1 = c^*$; the second home firm produces at marginal cost $c_2 = \alpha c_1$ ($\alpha > 0$). Assume that the demand in the third country is linear and examine how the optimal home export tax or subsidy changes with α.

10.2 Rivalry across markets

We now bring the different pieces together to consider the empirically more relevant case where home and foreign firms sell in both their local market and their rival's market. Since competition is now in 2 countries, we must distinguish between the cases of segmented and connected markets. In this section we consider not only the case where the number of firms is fixed, but also the case where that number is determined endogenously.

Segmented markets

We already know that when markets are segmented, marginal costs constant and the number of producers given, the equilibrium in one market does not depend on parameters of demand in the other market.[21] This means in particular that small policy changes that pertain to one market do not perturb an existing equilibrium in another market. More specifically, it entails that a home tariff will not affect a foreign market and, likewise, a home export tax or subsidy will not change the quantities sold in the home country. The latter signifies that our earlier results (pp. 404 and 406) relating to the effects of home export taxes and subsidies are the same regardless of whether or not the foreign based firms also export to the home market. Hence, the presence of home producers as well as home consumers only forces us to reconsider the effects of tariff policy.

Fixed number of firms

Recall from p. 397 that a tariff raises home welfare if the gain from capturing the profits of foreign firms in the form of tariff revenue exceeds the decline in the surplus of home consumers. Now, the profits of home firms are an integral part of home welfare and hence an additional term is added to the welfare expression. Formally:

$$W(\tau) = \left\{ \int_0^{Q_l + Q_x^*} p(v)dv - p(Q_l + Q_x^*)[Q_l + Q_x^*] \right\}$$

$$+ \frac{\tau}{1+\tau} Q_x^* p(Q_l + Q_x^*)$$

$$+ \{[p(Q_l + Q_x^*) - c]Q_l + [p^*(Q_x + Q_l^*) - c]Q_x - nF\}$$

where $Q_l(Q_l^*)$ and Q_x (Q_x^*) denote local sales and export sales by the home (foreign) industry. The first and second terms on the right-hand side of this expression are consumer surplus and tariff revenue, respectively. The third term represents the home industry profits. Differentiation yields:

$$\frac{dW(\tau)}{d\tau} = - \left[[Q_l + Q_x^*] \frac{dp}{d\tau} \right] + \frac{d}{d\tau} \left[\frac{\tau}{1+\tau} p Q_x^* \right]$$

$$+ \left[(p - c) \frac{dQ_l}{d\tau} + Q_l \frac{dp}{d\tau} \right] \tag{10.18}$$

Note that the second component of the third term cancels with the first component of the first term. This reflects that part of the decline in consumer surplus resulting from the tariff that is recouped in the form of higher profits by home firms.

On p. 397 we found that the welfare effect of a tariff is in general ambiguous, but that a small increase in the tariff starting from free trade increases home welfare. Since we now assume a home industry we have:

$$\left. \frac{dW(\tau)}{d\tau} \right|_{\tau=0} = -Q_x^* \frac{d[p/1+\tau]}{d\tau} + [p - c] \frac{dQ_l}{d\tau} > 0$$

The first term is the same as in (10.6) and thus positive for $MR' - p' < 0$. The second term is also positive since an increase in the tariff shifts the foreign reaction function downward resulting in higher Q_I and lower Q_x^*.[22] We conclude that the presence of a home industry does not modify the earlier finding that a small tariff benefits home welfare. The optimal tariff is different though since the welfare function now includes an additional term.

Problem 10.4: Assume that the home inverse demand is $p = a - b(Q_I + Q_x^*)$ and assume that $c = c^*$. The total number of home and foreign firms selling in the home market is $N(N = n + n^*)$. Holding N fixed, examine how the optimal tariff changes as a function of n.

It can be shown that in the case of a linear demand the welfare maximizing tariff is higher when the foreign marginal cost is lower. Specifically, when there is one home and one foreign firm, and competition is Cournot, one finds $-d\tau^0/dc^* = 1/2$, i.e. the optimal tariff τ^0 increases by one-half of the fall in the foreign marginal cost.[23]

Problem 10.5: Assume that there are 2 firms, 1 domestic and 1 foreign, supplying a home market with inverse demand given by $p = a - b(Q_I + Q_x^*)$. The unit cost common to both firms is c. Examine the effect on home welfare of a foreign subsidy equal to 50% of the marginal cost of exports assuming: (1) that the home country is a free trader; (2) that the home country takes the foreign subsidy rate as a given and subsequently sets an optimal tariff.

The change in foreign profits due to the home tariff is given by

$$\frac{d\pi^*(\tau)}{d\tau} = \left[\frac{p(Q_I + Q_x^*)}{1 + \tau} - c^* \right] \frac{dQ_x^*}{d\tau} + \frac{Q_x^*}{1 + \tau} \frac{dp/(1 + \tau)}{d\tau} < 0 \qquad (10.19)$$

Since the price received by foreign firms is in excess of marginal cost, foreign profits fall when the quantity of exports falls. This is captured by the first term in (10.19). The second term captures the effect on profits change attributable to the change in net price.

From (10.18) and (10.19) it follows that the change in world welfare flowing from a change in the home tariff is:

$$\frac{dW(\tau) + \pi^*(\tau)}{d\tau} = [p - c] \frac{dQ_I}{d\tau} + [p - c^*] \frac{dQ_x^*}{d\tau}$$

$$= [p - c] \frac{d(Q_I + Q_x^*)}{d\tau} + [c - c^*] \frac{dQ_x^*}{d\tau}$$

To interpret the latter expression consider first the case where $c = c^*$. We already know that $dQ_x^*/d\tau < 0$ and $dQ_l/d\tau > 0$. Since the slope of the home reaction function is larger than 1 in absolute value, i.e since $-1 > \partial Q_l/\partial Q_x^*$ we also know that $d(Q_l + Q_x^*)/d\tau < 0$.[24] Thus, the tariff lowers world welfare. The same is true when $c > c^*$. However, when foreign costs are higher than home costs ($c < c^*$), the home tariff may raise world welfare.

Problem 10.6: Assume a home and a foreign firm producing different varieties of the same product. Let the home demand for the home and foreign variety respectively be $Q_l = a - bp_l + kp_x$ and $Q_x^* = a - bp_x + kp_l$ ($b > k$) where p_l and p_x are the prices of the locally produced and the imported variety. Let the firms compete in prices. Examine the effect of an import tariff on the profits of both firms. Could the foreign firm gain from the tariff?

Variable number of firms

To study the effects of tariffs and subsidies when there is free entry we adopt the model of Chapter 9 (p. 337). We let firms engage in Cournot rivalry and we assume that they incur a transport cost τ on each unit exported. Since we assume segmented markets, the first-order conditions for profit maximization are determined independently for each market. Given this, the set of first-order conditions in the home country market, respectively, the foreign country market under free trade are[25]

$$p + q_l p'(Q_l + Q_x^*) - c = 0$$

(for a home firm in the home market)

$$p + q_x^* p'(Q_l + Q_x^*) - c^* - \tau = 0$$ (10.20a)

(for a foreign firm in the home market)

$$p^* + q_x p^{*'}(Q_x + Q_l^*) - c - \tau = 0$$

(for a home firm in the foreign market)

$$p^* + q_l^* p^{*'}(Q_x + Q_l^*) - c^* = 0$$ (10.20b)

(for a foreign firm in the foreign market)

Using (10.20a) and (10.20b), the zero profit conditions can be written:

$$\pi = -\frac{1}{p'}[p - c]^2 - \frac{1}{p^{*'}}[p^* - (c + \tau)]^2 - F = 0$$ (10.21a)

and

$$\pi^* = -\frac{1}{p'}[p - (c^* + \tau)]^2 - \frac{1}{p^{*'}}[p^* - c^*]^2 - F^* = 0$$ (10.21b)

Since there are n home and n^* foreign firms we also have

$$Q_l = nq_l \quad \text{and} \quad Q_x^* = n^* q_x^* \tag{10.22a}$$

$$Q_x = nq_x \quad \text{and} \quad Q_l^* = n^* q_l^* \tag{10.22b}$$

The demand functions and the conditions (10.20)–(10.22) jointly determine q_l, q_x, q_l^*, q_x^*, n, n^*, Q_x, Q_l, Q_x^*, Q_l^* and the prices p and p^*. We assume that the parameters of the model are such that in equilibrium $n > 0$ and $n^* > 0$.

To examine how trade policy perturbs this equilibrium we now assume that the two demands are linear and that the foreign market is λ times as large as the home market [i.e. $p^*(Q_l^* + Q_x) = p(Q_l^* + Q_x/\lambda)$]. Specifically,

$$p = A - [Q_l + Q_x^*] \tag{10.23a}$$

$$p^* = A - [(Q_x + Q_l^*)/\lambda] \tag{10.23b}$$

First order conditions are then

$$q_l = p - c \quad \text{and} \quad q_x = \lambda(p^* - c - \tau) \quad \text{(for a home firm)} \tag{10.24a}$$

$$q_l^* = \lambda(p^* - c^*) \quad \text{and} \quad q_x^* = p - c^* - \tau \quad \text{(for a foreign firm)} \tag{10.24b}$$

The different price combinations consistent with zero profits can be represented as in Figure 10.6. Consider first the profits of a home firm. When $p^* < c + \tau$ the foreign market cannot contribute positively to home firm profits and thus $\pi = 0$ obtains when $p = c + \sqrt{F}$. Similarly, a home firm will not sell in the home market when $p < c$ implying that a foreign price $p^* = c + \tau + \sqrt{F/\lambda}$ will be just sufficient to cover fixed and variable cost. It then follows from (10.21) that the locus of the price combinations that yield $\pi = 0$ must lie on a segment of a circle centered at $(c, c + \tau)$. The price combinations which yield $\pi^* = 0$ are similarly obtained and are also displayed in Figure 10.6. The zero profit equilibrium prices are given by the coordinates of E, the intersection of the zero profit loci.

Differentiation of (10.21) yields

$$\frac{dp^*}{dp}\bigg|_{\pi=0} = -\frac{q_l}{q_x} \quad \text{and} \quad \frac{dp^*}{dp}\bigg|_{\pi^*=0} = -\frac{q_x^*}{q_l^*}$$

upon use of (10.24). This implies that the circle $\pi = 0$ intersects the circle $\pi^* = 0$ from above when every firm sells more in its local market than in its exports market. This is in fact the case under the assumptions of the model.[26]

We are now ready to investigate the effect of a *specific* tariff which we assume to be small enough to preserve an equilibrium where $n > 0$ and $n^* > 0$. A small home tariff $d\tau$ (or small increase in the transportation cost from the foreign to the home country) changes (10.21b) to

$$\pi^* = -\frac{1}{p'}[p - (c^* + \tau + d\tau)]^2 - \frac{1}{p^{*'}}[p^* - c^*]^2 - F^* = 0.$$

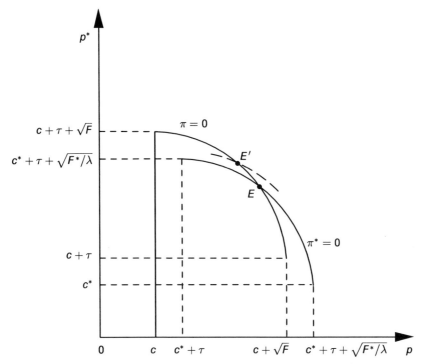

Figure 10.6 *Tariff under freedom of entry*

Graphically, this translates into a shift of the foreign firm's zero profit locus to the right, as shown by the dotted segment of a circle in Figure 10.6. The result is a new equilibrium E', at which the home price is *lower* and the foreign price is higher.

This is a surprising result. To gain some intuition consider the following thought experiment. Imagine that once the tariff is imposed the home consumer price and the number of home firms are frozen at their pre-tariff levels. Since the price received by a foreign firm in the home market must then fall below the frozen consumer price, the foreign firm's profit – which was initially zero – must become negative. In response, foreign firms will exit the industry. Exit, however, enhances home firm profits. Since home profits were initially zero they must now be positive. Now let the home consumer price and number of home firms become variable again. Positive home profits produce entry by home firms. The net effect of entry by home firms and exit by foreign firms is to lower the home price since home firms produce relatively more in the home market than in the foreign market. We find that the quantity response of the home industry to the tariff is stronger when the number of home firms is variable than when it is fixed. It is the strength of this response that causes the fall in the home price.

Welfare

Since profits are zero in equilibrium, home country welfare depends only on tariff revenue and consumer surplus, the latter declining in p. Since an increase in the home tariff lowers the home price, consumer surplus always increases in the tariff. The lowest home price is attained either when all the foreign firms have exited, or when they have ceased to export even though they continue to supply the foreign market.

For the special case where the social value of tariff revenue is zero, a positive relation between the tariff and consumer surplus implies that the optimal tariff is the prohibitive tariff. If the social value of tariff revenue is positive, as one normally assumes, a small tariff is even more desirable from a home welfare point of view but, a large tariff, let alone a prohibitive tariff, is not necessarily optimal. Indeed, any increase of the tariff beyond its revenue maximizing value means that losses in tariff revenue have to be set against gains in consumer surplus.

The effect of the home tariff on foreign welfare is immediate. As foreign profits are always zero, the change in foreign welfare equals the change in the surplus of foreign consumers. We know that this surplus is decreasing in the home tariff since the home tariff and the foreign price move in the same direction. Hence, foreign welfare is declining in the home tariff.

Finally, note that a specific home export subsidy shifts the $\pi = 0$ schedule in Figure 10.6 inward and therefore lowers the home price while it raises the foreign price. Hence, foreign welfare must be lower than in the absence of the subsidy. Home consumers clearly gain as the subsidy is increased since the home price falls, but government expenditure which enters home welfare with a negative sign, also increases. It can be shown that a small export subsidy increase the net welfare of the home country.[27]

Connected markets

When markets are connected rather than segmented as assumed to this point, quantities are not set independently in each country even when marginal costs are constant. Cournot firms decide on a total volume of output rather than on quantities for each country. They make this decision as if the total output by all other firms were given.[28]

In this section we examine first the effects of trade policy when the number of firms in each country is fixed. Then we explore in greater detail the case of free entry. We show in particular that the elimination of market segmentation removes the perverse effect of the tariff found above.

Fixed number of firms

When the number of firms is fixed and markets are connected, analysis of the effects of a tariff must account for the fact that an increase of the home price is accompanied by an increase of equal magnitude in the foreign price. The common home and foreign price is determined by the demand parameters and the trade policies of both countries. Using a framework that assumes Cournot behavior, linear demands, constant marginal costs, *specific* trade taxes and product differentiation across, but not within countries, it can be shown that the joint effect of the trade policies of two countries is a weighted average of the effects of the policy undertaken by each country, where the weights are the relative sizes of demand.[29] The implication of this weighting is that a tariff levied by one country alone is 'diluted', with the extent of dilution being larger the smaller the relative size of the tariff imposing country.

As to the welfare effects of trade policies, there now is a component not encountered in the segmented markets case: the impact of a home tariff on the home industry's profits derived from export sales. Since the home and foreign varieties are substitutes, the price of the home variety also increases in response to the increase in the consumer price of the imported variety. Since prices of each variety are equal in both markets, the home industry now derives a higher revenue from exports even if the exported quantity does not change. However, in response to the price increase of the home variety, home firms expand output, and part of the additional output is in fact exported.[30]

As in the case of segmented markets, a small unilateral home tariff increases home welfare. The total welfare effect has the following components: (a) an increase in the price that home consumers pay for both varieties; (b) a decrease in the net of duty (producer) price paid for the foreign variety and an increase in the export price of the home variety (both of which improve the home country's terms of trade); (c) an output increase by the home industry which raises home profits since marginal cost is lower than price.

Variable number of firms[31]

Consider again the case of free entry and maintain the assumption that the home and foreign industry produce varieties that are imperfect substitutes. The cost functions for home and foreign firms are respectively $C(q) = cq + F$ and $C^*(q^*) = c^*q^* + F^*$. Let the inverse demands for each of the two varieties be

$$p = a - bQ_l - kQ_x^* \quad \text{and} \quad \bar{p} = a - \frac{bQ_x}{\lambda} - k\frac{Q_l^*}{\lambda}$$

(for the home variety) (10.25a)

$$p^* = a - b\frac{Q_l^*}{\lambda} - k\frac{Q_x}{\lambda} \quad \text{and} \quad \bar{p}^* = a - bQ_x^* - kQ_l$$

(for the foreign variety) $\hspace{4cm}$ (10.25b)

where p and p^* denote the prices that consumers in the home and foreign country are paying for the locally produced variety, and $\bar{p}$ and $\bar{p}^*$ respectively denote the price that the foreign consumers pay for the home variety and, the price that the home consumers pay for the foreign variety. The Qs have the same interpretation as in earlier sections. Also assume $b > k$.

If the home country imposes a tariff and if transport cost is zero, the following conditions hold

$$p = \bar{p} \hspace{6cm} \text{(10.26a)}$$

$$p^* = \bar{p}^*/(1 + \tau) \hspace{4.5cm} \text{(10.26b)}$$

From (10.25) and (10.26) it follows that

$$p = a - b\frac{Q_l + Q_x}{1 + \lambda} - k\frac{Q_l^* + Q_x^*}{1 + \lambda}$$

and

$$p^* = a\frac{1 + \lambda}{1 + \tau + \lambda} - b\frac{Q_l^* + Q_x^*}{1 + \tau + \lambda} - k\frac{Q_l + Q_x}{1 + \tau + \lambda}$$

We assume that economies of scale are small enough to imply (almost) zero profits under free entry. If so, the slope of each firm's average cost curve must be equal in equilibrium to the slope of its perceived demand.[32] Since the inverse demand for the home variety is unaffected by the tariff it must follow that the quantity produced by the individual home firm does not change. Specifically, it implies that any change in the total production of the home variety occurs through adjustments in the number of firms. The inverse demand for the foreign variety, by contrast, becomes less steep when the tariff is raised. Hence output per foreign firm increases.

The equilibrium outputs per firm can be solved explicitly from the demands, the first-order conditions, and the zero profit conditions. These outputs are

$$q = \sqrt{F(1 + \lambda)/b}$$

and

$$q^* = \sqrt{F^*[1 + \tau + \lambda]/b}$$

Since output per home firm is unaffected by the tariff, the average cost does not change for home firms. Since the prices p and $\bar{p}$ are equal to average cost they do not change either. In contrast, the average cost set by each foreign firm is lower under the home tariff. Thus the net-of-duty price received by a foreign firm must also be lower. Under the home tariff, the price paid by home consumers for the foreign variety is

$$(1 + \tau)p^* = (1 + \tau)[c^* + F^* \sqrt{b/F^*(1 + \tau + \lambda)}].$$

This price is increasing in the tariff, unlike the foreign producer price which is decreasing in the tariff.[33]

Welfare changes are given by

$$\frac{dW}{d\tau} = -Q_x \frac{d(1 + \tau)p^*}{d\tau} + \frac{d(\tau p^* Q_x)}{d\tau}$$

with the first term representing the change in consumer surplus and the second the change in tariff revenue. For a small tariff we find

$$\left. \frac{dW}{d\tau} \right|_{\tau=0} = -Q_x \frac{dp^*}{d\tau} > 0$$

which implies that a small tariff benefits the home country.[34]

Problem 10.7: Determine for the case where demands are as in (10.25) how the tariff affects the consumption of both varieties as well as the number of home and foreign firms.

If we instead consider a home export tax, then $p = \bar{p}/(1 + \theta)$ and $p^* = \bar{p}^*$. The analysis proceeds along the same lines as for the tariff and can be summarized as follows: the price of the foreign variety is the same as under free trade; the home price of the home variety is lower whereas the foreign price of the home variety is higher than under free trade. Since an export subsidy can be viewed as a negative tax, we conclude that it raises the home price of the home variety and lowers the foreign price of the home variety. We also conclude that it leaves the price of the foreign variety unchanged in both markets and lowers output per firm in the home country.[35] A small subsidy unambiguously lowers home welfare since, in the present model, there are no foreign rents to capture even if total home output expands. Hence, home welfare declines as a result of the increase in average costs and the deterioration of the home country's terms of trade.

Finally we note that if the home and foreign produced variety are instead perfect substitutes (i.e. $b = k$), an arbitrarily small home tariff or export subsidy completely drives out the foreign industry. This rather peculiar outcome is due to the fact that if both home and foreign firms earned zero profits under free trade, foreign profits must be negative when home profits are zero under the tariff.

10.3 Extensions

Variable marginal cost

If marginal costs rise with the level of output then the quantity sold in one country is not independent of the quantity sold in another country even when markets are segmented. In particular, a change in the volume supplied to one market affects the marginal cost of supplying the other market. For example, when the home firm sets a tariff it also affects the exports of its home industry since the increased sales by home firms to home consumers affect the marginal cost of export sales. Likewise, an export subsidy will affect the price paid by home consumers. This, however, need not change our earlier findings. It can be shown, e.g. that when a single home and a single foreign firm sell into each other's market, and each government engages in trade policy, there will emerge a (Nash) equilibrium in which export subsidies by both countries are positive and welfare is lower than under free trade.[36]

Also, when marginal costs are decreasing, a home tariff may actually have the effect of promoting the exports of the good on which the tariff is levied.[37] The logic of this result is that a tariff, by increasing home sales of home firms at the expense of foreign firms, lowers the marginal cost of home firms and concomitantly raises the marginal cost of foreign firms. These cost changes in turn, shift the reaction functions in the foreign market in favor of home firms and this raises home firm export sales.

Monopolistic competition

The preceding sections assumed either that goods were homogeneous or that the number of varieties was given. We now consider the effect of trade policies that affect the number of varieties. As in Chapter 9, analysis of monopolistic competition requires that one specify the source of consumers' demand for variety. The two common approaches are 'love of variety' or 'most preferred variety'. Although the details of modeling differ between these approaches, the basic conclusions are that an increase in the number of varieties brought about by a policy intervention *may* constitute an additional source of welfare gains. In the 'love of variety' model this gain flows from the fact that any amount of spending on the differentiated good can be spread over a greater number of varieties; in the 'most preferred variety' model it derives from the opportunity given the 'average' consumer to purchase a variety that matches more closely a most preferred specification.

To illustrate, we briefly summarize a model by Lancaster (1991) in which he adopts his 'most preferred variety' approach.[38] This model assumes a small open economy which consumes 2 goods, one homogeneous and the other differentiated. The rest of the world is assumed to supply varieties of the differentiated good at prices which are fixed to the importing country. The foreign specifications are also given to the small economy and are equidistant from each other.[39] These assumptions rule out the possibility of gains flowing from policies that change the terms of trade or the foreign specifications. Consumers' ideal specifications are distributed uniformly over the product specification circle and, since the number of foreign varieties is finite, the utility obtained from a particular variety varies according to consumer type. Indeed, the utility in question depends on the distance between the consumer's most preferred specification and the specification of the variety purchased. Preferences are such that all consumers purchase either 1 unit of the differentiated good or none at all and, the prices of all foreign varieties are sufficiently low to ensure that all home consumers purchase a foreign variety if foreign varieties are the only ones offered for sale. It is also assumed that there potentially exists a domestic industry producing the same differentiated product. All potential home producers would, upon entering the market, produce a single variety and incur the same constant marginal and fixed cost.

Profit maximization requires that the specification of the local variety be chosen at the midpoint of the locations of the two foreign varieties.[40] Positive sales by local firms must therefore mean that some consumers whose ideal variety lies on the segment of the circle between the two adjacent foreign varieties enjoy an increase in surplus from shifting to the home variety. Since consumers always have the option of buying a foreign variety at the same fixed price, no consumer can lose from domestic entry as long as free trade prevails. Such entry under free trade has 2 welfare components: a gain in surplus racked up by consumers who switch to a better matched variety, and a gain or loss equal to the difference between the resource cost of producing the domestic variety and the resource cost of the displaced imports.

The circumstance under which a case for a tariff can be made is when domestic entry does not take place, notwithstanding the fact that it is socially beneficial. Such a situation may arise since the entrant cannot capture all the welfare gains resulting from consumers being able to purchase specifications better suited to their preferences. Indeed, while consumers located on the outer boundaries of an entrant's market area are indifferent between the home and the foreign variety, and hence indifferent to entry, the inframarginal consumers who upon entry would purchase the home variety would actually gain surplus. This is a social gain that cannot be seized by an entrant who does not price discriminate. An optimal tariff can fully correct for this 'market failure'. Under the assumptions of the model, the tariff can generate the welfare maximizing level of local production when foreign prices and market specifications are given.[41]

10.4 **Quantitative restrictions**

We now examine trade restrictions in the form of import quotas and VERs. We consider first the case where there is a single firm in the importing country but imports are supplied competitively. We then examine the case where firms in the importing country are price takers and market power resides solely with foreign firms. Lastly, we consider a duopoly setting with one home firm and one foreign firm. In all cases we contrast the outcomes under the quota to those arising under a tariff.

Recall from Chapter 5 that import quotas generate rents and that the allocation of these rents has an important bearing on the welfare effects of the quota. Here we assume that when the right to import under the quota is held by agents in the importing country, these agents act as perfect competitors with respect the purchase or sale of quota rights. We also assume that events unfold in the following sequence: first the government sets the level of permissible imports and only then do producers set their price or quantity. Any trading in quota licences, if it occurs, occurs last.

Domestic market power[42]

Figure 10.7 illustrates the domestic market for a homogeneous good where MC denotes the marginal cost of the home industry and DD' denotes domestic demand. Foreign supply is assumed infinitely elastic at the world price p^*. Assuming first that the domestic industry consists of perfectly competitive firms, we know from Chapter 5 that the imposition of an *ad valorem* tariff (τ) will raise the domestic price of imports and result in a new equilibrium domestic price equal to $(1 + \tau)p^*$. The increase in the domestic equilibrium price will raise home production from Q_1 to Q_2.[43]

Now let the home industry instead be a monopoly, in which case MC denotes the marginal cost curve of the monopolist. Under the tariff, the 'residual demand' (i.e. market demand *minus* foreign supply) facing the monopolist becomes the kinked curve VND since, at any local price higher than $(1 + \tau)p^*$, domestic consumers will demand only the imported good. Since marginal revenue equals price when demand is horizontal, the condition $MR = MC$ is still satisfied at point R in Figure 10.7.

Now assume that the tariff is replaced by a quota that limits imports to the quantity arising under the tariff. This quota alters the residual demand facing the monopolist as follows: For all prices below p^* the residual demand equals the market demand, while for all prices above p^* the residual demand equals the market demand *minus* the volume of imports specified by the quota. This new residual demand is shown as $DSTZ$ in

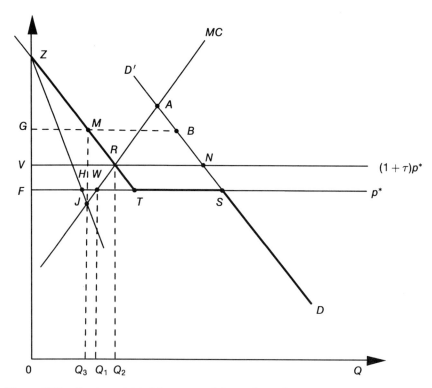

Figure 10.7 *Quota-restricted imports and domestic market power*

Figure 10.7 where the distance between T and S equals the distance between R and N. As shown, the marginal revenue associated with this residual demand intersects MC at a quantity Q_3. Since $Q_3 < Q_2$, home firm output is less, and the domestic price higher, that under the tariff. These different equilibria under the quota and the tariff arise since the quantity demanded from the monopolist under a quota no longer equals zero for prices larger than $(1 + \tau)p^*$.

We see that in the presence of a domestic monopoly, a quota that restricts imports to the same volume as the tariff yields an equilibrium different from the tariff. This applies even to the limiting case where the rate of duty is zero. In particular, a quota allowing the free trade import level raises the domestic price above p^*. Invoking a continuity argument, one can infer that shifting from free trade to a quota that allows imports somewhat in excess of free trade imports will also raise the domestic price above p^*.

Under the quota domestic welfare is lower than under the tariff. The loss in welfare due to the tariff is shown in Figure 10.7 as the area RTW. Under the quota consumer welfare falls from its free trade level by an amount given by the area *GBSF*. The value of importers' rents or government revenue from the sale of import licences is given by the area *MBST*, while the increase in home firm profits is equal to the area *GMHF* *minus* the area *HWJ*. Thus, replacing the tariff by a quota which allows the same volume of imports, lowers welfare by an amount represented by the area *JRM*.

Foreign monopoly

Now assume there is a single foreign firm and a fringe of competitive home firms selling in the home market. Let D in Figure 10.8 represent the residual demand facing this foreign monopolist [44] Assume that imports are initially subject to an *ad valorem* tariff τ. Under the tariff, the foreign firm with marginal cost MC^* faces the demand $D/(1 + \tau) \equiv D_\tau$, marginal revenue is MR_τ and the quantity exported is Q_τ. Home consumers pay the price $\hat{p}_\tau$, the foreign exporter receives the price p_τ and tariff revenue collected by the home government is $[\hat{p}_\tau - p_\tau]Q_\tau$.

If the tariff is now replaced by a quota which limits imports to Q_τ the residual demand facing the foreign firm becomes D for all quantities smaller

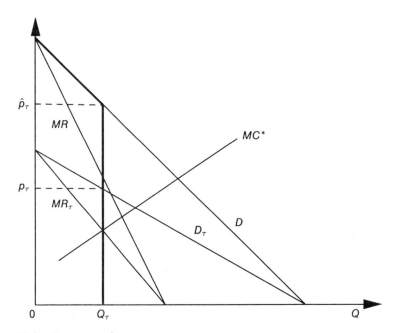

Figure 10.8   *Foreign market power*

than Q_τ and becomes vertical at Q_τ. Note that the downward sloping segment of MR lies above MC^* for all quantities smaller than Q_τ. Since exports cannot exceed Q_τ, they remain at the same level as under the tariff and the home consumer price is also the same. In this case the dif-ference between the quota and the tariff is that the foreign firm now receives the price $\hat{p}_\tau$.[45]

Since the producer price under the import quota equals the price paid by home consumers, import licences have zero value. This result contrasts with that of Chapter 5 regarding the effects of an import quota. Specifically, in competitive markets importers could earn positive rents from the quota since competition prevented the price charged by exporters from exceeding their marginal cost. In the present case, no quota rents are earned by any agent in the home country to partially offset the loss of consumer surplus.

The result that quota rights have zero value when the domestic market is supplied by a foreign monopoly appears to carry the implication that an import quota and a voluntary export restraint (VER) have the same welfare consequences.[46] However, this conclusion is correct only when the markets supplied by the foreign monopolist are segmented. If markets are not segmented a restrictive import quota may have a positive price. The reasoning is as follows.[47]

When markets are connected, raising price in the quota-restricted market implies that prices must rise in the other markets as well. It means in particular that if prices in the other markets were initially at their profit maximizing level, increasing price in the restricted market to capture the quota rents entails a sacrifice in terms of forgone profits elsewhere. More specifically, it implies that the profit maximizing producer price in the import restricting market will not be equal to the consumer price, if a slightly lower price would entail a sacrifice in profits in that market smaller than the gains the lower price would generate in other markets.

The preceding argument can be made more explicit with the aid of Figure 10.9 where demand $\bar{D}$ now represents the horizontal sum of the demands facing the foreign monopolist in all markets. For simplicity, it is assumed that the quota imposing home country demands at any price the same quantity as all other countries together. This assumption ensures that the home demand D coincides with $\overline{MR}$, the marginal revenue associated with $\bar{D}$.

Under free trade the monopolist sets the price p_1, the total quantity is $\bar{Q}_1$ and the quantity sold in the home country is Q_1, i.e. half of the total quantity. Now let the home country restrict imports to Q_1. The total demand facing the monopolist becomes AB_1E_1. Hence, marginal revenue is AG_1 for $Q < \bar{Q}_1$ and H_1R_1 for $Q > Q_1$. The monopolist therefore continues to produce the same quantity as under the tariff and sets the same price.

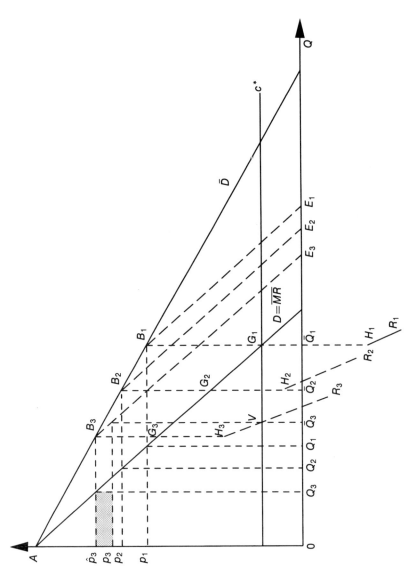

Figure 10.9 *Quota revenue when markets are connected*

If the quota is tightened to Q_2 the kink in the total demand slides upward, and the lower section of marginal revenue curve slides leftward. The demand is now AB_2E_2 and the associated marginal revenue is $AG_2H_2R_2$. Since the intersection with c^* occurs on the vertical segment of marginal revenue, the profits maximizing quantity is $\overline{Q}_2$ and the corresponding price is p_2. The producer price is still equal to the consumer price. Hence, quota rents remain zero.

Quota rents remain zero as long as the allowed imports are not much lower than the free trade quantity since this ensures that the cost to the exporter of raising price in the home market in terms of forgone profit in other markets continues to be small. However, as the quota is tightened one eventually reaches a point where c^* intersects marginal revenue on its lower, sloping, segment. Such is the case when the quota limits imports to Q_3. The demand is now AB_3E_3 and marginal revenue is $AG_3H_3R_3$. Marginal cost intersects marginal revenue at V and the profit maximizing quantity and producer price are respectively $\overline{Q}_3$ and p_3. However, the price which clears the home market for the quantity Q_3 is $\hat{p}_3$. Since the consumer price is now higher than the producer price, quota rents are positive. The value of the quota is $(\hat{p}_3 - p_3)Q_3$ i.e. the shaded area in Figure 10.9. From the home country's point of view, auctioning import licences is, in this case, superior to giving them away to a foreign government as would occur under a VER.

Problem 10.8: Assume that the demands in the home and the foreign country are linear and have the same elasticity when price is the same (as in Figure 10.9). Determine how the quota at which consumer price starts diverging from producer price, varies as a function of relative country sizes.

Home and foreign market power

Now assume a Cournot duopoly involving 1 home and 1 foreign firm.[48] Their free trade reaction functions r_f and r_f^* are shown in Figure 10.10 and the free trade equilibrium occurs at point R. Under a quota (or VER) the foreign reaction function becomes kinked. When the quota limit constrains imports to the free trade level, the foreign reaction function is FRH and the equilibrium remains as under free trade. This may appear startling in the light of the result found on p. 425, which showed that a quota allowing the quantity of free trade imports results in lower output by the home firm. Note though, that there is an important difference in behavioral assumptions. On p. 425 the home firm was a Stackelberg leader, i.e. it chose quantity taking into account the response of imports to that choice. Since that response is different under a quota which allows the free trade volume

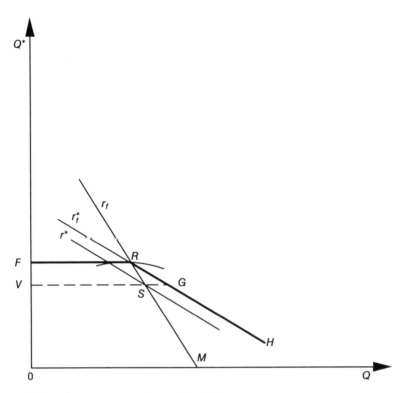

Figure 10.10   *Cournot competition with a VER*

of imports than under free trade (and under a tariff), the Stackelberg leader chooses a different quantity under the two scenarios. Under Cournot competition on the other hand, the home firm takes the quantity sold by its rivals as a given. Hence, if the quota-constrained exporter sells the same amount as under free trade, the optimal response of the home firm is to produce the free trade quantity.

A lower quota shifts the horizontal segment of the foreign reaction function downward. When the quota is more restrictive the foreign reaction function is *VGH*, and yields the same quantity equilibrium as an import tariff which lowers the foreign reaction function to r^*. Thus, under Cournot competition a tariff can be replaced by a quota which yields the same level of imports *and* the same output by both firms. Consumer prices must then also be the same.

Since a more restrictive quota slides the equilibrium point *S* downward along the reaction function r_f, it must increase the home firm's profits and decrease the exporter's profits. Under the standard assumption made in the earlier sections, r_f has slope steeper than a 45° line. Hence total quantity sold in the home market declines toward the monopoly quantity M as the quota is tightened. Hence the sum of profits earned by both firms increases as the equilibrium approaches the point M.

Problem 10.9: Use Figure 10.10 to show how a quota can be used to induce the home firm to produce the quantity it would have produced if it were a Stackelberg leader. Which tax or subsidy yields the same Stackelberg outcome?

The observation that the exporter's profits decline as the equilibrium shifts downward along r_f, suggests that foreign producers would always oppose having their exports cut back by a quota or even a VER. This in fact is true for Cournot competitors but may not be true for price setting firms.

To see why, consider Figure 10.11 where R is the free trade equilibrium since it is the intersection of the two price reaction functions r_f and r_f^*. The reaction functions are drawn under the assumptions that inverse demands

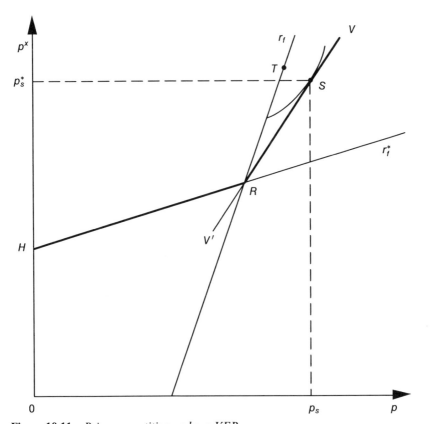

Figure 10.11 *Price competition under a VER*

are $p = a - bQ_l + kQ_x^*$ and $p^* = a - bQ_x^* + kQ_l (b > k)$ for the variety produced by the home respectively foreign firm, and that marginal costs are constant and equal for both firms.[49] The locus of price combinations p and p^* for which the demand for imports equals the free trade level of imports is shown as VV'. Clearly, VV' passes through R. It must also be flatter than r_f. To see why, note that for any upward movement along r_f, say from R to T, the imported quantity must fall since the foreign price increases more than the home price, and the former has a greater impact on the demand for the foreign variety. Thus, the increase in p^* that accompanies an increase in p must be smaller if the demand for the imported variety is to stay the same. The implication is that the upper segment of VV' must be located below r_f. Applying the same reasoning, one shows that the lower segment of VV' must be located above r_f.

Assume now that the home country sets a VER which limits exports to the free trade quantity. In that case, it must be true that for all price combinations located on r_f^* to the left of VV', the VER is not binding. Hence, the foreign firm's reaction function remains as under free trade. By contrast, for all price combinations on r_f^* to the right of R, the constraint is binding implying that the foreign reaction function is now HRV instead of r_f^*.[50]

If the home firm sets its price p first, (i.e. acts as a Stackelberg leader) and the foreign firm then chooses p^* in full knowledge of p (i.e acts as a Stackelberg follower) to ensure that it exports the quantity allowed under the VER, then the home firm will choose price to ensure an equilibrium at S, the point at which a home isoprofit curve is tangent to RV. The equilibrium involves the home firm choosing p_s and the foreign firm responding by choosing p_s^*. At S both prices are higher than under free trade. The home firm's profits are higher than under free trade and so are the profits of the foreign firm. The exporting firm gains from being restrained since it now sells the same quantity as under free trade but at a higher price.

By virtue of continuity it must be true as well that a VER which restricts exports slightly below the free trade level increases the foreign firm's profits. Hence Harris' (1985) point that voluntary export restraints may indeed be voluntary. The effect of a VER is not unlike that of collusive agreements to cut quantities in order to raise the price. This explains why VERs have been referred to as 'facilitating practices'.[51]

Endogenous product quality

None of the approaches discussed thus far considers how trade policies might affect product characteristics. To do so one needs to turn to that strand of the literature that considers the effect of trade polices on the quality of imports.

Quantitative restrictions in the form of quotas or VERs affect the quality of imports through two channels. The first is a shift in the composition of demands for individual products within the quota-restricted product category; the second is a change in the specifications of the individual products that make up the category.

Considering the composition effect first, we note if the quota raises the consumer price of each variety of a product by an equal amount – the amount of quota rent – this will have the effect of increasing the price of the more expensive varieties by less in *relative* terms than it increases the price of the lower priced varieties. Under reasonable assumptions about demand, the decline in the relative price of more expensive and, presumably, higher quality varieties, will tilt demand from the lower priced to the higher priced varieties.[52] A smaller relative increase in the price of the higher quality items is in fact assured when all prices are given to the country which imposes the quota. However, the same outcome need not follow when prices are not given since the producer prices will be adjusted taking the restrictiveness of the quota into account. Nonetheless, it is possible to show that reasonable restrictions on demand and cost yield an upgrading of quality through a change in the mix of quota constrained imports.[53]

As to changes in the quality of individual products, the intuition is that under quantity restrictions, firms will change specifications in order to increase the sales *value* derived from a given volume, since doing so increases the profit per-unit exported. This allows exporters to partially circumvent the quantitative restriction.[54] As in the case of the composition effect, some restrictions have to be imposed on cost and demand to formally derive quality upgrading of an individual product.[55]

The measurement of quality upgrading

Evidence of quality upgrading in response to quantitative restrictions can be found in several empirical studies.[56] The industry most extensively studied in this regard, both in the United States and in Europe, has been the automobile industry. Starting in the 1970s, Japanese exports of automobiles became subject to VERs. Exports to the US were restricted in 1981, and initially limited to 1.68 million units.[57] The 'voluntary' agreement followed earlier accords with the United Kingdom (1976) and France (1980) and preceded similar limitations on exports to the Benelux countries, West Germany and Sweden.[58]

The quality upgrading that ensued has been particularly noticeable in the case of exports to the US market. Table 10.1 provides summary information. The unit values which appear in row (1) are weighted averages of suggested retail prices of base models, with the quantities sold used as weights. From 1980 to 1985 the unit value rose by 55%, with over one-third of

Table 10.1[59]   *Prices and qualities of Japanese car imports in the United States, 1980–5*

	1980	1981	1982	1983	1984	1985
Cars						
Unit value	5175	6211	6834	7069	7518	8038
Price index	100.0	119.8	129.1	131.2	138.8	148.3
Unit quality	5124	5511	5896	6257	6488	6709
Quality index	100.0	107.4	112.8	117.3	121.3	125.4
Trucks						
Unit value	4937	6298	6419	6089	6261	6339
Price index	100.0	127.5	131.8	125.3	127.3	129.7
Unit quality	4943	5041	5275	5276	5274	5620
Quality index	100.0	102.1	106.4	105.5	104.7	112.3

Source: Feenstra (1988b).

the increase taking place between 1980 and 1981. This includes the combined effect of three changes: a primary price effect due to the VER and other factors such as inflation; a secondary price effect attributable to changes in the quality of individual models and, third, a price effect ascribable to a shift in the composition of demand from lower priced to higher priced models.

The price increase is more adequately measured by a price index calculated using constant weights between two years. This index, reported in row 2, shows a 48% increase from 1980 to 1985 with 60% of that increase taking place during the period 1980–2.[60] As this index still reflects the three effects on price just mentioned, we turn our attention to the econometric technique which identifies the portion of the price increase explained by quality upgrading.

The technique is known as hedonic regression and it explains changes in price by shifts in product characteristics. In the case of automobiles such characteristics are: horsepower, length, weight, gas mileage, width, etc. The basic idea behind hedonic regression is that consumers' demand ultimately depends on the services provided by a product, and that the number of services a product provides is a function of measurable characteristics.[61] Hence, price changes will reflect changes in characteristics. Hedonic regression extracts the effect of quality on price by identifying that effect with the variation in price explained by the change in product attributes alone. The residual part then is the pure price effect.

Alas, in the case of the car market, the unexplained part cannot be attributed to the VER alone. Prices in 1985 could also have been different from 1980 prices because of shifts in the cost of production and movements in exchange rates. These influences have to be netted out if one is to capture the price impact due solely to the VER.

To do so, one specifies an equation of the following form

$$p_m^t = \alpha^t + \exp\left(\beta^t + \sum_h \gamma_h^t Z_{mh}^t\right) + \varepsilon_m^t \tag{10.27}$$

where p_m^t is the list price of model m in year t and Z_{mh}^t measures characteristic h possessed by model m in year t. (10.27) allows for a *specific* price change due to the quota and captured by the coefficient α^t, and a *percentage* change due to other factors and picked up by the coefficient β^t.

However, because of multicollinearity, the coefficients α^t and β^t cannot be precisely estimated when data on the car market alone are used. Fortunately, this problem can be remedied by pooled regression on the prices of cars and trucks. Japanese truck imports were not subjected to a VER but to a 21% import tariff. This is a percentage change in price. In the absence of a quota one expects no additional specific price change. Hence, one can specify the hedonic equation for trucks with the term α omitted. Formally,

$$\hat{p}_m^t = \exp\left(\hat{\beta}^t + \sum_h \gamma_h^t \hat{Z}_{mh}^t\right) + \hat{\varepsilon}_m^t \tag{10.28}$$

where, except for the 'hat' which indicates that the variables pertain to trucks, the notation is the same as for cars.

(10.27) and (10.28) are then estimated from the pooled car and truck data subject to the cross-equation constraints $\beta_{1980} = \hat{\beta}_{1980}$ and $\beta^t = \hat{\beta}^t - 0.16$, where $t = 1981, 1982, \ldots 1984$. The number 0.16 captures the effect of the tariff levied on the imports of trucks in August 1980.[62]

Table 10.2 reports the estimated coefficient except the βs. The coefficients at the bottom of the table clearly indicate the important effect the VER has had on price. In 1983 and 1984 it increased the average price of a Japanese car at the retail level by more than $1000.

Once the coefficients are estimated they can be used to calculate the quality of individual models as the predicted price with the contribution of the dummies excluded (i.e. $\exp(\beta_{1980} + \sum_h \gamma_h^t Z_{mh}^t)$). The predicted qualities can then be averaged. The unit qualities reported in row 3 of Table 10.1 are obtained by averaging the qualities of the individual models using the quantities sold in each year as weights. Thus, variations reported in row 3 reflect the quality change of individual models *and* the shifts in demand across models. The quality index in row 4, by contrast, is calculated using constant weights. It therefore gives a measure of the change in quality of individual models.[63]

Rows 3 and 4 in Table 10.1 reveal that upgrading occurred both through a composition effect and through an increase in the quality of individual models. They also show that the increase in the quality of individual models alone accounted for more than half of the increase in price over the period

Table 10.2 *Hedonic regression for Japanese car and truck exports to the United States*

	Cars	Trucks
Constant	6.80*	7.01*
Weight (tons)	0.002	0.32*
Width (feet)	0.35*	0.11
Height (feet)	−0.16*	0.091
Horsepower (100)	0.70*	0.066
Transmission (5-speed or auto)	0.16*	0.081*
Power steering	0.073*	0.008
Air conditioning	0.17*	
Four-wheel drive		0.21*
α_{1981}	434	
α_{1982}	707*	
α_{1983}	1085*	
α_{1984}	1096*	
α_{1984}	256	

Starred variables are significant at the 95% level. The number of observations is 254 and $R^2 = 0.917$.
Source: Feenstra (1988b).

1980–85. The largest increases took place immediately following the VER. The same calculations carried out for trucks also reveal an increase in quality, but a more modest one. This suggests that the VER may not be the only factor explaining the quality upgrading of cars.

10.5 **Contingent protection**

'Contingent protection' refers to trade restrictions imposed in response to certain actions by foreign governments or foreign firms that the importing country deems injurious to the local industry. Two common types of contingent protection are tariffs applied on imports held to be dumped and tariffs levied on the import of goods that have benefited from export subsidies. The former are called anti-dumping tariffs, the latter counter-vailing tariffs.

'Dumping' is the sale of a good for export at a price below its normal value. 'Normal value' is defined as the comparable price of the same or similar product in the exporting country.[64] The difference between the export price and normal value is referred to as the 'margin of dumping'. Under GATT rules, the importing country may counter dumping with a duty against the parties found to engage in dumping, if the dumped imports have been or are likely to be a cause of injury to the home industry.[65] GATT provisions also limit the rate of antidumping duty to the margin of dumping. The decision to impose an antidumping duty may be suspended or terminated if the offending exporter revises export prices upwards or agrees to limit the volume of its exports.

Countervailing duties are intended to offset the effects of foreign subsidies. Current WTO rules permit an importing country to levy countervailing duties only against subsidies deemed *specific,* i.e. targeted at specific firms, industries or at specific activities. Subsidies conditional on export performance and subsidies that give producers incentives to use local inputs in preference to imported inputs are explicitly prohibited. Declared immune from any challenge under WTO rules are non-specific subsidies as well as a number of specific subsidies explicitly listed, e.g. certain forms of R&D assistance. The remaining subsidies, fall in a third category called 'actionable subsidies'. Prohibited and actionable subsidies can be opposed using a multilateral dispute resolution track (track I) or by means of countervailing duties (track II). If the latter route is chosen, procedures and remedies are very similar to those of antidumping. Specifically, a countervailing duty may be imposed only if the subsidized imports are shown to cause injury to the domestic industry, and the rate of duty may not exceed the rate of subsidy. Under WTO rules, antidumping and countervailing duties lapse after 5 years.

For modelling purposes, the differences between a conventional tariff and an antidumping or countervailing duty fall under the following headings: (1) Uncertainty of application (e.g. Will the local industry file a complaint? Will a determination of dumping or subsidy be made? How will the rate of duty compare to the margin of dumping?). (2) The time period between the initiation of an action and the application of a duty or the reaching of a settlement, if any. (3) The length of time during which the duty remains in effect. These characteristics of contingent protection are the basis of strategic interactions that display some striking differences from those of conventional tariffs.

Dumping and anti-dumping

Dumping can be classified as either persistent or sporadic. Sporadic dumping is generally coupled to downturns in the business cycle, while persistent dumping is thought to be associated with the application of market power.

Formal analyzes of sporadic dumping are relatively recent in the literature.[66] In this regard, Ethier (1982) shows that dumping, defined as pricing
below cost, can be profit maximizing for competitive firms in periods of low
demand if input prices are fixed in time and factor use cannot be adjusted
freely to fluctuations in demand.[67] Clarida (1993) shows that dumping (also
defined as below cost sales) can arise from the excessive numbers of new
firms which enter in periods of high demand. Gruenspecht (1988) demonstrates that in the presence of learning effects, the trade-off between current
and future costs can result in a positive calculated margin of dumping in the
current period, even if the present value of the margin is zero.[68]

Persistent dumping is traditionally viewed as the outcome of a foreign
firm discriminating between its local market and a foreign market.
Assuming that demand in the foreign market is more elastic than in the
local market, profit maximization implies that the firm will practice third
degree price discrimination if markets are segmented – that is, it will
maximize profits by setting a lower price in the foreign market.

Extension of this analysis to a setting which accounts for essential features
of the countermeasures that may be taken by the importing country are
Ethier and Fischer (1987), Dixit (1988a), Fischer (1992) and Reitzes (1993).
Below we consider the main conclusions of these studies by considering the
model of Fischer (1992).

Assume there are 2 firms, 1 home and 1 foreign. The home firm sells only
locally while the foreign firm sells in its own market and also exports to the
home market. The 2 markets are segmented, and the home and foreign firms
produce goods that are imperfect substitutes. Profits are maximized over a
2-period horizon. During the first period the home country does not impose
an antidumping duty. Nonetheless the existence of an antidumping law
affects each firm's first-period decision since it influences the probability that
an antidumping tariff will be levied in the second period.

Denote the inverse home demands for the home and foreign variety as
$p_l = p(Q_l, Q_x^*)$ and $p_x = p(Q_x^*, Q_l)$ respectively, where $\partial p_l / \partial Q < \partial p_l / \partial Q_x^* < 0$
and similarly for p_x. Unit costs are the same for both firms. The probability
that an antidumping tariff will be levied in the second period in response to
dumping in the first period is denoted $m(s)$ and $m'(s) > 0$. The variable 's'
subsumes all the factors relevant to such action, i.e. to a finding of dumping
and a finding of injury caused by dumping.

Let Δ^* be the difference between the second period profits earned by the
foreign firm under the antidumping and the no antidumping scenarios.
Similarly, let Δ represent the profit difference for the home firm under these
two scenarios. With π_t denoting the profits of the home firm in period t,
$[t = \{1,2\}]$ in the absence of an antidumping action, the expected second
period profit of the home firm is $E(\pi_2) = m(s)\Delta + \pi_2$. Similarly, the expected
second period profit for the foreign firm is $E(\pi_2^*) = m(s)\Delta^* + \pi_2^*$. Total

expected profits are therefore

$$E(\pi) = \pi_1 + E(\pi_2) = p_l Q_l - c Q_l + m(s)\Delta + \pi_2$$

(for the home firm)

$$E(\pi^*) = \pi_1^* + E(\pi_2^*) = p_x Q_x^* - c Q_x^* + m(s)\Delta^* + \pi_2^*$$

(for the foreign firm)

To analyze how the threat of a second period antidumping duty affects first period behavior we must first specify (1) whether firms choose price or quantity, (2) how firms' choices affect the probability of action in the second period and, (3) how these choices affect Δ and Δ^*.

We limit ourselves to the case of quantity setting firms (one of the cases explored by Fischer, 1992) and we let $s = Q_x^*/Q_l$, i.e. we assume that action is more likely if the home firm has a lower market share.[69] Under Cournot rivalry, the first-order conditions are

$$\frac{\partial E\pi}{\partial Q_l} = p(Q_l, Q_x^*) + Q_l \frac{\partial p(Q_l, Q_x^*)}{\partial Q_l} - c$$

$$+ \left[\Delta m'(s) \frac{\partial s}{\partial Q_l} + m(s) \frac{\partial \Delta}{\partial Q_l} \right] = 0 \qquad (10.29a)$$

$$\frac{\partial E\pi^*}{\partial Q_x^*} = p(Q_x^*, Q_l) + Q_x^* \frac{\partial p(Q_x^*, Q_l)}{\partial Q_x^*} - c$$

$$+ \left[\Delta^* m'(s) \frac{\partial s}{\partial Q_x^*} + m(s) \frac{\partial \Delta^*}{\partial Q_x^*} \right] = 0 \qquad (10.29b)$$

where the 2 terms in square brackets capture the expected effect of first period decisions on second period profits.

The first of these terms is negative in (10.29a) as well as in (10.29b) since $\Delta > 0$ and $\Delta^* < 0$ under an antidumping tariff. These terms show that the threat of an antidumping action gives each producer an incentive to reduce output. The benefit derived by the home firm from a lower first period output flows from the increased probability of antidumping action. The foreign firm draws the benefit from its decrease in exports from a lowering of the probability that antidumping action will be taken. Since taking account of the effect of contemporaneous quantity decisions on future profits is formally equivalent to an increase in marginal cost, it must shift both reaction functions downward. Hence, total quantity is lower than if antidumping action were ruled out. When $\Delta = -\Delta^*$ the equilibrium is symmetric and thus Q as well as Q^* must be lower in equilibrium.

If $\Delta < (>) \Delta^*$the market share of the home firm will be smaller (larger) than that of the foreign firm.

Now consider the second component in each bracketed term.[70] Since a higher margin of dumping is likely to result in a higher antidumping tariff, it is reasonable to consider that Δ and Δ^* will increase in absolute value when the home price of the foreign variety falls in response to an increase in Q_x^*. In the case of the foreign firm, this would provide an added incentive to decrease quantity. The home firm, by contrast, faces the following trade off: By restricting quantity it increases the probability of an antidumping action but, at the same time, it raises the home price of the foreign variety thereby lowering the margin of dumping. Since the margin, more often than not, will be chosen as the rate of antidumping duty, the home firm would prefer it to be found as high as possible. This is an incentive to *increase* output. The net effect of the two components of the bracketed term in (10.29a) on the quantity set by the home firm thus appears ambiguous.

To carry the analysis further requires that the terms Δ and Δ^* be given specific content, and that the relation between the rate of antidumping duty and s be made explicit. Specifically, one must model how antidumping action affects the difference between first and second period profits and how the antidumping tariff relates to the margin of dumping.[71]

Early settlement of anti-dumping cases

An antidumping petition is often withdrawn by the home industry before a determination of dumping is made. Such withdrawal is usually made upon a commitment by exporters to raise price by an agreed amount (called a price undertaking) or to restrict the volume of exports (a quantity undertaking). Stegemann (1990) reports that during the period 1980–8, the European Commission accepted price or quantity undertakings in 202 cases versus 60 cases in which an antidumping duty was imposed. Prusa (1992) found the number of cases suspended or terminated in the US in the early 1980s to be nearly equal to the number of cases in which duties were levied. He also found that US imports of products for which petitions were withdrawn displayed a decline similar to that of imports that were subjected to an antidumping duty. The inference one can draw from the latter observation is that a withdrawal of a petition should not be viewed as evidence of failure by the petitioning industry.

The finding that two parties would be willing to enter into an agreement if they knew with certainty the rate of antidumping duty to be levied absent an agreement is intuitive. Indeed, if the foreign firm were willing to set its price at the post-tariff consumer price, or alternatively, if it were willing to reduce its exports to the post-tariff level, the home firm would earn no less than under the duty. Exporters would be better off since they would pocket what would otherwise be government revenue. The undertaking route must therefore provide an opportunity for mutually beneficial bargaining.

Prusa (1992) shows that bargaining is also mutually beneficial when the outcome of the petition is not known with certainty. More importantly, he argues that the settlement process in an antidumping case is fundamentally different from a standard bargaining game in which players decide on the division of a 'pie' of given size. The settlement process provides a framework which facilitates the setting of prices which generate higher profits for all producers, home and foreign. The implication is that the initiation of an anti-dumping petition facilitates a cooperative outcome that approaches a collusive equilibrium. The major difference with collusion of the ordinary kind then, is that when an antidumping procedure is instrumental in reaching the agreement, the parties are immune from prosecution under competition law.

In this regard it is interesting to note that four industries (chemicals, steel, electrical and non-electrical machinery) accounted for more than two-thirds of EC antidumping petitions during the period 1980–9. Over the same period 30 anti-cartel cases were initiated (25% of all anti-cartel cases) dealing with products also involved in almost 100 antidumping cases (25% of all antidumping cases).[72]

Export subsidies and countervailing duties

On p. 414 the claim was made that when demand is linear the welfare maximizing response to a foreign subsidy is to raise the import tariff by an amount less than the subsidy. This raises the question whether a country which gains from subsidizing its exports when its trading partners adopt a free trade stance, still gains when the importing countries retaliate by imposing a countervailing duty (CVD).

This question can be examined in the framework of a game played over a T-period horizon.[73] At the beginning of the first period the foreign government sets an export subsidy which remains in effect for the entire duration of the game. The subsidy triggers a CVD action by the home country but, since procedures take time, the duty is imposed only at the beginning of the $(t + 1)$th period. It then stays in effect until the end of period T.

The game, solved by backward induction, unfolds as follows: during each period, 1 home and 1 foreign firm engage in Cournot competition and their quantity choices are affected by contemporaneous trade policies, i.e. the foreign subsidy in the first t periods and, the foreign subsidy plus the countervailing duty in the remaining $T - t$ periods. The tariff which maximizes home welfare is determined by a home government which views the foreign subsidy as a given but takes into account the effects of the tariff on firms' quantity choices in the post-tariff era. The final step is the determination of the foreign subsidy which maximizes foreign welfare. It is chosen by the foreign government taking into account the effects on the ensuing quantity equilibrium in the t retaliation-free periods, the coming countervailing response, and the quantity response by the 2 firms to the subsidy *and* the tariff in the final $T - t$ periods.

The effects of countervail can then be examined by verifying how the optimal subsidy is affected by: (1) the expeditiousness of the procedures;[74] (2) the effect of the GATT constraint which bounds the countervailing duty to the rate of subsidy.

This analysis is conducted in a framework which assumes linear demands and shows that the optimal subsidy is zero when retaliation is faster than some cut-off value and positive when it is slower. In the latter case the rate of subsidy is positively related to the delay in countervailing action. This can be explained as follows: from the foreign country welfare point of view, the benefits from profit shifting during the retaliation-free periods must be set against the losses suffered during the retaliation periods. This explains why the subsidization of exports becomes profitable only when retaliation is sufficiently delayed.

Also, one finds that the GATT constraint is always binding.[75] Comparing the equilibrium which emerges when the GATT constraint is imposed to the equilibrium which prevails when it is not, reveals 2 distinct effects. The first is that swifter retaliation is required for subsidization not to occur. This is due to a reduction in the losses (compared to free trade) during the retaliation periods. The second effect of the constraint is to lower the optimal subsidy rate in those cases where the retaliation delay is longer. The reason is that since the impact of retaliation is not as severe, a lower subsidy is sufficient to maintain the exporter's market share.

The conclusions that emerge are that CVDs reduce but not necessarily eliminate the profitability of export subsidies, and that a constraint on the amount of duty lessens the deterrence effect of countervailing tariffs.

Finally it must be stressed that a petition for countervail, just like an antidumping petition, may be withdrawn upon the successful negotiation of an undertaking between subsidized exporters and the home industry. As in the case of dumping examined earlier, such settlement has the potential to make both parties better off. Subsidization could therefore benefit the foreign economy not through profit shifting, but by triggering a CVD petition which produces a settlement that allows the exporting industry to earn a higher profit margin on a lower export volume.

10.6 Quantification: computable partial equilibrium modelling

Quantitative work on trade policy in oligopolistic markets has made extensive use of computable equilibrium models. As discussed in Chapter 5 the approach contains a sequence of steps. First, a model deemed to capture the essential strategic features of the industry is drafted. Second, the model is calibrated, i.e. parameter values of the model are determined to fit the observations of some chosen base year. These parameter values are established on the basis of external sources of information that typically include previous econometric work and engineering studies, and on the analyst's judgment. Finally, simulation exercises are performed on the fully identified model. These typically indicate how changes in policy, tariffs, for example, affect prices, quantities and welfare in a market.

In what follows we use Dixit's (1988b) pioneering study of the rivalry between American and Japanese automobile producers to illustrate the basic approach and the kind of results obtained.[76] The main goal of the Dixit (1988b) paper is to calculate the tariff and subsidy policies that would have been optimal in 1979 and 1980 as the import penetration of Japanese cars increased sharply, and to compare them with the policies that were in effect at the time. Since the approach is partial equilibrium only the car market is modelled and demands as well as costs are assumed given.[77] The model postulates that demands for American and Japanese automobiles by US consumers take the form

$$Q = A - Bp + Kp^*$$
$$Q^* = A^* - B^*p^* + Kp \tag{10.30}$$

where Q and p [Q^* and p^*] represent the quantity and the price at which the US [Japanese] made automobiles are sold in the United States. The parameters A, A^*, B, B^*, and K are positive and $BB^* - K^2 > 0$. The demand specifications (10.30) assume that US and Japanese cars are imperfect substitutes but that the varieties produced within each country are perfect substitutes. The inverse demands are

$$p = a - b - bQ - kQ^* \tag{10.31a}$$
$$p^* = a^* - b^*Q^* - kQ \tag{10.31b}$$

where $bb^* - k^2 > 0$. These demands are assumed to originate from a utility function of the form $u = U(Q, Q^*) + M$ where M is consumption of an aggregate numeraire good measured in real dollars and $U(Q, Q^*) = aQ + a^*Q^* - \frac{1}{2}[bQ^2 + b^*Q^{*2} + 2kQQ^*]$. Unit production costs are assumed to be constants, equal to c for the US and c^* for Japan. Markets are segmented.

In the presence of a (specific) subsidy σ to American producers and a (specific) tariff τ on US automobile imports from Japan, the per-firm profits earned on US sales are

$$\pi = [p(Q, Q^*) - (c - \sigma)]q$$

and

$$\pi^* = [p^*(Q, Q^*) - (c^* + \tau)]q^*$$

where q and q^* denote output per US and Japanese firm. Taking quantity as the decision variable, the first-order conditions for US and Japanese firms are, respectively,

$$p + q \frac{\partial p}{\partial q} = c - \sigma \quad \text{with} \quad \frac{\partial p}{\partial q} = \left(\frac{\partial p}{\partial Q} \frac{\partial Q}{\partial q} + \frac{\partial p}{\partial Q^*} \frac{\partial Q^*}{\partial q} \right) \qquad (10.32a)$$

$$p^* + q^* \frac{\partial p^*}{\partial q^*} = c + \tau \quad \text{with} \quad \frac{\partial p^*}{\partial q^*} = \left(\frac{\partial p^*}{\partial Q} \frac{\partial Q}{\partial q^*} + \frac{\partial p^*}{\partial Q^*} \frac{\partial Q^*}{\partial q^*} \right) \qquad (10.32b)$$

Under Cournot rivalry, $\partial p / \partial q = -b$ and $\partial p^* / \partial q^* = -b^*$. A more competitive market than Cournot would have conjectural variation terms $\partial Q / \partial q < 1$ and/or $\partial Q^* / \partial q < 0$ so that $0 > \partial p / \partial q > -b$. The same logic can be applied to interpret how the degree of competition would affect $\partial p^* / \partial q^*$.

Summing (10.32a) over individual firms and dividing the sum by the number of US firms which is denoted n, and then substituting from (10.31a) yields

$$(a - bQ - kQ^*) - Q\Psi = c - \sigma \quad \text{where} \quad \Psi = -\frac{1}{n} \frac{\partial p}{\partial q} \qquad (10.33a)$$

Similarly, for the Japanese industry,

$$(a^* - b^*Q^* - kQ) - Q^*\Psi^* = c^* + \tau \quad \text{where} \quad \Psi^* = -\frac{1}{n^*} \frac{\partial p^*}{\partial q^*} \qquad (10.33b)$$

The terms Ψ and Ψ^* are an aggregate version of the conjectural variation parameter discussed in Chapter 9. In the case of Cournot conduct the parameters are respectively equal to $-b/n$ and $-b^*/n^*$. For conduct more (less) competitive than Cournot $\Psi > (<) - b/n$ and $\Psi^* > (<) - b^*/n^*$. This means in particular that Ψ and Ψ^* yield the same equilibrium as would $\hat{n} = b/\Psi$ American firms and $\hat{n}^* = b^*/\Psi^*$ Japanese firms engaged in Cournot competition.

Calibration and interpretation

If the values of the parameters a, a^*, b, b^*, k as well as the two prices, quantities, costs and the tariff and subsidy were known, (10.33) could be solved for Ψ and Ψ^*. In fact not all parameters are known. Calibration is the procedure by which the unknown parameters are determined. Some of the external information used in the calibration can be put directly into (10.33), other information can be used only to infer restrictions on parameter values which appear as additional equations. The calibration of the Dixit model is as follows.

Quantities and values for imports and locally produced goods are obtained from trade and manufacturing tabulations and used to calculate unit values that proxy for prices. Trade policy variables are also known. Cost figures are more difficult to obtain. Dixit surveys a number of studies and chooses values for c and c^* in the range of available estimates.

The remaining external information serves to generate 3 additional equations which in combination with the 2 demand equations constitute a system from which the 5 parameters a, a^*, b, b^*, and k can be solved.

Using values of demand parameters from econometric and engineering estimates, Dixit concludes that the own price elasticity of total demand for automobiles is (about) unity. In the context of the model this is given the interpretation that an equiproportional change in prices of 1% by all firms changes aggregate car sales by 1%. That is, writing $p = p_0 P$ and $p^* = p_0^* P$ where p_0 and p_0^* are prices in a base period, and defining the quantity aggregate $Q = p_{u0} Q_0 + p_{j0} Q_j$, market elasticity can be written $-P dQ / Q dP = 1$. Using (10.30) and setting $P = 1$, the following equality follows: $Q[B P_0^2 + B^* p_0^{*2} - 2K p_0^2 p_0^{*2}] = 1$.

A second equation derives from the formula of the elasticity of substitution $d \log(Q/Q^*)/d \log(p/p^*)$ which, according to econometric estimates, equals 2. Developing this expression yields a second equation.[78]

Finally (10.30) can be used to derive $Q/Q^* = [A(1/p^*) - B(p/p^*) + K]/[A^*(1/p^*) + K(p/p^*) - B^*]$. Imposing the condition that Q/Q^* is a function of p/p^* alone at the initial equilibrium point requires that $\partial(Q/Q^*)/\partial(1/p^*) = 0$ at $p = p_0$ and $p^* = p_0^*$ and generates the final additional equation: $p_0[AK + A^* B] = p_0^*[A^* K + A B^*]$.

By solving the 5-equation system one obtains values for the 5 unknown parameters which can be inserted into (10.33) to yield values for Ψ and Ψ^*. These values in turn, are used to calculate $\hat{n}$ and $\hat{n}^*$, i.e. the number of Cournot equivalent US and Japanese firms that would have yielded the observed outcome.

Once the demand parameters have been identified, one can also, by imposing (instead of calculating) conjectural variation parameters derive the equilibria that would have prevailed if firms acted as Cournot or Bertrand competitors. The results of these calculations are displayed in Table 10.3.

Table 10.3 indicates that conduct was more competitive in 1980 than in 1979. It also shows that in each of these years the Cournot equivalent number of US firms was considerably larger than the actual number, implying that US firms were playing more competitive than Cournot firms.

Table 10.3 *Market conduct and policy calculations, 1979–83*

	1979	1980	1983
Cournot equivalent number of firms			
USA	10.17	19.12	13.85
Japan	4.46	10.49	4.16
US car prices ($)			
Actual	5951	6407	7494
Cournot conduct	7280	8099	9217
Bertrand conduct	5400	6100	7000
Japanese car prices ($)			
Actual	4000	4130	5239
Cournot conduct	4128	4525	5320
Bertrand conduct	3400	3800	4400

Source: Dixit (1988b).

Table 10.3 also compares the actual prices with the prices that would have prevailed if conduct had been Cournot or Bertrand. Finally, the 1983 numbers show the extent of collusion that would have been needed (in the absence of a VER) to replicate the equilibrium that was in fact observed under the VER. The second row of Table 10.3 indicates that the VER brought about the same equilibrium that would have obtained under increased collusion by the Japanese exporters. As shown, the number of Japanese Cournot equivalent firms dropped sharply from 1980 to 1983 and the actual price of Japanese cars, which in 1980 was about halfway between the price under Cournot and the price under Bertrand conduct, was close to Cournot in 1983. By contrast, collusion by the US manufacturers does not appear to have been greatly strengthened.

Since prices were above Bertrand levels, some monopoly power was present in the market, and thus there was *a priori* a role for tariffs and subsidies. The optimal intervention can be calculated since all the parameters of the model are now available. The optimal tariff and subsidy from the U.S point of view are obtained from the maximization of the welfare function

$$W = [U(Q, Q^*) - pQ - p^*Q^*] + [p - c + \sigma]Q + \tau Q^* - \sigma Q$$

where the first and second term respectively denote U.S consumer surplus and profits, while the last terms represent tariff revenues and subsidy payments. The optimal tariff and subsidy can be compared to the values of the trade policy variables in effect at the time. This is done in Table 10.4, first for the case when tariff policy alone is used, then for the case where the subsidy is the only instrument used and finally, for the case where both a

Table 10.4 *Optimal tariffs and subsidies, 1980*

Variable unit		Actual tariff	Optimum tariff	Optimum subsidy	Optimum tariff and subsidy
τ	$/car	100	298	0	211
σ	$/car	0	0	372	325
US consum.surp.	$billion	24.49	24.14	27.01	26.33
US profit	$billion	1.95	1.98	2.20	2.19
Japan profit	$billion	0.46	0.39	27.01	0.39
Tariff revenue	$billion	0.20	0.55	0	0.39
Subsidy cost	$billion	0	0	2.51	2.19
Total US welfare	$billion	26.64	26.66	26.70	26.71

Source: Dixit (1988b).

tariff and a production subsidy are utilized. In each of these cases the optimal policy is derived assuming that the values of Ψ and Ψ^* remain unaffected by the policy.

When both instruments are used, the subsidy serves the objective of eliminating the monopoly distortion and the tariff serves to shift profits from Japanese to US firms. When only one instrument is used it must serve both objectives. This explains why the optimal subsidy is higher when it is the only instrument than when two instruments are used. When $p = c$ a further increase in the subsidy creates a deadweight burden of the second-order from driving price below marginal cost, while the gains from profit shifting are of the first-order. Similarly, the tariff is higher when it is the only instrument used since the tariff also increases production in the US and the latter increases welfare since $p > c$. The calculated values show that if the tariff alone were used it would have been optimal to set it about three times higher than the tariff in effect at the time. Still, the estimated welfare gains of either policy alone or combined are small.[79]

Caveats

Subsequent papers have reexamined the effect of trade policy in the automobile market. Krishna *et al.* considered the US market for the period 1979–85. They specified a demand which allows product differentiation not just between countries but also within countries. They found that the conduct of US producers was *more* competitive than Bertrand. This can be explained as follows: If one assumes that the US producers sell homogeneous goods, then Bertrand behavior implies that price is equal to marginal cost and hence, any equilibrium with price in excess of marginal cost must be less competitive than Bertrand. With differentiation, however, Bertrand rivalry yields a positive mark-up and a finding that the actual mark-up is lower than the Bertrand mark-up would imply that conduct is more competitive than Bertrand.[80] Krishna *et al.* (1994) also found that it is optimal to subsidize imports. This should not come as a surprise since the demand in their model is very convex and this entails $MR' - p' > 0$. As in Dixit (1988b), the welfare effects are found to be small.

The numbers generated by computable models do evidently also depend on whether one assumes that the market under investigation is segmented or connected to other markets. In this regard, it should be noted that recent literature has criticized the sharp delineation between segmentation and connection by arbitrage as extreme, and not in conformity with actual practice. In response, an intermediate approach, modelled as a 2-stage game, has been proposed.[81] In the first stage, firms choose a total capacity or quantity, each taking as given the total capacity or quantity chosen by their rivals. In the second stage, output is distributed between markets conditional on output or capacity chosen at the first stage. The segmented market game played in the second stage may be either Cournot or Bertrand.[82] In models of this intermediate type, the effect of tariffs and subsidies spill over from one market to the other even when price differences are not arbitraged away.[83]

Finally, we must emphasize that the caveats discussed in Chapter 5 on the use of applied general equilibrium models apply equally to the partial equilibrium models. These models allow the analyst to quantify interactions between variables and to gain insights into firms' responses to policy changes, but they do not provide a test of theory. Results derived from calibrated partial equilibrium model are to be regarded with great caution. Sensitivity tests, such as changing marginal cost or elasticities, give some indication of robustness, but are difficult to interpret since they involve a recalibration of the model. For example, using a different value of cost will change in calculated value of the intensity of competition.

10.7 **Implications for trade policy**

This chapter's analysis of trade policy has drawn on the tools of industrial organization and has shown that intuitions stemming from perfectly competitive settings are likely to be misleading when markets are oligopolistic. Having worked one's way through a number of sections that underscored how export taxes or subsidies could be used to produce gains in the form of profit transfers, and which underlined why countries need not be large to derive favorable terms of trade effects from import tariffs, one may ask whether interventions in the trade arena designed to tilt in one's favor the outcome of oligopolistic interaction now enjoy theoretical support. Since much trade is conducted by corporations enjoying market shares that could be viewed as *prima facie* evidence of market power, this chapter's results beg the more general question whether the case in favor of free trade as a guiding principle for policy, has been significantly weakened.

The majority consensus emerging from the contributors to the literature on trade policy is that the case for interventionism is hardly strengthened by the findings summarized in this chapter.[84] The essence of their arguments is that while the existence of welfare improving policy prescriptions within the framework of *a* model is a necessary condition to recommend a deviation from free trade, it is not a sufficient one.

In the case of imperfect competition, there is first and foremost the issue of robustness. None of the models of rivalry examined in this chapter captures oligopolistic competition in all its complexity, but even a comparison of the simplest models shows that policy recommendations derived from the assumption of quantity competition can be radically different from those flowing from models which posit that price is the variable of choice. Even with Cournot competition, changing assumptions regarding freedom of entry or the segmentation of markets sometimes alters the type of policy that is optimal. Unfortunately, making a determination as to whether prices are equalized across markets, and to what extent entry is curbed is not a simple exercise.[85] The design of a policy that fits the circumstance of a particular industry so that it improves welfare with a high degree of probability must therefore impose information requirements unlikely to be met in practice.

These requirements multiply if one considers that, in addition to the risk of choosing the improper instrument, there is a danger of targeting the wrong industry. A policy whose aim it is to increase the contribution to welfare of one oligopolistic industry may lower overall welfare since binding endowment constraints may cause other oligopolistic industries to contract, lowering their contribution to welfare.[86] Overall optimization is even less likely when trade intervention is decided upon one industry at the time, as is likely if one tailors policy to changing circumstances.

Commitment problems cannot be overlooked. Consider, for example, a subsidy policy whose aim it is to generate investments that will expand the home production capacity and allow a home firm to capture a larger share of the world market. If the government is unable to credibly precommit to terminate its program at a particular date, the beneficiary has an incentive not to carry out all the investments that would allow it to capture the intended market share. If it expects that the factors and objectives that were instrumental in getting the subsidy started in the current period will play themselves out in similar fashion upon expiry of the current program if the objective is not fully met, it will invest less. Indeed, since under the credible commitment scenario, the last dollar invested must contribute a discounted future revenue stream of 1 dollar, it must be true that under a less than fully credible scenario, investment is less since a smaller capacity makes it more likely that the subsidy policy will be renewed.[87]

Even if a government could somehow resolve the information and commitment problems, its policy would not have the intended effects if trading partners attempted to exploit their own market power through the application of similar instruments. While free trade may not appear welfare maximizing under oligopoly for given policies of trading partners, one's own interventions may well trigger retaliatory actions that make all parties worse off than free trade.

Political economy considerations also weigh heavily against selective interventionism. The cost of lobbying to obtain the most favorable treatment is a resource cost that must be set against any eventual gain from intervention. Resources spent on lobbying are determined primarily by the redistributive effect of the policies one lobbies for.[88] The willingness to use strategic policy would amplify the wasteful spending of resources to obtain such transfers. Also, since the determination of trade policy is made through the political process, one must expect that small groups with a keen appreciation of their gains from protectionist measures will more successfully influence governments than the perhaps more numerous groups with more diffuse stakes. This is likely to affect the weighting of producers relative to consumers in the welfare function that elected officials will seek to maximize.

Finally, it must be stressed that by drawing a sharp delineation between home and foreign firms this chapter has passed over the policy implications of cross-ownership. Ownership by one country's residents of shares in a firm located in another country, complicates the welfare implications of tariffs and subsidies. The profits accruing to firms located in the home country are no longer in their entirety part of home welfare, whereas part of the profits of firms operating in foreign markets are part of home welfare.[89] Foreign shareholding also raises the possibility that firms located in different countries operate under common management and hence respond differently to trade policy than independent profit maximizers. This raises a new set of issues taken up in Chapter 11.

Notes

1. See, for example, Katrak (1979), Auquier and Caves (1979) and Brander and Spencer (1984).
2. Key references are Brander and Krugman (1983), Brander and Spencer (1984, 1985), Spencer and Brander (1983) and Eaton and Grossman (1986).

3. This section draws primarily on Brander and Spencer (1984, 1985), Eaton and Grossman (1986) and Helpman and Krugman (1989).

4. The analysis, except for some adjustments to the welfare analysis, is the same if one allows a home industry made up of price taking firms.

5. We assume here that utility is of the form $u = U(Q^*) + M$ where M is consumption of a numeraire good. This utility function is practical for welfare analysis since marginal utility of the numeraire good is constant which implies that welfare changes are exactly measured by the surplus method. The inverse demand is $p = U'(Q^*)$.

6. These results remain valid in the presence of price-taking foreign firms.

7. This latter assumption does affect the results, but allows us to use a simpler notation.

8. Since tax revenue is a purely internal transfer.

9. To show this, rewrite (10.7) as $p^* + Qp^{*\prime} - c - [\{1 - (1/n)\}Qp^{*\prime} - c\theta] = 0$ and set the term in square brackets equal to zero.

10. They are drawn assuming linear demand and equal marginal costs in both countries.

11. S must be a tangency point for otherwise a point on r_f^* slightly to the right of S would be more profitable for the home firm. The point R cannot be a tangency point since the home firm's isoprofit curves are horizontal at the point where they intersect r. Finally, since r_f^* is downward sloping and the isoprofit curve passing through R has zero slope at R, it must be that a point of tangency between r_f^* and an isoprofit curve is located as shown in Figure 10.3.

12. The reason is given in Chapter 9.

13. Note that we assume, in contrast to the homogeneous good analysis of Bertrand competition in Chapter 9, that each firm sells a different variety of the good.

14. See Tirole (1988, p. 209).

15. To determine that S is located to the northeast of R use the same reasoning as in the Cournot case.

16. Recall from Chapter 5 that with perfect competition each country's gains from trade are lower when all countries choose their optimal tariff then if all traded freely.

17. This yields a perfect Nash equilibrium, i.e. the components of the equilibrium strategies are themselves Nash equilibria in the subgames. The solution to such game is found by solving the problem backwards. First, firms' optimal decisions are determined for *given* government policies, then the policies themselves are chosen taking into account the effects they have on firm behavior.

18. Recall that this condition is satisified unless the demand is very convex.

19. The welfare maximizing taxes would yield the monopoly quantity.

20. Analyses of subsidies under different assumptions are found in de Meza (1986) and Neary (1994).

21. See Chapter 9 (p. 338).

22. For the foreign firm the tariff is formally equivalent to an increase in marginal cost.

23. This result is obtained by Dixit (1988a). Since an export subsidy is equivalent from the recipient's point of view to a decrease in cost it suggests that the optimal home

response to a foreign subsidy is a countervailing tariff. Countervail is further examined in Section 10.6.

24. See Chapter 9 (p. 333).

25. The model presented in this section follows Venables (1985).

26. Venables (1985) shows that for non-linear demands the slopes of the zero profit also bear this relationship to each other when $q_l > q_x^*$ and $q_l^* > q_x^*$. We know from p. 338 that this will be the case when $c < c^* + \tau$ and $c^* < c + \tau$.

27. See Venables (1985).

28. Section 9.1 has already pointed out that it does not matter whether firms actually deliver the good to individual markets or leave the cross-country allocation of the total quantity to be carried out by competitive arbitrageurs.

29. See Markusen and Venables (1988).

30. Similarly, a home export subsidy lowers the price of the home variety, resulting in a decline in the price of the imported variety.

31. The material in this section is based on Horstmann and Markusen (1986).

32. To see this note that substitution of the first order condition into the zero profit condition yields $-p' = F/q^2 = -d[F/q]/dq$.

33. A foreign *ad valorem* export tax would have the same effects. The effects are not the same, however, when the tariff is specific. See Markusen and Venables (1988).

34. Results are extended to more general demands and to specific tariffs and subsidies in Horstmann and Markusen (1986).

35. Note that an *ad valorem* subsidy increases the slope of the demand facing the subsidized firm. Hence, equality between the slope of the demand and average cost functions will occur at a lower output level. Markusen and Venables (1988) address the case where the taxes and subsidies are specific, rather than *ad valorem*. Since the slope of demands is unaffected by a specific tax or subsidy, average cost remains unchanged when such policy is used. Hence, output per firm remains the same and all changes in total quantity arise solely from the entry or exit of firms.

36. This is shown in Brander and Spencer (1985).

37. The argument is developed in detail in Krugman (1984).

38. Flam and Helpman (1987) provide an analysis using 'love of variety' preferences.

39. See Chapter 9 (p. 367 and 368).

40. It is assumed that fixed costs are high enough to exclude profitable production with 2 home varieties interposed between the same two foreign varieties.

41. This, however does not mean that all consumers gain. Since a tariff increases the price of imports it must impose a cost on those who continue to consume foreign brands once the tariff is levied. However, even those who buy the local brand do not necessarily gain relative to their pre-tariff position. The fact that they purchase the local brand merely reveals that they are better off doing so than buying a foreign variety at the post-tariff price.

42. This section based on Bhagwati (1965).

43. In what follows we consider only values of τ for which the tariff inclusive supply curve intersects the domestic demand below point A in Figure 10.7.

44. D is obtained by subtracting from consumer demand the quantity supplied by the competitive home industry.

45. This result is due to Shibata (1968).
46. Recall from Chapter 5 that under a VER the exporting country captures the rents generated by the export quota.
47. Krishna (1989, 1990, 1991) elaborates on this theme.
48. This case is examined by Hwang and Mai (1988).
49. See Harris (1985).
50. The foreign reaction function cannot be located below RV since profit maximization requires that the foreign firm dispose of its constrained exports at the highest possible price.
51. Krishna (1989) explores the effects of a VER in the framework of a price setting duopoly, but unlike Harris (1985) who assigns a leadership role to the home firm, she assumes that firms choose price simultaneously. She finds that there exists a mixed strategy equilibrium with the home firm alternating between a low price at which the constraint is binding and a high price at which it is not. She finds that a VER set at the free trade level of exports raises the profits of the foreign firm as well as the expected profits of the home firm.
52. Falvey (1979).
53. Krishna (1990).
54. This appears most clearly when actual demand is defined on services rendered and quality measures the number of units of service that can be rendered by the import restricted product.
55. Analyses can be found in Rodriguez (1979), Das and Donnenfeld (1987, 1989), Krishna (1987), Feenstra (1988b, 1993, 1995).
56. E.g. Aw and Roberts (1986) for footwear, Boorstein and Feenstra (1991) for steel, Faini and Heimler (1991) for textiles and clothing. Feenstra (1984, 1985, 1988b, 1993, 1995), de Melo and Messerlin (1988) for automobiles.
57. In the year preceding the VER Japanese car imports accounted for 21.2% of new passenger automobiles purchased in the United States. Once the VER was agreed upon, the Ministry of International Trade and Industry (MITI) determined the maximum allowable exports per individual firm (see Feenstra, 1985).
58. See de Melo and Messerlin (1988).
59. The numbers in the table and the analysis that follows are from Feenstra (1988b).
60. The index shown in row 2 is the Fisher Ideal index of change for each pair of years, i.e. the geometric mean of the Laspeyres index which uses first year quantities as weights, and the Paasche index which uses second year quantities as weights.
61. The demand originates from a utility function whose arguments are the product characteristics (see Lancaster, 1966, 1979).
62. The 21% rise in the tariff corresponds to 16% at the retail level. The year 1985 is dropped from the cross-equation constraint since an earlier testing of these constraints rejected the hypothesis that the coefficients were different by 0.16 for the year 1985.
63. The method used is the same as for the price index (see n. 60).
64. In the absence of such domestic price, normal value is defined as the comparable price for export to any third country or the cost of production in the country of

origin *plus* a reasonable addition for selling cost and profit. Under US law below cost selling is part of the definition of dumping.

65. Injury is assessed by such measures as the decline in production, capacity utilization, fall in market share, etc.

66. Other explanations for dumping include incomplete pass-through of exchange rate fluctuations (Leidy and Hoekman, 1988; Feinberg, 1989), consumption externalities (Flam, 1987) and exclusionary practices.

67. The fixed factor in Ethier's model is managerial labor. The granting of employment security to managers is profit maximizing since it allows employers to pay a lower wage.

68. This arises since a firm's costs depend not only on current output but on past accumulated output. Since, with learning, higher current output entails lower future costs, the cost relevant to the profit maximizing quantity choice is lower than current cost. The equilibrium price may therefore fall below current cost, which would be interpreted in the data as dumping.

69. This criterion links m to the probability of a finding of injury. An alternative would be to assume that s depends on the difference between the price of the foreign variety in the home market and in its market of origin. This would also link m to the probability that a determination of dumping will be made.

70. Fischer (1992) does not model this second term.

71. Reitzes (1993) pursues this approach, adopting a model in which producers take into account the effect of their quantity or price decision on the rate of antidumping duty. In contrast to Fischer (1992) Reitzes' model assumes that given dumping, the probability of antidumping action is not affected by marginal changes in firms' decision variables.

72. Messerlin (1990, 1995).

73. The model whose essential features are summarized below is Qiu (1995). (See also Collie, 1991.)

74. The earlier the retaliatory response, the lower t.

75. Qiu (1995) assumes that no conventional tariff is levied on the countervailable import.

76. Additional work on the automotive industry includes Krishna *et al.* (1994), Laussel *et al.* (1988), Smith and Venables (1988), Smith (1994) and Venables (1994). Examples of studies of strategic trade policy in other industries include Baldwin and Krugman (1988a), Klepper (1990), and Baldwin and Krugman (1988b).

77. Examples of general equilibrium models of imperfect competition are Harris (1985), de Melo and Robinson (1989), Nguyen and Wigle (1992).

78. Using (10.30) an elasticity of substitution equal to 2 implies $\{dp[B + K]/Q + dp^*[B^* + K]/Q^*\} = 2[(dp/p) - (dp^*/p^*)]$ where dp and dp^* can be taken as price differences between 2 years.

79. Laussel *et al.* (1988) applied Dixit's model to study competition between European and Japanese automobile producers. By and large their findings parallel those of Dixit. The tariff is found to be better than free trade, but the increase in domestic welfare is also found to be tiny. As in Dixit, subsidies are found to have a stronger effect, particularly in the UK market where the model suggested that competition was less intense than in other European countries.

80. See Brander (1995).
81. See Venables (1990, 1994) and Ben Zvi and Helpman (1992).
82. Under Cournot competition, firms allocate their predetermined total output across individual markets given sales by other firms in these markets. Under Bertrand, firms set prices in each market taking as given other firms' prices in these markets.
83. Venables (1990), for example, shows that the size of welfare gains from using tariffs and export subsidies in such 2-stage models lies between the gains attained for segmented and connected markets.
84. Of particular interest in this regard are Brander (1986), Grossman (1987), Krugman (1993), McCulloch (1993).
85. Evidence of this is provided by the experience of antitrust litigation where the issues of market delineation and entry barriers tend to be hotly contested. Furthermore, in actual practice one would also have to consider the possibility that the domestic market is connected to some foreign markets but not to others.
86. See Dixit and Grossman (1986).
87. This idea is developed by Tornell (1991).
88. See, e.g. Hillman and Riley (1989).
89. Using data on the foreign ownership of US industries and assuming a percentage US ownership of foreign industries Dick (1993) has shown that optimal subsidies are considerably lower than when cross-ownership is ignored.

References and additional reading

General

Ben Zvi, S. and Helpman, E. (1992), 'Oligopoly and Segmented Markets', in Grossman, G. (ed.), *Imperfect Competition and International Trade* (Cambridge, Mass. and London: MIT Press).

Bhagwati, J. (1971), 'The Generalized Theory of Distortions and Welfare', in Bhagwati, J.N., Mundell, R.A., Jones, R.W. and Vanek, Y. (eds), *Trade, Balance of Payments and Growth: Papers in International Economics in Honor of Charles P. Kindleberger* (Amsterdam: North-Holland), 69–90.

Bhagwati, J. (1982), 'Directly-Unproductive Profit-Seeking (DUP) Activities', *Journal of Political Economy*, 90, 988–1002.

Brander, J. A. and Krugman, P. (1983), 'A "Reciprocal" Dumping Model of Trade', *Journal of International Economics*, 15, 313–23.

Dixit, A.K. (1984), 'International Trade Policy for Oligopolistic Industries', *Economic Journal Conference Papers*, 94, 1–16.

Feenstra, R. (ed.) (1988a), *Empirical Methods for International Trade* (Cambridge, Mass.: MIT Press).

Flam, H. and Helpman E. (1987), 'Industrial Policy under Monopolistic Competition', *Journal of International Economics*, 22, 79–102.

Helpman, E. and Krugman, P.R. (1989), *Trade Policy and Market Structure* (Cambridge, Mass. and London: MIT Press).

Helpman, E. and Razin, A. (1991), *International Trade and Trade Policy* (Cambridge, Mass. and London: MIT Press).

Hillman, A.L. and Riley, J. (1989), 'Politically Contestable Rents and Transfers', *Economics and Politics*, 1, 1989, 17–39.

Hillman, A.L. and Ursprung, H.W. (1988), 'Domestic Politics, Foreign Interests and International Trade Policy', *American Economic Review*, 78, 729–49.

Horstmann, I. and Markusen, J.R. (1986), 'Up the Average Cost Curve: Inefficient Entry and the New Protectionism', *Journal of International Economics*, 20, 225–47.

Krishna, K. and Thursby, M. (1991), 'Optimal Policies with Strategic Distortions', *Journal of International Economics*, 31, 291–308.

Krugman, P.R. (1993), 'The Narrow and Broad Arguments for Free Trade', *American Economic Review*, 83(2), 362–6.

Krugman, P.R. and Smith, A. (eds) (1994), *Empirical Studies of Strategic Trade Policies* (Chicago and London: University of Chicago Press).

Markusen, J.R. (1981), 'Trade and the Gains from Trade with Imperfect Competition', *Journal of International Economics*, 11, 531–51.

McCulloch, R. (1993), 'The Optimality of Free Trade: Science or Religion?', *American Economic Review*, 83(2), 367–71.

Tirole, J. (1988), *The Theory of Industrial Organization* (Cambridge, Mass. and London: MIT Press).

Tornell A. (1991), 'On the Ineffectiveness of Made-to-Measure Protectionist Programs', in Helpman, E. and Razin, A. (eds), *International Trade and Trade Policy* (Cambridge, Mass. and London: MIT Press), 66–79.

Taxes and subsidies

Auquier, A.A. and Caves, R.E. (1979), 'Monopolistic Export Industry, Trade, Taxes, and Optimal Competition Policy', *Economic Journal*, 89, 559–81.

Baldwin, R.E. (ed.) (1988), *Trade Policy Issues and Empirical Analysis* (Chicago: University of Chicago Press).

Brander, J.A. (1995), 'Strategic Trade Policy', in Grossman, G. and Rogoff, K. (eds), *Handbook of International Economics* Vol. III, (Amsterdam: North-Holland), 1395–455.

Brander, J. and Spencer, B.J. (1984), 'Tariff Protection and Imperfect Competition', in Kierzkowski, H. (ed.), *Monopolistic Competition and International Trade* (Oxford: Oxford University Press).

Brander, J.A. and Spencer, B.J. (1985), 'Export Subsidies and Market Share Rivalry', *Journal of International Economics*, 18, 82–100.

Carmichael, C.M. (1987), 'The Control of Export Credit Subsidies and its Welfare Consequences', *Journal of International Economics*, 23, 1–19.

de Meza, D. (1986), 'Export Subsidies and High Productivity: Cause or Effects', *Canadian Journal of Economics*, 19, 347–50.

Dick, A.R. (1993), 'Strategic Trade Policy and Welfare', *Journal of International Economics*, 35, 227–49.

Dixit, A.K. and Grossman, G.M. (1986), 'Targeted Export Promotion with Several Oligopolistic Industries', *Journal of International Economics*, 21, 233–50.

Dixit, A.K. and Kyle, A.S. (1985), 'The Use of Protection and Subsidies for Entry Promotion and Deterrence', *American Economic Review*, 75, 139–52.

Eaton, J. and Grossman, G.M. (1986), 'Optimal Trade and Industrial Policy under Oligopoly', *Quarterly Journal of Economics*, 101, 383–406.

Gruenspecht, H.K. (1988), 'Export Subsidies for Differentiated Products', *Journal of International Economics*, 24, 331–44.

Katrak, H. (1979), 'Multinational Monopolies and Commercial Policy', *Oxford Economic Papers*, 29, 283–91.

Krugman, P.R. (1984), 'Import Protection as Export Promotion: International Competi-tion in the Presence of Oligopoly and Economies of Scale', in Kierzkowski, H. (ed.), *Monopolistic Competition and International Trade* (Oxford: Oxford University Press), 180–93.

Lancaster, K. (1991), 'The "Product Variety" Case for Protection', *Journal of International Economics*, 31, 1–26.

Markusen, J.R. and Venables, A.J. (1988), 'Trade Policy with Increasing Returns and Imperfect Competition: Contradictory Results from Competing Assumptions', *Journal of International Economics*, 24, 299–316.

Richardson, J.D. (1989), 'Empirical Research on Trade Liberalization with Imperfect Competition', *NBER Working Paper*, 2883.

Neary, J.P. (1991), 'Export Subsidies and Price Competition', in Helpman, E. and Razin, A. (eds), *International Trade and Trade Policy* (Cambridge, Mass.: MIT Press) 80–95.

Neary, J.P. (1994), 'Cost Asymmetries in International Subsidy Games: Should Governments Help Winners or Losers?', *Journal of International Economics*, 77, 197–218.

Spencer, B.J. and Brander, J.A. (1983), 'International R and D Rivalry and Industrial Strategy', *Review of Economic Studies*, 50, 707–22.

Venables, A.J. (1985), 'Trade and Trade Policy with Imperfect Competition: The Case of Identical Products and Free Entry', *Journal of International Economics*, 19, 1–19.

Venables A.J. (1990), 'International Capacity Choice and National Market Games', *Journal of International Economics*, 29, 23–42.

Quantitative restrictions

Aw, B. and Roberts, M. (1986), 'Estimating Quality Change in Quota Constrained Markets: The Case of US Footwear', *Journal of International Economics*, 21, 45–60.

Bhagwati, J.N. (1965), 'On the Equivalence of Tariffs and Quotas', in Baldwin, R.E. *et al.* (eds), *Trade Growth and the Balance of Payments – Essays in Honor of Gottfried Haberler* (Chicago: Rand McNally), 53–67.

Bhagwati, J.N. (1968), 'More on the Equivalence of Tariffs and Quotas', *American Economic Review*, 58, 481–5.

Boorstein, R. and Feenstra, R.C. (1991), 'Quality Upgrading and its Welfare Cost in US Steel Imports, 1969–1974', in Helpman, E. and Razin, A. (eds), *International Trade and Trade Policy* (Cambridge, Mass.: MIT Press), 167–86.

Das, S.P. and Donnenfeld, S. (1987), 'Trade Policy and its Impact on Quality of Imports', *Journal of International Economics*, 23, 77–95.

Das, S. and Donnenfeld, S. (1989), 'Competition and International Trade: Quantity and Quality Restrictions', *Journal of International Economics*, 27(4), 299–318.

de Melo, J. and Messerlin, P.A. (1988), 'Price, Quality and Welfare Effects of European VERs on Japanese Autos', *European Economic Review*, 32, 1527–46.

de Melo, J. and Winters, L.A. (1993), 'Price and Quality Effects of VERs Revisited: A Case Study of Korean Footwear Exports', *Journal of Economic Integration*, 8(1), 33–57.

Faini, R. and Heimler, A. (1991), 'The Quality of Production of Textiles and Clothing and the Completion of the Internal Market', in Winters, L.A. and Venables, A. (eds), *European Integration: Trade and Industry* (Cambridge University Press).

Falvey, R. (1979), 'The Comparison of Trade Within Export-Restricted Categories', *Journal of Political Economy*, 87(5), 1142–65.

Feenstra, R.C. (1985), 'Automobile Prices and Protection: The US–Japan Trade Restraint', *Journal of Policy Modeling*, 7(1), 49–68.

Feenstra, R.C. (1988b), 'Quality Change under Trade Restraints in Japanese Autos', *Quarterly Journal of Economics*, 103(1), 131–46.

Feenstra, R.C. (1993), 'Measuring the Welfare Effect of Quality Change: Theory and Application to Japanese Autos', *NBER Working Paper*, 4401.

Feenstra, R.C. (1995), 'Estimating the Effects of Trade Policy', in Grossman, G. and Rogoff, K. (eds), *Handbook of International Economics* (New York: Elsevier Science).

Harris, R. (1985), 'Why Voluntary Export Restraints are "Voluntary"', *Canadian Journal of Economics*, (4), 799–809.

Hwang, H. and Mai, C.-C. (1988), 'On the Equivalence of Tariffs and Quotas under Duopoly: A Conjectural Variations Approach', *Journal of International Economics*, 24, 373–80.

Krishna, K. (1987), 'Tariffs versus Quotas with Endogenous Quality', *Journal of International Economics*, 23, 97–122.

Krishna, K. (1988), 'The Case of the Vanishing Revenues: Auction Quotas with Oligopoly, National Bureau of Economic Research Inc.', *Working Paper*, 2723.

Krishna, K. (1989), 'The Case of the Vanishing Revenues: Auction Quotas with Monopoly, National Bureau of Economic Research Inc.', *Working Paper*, 2840.

Krishna, K. (1990a), 'The Case of Vanishing Revenue: Auction Quotas with Monopoly', *American Economic Review*, 80(4), 828–37.

Krishna, K. (1990b), 'Protection and the Product Line', *International Economic Review*, 31(1), 87–102.

Krishna, K. (1991), 'Making Altruism Pay in Auction Quotas', in Helpman, E. and Razin, A. (eds), *International Trade and Trade Policy* (Cambridge, Mass. and London: MIT Press), 46–65.

Lancaster, K. (1966), 'A New Approach to Consumer Theory', *Journal of Political Economy*, 74, 132-57.

Lancaster, K. (1979), *Variety, Equity, and Efficiency* (New York: Columbia University Press).

Rodriguez, C. (1979), 'The Quality of Import and the Differential Welfare Effects of Tariffs, and Quality Controls as Protective Devices', *Canadian Journal of Economics*, 22(3), 439–49.

Shibata, H. (1968), 'A Note on The Equivalence of Tariffs and Quotas', *American Economic Review*, 58, 137–42.

Contingent protection

Bellis, J-F. (1990), 'The EEC Antidumping System', in Jackson, J. H. and Vermulst, E.A. (eds), *Antidumping Law in Practice: A Comparative Study* (London: Harvester Wheatsheaf).

Boltuck, R. and Litan, R.L (eds) (1991), *Down in the Dumps: Administration of the Unfair Trade Laws* (Washington, DC: Brookings Institution).

Clarida, R.H. (1991), 'Entry, Dumping, and Shakeout', *American Economic Review*, 83(1), 181–202.

Collie, D. (1993), 'Export Subsidies and Countervailing Tariffs', *Journal of International Economics*, 31, 309–24.

Dixit, A. (1988a), 'Anti-Dumping and Countervailing Duties under Oligopoly', *European Economic Review*, 32, 55–68.

Ethier, W.J. (1982), 'Dumping', *Journal of Political Economy*, 90(3), 487–506.

Ethier, W.J. and Fisher, R.D. (1987), 'The New Protectionism', *Journal of Economic Integration*, 2(2), 1–11.

Feinberg, R.M. (1989), 'Exchange Rates and "Unfair Trade"', *Review of Economics and Statistics*, 71, 704–7.

Finger, J.M. (1993), 'The Origins and Evolution of Antidumping Regulation', in Finger, J.M. (ed.), *Antidumping: How it Works and Who Gets Hurt* (Ann Arbor: University of Michigan Press).

Fischer, R.D. (1992), 'Endogenous Probability of Protection and Firm Behavior', *Journal of International Economics*, 32, 149–63.

Flam, H. (1987), 'Reverse Dumping', *European Economic Review*, 31, 82–8.

Gruenspecht, H.K. (1988), 'Dumping and Dynamic Competition', *Journal of International Economics*, 25, 225–48.

Jackson, J. (1989), *The World Trading System: Law and Policy of International Economic Relations* (Cambridge, Mass. and London: MIT Press).

Jackson, J.H. and Vermulst, E.A. (eds) (1990), *Antidumping Law and Practice: A Comparative Study* (London: Harvester Wheatsheaf).

Leidy, M.P. and Hoekman, B.M. (1988), 'Production Effects of Price- and Cost-Based Anti-Dumping Laws under Flexible Exchange Rates', *Discussion Paper* 224, Research Seminar in International Economics (University of Michigan).

Marvel, H.P. and Ray, E.J. (1995), 'Countervailing Duties', *The Economic Journal*, 105, 1576–93.

Messerlin, P. (1990), 'Anti-Dumping Regulation or Pro-Cartel Law? The EC Chemical Cases', *World Economy*, 13(4), pp. 465–92.

Messerlin, P. and Reed, G. (1995), 'Antidumping Policies in the United States and the European Community', *Economic Journal*, 105, 1565–75.

Prusa, T.J. (1992), 'Why are so Many Antidumping Petitions Withdrawn?', *Journal of International Economics*, 33, 1–20.

Prusa, T.J. (1994), 'Pricing Behavior in the Presence of Antidumping Law', *Journal of Economic Integration*, 9(2), 260–89.

Qiu, L.D. (1995), 'Why Can't Countervailing Duties Deter Export Subsidization?', *Journal of International Economics*, 39, 249–72.

Reitzes, J.D. (1993), 'Antidumping Policy', *International Economic Review*, 34(4), 745–63.

Seade, J., 'On the Effects of Entry', *Econometrica*, 48(2), 479–89.

Spencer, B.J. (1993), 'Capital Subsidies and Countervailing Duties in Oligopolistic Industries', *Journal of International Economics*, 24, 45–69.

Staiger, R.W. and Wolak, F.A. (1989), 'Strategic Use of Antidumping Law to Enforce Tacit International Collusion', *Working Paper*, 3016, National Bureau of Economic Research.

Stegemann, K. (1990), 'EC Anti-Dumping Policy: Are Price Undertakings a Legal Substitute for Illegal Price Fixing?', *Weltwirtschaftliches Archiv*, 126(2), 268–97.

US International Trade Commission (1990), *The Economic Effects of Antidumping and Countervailing Duty Orders and Suspension Agreements*, Investigation, 332–44, Publication 2900 (Washington DC).

Computable models

Baldwin, R. and Krugman, P.R. (1988a), 'Market Access and International Competition: A Simulation Study of 16K Random Access Memories', in Feenstra, R. (ed.), *Empirical Methods for International Trade* (Cambridge, Mass.: MIT Press), 171–97.

Baldwin, R. and Krugman, P.R. (1988b), 'Industrial Policy and International Competition in Wide-Bodied Jet Aircraft', in Baldwin, R. (ed.), *Trade Policy Issues and Empirical Analysis* (Chicago: University of Chicago Press), 45–71.

Brander, J. (1986), 'Rationales for Strategic Trade and Industrial Policy', in Krugman, P.R. (ed.), *Strategic Trade Policy and the New International Economics* (Cambridge, Mass.: MIT Press), 213–6.

de Melo, J. and Robinson, S. (1989), 'Product Differentiation and the Treatment of Foreign Trade in Computable General Equilibrium Models of Small Economies', *Journal of International Economics*, 27, 47–67.

Dixit, A. (1988b), 'Optimal Trade and Industrial Policies for the US Automobile Industry', in Feenstra, R. (ed.), *Empirical Methods for International Trade Policy* (Cambridge, Mass.: MIT Press), 161–65.

Grossman, G. (1987), 'Strategic Export Promotion: A Critique', in Krugman, P.R. (ed.), *Strategic Trade Policy and the New International Economics* (Cambridge, Mass.: MIT Press).

Harris, R. (1984), 'Applied General Equilibrium Analysis of Small Open Economies with Scale Economies and Imperfect Competition', *American Economic Review*, 74, 1016–32.

Klepper, G. (1990), 'Entry into the Market for Large Transport Aircraft', *European Economic Review*, 34, 775–803.

Krishna, K., Hogan, K. and Swagel, P. (1994), 'The Non-optimality of Optimal Trade Policies: The US Automobile Industry Revisited, 1979–85', in Krugman, P.R. and Smith, A. (eds), *Empirical Studies of Strategic Trade Policies* (Chicago and London: University of Chicago Press), 11–40.

Laussel, D., Montet, C. and Peguin-Feisolle, A. (1988), 'Optimal Trade Policy under Oligopoly: A Calibrated Model of the Europe–Japan Rivalry in the EEC Car Market', *European Economic Review*, 32, 1547–66.

Nguyen, T.T. and Wigle, R.M. (1992), 'Trade Liberalization with Imperfect Competition: The Large and the Small of It', *Journal of International Economics*, 36, 17–33.

Norman, V.D. (1989), 'Trade Policy under Imperfect Competition, Theoretical Ambiguities–Empirical Regularities?', *European Economic Review*, 33, 473–9.

Smith, A. (1994), 'Strategic Trade Policy in the European Car Market', in Krugman, P.R. and Smith, A. (eds), *Empirical Studies of Strategic Trade Policies* (Chicago and London: University of Chicago Press), 67–81.

Smith, A. and Venables, A.J. (1988), 'Completing the Internal Market in the European Community: Some Industry Simulations', *European Economic Review*, 32, 1501–26.

Smith, A. and Venables, A.J. (1991), 'Counting the Cost of Voluntary Export Restraints in the European Car Market', in Helpman, E. and Razin, A. (eds), *International Trade and Trade Policy* (Cambridge, Mass. and London: MIT Press).

Venables, A.J. (1994), 'Trade Policy under Imperfect Competition: A Numerical Assessment', in Krugman, P. and Smith, A. (eds), *Empirical Studies of Strategic Trade Policy* (Chicago and London: University of Chicago Press).

■ *Chapter 11* ■

Multinational Production

11.1 The multinational enterprise	*11.3* The choice between multinational and uninational production
11.2 Firm-specific assets and internalization: the OLI framework	*11.4* Multinational enterprises and trade in general equilibrium
	11.5 Empirical evidence

As shown in Chapter 9, theoretical explanations of the empirically important phenomena of intra-industry trade (IIT) required that we abandon the assumption of perfectly competitive markets. While trade models with imperfectly competitive markets expand our understanding of intra-industry trade and other issues, these models assume, as do the traditional models, that each firm undertakes production in only one country. This assumption, however, runs counter to readily observed facts of modern international commerce.[1] Hence, just as the empirical phenomena of intra-industry trade cast a shadow on models based on perfect competition, the existence of multinational enterprises – that is, firms who own and undertake production in more than one country – casts a shadow on the assumption of single-country firms. The assumption of single country firms is further questioned by the observation that a sizable portion of intra-industry trade is actually intra-firm trade – that is, trade across national borders but within the confines of a single firm.

In this chapter, the issue of intra-firm trade is considered as part of a much broader question: what is the basis for the common ownership and control that links establishments in different countries into one entity called the multinational enterprise (MNE)?[2] We begin by considering the very notion of a MNE and review data on the extent of multinational activity. We explore the essence of a large literature that explains the basis for MNEs in terms of three 'advantages': ownership, location and internalization. Dubbed 'OLI', this framework has been the main theoretical framework for discussing the basis for MNEs. More recent attempts to rigorously model the basis for MNEs in the context of trade theory with imperfectly competitive markets are examined next. In this regard, we consider the roles of oligopolistic interaction and also trade barriers as explanations for transnational production. We then delve further into the link between MNEs and trade theory by examining how factor endowments affect production and trade when firms can be transnational. The chapter concludes with a review of some empirical work that ties together many of the ideas discussed in earlier sections.

11.1 The multinational enterprise

A MNE is operationally defined as a firm that owns and controls productive assets located in more than one country. While the notions of common ownership and control appear simple enough, there is in fact no sharp divide between a multinational and a uninational enterprise. Rather, the passage from one form to the other is more in the nature of a continuum. Equity participation among incorporated establishments can range anywhere between 0% and 100%, and asserting common ownership is a matter of definition, not theory. Control is similarly fuzzy since the autonomy of establishments under common ownership is also a matter of degree. Any percentage ownership may be combined with varying degrees of autonomy granted to individual establishments.

Statistical agencies use the criterion of ownership to distinguish between multinational and uninational enterprises since, unlike control, ownership is easily quantifiable. Even so, the degree of ownership that qualifies an enterprise as multinational in the data may differ between statistical agencies.[3] In contrast, theoretical work tends to distinguish MNEs from uninational enterprises on the basis of control. Specifically, a firm is multinational if it has establishments in at least two countries and the prices, quantities or other decision variables are determined in each location through a process of joint profit maximization.

Why multinational?

After settling on a definition, any discussion of MNEs must then turn to the question: 'Why multinational – that is, why is production in one country undertaken by an entity controlled by another entity located in a different country?' That such a question is raised in the first place attests to the belief that familiarity with local business practices, consumer preferences and labor market conditions is an important asset which gives local firms an edge over foreign transplants. From this it follows that a foreign firm, less familiar with the local terrain must, in order to sustain the rivalry of local enterprises, possess some other advantages, not shared by local firms. But this is only part of the story. Even if a foreign based firm possessed advantages that would allow it to thrive in a foreign environment, this by itself would not imply that the most profitable route to exploit these advantages is by setting up a foreign plant. That is, to explain the prevalence of multinational activities one must also explain why foreign subsidiaries are established when other alternatives to supply foreign markets, such as exporting, licensing and joint venture, are available.

There exists a large body of literature that addresses such questions in a framework known as 'OLI' which, as we saw above, stands for ownership advantages, locational advantages and internalization advantages.[4] Ownership advantages allow a firm to overcome the disadvantages of a foreign location. Locational advantages (e.g. input costs, oligopolistic interaction, trade policy) make it more profitable to produce in a country than to export to it. Internalization advantages make it more profitable to undertake production oneself than to deal with a foreign partner who is more familiar with the local environment.

Ownership and internalization advantages are the core explanation for the existence of MNEs in the OLI framework. These two advantages are postulated to derive from at least one of the following two sources: (1) the existence of a common cost incurred at the firm, but not the plant level so that, as these costs become large, multiplant production becomes cheaper relative to expanding production in a single plant; (2) the existence of firm-specific, knowledge based assets.

Although conceptually different, joint costs and firm-specific advantages are empirically related. Specifically, the advantages attributed to MNEs are to be found in the realm of technological know-how, organizational skills and brand recognition. These intangible assets possess a characteristic of 'jointness' that permits their use in one location with little or no cost in terms of forgone production or profits at other locations. Section 11.3 will discuss these issues in greater detail.

Multinational activity

Foreign direct investment

The unprecedented growth of international trade flows over the last decades has been matched by a no less dramatic surge in the activities of multinational enterprises. A common measure of such activity is foreign direct investment (FDI), measured as either a flow or a stock. For balance of payment purposes, the International Monetary Fund (IMF) defines FDI as the acquisition, by an entity resident in one country, of a lasting interest in an entity resident in another country. Measured direct investment flows cover the initial and subsequent transactions between these entities including, new equity purchased or acquired by other means, reinvested earnings by the controlled firms, and loans from the controlling to the controlled entity.

FDI stocks are calculated by accumulating annual FDI flows over time. These flows are classified into outflows and inflows. Inflows are direct investments undertaken by foreign based MNEs in the recipient or host country; outflows are investments that home based MNEs undertake in foreign countries.

World inflows of FDI represented 1.1% of world gross fixed capital formation in 1960. 30 years later this percentage had risen to 3.5%. The growth of multinational involvement is further evidenced in Table 11.1 which shows a 25-fold increase in the stock of capital held by foreign affiliate firms between 1961 and 1990, a period over which the total value of world exports by all firms multiplied 26 times.

Not only has the level of multinational activity increased over the past few decades, there has also been a change in its sectoral composition. Since the mid-1970s, the share of foreign assets in services has grown, while the share of these assets in manufacturing has declined. Over half of the stock of outward FDI held by German, Japanese and US parents in 1991 was in the tertiary sector.[5] Also, the channel through which FDI is being carried out has undergone changes. Whereas in the past foreign direct investment was mainly greenfield investment, it is now increasingly being carried out in the form of mergers and purchase of going concerns.[6]

The developed countries are the main sources and destinations of FDI. In 1994 they accounted for 83% of outflows and 59% of inflows. Total outflows in that year were $230 billion. The United States remains a dominant supplier of FDI, but its share of world outward investment has been falling. From 57.6% of outward FDI flows in 1960 the US share declined to 19.8% in 1994. The US share of the outward stock,[7] still at 42% in 1980 fell to 25.3% in 1994. In contrast, the portion of the world stock of outward FDI held by Japanese parents rose from 3.0 to 11.8% over the same period, while the share held by parents located in current EU member countries rose from 40.7 to 44.6%.[8]

Table 11.1 *Value of world merchandise exports and stock of FDI, 1961–90 (US$ billion)*[a]

	1961	*1975*	*1990*
World exports	134	878	3485
World stock of FDI	68	264	1675

Note:
[a] Stocks are averages of inward and outward FDI stocks.

Sources: Hummels and Stern (1994), UNCTAD (1994).

The US has also become an important recipient of FDI. Its share of world inward FDI flows rose from 7.2% in 1972 to 23% on average over the period 1988–92. Its share of the inward stock rose from 16.5% in 1980 to 21.5% in 1994. The Japanese portion of world inward stock has remained low, falling from 6 to 2% between 1980 and 1992. The EC share has remained relatively stable, rising from 35% in 1980 to 39.4% in 1992.[9]

The United States, historically a net supplier of FDI, is now a net recipient. US inflows of FDI were twice as large as US outflows between 1982 and 1987, and were 1.5 times as large during the period 1988–92.

While the US is the largest recipient of FDI, the role of foreign owned firms in the US economy remains small when compared to other major industrialized countries except Japan, as is shown in Table 11.2.

Table 11.2   *Relative importance of foreign-owned firms, selected countries, 1986*[a]

	% share of foreign-owned firms in		
Country	Total sales	Total manufacturing employment	Total assets
USA	10	7	9
Japan	1	1	1
West Germany	27	21	NA
France	18	13	17
UK	20	14	14

Source: Julius and Thomsen (1988, as cited in Graham and Krugman, 1993).

Although balance of payment data on FDI flows are the most frequently used measure of multinational activity, these data are not without defects. For example, direct borrowing by affiliates in the open market is not counted as FDI even when the loans are guaranteed by the foreign parent. Since this means that a (parent) firm can become a multinational, or expand its existing foreign operations, without there being a matching transfer of financial capital, the measured FDI flows do in fact underestimate the accumulation of FDI. This downward bias is further reflected in the calculation of FDI stocks which excludes capital gains, such as those arising from inflation.[10] This imparts a downward bias to the estimated value of old investment relative to recently acquired assets hence to estimated FDI stocks. Despite these drawbacks, FDI flows and FDI stocks continue to be used as a measure of multinational activity, primarily because alternative data, such as sales by foreign affiliates, are available only for a limited number of countries and at infrequent intervals.[11]

Foreign affiliate trade

Issues concerning a firm's choice between exporting and establishing a local plant to supply foreign markets require consideration of trade. In this regard, it is important to note that trade by MNEs is not a notion devoid of ambiguity. A very inclusive definition of MNE-related trade is trade where either a parent or an affiliate of an MNE participates as a buyer or seller. By this broad definition, over 99% of total US international trade in 1982 would be considered trade by multinational firms.[12] Alternatively, one could define MNE trade as including only those transactions where a parent alone or an affiliate alone participates as a buyer or seller. Under the former 83% of US merchandise trade in 1982 was multinational, under the latter it was 51%. A fourth definition would limit MNE-related trade to the transactions between a parent and an affiliate. Under this definition 34% of US trade in 1982 was MNE-related trade.

Table 11.3 shows the significance of intra-firm shipments in total trade for the United States and other countries. It must be stressed, though, that only a small percentage of sales by US subsidiaries involves intrafirm transactions. The lion's share of sales – about two-thirds of the total – are destined for the market in which the subsidiary is located.[13]

Table 11.3 *Intra-firm trade as % of total trade, 1976–93*

Country (year)	Share of exports (%)	Share of imports (%)
USA (1993)	36	43
UK (1984)	29	51
Sweden (1994)	38	9
Belgium (1976)	53	48
France (1993)	34	18
Japan (1993)	25	14

Source: Dunning (1992, as cited in Cantwell, 1994 and UNCTAD, 1996).

In Chapter 1 we introduced the Grubel–Lloyd (GL) index of intra-industry trade (IIT) and of intra-industry FDI. A similar index can be used to measure the extent of intra-industry affiliate sales (IIAS). Such sales are said to take place when foreign based affiliates of home parents sell a commodity in foreign markets (outward affiliate sales) while the same commodity is sold in the home market by home-based foreign-owned affiliates. The index is

$$IIAS_j = \frac{\sum_i \min(IAS_{ij}, OAS_{ij})}{\sum_i \min(IAS_{ij} + OAS_{ij})} \times 100$$

where IAS_{ij} denotes inward sales of commodity j by affiliates owned by parents in country i and OAS_{ij} are outward sales of commodity j by affiliates located in country i and owned by home parents. The indices for the five industries with the largest sum of outward and inward sales US are reported in Table 11.4.

Table 11.4   *Index of US IIAS and IIT, 1989*

Industry	IIAS index	ITT index
Industrial chemicals & synthetics	47	50
Drugs	23	63
Integrated petroleum refining & extraction	12	29
Computer & office equipment	19	44
Motor vehicles & equipment	7	14

Source: Brainard (1993b).

11.2   Firm-specific assets and internalization: the OLI framework

Firm-specific, knowledge-based assets

The OLI framework views intangible assets such as intellectual property, organizational skills, reputation and brand recognition as the primary sources of advantage that allow a foreign based firm to compete against local firms in the latter's home market.[14] The advantage these assets confer on the foreign firm derives from the fact that their use in one location in no way diminishes the contribution they can make to production and profits in other locations. Moreover, the transfer of knowledge to an establishment located in another country is inexpensive when compared to its *de novo* acquisition. Know-how embodied in blueprints and patented chemical formulas travels fast and at relatively little cost. The transfer of know-how relating to the organization of manufacturing processes demands more time and effort of engineers and managers, yet it remains inexpensive when compared to alternative means of learning. While it is also true that consumer recognition and marketing techniques developed for one market do not spill over fully to another country, it remains true as well, that adaptation to local conditions tends to be less costly than new creation.

Several empirical studies have examined the hypothesis of a relationship between the level of multinational activity and intangible assets as suggested by the OLI framework. These studies typically regress a measure of multinational activity on variables that proxy for various intangible assets a firm might posses. An early representative of this literature is Horst (1974) which, using cross-industry data, found that local production by Canadian subsidiaries of US parents are increasing in the US R&D intensity of the industry to which the subsidiary belongs.[15]

A more recent example is the study by Kravis and Lipsey (1992) which explores the relationship between firm-specific knowledge-based assets and world export shares of US based establishments, US MNEs, MNE parents and MNE affiliates. Table 11.5 reports a sample of their results.

The independent variables are industry characteristics, of which the first three are factor proportion measures and the last two are proxies for intangible firm-specific assets which presumably give an MNE an advantage wherever it produces.

The explanatory power of the factor proportions variables can be expected to be higher for the non-MNEs than for the MNEs since the ties of dependence of the latter on home country factors of production is weaker.

Table 11.5 *Explaining US shares in world manufactures exports*

Dependent variable (as share of world exports)	Independent variables					
	Capital	Labor	Human capital	Advertising	R&D	R^2
US exports	−0.08	−0.82	4.02	−1.39	0.94	0.48
	(1.2)	(2.2)	(3.8)	(2.6)	(2.6)	
US MNE exports	−0.14	−1.40	5.24	1.03	2.55	0.53
	(1.2)	(1.9)	(2.7)	(1.0)	(3.8)	
US parent exports	−0.12	−1.00	3.16	−0.18	1.25	0.52
	(1.9)	(2.8)	(3.1)	(0.3)	(3.6)	
Affiliate exports	−0.02	−0.32	2.08	1.21	1.29	0.37
	(0.3)	(0.7)	(1.6)	(1.8)	(2.9)	

Notes:

t-statistics in parentheses. Intercept estimates not shown. The data are 1997 and 1982 data for 28 industries pooled for the purposes of estimation. *Capital* = parent property plant, and equipment per $ of sales; *Labor* = parent employment multiplied by the average wage of unskilled workers in the United States, per $ of sales; *Human capital* = average human capital per worker multiplied by employment in the industry in the United States per $ of sales. Human capital is measured as the product of the number of workers in the 2 highest skill occupational classes and the average human capital worker in that class, measured by the difference in the United States between the wages of workers in that class and the wages of unskilled workers; *Advertising* = advertising expenditure per $ of business receipts; *R&D* = parent R&D expenditure per $ of sales.

Source: Kravis and Lipsey (1992).

This presumably explains why the negative correlation between physical labor and export performance is stronger for all US based firms (row 1) and for US parents (row 3) than for MNEs as a whole (row 2) and foreign affiliates (row 4).[16]

The variables which display a consistent positive influence across all four equations are human capital and R&D intensity. The latter variable, however, has larger coefficients when the dependent variable is the export share of MNEs than when it is the export share of all US based firms. Estimation results also show that in contrast to R&D intensity which correlates strongly and positively with parents' shares, affiliates' shares and total US shares, advertising intensity relates negatively to the export performance of US based firms. Advertising intensity adds to the export share of MNEs as a whole. This, however, is due only to a positive effect on affiliates' export performance. It suggests that American MNEs exploit the advantages that flow from brand recognition by transferring production to foreign plants rather than through exports from their home base.[17]

While these findings are consistent with the hypothesis that intangible knowledge-based firm-specific assets play a central role in foreign investment, a clearer grasp of their role in overcoming the disadvantage due to less familiarity with a host market can be obtained by distinguishing between investments in different markets. Specifically one can hypothesize that if ownership of knowledge-based assets is critical in overcoming handicaps flowing from less intimacy with a host country, then observed ownership should vary according to the knowledge that foreign investors have of host countries.

This hypothesis has been investigated by Belderbos and Sleuwaegen (1996), who argue that the presence of Japanese trading houses in South Asian countries gives Japanese firms advantages in terms of market intelligence that they do not enjoy in Western markets. Host country government support in South Asian countries and the absence of strong local competition also suggest a lesser role for firm-specific advantages than in Western markets. Using a multinomial logit model, Belderbos and Sleuwaegen show that the probability that a Japanese enterprise become West-bound rather than Asia-bound or remain uninational is positively correlated to the following variables: R&D intensity, sales cost intensity measured as the sum of sales force expenditure and advertising outlays as a percentage of sales (a proxy for reputation and marketing know-how), and human resource intensity defined as labor cost of non-factory employees as a fraction of total labor cost (a proxy for the availability and quality of staff that can be expatriated to facilitate the transfer of organizational skills). They also find all three variables significantly related to the probability that a Japanese firm becomes West-bound. By contrast, only the human resource variable exerts a significant influence on the probability that a Japanese firm becomes Asia-bound.

Further evidence on the role of knowledge-based assets in overcoming the handicap of unfamiliarity with a foreign environment is provided by Pugel *et al.* (1996), who focus on the role played by knowledge-based assets owned by the *host country's* industries. Considering Japanese investment in the United States, they regress the share of employment in US industries accounted for by subsidiaries of Japanese parents against the R&D intensity of the industry in the US as well as in Japan, and against the advertising intensity of the industry in each country.[18] They find that the share of US employment attributable to Japanese subsidiaries correlates positively with Japanese R&D and advertising intensity, but that US R&D intensity has no significant effect. They attribute this to the fact that possession of important intangible assets by host country firms may act both as a repellent and a lure for foreign firms. That is, such assets may attract firms who expect that setting up a local subsidiary will speed up the acquisition of local knowledge that can then be exploited in other markets. Pugel and his co-authors maintain that, in the case of US R&D, neither the repelling nor the attracting effect dominates. Interestingly, they also find that US advertising has a negative and significant coefficient. They ascribe this to the fact that reputation reflected in established brand names cannot be easily imitated or duplicated. Hence reputation cannot act as lure which would indicate that the deterrence effect dominates.

Overall these studies confirm the central role of know-how in the decision to engage in FDI. They also support the idea that possession of knowledge-based assets is all the more critical the stronger the capabilities of host country firms. Finally, one notes as well that knowledge-based assets frequently appear among entry barriers commonly cited in the industrial organization literature. It is hardly surprising therefore, to find a positive correlation between market concentration and measures of multinational production.[19]

Internalization and transnational production

While the empirical evidence indicates that firm-specific, knowledge-based assets correlate positively with MNE activity, the mere possession of knowledge-based advantages does not imply that the most profitable way to exploit them is to set up production facilities in a foreign country. Why not simply transfer such knowledge to local firms in order to overcome the lack of familiarity with the local market? Wouldn't the surplus to be shared among the transferor and transferee be larger than the surplus derived by establishing one's own production facilities?

Clearly, a central factor governing the choice between the licensing of know-how and its internal exploitation is the cost of transferring that knowledge. In this regard, the available evidence tends to indicate that transfers between establishments under common ownership are less costly than arm's length technology transfers. Teece (1977) concluded on the basis of survey data that transfers by multinationals to joint venture partners are on average 5.1% more costly than transfers to wholly-owned subsidiaries, while transfers to independent licensees cost about 8.7% more than transfers to subsidiaries.[20] However, the transfer cost is only one of the factors that determine whether the technology will be licensed to an outsider or exploited internally. Licensing carries additional costs that flow from the opportunistic exploitation of information asymmetries. The sources of some of these costs are discussed below.

First, there is the need to reveal during the initial stage of negotiation certain aspects of the technology to potential licensees, probably firms in the same or a related industry. There is always the risk that a potential licensee will reject the deal and make use of the information in his or her own enterprise, or will reveal it to others.

A second set of problems relate to agency issues. A licensee may produce several goods under licence and the effort devoted to an individual product can hardly be monitored by the licensor. Also, the licensee is likely to have better information about consumers in the local market than the licensor and may be reluctant to reveal that information in order to exploit it for his or her own benefit.[21]

There is the risk that the licensee will skimp on quality and destroy the licensor's capital embodied in reputation. This idea is explored in Horstmann and Markusen (1987) in the framework of a model that assumes that the MNE possesses a technology which makes it possible to produce either high or low quality, the former at greater cost than the latter. The essence of their model is a follows: in the absence of a technology transfer, potential licensees – of which there are many – are capable of producing only low quality. It is assumed that, prior to purchase, consumers who purchase from an unknown seller cannot ascertain whether the quality of the product being offered to them is high or low. However, consumers become aware that a particular seller has been licensed to produce the high quality product – possibly because that seller uses a brand name. They are then willing to pay a higher price for the product sold by the licensed firm than for a product sold by unlicensed producers. This, however, applies only as long as the licensee maintains the reputation of a high quality producer. If the licensee violates the commitment to high quality by lowering quality in any one period, consumers become aware of this in the next period. As soon as they do, the licencee's reputation as a high quality producer is lost forever.

The basic insight of the model can now be shown. Let the licensee's per-period profit derived from the production of high quality be denoted π_h and let π_l be the profit obtained in the single period when the licensee produces low quality while still maintaining reputation as a high quality producer. Since, during that single period, the licensee collects the price of high quality product while incurring the cost of producing low quality, it must be true that $\pi_h < \pi_l$. In subsequent periods though, the profits of the cheater are zero since in the eyes of consumers there is no longer anything that would distinguish him from producers who have never been licensed. Hence, the condition which ensures that the licensee maintains quality is:

$$\frac{\pi_h - g}{i} > \pi_l - g \quad \Leftrightarrow \quad g < \frac{\pi_h - i\pi_l}{1 - i} \qquad (11.1)$$

where i is the interest rate in the country of the licensee, and g is the fixed per-period payment made by the licensee while the licensing contract is in effect. The left-hand side of (11.1) is the present value of the infinite stream of profits derived from producing high quality, whereas the right-hand side is the 1-period profit from cheating. (11.1) implies that if the licensor sets g equal to π_h – which is the payment that would leave the licensor indifferent between licensing and internal production if he could produce at the same cost as the licensee – the licensee will cheat. Profitable licensing is therefore possible only when the profit that the owner of the technology can obtain by producing himself is sufficiently lower than the profit a licensee could obtain by producing high quality.

To determine the conditions under which licensing rather than local production by the owner of the technology will take place, we let Π denote the profits the potential licensor would earn from own production. The condition that must be satisfied in order to make the owner of the technology better off under a licensing contract is $\Pi < g$. However, g must also satisfy (11.1) if the licensee is not to cheat on quality. Hence there will be room for licensing and quality maintenance if

$$\frac{\pi_h - i\pi_l}{1 - i} > \Pi \qquad (11.2)$$

When (11.2) holds, the owner of the technology can give a licensee a portion of the rent that is sufficient to induce high quality maintenance and still earn higher profits than by undertaking himself production in the foreign market.

11.3 The choice between multinational and uninational production

Once a firm has decided to internalize its operations it still faces the choice of how to supply both its home and foreign markets. That is, should the firm produce in its home country and export to foreign markets or supply foreign markets from a plant located in a foreign country? In the latter case, the firm could also choose to supply its home market by importing from its foreign plants. Below we discuss the factors determining these decisions starting with the case where the firm is a monopolist and there are no taxes on profits and no impediments to trade. We then introduce tariffs and corporate taxes and examine how the influence the firm's location decisions. Finally, we consider oligopolistic interaction and the use of multinational production as a method for deterring the entry of potential rivals.

The case of monopoly

Transportation costs

Consider two markets; a home market with L consumers and a foreign market with L^* consumers. All consumers have identical preferences and incomes so that at any price the quantity demanded in the foreign country is L^*/L times as large as the quantity demanded by home consumers. Let the demands in the home and foreign countries be given by

$$q = L(a - p) \quad \text{and} \quad q^* = L^*(a - p^*) \tag{11.3}$$

Assume that export sales must incur a per-unit transport cost τ.[22] The firm chooses between the following options: (a) to supply both markets from a home plant; (b) to supply both countries from a foreign plant; (c) to supply each market from a local plant. In the absence of strategic considerations the profit maximizing choice is determined solely by the magnitude of tariff payments relative to production costs. The latter have too components. Marginal production costs (c) are constant and equal in both countries; fixed costs differ between countries. Letting F and F^* denote home and foreign fixed costs per *plant*, the profits associated with each option can be written:

(a) Production in a home plant alone:[23]

$$[(a - c)^2 L + (a - c - \tau)^2 L^*]/4 - F$$

(b) Production in a foreign plant alone:

$$[(a - c - \tau)^2 L + (a - c)^2 L^*]/4 - F^*$$

(c) Production in a home and a foreign plant:

$$[(a - c)^2 (L + L^*)]/4 - F - F^*$$

It is easily checked that the difference between the home and the foreign price is smaller than τ regardless of whether production takes place in one country or in both. Indeed, since marginal cost is assumed to be the same in all locations, price will necessarily be the same in both countries if option (c) is chosen. If on the other hand a single plant is used to supply both markets, part of the transport cost will be absorbed. Thus, in either case markets will be segmented in equilibrium.

For a given transport cost, the choice among the three options will depend on market sizes. This is illustrated in Figure 11.1 for the case where $F > F^*$. When the combination L and L^* lies above (below) the line passing through A and B, the firm earns higher (lower) profits by locating in the home country alone than by locating in the foreign country alone. It earns higher (lower) profits by producing in both countries than in the home country alone if

$$L^* > (<) \, 4F^*/\bar{\tau}^2 \quad \text{where } \bar{\tau}^2 \equiv [(a-c)^2 - (a-c-\tau)^2]$$

Similarly, profits are higher (lower) when producing in both countries than in the foreign country alone when $L > (<) \, 4F^*/\bar{\tau}^2$.

Putting these conditions together one derives the range of country sizes for which profits (a), (b) or (c) are profit maximizing. These are shown in Figure 11.1. An increase in transportation cost brings point B closer to the origin implying that a 2-plant firm is more profitable for smaller country sizes. Increasing the fixed cost F reduces the size of the area for which production takes place in the home country alone, and increases the sizes of the areas in which production is concentrated either in the foreign country alone or

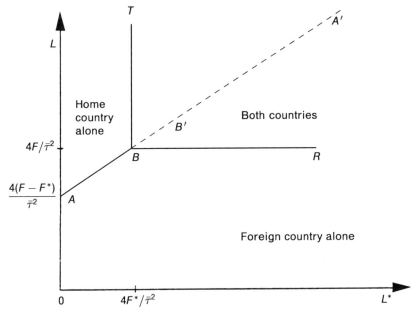

Figure 11.1 *Transportation cost and the choice of production sites*

in both countries. It is also apparent from Figure 11.1 that an equiproportional increase of F and F^* shifts B upward along the line AA'. This indicates that the range of country sizes that calling for a 2-plant solution is getting smaller.

Problem 11.1: Assume that demands are given by (11.2). Construct a similar partition as in Figure 11.1 assuming that the (constant) marginal costs rather than fixed costs differ across countries.

Policy interventions and transfer pricing

We now look at the joint effects of a tariff and a corporate income tax as determinants of plant location.[24] The interaction between these policy instruments raises the issue of transfer pricing, i.e. the setting of prices on intrafirm transactions to minimize the bite of trade and income taxes on the firm's global profits.[25]

According to internationally agreed principles, the dutiable value must be the arm's-length price. Nonetheless exporters have some elbow room when declaring a value for duty. This manoeuvring space derives from the fact that comparable arm's length prices may not exist or, when they do exist, customs authorities may be unable or unwilling to find out what they are. By declaring a high value for duty the firm increases the tariff payments it must make. However, since a higher import price shifts profits from the importing country to the exporting country, the total tax burden will fall if profits declared in the importing country are more heavily taxed than profits realized in the exporting country. Whether the exporter is better off declaring a low or a high value for duty therefore depends on the rate of duty relative to the difference in taxation rates.[26]

To examine the effects of tariffs and taxes we let τ and τ^* denote the *ad valorem* tariff rates in the home and the foreign country and, similarly, we let T and T^* denote, respectively, the share of the firm's profit earned in the home country and the foreign country that is eventually paid to some tax authority.[27] Denote the transfer prices set by a home respectively foreign plant as R and R^* and assume that these prices must lie in an interval $[R_{min}, R_{max}]$. Imposing such constraint is reasonable when pricing outside this interval would trigger an investigation by customs authorities which is more costly to the firm than declaring a value for duty within the interval.

Assuming that marginal cost is c regardless of the location of production, the net of tax profits associated with the three options discussed above are

(a) For a home plant alone:

$$\pi_a = (1 - T)[(p - c)q + (R - c)q^* - F] + (1 - T^*)[p^* - R(1 + \tau^*)]q^*$$

(b) For a foreign plant alone:

$$\pi_b = (1 - T)[p - R^*(1 + \tau)]q + (1 - T^*)[(R^* - c)q + (p^* - c)q^* - F^*]$$

(c) For two plants:

$$\pi_c = (1 - T)[(p - c)q - F] + (1 - T^*)[(p^* - c)q^* - F^*]$$

The analysis below contrasts options (a) and (c). It is left to the reader to examine how adding option (b) will affect the firm's location decision.

Differentiation of π_a shows that R must be chosen such that

$$R = R_{max} \quad \text{when } (1 + \tau^*) < (1 - T)/(1 - T^*)$$

and

$$R = R_{min} \quad \text{when } (1 + \tau^*) > (1 - T)/(1 - T^*)$$

With respect to quantities, the first-order conditions are:

$$MR(q) = c$$

and

$$MR^*(q^*) = c\frac{1 - T}{1 - T^*} - R\left[\frac{1 - T}{1 - T^*} - (1 + \tau^*)\right]$$

Since differentiation of π_a *and* π_c with respect to q yields the same expression, we know that the quantity sold in the home market is the same under option (a) as under option (c).

To compare profits under option (a) to those of option (c), for the general case where $T \neq T^*$, we solve the first-order conditions for q and q^* for the particular case where demands are given by (11.3). Defining $\Delta \equiv (1 - T)/(1 - T^*)$, it is straightforward to show that the profits associated with options (a) and (c) are given by:

$$\pi_a^0 = (1 - T)[(a - c)^2 L/4 - F] + (1 - T^*)$$

$$\times [(a - \Delta c) - R(1 + \tau^* - \Delta)]^2 L^*/4$$

$$\pi_c^0 = (1 - T)[(a - c)^2 L/4 - F] + (1 - T^*)[(a - c)^2 L^*/4 - F^*]$$

In contrast to the previous section, zero fixed costs no longer imply that profits are highest when each market is supplied by a local plant. To illustrate, we consider the case $F^* = 0$. Under zero fixed cost for a foreign plant, we have:[28]

$$[\pi_c^0 - \pi_a^0] > 0 \quad \text{when } c(1 - \Delta) - R(1 + \tau^* - \Delta) < 0 \tag{11.4}$$

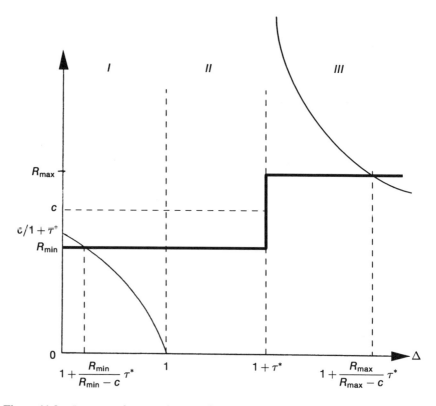

Figure 11.2   *Location choice under transfer pricing*

To explore the implications of (11.4) we consider Figure 11.2, which displays the optimal transfer price as the (bold line) step function bounded by R_{min} and R_{max}. We have three possibilities: $\Delta < 1$ which corresponds to area *I* in Figure 11.2; $1 < \Delta < 1 + \tau^*$ which corresponds to area *II*; and $1 + \tau^* < \Delta$ which is represented by area *III*.

Using (11.4) we find

Case 1: $\Delta < 1$ ensures that (11.4) is satisfied for

$$R > c(1 - \Delta)/(1 + \tau^* - \Delta)$$

The combinations of R and Δ which satisfy this condition are located above the hyperbola shown in area *I* of Figure 11.2. Option (a) will be chosen only when $\Delta < 1 + (R_{min}/(R_{min} - c))\tau^*$ a condition which holds only if $c/1 + \tau^* > R_{min}$. By contrast, when $\Delta > 1 + (R_{min}/(R_{min} - c))\tau^*$ the 2-plant solution generates higher profits than a home plant alone.

Case 2: $1 < \Delta < (1 + \tau^*)$ ensures that (11.4) is satisfied for any positive R. The 2-plant solution is always profit maximizing when Δ belongs to this interval.

Case 3: $1 + \tau^* < \Delta$, a condition under which (11.4) is satisfied for $R < c(1 - \Delta)/(1 + \tau^* - \Delta)$. The combinations of R and Δ which satisfy (11.4) are now located below the hyperbola displayed in area *III* of Figure 11.2. Hence, the 2-plant solution is preferred when $\Delta < 1 + (R_{max}/(R_{max} - c))\tau^*$, otherwise the home plant alone is profit maximizing.

We see that when the taxation of profits in the home county is very low compared to the taxation of profits realized in the foreign country, a home plant alone is optimal. As the tax rates becomes more equal the dominant option is to establish a plant in each location. However, one cannot exclude the possibility that for a very high home taxation rate it becomes optimal again to concentrate production in the home country. This rather particular result arises when the minimum transfer price allows the firm to declare losses on exports. These losses are then set against profits derived from local sales.[29]

Empirical evidence

Empirical studies on the effect of the tariff and on transfer pricing include Horst's (1972) study of US and Canadian firms and Grubert and Mutti's (1991) study of US MNE activity across 33 countries. Horst found that US exports to Canada as a proportion of US exports *plus* production of US-owned Canadian subsidiaries were negatively related to the Canadian tariff. A similar relationship was found in the case of sales to the United Kingdom and to the EC. In their broader sample of 33 countries, Grubert and Mutti found evidence of income shifting by US MNEs into low tax countries. In addition, host country corporate income tax rates appeared to have a large and significant negative impact on export sales by local US-owned subsidiaries to third countries, but not on local sales. They also found tariffs to be unrelated to affiliates' exports to third countries but positively related to local sales.[30]

Oligopolistic interaction and entry deterrence

Modeling MNE behavior in oligopolistic environments introduces new considerations in the export versus foreign production decision. In particular, it is possible that foreign production becomes a preferred option even when cost and trade policy variables might otherwise dictate exporting. A simple model can be used to illustrate this point.[31]

Assume a home firm which has already incurred a firm-specific sunk cost G, as well as a plant-specific fixed cost F to produce in a plant located in its home market.[32] The home firm's output is sold locally and in a foreign market. There also is a foreign firm which, by incurring the same firm-specific (G) and plant-specific (F) fixed costs as the home firm, can compete with the home firm in the foreign country. It is assumed that, should the foreign firm undertake production, it does not export to the home country.

The game unfolds as follows. In the first stage the home firm decides whether or not to establish a subsidiary in the foreign country. If it does, it incurs an additional fixed cost F; if it does not, it serves the foreign market through exports. By choosing to export the firm incurs a transport cost but saves the fixed plant cost. It is assumed that the home firm's sales to the foreign market are profitable regardless of the method of supply (exports or local production) chosen by the home firm.

In the second stage the foreign firm decides whether to enter the foreign market. Once both entry decisions have been made, the 2 firms engage in Cournot competition to determine output quantities.[33] It is assumed that the entry decisions are made taking into account their effect on the subsequent quantity equilibrium. Finally, it is assumed that marginal costs are constant and that markets are segmented. This allows for a determination of the quantity equilibrium as a function of foreign demand parameters only.

Figure 11.3 displays the reaction function of the foreign firm (r^*) as well as the reaction of the home firm when it chooses to export (r_E) and when it establishes a plant in the foreign country (r_{MNE}). The reaction function r_E is located below r_{MNE} since a tariff is assumed to be levied on exports sales and is therefore part of the home firm's marginal cost.

Let $\tilde{\pi}$ and $\tilde{\pi}^*$ denote *variable profit* (i.e. the difference between revenue and variable cost) of the home and foreign firm, respectively. Then the quantity equilibrium is located at point H or point J in Figure 11.3 depending on the option chosen by the home firm. It is clear from Figure 11.3 that opting for foreign production has, from the home firm's perspective, the advantage of bringing about a lower equilibrium output by the foreign firm.

Consider first the case where the foreign firm's profits at point $J(\tilde{\pi}_J^*)$ are positive. Since the equilibrium at H yields higher profits to the foreign firm than the equilibrium at point J, it must be true that the foreign firm's profits at H are also positive. This in turn, implies that entry by the foreign firm takes place regardless of the option chosen by the home firm. The home firm chooses to export if $\tilde{\pi}_J - G \leq \tilde{\pi}_H$, otherwise it establishes a plant in the foreign country. Conversely, if the profits of the foreign firm are negative at H then they must also be negative at J. Hence, the foreign firm will not enter regardless of the option chosen by the home firm. The home firm will choose

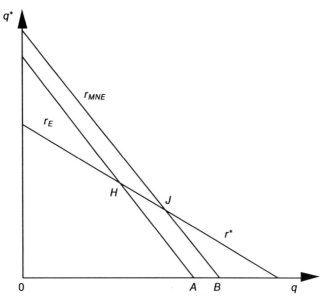

Figure 11.3 *Local production and entry deterrence*

to export if and only if $\tilde{\pi}_B - G \leq \tilde{\pi}_A$, i.e. if its monopoly profits from exporting are larger than its monopoly profits from producing in the foreign country.

The most interesting case is where $\tilde{\pi}_H^* - F - G > 0 > \tilde{\pi}_J^* - F - G$ and $\tilde{\pi}_B - G \leq \tilde{\pi}_A$. In this case, entry by the foreign firm can be profitable but only if the home firm chooses to export. At the same time, exporting is more profitable to the home firm if the foreign firm chooses not to enter. When these conditions hold, the optimal decision for the home firm is to make an irrevocable commitment to produce in a foreign subsidiary if $\tilde{\pi}_B - G > \tilde{\pi}_H$ holds, and to export otherwise.

Horstmann and Markusen (1992) explore a related model in which a home and a foreign firm decide between the following: (a) not entering; (b) entering with one plant supplying both markets; (c) entering with 2 plants, each supplying local consumers. In contrast to the preceding model, entry decisions in the Horstmann and Markusen model are made simultaneously in the first stage of the game. Three equilibria are then possible: (1) a classical duopoly with 2 single-plant firms; (2) a monopoly with 1 plant in each country; (3) a duopoly where both firms have plants in the 2 countries. Roughly speaking, a market structure of type (1) emerges when plant-specific costs (F) are large relative to firm-specific and transport costs (or tariffs). An equilibrium of type (2) arises when transport- and firm-specific costs are so high that 2 firms cannot to be profitable. Type (3) structures emerge with low plant specific costs.

Trade interventions and firm structure

The models of oligopolistic interaction underscore the fact that one cannot take firm structure as a given when determining the optimal trade intervention. For example, returning to Figure 11.3, it is clear that increasing the tariff widens the gap between the r_E and r_{MNE}. In particular, starting from a low tariff rate, the initial effect of a tariff increase will be to reduce export sales. However, once a critical level of the tariff is attained, the tariff is 'jumped', that is, the firm ceases to export and instead supplies the foreign market via local production. This critical level of the tariff may lie far below the rate that maximizes welfare if the possibility of tariff jumping were ruled out.

Allowing the tariff to be jumped suggests that small changes in the tariff rate may bring about discontinuous shifts in prices, quantities and market structure. The existence of such discontinuities, however, appears to hinge on either there being few firms in the industry, or on having most or all firms jump the tariff at the same time. The following example provides some intuition in regard to the factors which determine whether discontinuous jumps at the industry level will occur.

Let there be n_x firms that supply a market through exports, and incur a specific tariff or transport cost τ by doing so. Let there be n_y firms supplying the same market from a local plant. The inverse demand is $p = a - Q$ with $Q = (n_x q_x + n_y q_y)$ where q_x and q_y denote respectively the quantity sold by an individual exporter and local producer. The marginal production cost of exporters and local producers are respectively c_x and c_y. Hence, the marginal cost of exporting is $c_x + \tau$. In addition, local producers incur a fixed cost per plant F which is not incurred by exporters. Under Cournot rivalry, the first-order conditions for exporters and local plants are respectively:

$$a - (n_x + 1)q_x - n_y q_y (c_x + \tau) = 0$$

and

$$a - n_x q_x - (n_y + 1)q_y - c_y = 0$$

Using these conditions it is straightforward to show that the profits from exporting and local production are, respectively:

$$\pi_x = \{[a - (n_y + 1)(c_x + t) + n_y c_y]/[n_x + n_y + 1]\}^2$$
$$\pi_y = \{[a - (n_x + 1)c_y + n_x(c_x + \tau)]/[n_x + n_y + 1]\}^2 - F$$

Hence, $\text{sign}[\pi_y - \pi_x] = \text{sign}\{-F^{1/2} - [c_y - (c_x + \tau)]\}$ This indicates that when marginal production costs are constant, either all firms choose to be exporters or all choose to become multinational. To obtain an interior equilibrium in which some firms export and others are multinational it is necessary to have $-F^{1/2} - [c_y - (c_x + T)] = 0$ in equilibrium.[34] This outcome requires that costs (fixed, variable or both) increase with the quantity of output produced in a country. If so, the establishment of plants in the country where costs are initially lower will bring about an increase in cost which may eventually attain a level which makes firms indifferent between producing in only 1 or in the 2 countries. If such equilibrium is attained one may observe some firms producing in one country, while others produce in both. This type of equilibrium is explored more fully in the general equilibrium analysis presented below.

Problem 11.2:   Take the example above. Let $N = n_x + n_y$ where N is fixed. Assume that $F(n_y) = (4 + n_y)F/4$ but that neither c_x nor c_y depend on the number of firms in a particular location. Find parameter values such that n_x and n_y are positive when firms are free to choose their mode of market penetration. Examine how the share of sales accounted for by exports changes as a result of small changes in N. Treat the number of firms as a continuous variable.

11.4 Multinational enterprises and trade in general equilibrium

We now consider MNEs in the context of the traditional general equilibrium trade model. In this framework, we examine how country characteristics may affect production and trade patterns when firms can, but need not, produce by combining inputs that are located in different countries. To understand the different factors that underlie the establishment of foreign subsidiaries and the observation of intra-firm trade, it is important to distinguish vertically from horizontally integrated firms. The former have establishments in one country that supply inputs to affiliated establishments in other countries. By definition, vertically integrated firms engage in intra-firm trade. Horizontally integrated firms have establishments in different locations that produce the same or similar product. Horizontally integrated firms may, but need not, engage in intra-firm trade.[35] Below we consider the role of factor endowments in determining firms' decision to locate different stages of the production process in different countries. We then turn to the case of horizontally integrated MNEs and we discuss the roles of endowments in deciding the composition of industry as between uninational and multinational enterprises.[36]

Factor endowments and vertically integrated multinationals

We consider the Helpman (1984) and Helpman and Krugman (1985) model in which vertically integrated firms decide whether to locate all stages of their production in a single country or to locate upstream operations in one country and downstream activities in another. The model assumes an economy with 2 producing sectors: food and manufactures. Manufactures come in different varieties and are produced using four types of inputs: labor, capital, intermediate inputs, and 'headquarters' services'. 'Headquarters' services', a convenient label for intangible assets such as know-how and reputation, are produced as a first-stage activity that uses only labor and capital as inputs. In the next production stage, labor and capital are combined with headquarters' services to make an intermediate input. The latter is best thought of as a collection of components. The last production stage uses labor, capital, headquarters' services and intermediate inputs to produce a final, consumable, product.

Intermediate inputs as well as headquarters' services are not generic but are instead firm-specific and, since each firm produces a single variety, they are also variety-specific. This means that each variety of intermediate input and headquarters' services can only be used as an input in the production of the final good variety for which they were originally designed.

This specificity of headquarters' services and of intermediates exposes arm's length transactions in these inputs to contracting problems that flow from opportunism.[37] The basic problem of exposure to opportunism is that the intended user of specialized inputs has an incentive to renege on the contract with the supplier once the latter has incurred a sunk cost. Since the inputs, once specialized, have no value to a firm producing a different variety, the buyer finds herself in a situation where she can demand better terms alleging that some contractual term has not been met. The writing of contracts which address the potential for opportunism is costly, and while some contractual provisions will mitigate the problem, they are unlikely to eliminate it. By integrating the production of headquarters' services, intermediates and downstream transformation activities within a single firm the vulnerability due to the opportunism of others is avoided.

The model also assumes that labor and capital are immobile across borders but that manufacturing firms may combine firm-specific headquarters' services or intermediates produced in one country with capital and labor located in another country. As an input in the production of intermediates and the final good, headquarters' services are assumed to be equally productive regardless of the location of the downstream production stages. Similarly, intermediates are assumed to be equally productive when used in the manufacture of the final good, regardless of the country in which the intermediates are combined with the three other inputs.

A further assumption is that while there exist many potential varieties of the final good, each variety has the same cost structure. The cost functions associated with the production of headquarters services and intermediates are $C^H(w, r, h)$ and $C^Z(w, r, h, z)$ respectively, where h denotes the amount of headquarters' services and z is the amount of intermediates. Both inputs are produced under increasing returns to scale with C^Z increasing in z and declining in h.[38] The cost of final assembly is $C^P(w, r, h, z, q)$ where q denotes the quantity of final output produced by the firm. Final stage production also exhibits increasing returns to scale.

Assuming there are no impediments to trade (e.g. no transport costs or tariffs), the total cost incurred by a manufacturing firm is the sum of the three aforementioned components. When the rewards paid to capital and labor are the same at each production stage, total cost is:

$$C(w, r, q) = \min_{h,z}[C^P(w, r, h, z, q) + C^Z(w, r, h, z) + C^H(w, r, h)] \quad (11.5)$$

where, at the margin, the cost of an expansion of headquarters' services and intermediates must equal the downstream cost savings that such an expansion brings about.

The assumption of increasing returns to scale at each of the three stages implies that the cost incurred in producing either headquarters' services, the intermediate input or the final product will be lowest when all activities at a given stage are consolidated in a single plant.[39] By contrast, there is nothing in the model that would also make it more advantageous to concentrate different stages in the same plant. Since tariffs and transportation costs are assumed to be zero, minimization of total cost requires that the firm carry out an individual production stage in the country where factor prices make it the low cost site for that stage.

The remaining assumptions of the model are as in Section 9.4 (p. 364). Specifically, consumer preferences are homothetic and equal across countries; demands for all individual varieties are the same. Firms in the manufacturing sector produce a single variety and equate marginal cost to marginal revenue. Freedom of entry in food and manufactures brings about equality between price and average cost. Food, the numeraire good, is assumed to be produced under conditions of constant returns to scale using labor and capital as inputs. Only locally available labor and capital can be used to produce food, and perfect competition in the food sector ensures that food producers earn zero profits in equilibrium.

Given the above assumptions, the first-order and zero profit conditions together with the market clearing conditions for factor markets and final good markets[40] determine the output of each industry, the number of varieties produced and the prices of goods and factors. As in Chapter 9, the equilibrium of the integrated economy with all factors internationally mobile can serve as the baseline against which alternative equilibria can be compared. In the present context, we wish to establish the conditions under which firms will concentrate all production stages in a single country, and conditions under which different production stages will be located in different countries.

To address this issue, Figure 11.4 displays factor employment vectors for the integrated economy with OQ_1^w and OQ_2^w denoting world factor utilization in food and manufacturing. Figure 11.4 is drawn under the assumption that the manufacturing sector is capital-intensive. The vectors OH^w, H^wZ^w and $Z^wQ_2^w$ represent factor usage for each of the 3 production stages in the manufacturing industry. It is assumed that the production of headquarters' services is the most capital-intensive stage, its intensity being given by the slope of OH^w. Final assembly is the least capital-intensive, where this intensity is expressed by the slope of $Z^wQ_2^w$. The slope of H^wZ^w shows the capital intensity of intermediates production. Thus, OQ_2^w stands for the sum of direct and indirect employment in manufacturing.

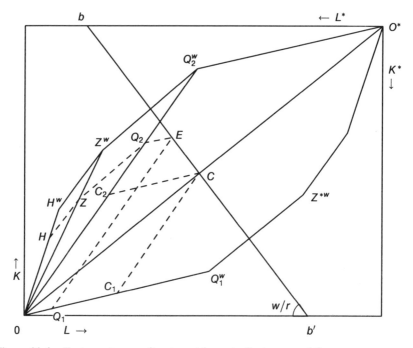

Figure 11.4 *Factor price equalization with vertically integrated firms*

If food and manufactures were the only goods traded, then the factor price equalization set would be the parallelogram $OQ_2^w O^* Q_1^w$. However, when headquarter services and intermediates are also tradeable, the FPE set includes the areas $OH^w Z^w Q_2^w$ and $O^* H^{*w} Z^{*w} Q_1^w$. This enlarged area is in fact the FPE set when firms can become multinational. Since the number of goods exceed the number of factors, factor price equalization is consistent with a great many production configurations. In the present context this means that for any endowment allocation inside the FPE set, the quantities, prices and number of varieties in the integrated economy can be reproduced with different degrees of foreign engagement.[41]

To limit the number of possible configurations, we adopt the following rule: whenever several equilibria are possible, we choose the equilibrium which minimizes the extent of foreign involvement. Specifically, this requires that firms do not decentralize their activities when the cost of factors is the same in both countries.[42] In addition, it is assumed that if factor cost differences dictate multiplant production, then third stage assembly is separated from upstream stages before the intermediate stage is disconnected from the production of headquarters services. Helpman and Krugman (1985) state that this latter assumption is justified on the grounds that it is more costly to separate the production of middle products from the 'center' than to separate finished product lines since middle products call for know-how more readily available at the 'center' stages.

Consider now an endowment point such as E located in Figure 11.4 above the diagonal and within the parallelogram $OQ_2^w O^* Q_1^w$. The home country's factor use in manufacturing is given by the vector OQ_2 which decomposes into headquarters factor use OH and intermediate and final assembly use, HZ and ZQ_2 respectively. Since the endowment point lies in the parallelogram $OQ_2^w O^* Q_1^w$, trade in food and final manufactures alone can equalize factor prices. Since there are no cost savings from engaging in multiplant production, the assumption that foreign involvement is minimized implies that all manufacturing firms are uninational. Hence, in equilibrium, each country produces intermediates as well as headquarters' services in proportion to final stage assembly. The home country is a net exporter of fully finished differentiated manufactures and an importer of food. This is seen in Figure 11.4 which shows $OQ_2 > OC_2$ and $OQ_1 < OC_1$ where the consumption vectors are constructed as in Chapter 9.[43] Note that as in Chapter 9, there is intra-industry trade (IIT) in manufactures since consumers in both countries consume all varieties. All manufacturing stages are concentrated in uniplant firms that use the production techniques of the integrated equilibrium. The factor content of trade is given by the vector EC.

Consider now the endowment point $\hat{E}$ outside the area $OQ_2^w O^* Q_1^w$ as shown in Figure 11.5. In this case, trade in food and final goods alone no

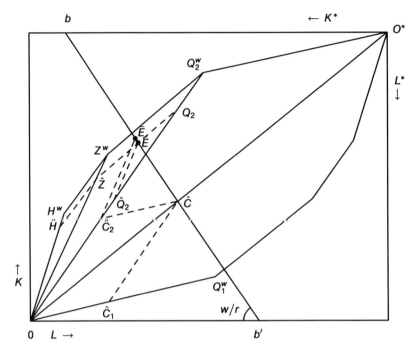

Figure 11.5 *Multinational production with intra-firm trade*

longer equalizes factor prices. Since the home country is capital-rich, it is assumed that wages (in the absence of foreign production) are lower in the foreign country and capital rentals higher.[44] This has two consequences: it provides an incentive for home firms to carry out final assembly in the foreign country, and it brings about home country specialization in the production of manufactures.

The equilibrium which reproduces the integrated equilibrium with the minimum foreign involvement is obtained as follows. Draw through $\hat{E}$ a line parallel to $Z^w Q_2^w$ to yield the points $\hat{Z}$ and Q_2. Through $\hat{Z}$, draw a line parallel to $H^w Z^w$ and label $\hat{H}$ its intersection with OH^w. The allocation of labor and capital in the home country is now as follows: $O\hat{H}$ in the production of headquarters services, $\hat{H}\hat{Z}$ in the production of intermediates, and $\hat{Z}\hat{E}$ in third-stage final assembly.

Home produced headquarters services and intermediates are used by home firms in the third stage of production, in combination with foreign labor and capital in the amount given by $\hat{E}Q_2$. Thus home firms are multinational and the final stage production is carried out by some firms in the home country and by others in the foreign country. The latter engage in intra-firm trade in intermediates. Since some third-stage production takes place in the foreign country, the number of varieties produced in the home country is less than the number of home firms; conversely, the number of foreign varieties exceeds the number of foreign firms. Employment by foreign firms is $Q_2Q_2^w$ in manufactures and $O^*Q_2^w$ in the food industry.[45] The home country produces no food.

Since consumers consume all varieties regardless of country of residence, there is again 2-way trade in manufactures. With the endowment point at $\hat{E}$, the home country is a net exporter of final manufacturing output as well as of intermediates and headquarters' services. This follows from the fact that $O\hat{Q}_2 > O\hat{C}_2$, where the term on the left represents the amount of final output of manufactures produced in the home country and the term on the right represents consumption of manufactures. The exports of final assemblies could be arm's-length or intra-firm, while the exports of intermediates and headquarters' services are only intra-firm.

As the endowment point slides further upward along the iso-income line bb', the production point $\hat{Q}_2$ approaches the consumption point $\hat{C}_2$. Eventually one has $O\hat{Q}_2 = O\hat{C}_2$. The endowment in question is represented as point $\bar{E}$ in Figure 11.5. For endowments even further from the diagonal, the home country continues to export final assemblies since it still engages in third-stage assembly and foreign consumers will always purchase home

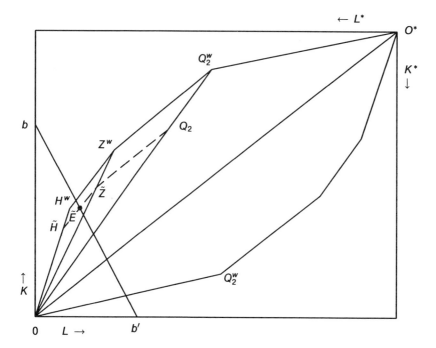

Figure 11.6 *Trade in headquarters' services*

varieties. However, the home country is now a *net* importer of final assemblies. It does, however, remain an exporter of intermediates and of headquarters' services. Since the home country does not produce food, all its demand for food is met by imports.

As the foreign country becomes even more capital rich, the endowment point may eventually cross into the triangle OH^wZ^w. One such endowment point is shown as $\tilde{E}$ in Figure 11.6. Now, even shifting all final assembly to the foreign country is not sufficient to equalize factor prices. Hence, intermediate production is also transplanted to the foreign country. The production allocation that minimizes foreign involvement and achieves factor price equalization is when the quantity $O\tilde{H}$ of home factors is allocated to the production of headquarters services and the quantity $\tilde{H}\tilde{E}$ of home factors is allocated to the production of intermediates. Finally, all middle products, regardless of whether they are produced at home or abroad are combined with headquarters' services and foreign labor and capital for final assembly in foreign plants. No third-stage production at all is taking place in the home country. Total employment of factors by home manufacturing firms is given by OQ_2 and home country employment is $O\tilde{E}$. Again, the home country imports all the food it consumes, as well as all final assemblies. All home exports are intra-firm, and consist of intermediates and headquarters' services.

Whether the endowment $\tilde{E}$ also generates intra-industry trade is a matter of definition. If intra-industry trade is defined as 2-way trade in products produced with identical factor intensities, then intra-industry trade is absent. In contrast, if intra-industry trade is defined as trade carried out by establishments classified as belonging to the same industry or product category, then the export of intermediates associated with the import of final assemblies qualifies as intra-industry trade.

Transport costs and horizontally integrated multinationals

While the previous section provides a setting in which multinational firms emerge endogenously, the assumptions of zero transport costs and increasing returns to scale at each stage only allow different stages of a firm's production to be located in different countries. Hence, the model cannot address the empirical fact of horizontally integrated firms. The model also permits unidirectional trade in headquarters' services where the importance of this trade relates positively to a disparity in relative endowments. However, the model is unable to address the observation that a country can be a source country of parent firms (with subsidiaries abroad) and the host country of affiliates of foreign parent firms. Therefore, the model is unable to account for the disproportionate role of multinational activity among rich countries.

The reconciliation of theory with these empirical observations is the subject of recent work by Markusen (1995) and Markusen and Venables (1995, 1996). Their models are similar to the general equilibrium models examined in Chapter 9 but with two major differences. First, firms in the differentiated sector have the option of becoming multinational by incurring the fixed cost per plant twice: once per country. Second, transport costs are incurred on export sales of the differentiated good. Uninational firms (i.e. firms with one plant located anywhere) incur transport costs while multinationals do not.

The presence of transport costs complicates the analysis considerably since it causes the factor price equalization set to become one-dimensional. This comes from the fact that reallocations of production in response to shifts in endowments induce changes in the amount of resources consumed in transportation. Since the total amount of resources is fixed, this must result in a change in aggregate output. Hence, when transport costs are positive, the cross-country allocation of production is no longer determined by endowments alone but is a function of the endowment allocation *and* the distribution of consumer expenditure across countries. The effect of transportation costs is to skew the production of manufactures towards the country with the larger expenditure.

Since the standard technique for constructing production and consumption vectors under factor price equalization is no longer applicable, numerical techniques are used instead to partition the endowment box into regions that correspond to different equilibrium configurations of multinational and uninational firms. While the size and the shape of the regions depends very much on the values of the variable transport cost and the fixed cost per plant, the following picture emerges.

The smaller is the difference in relative endowments and the smaller the difference in country sizes, the more preponderant is the presence of multinationals in the differentiated industry. When relative endowments and country sizes are equal or nearly equal, all manufacturing firms are multinational in equilibrium. By moving the endowment away from the centre of the box, one eventually enters regions where multinational and uninational firms coexist. Depending on the direction of the move, the region entered can have uninational firms located in only one country or in both countries. As the endowment point is placed even further from the centre of the box one eventually enters regions where all production in the differentiated sector is carried out by uninational firms. Depending on the location of endowment point, uninational firms in the manufacturing industry are located in the 2 countries or in 1 country only.

These observations suggest, consistent with empirical observation, that the more similar countries are in terms of absolute and relative endowment the more likely it is that they will harbor plants of the same multinational firm. Moreover, the model implies that at the centre of the box, where relative and absolute endowment are similar, the composition of trade is skewed towards intra-industry affiliate sales. The model is also consistent with 2-way foreign investment, although in Markusen and Venables (1996), for example, there is nothing that identifies one plant as a parent and the other as a subsidiary.

11.5 **Empirical evidence**

The different issues discussed in this chapter are brought together in an empirical study by Brainard (1993a). This study is interesting because unlike earlier studies it addresses many of the hypotheses about MNEs using a single data set. The data consist of pooled observations on the 1989 trade and affiliates sales between the US and 27 countries in each of 64 industries.

The hypotheses tested by Brainard pertain to outward and inward activity, but we report on the former only. Total outward activity in industry j and country i is defined as the sum of US exports of commodity j to country i and sales by US-owned foreign subsidiaries located in country i and belonging to industry j. The results we report concern primarily the effects of a number of variables on the composition of outward activity as between trade and affiliate sales. The variables in question fall within three categories.

First, endowment variables. The model of vertical foreign expansion would have us expect that multinational activity is more prevalent than trade among country pairs with larger endowment differences, whereas the model of horizontal integration suggests the opposite.[46] Since the United States has among the highest *per capita* incomes and is in all cases the market of origin or destination, endowment differences can be proxied by *per capita* incomes.[47] A related variable which proxies for changes in relative production cost associated with macroeconomic factors is the depreciation of the US dollar *vis-à-vis* the destination currency between 1985 and 1989. One would expect sales by subsidiaries of US parents to be lower relative to US exports, everything else being equal, when the destination country has experienced a currency appreciation relative to the dollar.

Second, proximity and scale variables. The former include transportation costs, distance and barriers to trade. According to theory these should favor sales by subsidiaries in foreign locations at the expense of exports. Higher barriers to foreign investment, by contrast, should augment trade at the expense of affiliate sales. Theory also indicates that sales by foreign affiliates should be more prevalent when economies of scale at the plant level are weaker and the destination market is larger. Finally, to the extent that profits from exports are reported and taxed in the country of origin rather than the country of destination, US firms should, all else being equal, favor the export mode of market penetration when profits in the destination country are more heavily taxed.

The third and last category of variables are those that proxy for ownership of intangible assets, capturing firms' ability to engage in multinational activity.

The sample of estimation results reported in Table 11.6 relates the aforementioned variables to two measures of outward and inward activity: the first is the probability of observing positive affiliate sales,[48] the second is the share of outward activity accounted for by affiliate sales in those cases where the share is positive.

The estimation results display a strong positive correlation between the likelihood of observing outward affiliate sales and the size of the foreign country as measured by its GDP. They also indicate a strong negative correlation with distance. This is a correlation similar to that found in a gravity equation where the dependent variable is the volume of bilateral trade. The negative effect of scale economies on the probability of engaging in multinational activity is also in line with expectations. The negative sign appears as well in the equation which explains the affiliates' share, and presumably reflects the fact that the larger the scale economies the higher the proportion of industry members who choose exports as the preferred mode of foreign market penetration.

The results on trade barriers are mixed. While openness to investment and tariffs have signs that accord with expectations, the proxy for NTBs appears unrelated to both dependent variables. Transport costs also appear not to be a determinant of the likelihood of observing multinational production. However, they are correctly signed and significant in the share equation which does not include distance as an explanatory variable. The tax coefficient in the share equation diverges from the predicted sign and is significant.

The *per capita* income coefficient is significant only in the share equation. The fact that it is positive lends support to the Markusen and Venables (1996) model of horizontally integrated MNE production rather than to the Helpman and Krugman model (1985) of vertically integrated MNE production. The coefficient on the exchange rate also has the predicted sign in both equations.

Overall, the results also confirm the earlier findings in regard to the prominent role played by proprietary advantages flowing from intellectual property. They also indicate that the effect of *per capita* income differentials on intra-industry affiliates' sales are of the same sign as their effect on intra-industry trade. By and large, they also indicate that trade barriers play a role in accordance with theory.

Table 11.6 *Regression estimates for outward direct investment*

Explanatory variable	Dependent variable	
	Probability of subsidiary sales	Subsidiary share of total activity
Intercept	1.434	−0.646
Transport costs	0.122	0.195
	(0.38)	(3.33)
Foreign tariff	0.105	0.166
	(1.71)	(2.12)
Openness to trade	0.884	−0.356
	(1.55)	(−0.84)
Openness to investment	0.944	2.186
	(2.23)	(5.60)
Plant scale economies	−0.173	−0.154
	(−3.68)	(−4.42)
Per capita income	0.044	0.761
	(0.26)	(4.99)
US$ depreciation in foreign market	−0.179	−0.287
	(−2.02)	(3.84)
Tax rate	−0.178	0.927
	(−0.42)	(2.20)
GDP	0.479	–
	(8.54)	
US industry R&D intensity	0.545	–
	(10.10)	
Distance	−0.697	–
	(−3.59)	

Notes:

Obs. = 1126 (RHO = 0.122 (0.84))

Loglikelihood = −1572; % positive obs = 73.7

Transport costs are calculated as freight and insurance charges divided by import values. US and foreign tariffs are aggregated into 3-digit SIC categories. Plant scale economies are proxied by the number of production employees in the median plant in each industry. Corporate tax burdens are proxied by corporate tax rates. In the absence of data on non-tariff barriers, use is made of indices of openness to trade and openness to investment based on surveys which ask managers to rank countries with respect to these characteristics. R&D is research expenditures as a % of sales of the US industry.

Source: Brainard (1993a).

Notes

1. Rugman (1988), for example, estimated that the 500 largest multinationals controlled about half of the world's trade flows.
2. MNEs are commonly described as comprising a parent and one or more affiliates (or subsidiaries); the parent is defined as the establishment that owns and exercises control over its affiliates.
3. For example, the US Bureau of Economic Analysis publishes separate data for majority-owned foreign subsidiaries of US parents and for affiliates, where the latter are defined as establishments with at least 10% non-US ownership.
4. See Dunning (1981).
5. UNCTAD (1994), Table III.6.
6. UNCTAD (1994), Table III.6.
7. That is, the stock held abroad by US residents.
8. Calculated from UNCTAD (1994, 1996).
9. Among individual EC members. France's share increased from 4.4 to 6% over the same 12-year period. Spain's share rose from 1 to 5% and the UK share fell from 12.5 to 8.5%.
10. See Graham and Krugman (1993).
11. Graham and Krugman (1993) suggest that direct evidence on the role of foreign-controlled firms, if available, should be used to establish a baseline for MNE activity and that balance of payments data should then be used as an indicator of recent developments.
12. The different definitions and the detail of the calculation appear in Hipple (1990).
13. Eden (1994).
14. Caves (1971, 1996) provides an extensive discussion of each of these factors.
15. R&D intensity is defined as R&D expenditures per dollar of sales and acts as a proxy for technological know-how capital.
16. Affiliate exports can be expected to reflect the firm-specific characteristics as well as characteristics of the host country.
17. This accords with other findings that advertising intensity encourages local production at the expense of exports. See, e.g. Caves (1980) and Owen (1982).
18. Employment is chosen instead of value added because data are available at a higher level of disaggregation.
19. For example, Pugel (1978), Parry (1978), Deane (1970), and Caves *et al.* (1980).
20. The costs in question concern the organization and operation of production processes, quality control and various other manufacturing procedures.
21. This idea is explored in Horstmann and Markusen (1996), who posit that the licensee observes the states of demand in the host country whereas the licensor only knows the probabilities that demand will be high or low. The optimal level of sales by the licensee is larger when demand is high than when demand is low. However, the licensee's utility is decreasing in effort. In order to induce the licensee to reveal the state of demand to the licensor when demand is high, and to make him deliver the amount of effort that is optimal under this circumstance,

the licensor must insure that the licensee, by telling the truth and delivering high effort under high demand, earns rents at least as high as those she earned by declaring that demand is low when it is in fact high. This, however, lowers the portion of the rents captured by the owner of the technology and thereby provides an incentive for carrying out production internally.

22. As in Chapter 9 we use the same notation for a specific transportation cost as for a specific tariff.

23. Note that options (a) and (b) assume that $(a - c) > \tau$ since otherwise a plant located in one country could not profitably supply consumers in the other country.

24. There are, of course, a great many other policies (e.g. competition laws, labor market policies and foreign exchange restrictions) that affect the location decision. The interaction of policies adopted in different jurisdictions also matters. For example, the impact of host country corporate income tax rates will depend on the tax policies of the parent firm's home country. For example, the country may exempt income taxed abroad from further taxation, grant tax credits for taxes paid abroad, or merely allow foreign taxes to be deducted for taxable income.

25. Pioneering work in this area is Horst (1971).

26. Strictly speaking, the practice of under- or over-involving as represented by transfer pricing does not require that the buying and the selling take place among affiliates of the same enterprise. However, common ownership and management presumably make it easier and less risky to engage in price manipulations designed to lower total tax burdens.

27. Subsumed in T and T^* are regulations concerning tax rates, depreciation schedules, deferral and tax conventions between the home and the foreign country.

28. Setting $F^* = 0$ eliminates L^* as a determinant of plant location.

29. In our example, the bounds on transfer prices are assumed to be fixed. Samuelson (1982) and Eden (1985) model the case where the bounds are determined endogenously. Kant (1988) assumes that the probability that penalties will be imposed for over- and under-invoicing increases with the distance between the transfer price and the arms-length price. The latter allows outcomes where the transfer price is in the interior rather than a boundary of the admissible interval.

30. The tariffs in question were weighted averages of tariff rates of manufactures.

31. This model is based on Smith (1987). Horstmann and Markusen (1987) examine a related model in which foreign demand grows over time and the home firm decides if and when to establish a foreign subsidiary in the foreign market.

32. The sunk cost G can be viewed as the cost of acquiring the knowledge based capital.

33. Smith (1987) also investigates an alternative sequencing in which the foreign firm decides upon entry before the home firm.

34. At least when the number of firms is large.

35. While a useful distinction, horizontal and vertical relationships are often intertwined since, in reality, plants located in different countries carry out similar assembly work while procuring components from each other.

36. The general equilibrium theory of production by vertically integrated MNEs has been developed primarily by Helpman (1984), Helpman and Krugman (1985). The main sources for horizontally integrated MNEs are Markusen (1995) and Markusen and Venables (1995, 1996). Ethier (1986) focuses on the general equilibrium aspects of internalization and considers the question of how country characteristics influence a firm's decision to exploit knowledge based asset advantages either internally or through alternative means.
37. A detailed discussion of the issues raised by opportunism is found in Williamson (1985).
38. The costs C^H, C^p and C^z may include a fixed component.
39. This strengthens the incentive for vertical integration by suggesting that in its absence arm's-length transactions would also be plagued by problems of bilateral monopoly.
40. The demand for labor and capital includes the demands at each of the three production stages.
41. Since there are more goods than factors the pattern of trade is indeterminate (see Section 7.6, p. 276). This means in particular that the equilibrium of the integrated economy could be duplicated with manufacturing firms using only home capital and labor to produce headquarters' services, intermediates and final assembly, or with some or all manufacturing firms using primary factors in both countries.
42. One justification for this is to assume that separating the stages is costly but that such costs are small and not explicitly modelled.
43. Note that since there are no pure profits in the economy, the consumption point lies on the factor income line.
44. When the production technology is homothetic this can be proven.
45. A food producing firm is foreign if it employs factors located in the foreign country. A manufacturing firm is labeled foreign if it produces headquarters services in the foreign country.
46. The Brainard (1993a, 1993b) papers do in fact predate the general equilibrium models of horizontal integration. This explains why she claims that the factor proportions explanation is supported by the data if the extent of multinational activity between country pairs is found to be positively related to endowment differences.
47. As pointed out in Section 9.5 (p. 380), it may also be related to simliarity in tastes.
48. The dependent variable is a dummy variable which takes the value of 1 if affiliate sales are positive and 0 otherwise.

References and additional reading

General

Cantwell, J. (1994), 'The Relationship between International Trade and International Production', in Greenaway, D. and Winters, A. (eds), *Surveys in International Trade* (Cambridge, Mass. and Oxford: Blackwell).

Caves, R.E. (1996), 'Multinational Enterprise and Economic Analysis', *Cambridge Surveys of Economic Literature*, 2nd edn (Cambridge: Cambridge University Press).

Dunning, J.H. (1981), *International Production and the Multinational Enterprise* (London: Allen & Unwin).

Dunning, J.H. (1992), *Multinational Enterprises and the Global Economy* (Wokingham: Addison-Wesley).

Froot, K.A. (1993), *Foreign Direct Investment* (Chicago and London: University of Chicago Press).

Graham, E.M. and Krugman, P.R. (1993), 'The Surge in Foreign Investment in the 1980s', in Froot, K.A. (ed.), *Foreign Direct Investment* (Chicago and London: University of Chicago Press), 13–36.

Hillman, A.L. and Ursprung, H.W. (1993), 'Multinational Firms, Political Competition and International Trade Policy', *International Economic Review*, 34(2), 347–63.

Hipple, F.S. (1990), 'The Measurement of International Trade Related to Multinational Companies', *American Economic Review*, 80(5), 1263–70.

Hummels, D.L. and Stern, R.M. (1994), 'Evolving Patterns of North American Merchandise Trade and Foreign Direct Investment, 1960–1990', *The World Economy*, 17(1), 5–31

Julius, D. and Thomsen, S. (1988), 'Foreign-Owned Firms, Trade, and Economic Integration', *Tokyo Club Papers*, 2(1), 151–74.

Lipsey, R.E. (1990), 'Foreign Direct Investment in the United States: Changes over Three Decades', in Froot, K.A. (ed.), *Foreign Direct Investment* (Chicago and London: University of Chicago Press), 113–72.

Markusen, J.R. (1995), 'The Boundaries of Multinational Enterprises and the Theory of International Trade', *Journal of Economic Perspectives*, 9(2), 169–89.

Pugel, T.A. (1978), *International Market Linkages and US Manufacturing: Prices, Profits and Patterns* (Cambridge, Mass.: Ballinger).

Rugman, A. (1988), 'The Multinational Enterprise', in Walter, I. and Murray, T. (eds), *Handbook of International Management* (New York: Wiley).

UNCTAD (1994, 1996), *World Investment Report, Transnational Corporations, Employment and the Workplace* (New York and Geneva: United Nations).

Vernon R. (1993), 'Where are the Multinationals Headed?', in Froot, K.A. (ed.), *Foreign Direct Investment* (Chicago and London: University of Chicago Press), 57–84.

Firm-specific assets and internalization

Belderbos, R. and Sleuwaegen, L. (1996), 'Japanese Firms and the Decision to Invest Abroad: Business Groups and Regional Core Networks', *Review of Economics and Statistics*, 28(2), 214–21.

Caves, R.E. (1971), 'International Corporations: The Industrial Economics of Foreign Investment', *Economica*, 38, 1–27.

Ethier, W. (1986), 'The Multinational Firm', *Quarterly Journal of Economics*, 101, 805–33.

Ethier, W. and Horn, H. (1990), 'Managerial Control of International Firms and Patterns of Direct Investment', *Journal of International Economics*, 28, 25–45.

Grubaugh, S.G. (1987), 'Determinants of Direct Foreign Investment', *Review of Economics and Statistics*, 69, 149–52.

Gruber, H., Mehta, D. and Vernon, R. (1967), 'The R&D Factor in International Trade and International Investment of US Industries', *Journal of Political Economy*, 75, 20–37.

Horstmann, I.J. and Markusen, J.R. (1987), 'Licensing vs. Direct Investment: A Model of Internalisation by the MNE', *Canadian Journal of Economics*, 20, 464–81.

Horstmann, I.J. and Markusen, J.R. (1996), 'Exploring New Markets: Direct Investment, Contractual Relations and the Multinational Enterprise', *International Economic Review*, 37, 1–19.

Pugel, T. A., Kragas, E.S. and Kimura, Y. (1996), 'Further Evidence on Japanese Direct Investment in US Manufacturing', *Review of Economics and Statistics*, 208–13.

Teece, D.J. (1977), 'Technology Transfer by Multinational Enterprise: An Assessment', *Economic Journal*, 87, 242–61.

Teece, D.J. (1986), 'Transaction Cost Economics and the Multinational Enterprise: An Assessment', *Journal of Economic Behavior & Organization*, 7(1), 21–46.

Williamson, O.E. (1985), *The Economic Institutions of Capitalism* (New York: Free Press).

Trade barriers and multinational production

Brainard, S.L. (1993a), 'An Empirical Assessment of the Proximity–Concentration Tradeoff between Multinational Sales and Trade', *NBER Working Paper Series*, 4580.

Brainard, S.L. (1993b), 'An Empirical Assessment of the Factor Proportions Explanation of Multinational Sales', *NBER Working Paper Series*, 4583.

Caves, R.E., Porter, M.E. and Spence, A.M. (1980), with Scott, J.T. *Competition in the Open Economy: A Model Applied to Canada* (Cambridge, Mass.: Harvard University Press).

Eden, L. (1985), 'Microeconomics of Transfer Pricing', in Rugman, A.M. and Eden, L. (eds), *Multinationals and Transfer Pricing* (New York: St Martin's Press), 13–46.

Eden, L. (1994), *Multinationals in North America* (Eden, Calgary: University of Calgary Press).

Ethier, W. (1986), 'The Multinational Firm', *Quarterly Journal of Economics*, 806–833.

Grubert, H. and Mutti, J. (1991), 'Taxes, Tariffs and Transfer Pricing in Multinational Corporate Decision Making', *Review of Economics and Statistics*, 79, 285–93.

Horst, T. (1971), 'The Theory of the Multinational Firm: Optimal Behavior under Different Tariff and Tax Rates', *Journal of Political Economy*, 79, 1059–72.

Horst, T. (1974), 'The Industrial Composition of US Exports and Subsidiary Sales to the Canadian Market', *American Economic Review*, 62, 37–45.

Kant, Ch. (1988), 'Endogenous Transfer Pricing and the Effects of Uncertain Regulation', *Journal of International Economics*, 24, 147–57.

Kravis, I.B. and Lipsey, R.E. (1992), 'Sources of Competitiveness of the United States and its Multinational Firms', *Review of Economics and Statistics*, 74(2), 193–201.

Samuelson, L. (1982), 'The Multinational Firm with Arms' Length Transfer Price Limits', *Journal of International Economics*, 13, 365–74.

MNEs and oligopoly

Deane, R S (1970), *Foreign Investment in New Zealand Manufacturing* (Wellington: Sweet and Maxwell).

Horstmann, I.J. and Markusen, J.R. (1987), 'Strategic Investments and the Development of Multinationals', *International Economic Review*, 28, 109–21.

Horstmann, I.J. and Markusen, J.R. (1992). 'Endogenous Market Structures in International Trade (Natura Facit Saltum)', *Journal of International Economics*, 32, 109–29.

Hymer, S. (1976), 'The International Operations of National Firms: A Study of Foreign Direct Investment', PhD dissertation (Cambridge, Mass.: MIT Press).

Parry, T.G. (1978), 'Structure and Performance in Australian Manufacturing, with Special Reference to Foreign-Owned Enterprises', in Kasper, W. and Parry, T.G. (eds), *Growth, Trade and Structural Change in an Open Australian Economy* (Kensington, Australia: Centre for Applied Economic Research). 173–99.

Roy, S. and Viaene, J.-M. (1998), 'On Strategic Vertical Foreign Direct Investment', *Journal of International Economics*, forthcoming.

Smith, A. (1987), 'Strategic Investment, Multinational Corporations and Trade Policy', *European Economic Review*, 31, 89–96.

MNEs and trade in general equilibrium

Helpman, E. (1984), 'A Simple Theory of International Trade with Multinational Corporations', *Journal of Political Economy*, 92, 451–71.

Helpman, E. and Krugman, P.R. (1985), *Market Structure and Foreign Trade* (Cambridge, Mass. and London: MIT Press).

Markusen, J.R. and Venables, A.J. (1995), 'Multinational Firms and the New Trade Theory', *NBER Working Paper*, 5036.

Markusen, J.R. and Venables, A.J. (1996), 'The Theory of Endowment, Intra-Industry and Multinational Trade', *NBER Working Paper*, 5529.

PART IV

Special Topics

■ *Chapter 12* ■

Economic Integration

Since the mid-1980s there has been a surge of regional trade agreements (RTAs) around the globe. In 1992 there were 34 integrated areas and, since then, 29 new agreements have been notified to the GATT and the WTO.[1] For example:

- The European Community's 1992 internal market program,
- The accession of Austria, Finland and Sweden into the European Community (EC),
- The Canada–US Free Trade Agreement (CUSTA) which was extended to the North American Free Trade Agreement (NAFTA) in December 1992 by including Mexico,
- The Mercosur Agreement between Argentina, Brazil, Paraguay and Uruguay for a customs union,
- The Australia–New Zealand Closer Economic Relations Trade Agreement (ANZCERTA),
- Commitments to an ASEAN (Association of South-East Asian Nations) Free Trade Agreement.

Agreements such as these are the most notable, but many new initiatives for special association agreements within Europe, Asia and the two American continents are currently being negotiated.

Through a RTA, a group of countries agrees to enjoy freer international economic relations among themselves. In the extreme, this allows for the free movement of goods and services, capital, and labor within the integrated area. However, the institutional arrangements under which countries open their borders will differ in reality. The following describes in increasing degree of intensity the various schemes of integration.

In a *free trade area*, member countries eliminate tariffs among themselves but maintain individual tariff schedules on imports from non-member countries. As members maintain their own external tariff, imports could enter through the member country with the lowest tariff and then be re-exported to other members. Member countries therefore agree to 'rules of origin' that determine whether a good is eligible for a tariff-free treatment. These rules often require that goods contain a high percentage of domestic content to prevent the simple repackaging of goods. The NAFTA fits this definition.[2]

In a *customs union (CU)*, members also eliminate tariffs among themselves but establish a common external tariff (CET) against non-members. Customs revenues accrue either to a common fund or to each member's Treasury.[3]

A *common market* allows the free movement of capital and persons in addition to the requirements of a customs union. The European Union (EU) comes closest to this definition.

Finally, in an *economic union*, members of a common market unify all other economic (fiscal, monetary) and socio–economic (labor, social security) policies. While this is the ultimate goal of the EU, only Belgium and Luxembourg have unified their monetary policy (since 1921). The United States is an economic union.

It seems *a priori* that RTAs are a good thing because they represent a move toward freer trade. However, a common feature of these agreements is the discriminatory treatment which favors members relative to non-members. For example, goods imported from member countries face a zero tariff while similar goods imported from non-member countries face a positive tariff. Given this, the analysis of the pros and cons of economic integration has largely focused on the relative merits of two concepts of the theory, namely, trade creation and trade diversion, each with different welfare implications. Building upon these results, Kemp and Wan (1976) have proved one of the main theorems in the field to give a rationale for the gradual enlargement of a customs union until all countries of the world are included.

This chapter will take up these issues, discuss the economic rationale for the integration of both product and factor markets and examine the empirical evidence. In this regard we use the theory to highlight the simulation results on the NAFTA and to review what is meant by 'new regionalism'.

12.1 The theory of integration

Basic concepts

Trade creation and trade diversion

The traditional treatment of economic integration considers a customs union (CU)[4] and focuses on two central concepts, namely, trade creation and trade diversion.[5] Trade creation is the trade created within the CU when production in member countries is replaced by imports from a more efficient producer in the union. Trade diversion is the amount of trade diverted by the CU when imports from an outsider are replaced by imports from a less efficient union producer.

The trade creating and trade diverting effects of a CU are illustrated in Figures 12.1 and 12.2, respectively. The exposition builds on a method of analysis already set out in Chapter 5. Consider a single good and 3 countries: the home country (H), the partner country (P) and the outside

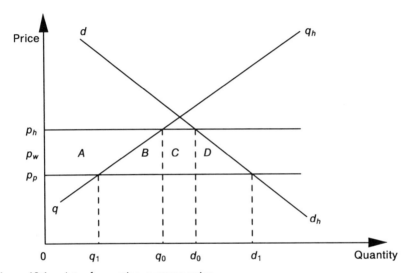

Figure 12.1 *A trade-creating customs union*

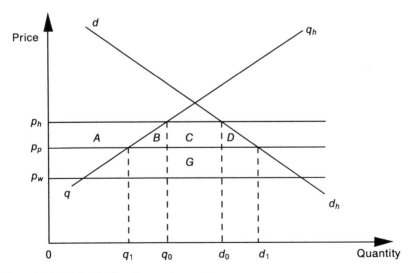

Figure 12.2 *A trade-diverting customs union*

world (W). The home country, assumed small compared to P and W, faces infinitely elastic supply at prices p_p and p_w, respectively. The home country's supply is indicated by the line qq_h in each figure while the line dd_h represents the home country's demand for the commodity. Before H forms a CU with P, H is assumed to have imposed a non-prohibitive, non-discriminatory, *ad valorem* tariff τ on imports from both P and W.

Assume that P is the least-cost supplier, (i.e. $p_p < p_w$). Before the formation of the CU, the domestic price of imports from P is $p_h = p_p(1 + \tau)$. From Figure 12.1, it is clear that at this price, H produces q_0, consumes d_0 and imports $(d_0 - q_0)$ from P. Now let H form a CU with P. The price of imports from P now drops to p_p and implies a fall in home's production to q_1, an increase in home's consumption to d_1 and a rise in its imports from P to $(d_1 - q_1)$. The sum of the distances $q_0 q_1$ and $d_0 d_1$ represents the amount of trade created by the CU. The welfare implication is a loss in the surplus of home producers equal to area A, a loss in tariff revenue measured by area C, and a gain in consumers' surplus measured by area $A + B + C + D$. The net welfare gain is therefore area B and D which is positive. Hence, a trade creating CU benefits the home country. The more elastic are the lines qq_h and dd_h, and the higher is τ, the larger are areas B and D and the larger net welfare gain from joining the union.

If W is instead the least-cost source of foreign supply (i.e. $p_w < p_p$), the CU will be trade diverting. This is shown in Figure 12.2. This figure is similar to Figure 12.1 except that the roles of prices p_p and p_w have been reversed. Before the formation of a CU, the domestic price of imports from W is $p_h = p_w(1 + \tau)$, the home country consumes d_0 of which q_0 is domestically produced and $(d_0 - q_0)$ is imported from W. If a CU is now formed between H and P, then all imports previously supplied by W will be imported from P at the lower price p_p. This is the pure trade diverting effect of the CU. However, since $p_p < p_w(1 + \tau)$, the volume of imports increases from $q_0 d_0$ to $q_1 d_1$. Hence, there is also trade creation. The decline in the price decreases the producer surplus of home producers by area A, but increases consumer surplus by the amount equal to area $A + B + C + D$. Areas C *plus* G show the loss of tariff revenue formerly collected on imports from W. The net effect on the home country's welfare is then area B and D *minus* G which is indeterminate. Hence, a net welfare loss occurs if area G is larger than area B and D. If it is not so then we have an example in which a trade diverting CU is beneficial to the home country.

Trade modification

Trade modification means the change in trade with non-member countries due to the elimination of tariffs on goods traded only within the CU.[6]

Assuming that imported goods into the CU are different from those produced within the CU, trade modification claims that the trade flows between member countries could be complementary to those from non-member countries, instead of perfect substitutes as assumed in trade diversion.

Trade modification departs from trade diversion in the following way. Suppose, as an example, that H imports automobiles from P and tyres from W. Upon the abolition of tariffs between H and P, home automobile imports from P increase and tyre imports from W are likely to rise as well. As a result, the bilateral trade flow between H and P is complementary to that between H and W. Call this positive trade modification.

Trade modification resembles trade diversion as follows. Suppose that H imports compact cars from P and full size cars from W. If H abolishes its tariffs on cars from P, imports of compact cars from P increase, partly at the expense of full size cars from W. As a result, the bilateral trade flow between H and P is a substitute to that between H and W as in trade diversion (but for different reasons). Call this negative trade modification.

Problem 12.1: Consider a non-preferential tariff reduction such that the tariff inclusive domestic price equals p_p in Figure 12.2. Show that this multilateral tariff reduction is superior to the formation of a CU between H and P.

Empirical results

Figure 12.2 has illustrated that the economic desirability of a CU depends on the extent of trade diversion. Measurement of the latter is therefore an important empirical question. Many empirical studies took on the issue, three of which, each with a different emphasis, will be discussed here.

Measuring the net welfare effects of a CU is easily done for a single commodity. As shown in Figure 12.2, the negative effect of pure trade diversion is given by area G which can be estimated as:

$$\text{Area } G = (p_p - p_w)(d_0 - q_0) \tag{12.1}$$

Likewise, the positive welfare effects of trade creation can be approximated by:

$$\text{Area } B = \frac{(p_h - p_p)(q_0 - q_1)}{2} \equiv \varepsilon q_0 \frac{(p_h - p_p)^2}{2} \tag{12.2}$$

$$\text{Area } D = \frac{(p_h - p_p)(d_1 - d_0)}{2} \equiv -\eta d_0 \frac{(p_h - p_p)^2}{2} \tag{12.3}$$

where $p_h = p_w(1 + \tau)$ is assumed to be unity, ε is the price elasticity of supply ($\varepsilon > 0$), and η is the price elasticity of demand ($\eta < 0$). Adding (12.2) and (12.3) and subtracting (12.1), we can write:

$$\text{Area } (B + D - G) = [p_w\tau - (p_p - p_w)]^2(\varepsilon q_0 - \eta d_0)/2$$

$$- (p_p - p_w)(d_0 - q_0) \qquad (12.4)$$

Several inferences can be made from (12.4) about the likelihood that a trade-diverting CU is welfare improving. Welfare in (12.4) is increasing in a number of parameters: (1) the more elastic is the demand and supply curve; (2) the lower the difference in production efficiency between P and W (the closer p_p is to p_w); (3) the higher is τ, and (4) the lower the pre-union level of outside imports ($d_0 - q_0$) relative to domestic demand or supply. This is largely the method followed by Johnson (1958) to approximate the sectoral effects of the UK accession to the European Free Trade Agreement (EFTA).[7]

Although the above method of measurement is useful, it assumes that imports and domestic production are perfect substitutes. However, in a world of many commodities, goods might be imperfect substitutes and trade diversion for some commodities could be offset by positive trade modification for the others. There is therefore the empirical question of whether trade flows within the CU are substitute or complementary to those from outsiders. If found complementary, then the negative welfare effects of trade diversion may not exist.

To examine whether bilateral trade flows are substitutes or complements, Viaene (1982) estimated the following system of equations for Spain's bilateral import flow from 7 EC countries and the rest of the world (ROW)[8]:

$$m_{lt} = \beta_l^1 AV_t + \beta_l^2 CU_t + \beta_l^3 p_{lt} + \alpha_l \sum_{i \neq l} m_{it} + u_{lt} \qquad (12.5)$$

where

$m_{lt} = $ Spain's real aggregate imports from country l at time t
$m_{it} = $ Spain's real aggregate imports from country i ($i \neq l$)
$AV_t = $ Spain's real gross value added in agriculture and industry
       (a measure of aggregate activity)
$CU_t = $ rate of capacity utilization of the Spanish economy
       (pressure of demand variable)
$p_{lt} = $ region l's export price (including tariffs) relative to Spain's
       domestic price
$u_{lt} = $ disturbance term.

The parameter α_l measures the dependency of Spain's bilateral import flow from country l with the sum of all other bilateral import flows, $\sum m_i$. If the effect of a change of ($\sum m_i$) on m_l is positive ($\alpha_l > 0$), the flows are complementary and if negative ($\alpha_l < 0$), the flows are substitutes.

The system of 8 bilateral import equations was estimated using Three Stage Least Squares (3SLS) on annual data for the period 1961–77. Table 12.1 presents the estimates of α_l and the implied elasticity values. The results show evidence of interdependencies in Spain's imports from all sources. The positive values (except for UK–Ireland) indicate that each country's bilateral exports to Spain are all complementary with respect to the aggregate of the other bilateral flows. Most notably, Spain's imports from the ROW are complementary with those from EC countries. Hence, if trade between Spain and the EC expands as a result of a CU then Spain's imports from the ROW would also expand. The possibility of trade diversion is therefore not supported by the data.

Estimates of trade creation and diversion can also be made by looking at changes in the sources of supply of goods to EC countries. Jacquemin and Sapir (1988) investigate this issue for total manufactures over the period 1973–84. They first compute a country's apparent consumption (d) as the

Table 12.1   *Substitution and complementarity of Spain's bilateral import flows, 1961–77*

	Value	Elasticity
Belgium–Lux	0.0117 (2.795)	0.528
Denmark	0.0027 (1.539)	0.397
France	0.0293 (2.750)	0.281
Germany	0.0393 (2.159)	0.287
Italy	0.0163 (1.960)	0.286
Netherlands	0.0230 (4.883)	0.786
UK–Ireland	−0.0145 (−1.616)	−0.191
Rest of world	0.7708 (3.278)	0.505

Note:
t-statistics in parentheses.
Source: Viaene (1982).

sum of domestic production net of exports $(q - x)$, intra-EC imports (m^i) and extra-EC imports (m^*) and then examine the following relationship:

$$\frac{(q - x)}{d} + \frac{m^i}{d} + \frac{m^*}{d} = 1 \tag{12.6}$$

(12.6) simply adds the share of each component of apparent consumption: the domestic share (production *minus* exports), a partner share (second term) and an outside share (third term). The empirical counterpart of (12.6) is given in Table 12.2 for Germany, France and the United Kingdom.

Trade creation should be reflected by a fall in the share of consumption that is supplied by a country's domestic producers. Column (1) of Table 12.2 shows that this is the case for all countries, although the evolution as well as the starting and ending percentages vary across countries. Column (2) indicates that the share of intra-community trade rises for all countries. Trade diversion should be reflected by a decrease in the share of EC imports from countries outside the EC. The values in column (3) of Table 12.2 indicates that just the opposite occurred for Germany and France. The United Kingdom shows an erratic pattern but no indication of a decrease. Overall, the results are indicative of trade creation with member countries and positive trade modification with non-member countries and again exclude trade diversion on the aggregate.

Table 12.2   *Share of domestic production, intra-EEC imports and extra-EEC imports in apparent consumption,[a] 1973–84*

	Germany			France			UK		
Year	(1)	(2)	(3)	(1)	(2)	(3)	(1)	(2)	(3)
1973	85.2	8.7	6.2	81.6	12.3	6.1	78.7	7.5	13.8
1974	84.8	8.8	6.4	79.5	13.2	7.3	75.7	9.2	15.1
1975	84.2	9.2	6.5	81.5	12.1	6.4	79.4	8.4	12.3
1976	82.8	9.8	7.3	79.1	13.7	7.2	77.2	9.5	13.3
1977	82.2	10.1	7.7	78.5	13.9	7.5	76.8	10.0	13.2
1978	81.8	10.3	7.9	78.4	14.1	7.4	76.3	10.3	13.4
1979	80.9	10.7	8.4	77.2	14.7	8.2	75.2	11.2	13.6
1980	79.5	11.0	9.5	76.8	14.4	8.8	74.8	10.8	14.4
1981	78.5	11.1	10.4	76.0	14.7	9.3	76.5	11.2	12.3
1982	77.8	11.6	10.6	74.9	15.5	9.6	75.5	11.9	12.6
1983	77.5	11.8	10.8	74.4	15.7	9.9	73.4	13.1	13.5
1984	75.9	12.1	12.0	73.1	16.3	10.6	71.4	13.7	14.9

Notes:
[a] (1) = Domestic production, (2) = Intra-EEC imports, (3) = Extra-EEC imports. Numbers are % (scale 100) of apparent consumption.
Source: Jacquemin and Sapir (1988).

The terms of trade argument

A large customs union

We now examine the implications of terms of trade changes. Consider the following 2-good economies: H (home), P (partner) and W (the rest of the world). The international equilibrium for good 2 is depicted in Figure 12.3. The curve x_w is non-CU supply of good 2 and the curve m_{cu} is the sum of both home and partner import demands for good 2. Hence, the equilibrium is at point a with imports m_f from W and price p_w (relative price of good 2).

Though in isolation H and P are assumed too small to affect their terms of trade with W, together in the CU they may have enough market power to affect the equilibrium price. This case is illustrated in Figure 12.3. Because x_w is upward sloping, the marginal cost of imports to the CU exceeds the supply price. This is so because if the CU were to import 1 less unit, it would save its price p_w. But it would also force down this price and save on what is still imported, the saving being represented by the distance ad.

This is formally shown by writing the supply curve in inverse form as $p = p(x_w)$. Then the cost of imports equals $x_w p(x_w)$. The marginal cost of imports is $p(x_w) + x_w[dp(x_w)/dx_w]$, and can be rewritten as:

$$MC = p(x_w)[1 + (x_w/p(x_w))(dp(x_w)/dx_w)]$$

$$= p(x_w)[1 + 1/f^*] \tag{12.7}$$

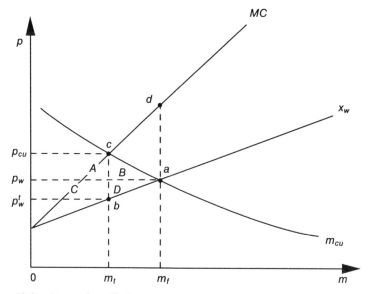

Figure 12.3 *External tariff of a customs union*

where f^* is the elasticity of export supply. This marginal cost of imports to the union is shown as the MC curve in Figure 12.3. At point a, the import price p_w is less than the marginal cost of m_f units. Hence, by restricting its demand for imports, the CU reduces the equilibrium relative price of imports and will continue to restrict its demand until point c where the internal price in the union equals the marginal cost.

One way to restrict trade is with an *ad valorem* tariff τ. The internal price of the union is then $p_{cu} = p_w(1 + \tau)$. The solution for τ is obtained by setting the internal price p_{cu} equal to the marginal cost of imports (12.7):

$$\tau = \frac{1}{f^*}$$

The solution for τ is just the optimum tariff formula. Hence, it is optimal for the CU to restrict trade with respect to outsiders and to do it by imposing a CET that corresponds to the optimal tariff. The CU then achieves a maximum welfare gain for the CU as a whole. Building on the analysis set out in Chapter 5, the welfare gain of this policy to the CU is measured by area C *minus* area B. The welfare loss to W equals area C and D. The net loss in world welfare equals the sum of areas B and D.

Empirical findings

Petith (1977) tested for terms of trade effects associated with the elimination of tariffs and the establishment of the CET in connection with the formation of the EC in 1958. Table 12.3 shows his calculated terms of trade changes ($\hat{p}$) and their effects on the gross national product ($\hat{G}$) of Germany and France.

Table 12.3 *The EC and the terms of trade, 1958*

	$E/e = 2.4$		$E/e = 2.8$		$E/e = 8.8$	
	$\hat{p}$	$\hat{G}$	$\hat{p}$	$\hat{G}$	$\hat{p}$	$\hat{G}$
Germany	2.6	0.39	3.1	0.47	7.4	1.2
France	3.6	0.27	4.2	0.32	8.9	0.66

Notes:
$\hat{p} = \%$ change in the terms of trade *vis-à-vis* non-EC world; $\hat{G} = \%$ change in GNP resulting from $\hat{p}$; $E/e =$ ratio of elasticity of substitution between internal and external sources of imports (E) relative to that between all imports and domestic goods (e).
Source: Petith (1977).

The magnitudes of $(\hat{p})$ and $(\hat{G})$ depend primarily on the parameter E/e which is the elasticity of substitution between imports from partner countries and imports from outsiders (E) relative to the elasticity of substitution between imports from all sources and domestic goods (e). The greater is E relative to e, the larger is the restriction in demand for outside goods arising from the CU and therefore the larger is the improvement in each member's terms of trade.

For the indicated range of values for E/e (drawn from the empirical literature) Germany's terms of trade improved between 2.6% and 7.4% while France's terms of trade improved between 3.6 and 8.9%. The effects of the terms of trade changes on GNP range from 0.39 to 1.2% for Germany and from 0.27 to 0.66% for France. When these results are compared with other effects of economic integration (see Table 12.4, p. 515), terms of trade improvements are one of the major effects of the formation of the EC.

Intra-union income transfers

A customs union may provide financial arrangements and cross-country compensatory payments among its members to compensate for the uneven distribution of gains. These payments are normally financed from revenue generated by the union's CET. Below we first describe the theory underlying the transfer process and then present empirical findings related to this issue.

The Kemp–Wan proposition

Kemp and Wan (1976) provide conditions under which a set of countries may form a Pareto-improving CU. The result is appealing because it gives an incentive for the gradual enlargement of a CU until all countries are included and hence free trade prevails in the world.

Proposition 12.1 (Kemp–Wan):   There exists a common set of tariffs and a system of lump-sum compensatory payments, involving only members of the union, such that there is an associated tariff-ridden competitive equilibrium in which each individual, whether a member of the union or not, is not worse off than before the formation of the union.[9]

The analysis is a general equilibrium description of CU formation. The result assumes any number of countries and commodities and permits there to be trade restrictions and costs of transport. The theorem states that a CU, if properly defined, can potentially be world Pareto-improving. Welfare gains arise from trade creation between members of the union while avoiding trade diversion with the rest of the world. What is required is for the CU to adjust its CET so as to leave trade with the rest of the world the same as before the formation of the CU. The terms of trade and welfare of outsiders will then remain unchanged. The result also requires income transfers between countries such that no member of the union is worse off after the union.

Quantification

Upon the formation of a CU, tariff revenues formally collected by individual member countries are instead channelled to a common fund. This fund is then used for redistributing income across member countries through regional development programs and various social projects. On balance, each member country can determine its net payment to the rest of the union, whether positive or negative. As suggested by the Kemp–Wan proposition, a testable hypothesis is whether the actual system of payments within a CU ensures that each member's post-union level of satisfaction is at least equal to its pre-union level. This is precisely the question Grinols (1984) investigated for Great Britain's entry into the EC.

To understand Grinols' analysis, let the production possibility curve for a country considering joining a CU be given by $T_1 T_2$ in Figure 12.4. Good 1 is on the vertical axis, good 2 on the horizontal axis. Prior to joining the CU, the represented economy is assumed to have levied a non-discriminatory tariff, so that the initial tariff-ridden equilibrium involves production at point a, consumption at point a', and a level of welfare u_0.

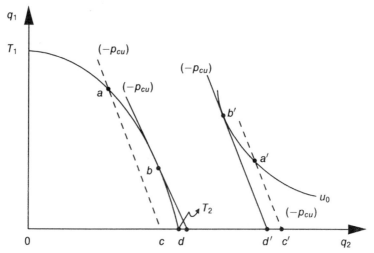

Figure 12.4   *The transfer analysis*

Upon joining the union, the country adopts the union's CET which implies the new equilibrium terms of trade p_{cu}. At this price, a transfer to this economy equivalent to the distance cc' is necessary to achieve the pre-accession welfare level u_0. The CU brings, however, gains from substitution in production and in consumption. At the price p_{cu}, production shifts from good 2 to good 1 until the tangency point b. Likewise, substitution in consumption leads to the new consumption point b'. Considering these two gains, the theoretical transfer guaranteeing the welfare level u_0 is dd'. Therefore, the following difference assesses whether Great Britain's entrance into the EC was welfare improving:

$$T - dd' \gtreqless 0 \tag{12.8}$$

In this expression, T is the actual net transfer in pounds from the EC to Britain and dd' is the theoretical transfer. If (12.8) is positive (negative), then the welfare improved (deteriorated). Grinols computed the annual value of (12.8) over the period 1972–80. On average over the period, the loss to Britain amounts to more than 1.5% of its GDP. In some years, Britain would have been better off by as much as 3 to 4% of GDP by not entering the EC.

Table 12.4 presents two other studies on joining the EC. Both assume perfect competition and model the transfer payments explicitly. However,

Table 12.4 *Numerical effects of integration policies, 1977 and 1982*

Authors	Policy change and method[a]	Results
Miller and Spencer (1977)	UK accession to the EC General equilibrium model for the United Kingdom, the EC, the Commonwealth and the Rest of the world; *ex ante* static approach	*Welfare UK:* −1.8%[b]
Viaene (1982)	Spain joining the EC Macroeconomic model for Spain with neoclassical features and complementarity of the bilateral trade flows between Spain and EC members, the United States and the Rest of the world; *ex ante* dynamic approach	*GNP Spain:* −0.3%

Notes:
[a] Terms of trade effects with non-members are excluded.
[b] This figure assumes a net transfer of 90% of British tariff proceeds to the EC.

terms of trade changes with third countries are ignored and hence also are potential gains from increased market power. Both studies confirm Grinols' result that joining the EC involved a loss in national income. This negative conclusion is also shared by most models of integration that were constructed in the late 1970s and early 1980s under the paradigm of perfect competition.

Economies of scale

We now consider whether economies of scale, assumed to be internal to firms, strengthen the argument in favor of economic integration. The scale economies treatment of a customs union is not very different from that of trade policy of Chapter 10. Results are usually specific to particular models which are representative of particular market structures. Given this, the aim of this section is to construct a minimal model where the concepts relevant to scale economies are introduced and the familiar concepts of trade creation and trade diversion are discussed and judged as relevant in the present context (Corden, 1972).[10]

Consider the market for a single homogeneous good in our 3-country model i.e. H, P, which will form a union, and country W. Assume the good is initially or potentially supplied by a single firm in each of the union countries. Country W can supply units of this good at fixed price p_w, the constancy of p_w implying insignificant economies of scale in W resulting from the union. The average cost curve of each firm in each union country is

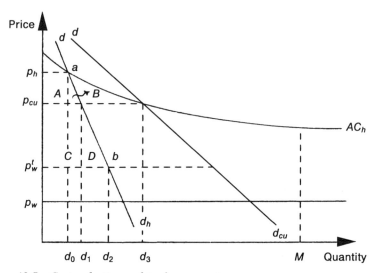

Figure 12.5   *Cost reduction and trade suppression*

assumed to lie above p_w so that no firm exports to W. In this framework we now explore the concepts of cost reduction and trade suppression associated with market integration. The single-country analysis of these effects is illustrated in Figure 12.5, that of the 2-country, involving H and P, in Figure 12.6.

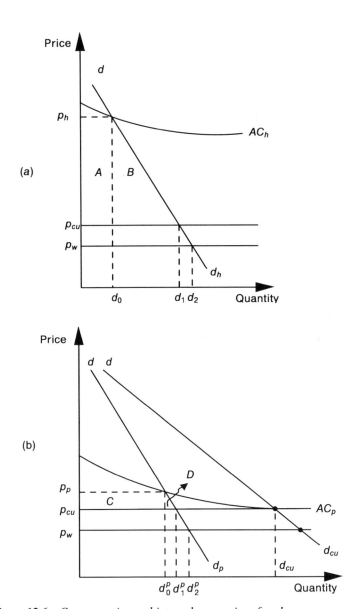

Figure 12.6 *Customs union and internal economies of scale*

Cost reduction and trade suppression

Figure 12.5 shows the declining average cost curve of the home producer where point M defines the minimum efficient size. Home demand before and after the formation of the CU is denoted, respectively, as dd_h and dd_{cu}. The latter is the sum of H and P demand.

As $AC_h > p_w$ everywhere, production is profitable only if the country levies a tariff. The tariff rate is 'made-to-measure' such that the tariff inclusive import price just equals the average cost. This tariff inclusive price is also the price p_h the profit maximizing firm charges in order to prevent imports. If $p_h < AC_h$ the firm would exit the market and the whole of home's consumption would be imported. If $p_h > AC_h$, the firm would potentially earn positive profits but there would be imports and no domestic production. Without integration, equilibrium is at point a with d_0 being the quantity consumed and produced by the home firm. With integration, equilibrium occurs at the intersection of AC_h and dd_{cu} at the equilibrium price p_{cu}. The CET that guarantees CU production can be lower than before integration. The welfare gain to home consumers corresponds to the area A and B. This gain arises from the cost reduction resulting from a larger internal market. The initial consumption d_0 is now obtained at the lower price p_{cu}, the associated gain corresponding to area A. An extra quantity is also purchased at this lower price, on which area B of consumer surplus is obtained.

Consider now the case where a tariff lower than the made-to-measure tariff is applied. Equilibrium is initially at point b with d_2 imported from W at the tariff inclusive price $p_w^t = p_w(1 + \tau)$. Upon market integration, the equilibrium price is p_{cu}. Provided the CET is made-to-measure a home producer could enter the market, produce d_1 for the home country and export $d_1 d_3$ to P. If so, cheaper imports from W will be replaced by dearer domestic production which leads to a loss in domestic consumer surplus equal to area C and D. This is the trade suppression effect.

Problem 12.2: The above framework raises the issue of government trade policy in the presence of domestic monopoly. Show the non-equivalence of tariffs and import quotas in Figure 12.5. Compare this situation to that in which the monopolist produces under conditions of increasing costs.

2-country analysis

Consider now the case of 2 countries. The H and P markets are represented by panels (a) and (b) of Figure 12.6, respectively. In Figure 12.6, H's demand is dd_h, P's demand is dd_p and the union demand is dd_{cu}, the horizontal sum of dd_h and dd_p. Both H and P are assumed to face price p_w from W. The home firm is assumed to be the least efficient producer.

Given this, the welfare consequences of a CU depend on the pre-union market structure. Of the several cases that can arise, we investigate here the one in which there is initial production in both union countries. This is only possible if both countries initially levy made-to-measure tariffs, H's tariff being larger than P's. Market structures that generate less favorable outcomes are left as an exercise (see Problems 12.3 and 12.4).

The post-union equilibrium is given by the intersection of AC_p and the union's aggregate demand dd_{cu}. Total union production and consumption is d_{cu} at the internal union price p_{cu}. The CET can be less than the 2 initial tariffs and since $p_{cu} < AC_h$, the home firm exits the union market which is then captured by P's firm.

Home's initial production d_0 is replaced by cheaper imports from P which generates the familiar trade-creation gain equal to area A. The lower union price p_{cu} induces increased consumption $d_0 d_1$ and a welfare gain equal to area B. The total home gain equals area A and B. The partner country's welfare gain corresponds to the area C and D which is the gain from cost reduction.

Problem 12.3: Assume instead that P is the only producer of the good. Using Figure 12.5, determine the welfare gains or losses arising from a CU and compare your results with those given in the text. Identify trade diversion in this context.

Problem 12.4: Characterize the welfare consequences of a CU for each participating country if only the home firm produces. Identify trade suppression and its welfare effects.

12.2 Factor markets

The previous sections have focused on the new movements of goods created by a new RTA. However, a customs union can also permit factor mobility between union countries. The EC, for example, has gone beyond the ideas of a customs union to allow for the overall right of establishment in member countries, becoming thereby a common market.

This section considers one possible method of analyzing the general problem of factor mobility (MacDougall, 1960). We first consider the case of full capital mobility with labor immobile and then labor mobile with capital immobile. The primary emphasis of this section is on intuitive arguments and on simple geometric expositions borrowed from Section 6.1.

More rigorous proofs of the results are discussed in Ruffin (1984) and in Wong (1995). Though our framework restricts itself to integrated areas, the analysis can be used to interpret the broader issues of international migration and of firm relocation. As factor mobility affects the level and distribution of income of participating countries, the analysis of this section identifies also the groups of primary factors that would favor and oppose such mobility and, therefore, can give a political economy interpretation to the design of the various institutional agreements.

Capital mobility

Assume that H and P will form a common market and that W does not allow for the free movement of capital (and persons). Each country of the common market produces a single good by means of two primary factors, capital K and labor L. The production functions, $F(K_h, L_h)$ and $F(K_p, L_p)$ respectively, are neoclassical (see pp. 116–18) and have similar functional forms. The national capital–labor ratios are assumed different with H being relatively more capital-abundant than P, that is $(K_h/L_h) > (K_p/L_p)$.

The left and right vertical axes of Figure 12.7 measure capital's real return in H and P, r_h and r_p respectively. The capital stock of both countries is measured by the distance OO^* along the horizontal axis. Any point of this axis denotes an allocation of capital between the two countries. In the absence of capital mobility, OK_0 is owned by H and K_0O^* is owned by P.

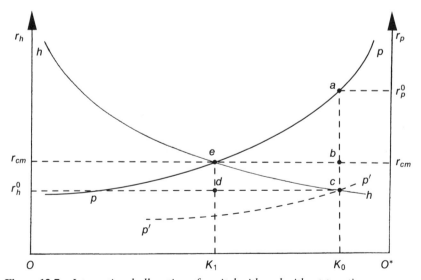

Figure 12.7 *International allocation of capital with and without taxation*

The curves hh and pp, drawn with reference to origins O and O^* respectively, relate the capital stock to the physical marginal product of capital in each country. By definition, each curve is drawn holding fixed a country's stock of labor. Each curve is a decreasing function of the capital–labor ratio owing to diminishing marginal returns. Factors in each country are fully employed as long as the real rental rates equal the marginal products. The initial allocation of the factor endowments therefore implies $r_h^0 < r_p^0$ and also $w_h^0 > w_p^0$.

Total home output produced with capital OK_0 is equal to the area under the curve hh up to K_0. To see this, consider:

$$\int_0^{K_0} F_K(K_h, L_h)dK_h = F(K_0, L_h) - F(O, L_h) = F(K_0, L_h) \qquad (12.9)$$

where $F_K(\cdot)$ is the marginal product of capital and $F(O, L_h) = 0$ since it is a property of neoclassical production functions that a single factor does not produce any output in the absence of the other.[11] Under our assumptions, the part of output that goes to domestic capital owners equals the real rental rate times the capital stock, $(r_h^0 \times OK_0)$. The part of output that goes to labor is the remaining area under each curve. The partner country's output and income distribution are obtained by analogy.

Integration with full capital mobility

Upon the opening of trade between the two countries, a same price will prevail and no trade will take place unless to accommodate for other items in the balance of payments (in this context, the interest service on foreign capital). Integration becomes, however, meaningful if capital mobility is introduced. Capital flows from the low return to the high return country, that is from H to P until factor price equalization is achieved at point e in Figure 12.7. The quantity K_0K_1 of domestically owned capital has been transferred to P.[12]

This reallocation of capital raises P's production by eaK_1K_0 and reduces home's production by ecK_0K_1. The net effect is an increase in union output and welfare that corresponds to area eac. Of the total gain, ebc accrues to H and eab to P. The home country's welfare gain is the income generated by K_0K_1 units of its capital now working in P, area ebK_0K_1, *less* the loss in domestic product caused by the displacement of these units abroad, area ecK_0K_1.[13] The partner country's welfare gain equals the difference between the gain in its output *less* the return to H's capital that works in partner country.

While each country has a net benefit, some groups within each country are worse off. Since home's capital–labor ratio decreases, its real wage rate and real rental rate move in opposite directions. Conversely labor gains and capital loses in P since P's capital–labor ratio increases.

Problem 12.5: Apply the analysis of capital mobility to determine the groups of primary factors in Mexico and the United States that would oppose or favor full capital mobility made possible by the Free Trade Agreement between these countries.

Taxation

Though some capital flows are observed between wealthy and poor countries, the bulk of capital flows are among the former ones. An intriguing question is why more capital does not flow from rich countries, such as Germany, the United States into poorer countries like Spain, Portugal, Mexico until capital–labor ratios, and hence wages and capital returns, are equalized.

One reason advanced in the literature is that the simple framework of this section clearly overstates the actual difference in marginal products of capital. A claim is that the assumptions on technology of our model must be amended to account for differences in human capital and in the external benefits of human capital (Lucas, 1990).

The different regimes of taxation of capital income introduce distortions in the allocation of international investments as well. Table 12.5 summarizes the statutory corporate income tax rates in the 12 EC countries. Table 12.5 suggests that there is considerable variation in these rates. Suppose a tax rate of ac/aK_0 in Figure 12.7 is imposed in P while capital is not subject to a tax in H. Private investors who react to after-tax returns are only interested in the line $p'p'$ which is obtained by a $ac/aK_0\%$ downward shift of the curve pp. Starting from the free mobility equilibrium point e, the result of this foreign tax is the repatriation of H capital working in P until point c where the after-tax returns are equalized. An amount K_1K_0 of domestically-owned capital returns in H. Despite free mobility of capital a differential in gross marginal products prevails and corresponds to that before capital mobility was permitted. The global loss due to foreign taxation corresponds to area eac and completely offsets the initial gain due to the free mobility of capital. The effect of the tax is therefore to duplicate the pre-mobility allocation of capital stocks.[14]

Problem 12.6: In analogy to the optimal tariff argument, show that it pays the capital exporting country to restrict incipiently its capital exports by raising an optimum tax rate on capital movements. Indicate the losses for the foreign country.

Table 12.5 *Statutory corporate tax rates, 1989 (%)*

	Central government	*Central and local government*[1]
Belgium	43	43
Denmark	50	50
France	39	39
Germany	56/36/[2]	62/45/[2]
Greece	35[3]	35[3]
Ireland	10[4]	10[4]
Italy	36	46
Lux.	37[5]	43
Netherlands	35	35
Portugal	36.5	40
Spain	35	36[6]
UK	35	35

Notes:
1. Net rates.
2. Split rate system: first rate applies to retained earnings, second rate to distributed earnings.
3. Rate for industrial companies quoted on the Athens Stock Exchange.
4. Rate for industrial companies, to remain in effect until the end of the year 2000. The standard rate for other companies is 43%.
5. Including a 2% surcharge (deductible) for the employment funds.
6. Includes the surcharge for the chamber of commerce.
Source: Tanzi and Bovenberg (1989).

Labor mobility

In the preceding analysis we allowed capital to be internationally mobile and labor to be immobile. Below we analyze the case of no capital but full labor mobility.[15] The analysis, though seemingly related to that of capital mobility, leads to different welfare conclusions. In addition, the adjustment on the labor market is often constrained by a binding wage floor.

Asymmetries

Figure 12.8 depicts the optimal allocation of labor, holding fixed the allocation of capital. The left and right vertical axes measure labor's real wage in *H* and *P*, respectively. Total labor of both countries is measured by

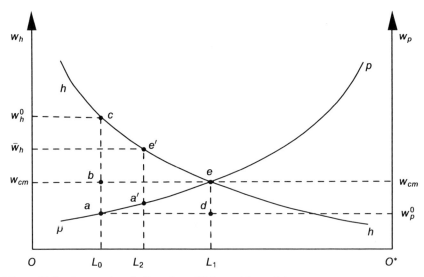

Figure 12.8   *International allocation of labor with a minimum wage*

the distance OO^* along the horizontal axis. The initial allocation of labor between H and P is assumed to be such that OL_0 and L_0O^* workers are in H and P, respectively. Curves hh and pp, drawn with reference to origins O and O^* respectively, are now labor's physical marginal product in each country. The law of diminishing returns implies that the marginal product of labor is higher in the labor-scarce economy ($w_h^0 > w_p^0$). If labor mobility is allowed, immigration will then occur only to the labor-poor country, and will continue until point e where capital–labor ratios, real wages and real capital returns are equalized. At point e, H absorbs the quantity L_0L_1 of P labor and the new equilibrium real wage is w_{cm}. Given this, H production increases by the area ecL_0L_1 but, against this increase, there is a less than offsetting wage bill paid to migrants given by the area ebL_0L_1, thus yielding a home gain of ecb. This gain accrues exclusively to home capitalists who also absorb the real wage loss of home labor, the area $cbw_{cm}w_h^0$.

As the real wage in P has increased from w_p^0 to w_{cm}, partner labor whether migrants or non-migrants, gains at the expense of partner capitalists. Whether this translates in an overall gain in P depends on whether the labor units L_0L_1 productive in H are border workers or migrants who reside in H. The distinction is important because it affects the composition of national incomes and determines under which jurisdiction, i.e. tax system, these labor units fall. In the former case, national income in P increases by eba, that is the difference between the repatriated wage bill ebL_0L_1 and the loss in P output eaL_0L_1. In the latter case, area ebL_0L_1 is part of the domestic product of H that then appropriates all the allocation gains. Those who are left behind in *P* face an uncompensated aggregate loss corresponding to the area *eda*. Partner country, essentially partner capital, is a net loser from this type of labor mobility.

Wage floor and illegal immigration

Suppose instead that *H* subjects its entire labor market to a minimum wage floor. Define this minimum wage by $\overline{w}_h$ in Figure 12.8. If labor mobility is free, home firms will hire partner labor until the marginal product of labor equals $\overline{w}_h$. The direct effect of the wage floor is to restrict the number of immigrants to L_0L_2 compared to L_0L_1 before. A differential in marginal products will therefore remain, indicating that though gains are realized they are not exhausted.

Though further potential gains can be realized by lowering $\overline{w}_h$, these gains do not accrue to all groups in the society. Home labor sees its marginal product decline with immigration and will therefore object against a lower $\overline{w}_h$. In contrast, the marginal product of home capital increases with immigration and owners of capital will therefore favor a lowering of $\overline{w}_h$. If this is not possible, capital owners would then be prepared to hire illegal immigrants at a marginal product lower than $\overline{w}_h$.

12.3 Facets of economic integration: the NAFTA

Recent years have seen a wave of regionalism in North America starting with the Canada–US Free Trade Agreement (CUSTA) in 1988 and extended to the NAFTA in December 1992 by including Mexico. The latter agreement reduces and ultimately eliminates most of the barriers to trade and investment (but not to investments in Mexican oil industry) among Canada, Mexico and the United States. The prospect of the NAFTA stimulated a large amount of research on its potential effects, mainly on trade, income and welfare of the participating countries. The quantitative assessment of these effects was typically made using Applied General Equilibrium Models (AGE).[16] Tables 12.6–12.8 list some of the results generated by these models.

An interesting feature of the NAFTA is that member countries are currently at widely different stages of economic development and the countries have different relative supplies of physical and human capital. One must therefore expect the efficiency gains brought about by free trade and investment to arise from different reasons. Between Canada and the United States, gains from freer trade should reflect gains from economies of scale

Table 12.6   *The NAFTA and income: static models with CRS*[a]

	Tariffs and NTBs (1)	Tariffs, NTBs and Mex. K-inflow[b] (2)	Tariffs, NTBs, Mex. K-inflow and endog. migration (3)
Mexico			
Wage[c] R	−0.2	9.2	4.7
UW	−0.2	9.2	4.7
S	1.0	7.4	7.7
WC	1.0	8.8	9.1
Rent	1.1	−1.2	−0.9
Real income	0.3	6.4	6.8
USA			
Wage R	0.3	−0.4	1.8
UW	0.4	0.7	1.8
S	0	0.1	0.0
WC	0	0.3	0.2
Rent	0	1.2	1.1
Real income	0	0.1	0.1

Notes:
[a] % change with respect to no integration.
[b] A 7.6% increase in Mexican capital stock.
[c] R = rural; UW = urban unskilled; S = skilled; WC = white collar.
Sources: Hinojosa-Ojeda and Robinson (1991, cited in Brown, 1992).

and reduction in monopoly power of firms. Between Mexico and its partners, efficiency gains should emerge from increased specialization and a reallocation of resources along the lines of comparative advantage.

Table 12.6 reports the results of three scenarios based on a static model with constant returns to scale (CRS). Column (1) depicts the NAFTA simply as a removal of tariffs and NTBs. The estimated welfare changes are therefore the result of intersectoral specialization and the removal of consumption distortions. These results reflect the concepts of trade creation and trade diversion of Section 12.1, a difference being that AGE models take explicit account of the factor supplies constraints. The results are indicative of a general consensus on the static trade effects of the NAFTA, namely that the effects are small for both Mexico and the United States. One reason for

Table 12.7   *The NAFTA and income: static models with IRS[a]*

	Tariffs and NTBs (1)	Tariffs, NTBs and Mex. K-inflow[b] (2)
Canada		
Real wage	0.4	0.5
Rent	0.4	0.5
Real income	0.7	0.7
Terms of trade	−0.5	−0.5
Mexico		
Real wage	0.7	9.3
Rent	0.6	3.3
Real income	1.6	5.0
Terms of trade	−0.1	−2.5
USA		
Real wage	0.2	0.2
Rent	0.2	0.2
Real income	0.1	0.3
Terms of trade	0.2	0.0

Notes:
[a] % change with respect to no integration.
[b] 10% increase in Mexican capital stock.
Source: Brown *et al.* (1992, cited in Brown, 1992).

Table 12.8   *The NAFTA and income in Mexico: a dynamic model (% change over base steady state)*

Complete liberalization	2.6
Liberalization and interest rate reduction (from 10% to 7.6%)	8.1

Source: Young and Romero (1992, cited in Brown, 1992).

this outcome is that restrictions on trade between the United States and Mexico are already low except in sensitive sectors (textile). Columns (2) and (3) allow for, respectively, international capital mobility and for international capital and labor mobility. In essence, these two columns are a quantification of the theoretical analysis of Section 12.2. The capital inflow into Mexico promises to raise its income. The consequences of migration are less obvious, except for certain types of labor. The results suggest that capital is a major constraining factor in the Mexican economy.

Table 12.7 considers the first two scenarios but assumes increasing returns to scale (IRS) and imperfectly competitive market structures. The essential feature of the model is monopolistic competition with free entry of firms and downward sloping average cost curves. Column (1) of Table 12.7 indicates that non-competitive market structures considerably raise the gains from the NAFTA for Mexico (1.6%). Compared to Table 12.6, this extra gain is essentially the result of increased scale economies due to the larger market.[17] Column (2) of Table 12.7 corroborates the powerful effects of foreign direct investment on the Mexican economy shown by the perfectly competitive model.

Finally, Table 12.8 shows the results of a dynamic model that studies the questions of the NAFTA in the context of intertemporal utility and profit maximization. The reported model is a neoclassical model of growth for Mexico with an emphasis on the capital goods market.[18] As the NAFTA removes the tariff on foreign capital goods (assumed to be perfect substitutes of domestic goods), the steady-state level of Mexican GDP is raised by 2.6%. If, in addition, Mexico were in a position to reduce its real interest rate (from 10 to 7.6%), this percentage would become 8.1%. These results stress once again that the rules governing capital flows are as important as the rules guiding the flow of goods.

12.4 **New regionalism**

It is clear from Figure 12.3 that the CU's optimal tariff creates a welfare loss for W. We might therefore expect W to retaliate unless it consists of a number of small countries which are unable to organize. The possibility of retaliation gives rise to the debate about the overall desirability of increased regionalism.

In particular two intriguing questions have been raised: (1) Would the division of the world into regional blocs be expected to lead to global trade conflicts and therefore lower welfare? (2) Do regional agreements compete with or complement the multilateral trading system personified by the WTO? A large number of inspiring papers have contributed to these issues and their answers, to be reviewed here, have been mixed.

Retaliation and global trade wars

The case of retaliation as a result of a CU amounts to solving a non-cooperative tariff game. A first reaction curve indicates the CU's welfare maximizing tariff response for a given value of W's tariff. Conversely, the other reaction curve depicts W's optimal tariff response for given values of CU's tariff. Assuming each reaction curve is downward sloping, the point of intersection determines the Nash equilibrium values of the tariffs and hence also international trade.[19] A robust outcome of this non-cooperative game is that post-retaliation tariffs will typically be higher for larger countries and that a Nash tariff war will not eliminate trade (Johnson, 1953). However, this outcome does not hold when other instruments of commercial policy are the strategic variable. For example, Rodriguez (1974) and Tower (1975) show that trade will be asymptotically reduced to zero if import or export quotas, and not tariffs, are used. More recently, Krugman's (1991) model confirms that, as trade blocs simultaneously form, higher external barriers and lower world welfare will be observed.

The above results on retaliation imply that, as new RTAs form, global trade conflicts may emerge which would endanger the postwar cooperation in international trade. A number of contributions to the game-theoretic international trade literature do not, however, support the idea of a global trade war, for essentially two reasons (Perroni and Whalley, 1996). First, a large share of the new RTAs take the form of free trade areas which, unlike a CU, do not coordinate their external tariff policy. Hence, the retaliatory power of outsiders is not exacerbated (Kennan and Riezman, 1990). Second, trade retaliation in reality is episodic and more of the form of a single retaliatory exchange while non-cooperative tariff games assume that retaliation continues until the Nash outcome is reached. Episodic trade conflict is a feature of recent work on infinitely repeated games that search for conditions under which two countries can sustain freer trade given that they determine trade policies non-cooperatively (Dixit, 1987; Riezman, 1991). In these models, even if cooperation can be sustained over time, periodic reversions to high tariffs will occur in order to provide renewed incentives for countries to cooperate.

Regionalism versus multilateralism

An important clue for understanding the emergence of 'new regionalism' is the different nature of the new RTAs compared to the traditional formation of customs unions like the EC or Mercosur. In particular, the new RTAs consist of individual countries or groups of countries that wish to join an existing integrated area, either the EC or the United States. This has been termed the 'hub and spoke' structure of integration (Wonnacott, 1990). Also, applicant countries are relatively small and at widely different stages of economic development. For example, *per capita* GDP of Mexico was 2490 US$ in 1990, compared to 22 055 US$ and 21 527 US$ for, respectively, the United States and Canada. Potential new-comers from Central and East Europe have only a quarter of the purchasing power of the present EC average. Finally, large countries usually obtain asymmetric concessions from smaller countries in the regional negotiations which are willing to undergo drastic economic and social reforms.

Against this background, recent literature offers some insight into the question of whether the formation of RTAs harms or helps multilateral trade cooperation. So far, answers have been mixed. On the one hand, Bagwell and Staiger (1993) show that during the transition to a free trade area tariffs may temporarily rise. On the other hand, Ethier (1996) argues that RTAs give newcomers a marginal advantage compared to non-participating small countries in attracting foreign direct investments which then gain access to a large market. This argument is in line with the simulation results of Tables 12.6 and 12.7 which underline the importance of capital as a major constraining factor in most applicant countries.

12.5 **Concluding remarks**

How much is a country willing to pay in order to enjoy free trade with a specified group of countries? Each member state of an integrated area has asked itself this question and evaluated the benefits a country expects to reap from integration. The customs union theory presents a number of arguments in favor or against economic integration within the framework of economic theory but does not, however, provide clear cut answers. It is mostly an empirical question.

A difficulty with traditional customs union theory and with its extensions to include scale economies is that the field is too broad, with too many particular conclusions to different specifications to be comprehensively treated in a consistent manner. Another criticism is the small number of results. Several reasons have been advanced to explain this lack of progress. First, a difficulty with the customs union theory is that it starts from a distorted initial situation and struggles with the complexity of welfare comparisons inherent in second best analyses. Second, the focus of economic integration is on the customs union. But no convincing argument has been advanced as to the superiority of this form of integration compared to, let us say, a multilateral reduction of trade barriers. Moreover, it remains unclear whether free trade areas represent a net movement towards freer trade since they adopt rules of origin that govern trade within the area. Third, the focus of the theory has been on the static concepts of trade creation/diversion while the bulk of the effects of economic integration seem to come instead from economies of scale and factor mobility. Lastly, unlike other branches of economics, the customs union theory has not evolved in response to empirical research. So, the theory keeps emphasizing the theoretical effects of trade diversion whereas empirics hardly finds any support for this concept. In the light of theoretical uncertainty in connection with the welfare effects, there is a clear need for improved links between theory and data and for renewed empirical investigations of the questions raised by economic integration.

Notes

1. See de la Torre and Kelly (1992) for a list of regional integration areas. See also Sampson (1996).
2. The NAFTA also liberalizes, to some degree, investment among members.
3. Article XXIV of GATT spells out the principles for both customs unions and free trade areas. See McMillan (1993) for an interpretation of this Article.
4. The formation of a CU attracted great attention among economic theorists, and several books and interpretive survey articles appeared on the subject. See e.g. Lipsey (1960), Krauss (1972), Michaely (1977), Hansen *et al.* (1992).
5. This terminology is from Viner (1950). The concepts used here derive, however, from Johnson (1962) who includes both production and consumption effects whereas Viner focuses on the former only.
6. The terminology is from Ethier and Horn (1984).
7. (12.4) also suggests that the ideal partners for the home country to form a CU should be those whose production efficiency approaches that of the outside world. This suggests that the CU should contain a large number of countries since it is more likely to find a partner country whose price is close to the world price.
8. Greece had almost no trade with Spain over the sample period and was therefore excluded from the list of EC member countries.
9. See Kemp and Wan (1976) for a detailed list of assumptions and the proof of the proposition.
10. The analyses of this section involve scenarios where only trade barriers change, in contrast to Chapter 10 which also considers market segmentation and its counterfactual, full market integration.
11. The interpretation of (12.9) is trivial. The marginal product of a factor is the derivative of output with respect to that factor so that output is the integral of this marginal product.
12. Helpman and Razin (1983) have shown that in economies with sectors which produce differentiated goods under increasing returns to scale, international capital movements may flow in the wrong directions, thereby harming the host as well as the investing country.
13. The gains derive from the difference between national income and domestic product. Both concepts are similar in absence of factor mobility but differ under mobility. For example, the post-mobility domestic product is reduced to the area under the *hh* curve up to point *e* while the post-mobility national income increases by the area *ebc*.

14. Political risk is also an important factor in limiting capital flows. This could be interpreted as a foreign tax, this tax being equivalent to a risk premium associated to the risky country.

15. Numerous alternative policies could be considered. Such policies include trade in goods and in factors (Wong, 1983), and the choice between labor and capital mobility (see, e.g. Ramaswami, 1968; Bhagwati and Srinivasan, 1983; Calvo and Wellisz, 1983; Cheng and Wong, 1990; Wong, 1995).

    A related problem is the brain drain that is so important in growth strategies of poorer countries (see, e.g. Bhagwati and Hamada, 1974 for a model of the brain drain; Findlay and Kierzkowski, 1983 for a model of the reverse brain drain).

16. See, e.g. Lustig *et al.* (1992) for a collection of papers on several areas of NAFTA. In this collection, Brown (1992) provides a detailed survey of the structure of the AGE models that have been used to assess the impact of NAFTA. See also Srinivasan *et al.* (1993), Francois and Shiells (1994).

17. Harris (1984), Harris and Cox (1984) were the first to show that AGE models with non-competitive market structure and scale economies generate much larger gains from trade liberalization policy than earlier AGE models with perfect competition and constant returns to scale. Harris (1984) shows also that, at the industry level, both models yield dramatically different results. The hypothesis of no correlation between industry effects of both models is accepted at the 99% level of significance.

18. Brada and Méndez (1988) have empirically tested the dynamic effects of integration. The latter do exist but have a relatively insignificant explanatory power on the growth of member countries' output. Chapter 14 provides other links between economic integration and growth in the context of endogenous growth theory.

19. Johnson (1953) and Riezman (1982, 1985) address the issue of multiple equilibria in this setting.

References and additional reading

Customs union theory

Bliss, A. (1994), *Economic Theory and Policy for Trading Blocks* (Manchester: Manchester University Press).

Cooper, C.A. and Massell, B.F. (1965), 'Towards a General Theory of Customs Unions for Developing Countries', *Journal of Political Economy*, 73, 461–76.

Corden, W.M. (1972), 'Economies of Scale and Customs Union Theory', *Journal of Political Economy*, 80(3), 465–75.

Ethier, W.J. and Horn, H. (1984), 'A New Look at Economic Integration', in Kierzkowski, H. (ed.), *Monopolistic Competition and International Trade* (Oxford: Clarendon Press), 207–29.

Hansen, J.D., Heinrich, H. and Nielsen, J.W.-M. (1992), *An Economic Analysis of the EEC* (London: McGraw-Hill).

Hine, R.C. (1994), 'International Economic Integration', in Greenaway, D. and Winters, L.A. (eds), *Survey in International Trade* (Oxford: Basil Blackwell), 234–72.

Johnson, H. (1962), 'The Economic Theory of Customs Union', in Johnson, H. (ed.), *Money, Trade and Economic Growth* (London: George Allen & Unwin).

Kemp, M.C. and Wan, H.Y. (1976), 'An Elementary Proposition Concerning the Formation of Customs Unions', *Journal of International Economics*, 6, 95–7.

Krauss, M.B. (1972), 'Recent Development in Customs Union Theory: An Interpretive Survey', *Journal of Economic Literature* (June), 413–36.

Lipsey, R.G. (1960), 'The Theory of Customs Unions – A General Survey'. *Economic Journal*, 70, 496–513.

McMillan, J. (1993), 'Does Regional Integration Foster Open Trade? Economic Theory and GATT's Article XXIV', in Anderson, K. and Blackhurst, R. (eds), *Regional Integration and the Global Trading System* (New York: Harvester Wheatsheaf), 292–310.

Michaely, M. (1977), *Theory of Commercial Policy* (Chicago: University of Chicago Press).

Viner, J. (1950), *The Customs Union Issue* (New York: Stevens & Sons).

Wonnacott, P. and Wonnacott, R. (1981), 'Is Unilateral Tariff Reduction Preferable to a Customs Union? The Curious Case of the Missing Foreign Tariffs', *American Economic Review*, 71, 704–13.

Wooton, I. (1986), 'Preferential Trading Arrangements: An Investigation', *Journal of International Economics*, 21, 81–97.

Empirics of customs unions

Baldwin, R. *et al.* (1992), *Is Bigger Better? The Economics of EC Enlargement* (London: Centre for Economic Policy Research).

Brada, J.C. and Méndez, J.A. (1988), 'An Estimate of the Dynamic Effects of Economic Integration', *Review of Economics and Statistics*, 70(1), 163–8.

De la Torre, A. and Kelly, M.A. (1992), 'Regional Trade Arrangements', *International Monetary Fund, Occasional Paper*, 93 (March).

Flam, H. (1992), 'Product Markets and 1992: Full Integration, Large Gains?', *Journal of Economic Perspectives*, 6(4), 7–30.

Grinols, E.J. (1984), 'A Thorn in the Lion's Paw: Has Britain Paid Too Much for Common Market Membership?', *Journal of International Economics*, 16, 271–293.

Jacquemin, A. and Sapir, A. (1988), 'European or World Integration?', *Weltwirtschaftliches Archiv*, 124(1), 127–38.

Johnson, H.G. (1958), 'The Gains from Freer Trade with Europe: An Estimate', *Manchester School*, 26, 247–55.

Miller, M.H. and Spencer, J.E. (1977), 'The Static Economic Effects of the UK Joining the EEC: A General Equilibrium Approach', *Review of Economic Studies*, 136, 71–94.

Petith, H.C. (1977), 'European Integration and the Terms of Trade', *Economic Journal*, 87, 262–72.

Smith, A. and Venables, A.J. (1988), 'Completing the Internal Market in the European Community: Some Industry Simulations', *European Economic Review*, 32, 1501–25.

Viaene, J.-M. (1982), 'A Customs Union Between Spain and the EEC', *European Economic Review*, 18, 345–68.

Willenboekel, D. (1994), *Applied General Equilibrium Modelling: Imperfect Competition and European Integration* (Chichester: John Wiley).

Winters, L.A. and Venables, A.J. (1991), *European Integration: Trade and Industry* (Cambridge: Cambridge University Press).

International factor mobility

Bhagwati, J.N. and Hamada, K. (1974), 'The Brain Drain, International Integration of Markets for Professionals and Unemployment: A Theoretical Analysis', *Journal of Development Economics*, 1, 19–42.

Bhagwati, J.N. and Srinivasan, T.N. (1983), 'On the Choice between Capital and Labour Mobility', *Journal of International Economics*, 14, 209–21.

Calvo, G. and Wellisz, S. (1983), 'International Factor Mobility and National Advantage', *Journal of International Economics*, 14, 103–14.

Cheng, L.K. and Wong, K.Y. (1990), 'On the Strategic Choice between Capital and Labor Mobility', *Journal of International Economics*, 28, 291–314.

Findlay, R. and Kierzkowski, H. (1983), 'International Trade and Human Capital: A Simple General Equilibrium Model', *Journal of Political Economy*, 91, 957–78.

Helpman, E. and Razin, A. (1983), 'Increasing Returns, Monopolistic Competition, and Factor Movements: A Welfare Analysis', *Journal of International Economics*, 14, 263–76.

Lucas, R.E. (1990), 'Why Doesn't Capital Flow from Rich to Poor Countries?', *American Economic Review*, 80(2), 92–6.

MacDougall, G.D.A. (1960), 'The Benefits and Costs of Private Investment from Abroad: A Theoretical Approach', *Economic Record*, 36, 13–35.

Ramaswami, V.K. (1968), 'International Factor Movement and the National Advantage', *Economica*, 35, 309–10.

Ruffin, R.J. (1984), 'International Factor Movements', in Jones, R.W. and Kenen, P.B. (eds), *Handbook of International Economics*, Vol. I (Amsterdam: North-Holland), 237–88.

Tanzi, V. and Bovenberg, A.L. (1989), 'Is There a Need for Harmonizing Capital Income Taxes within EC Countries?' (Washington, DC: International Monetary Fund), mimeo.

Wong, K.Y. (1983), 'On Choosing Among Trade in Goods and International Capital and Labor Mobility: A Theoretical Analysis', *Journal of International Economics*, 14(3/4), 223–50.

Wong, K.Y. (1995), *International Trade in Goods and Factor Mobility* (Cambridge, Mass.: MIT Press).

Free trade agreements

Brown, D.K. (1992), 'The Impact of a North American Free Trade Area: Applied General Equilibrium Models', in Lustig, N., Bosworth, B.P. and Lawrence, R.Z. (eds), *North American Free Trade: Assessing the Impact* (Washington, DC: Brookings Institution), 26–68.

Brown, D.K., Deardorff, A.V. and Stern, R.M. (1992), 'A North American Free Trade Agreement: Analytical Issues and a Computational Assessment', *The World Economy*, 15, 11–30.

Francois, J.F. and Shiells, C.R. (1994), *Modelling Trade Policy: Applied General Equilibrium Assessments of NAFTA* (Cambridge: Cambridge University Press).

Harris, R. (1984), 'Applied General Equilibrium Analysis of Small Open Economies with Scale Economies and Imperfect Competition', *American Economic Review*, 74(5), 1016–32.

Harris, R. and Cox, D. (1984), *Trade, Industrial Policy, and Canadian Manufacturing* (Toronto: Ontario Economic Council Research Study).

Hinojosa-Ojeda, R. and Robinson, S. (1991), 'Alternative Scenarios of US–Mexico Integration: A Computable General Equilibrium Approach', *Working Paper*, 609 (University of California, Berkeley).

Lustig, N., Bosworth, B.P. and Lawrence, R.Z. (1992), *North American Free Trade: Assessing the Impact* (Washington, DC: Brookings Institution).

Srinivasan, T.N., Whalley, J. and Wooton, I. (1993), 'Measuring the Effects of Regionalism on Trade and Welfare', in Anderson, K. and Blackhurst, R. (eds), *Regional Integration and the Global Trading System* (New York: Harvester Wheatsheaf), 52–79.

Young, L. and Romero, J. (1992), *Steady Growth and Transition in a Dynamic Dual Model of the North American Free Trade Agreement* (Austin: University of Texas).

Retaliation and trade warfare

Coneybeare, J.A.C. (1987), *Trade Wars: The Theory and Practice of International Commercial Rivalry* (New York: Columbia University Press).

Dixit, A. (1987), 'Strategic Aspects of Trade Policy', in Bewley, T.F. (ed.), *Advances in Economic Theory: Fifth World Congress* (Cambridge: Cambridge University Press), 329–62.

Johnson, H.G. (1953), 'Optimum Tariffs and Retaliation', *Review of Economic Studies*, 21, 142–53.

Kennan, J. and Riezman, R. (1990), 'Optimal Tariff Equilibrium with Customs Unions', *Canadian Journal of Economics*, 23(1), 70–83.

Krugman, P.R. (1991), 'Is Bilateralism Bad?', in Helpman, E. and Razin, A. (eds), *International Trade and Trade Policy* (Cambridge, Mass.: MIT Press), 9–23.

Perroni, C. and Whalley, J. (1996), 'How Severe is Global Retaliation Risk under Increasing Regionalism?', *American Economic Review Papers and Proceedings*, 86(2), 57–61.

Riezman, R. (1982), 'Tariff Retaliation from a Strategic Viewpoint', *Southern Economic Journal*, 48, 583–93.

Riezman, R. (1985), 'Customs Unions and the Core', *Journal of International Economics*, 19, 355–65.

Riezman, R. (1991), 'Dynamic Tariffs with Asymmetric Information', *Journal of International Economics*, 30(3/4), 267–83.

Rodriguez, C.A. (1974), 'The Non-Equivalence of Tariffs and Quotas Under Retaliation', *Journal of International Economics*, 4, 295–8.

Tower, E. (1975), 'The Optimum Quota and Retaliation', *Review of Economic Studies*, 42, 623–30.

Regionalism versus multilateralism

Bagwell, K. and Staiger, R.W. (1993), 'Multilateral Tariff Cooperation during the Formation of Regional Free Trade Areas', *National Bureau of Economic Research, Working Paper*, 4364.

Bond, E. and Syropoulos, C. (1993), 'Trading Blocs and the Sustainability of Interregional Cooperation', *Department of Economics Discussion Paper*, 93-17, University of Birmingham.

Ethier, W.J. (1996), 'Regionalism in a Multilateral World', *Working Paper*, International Economics Research Center, University of Pennsylvania.

Sampson, G.P. (1996), 'Compatibility of Regional and Multilateral Trading Agreements: Reforming the WTO Process', *American Economic Review Papers and Proceedings*, 86(2), 88–92.

Wonnacott, R. (1990), *US Hub-and-Spoke Bilaterals and the Multilateral Trading System* (Toronto: Howe Institute).

■ Chapter 13 ■

Exchange Rates and International Trade

The collapse of the Bretton Woods system of fixed exchange rates in 1973 raised theoretical and empirical issues about the consequences of flexible exchange rates for international trade. Of specific interest was the effect that increased exchange rate volatility may have on the level of trade and the role of the forward exchange market in this context. However, international trade theory has little say about such effects since it traditionally restricts itself to models in which no nominal exchange rate is defined.[1] On the other hand, models of the international monetary theory rarely address issues of trade patterns. Recent research attempts to connect these two fields by incorporating the nominal exchange rate in trade models. These research efforts can be viewed as a step taken by the international trade literature to reconsider its assumptions about imperfect competition, capital and exchange rate markets.

This chapter examines topics that attempt to link the exchange rate to international trade. In this context, we consider four issues. Section 13.1 first considers the role of exchange rates in a partial equilibrium framework and derives the so-called separation and full hedging propositions. Section 13.2 looks at the choice of invoice currency. Section 13.3 analyzes the factors affecting the pass-through from exchange rates to import prices. Finally, Section 13.4 treats the concept of hysteresis.

13.1 Trade and exchange rate volatility

The exporter's risk bearing optimum

Consider the problem of a risk averse domestic firm which produces a single product for export. A production level q entails a cost $C(q)$ where the cost function $C(\cdot)$ is assumed to be strictly convex, increasing and twice differentiable, i.e. $C' = \partial C/\partial q > 0$, $C'' = \partial^2 C/\partial q^2 > 0$ and $C(0) = 0$, primes denoting partial differentiation. Markets are assumed competitive and the world price of the product, expressed in foreign currency, is p^*.

A characteristic of international trade is the practice of extending trade credit. Once goods are delivered, the exporter allows the foreign buyer to defer payment until a fixed future date. Thus, there are two dates, one on which goods are produced and delivered, and one on which they are paid for. The exporter's receipts in domestic currency are given by $\tilde{e}p^*q$ where $\tilde{e}$ is the unknown future spot exchange rate. The exchange rate is defined as the domestic currency price of the foreign currency and the tilde refers to the random nature of the future spot rate. The exporter can cover the exchange rate uncertainty arising from his foreign currency exposure by selling an amount k of foreign currency forward at the known forward exchange rate e_f. This forward transaction will add $(e_f - \tilde{e})k$ to his local currency profits. Given this, the exporter's profit function on the date at which payment is received can be written:

$$\tilde{\Pi} = \tilde{e}p^*q - C(q) + (e_f - \tilde{e})k \tag{13.1}$$

The exporter will choose q and k so as to maximize the expected utility of profits $EU(\tilde{\Pi})$, where E is the expectations operator. $U(\cdot)$ is a strictly concave, increasing and differentiable von Neumann–Morgenstern utility function defined over the exporter's profits $\tilde{\Pi}$. The first-order conditions for this maximization problem are:

For q: $EU'(\tilde{\Pi})[\tilde{e}p^* - C'(q)] = 0$ \hfill (13.2)

For k: $EU'(\tilde{\Pi})[e_f - \tilde{e}] = 0$ \hfill (13.3)

where $U'(\cdot)$ is the marginal utility and $EU'(\tilde{\Pi}) > 0$. Using (13.3) to substitute for $\tilde{e}$ in (13.2) gives the solution for the optimal level of export:

$$e_f p^* = C'(q) \tag{13.4}$$

The optimal level of export is chosen so as to equate the marginal cost of production to the domestic currency price of q. Hence, the optimal output level is independent of both the distribution of the exchange rate $\tilde{e}$ and the exporter's attitute toward risk. This result is known as the 'separation proposition'. The implication is that any two firms with the same cost function but with different attitudes toward risk, and with different probability beliefs about the future exchange rate, will produce the same level of output. This is the important contribution of a forward market.[2]

A second result, known as the 'full hedging proposition', states that if the forward exchange market is unbiased, namely $E\tilde{e} = e_f$, then the value of the optimal forward contract is $p^*q = k$. To demonstrate this result, note that strict concavity of $U(\cdot)$ implies $\text{cov}[\tilde{\Pi}, EU'(\tilde{\Pi})] \leq 0$, with equality holding when profits $\tilde{\Pi}$ are not random. Making use of (13.1)–(13.3) we have:

$$\text{cov}[\tilde{\Pi}, EU'(\tilde{\Pi})] = -EU'(\tilde{\Pi})[(p^*q - k)(E\tilde{e} - e_f)] \leq 0 \qquad (13.5)$$

(13.5) implies:

$$(p^*q - k)(E\tilde{e} - e_f) \geq 0 \qquad (13.6)$$

The difference $(E\tilde{e} - e_f)$ is the risk premium and indicates the extent to which the exporter's expectation of the future exchange rate deviates from the market forward rate. When $(E\tilde{e} - e_f)$ is positive, the difference is called a normal backwardation. When negative, this expression is a cotango, when zero, an unbiased forward market. In the latter case, i.e. $E\tilde{e} = e_f$, (13.6) is zero and profits $\tilde{\Pi}$ are no longer random. From (13.1), the necessary condition for profits to be non-random is:

$$p^*q = k \qquad (13.7)$$

which states that the exporter hedges his export transaction completely. If $E\tilde{e} \gtrless e_f$ then from (13.6) it follows that $p^*q \gtrless k$, that is the exporter sells a smaller or greater amount of foreign exchange than his foreign currency receipts. If the forward market is biased, it is optimal for the exporter to speculate on the forward exchange market by taking a short or long position depending on whether the risk premium is respectively negative or positive.

An example

Assume a trading house which buys commodities on the domestic market and resells them abroad. Further assume that the trading house faces the following inverse supply function for domestic goods: $p = d + q/2$, where d is a constant and q is the quantity purchased at home and sold abroad. The value of domestic purchases is then $dq + q^2/2$. The trading house receives a price p^* in foreign currency on each unit exported and hence earns a total of $\tilde{e}p^*q$ in domestic currency. The profit function of the trading house is then:

$$\tilde{\Pi} = \tilde{e}p^*q - dq - q^2/2 + (e_f - \tilde{e})k \qquad (13.8)$$

where k is the amount of forward foreign currency sold at the forward rate e_f.

For analytical convenience, let this exporter's *ex ante* probability beliefs about the value of $\tilde{e}$ be described by a normal probability density function. The distribution has mean $E\tilde{e}$ and variance σ^2, where these values are conditional on the exporter's information set on the decision date. Since $\tilde{e}$ is normally distributed, profits are also normally distributed with mean $E\tilde{\Pi}$ and variance var $\tilde{\Pi}$. Suppose that $U(\tilde{\Pi}) = -e^{-\alpha\tilde{\Pi}}$ where $\alpha = -U''(\tilde{\Pi})/U'(\tilde{\Pi})$

is the measure of (constant) absolute risk aversion.[3] Expected utility can then be written as $EU(\tilde{\Pi}) = -e^{\alpha(E\tilde{\Pi} - (\alpha/2)\,\text{var}\,\tilde{\Pi})}$ given our assumption of normality.[4] Hence, maximizing $EU(\tilde{\Pi})$ is equivalent to maximizing:

$$EV = E\tilde{\Pi} - \frac{\alpha}{2}\,\text{var}\,\tilde{\Pi} \tag{13.9}$$

(13.9) is the traditional mean–variance utility function. Maximizing (13.9) with respect to q and k gives the following optimal solutions:

$$q = p^* e_f - d \tag{13.10}$$

$$k = p^* q - \frac{E\tilde{e} - e_f}{\alpha\sigma^2} \tag{13.11}$$

In (13.10) q does not depend on α or σ^2, which corroborates the separation result (13.4). A change in the forward rate, however, will affect the trade level of q according to the conventional terms of trade analysis. (13.11) shows that the optimal hedge has two components, the sale of forward currency for trade purposes and speculation. The latter component, $(E\tilde{e} - e_f)/\alpha\sigma^2$, adds or subtracts from the trade component depending on the sign of the risk premium, i.e. $(E\tilde{e} - e_f)$. Contrary to popular belief, it does not take risk-loving agents to get speculative positions. The amount of speculation is decreasing in α and σ^2 but increasing in the risk premium. If the risk premium is zero, the full hedge result, i.e. $k = p^* q$, obtains.

Inserting (13.10) and (13.11) in (13.8) and then computing (13.9) gives the level of expected utility at the optimum:

$$EV = \frac{q^2}{2} + \frac{(E\tilde{e} - e_f)^2}{2\alpha\sigma^2} \tag{13.12}$$

The first term in (13.12) is the expected utility attached to international trade while the second is the expected utility from speculation. The speculation term vanishes if the forward market is unbiased. If, in addition, the separation result holds, the exporter avoids exchange risk altogether and is indifferent between a fixed or flexible exchange rate regime.

This last conclusion is counter to the popular conjecture that increased exchange rate volatility reduces the volume of trade. However, there are situations in which this conjecture is obtained, two of which are pursued here. The first considers the absence of a forward market; the second questions the exogeneity of the forward rate (Viaene and de Vries, 1992).

Problem 13.1: Consider the case of a trading house which imports commodities from abroad and retails them locally. The trading house faces the domestic demand function $p_m = a - q_m/2$. Assume further each unit of the imported commodity costs a fixed foreign currency price p^*_m. Assuming a mean–variance utility function for the importer, derive the optimal solution for the level of imports q_m and for the hedge k_m. Discuss the implications of the separation and full hedging results for the importer's level of expected utility.

Problem 13.2: Consider the case of a speculator who has initial wealth W_s. The speculator allocates this wealth among domestic assets, which earn the interest rate r (covered interest parity is assumed to hold), and by open positions in exchange markets with a view to profiting from the discrepancy between the current forward rate and his expected future spot rate. The speculator's future wealth is then:

$$\tilde{W}_s = (1 + r)W_s + (e_f - \bar{e})k_s$$

Assuming a mean–variance utility function, derive the optimal amount of forward sales k_s so as to maximize the speculator's expected utility of future wealth. Check that the second-order condition for an interior maximum is not violated for risk-loving speculators.

No forward market

This situation relates to the case when the trading firm has no access to a forward exchange market. This applies to many developing and transitional economies where well developed foreign markets do not exist and to industrial countries where the access to the market is too costly. If the firm does not have access to a forward market then k in (13.8) is zero. Maximizing (13.9) with respect to q only gives:

$$q = \frac{p^* E\tilde{e} - d}{1 + \alpha\sigma^2} \tag{13.13}$$

which compares to (13.10). Consider a mean-preserving spread change, that is a higher volatility of the exchange rate (a higher σ^2) while maintaining the mean $E\tilde{e}$ constant. By (13.13), this change lowers the level of trade and the exporter's expected utility.

A general equilibrium analysis

The separation proposition derived in (13.4) is a partial equilibrium outcome and does not generally hold in the general equilibrium sense that the aggregate net supply of forward currency determines e_f. To see this, consider the market clearing condition on the forward market and assume that the number of exporters, importers and speculators is n, m and s, respectively. All agents are assumed to have the same degree of risk aversion $\alpha > 0$. Adding the amounts of forward foreign currency sales by exporters (see (13.11)), importers (see Problem 13.1) and speculators (see Problem 13.2) and solving for the equilibrium forward rate gives:

$$e_f = E\tilde{e} - \Omega\sigma^2(TB + F) \tag{13.14}$$

where $\Omega = \alpha/(m + n + s)$ measures aggregate risk aversion, TB is the trade balance and F is a term that represents exogenous forward currency sales by the central bank.[5] The solution in (13.14) expresses the forward rate in terms of the expected exchange rate, the risk aversion parameter, the conditional variance of $\tilde{e}(\sigma^2)$ and the net foreign currency exposure of the economy $(TB + F)$. A striking implication of this framework is that a change in the volatility will have opposite effects on imports and exports. The intuition behind this result is that importers and exporters are on opposite sides of the forward market. An increase in σ^2 in (13.14) causes, *ceteris paribus*, the forward rate to increase (assuming $(TB + F) < 0$) which increases exports (see 13.10) and decreases imports (see Problem 13.1). Who gains or loses from this increase in exchange risk therefore depends on the net aggregate foreign currency exposure $(TB + F)$: if negative, exporters gain and importers lose and vice versa.[6]

Empirical results

Several empirical studies have examined the hypothesis that increases in exchange rate volatility reduce trade. The results differ depending on whether the analysis assumes the existence of a well developed forward market. Studies of developing countries in which forward markets are absent generally find a negative relationship between trade and exchange rate volatility (Coes, 1981). For countries with forward markets, no consistent link between volatility and trade has been found. Table 13.1 summarizes these mixed results by showing the elasticity of US bilateral trade flows to exchange rate volatility. This elasticity is obtained by regressing US bilateral trade flows on a measure of the volatility of the bilateral exchange rate with each partner country.[7] The estimated coefficients are of either sign and are often not significantly different from zero. The number of negative elasticities increases, however, as the estimation becomes more and more restricted to the floating rate period.[8] Despite this, all these studies indicate that a decrease in the mean level of the exchange rate (an appreciation) does reduce trade (not shown).

Table 13.1   *Effects of increasing exchange rate volatility on US bilateral trade flows, 1965–83*

	Cushman (1983) 1965–77		IMF (1984) 1965–82		Cushman (1988) 1974–83	
US exports to						
UK	0.080	(2.71)	−0.01	(−0.81)	−0.086	(−4.27)
Netherlands					−0.040	(−1.31)
France	−0.065	(−3.02)	0.03	(3.01)	−0.043	(−0.75)
Germany	0.019	(1.24)	−0.004	(−0.67)	−0.034	(−1.16)
Canada	−0.036	(−3.45)	−0.01	(−0.58)	−0.055	(−2.44)
Japan	−0.058	(−2.89)	0.03	(3.56)	0.064	(2.01)
US imports from						
UK	0.031	(1.48)	0.001	(0.11)	−0.132	(−2.54)
Netherlands					−0.099	(−2.98)
France			−0.01	(−1.21)	−0.091	(−2.46)
Germany	0.032	(1.41)	−0.003	(−0.32)	0.086	(1.78)
Canada	−0.037	(−3.15)	0.01	(0.42)	−0.125	(−2.40)
Japan	−0.057	(−2.41)	−0.29	(−2.96)	−0.086	(−2.24)

Note:
Elasticities (and *t*-ratios) of US bilateral trade flows with 6 countries with respect to bilateral exchange rate volatility.
Source: Cushman (1988).

13.2 The choice of the invoice currency

Apart from the product price and the forward rate, the currency in which an invoice is denominated has an important influence on the conduct of international trade. In choosing the currency of invoice one also chooses which of the two parties to the transaction bears the risk of the exchange rate fluctuations, namely the party whose receipts and costs are not labelled in the same currency. For example, in (13.1), the exporter's receipts are denominated in foreign currency while his or her costs are denominated in local currency. Hence it is optimal for the exporter to hedge against exchange rate risk.

An empirical regularity relating to the choice of invoice currency is Grassman's (1973) empirical observation that trade is usually invoiced in the exporter's currency. More recent data are given in Table 13.2. This empirical finding has been revisited by several authors (e.g. Black, 1985). Deviations from this finding are also well recorded (Basevi *et al.*, 1985). Explanations for why invoicing is predominantly in the exporter's currency have not received much attention. Bilson (1983) offers a macroeconomic explanation;

Table 13.2   *Share of trade contracts denominated in domestic and foreign currency,*
1976 (% of total)

	Own currency		US $	
	x	*m*	*x*	*m*
USA	90	–	90	–
Germany	87	42	5	31
Switzerland (1977)	83	41	7	–
UK (1977)	69	–	17	–
France	68	32	9	29
Sweden	67	26	14	22
Austria	55	25	10	16
Denmark	54	25	12	23
Netherlands	50	31	13	23
Belgium	47	26	12	25
Italy	39	16	31	43
Finland	16	–	22	–
Japan	30	1–2	68	90
New Zealand	20–30	–	75	70–80
Latin America	0	0	85	–
OPEC	0	0	95	–
Others	0	0	70	–

Notes:
x = Exports; m = Imports; – = Not available.
Source: Scharrer (1979, cited in Black, 1985).

Giovannini (1988) derives a result that depends on whether profits of a risk
neutral exporter are a concave or a convex function of the exchange rate;
Fukuda and Cong (1994) argue that demand conditions in the foreign
markets explain the choice of invoice currency by Japanese exporters;
Viaene and de Vries (1992) advance as an explanation the strategic non-
cooperative bargaining between exporters and importers.

The hedge decision

To examine the issues involved consider the analysis of Viaene and de Vries
(1992), in which a domestic exporter and a foreign importer have agreed to
trade 1 unit of a commodity. The exporter charges the price p in his or her
currency and charges p^* in foreign currency. Assuming that the domestic

currency is the exporter's currency in which his or her profits are expressed and maximized, the expression for the exporter's profit is:

$$\tilde{\Pi} = \lambda p + (1 - \lambda)\tilde{e}p^* - c + (e_f - \tilde{e})k \tag{13.15}$$

where $\tilde{e}$ is the future domestic price of foreign currency; e_f is the forward rate, k is the net supply of forward foreign currency, and c is the per-unit production cost in domestic currency. Due to trade credit, the exporter will receive $\lambda p + (1 - \lambda)\tilde{e}p^*$ in the future, where λ is the invoice parameter indicating the proportion of domestic currency receipts. To shield himself from the uncertain future spot rate, the merchant can take a hedge k by buying or selling foreign currency forward.

Denote the mean and variance of $\tilde{e}$ as $E\tilde{e}$ and σ^2, respectively, and assume further that the exporter maximizes the mean–variance utility function (13.9) with respect to k. The optimal hedge is then:

$$k = [e_f - E\tilde{e}]/\alpha\sigma^2 + (1 - \lambda)p^* \tag{13.16}$$

and the level of expected utility is:

$$EV = \tfrac{1}{2}[e_f - E\tilde{e}]^2/\alpha\sigma^2 - c + \lambda p + (1 - \lambda)e_f p^* \tag{13.17}$$

Note that the exporter hedges only a part of his or her exposure unless the risk premium is zero, i.e. $e_f = E\tilde{e}$ when the exporter hedges completely. Even without foreign currency risk, i.e. $\lambda = 1$, a risk averse exporter will still undertake a favorable bet: $k = (e_f - E\tilde{e})/\alpha\sigma^2$.

Now consider the case in which the invoice parameter is not exogenous but can instead be determined by the exporter. Since expected utility (13.17) is now a function in λ, differentiation gives:

$$\frac{\partial EV}{\partial \lambda} = p - e_f p^*$$

Since EV is linear in λ, EV increases (decreases) with λ as p exceeds (is less than) $e_f p^*$. Since the relevant domain of λ is restricted to the interval $[0, 1]$, 3 solutions to the above equation may prevail. First, if $p = e_f p^*$, then any $0 \le \lambda \le 1$ generates the same expected utility and the choice of the invoice currency is irrelevant. Second, if $p > e_f p^*$, then $\partial EV/\partial\lambda > 0$ for $0 \le \lambda \le 1$ and expected utility attains its maximum at the corner solution $\lambda = 1$. Third, if $p < e_f p^*$, then $\partial EV/\partial\lambda < 0$ and expected utility attains its maximum at $\lambda = 0$. If we exclude the case $p = e_f p^*$ and focus on $p < e_f p^*$ or $p > e_f p^*$ (when $\lambda = 0$ or 1) then we need to ask which case, $\lambda = 0$ or $\lambda = 1$, will be the observed outcome? To answer this question, we must introduce the preferences of the importer. If the foreign importer sells the imported product in his or her local market at a price expressed in his or her own currency, then it can be shown (see Problem 13.3) that when $p > e_f p^*$, it is optimal for the importer to set $\lambda = 0$, i.e. the importer would prefer to pay in his or her own currency. However, this conflicts with the exporter's preferences and it is possible by a similar reasoning to show that the conflict holds when $p < e_f p^*$. Hence, how can we resolve the conflict over the invoice parameter between the importer and exporter? One way is to apply models of non-cooperative bargaining that discuss the partition of a melting cake between two parties (Rubinstein, 1982; Sutton, 1986; Rubinstein, 1987).

Problem 13.3:   Consider a foreign importer who retails imports on his local market at a price v^*. The importer has the following profit function:

$$\tilde{\Pi}^* = v^* - \lambda \frac{p}{\bar{e}} - (1 - \lambda)p^* + \left(\frac{1}{\bar{e}} - \frac{1}{e_f}\right) k^*$$

where the '*' denotes variables denominated in the importer's currency. Maximize (13.9) to find the importer's optimal hedge k^*, and level of expected utility. Show that the importer and exporter disagree about the value of λ.

Sequential bargaining

Imagine that both parties bargain over the value of an invoice parameter by alternating bids until an agreement is reached. Depending on the specifics of the commodity being traded we distinguish between 2 cases. The first case presumes that the bargaining over λ can be studied in isolation from market considerations. For example, this could arise in the case of trade in non-standardized commodities such as capital goods where the option of finding another importer or exporter is very costly. However, for trade in standardized commodities, market considerations have to be taken into account, because each party can opt out and contact a new partner.

In the first case, assume that each party, in turn, makes an offer in terms of λ and the other party may agree to the offer or reject it. If the other party accepts, the game ends; if the offer is rejected, a counteroffer is made at the next stage; and so on, with no limit on the number of repetitions of the process. As time is an important factor in international trade, each party discounts the final agreement by a discount factor, δ_x and δ_m for the exporter and importer respectively $(\delta_x, \delta_m < 1)$.[9] The discount factors provide an incentive for the players to reach an agreement.

It was shown by Rubinstein (1982) that, in this game, the agreement is immediate and that there is a unique partition which can be supported as a subgame perfect equilibrium.[10] To show this,[11] consider the subgame beginning with an offer made by the exporter at time $t = 2$. Let $\hat{\lambda}$ be this offer which represents the supremum of the invoice parameter the exporter can expect in this game. Then, $\delta_x \hat{\lambda}$ is the discounted value of this parameter to the exporter at time $t = 1$. Hence, any offer at time $t = 1$ by the importer which gives the exporter a share less than $\delta_x \hat{\lambda}$ will certainly be rejected by him at period 2. So the invoice parameter the importer can obtain cannot be more than $(1 - \delta_x \hat{\lambda})$. This discounted at time $t = 0$ gives $\delta_m(1 - \delta_x \hat{\lambda})$. At time $t = 0$, any offer by the exporter which gives the importer a share of the trade contract in his or her currency less than $\delta_m(1 - \delta_x \hat{\lambda})$ will certainly be rejected at period 1. Hence, the exporter will obtain at most a share in own currency equal to $(1 - \delta_m(1 - \delta_x \hat{\lambda}))$. However, this must equal $\hat{\lambda}$ which solves for the equilibrium value $\hat{\lambda} = (1 - \delta_m)/(1 - \delta_m \delta_x)$. The importer receives $1 - \hat{\lambda}$. This is the solution reported in Table 13.3.

The result has the feature that the more patient a player ($\delta_x \rightarrow 1$ or $\delta_m \rightarrow 1$), the greater his share in own currency. There is also a first-mover advantage: for example, when $\delta_x = \delta_m = \delta$, then $\hat{\lambda} = 1/(1 + \delta)$. The party that goes first will therefore have an advantage over the party that goes second since more than half of the trade transaction will be invoiced in the first party's currency.

When market considerations matter, it can be shown that the currency of exporters dominates if importers outnumber exporters, since exporters will have some monopoly power. A concrete example helps to illustrate the bargaining power of exporters. The Netherlands had 7701 registered exporters and 9406 registered importers in 1987. Of these, 2923 firms produced and exported manufactured goods directly, while 723 firms produced and imported manufactured goods directly. The rest of the firms were trading

Table 13.3   *The invoice parameter*[a]

	$\hat{\lambda}$	$1 - \hat{\lambda}$
$0 < \delta_x, \delta_m < 1$[b]	$\dfrac{1 - \delta_m}{1 - \delta_x \delta_m}$	$\dfrac{\delta_m(1 - \delta_x)}{1 - \delta_x \delta_m}$
$\delta_x \rightarrow 1$	1	0
$\delta_m \rightarrow 1$	0	1
$\delta_x = \delta_m = \delta$	$\dfrac{1}{1 + \delta}$	$\dfrac{\delta}{1 + \delta}$

Notes:

[a]Table 13.3 presents the equilibrium solution $\hat{\lambda}$ conditional upon $p > p^* e_f$ and the exporter having the advantage of making the first offer. The exporter receives $\hat{\lambda}$ and the importer $1 - \hat{\lambda}$. If the importer is the first proposer, the two outcomes have to be interchanged.

[b]δ_x, δ_m represent the discount factors of the exporter and importer, respectively.

houses, focusing either on exports or on imports. Production of manufactures is therefore concentrated, while trading activities are spread across a larger number of distributors, and hence importers. Producers that export have a bargaining advantage over the importer since they have a better chance of finding another partner if a deal cannot be made. This analysis is consistent with Grassman's (1973) finding on the use of exporter's currency.

13.3 Prices and exchange rates

The large fluctuations of exchange rates in the last two decades have drawn attention to the pricing policies of international firms. To remain competitive, exporting firms are thought to respond incompletely to exchange rate movements by adjusting their export prices and their mark-up over marginal cost. This phenomenon is termed 'exchange rate pass-through' (EPT). Considerable theoretical and empirical research has examined the pricing policies by firms and the differences in the behavior of US and foreign firms. The results have often been used to explain the persistent US trade deficit in spite of the large depreciation of the US dollar starting in the mid-1980s. The argument is that prices and trade volumes of imperfectly competitive industries react less to exchange rate movements than would competitive ones.[12]

Concepts and definitions

The concept of EPT can be best seen by focusing on the pricing behavior of firms which produce both for export and the domestic market. Firms sell in the domestic market at the price p_d and in the export market at the foreign currency price p^*. Firms are assumed to be interested in their domestic currency profits. The relevant price is then the domestic currency price of exports, i.e. $p = ep^*$ where the exchange rate e is the domestic currency price of foreign currency. Expressing $p = ep^*$ in relative changes and dividing by $\hat{e}$ gives two related measures of EPT:

$$\varepsilon = 1 + \varepsilon^* \tag{13.18}$$

The first, $\varepsilon = \hat{p}/\hat{e}$, is the elasticity of the domestic currency export price with respect to the exchange rate. The second, $\varepsilon^* = \hat{p}^*/\hat{e}$, is the elasticity of the foreign currency export price with respect to the exchange rate. EPT can be measured by either ε or ε^*, (13.18) indicating the relationship between them.[13]

EPT is complete, incomplete or perverse if a depreciation of the exporter's currency $(\hat{e} > 0)$ causes the domestic currency price of exports to be unchanged $(\varepsilon = 0)$, to increase $(\varepsilon > 0)$ or to decrease $(\varepsilon < 0)$. Complete EPT implies that firms maintain own-currency prices and profit margins on their foreign sales constant and mechanically pass any exchange rate change through to buyers. Incomplete EPT implies that exporters absorb some portion of an exchange rate change in their mark-up of price over marginal cost. When the exchange rate depreciates ($\hat{e} > 0$) firms experience rising margins and when the exchange rate appreciates ($\hat{e} < 0$) falling margins. A perverse EPT is theoretically justified when firms seek to increase their market share abroad (Froot and Klemperer, 1989).

The concept of 'pricing to market' (PTM) refers to the case in which exporting firms charge a different price in home and foreign markets.[14] In terms of the above framework, this implies that p and p_d need not be the same. While some natural dispersion in prices is expected when there are transport costs, if prices still differ after correcting for these, then the residual can reflect ineffective spatial commodity arbitrage[15] or segmented markets.[16]

The exchange rate pass-through under oligopoly

To understand the analytics of EPT, we consider a model of oligopoly of firms in a foreign market due to Dornbusch (1987). This model assumes a single homogeneous commodity and a linear demand for this good:

$$d^* = a^* - b^* p^* \qquad (13.19)$$

where d^* is foreign market demand, p^* the price denominated in the currency of the foreign market, a^* and b^* constants with a^* capturing the non-price determinants of demand. The foreign market is supplied by n^* foreign firms (indexed i), selling the quantity q_i^* in their local market and by n domestic firms (indexed j) exporting the quantity x_j. It is assumed that: (1) all firms adopt a Cournot quantity strategy, (2) there are barriers to entry so that the number of firms is fixed and (3) markets are segmented so that we need only focus on prices and quantities in the foreign market.

A foreign firm seeks to maximize its foreign currency profits:

$$\Pi_i^* = (p^* - c^*)q_i^* \qquad i = 1, \ldots, n^*$$

where c^* is the foreign firm's constant marginal cost of production. In contrast, a domestic exporting firm maximizes domestic currency profits:

$$\Pi_j = (ep^* - c)x_j \qquad j = 1, \ldots, n$$

where c is the domestic firm's constant marginal cost. Since aggregate sales across firms sum to market demand, profit maximization by foreign firm i and domestic firm j with respect to output gives rise to the following reaction functions:

$$a^* - (n^* + 1)q^* - nx - b^* c^* = 0 \qquad (13.20)$$

$$a^* - n^* q^* - (n + 1)x - \frac{b^* c}{e} = 0 \qquad (13.21)$$

where symmetry within each group of firms ($x_j = x, \forall_j; q_i^* = q^*, \forall_i$) is assumed. Given this, the reaction functions give the optimal behavior of the representative firm of each group. These functions are depicted in Figure 13.1, the domestic firm's reaction curve being RC, the foreign being R^*C^*.

Solving (13.20) and (13.21) yields the Cournot–Nash equilibrium solution for domestic exports and foreign production:

$$q^* = \frac{1}{(n + n^* + 1)} \left[a^* - (n+1)b^*c^* + nb^* \frac{c}{e} \right] \tag{13.22}$$

$$x = \frac{1}{(n + n^* + 1)} \left[a^* + n^*b^*c^* - (n^*+1)b^* \frac{c}{e} \right] \tag{13.23}$$

The output supplies depend on the marginal costs in foreign currency. By (13.19), the equilibrium price in the foreign market is:

$$p^* = \frac{1}{(n + n^* + 1)} \left[\frac{a^*}{b^*} + n^*c^* + n \frac{c}{e} \right] \tag{13.24}$$

The industry price depends on a (weighted) sum of the marginal costs in foreign currency of all firms in the market.

A devaluation of the exporters' currency (or equivalently an appreciation of the foreign currency ($\hat{e} > 0$)) will shift the exporters' reaction curve RC to the right in Figure 13.1. The new Cournot–Nash equilibrium is A', which implies an increase in the market share of exporting firms and a decrease in the market share of foreign firms. The industry price declines, as is seen from (13.24) since an increase in the supply of exports more than offsets the reduction in foreign supply. Hence, a devaluation has an interpretation

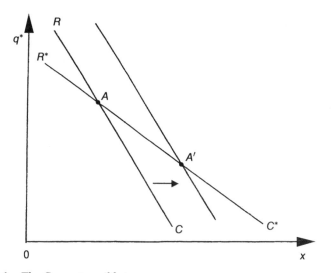

Figure 13.1   *The Cournot equilibrium*

similar to that of a domestic export subsidy while an appreciation has an interpretation similar to that of a foreign tariff on imports.[17]

A key result of this analysis is an expression for the EPT measure, defined by ε in (13.18):

$$\varepsilon = 1 - \frac{n}{(n + n^* + 1)} \frac{c}{ep^*} \tag{13.25}$$

This indicates that the EPT has 2 determinants in this model: the relative number of exporting firms and the ratio of marginal cost to the domestic currency price of exports. Noting that $\partial \varepsilon / \partial n < 0$ and $\partial \varepsilon / \partial n^* > 0$ (13.25) allows a comparison of EPT expressions for different assumptions about market structure. A limiting case is when the number of foreign firms relative to the number of home exporting firms is low ($n \to \infty$). Foreign firms are then price takers and EPT is complete ($\varepsilon = 0$). If the number of foreign firms is instead large ($n^* \to \infty$) then domestic exporters are price takers and $\varepsilon = 1$. The cases $n^* = 0$ and $n = 1$ correspond to the case of a monopoly and imply $\varepsilon = 1 - c/2ep^*$ so that EPT is incomplete ($\varepsilon > 0$).

Assuming forms of imperfect competition different from that assumed here yields other expressions for EPT than (13.25). These expressions imply that, besides the role of market structure contained in (13.25), the theoretical value of ε depends on (1) the functional form of demand (Dornbusch, 1987; Feenstra, 1989); (2) the functional form for costs (Cheffert, 1994) and (3) the degree of product substitutability in foreign markets (Dornbusch, 1987).

Empirical studies of EPT have, however, not been able to devise tests that can discriminate between these alternative determinants of the value of ε. In particular, a testing of the significance of ε is not a proper test of which theory underlies any particular value of ε. Since one cannot test the theory underlying ε, studies instead focus on the sign of ε and whether it significantly differs from zero. A positive and significant ε indicates incomplete EPT while an insignificant ε is indicative of complete EPT.

Problem 13.4: Consider the oligopoly situation in the foreign market as sketched in the main text, except now replace the n domestic exporting firms by n foreign affiliates of home based multinationals. Foreign affiliates have costs that consist of inputs purchased from the parent company at home (intra-firm trade) and of costs in foreign currency terms incurred in the foreign country. Assuming constant marginal costs, how does an exchange rate change affect the equilibrium quantity allocation between foreign firms and foreign affiliates? What is the effect of an exchange rate change on the industry price p^*?

Test of the PTM hypothesis

Analyses of the PTM hypothesis focus on how the ratio of own-currency export price relative to domestic price compares across industries and countries, how it evolves over time, and how it responds to changes in the exchange rate. Marston (1990) undertakes such a test using data on pricing by Japanese manufacturing firms in export and domestic markets.[18] In particular, he looks at the relative price (ep^*/p_d) for 17 Japanese final products over the period from February 1980 to December 1987 and relates this ratio to changes in real exchange rates, real wages and other factors like market structure and industrial production.

The parameter of interest is the PTM elasticity which measures the sustained effect of a rise in the real exchange rate (a depreciation) on the ratio of export to domestic prices. The estimates obtained ranged in size from 0.406 (trucks) to 1.03 (tyres and tubes) for 8 products consisting of transport and tractor equipment and from 0.278 (microwave ovens) to 1.11 (amplifiers) for 9 consumer products. 2 coefficients were not significantly different from zero (small trucks, cameras). All elasticities were positive, indicating that a yen depreciation (appreciation) leads Japanese firms to raise (lower) their domestic currency export price relative to their domestic price, evidence of pricing to market. For example, the PTM elasticity of 0.406 for trucks indicates that a rise in the real exchange rate by 1% raises the export–domestic price ratio by 0.406%.

13.4 Hysteresis

The preceding analysis has focused on the short-run effects of exchange rate changes. However, it is conceivable that entry and exit of firms in response to sufficiently large real exchange rate shocks can have lasting effects on the market structure, prices and trade volumes.

Models that explore the longer-term effects of exchange rate changes use the concept of hysteresis. Hysteresis is defined as:

> an effect that persists after the cause that brought it about has been removed. The argument is that firms must incur sunk costs to enter new markets, and cannot recoup these costs if they exit (Dixit, 1989b, p. 205).

The possibility of hysteresis arising from exchange rate shocks was put forward by Baldwin (1988). Baldwin and Krugman (1989) expand this analysis while Dixit (1989a, 1989b) examines hysteresis using the theory of option pricing to analyze investment decisions.[19] These models examine entry and exit decisions of domestic firms in a foreign market. Specifically, firms are assumed to incur a sunk capital cost to enter the market and a fixed maintenance cost to stay active in the market. Sunk costs include the costs of adapting the product to local market conditions (e.g. health and safety regulations, product launching through advertising, and setting up a distribution, sales and service network). Maintenance costs are necessary to prevent sunk assets from disappearing and, hence, the firm from exiting.[20]

Entry and exit conditions

To illustrate hysteresis, consider the model of the previous section, characterized by the solutions (13.22)–(13.25). Note that the equilibrium profit of each domestic firm is $\Pi = ex^2/b^*$ when denominated in domestic currency and $\Pi/e = x^2/b^*$ when denominated in foreign currency. Assume for simplicity that $b^* = 1$ and that firms have static expectations about the exchange rate. Let F be the cost to enter the foreign market and X be the maintenance cost, both being measured in foreign currency. Given this, we consider the export decision of domestic firms under alternative outcomes of profits (and, hence, about the exchange rate):

$$\begin{cases} \text{If } x^2 > F, \text{ enter the foreign market} \\ \text{If } x^2 < X, \text{ abandon the foreign market if already entered} \end{cases} \quad (13.26)$$

The optimal decision rule (13.26) involves 2 trigger values of profits, F and X with $F > X$. A domestic firm should enter the foreign market if x^2 rises above F and should abandon the market if x^2 falls below X. Hence, it must be the case that in equilibrium:

$$F \geq x^2 \geq X \quad (13.27)$$

This relation establishes a range of profits and exchange rates within which the number of firms in the foreign market is constant. Within this range, it is optimal for firms to maintain their current position. Assume that the solution given by (13.22)–(13.24) satisfies (13.27), with inequalities holding strictly. Also, assume that n^* is constant, but that the number of domestic firms may change in response to profits to be earned. A period-by-period Cournot–Nash equilibrium can then be computed.

Figure 13.2 depicts the decision rules given by (13.27). The curves FF and XX give the combinations of e and n such that $x^2 = F$ and $x^2 = X$, respectively. Making use of (13.23), one obtains:

$$n = \frac{1}{\sqrt{F}} \left[a^* + n^* c^* - (n^* + 1) \frac{c}{e} \right] - n^* - 1 \qquad FF \text{ curve}$$

$$n = \frac{1}{\sqrt{X}} \left[a^* + n^* c^* - (n^* + 1) \frac{c}{e} \right] - n^* - 1 \qquad XX \text{ curve}$$

The XX curve lies to the right of the FF curve because, for a given exchange rate, a lower level of profit can only be achieved by a higher number of domestic firms. Between these 2 curves, one has the zone of inaction.[21] Both

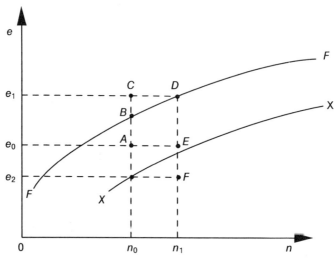

Figure 13.2   *Equilibrium range of firms*

curves are increasing (at a decreasing rate). Starting from any point on *FF*, a rise in profits following a depreciation of the domestic currency (an increase in *e*) has to be offset by entry in order to maintain profits at *F*. Alternatively, starting from any point on *XX*, an appreciation leads to a decline in profits below *X* and leads firms to exit the market until the equality of profits with *X* is re-established.

Exchange rate surprises

In this framework we can consider a sequence of unexpected changes in the exchange rate and analyze their effect on market structure in the foreign country. Starting from point *A* in Figure 13.2, a small exchange rate depreciation that brings the exchange rate, let us say, to *B* does not affect market structure. The level of exports of existing domestic firms increases and the foreign price p^* falls as a consequence of the reduction in the domestic marginal cost measured in foreign currency. In contrast, a larger exchange rate depreciation to e_1 alters the market structure and the new equilibrium to point *D*. At *D*, $(n_1 - n_0)$ new domestic firms have entered the foreign market. If the shock subsequently reverses itself (point *E*) the initial market structure is not restored. The number of firms remains higher than before since the exchange rate appreciation is not large enough to induce exit of firms. The initial market structure will only be restored if the exchange rate were e_2. If *E* is compared to *A*, the new equilibrium *E* is characterized by an increase in the market share of exporting firms and a decrease in the market share of foreign firms. Domestic firms export less per firm but the total volume of exports has increased. Foreign firms sell less in their local market, both individually and in the aggregate. Industry price declines since the increase in exports more than offsets the reduction in foreign supply. The measure of value of EPT is also smaller.[22]

Empirical results

Models producing hysteresis have been put forward to explain the puzzling observations about the US trade balance. From 1980 to the end of 1984, the real value of the US dollar appreciated sharply but the volume of imports began to rise after a long lag, only at the start of 1983. Starting from the first quarter of 1985, 2 years of continuous depreciation reduced the real value of the dollar back to its 1978 level. During these two years, there was only a slight increase in real import prices and import volumes did not decrease. Hence, the US trade balance did not improve. Schematically, in our context, if one considers the US as the foreign market, the cycle of the US dollar could be represented in Figure 13.2 by the move of the exchange rate from e_0 to e_1 and back.

Three approaches to empirically test for hysteresis have been undertaken. The first involves the search for structural breaks in the EPT measures. The preceding model implies that the EPT elasticity changes over time but that large exchange rate movements would cause structural breaks in the relationship, like those observed by the passing of trigger values (in Figure 13.2, movement from A to C, D and E). Baldwin (1988) presents evidence that the EPT relationship shifted in the 1980s, although no structural break could be found for import volumes. A second test looks at whether cumulative changes in the exchange rate determine trade flows. Under this hypothesis, imports should depend on the history of exchange rate changes. This contrasts with the traditional view that only the current level of the exchange rate matters. Tests of this conjecture using US data do not support this hypothesis (Parsley and Wei, 1993). The third test derives from an analogy with financial options. According to this interpretation, as volatility increases, one would expect time series estimates to show (1) a negative effect on entry due to larger exchange rate uncertainty (see n. 15), and (2) increased unresponsiveness of trade flows to exchange rate changes. Results based on US data support the former interpretation of hysteresis effects (Campa, 1993) but not the latter (Parsley and Wei, 1993).

13.5 Concluding remarks

This chapter has discussed some of the issues linking exchange rates and international trade. This area of study departs from traditional trade theory by relying on assumptions about imperfect competition and biased and unbiased exchange rate markets.

The central points to be drawn from this analysis are first the behavioral differences between importers and exporters. Importers are traditionally grasped as the mirror image of exporters for reasons based on the conventional terms of trade analysis. But this chapter has shown that differences in the behavior of exporters and importers go beyond the differentiated response of trade flows to exchange rate changes. The effects of a change in volatility on importers and exporters, for example, are opposite to each other. If the choice of the exchange rate regime (fixed versus flexible) is a political issue, importers and exporters will support different political candidates. Also, the expectation formation of exporters and importers usually go in opposite directions.

Second, empirical examination has not kept pace with the theoretical developments. The topic is also marked by conflicting empirical findings. Given this, the results to date suggest a sizable agenda for further research. In particular, there is a general need for the standard results of the literature to be reinterpreted and nested in an unifying framework. This would facilitate the task of empirically formulating nested hypotheses and the identification of those parts of the theory that are at stake.

Notes

1. A major exception is Dornbusch *et al.* (1977).
2. The separation result has been derived by Danthine (1978), Holthausen (1979), and Feder *et al.* (1980) in a closed-economy model of the firm under price uncertainty. Ethier (1973), Baron (1976) and Kawai (1981) derived the same result in an open-economy model, Kawai and Zilcha (1986) under price and exchange rate uncertainty.
3. The condition $\alpha > 0$ implies risk aversion; $\alpha = 0$ risk neutrality and $\alpha < 0$ risk loving.
4. See Hirschleifer and Riley (1992, Chapter 2) for the precise conditions which allow a conversion of $EU(\tilde{\Pi})$ into a function only of $E\tilde{\Pi}$ and var $\tilde{\Pi}$ and for the errors which are made by the approximation.
5. It is assumed for expository purposes that $E\tilde{e}$ and σ^2 in (13.14) are the same across agents. In practice, market participants are, however, heterogeneous. In an analysis of panel data of bi-weekly surveys on the yen/dollar exchange rate expectations, Ito (1990) finds that traders are characterized by wishful expectations: exporters expect a yen depreciation (relative to others) and importers expect a yen appreciation (relative to others).
6. This result has implications for the political choice of exchange rate regimes since there is a conflict of interest among exporters, importers and speculators over the desired degree of exchange rate flexibility (Ruland and Viaene, 1993).

7. The results are sensitive to the measure which proxies the conditional variance of $\tilde{e}$. See Perée and Steinherr (1989) for a justification and a comparison of these proxies.

8. See also, e.g. Brada and Méndez (1988), Hooper and Kohlhagen (1978), Gotur (1985), Kenen and Rodrik (1986), Bailey *et al.* (1986), Thursby and Thursby (1987), De Grauwe and Verfaille (1988), Perée and Steinherr (1989), and Sapir and Sekkat (1995) for other empirical findings.

9. Discounting is measured by the discount rate (the r notation) or the discount factor (the δ notation). The discount rate is analogous to the rate of time preference, r, and the discount factor is $\delta = 1/(1 + r)$. No discounting is equivalent to $r = 0$ and $\delta = 1$.

10. A subgame perfect equilibrium is a Nash equilibrium for the whole game and its restriction to any subgame must also be a Nash equilibrium (see Gibbons, 1992).

11. The proof is that of Sutton (1986).

12. See Goldberg and Knetter (1997) for an updated review of the theoretical and empirical literature.

13. If the exchange rate e is instead defined as the units of foreign currency per-unit of domestic currency (so a domestic devaluation is a decrease in e), then the relationship between export prices in domestic and foreign currency becomes $p = p^*/e$. Taking relative changes and dividing by $\hat{e}$ gives alternative measures of EPT: $\eta + 1 = \eta^*$, where $\eta = \hat{p}/\hat{e}$ and $\eta^* = \hat{p}^*/\hat{e}$. The latter expressions and (13.18) give 4 ways to measure EPT altogether. One difference between these alternative measures is that ε^* will generally be non-positive while η^* is non-negative ($\eta^* = -\varepsilon^*$). The literature has indiscriminately discussed these four measures to characterize the same thing, i.e. the pricing behavior of trading firms, and has led to some confusion in the interpretation and comparison of theoretical and empirical results. In what follows we consider (13.18) only.

14. See Krugman (1987).

15. For a large number of countries, there are usually official and unofficial barriers to international arbitrage in many commodities. Krugman (1987) cites the example of German automobiles.

16. Markets are segmented if firms are able to discriminate between countries, i.e. if they are able to set different prices and different mark-ups in different countries (see Chapter 10).

17. Feenstra's (1989) empirical study is unable to reject the hypothesis that there is a symmetric response of import prices to a change in exchange rate and to a change in import tariff. Hence, research on EPT turns out to be also useful in estimating industry effects associated with trade policy.

18. See Knetter (1992) for an international comparison of PTM behavior.

19. For a review of the recent literature on the analysis of investment decisions under uncertainty, see Dixit (1992), Dixit and Pindyck (1994).

20. The oligopoly model of this section explains the main features of hysteresis but it is too simple in several ways. First, it is static in that firms take a period-by-period decision to enter or to exit. Recent models examine, in contrast, the intertemporal decision making by firms. Decisions are then forward looking, with firms rationally computing equilibria in future periods and using this to

infer their current period entry or exit decisions. These models convey a broader meaning to exit costs which then include the severance pay that is often part of wage settlements on labor markets.

21. Dixit (1989a) has shown that the zone of inaction, i.e. the vertical difference between the *FF* and *XX* curves, is increasing with the degree of exchange rate uncertainty.

22. The results are obtained taking the partial derivatives of (13.22)–(13.25) with respect to n, assuming $c^* = c/e$ and $a^* - c/e > 0$, the last condition guaranteeing a positive profit margin for domestic firms in oligopoly.

References and additional reading

International trade and exchange rates: theory

Baron, D.P. (1976), 'Flexible Exchange Rates, Forward Markets and the Level of Trade', *American Economic Review*, 66, 253–66.

Danthine, J.-P. (1978), 'Information, Futures Prices and Stabilizing Speculation', *Journal of Economic Theory*, 17, 79–98.

Dornbusch, R., Fischer, S. and Samuelson, P.A. (1977), 'Comparative Advantage, Trade, and Payments in a Ricardian Model with a Continuum of Goods', *American Economic Review*, 47(5), 823–39.

Ethier, W. (1973), 'International Trade and the Forward Exchange Market', *American Economic Review*, 63, 494–503.

Feder, G., Just, R.E. and Schmitz, A. (1980), 'Futures Markets and the Theory of the Firm under Price Uncertainty', *Quarterly Journal of Economics*, 95, 317–28.

Holthausen, D.M. (1979), 'Hedging and the Competitive Firm under Price Uncertainty', *American Economic Review*, 69, 989–95.

Kawai, M. (1981), 'The Behaviour of an Open Economy Firm under Flexible Exchange Rates', *Economica*, 48, 45–60.

Kawai, M. and Zilcha, I. (1986), 'International Trade with Forward-Futures Markets under Exchange Rate and Price Uncertainty', *Journal of International Economics*, 20, 83–98.

Ruland, L.J. and Viaene, J.-M. (1993), 'The Political Choice of the Exchange Rate Regime', *Economics and Politics*, 5, 271–83.

Viaene, J.-M. and de Vries, C.G. (1992), 'International Trade and Exchange Rate Volatility', *European Economic Review*, 36, 1311–21.

Viaene, J.-M. and Zilcha, I. (1998), 'The Behavior of the Competitive Exporting Forum under Multiple Uncertainty', *International Economic Review*, forthcoming.

International trade and exchange rate volatility: empirical studies

Bailey, M.J., Tavlas, G.S. and Ulan, M. (1986), 'Exchange Rate Variability and Trade Performance: Evidence for the Big Seven Countries', *Weltwirtschaftliches Archiv*, 3, 466–77.

Brada, J.C. and Méndez, J.A. (1988), 'Exchange Rate Risk, Exchange Rate Regime and the Volume of International Trade', *Kyklos*, 41, 263–80.

Coes, D. (1981), 'The Crawling Peg and Exchange Rate Uncertainty', in Williamson, J. (ed.), *Exchange Rate Rules: The Theory, Performance and Prospects of the Crawling Peg* (New York: St. Martin's Press), 113–36.

Cushman, D.O. (1983), 'The Effects of Real Exchange Rate Risk on International Trade', *Journal of International Economics*, 15, 45–65.

Cushman, D.O. (1988), 'US Bilateral Trade Flows and Exchange Risk during the Floating Period', *Journal of International Economics*, 24, 317–30.

De Grauwe, P. and Verfaille, G. (1988), 'Exchange Rate Variability, Misalignment and the European Monetary System', in Marston, R.C. (ed.), *Misalignment of Exchange Rates: Effects on Trade and Industry* (Chicago: University of Chicago Press), 77–103.

Gotur, P. (1985), 'Effects of Exchange Rate Volatility on Trade', *IMF Staff Papers*, 32, 475–512.

Hooper, P. and Kohlhagen, S.W. (1978), 'The Effect of Exchange Rate Uncertainty on the Prices and Volume of International Trade', *Journal of International Economics*, 8, 483–511.

International Monetary Fund (1984), 'Exchange Rate Volatility and World Trade', *Occasional Paper*, 28 (Washington, DC: IMF Research Department).

Ito, T. (1990), 'Foreign Exchange Rate Expectations: Micro Survey Data', *American Economic Review*, 80(3), 434–49.

Kenen, P.B. and Rodrik, D. (1986), 'Measuring and Analyzing the Effects of Short-Term Volatility in Real Exchange Rates', *Review of Economics and Statistics*, 68, 311–15.

Perée, E. and Steinherr, A. (1989), 'Exchange Rate Uncertainty and Foreign Trade', *European Economic Review*, 33, 1241–64.

Sapir, A. and Sekkat, K. (1995), 'Exchange Rate Regimes and Trade Prices: Does the EMS Matter?', *Journal of International Economics*, 38(1/2), 75–94.

Thursby, J.G. and Thursby, M.C. (1987), 'Bilateral Trade Flows, the Linder Hypothesis, and Exchange Risk', *Review of Economics and Statistics*, 69, 488–95.

The invoice currency

Basevi, G., Cocchi, D. and Lischi, P.L. (1985), 'The Choice of Currency in the Foreign Trade of Italy', *Research Paper*, 17 (University of Bologna).

Bilson, J.F.O. (1983), 'The Choice of an Invoice Currency in International Transactions', in Bhandari, J.S. and Putnam, B.H. (eds), *Economic Interdependence and Flexible Exchange Rates* (Cambridge, Mass.: MIT Press), 384–402.

Black, S.W. (1985), 'International Money and International Monetary Arrangements', in Jones, R.W. and Kenen, P.B. (eds), *Handbook of International Economics*, Vol. II (Amsterdam: North-Holland), 1153–94.

Fukuda, S.-I. and Cong, J. (1994), 'On the Choice of Invoice Currency by Japanese Exporters: The PTM Approach', *Journal of the Japanese and International Economies*, 8, 511–29.

Giovannini, A. (1988), 'Exchange Rates and Traded Goods Prices', *Journal of International Economics*, 24, 45–68.

Grassman, S. (1973), 'A Fundamental Symmetry in International Payment Patterns', *Journal of International Economics*, 3, 105–16.

Scharrer, H.E. (1979), 'Die Wahrungsstruktur im Welthandel', Wirtschaftsdienst.

Viaene, J.-M. and de Vries, C.G. (1992), 'On the Design of Invoicing Practices in International Trade', *Open Economies Review*, 3, 133–42.

Exchange rate pass-through

Cheffert, J.-M. (1994), *Exchange Rate and Prices in Models of Imperfect Competition*, PhD thesis (University of Namur, Belgium).

Dornbusch, R. (1987), 'Exchange Rates and Prices', *American Economic Review*, 77(1), 93–106.

Feenstra, R. (1989), 'Symmetric Pass-Through of Tariffs and Exchange Rates under Imperfect Competition: an Empirical Test', *Journal of International Economics*, 27, 25–45.

Fisher, E. (1989), 'A Model of Exchange Rate Pass-Through', *Journal of International Economics*, 26, 119–37.

Froot, K. and Klemperer, P. (1989), 'Exchange Rate Pass-Through When Market Share Matters', *American Economic Review*, 79(4), 637–54.

Goldberg, P.K. and Knetter, M.M. (1997), 'Goods Prices and Exchange Rates: What Have We Learned?', *Journal of Economic Literature*, 35(3), 1243–72.

Hooper, P. and Mann, C. (1989), 'Exchange Rate Pass-Through in the 1980s: The Case of US Imports of Manufactures', *Brookings Papers on Economic Activity*, 1, 297–337.

Knetter, M.M. (1989), 'Price Discrimination by US and German Exporters', *American Economic Review*, 79(1), 198–210.

Knetter, M.M. (1992), 'International Comparisons of Pricing-to-Market Behavior', *American Economic Review*, 83(3), 473–86.

Krugman, P.R. (1987), 'Pricing to Market When the Exchange Rate Changes', in Arndt, S.W. and Richardson, J.D. (eds), *Real-Financial Linkages Among Open Economies* (Cambridge, Mass.: MIT Press), 49–70.

Marston, R. (1990), 'Pricing to Market in Japanese Manufacturing', *Journal of International Economics*, 29, 217–36.

Rangan, S. and Lawrence, R.Z. (1993), 'The Responses of US Firms to Exchange Rate Fluctuations: Piercing the Corporate Veil', *Brookings Papers on Economic Activity*, 2, 341–79.

Hysteresis

Baldwin, R. (1988), 'Hysteresis in Import Prices: The Beachhead Effect', *American Economic Review*, 78(4), 773–85.

Baldwin, R. and Krugman, P.R. (1989), 'Persistent Trade Effects of Large Exchange Rate Shocks', *Quarterly Journal of Economics*, 104(4), 633–54.

Campa, J.M. (1993), 'Entry by Foreign Firms in the United States under Exchange Rate Uncertainty', *Review of Economics and Statistics*, 75(4), 614–22.

Dixit, A. (1989a), 'Entry and Exit Decisions under Uncertainty', *Journal of Political Economy*, 97(3), 620–38.

Dixit, A. (1989b), 'Hysteresis, Import Penetration and Exchange Rate Pass-Through', *Quarterly Journal of Economics*, 104(2), 205–28.

Dixit, A. (1992), 'Investment and Hysteresis', *Journal of Economic Perspectives*, 6(1), 107–32.

Dixit, A. and Pindyck, R.S. (1994), *Investment under Uncertainty* (Princeton: Princeton University Press).

Krugman, P.R. and Baldwin, R. (1987), 'The Persistence of the US Trade Deficit', *Brookings Paper on Economic Activity*, 1, 1–55.

Parsley, D.C. and Wei, S.-J. (1993), 'Insignificant and Inconsequential Hysteresis: The Case of US Bilateral Trade', *Review of Economics and Statistics*, 75(4), 606–13.

Venables, A.J. (1990), 'Microeconomic Implications of Exchange Rate Variations', *Oxford Review of Economic Policy*, 6(3), 18–27.

Non-cooperative bargaining models

Rubinstein, A. (1982), 'Perfect Equilibrium in a Bargaining Model', *Econometrica*, 50, 97–110.

Rubinstein, A. (1987), 'Perfect Equilibrium in a Market with Decentralized Trade and Strategic Behaviour: An Introduction', *Theoretical Economics Discussion Paper Series*, 87/147 (London School of Economics).

Rubinstein, A. and Wolinsky, A. (1985), 'Equilibrium in a Market with Sequential Bargaining', *Econometrica*, 53, 1133–50.

Sutton, J. (1986), 'Non-Cooperative Bargaining Theory: An Introduction', *Review of Economic Studies*, 53, 709–24.

Game theory and information

Gibbons, R. (1992), *Game Theory for Applied Economists* (Princeton: Princeton University Press).

Hirschleifer, J. and Riley, J.G. (1992), *The Analytics of Uncertainty and Information* (Cambridge: Cambridge University Press).

■ Chapter 14 ■

Growth and International Trade

The achievement of sustained economic growth has been one of the principal objectives of economic policies of the postwar years. Economic growth is seen as a solution to a variety of economic problems, and it is therefore not surprising that the analysis of its determinants has been one of the dominant topics in economic theory.[1]

During the past decades, the achievement by the developed, but mainly the developing world has been remarkable as evidenced by the rising trend of *per capita* income and consumption. *Per capita* consumption increased by more than 70% and broader measures of well-being also increased substantially (World Bank, 1990). Against this background of achievement, many have emphasized the costs of economic growth in terms of its effects upon the environment and the availability of exhaustible resources, and have also pointed out that more than 1 billion people in the developing world are still living in poverty.

The policy experience of developing and developed countries motivates much of the research activities dealing with economic growth. The process of theory construction usually starts with a summary of stylized facts which are regarded as relevant to the problem of economic growth, and the theoretical model is then made consistent with these facts.

This chapter examines the models that form the basis for much of the intuition economists have about growth. However, our focus will be on those issues that relate specifically to international trade. Although domestic policies are often the essential ingredients of a strategy for improving growth, international factors are generally assigned an important role. This chapter discusses several frameworks that trace the implication of international factors for growth. Section 14.1 starts by discussing the issues raised by the Harrod–Domar model of growth and its open economy extension, the 2-gap model. Section 14.2 then addresses the neoclassical model of growth and the issue of income convergence. Section 14.3 extends the analysis to the more complex 2-sector models of the literature. These latter models incorporate features such as relative prices (absent in the simpler models) which enable us to discuss the triangular relationship between growth, welfare and the terms of trade. Finally we examine the endogenous growth literature.

14.1 The Harrod–Domar model of growth

Modern theories of economic growth emanate from the seminal writings of Harrod (1939) and Domar (1946). Their contributions contain the crucial idea that economic growth relates to the determinants of aggregate saving and investment. The formalized body of work stemming from these contributions is called the Harrod–Domar (H–D) theory of growth.[2] Though simple, the H–D theory contains a structure whose insights will serve as useful background when more sophisticated issues are addressed. This section first outlines the H–D theory for the case of an isolated economy and then discusses an open economy. The latter is the so-called 2-gap model, a theory that identifies whether growth is limited by a domestic savings gap or a foreign exchange gap. As the 2-gap model has been applied to more countries than any other model it seems natural to concentrate on its main ideas and implications.

The foundation

The isolated economy version of the H–D theory describes essentially a 1-sector economy. The economy's ratio of capital to labor employed is defined as $k_t = K(t)/L(t)$, where $K(t)$ denotes the stock of capital and $L(t)$ the labor force available at time t. The rate of growth of $k(t)$ equals the difference between the rate of growth of capital and of labor:

$$\frac{\dot{k}(t)}{k(t)} = \frac{\dot{K}(t)}{K(t)} - \frac{\dot{L}(t)}{L(t)} \tag{14.1}$$

where the dot over a variable signifies the instantaneous rate of change of that variable with respect to an infinitesimal increase in time, i.e. $\dot{k}(t) = dk(t)/dt$.[3]

Gross investment is capital accumulation *plus* depreciation:

$$I = \dot{K} + \mu K \tag{14.2}$$

where $\mu > 0$ is the depreciation rate. Dividing both sides of (14.2) by K gives:

$$\frac{\dot{K}}{K} = \frac{I}{K} - \mu \tag{14.3}$$

Equilibrium in a closed economy with no government expenditure requires equality between saving and investment. The saving function determines the division of total output Y between output to be consumed and output for accumulation. Assuming a constant fraction s ($0 < s < 1$) of total output is saved for investment purposes, (14.3) can be written:

$$\frac{\dot{K}}{K} = \frac{sY}{K} - \mu \tag{14.4}$$

The labor force is assumed to grow at the constant exogenous growth rate n:

$$\frac{\dot{L}}{L} = n \tag{14.5}$$

After substitution of (14.4) and (14.5), (14.1) can be rewritten:

$$\dot{k} = sy - (\mu + n)k \tag{14.6}$$

where $y = Y/L$ is output per worker. (14.6) is an equation of motion for k which describes the accumulation of capital per worker available after equipping the new labor and providing for depreciation.

The technology of the economy is assumed to take the fixed coefficient form:

$$Y = \min\left[\frac{K}{a}, \frac{L}{b}\right] \tag{14.7}$$

where a and b are the capital–output and labor–output ratios, respectively. This technology implies the absence of substitution between capital and labor: total output is either $Y = K/a$ or L/b.[4] The per-worker form of (14.7) can be simply written as:

$$y = \min\left[\frac{k}{a}, \frac{1}{b}\right] \tag{14.8}$$

Given this, and assuming $k < a/b$, (14.6) becomes:

$$\dot{k} = \left(\frac{s}{a} - \mu\right)k - nk \tag{14.9}$$

In Harrod's terminology $(s/a - \mu)$ is the warranted rate of growth and n the natural rate of growth. The warranted rate of growth is the exogenous growth rate of output and of capital such that aggregate investment equals aggregate saving. To see this, consider total output which is $Y = K/a$ since

$K < aL/b$ by assumption. Applying the rate of change notation gives $\dot{Y}/Y = \dot{K}/K$. Using this and (14.4) one obtains:

$$\frac{\dot{Y}}{Y} = \frac{\dot{K}}{K} = \frac{s}{a} - \mu \qquad (14.10)$$

As (14.10) indicates, the rate of growth of output must equal the ratio of the saving propensity, s, to the capital–output ratio, a, net of the depreciation rate μ. Since the parameters s, a and μ are fixed, growth is exogenous in this model.

The steady-state solution to (14.9) requires that $\dot{k} = 0$ and hence involves a comparison between n and $(s/a - \mu)$. 3 cases arise. If $(s/a - \mu) < n$, the natural rate exceeds the warranted rate and there is redundancy of labor in the economy. As the extent of this redundancy grows the capital–labor ratio decreases and becomes zero in the limit. If $(s/a - \mu) > n$, the capital stock grows faster than the labor force implying that $K > aL/b$ and $Y = L/b$. Capital becomes the redundant factor. However, the steady-state equilibrium which is obtained by substituting $y = 1/b$ in (14.6), is unique and stable at $\bar{k} = s/b(n + \mu)$. Finally, when $(s/a - \mu) = n$, the razor's edge case, the capital stock and labor supply grow at a common rate. An entire range of equilibria is then possible, each involving full employment of both factors. However, the likelihood of this last case is low since the parameters involved in the comparison are exogenous and unrelated.

The 2-gap model

The H–D theory emphasizes domestic savings as the major constraint on the growth rate of an economy. If the constraint is somewhat relaxed by raising the propensity to save, the result will be a rise in the growth rate of both capital and output. The experience of the developing countries in the 1980s, and of transition economies in the 1990s, suggests however a different emphasis. In these cases, growth was also constrained by a limited supply of foreign exchange. The open economy version of the H–D model incorporates this foreign exchange constraint and enables one to identify whether growth is limited by a domestic savings gap or a foreign exchange gap.[5]

Consider a small open economy and assume that, at the given terms of trade, the economy is completely specialized (a corner solution on the production possibility curve) in the production of a single commodity. This commodity is both consumed and exported in exchange for an imported capital good. Technology is of the fixed coefficient form (14.7) and it is assumed that $K < aL/b$. Hence, labor is redundant and domestic output depends only on the capital stock. Given this, output and the capital stock grow at the same rate, the latter given by the ratio of investment over the capital stock as in (14.3), assuming $\mu = 0$ for simplicity. Domestic investment comprises capital imports as well as domestic output which must be combined in fixed proportion.

Panel (a) of Figure 14.1 depicts this economy. The vertical axis measures imports of capital goods while the horizontal axis measures the supply of

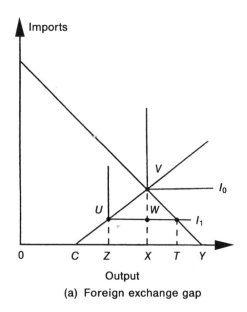

(a) Foreign exchange gap

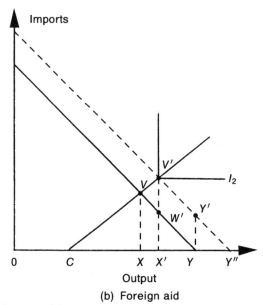

(b) Foreign aid

Figure 14.1   *The 2-gap model*

domestic output and its distribution among end-uses. Total output OY is allocated to consumption OC and savings CY according to a constant average propensity to save. The downward-sloping line VY gives the price of domestic ouput relative to imports. The slope of the ray from C through point V gives the ratio of imported inputs to domestic goods needed to achieve a level of domestic investment. Any point along this ray gives a different level of investment (and therefore of future output growth), the level increasing as one moves away from C. The economy depicted in panel (a) can sustain a level of investment I_0 which requires CX of domestic goods for investment and an amount XY of exported domestic goods to finance the imports VX.

Suppose that, because of a lack of foreign exchange reserves, imports of capital goods are limited to UZ. This can arise if exports are limited to TY (as a result of, for example, a reduction in foreign demand for this economy's product or of a loss of domestic resources in exporting the commodity – e.g. spoilage, inefficiency, ...). Lower imports imply a decrease in the domestic component of investment to CZ, a lower level I_1 of domestic investment and, hence, an excess supply of savings equal to ZT. The foreign exchange gap is VW.

Now consider panel (b) of Figure 14.1, which assumes that the economy has a target growth rate that corresponds to the investment level I_2. What would be the *ex ante* capital requirements implied by this targeted growth? The domestic component of investment would be CX' and the amount of imported inputs $V'X'$. An amount $X'Y''$ of exported domestic goods is therefore required to pay for these imports. Since the supply of output is OY, this economy would have a domestic savings gap of YY'' or, equivalently, a foreign exchange gap of $V'W'$. Therefore, the economy cannot achieve the targeted rate of growth unless the propensity to save is increased by shifting a proportion YY'' of domestic output from consumption to exports. Another solution would be foreign aid equal to the amount $V'W'$. Such aid would imply a decrease in exports to $X'Y$ as the proportion XX' of domestic output shifts from exports to the domestic component of investment.

Empirical implementation

Implementing the 2-gap model involves estimating the physical quantity of investment under two different specifications: the savings constrained regime and the import constrained regime. However, only one *ex post* observation on investment is available and in addition, it is not known *a priori* which regime generated this observation. An identification problem therefore arises and consists of determining which constraint holds at different times.

Estimation is similar to that of markets in disequilibrium and amounts to computing the probability that any observation comes from a particular regime.

Gersovitz (1982) estimated the 2-gap model for Argentina, Columbia, Ecuador, Guatemala and Peru using yearly observations over the period 1950–78. The results of estimation indicate that for approximately 55% of all observations, the probability of a savings constrained regime exceeded 0.5. This seems to suggest that investment in those countries is less likely to be constrained by imports than by domestic savings. Nevertheless, import constrained regimes are frequently observed. The case of Ecuador is interesting in that it is the only country in the sample with important oil exports. As expected, the estimation results show evidence of import constrained growth that is followed, after the major oil shocks, by saving constrained growth.

Problem 14.1:   The literature has criticized the 2-gap literature for its neglect of relative prices. Consider a deterioration in the terms of trade in Figure 14.1. What are the implications for the composition and growth of domestic output?

14.2 The neoclassical model of growth

The neoclassical model of growth can be said to stem from two papers, by Solow (1956) and Swan (1956). This model extends the H–D model by allowing substitution between capital and labor in the aggregate production function.

The fundamental equation

Specifically retaining (14.1)–(14.6), the neoclassical model of growth replaces the technology of the economy of (14.7) by:

$$Y = F(K, L) \tag{14.11}$$

which is a continuous, constant returns to scale (CRS), aggregate production function whose properties are discussed in Chapter 4. The per-worker form of (14.11) is:

$$y = f(k) \tag{14.12}$$

Given this, the law of motion of the capital–labor ratio (14.6) can be rewritten as:

$$\dot{k} = sf(k) - \lambda k \tag{14.13}$$

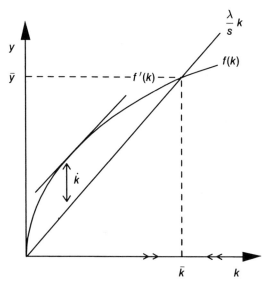

Figure 14.2   *Neoclassical growth*

where $\lambda = \mu + n$. (14.13) is called the fundamental differential equation of neoclassical economic growth, a representation of which is shown in Figure 14.2. From (14.13) there exists a steady-state (balanced growth) solution for capital intensity $\bar{k}$ at which the economy will be at rest, i.e. at $\dot{k} = 0$. Existence of this equilibrium is ensured by the following conditions, known as the Inada conditions:

$$\begin{cases} f(0) = 0 & f(\infty) = \infty \\ f'(0) = \infty & f'(\infty) = 0 \end{cases} \tag{14.14}$$

Uniqueness and global stability are guaranteed by:

$$f'(k) > 0 \qquad f''(k) < 0 \qquad \text{for } 0 < k < \infty \tag{14.15}$$

At $\bar{k}$, capital and labor grow at the same rate (i.e. n) and, by the assumption of constant returns to scale, real output also grows at this rate. Output per worker and the capital–income ratio are therefore constant.[6]

Technical progress

The neoclassical model of growth is suitable for extension in a number of different directions. An important extension is the inclusion of technical progress which the literature has examined at great length. This produced the well known Harrod, Hicks and Solow taxonomic classifications of technical progress (Jones, 1975). An important conclusion of this literature is that technical progress must be labor-augmenting for the neoclassical model to have a steady state with constant growth rates. The model in this form is also able to duplicate a number of stylized facts of growth.

To obtain a simple representation of technical progress in the neoclassical model, retain (14.1)–(14.6) but replace the aggregate production function (14.11) by:

$$Y = F(K, A(t)L) \tag{14.16}$$

with

$$\dot{A}(t)/A(t) = m$$

Technical progress is represented by the term $A(t)L$, which measures effective labor units. If m, the relative rate of change of A, is positive then technical change is said to be labor-augmenting and advances at the constant exogenous rate m.

If we redefine output per effective unit of labor as $y = Y/A(t)L$ and the capital intensity as $k = K/A(t)L$, the analysis will follow exactly the same lines as the model without technical progress with $A(t)L$ replacing L throughout:

$$\frac{\dot{k}}{k} = \frac{\dot{K}}{K} - \frac{\dot{L}}{L} - \frac{\dot{A}}{A} = \frac{sY}{K} - (\mu + n + m) \tag{14.17}$$

and the fundamental equation (14.13) becomes:

$$\dot{k} = sf(k) - (\mu + n + m)k \tag{14.18}$$

The new steady-state value $\bar{k}$ is found by setting $\dot{k}$ in (14.18) equal to zero to obtain:

$$f(\bar{k}) = \frac{(\mu + n + m)}{s} \bar{k} \tag{14.19}$$

Hence, the neoclassical growth model implies the existence of automatic forces that will lead an economy to its steady state, determined by the parameters n, m, s and μ. Note that initial conditions are immaterial in determining either the steady-state capital intensity or the steady-state growth rate, but these conditions are nevertheless important for the transition to the steady state. This latter point is readily reflected by dividing both sides of (14.18) by k, and then taking the derivative with respect to k:

$$\frac{\partial(\dot{k}/k)}{\partial k} = \frac{s}{k}\left[f'(k) - \frac{f(k)}{k}\right] < 0 \tag{14.20}$$

This derivative is negative by the adding-up property of neoclassical production functions. Hence, the growth rate $(\dot{k}/k)$ is unambiguously larger for lower values of the initial capital–labor ratio. A similar result obtains for the growth rate of output per unit of effective labor ($\dot{y}/y$). To show this, consider first the following approximation:

$$\dot{y} = f'(k)\dot{k} \tag{14.21}$$

(14.21) implies:

$$\frac{\dot{y}}{y} = \frac{kf'(k)}{f(k)} \frac{\dot{k}}{k} = \Omega \frac{\dot{k}}{k} \tag{14.22}$$

where $\Omega = kf'(k)/f(k)$ is capital's share of national income (provided that capital earns its marginal product). If the production function took the Cobb–Douglas form, then Ω would be constant and therefore independent of k. The growth path of y then mimics that of k and the derivative of $\dot{y}/y$ with respect to k is, as in (14.20), negative.

Speed of convergence

Another characteristic of the neoclassical growth model is the so-called speed of convergence, which is the speed at which the economy approaches its steady state. To develop this concept, begin by taking the first-order Taylor expansion of (14.18) around $\bar{k}$:

$$\dot{k} = [sf'(\bar{k}) - (\mu + n + m)](k - \bar{k})$$

Substitute for s using the steady-state condition (14.19):

$$\dot{k} = -\beta(k - \bar{k}) \tag{14.23}$$

where $\beta = (1 - \bar{\Omega})(\mu + n + m)$ and $\bar{\Omega}$ is the steady-state capital share. Parameter β is the speed of convergence and indicates how rapidly the stock of capital per effective worker approaches its steady-state value. Analogous to (14.22), income per effective worker (y) also converges to its steady state ($\bar{y}$) at the rate β. To see this, consider the following approximation to the change in *per capita* output:

$$y - \bar{y} = f'(\bar{k})(k - \bar{k})$$

which, using (14.21) and (14.23), leads to:

$$\dot{y} = -\beta(y - \bar{y}) \tag{14.24}$$

It is clear from (14.23) and (14.24) that the convergence coefficient β is independent of the production function and of the saving rate. The latter nevertheless affects $\bar{k}$ and $\bar{y}$.

The inclusion of labor-augmenting technical progress does not greatly affect the analytical complexity of the model, but does produce conclusions that are often in line with several of the stylized facts of growth experiences (see, e.g. Romer, 1989; Mankiw, 1995). Though some are already known, it is worth summarizing the main predictions of the model:

(1) An economy with a population growth rate n and a labor-augmenting technical improvement that proceeds at the exogenous rate m converges towards a steady growth path where the growth rates of output and capital are equal to $(n + m)$ and the capital–output ratio is constant.
(2) The ratio of capital to labor in natural units grows at the rate m.
(3) The real return to capital is constant and the real wage grows at the rate m, which is also the rate of growth of labor productivity.
(4) The shares of labor and of capital in national income are constant.
(5) Consumption *per capita* grows at the rate m.
(6) The steady-state level of income depends positively on the rate of saving and negatively on the rate of population growth and the depreciation rate.
(7) The rate of output growth is independent of the rate of saving.
(8) In the long run the economy approaches a steady state that is independent of initial conditions.

The above predictions constitute a set of hypotheses that can be evaluated using time series and cross-section data. The empirical evidence indicates that only hypotheses (1)–(6) pass the test of the data, the remaining two being questionable. Contrary to prediction (7), the data show a strong correlation between growth rates and saving rates across countries. The theorists nonetheless maintain prediction (7) by making the claim that most observations are recorded off the steady state and therefore describe the transitional dynamics of a growing economy.

Problem 14.2:   Derive formally the predictions of the neoclassical growth model with labor-augmenting technical improvement.

Convergence

The independence of the steady state with respect to initial conditions (prediction (8)) is related to the broader topic of convergence. Consider a group of isolated economies which are assumed to differ in terms of their initial capital intensity but are structurally similar in the sense that the production functions and underlying parameters of the neoclassical growth model are the same. Then, comparing the growth performance of these economies, we may infer the following. First, from (14.19), these economies will have the same steady-state capital intensity and growth rate. Second, reinterpreting (14.20) in this context, the more backward economies (those with relatively lower capital intensity) will have to grow faster than the rich ones in order to converge to those with higher capital intensities. Third, from (14.23) and (14.24), the economies will have the same speed of convergence β. This last inference is the essence of what is called the absolute convergence hypothesis.

This hypothesis has been extensively tested. The main finding is that absolute convergence is generally accepted for a group of homogeneous countries but does not occur in a large cross-section of countries. In the latter case a conditional form of convergence has been applied instead, controlling for the heterogeneity of characteristics of countries. These tests involve 3 questions: Is there a negative correlation between the initial level of income and the following growth experience? What is the speed of convergence? Is the process of convergence adequately described by the neoclassical growth model of the preceding section?

In an attempt to provide answers to the first two questions, Barro and Sala-i-Martin (1995) estimate the speed of convergence for US states using a specification of the form:

$$\frac{1}{T} \log\left(\frac{y_{iT}}{y_{i0}}\right) = a - \frac{(1 - e^{-\beta T})}{T} \log y_{i0} + \mu_{i0,T} \tag{14.25}$$

where y_{i0}, y_{iT} represent the *per capita* income in state i at time 0 and T respectively, T is the length of interval, β is the speed of convergence and $\mu_{i0,T}$, is the error term. Barro and Sala-i-Martin include other structural variables (not shown) to account for the heterogeneity of states.[7] Using non-linear estimation techniques, they provide estimates of β for the period 1880–1990 and for a number of subperiods. The point estimate of β for the whole sample is 0.0174 (standard error $= 0.0026$); for the period 1960–70, it is 0.0246 (standard error $= 0.004$). The main conclusion is that states within the United States tend to converge to their steady states at a speed of about 2% per year.

The third hypothesis is whether the observed process of convergence is described by the neoclassical growth model. To examine this issue, the theoretical definition in (14.23) is used to construct an estimate of β and this constructed value is compared to the regression estimate of β. In the United States, for example, the following parameter values are observed: $\overline{\Omega} = 0.33$, $n = 0.01$, $m = 0.02$ and $\mu = 0.03$. As a result, the constructed β is 0.04, which is twice as high as the estimate of β convergence of roughly 0.02. Hence, the neoclassical growth model in its present form predicts a speed of convergence that is twice that favored by the data. This divergence has led the theoretical literature to include, besides physical capital, factors like human capital which increase the value of $\overline{\Omega}$ and hence decrease that of constructed β (Mankiw, 1995).

Welfare: the Ramsey problem

The discussion thus far has focused on the production technology and ignored household behavior except for the exogenously given saving rate s. However, for different values of the saving rate the neoclassical model will approach different steady-state values for the levels of the variables even though the steady-state rate of growth will remain the same. Among the various saving rates, there will exist one rate for which steady-state *per capita* consumption achieves a maximum. To determine this welfare maximizing rate of savings we need an explicit analysis of household behavior in which the saving rate (s) is treated as endogenous.

This is the problem of a central planner who wants at time $t = 0$ to maximize the discounted sum of utility from current and future consumption of an infinitely lived representative agent (e.g. a dynasty):[8]

$$\max_{d(t)} W_0 = \int_0^\infty e^{-\rho t} U(d(t))\, dt \tag{14.26}$$

subject to

$$\dot{k} = f(k) - d - nk \tag{14.27}$$

together with the constraints $k(0) = k_0$; $k(t)$, $d(t) \geq 0$ and $0 \leq d(t) \leq f(k(t))$ for all t. Here, one assumes $\mu = m = 0$ for simplicity so that k and d are, respectively, capital and consumption per unit of natural labor ($k = K/L, d = D/L$). Parameter ρ is the rate of time preference. When $\rho > 0$, the consumer gives less weight to future consumption relative to current consumption in terms of utility. Finally, (14.27) states that output is divided between investment, consumption and equipping new labor.

The maximization problem (14.26) involves a choice at each point in time of how national output should be split between consumption and investment (savings), the latter going to produce more output in the future. This control problem is solved by using the maximum principle technique.[9] In this regard, the present value Hamiltonian is:

$$H(t) = e^{-\rho t}\{U(d(t)) + \nu(t)[f(k(t)) - d(t) - nk(t)]\} \tag{14.28}$$

where $\nu(t)$ is the costate variable associated with the state variable k.[10] The necessary and sufficient conditions for an interior maximum under general assumptions on the utility and production functions imply:

$$\frac{\partial H(t)}{\partial d(t)} = 0$$

$$\frac{d e^{-\rho t} \nu(t)}{dt} = -\frac{\partial H(t)}{\partial k(t)}$$

$$\lim_{t \to \infty} k(t)\nu(t)e^{-\rho t} = 0$$

Given (14.28), the first 2 conditions imply:

$$\nu = U'(d) \tag{14.29}$$

$$\frac{\dot{\nu}}{\nu} = -[f'(k) - (n + \rho)] \tag{14.30}$$

From (14.29), we have:

$$\frac{\dot{\nu}}{\nu} = \frac{d\,U''(d)}{U'(d)}\frac{\dot{d}}{d} \tag{14.31}$$

where $dU''(d)/U'(d)$ is the contemporaneous elasticity of marginal utility with respect to consumption. Hence, the differential equation for the costate variable (ν) can be written as a function of the differential equation in the control variable (d).

A conventional assumption is that utility has the iso-elastic form:

$$U(d) = \frac{d^{1-\theta}}{(1-\theta)} \qquad \text{for } \theta > 0, \theta \neq 1$$

$$= \ln d \qquad \text{for } \theta = 1 \tag{14.32}$$

so that the elasticity of $U'(d)$ with respect to d is a constant, $-\theta$ ($\theta \neq 1$). This utility function implies also a constant intertemporal elasticity of substitution $1/\theta$.

Rewriting (14.31) taking (14.32) into account and substituting in (14.30) gives:

$$\frac{\dot{d}}{d} = \frac{f'(k) - (n + \rho)}{\theta} \tag{14.33}$$

By the maximum principle, if the paths $\{\bar{d}(t)\}$ and $\{\bar{k}(t)\}$ are optimal, they must satisfy the differential equations (14.27) and (14.33). The latter, with $\dot{d}$ equal to zero, gives the value of $\bar{k}_m$ in the steady state:

$$f'(\bar{k}_m) = n + \rho \tag{14.34}$$

Hence, among all paths of balanced growth, the one yielding the highest consumption per worker is achieved by the path on which the marginal product of capital equals the sum of the growth of labor and the rate of time preference. The corresponding consumption *per capita* is obtained from (14.27):

$$\bar{d}_m = f(\bar{k}_m) - n\bar{k}_m$$

Two additional points. First, the solution $\bar{k}_m$ is called the 'Modified Golden Rule' capital intensity. The 'Golden Rule' condition is $f'(\bar{k}_g) = n$.[11] (14.34) therefore modifies the 'Golden Rule' by allowing for a non-zero rate of time preference ($\rho \neq 0$). We have $(\bar{k}_g - \bar{k}_m) \geq 0$ for $\rho \geq 0$ and the difference increases with the rate of time preference. Second, it has been shown that, under certain conditions, the optimal path for a decentralized economy is also that of the centralized economy (Blanchard and Fischer, 1989, Chapter 2). The condition on capital intensity that maximizes steady-state *per capita* consumption is then obtained from the equality between the interest rate and the sum of n and ρ. Given this equivalence result, the literature interchanges the interest rate and marginal product of capital.

14.3 2-sector models

2-sector models of economic growth are viewed as a natural extension of the simpler 1-sector models examined above. 2-sector models incorporate features such as relative commodity prices which are absent in single-sector models but are important to international trade.[12] Below we first consider the comparative statics of growth by showing the so-called immiserizing growth result. We then illustrate some of the difficulties encountered in progressing from single-sector models to more complex dynamic 2-sector, 2-country models.

Immiserizing growth

A major result deriving from the comparative statics of growth in a 2-sector model is the Rybczynski theorem. This basic proposition compares production equilibria at constant commodity prices after factor supplies have changed.[13] When commodity prices are allowed to change a striking result emerges: an open economy experiencing growth can be 'immiserized', that is, worse off. The possibility of immiserizing growth was first demonstrated by Bhagwati (1958). Here we first illustrate the conditions for immiserizing growth in the context of the standard $2 \times 2 \times 2$ model of Chapter 4 and then discuss a few empirical findings regarding this proposition.

The necessary condition

Consider the condition for international trade equilibrium prior to growth of one of the primary factors. By Walras' Law, it suffices to consider the market clearing condition for 1 of the 2 goods of this model. Let us consider the market for commodity 2 which is assumed to be the labor-intensive commodity and to be imported by the capital-rich domestic economy. The market clearing condition in this case is:

$$x_2^*(p_w) + q_2(p_w, h) - h_2(p_w, u_0) = 0 \tag{14.35}$$

where x_2^*, q_2 and h_2 are the net foreign supply, the domestic supply and the domestic (compensated) demand for good 2, respectively; the parameter h is an index of primary factors, i.e. $h = K,L$; u_0 is the utility level achieved prior to growth and p_w is the international price of good 2 relative to good 1 or the inverse of the domestic country's terms of trade. Total differentiation of (14.35) gives Bhagwati's expression for immiserization:

$$\left(a_1 \frac{q_2}{h_2} \hat{h} + a_2 \frac{q_2}{h_2} \hat{p}_w + a_3 \hat{p}_w \right) + f^* \frac{x_2^*}{h_2} \hat{p}_w \qquad (14.36)$$

where the '$\hat{\ }$' symbol over a variable denotes the relative change in that variable starting from the initial situation, $a_1 = (h/q_2)(\partial q_2/\partial h)$ is the output elasticity of a change in factor supply ($h = K, L$), $a_2 = (p_w/q_2)(\partial q_2/\partial p_w)$ is the price elasticity of domestic supply, $a_3 = -(p_w/h_2)(\partial h_2/\partial p_w)$ is the compensated demand elasticity, and $f^* = (p_w/x_2^*)(\partial x_2^*/\partial p_w)$ is the price elasticity of foreign supply of imports. Note that a_2, $a_3 > 0$ and $a_1, f^* \lessgtr 0$. Immiserizing growth occurs when (14.36) is negative. An important component of (14.36) is $\hat{p}_w$, the so-called 'zero gain' terms of trade change, which represents the change in the international price that, once growth has occurred, enables consumers to maintain their pre-growth level of utility u_0. Since nothing guarantees that this 'zero gain' price will be the market clearing price on world markets, immiserization will occur if there remains a residual excess demand. Indeed, in this case, the relative price of good 2 must increase which is a deterioration of the terms of trade and, hence, a loss in national welfare that outweighs the welfare gain from factor growth.

The term outside parentheses in (14.36) gives the change in imports supplied from abroad as the result of the terms of trade change $\hat{p}_w$. The terms in parentheses in (14.36) represent the total change in the net domestic supply of good 2. This change is composed of 3 terms: the change in production of good 2 due to growth $\hat{h}$, the change in the production of good 2, and the change in consumption of good 2, both due to the price change $\hat{p}_w$. Given this, consider a 'zero gain' decline in the terms of trade, i.e. $\hat{p}_w > 0$. Since the elasticities a_2 and a_3 are positive, the necessary condition for (14.36) to be negative is that either f^* or a_1 or both must be negative. A negative f^* indicates that part of the foreign supply curve is backward bending. A negative a_1 is indicative of factor growth that reduces output of competitive imports. This would be the case if, for example, capital were to increase in supply in a capital-rich economy since, by the Rybczynski theorem, output of the labor-intensive industry would decrease.

The immiserizing growth outcome is illustrated in Figure 14.3. Pre-growth production, consumption and welfare are at A, A' and u_0, respectively. The initial terms of trade is given by the price line AA' (not drawn). At this price, an increase in capital will cause an outward shift of the production

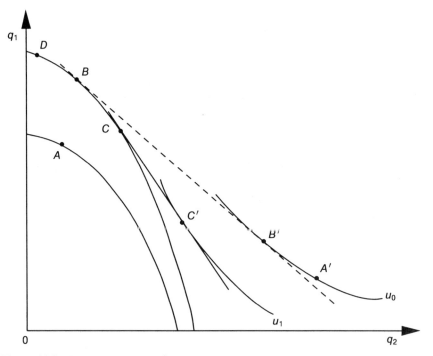

Figure 14.3   *Immiserizing growth*

possibility curve with D as the new production point. After growth, the price line BB' gives the zero gain price that maintains consumers on u_0. If, at the price BB', there exists a global excess demand for good 2, the terms of trade will deteriorate further to, say, CC'. At this post-growth price, production and consumption are at C and C', respectively. The result is a decline in national welfare from u_0 to u_1.

Empirical implications

The immiserizing growth result has tantalizing implications for economic growth. On the one hand, there is the so-called Prebisch–Singer hypothesis that postulates that LDCs' terms of trade are characterized by a negative long-term trend. These economies are therefore claimed to be 'immiserized' because the national income effects of growth are offset by the deterioration of the terms of trade. On the other hand, others claim that there is no strong trend in the terms of trade. For example, Krugman (1989) argues that a country's pattern of specialization at any point in time is largely arbitrary since it is largely determined by increasing returns to scale (IRS) rather than comparative advantage. Fast growing countries therefore expand their share of world markets not by reducing the relative price of their goods, but by expanding the range of goods they produce and export.

The basis for a negative decline in LDCs' relative export prices is asserted to be due to several factors. A first cause is found in the composition of LDCs' trade with industrialized countries, schematically typified as the exchange of primary commodities for manufactures. Demand for LDCs' products is assumed quite inelastic as they are often necessities; supply of these products is assumed inelastic as well, since supply can only be varied after a long time lag. A second cause is seen in the development of new products in industrialized countries that constantly substitute for primary products. In addition, a third cause stems from the less competitive market structure of manufactures, which would be conducive to oligopoly pricing. Given that export supply is inelastic, so runs the argument, a structural decline in demand for primary products causes a large drop in the relative price of these commodities. Likewise, given that import demand is inelastic, any growth that increases LDCs' production of primary products leads to a large decrease in relative prices as well. While this argument is easy to understand in its own right, it is based on guesstimates of price elasticities of trade and also abstracts from the signals provided by markets in guiding economic activities. In fact, the evidence indicates no pervasive decline in the terms of trade of developing countries. For example, Cuddington's (1992) study of 26 individual commodity prices relative to manufactured goods over the period 1900–83 found that only 5 of the 26 prices had significant negative trends. 16 were trendless and the remaining 5 had positive trends.

Further evidence is provided by Krugman (1989), who develops and tests a formal model that supports the idea that no strong trend in the terms of trade should be expected. The analysis starts by writing the standard trade balance identity of a $2 \times 2 \times 2$ model as:

$$b = m_1^*(Y^*, p) - pm_2(Y, p)$$

where b denotes the domestic trade balance in terms of good 1, m_1^* and m_2 are foreign imports of good 1 and domestic imports of good 2 respectively, Y and Y^* are domestic and foreign national incomes measured in terms of good 1, and p is the price of good 2 in terms of good 1, i.e. the inverse of the domestic terms of trade. It is implicitly assumed that the domestic economy exports good 1 in which it has a comparative advantage in exchange for good 2 in which it has a comparative disadvantage.

Differentiating totally and keeping a zero trade balance we obtain:

$$\hat{p} = \frac{\zeta \hat{Y} - \zeta^* \hat{Y}^*}{(\eta + \eta^* - 1)}$$

in which ζ and ζ^* are the income elasticities of demand for good 1 and good 2 respectively, and η and η^* are the (partial equilibrium) price elasticities.

The denominator is positive by the Marshall–Lerner stability condition. By the above formula, there will be a trend in the terms of trade unless

$$\frac{\zeta^*}{\zeta} = \frac{\hat{Y}}{\hat{Y}^*}$$

which is referred to as the '45 degree rule'. Otherwise, the analysis relates trends in the terms of trade to different income elasticities or to different long-term rates of growth. For example, a more rapidly growing domestic economy is expected to experience, *ceteris paribus*, a deterioration in its terms of trade because it is forced to reduce the price of its exports in order to sell higher quantities.

Regressing estimates of income elasticities in world trade on the growth rates of corresponding countries over the period 1955–65, Krugman (1989) obtains the following surprising result:

$$\ln \frac{\zeta^*}{\zeta} = -1.81 + 1.210 \ln \left(\frac{\hat{Y}}{\hat{Y}^*} \right)$$
$$(0.208)$$

$$R^2 = 0.754 \qquad SEE = 0.211$$

This regression result establishes a systematic relation between the ratio of income elasticities in trade and the ratio of rates of growth. The estimated parameter of the ratio of growth rates is positive and not significantly different from unity. The same result seems to persist in more recent periods. Hence, the 45 degree rule that turned out to be unlikely *a priori* becomes an empirical regularity: fast growing economies tend to face high income elasticities for their exports and low income elasticities for their imports, making trend changes in the terms of trade unnecessary. Krugman appeals to the models of monopolistic competition (see Chapter 9) to show that fast growing countries expand their share of world markets by expanding the range of goods produced, rather than by reducing their export prices.

Dynamic models

2-sector models provide a gain in realism by allowing relative prices to feature explicitly, but there is added complexity because existence, uniqueness and stability of balanced growth paths of economies in isolation cannot be proved for all combinations of assumptions. Even more serious difficulties arise once international trade is introduced. In this section we describe the dynamic 2-factor, 2-sector model and then illustrate the difficulties encountered in order to show existence of balanced growth paths of economies that are isolated, and open to international trade.

Features of the models

Many of the assumptions of a dynamic 2-sector model are identical to those of the static 2-sector model of Chapter 4 and therefore require little discussion. The model can be set out as follows. The production relationships describing the supply side are the 8 equations (4.6), (4.11), (4.12), (4.13) and (4.15) that solve for the 8 endogenous variables $\{q_j, k_j, \lambda_j, w, r\}$ in terms of the economy's factor supplies $\{K, L\}$ and commodity prices p_j. The symbols are defined such that j represents the commodity subscript $(j = 1, 2)$, q_j is output of commodity j, k_j is industry j's capital–labor ratio, λ_j is the proportion of the labor force allocated to sector j, w is the wage rate and r the rental rate both expressed in terms of the numeraire assumed to be good 1. Note these equations cover only the supply side of the economy. To also solve for the equilibrium commodity prices we must add demand.

To that end an extreme savings function is assumed in which the propensity to save out of profits is 1 and the propensity to save out of wages is 0.[14] Let good 1 be the consumption good and good 2 the capital good. The specification of demand implies the following equalities for demand and supply of the 2 goods:

$$wL = (q_1 + m_1) \tag{14.37}$$

$$rK = p(q_2 + m_2) \tag{14.38}$$

where m_j is the volume of imports of the jth good and $p = p_2/p_1$ is the relative price of investment goods. (14.37) and (14.38) indicate that wage income equals the sum of output and imports of the consumption good and that total profits (rK) equal the value of output *plus* imports of the capital good.

Solving (14.38) for m_2 and making use of (4.12) gives the expression for the import demand function for the second good:

$$m_2 = L\left[\frac{rk}{p} - \left(\frac{k - k_1}{k_2 - k_1}\right)f_2(k_2)\right]$$

Since r and k_j are functions of p and k, the import function can be rewritten in the general form:

$$m_2 = Lm_2(p, k)$$

The basic income identity, i.e. $wL + rK = p_1q_1 + p_2q_2$, applied to (14.37) and (14.38) implies the balance of payments condition:

$$m_1 + pm_2 = 0$$

Since the imports of goods by one country are the exports from the other country (indicated by '*'), we have:

$$m_1 + m_1^* = 0$$

$$m_2 + m_2^* = 0$$

The equilibrium terms of trade will be determined so as to clear the international market:

$$m_2(p,k) + \frac{L^*}{L} m_2^*(p,k^*) = 0 \tag{14.39}$$

where m_2^* is the foreign import function. At any instant of time, the above equations together with those of the foreign country are simultaneously satisfied and solve under general conditions for a unique momentary equilibrium corresponding to any initial factor endowments in both countries. It suffices now to describe the time paths of capital accumulation in both countries.

Given our assumptions, the rate of change of the domestic capital stock is:

$$\dot{K} = (q_2 + m_2) - \mu K$$

From (14.38) we have $q_2 + m_2 = rK/p$ and, if capital is paid its value marginal product, we have:

$$\dot{K} = f_2'(k_2)K - \mu K$$

In *per capita* terms, this leads to:

$$\frac{\dot{k}}{k} = f_2'(k_2) - (n + \mu) \tag{14.40}$$

which is the fundamental equation of the 2-sector model of the domestic economy. That of the foreign economy is obtained by analogy:

$$\frac{\dot{k^*}}{k^*} = f_2'(k_2^*) - (n^* + \mu^*) \tag{14.41}$$

Note that even if both countries use the same production function, the other parameters need not be the same.

Closed economy

The above model simplifies for the case of an economy in isolation since $m_1 = m_2 = 0$. Consider for example the fundamental equation (14.40). A balanced growth path for the domestic economy implies that $\dot{k} = 0$ which entails $f_2'(k_2) = n + \mu$. Hence, balanced growth implies that the marginal product of capital in the capital goods industry must equal the sum of the rates of depreciation and labor force growth. The principal condition for balanced growth in 2-sector models is therefore similar to that derived for the single-sector model (see (14.34)).

An important difference is stability. From (14.40) it is clear that $\dot{k}/k > 0$ when $f_2'(k_2) > n + \mu$ and vice versa. However, if k is rising, the marginal product f_2' must be falling so that it will eventually equal $n + \mu$. By the properties of neoclassical production functions this will only be the case if k_2 is increasing as well. Hence, whatever the initial factor endowments, the 2-sector economy will gravitate to the balanced growth path if k and k_2 move in the same direction. However, since $k = \lambda_1 k_1 + \lambda_2 k_2$, this is not necessarily the case since some changes in k_1 and λ_1 can prevent this comovement between k and k_2. The literature has therefore produced a sufficient condition for stability saying that, whatever the initial conditions, the economy gravitates to the balanced growth path if $k_1 \geq k_2$ for all values of w/r (Uzawa, 1961).

The international economy

To show the existence of a world steady-state equilibrium one needs to consider the laws of motion (14.40), (14.41) together with the international market clearing condition (14.39). A world steady state is achieved when $\dot{k} = \dot{k}^* = 0$. Oniki and Uzawa (1965), Bardhan (1965) and Atsumi (1971) have characterized the existence result and the sufficient conditions for stability. For example, Bardhan (1965) has shown that, when both the countries are incompletely specialized, the sufficient conditions for stability are that either consumer goods are more capital-intensive than capital goods or the elasticities of factor substitution are equal to or greater than unity in both sectors in both countries.

14.4 Endogenous growth

The neoclassical model is made consistent with the stylized facts of economic growth by introducing labor-augmenting technical progress into the aggregate production function. Long-run growth of *per capita* income then corresponds to that of the exogenously given growth rate of the labor-augmenting factor.

However, even the labor-augmenting version of the neoclassical model fails to fully account for the perpetually rising standards of living and the wide cross-country dispersion in both the levels and rates of growth of *per capita* income. Also, the exogeneity of technical progress must be seen as an analytical convenience rather than a serious representation of reality.

These shortcomings have stimulated the development of endogenous growth models. The models stem from the contributions by Romer (1986) and Lucas (1988). These models share the property that

economic growth is an endogenous outcome of an economic system, not the result of forces that impinge from outside'. (Romer, 1994, p. 3)

In these types of model growth can be endogenously driven (1) by growth in human capital that may involve knowledge spillovers (Romer, 1986) or may not (Lucas, 1988; Rebelo, 1991) or (2) by technological innovation (Romer, 1990; Grossman and Helpman, 1991).[15]

Basics

A common characteristic of endogenous growth models is that growth may be unbounded because the return to investment in broad capital (i.e. both human and physical capital) may not diminish as an economy develops. This fact is illustrated by (14.33). This relationship indicates clearly that the growth in *per capita* consumption can be sustained ($\dot{d}/d > 0$) only if the marginal product of capital $f'(k)$ stays perpetually above the level given by the sum of n and ρ.

The basic ingredients of endogenous growth models can be illustrated by the following simple representation of technology:

$$y(t) = f(k(t), h(t)) = Ak(t)^{\alpha}h(t)^{1-\alpha} \qquad 0 < \alpha < 1 \qquad (14.42)$$

where $y(t)$ is output per worker, $k(t)$ and $h(t)$ are 2 factors of production (i.e. physical and human capital per worker), A is a productivity parameter and α is the share parameter of the k factor. The single commodity is produced either for consumption or for accumulation of the stock of the k factor. Most models specify a law of motion for the h-factor as well.

Given (14.42), the marginal product of the k factor is readily obtained:

$$f'_k = \alpha A \left(\frac{h(t)}{k(t)} \right)^{1-\alpha} \qquad (14.43)$$

where $f'_k = \partial f / \partial k$. It is clear from (14.43) that $\partial f'_k / \partial k < 0$ and $\partial f'_k / \partial h > 0$. Hence, whether the marginal product of the k factor in (14.43) decreases as $k(t)$ accumulates depends on the offsetting impact from the accumulation of the h factor. If the h factor is accumulated no slower than the k factor, f'_k will not be decreasing and consequently, long-run growth can be sustained.

Growth driven by knowledge spillover

Consider the following illustration which assumes a competitive equilibrium with external scale economies (Romer, 1986). The motivation for this model is the idea that private knowledge is an intangible capital input in the production of the firm that may have an external spillover effect. Thus, $A(E)F(K_j, L_j, e_j)$ could represent the production technology available to firm j with capital K_j, labor L_j, the private stock of knowledge e_j and the public stock of knowledge E. In the simplest version of the model, E is assumed to increase one-for-one with e_j and the stock of capital is taken to be an index of acquired knowledge ($e_j = K_j$).[16] Assuming identical firms and that $F(\cdot)$ is homogeneous of degree 1, aggregation over all firms gives the aggregate production function $A(K)F(K, L)$. If $F(\cdot)$ is Cobb–Douglas, and if the accumulation of public knowledge exhibits diminishing returns, i.e. $A(K) = K^\delta$ with $0 < \delta < 1$, aggregate output takes the form $A(K)F(K, L) = K^\delta K^\alpha L^{1-\alpha}$, or in per-worker terms:

$$y = f(k, L) = k^{\alpha+\delta} L^\delta \tag{14.44}$$

where $k = K/L$. The marginal product of capital then becomes:

$$f'_k = (\alpha + \delta)\left(\frac{L^\delta}{k^{1-\alpha-\delta}}\right) \tag{14.45}$$

Assume a constant labor force ($n = 0$). If $\alpha + \delta$ is less than 1, the marginal product f'_k is decreasing in k and as in the neoclassical model, the steady state $\bar{k}$ is given by (14.34). Growth of output will be zero in this case. If $\alpha + \delta$ is equal to 1, $f'_k = (\alpha + \delta)L^\delta$ in (14.45) and using (14.33), this economy will always be along a constant steady-growth path given by $\dot{d}/d = [(\alpha + \delta)L^\delta - (n + \rho)]/\theta$. If $\alpha + \delta$ is greater than 1, the marginal product of capital is increasing rather than decreasing in k, so that the *per capita* capital stock can grow without bound. *Per capita* output and consumption can grow without bound as well. The level of *per capita* output in different countries need not converge in this case.[17]

Growth driven by industrial innovation

The innovation approach to endogenous growth theory describes the pace of technological progress as the outcome of deliberate investment decisions by profit seeking firms. Firms undertake R&D investments when they see an opportunity to earn profits on their research efforts. The amount of profits earned depends on the market structure. In this context, profit seeking firms will aim their research strategies at three tasks: improving the quality of existing products (Grossman and Helpman, 1991, Chapter 4), improving the

methods of production (Aghion and Howitt, 1992), or expanding the variety
of goods (Romer, 1990; Grossman and Helpman, 1991, Chapter 3 and
Chapter 9). Here we will only discuss the models of product variety.

Define $d(t)$ as the consumption of a single good at time t. In many models,
consumption $d(t)$ is modelled as the assembly of $n(t)$ differentiated inputs
which are imperfect substitutes to each other:

$$d(t) = \left[\int_0^{n(t)} q_j(t)^\alpha dj \right]^{1/\alpha} \qquad 0 < \alpha < 1 \qquad (14.46)$$

where q_j denotes consumption of good j that has been developed and
produced by a research firm in the economy and $n(t)$ is the number of input
designs available at time t. Specification (14.46) is a reinterpretation of the
Dixit–Stiglitz 'love of variety' utility function discussed in Chapter 9. The
properties of (14.46) are central to this approach of endogenous innovation.
The parameter α is a monotone transformation of the (constant) elasticity of
substitution which is $\varepsilon = 1/(1 - \alpha) > 1$. Also, the assembly of $d(t)$ exhibits
CRS in the inputs (for given $n(t)$). More importantly, the productivity of
primary factors of the economy rises with the number of varieties $n(t)$. To
see this, assume all inputs are symmetric, i.e. $q_j(t) = q(t)$. Then $d(t) =
n(t)^{1/\alpha} q(t)$. It is further assumed that the production of $q(t)$ requires 1 unit of
a single primary factor which we take to be labor. Hence, total employment
equals $n(t)q(t)$ and the average productivity of labor is $d(t)/n(t)q(t) =
n(t)^{-(1-1/\alpha)}$, which increases with $n(t)$ if $\alpha < 1$.

The representative consumer's consumption decision involves a 2-stage
procedure. In the first stage, the consumer maximizes an instantaneous
utility function subject to an instantaneous budget constraint. Assume that
the instantaneous utility function is logarithmic as in (14.32), i.e. $\ln d(t)$. The
first-order conditions for utility maximization subject to the instantaneous
budget constraint imply:

$$S(t) = \int_0^{n(t)} p_j(t) q_j(t) \, dj \qquad (14.47)$$

From this, one obtains the set of demand functions:

$$q_j(t) = \frac{S(t) p_j^{-\varepsilon}(t)}{\int_0^{n(t)} p_i(t)^{1-\varepsilon} di} \qquad (14.48)$$

With symmetric goods, (14.48) implies that $q(t) = S(t)/p(t)n(t)$ and (14.46)
implies that $d(t) = S(t)/p_d(t)$ where $p_d(t) = p(t)n(t)^{(\alpha-1)/\alpha}$.

Substituting the optimal input demands (14.48) into (14.46) and then
the obtained result into the utility function, the second stage involves the
household maximizing indirect utility over an infinite horizon subject to an

intertemporal budget constraint. That is, the problem is to choose the path $S(t)$ that maximizes utility over an infinite horizon:

$$U(\tau) = \int_{\tau}^{\infty} e^{-\rho(t-\tau)}(\log S(t) - \log p_d(t)) \, dt \qquad (14.49)$$

subject to an intertemporal budget constraint (not shown) that states that the present value of spending is not greater than the sum of household's holding of assets and the present value of labor income. Borrowing and lending are allowed at the nominal interest rate $r(t)$. By normalizing expenditure so that $S(t) = 1$ for all t, the solution to this maximization problem implies that the nominal interest rate is equal to the subjective discount rate for all t:

$$r(t) = \rho \qquad (14.50)$$

This is related to the discussion of the modified golden rule for a decentralized economy in the absence of depreciation and population growth (see (14.34)).

On the production side producers undertake 2 distinct tasks. They manufacture the known inputs and undertake the development of new designs. It is assumed that each single product design is produced by a single firm. Further, the production of existing products is characterized by CRS and requires 1 unit of labor per unit of output. Given this and the product demand (14.48), the profit maximization rule for the assumed monopolist amounts to equating marginal revenue and marginal cost, $p_j(t)\alpha = w(t)$ where $w(t)$ is the nominal wage. Consequently, for a unique wage, all suppliers of products charge the same price $p(t) = w(t)/\alpha$ and, by (14.48), sell the same quantity. This pricing strategy yields operating profits per design of:

$$\Pi(t) = p_j(t)q_j(t) - wq_j(t) = \frac{(1-\alpha)}{n(t)} \qquad (14.51)$$

after making use of (14.48) and assuming $S(t) = 1$ and symmetric demands. Operating profits are therefore decreasing in the number of designs.

Growth in this economy is driven solely by the increase in the set of available inputs. The development of new input designs takes several forms. Based on the nature of knowledge capital created by research, the following three cases have been considered.

Knowledge capital as private good

To invest in R&D is, in this case, a deliberate decision by the entrepreneur who fully appropriates the returns. The production of new designs follows:

$$\dot{n} = \frac{L_n}{a} \qquad (14.52)$$

where L_n is the amount of labor devoted to R&D, a is the labor requirement in the production of one design and the time subscript is omitted. Research activities are assumed perfectly competitive and firms hire research labor until:

$$w = \frac{v}{a}$$

where v is a claim to the stream of profits that accrues to a new design. This relationship expresses the equality between the value marginal product of labor (v/a) and the nominal wage. The variables w and v are in turn determined in general equilibrium.

Asset market equilibrium requires the following arbitrage condition to be satisfied:

$$\Pi + \dot{v} = rv \qquad (14.53)$$

The right-hand side of (14.53) gives the return to a riskless investment of size v. Alternatively, this amount could be invested in equities so the left-hand side of (14.53) gives the return to owners of the firm that consists of dividends Π and the capital gains $\dot{v}$ equity holders expect to earn on their assets. This arbitrage condition is crucial for explaining why the steady-state relative rate of innovation $(g \equiv \dot{n}/n)$ in the economy is zero:[18]

$$g = 0 \qquad (14.54)$$

Why? The steady state requires $\dot{v}/v = 0$. As the product variety expands, profit per product declines according to (14.51). The profit rate Π/v is driven to the nominal interest rate, which equals the rate of time preference. The research incentive, and hence growth, is then no longer maintained.

Knowledge capital as national public good

Firms are not always able to fully appropriate the returns to their investments. A reason might be that property rights associated with new designs are not well defined since some of the research results leak out into the pool of public knowledge. This idea is expressed by the following expression for the production of input designs:

$$\dot{n} = \frac{L_n n}{a} \qquad (14.55)$$

This indicates that new designs are produced using research labor L_n and the existing stock of knowledge. Here, the total number of existing product designs (n) proxies for the stock of knowledge, the latter having a positive external effect on the production of new designs. Since the positive spillover of n causes the cost of producing new designs to decline, the profit rate is no longer driven to the nominal interest rate and the research incentive is maintained. It can be shown that the relative rate of innovation is in this case:

$$g = (1 - \alpha) \frac{L}{a} - \alpha\rho \tag{14.56}$$

where L is the total labor supply. Growth of total output in the economy, being proportional to g, is sustained as well.

Knowledge capital as international public good

If the international diffusion of research results is permitted (but not trade) then the stock of knowledge available to firms investing in new product designs is augmented by the stock of foreign knowledge as long as there is no duplication. The production function in this case remains (14.55) but the positive externality from foreign research is now interpreted as $n + \Psi n^*$, where n^* stands for the set of available foreign products and Ψ for the fraction of foreign products unknown to domestic firms ($0 \leq \Psi \leq 1$). In this case, the relative rate of innovation becomes:

$$g = (1 - \alpha) \frac{(L + \Psi L^*)}{a} - \alpha\rho \tag{14.57}$$

where L^* is the foreign labor force. Comparing (14.56) to (14.57), the latter is not smaller, and is greater for any $\Psi > 0$. With $\Psi = 0$ (i.e. a complete duplication of research results in both countries) diffusion would not augment the autarky stock of knowledge.

In the case of both international trade and knowledge diffusion, the following result obtains:

$$g = (1 - \alpha) \frac{(L + L^*)}{a} - \alpha\rho \tag{14.58}$$

This result is equivalent to (14.57) with $\Psi = 1$, that is no duplication. National firms that are part of an integrated area avoid duplication of research and the stock of knowledge thereby reaches a maximum.

Empirical results

Growth empirics

There exists a vast literature that uses cross-country regressions to search for empirical linkages between the long-run *per capita* growth rate and the set of explanatory variables suggested by theory. Besides the initial level of real GDP *per capita* used to test the convergence hypothesis discussed earlier, the empirical literature suggests that growth rates in income per person depend positively on the investment share of GDP, on various measures of human capital (like initial secondary school enrolment rates) and depend negatively on the average annual rate of population growth. Altogether, these 4 variables explain about half of the cross-section variance in growth rates. A significant portion of the residual is explained by a variety of indicators of economic policy, political and institutional characteristics. For example, countries with political instability (proxied by the number of political upheavals) and market distortions (proxied by, e.g. measures of trade barriers or the black market exchange rate premium) tend to have lower growth rates. In contrast, countries with better developed financial markets (measured by the size of liquid assets relative to income) tend to have higher growth rates.

The robustness of the results in this literature is, however, hampered by correlation among the explanatory variables themselves. For example, Levine and Renelt (1992) and Levine and Zervos (1993) examine the extent to which the conclusions from existing studies are robust or fragile to small changes in the set of variables. Concerning growth and trade links, these studies identify a robust 2-link chain. On the one hand, there is a positive, robust correlation between growth and the share of investment in GDP. On the other hand, there is a positive and robust correlation between the investment share and the ratio of international trade (whether measured by the ratio of exports or imports to GDP). These findings emphasize the link between growth and the degree of openness in general, the causation running from trade to growth. The hypothesized channels through which this happens is that transfers of technology enhance the allocation and accumulation of resources.

Estimates of spillovers

Several recent papers assess the national and international spillovers required to generate endogenous growth. Coe and Helpman (1995) study the relationship between R&D and productivity between 1971 and 1990 using 22 countries (21 OECD countries plus Israel) as representative of the industrial North. Coe *et al.* (1997) provide estimates of these effects for a group of 77 developing countries from Africa, Asia, Latin America, and the Middle East. Both studies start by computing, for each country, a measure of total factor productivity (TFP):

$$\log TFP = \log Y - \Omega \log K - (1 - \Omega) \log L$$

where Ω is the share of capital in GDP. TFP gives a measure of the gains in output which cannot be attributed to extra labor or capital, i.e. essentially the assortment of intermediate inputs. From the preceding section, it is known that the measure of available inputs expands as a result of R&D investment. The empirical work is therefore performed by linking log TFP to measures of own (for developed countries only) and foreign R&D stocks and a set of other variables.

The estimates obtained suggest that industrial countries enjoy substantial benefits from R&D done within their national boundaries and from R&D done by their trade partners. In most of the smaller countries, foreign R&D has a larger impact on total factor productivity than does domestic R&D. International spillovers of R&D are, however, not confined to the group of industrial countries but are equally large for developing countries. In 1985–90, a 1% rise in US' R&D stock increases the TFP of developing countries by an average of 0.04%. This last figure becomes 0.02% if Europe's R&D stock increases by 1%, 0.01% for Japan. How can one country's R&D benefit foreigners? The authors suggest international trade as a main transmission channel. International trade stimulates cross-border learning of production methods, product designs and organizational methods. Furthermore, international trade enables countries to acquire technology embodied in inputs, and eventually, to copy foreign technologies that then make their own industries more efficient.

In a different setting, Irwin and Klenow (1994) use quarterly, firm-level data on seven generations of dynamic random access memory (DRAM) semiconductors over 1974–92 to find evidence of learning rates. They show that, on average, unit production costs fall by 20% every time cumulative output doubles.[19] They reckon also that when a firm (American or Japanese) makes an extra semiconductor, the spin-offs for other firms are worth about 1-third of the first firm's gains. Learning spillovers are found to be just as much between firms in different countries as between firms within a given country. Equally important is the finding that the transmission of learning from one generation of semiconductors to the next is very weak. This last evidence implies that the effects of industrial policies aimed at stimulating a particular generation of semiconductors would likely be short-lived.

14.5 Concluding remarks

An important contribution of new growth models is the endogenization of technological change. The thinking about how technology change comes about and how it affects a country's productivity is important to this process. Many theoretical results stress the link between a country's growth, its R&D investment and its rate of innovation. Much of the current debate is on whether the efforts of research labs are private knowledge to the active firm or whether this knowledge leaks to the pool of domestic and foreign knowledge. Recent empirical evidence suggests the existence of large spillovers within and outside national boundaries.

The evidence that spillovers are international in scope makes national policy recommendations more complex than initially thought. The set of optimal policy rules, if any, aimed at stimulating high tech industries have to be modified by taking into account of the fact that firms in other countries may benefit as well. Though the empirical results are not totally informative about the underlying transmission mechanism of spillovers, the existence of such spillovers is consistent with the recent trends toward improved protection of intellectual property rights.

Notes

1. The study of economic growth was nevertheless dormant for about two decades until being reawakened in the mid-1980s. It is now such an exploding field of research that a new scholarly journal has been created to serve as the main outlet for new developments (*Journal of Economic Growth*, Kluwer, first issue March 1996) and entire books are necessary to discuss the field thoroughly (see, e.g. Grossman and Helpman, 1991; Barro and Sala-i-Martin, 1995). Surveys with a more selective scope have also appeared (see, e.g. Mankiw, 1995).
2. See, e.g. Burmeister (1980) for a detailed review of the literature.
3. We henceforth drop the time subscript unless needed for clarity.
4. This specification of the technology implies some unemployment of either capital or labor. For example, if $Y = K/a$, then some labor is redundant since employment bK/a is less than the endowment L. This implies that, unlike the neoclassical model of growth, the steady state is not independent of initial conditions.
5. The material of this section partly depends on Findlay (1984) which contains both an exposition and a critique of the 2-gap model.
6. Starting from an early development stage, a country can grow at a rate different from n in the transition towards the balanced growth path.
7. There are two tests of conditional convergence applied to cross-sections of heterogeneous countries. The first test, called β convergence, consists of estimating, as in (14.25), the parameter β. The second but weaker test of convergence is σ convergence. Convergence occurs in this case if the cross- sectional dispersion of countries, measured by the standard deviation of the logarithm of *per capita* income across the group, declines over time. Next to β and σ convergence, there exist tests of convergence applied to time series (see, e.g. Bernard and Durlauf, 1995).
8. See the initial contribution by Ramsey (1928) and the later developments by Cass (1965) and Koopmans (1965).

9. In this control problem, k is called the state variable; d the control variable; (14.27) is the equation of motion and k_0 is the boundary condition. See, e.g. Blanchard and Fischer (1989, Chapter 2) or Intriligator (1971, Chapter 4) for more details.

10. The costate variable is interpreted as the shadow price of additional capital per worker measured in utility units.

11. With depreciation $(\mu \neq 0)$, (14.34) would become $f'(\bar{k}_m) = n + \rho + \mu$ and the Golden Rule condition $f'(\bar{k}_g) = n + \mu$.

12. Relative prices matter as well in single-sector models with borrowing and lending between countries. In this framework, intertemporal trade arises on the basis of differences in autarkic relative prices of present goods in terms of future goods, or 1 plus the autarkic rate of interest. See Blanchard and Fischer (1989) for applications on issues of saving and current account deficit/surplus.

13. This proposition has been shown in the 2-good, 2-factor context of Chapter 4 and extended to arbitrary numbers of goods and factors in Chapter 7.

14. Various specifications of demand have been used in the literature. For example, Atsumi (1971) assumes that a portion b_j of wage payments is spent on the jth good, i.e. $b_1 + b_2 = 1$ (in the text we assume $b_2 = 0$ for simplicity); Oniki and Uzawa (1965) assume that a constant fraction of GNP is saved and the rest is consumed; Bardhan (1965) assumes that wage income is totally consumed and part or all of rental income is saved.

15. There exist other classes of endogenous growth models dealing with, for example, public infrastructure (Barro, 1990) and taxation.

16. The model describes a process of knowledge accumulation by investing: learning by investing. Next to this, a strand of the literature, starting with Arrow (1961), places emphasis on on-the-job accumulation of human capital: learning by doing. Lucas (1993) uses learning rates in connection with international trade to explain episodes of very rapid income growth.

17. This model brings out a way in which government intervention affects an economy's growth rate. Because of the external spillover effects of the public stock of knowledge, a firm making investments raises the productivity of other investments, but these revenues cannot be appropriated by the active firm. A subsidy on the private use of capital would enable the economy to achieve the social optimum.

18. See Grossman and Helpman (1991, Chapter 3, Chapter 9) for the formal derivation of this and subsequent results.

19. The learning rate is the rate at which costs fall with each doubling of cumulative output. In this context, the learning rate is 20%.

References and additional reading

The foundation of economic growth

Arrow, K.J. (1961), 'The Economic Implications of Learning by Doing', *Review of Economic Studies*, 29, 155–73.

Atsumi, H. (1971), 'The Long-Run Offer Function and a Dynamic Theory of International Trade', *Journal of International Economics*, 1, 267–99.

Bardhan, P.K. (1965), 'Equilibrium Growth in the International Economy', *Quarterly Journal of Economics*, 79, 455–64.

Bhagwati, J. (1958), 'Immizerising Growth: A Geometric Note', *Review of Economic Studies*, 25, 201–5.

Blanchard, O.J. and Fischer, S. (1989), *Lectures on Macroeconomics* (Cambridge, Mass.: MIT Press).

Burmeister, E. (1980), *Mathematical Theories of Economic Growth* (New York: Macmillan).

Cass, D. (1965), 'Optimal Growth in an Aggregative Model of Capital Accumulation', *Review of Economic Studies*, 32, 233–40.

Domar, E.D. (1946), 'Capital Expansion, Rate of Growth and Employment', *Econometrica*, 14, 137–47.

Harrod, R.F. (1939), 'An Essay in Dynamic Theory', *Economic Journal*, 49, 14–33.

Intriligator, M.D. (1971), *Mathematical Optimization and Economic Theory* (Englewood Cliffs: Prentice Hall).

Jones, H.G. (1975), *An Introduction to Modern Theories of Economic Growth* (London: Nelson).

Koopmans, T.C. (1965), 'On the Concept of Optimal Economic Growth', in *The Econometric Approach to Development Planning* (Amsterdam: North-Holland), reissue of Pontificae Academiae Scientiarum Scripta Varia, 28 (1965), 225–30.

Oniki, H. and Uzawa, H. (1965), 'Patterns of Trade and Investment in a Dynamic Model of International Trade', *Review of Economic Studies*, 32, 15–38.

Ramsey, F.P. (1928), 'A Mathematical Theory of Saving', *Economic Journal*, 38, 543–59.

Solow, R.M. (1956), 'A Contribution to the Theory of Economic Growth', *Quarterly Journal of Economics*, 70, 65–94.

Swan, T.W. (1956), 'Economic Growth and Capital Accumulation', *Economic Record*, 334–61.

Uzawa, H. (1961), 'On a Two-Sector Model of Economic Growth', *Review of Economic Studies*, 29, 40–7.

Endogenous growth

Aghion, P. and Howitt, P. (1992), 'A Model of Growth through Creative Destruction', *Econometrica*, 60(2), 323–51.

Barro, R.J. (1990), 'Government Spending in a Simple Model of Endogenous Growth', *Journal of Political Economy*, 98, S103–125.

Grossman, G.M. and Helpman, E. (1991), *Innovation and Growth in the Global Economy* (Cambridge, Mass.: MIT Press).

Lucas, R.E. (1988), 'On the Mechanics of Economic Development', *Journal of Monetary Economics*, 22, 3–42.

Lucas, R.E. (1993), 'Making a Miracle', *Econometrica*, 61, 251–72.

Rebelo, S. (1991), 'Long-Run Policy Analysis and Long-Run Growth', *Journal of Political Economy*, 99, 500–21.

Romer, P.M. (1986), 'Increasing Returns and Long-Run Growth', *Journal of Political Economy*, 94, 1002–37.

Romer, P.M. (1989), 'Capital Accumulation in the Theory of Long-Run Growth', in Barro, R.J. (ed.), *Modern Business Cycle Theory* (Cambridge, Mass: Harvard University Press).

Romer, P.M. (1990), 'Endogenous Technological Change', *Journal of Political Economy*, 98, S71–102.

Romer, P.M. (1994), 'The Origins of Endogenous Growth', *The Journal of Economic Perspectives*, 8(Winter), 3–22.

Empirical studies

Barro, R.J. and Sala-i-Martin, X. (1992), 'Convergence', *Journal of Political Economy*, 100, 223–51.

Barro, R.J. and Lee, J.-W. (1994), 'Losers and Winners in Economic Growth', *World Bank Economic Review* (Supplement), 267–314.

Bernard, A.B. and Durlauf, S.N. (1995), 'Convergence in International Output', *Journal of Applied Econometrics*, 10, 97–108.

Coe, D.T. and Helpman, E. (1995), 'International R&D Spillovers', *European Economic Review*, 39, 859–87.

Coe, D.T., Helpman, E. and Hoffmaister, A.W. (1997), 'North–South R&D Spillovers', *Economic Journal*, 107, 134–49.

Cuddington, J.T. (1992), 'Long-Run Trends in 26 Primary Commodity Prices: A Disaggregated Look at the Prebisch–Singer Hypothesis', *Journal of Development Economics*, 39, 207–27.

Irwin, D.A. and Klenow, P.J. (1994), 'Learning-by-Doing Spillovers in the Semiconductor Industry', *Journal of Political Economy*, 102(6), 1200–27.

Krugman, P.R. (1989), 'Differences in Income Elasticities and Trends in Real Exchange Rates', *European Economic Review*, 33, 1031–54.

Lee, D.W. and Lee, T.H. (1995), 'Human Capital and Economic Growth: Tests Based on the International Evaluation of Educational Achievements', *Economics Letters*, 47, 219–25.

Levine, R. and Renelt, D. (1992), 'A Sensitivity Analysis of Cross-Country Growth Regressions', *American Economic Review*, 82, 942–63.

Levine, R. and Zervos, S.J. (1993), 'What We Have Learned about Policy and Growth from Cross-Country Regressions', *American Economic Review, Papers and Proceedings*, 83, 426–30.

Wolf, H.C. (1994), 'Growth Convergence Reconsidered', *Weltwirtschaftliches Archiv*, 130, 747–59.

World Bank (1990), *World Development Report: Poverty* (Oxford: Oxford University Press).

2-gap model

Findlay, R. (1984), 'Growth and Development in Trade Models', in Jones, R.W. and Kenen, P. B. (eds), *Handbook of International Economics, Vol. I* (Amsterdam: North-Holland), 185–236.

Gersovitz, M. (1982), 'The Estimation of the Two-Gap Model', *Journal of International Economics*, 12, 111–24.

Van Wijnbergen, S. (1986), 'Macroeconomic Aspects of the Effectiveness of Foreign Aid: On the Two-Gap Model, Home Goods Disequilibrium and Real Exchange Rate Misalignment', *Journal of International Economics*, 21, 123–36.

Other

Barro, R.J. and Sala-i-Martin, X. (1995), *Economic Growth* (New York: McGraw-Hill).

Mankiw, N.G. (1995), 'The Growth of Nations', *Brookings Papers on Economic Activity*, 1, 275–326.

■ *Appendix* ■

Data Methods and Sources

A.1 Trade flows	*A.3* Country characteristics
A.2 Industry characteristics	*A.4* Other data and sources

This Appendix discusses aspects of the data commonly used in applied analyses of trade and indicates sources for these data.[1] Until recently, the collection of internationally comparable data was a daunting task, often because the data were presented only in published form and the translation to electronic form was tedious and expensive. In addition, the published data were often not reported at the level of detail actually available. Only by special arrangement (contract work, etc.) could the more detailed data be obtained and even then further dissemination was restricted. However, most international organizations now make their data available, for a price, in electronic form (e.g. magnetic tape, CD or diskette). The publications office of any given organization provides a list of available data bases and their form. In addition, a phone call to the relevant statistical or research division of an organization can often turn up unadvertised data bases. Hence, locating unique data bases is still an art, despite the greater availability of international data, and a little effort in this respect can prove rewarding.

All international organizations now have World Wide Web (WWW) sites and a little 'browsing' of the Internet yields considerable information. Where possible, the following discussion notes Internet addresses of organizations and others who are potential sources of data. Those who wish to start immediately can go to one or all of the following three 'compendium' sites that offer links to international organizations and data, as well as other information of interest to economists:

- http://econwpa.wustl.edu/EconFAQ/EconFAQ.html
- http://www.helsinki.fi/WebEc/
- http://www.lib.umich.edu/libhome/Documents.center/stats.html

Before proceeding with the discussion of data we note an important new source of international data. Professors Harry Bowen, Robert Feenstra and Robert Lipsey have, with funding from the US National Science Foundation, conducted a project that now makes available a number of data sets on trade and related international variables on compact disk (CD) at nominal cost. Information on obtaining these data can be found on the WWW site of the National Bureau of Economic Research (http://www.nber.org).

A.1 Trade flows

The principle source of internationally comparable trade data is the United Nations (http://www.unicc.org). These data derive from UN member countries who submit their trade data to the United Nations Statistical Office (http://www.un.org/Depts/unsd/). The United Nations then processes and maintains these data which are classified according to the Standard International Trade Classification (SITC) system.

The SITC system

The SITC system consists of increasingly disaggregated levels of product categories, beginning from the 1-digit *section* level down to the 5-digit *item* level. Revisions to the SITC occur as the importance of products changes and new product categories are added. The current version, SITC Revision 3, consists of 10 1-digit *sections*, 75 2-digit *divisions*, 265 3-digit *groups*, 1038 4-digit *subgroups* and 3126 5-digit *items*. Table A.1 shows the product category headings at the 1-digit section level of the SITC. Sections 0–4 comprise agricultural products and raw material while 5–8 are considered to be semi-finished and finished manufactured goods. Section 9 refers to special

Table A.1   *Product category headings at the section level of the SITC*

Section	Description
0	Food & Live Animals
1	Beverages & Tobacco
2	Crude Materials, Excluding Fuels
3	Mineral Fuels, Lubricants & Related Materials
4	Animal and Vegetable Oils, Fats & Waxes
5	Chemicals
6	Manufactured Goods
7	Machinery & Transport Equipment
8	Miscellaneous Manufactured Goods
9	Goods not Classified by Kind

transactions such a movements of non-monetary gold, and also 'hidden' transactions typically related to the sale of military weaponry. A full listing of SITC Revision 3 is available at the WWW site http://pacific.commerce.ubc.ca/trade.

In principle, the value of transactions recorded at higher levels of aggregation of the SITC should equal the sum of transactions at lower levels of aggregation. In reality, the total at higher levels may exceed the sum of lower-level items since transactions below US$1000 are usually not reported. In addition, a UN member country has complete discretion as to the data it reports to the United Nations. For example, a country may choose to not report amounts at lower levels of aggregation for reasons of disclosure or a lack of funds for data collection and processing.

For applied work it is important to recognize that the SITC is a product based, not an industry based, classification. Hence, each SITC category necessarily involves some aggregation of products produced by different industries. As noted in Chapter 1, this can create problems when one attempts to develop empirical measures that conform to the industry constructs hypothesized by trade theory. More generally, any analysis that must link trade flows to their industry of origin will require a concordance between the SITC system and the relevant industrial classification (see Section A.2).

Trade reporting systems

Countries generally use one of two systems for recording their trade flows: the general and the special trade system. The difference between these systems is the definition of the statistical boundary. Under the general trade system any commodity that crosses the national frontier of the country is recorded. Under the special trade system any commodity that crosses the customs boundary is recorded. Neither system reports 'direct transit trade', which refers to the movement of commodities across national frontiers solely for transport.

Recorded exports under the general trade system consist of:

(1) exports of national products
(2) exports from customs-bonded manufacturing plants
(3) nationalized exports
(4) exports from customs-bonded warehouses and free areas.

Most countries aggregate these 4 categories into 2 categories, national exports and re-exports, when reporting their trade data. National exports consist of items (1) and (2) above while re-exports consist of items (3) and (4). National exports therefore consist of goods produced solely domestically and goods imported but which undergo some physical transformation. Re-exports consist of commodities that are imported and then exported in essentially the same physical condition. However, re-exports can contribute to a country's GDP since activities such as warehousing, repackaging, blending and other simple processing of goods (not involving a transformation of the commodity) represent value added by domestic factors of production.

Recorded imports under the general trade system consist of:

(1) imports entering directly from home consumption or use
(2) imports into customs-bonded manufacturing plants
(3) imports into customs-bonded warehouses and free areas.

Exports from, and imports into, customs-bonded warehouses and free areas are what is commonly called entrepôt trade. As noted in Chapter 1, entrepôt trade can represent a sizable fraction of a country's total exports.

The primary difference between the general trade system and the special trade system is that the latter excludes entrepôt trade. Thus, exports recorded under the special trade system consist of:

(1) exports of national produce
(2) exports from customs-bonded manufacturing plants
(3) nationalized exports.

Recorded imports under the special trade system are

(1) imports entering directly from home consumption or use
(2) imports into customs-bonded manufacturing plants
(3) imports withdrawn (inward) from customs-bonded warehouses and free areas.

The exclusion of entrepôt trade implies that a country's recorded exports and imports are less than they would be if recorded under the general trade system. Hence, export and import volumes can differ across counties due to differences in their system of trade reporting. A further issue is that some countries that report under the general trade system report national exports but not their re-exports. Hence, the country's total exports are under-reported whereas its total imports include the value of any goods ultimately re-exported. This difference can bias measures such as net exports or revealed comparative indexes that use ratios of exports and imports.

Aside from differences in reporting systems, trade figures can be biased for a number of reasons. For example, the United States does not record as imports goods produced in Mexico under the *maquiladora* program. In addition, for political reasons, Taiwan's trade is not openly published by the United Nations. In such cases, analysts often resort to 'backing-out' the data by using the mirror image data of partner countries. For example, data on US imports from Mexico are measured by Mexico's data on its exports to the United States. Similarly, data on Taiwanese exports are obtained by adding the data on partner country imports from Taiwan. Note that the use of partner country data contains a bias since exports are usually measured f.o.b. (free-on-board) while imports are measured c.i.f. (cost-insurance-freight), and the latter values normally exceed the former.[2]

Sources

Commodity trade data are maintained by the United Nations in its COMTRADE data base. Extracts from this data base are published in the UN *Yearbook of International Trade Statistics* and UN *Commodity Trade Statistics, Series D*. The difference between these two publications is the level of commodity and partner country detail, the latter being the more detailed source. The *Yearbook* data is available on CD while the *Series D* data are available on microfiche. The UN Statistical Office will also provide more detailed data in electronic form but the cost is very high – a full extract could cost well over US$100 000.[3] An alternative and cheaper source of these data is Statistics Canada (http://www.statcan.org.) who has licensed the UN data for sale on CD. Statistics Canada (StatCan) performs some additional processing of the UN data and aggregates the SITC commodity detail into about 600 SITC-related categories but does retain full partner country coverage. An even better source of these data is the US National Science Foundation project of Professors Bowen, Feenstra and Lipsey which makes the StatCan data available on CD and even extend (backward) the coverage of the StatCan data from 1980–92 to 1970–92.

Other sources of trade data include: the International Monetary Fund's (http://www.imf.org) *Direction of Trade*, which reports aggregate bilateral trade flows of its member countries; the Organization for Economic Co-operation and Development (OECD, http://www.oecd.org), which publishes *Import–Export Microtables* on microfiche which contain annual trade data of OECD countries with individual partner countries to the 5-digit SITC level; and the European Statistical Agency (EuroStat) (http://europa.eu.int/en/comm/eurostat). Like the IMF and OECD, EuroStat data only cover the trade of its member countries.

Table A.2   *International standard industrial classification (ISIC)*
(3-digit level)

ISIC	Description
300	Total Manufacturing
311	Food products
313	Beverages
314	Tobacco
321	Textiles
322	Wearing apparel, except footwear
323	Leather products
324	Footwear, except rubber or plastic
331	Wood products, except furniture
332	Furniture, except metal
341	Paper and products
342	Printing & publishing
351	Industrial chemicals
352	Other chemicals
353	Petroleum refineries
354	Miscellaneous petroleum & coal products
355	Rubber products
356	Plastic products
361	Pottery, china, earthenware
362	Glass and products
369	Other non-metallic mineral products
371	Iron & steel
372	Non-ferrous metals
381	Fabricated metal products
382	Machinery, except electrical
383	Machinery, electric
384	Transport equipment
385	Professional & scientific equipment
390	Other manufactured products

A.2 Industry characteristics

Internationally comparable data on industry characteristics is published according to the International Standard Industry Classification (ISIC). Table A.2 shows the industry categories at the 3-digit level of the ISIC. The 4-digit level of the ISIC roughly matches the 3-digit level of the SITC. UN publications that describe the SITC or ISIC indicate the relationship between these systems of classification. However, the mapping is not one-to-one – that is, a given SITC category may contain products produced by several ISIC industries. Empirical studies routinely adopt the 3-digit SITC level as equivalent to the industry definitions of the ISIC.

Production and inputs

The United Nations Industrial Development Organization (UNIDO, http:// www.unido.org) publishes data on production and expenditures on factor inputs in its annual publication *International Yearbook of Industrial Statistics*. These data cover industry variables such as value added, output, wages and salaries, gross fixed capital formation (all in current prices), number of establishments, employment, females employed and production indexes for the 29 3-digit ISIC manufacturing sectors. UNIDO makes these data available on diskette. The OECD's STAN (STructural ANalysis) data base contains similar data for OECD member countries and covers 49 ISIC-related sectors from 1972 to 1991. The STAN data base includes export and import data for each sector and is cheaper than its UNIDO counterpart, but covers fewer countries.

Input–output data

Calculation of the factor content of trade required for tests of the factor abundance theory (see Chapter 8) require data organized in the form of national input–output (I–O) tables. The international comparability of I–O tables is hampered since these tables are constructed using national systems of industry classification. Except as noted below, no supranational agency has yet seen fit to maintain detailed national I–O tables on a consistent basis (or at least make them publicly available). Hence, the main source of detailed I–O tables must remain the national statistical agency responsible for their construction.

In the United States, I–O tables are available in electronic form from the Bureau of Economic Analysis, US Department of Commerce (http:// www.bea.doc.gov) and are published in its *Survey of Current Business.*

The OECD *Input–Output Database* provides comparable I–O tables on diskette in both current and constant prices for 10 OECD countries: Australia, Canada, Denmark, France, Germany, Italy, Japan, the Netherlands, the United Kingdom and the United States, at several points in time from 1970 to 1990. The tables are defined for 36 sectors according to ISIC Revision 2. Similar tables are available from the Global Trade and Analysis Project (GTAP) at Purdue University (http://www.agecon.purdue.edu/gtap/). GTAP is primarily concerned with the development and maintenance of applied general equilibrium (AGE) models and data. The GTAP data base contains individual country I–O tables covering 37 sectors. Concordances between the ISIC and the GTAP sector definitions are also provided. The base year for these data is 1992. One should expect the growing use of AGE models to lead to more efforts to construct internationally comparable and detailed I–O tables.

Concordances

A concordance provides a link between different systems of classification. As noted, the United Nations publishes concordances between the SITC and the ISIC. However, these concordances do not contain weights that indicate, for example, the fraction of a given SITC category that should be allocated to a given ISIC category or vice versa. The national statistical agency responsible for submitting its country's trade or industry data to the United Nations maintains (unweighted) concordances between the national systems of commodity or industry classification and the relevant international systems. For example, EuroStat has concordances between the NACE[4] and the ISIC while the US Bureau of the Census (http://www.census.gov) has concordances between the US SIC and the ISIC (as well as the SITC and the Harmonized System). These concordances can be obtained by contacting the appropriate national statistical agency.

One additional need for a concordance arises when creating a long time series of data since a given classification system undergoes change over time. For example, long time series of trade data are usually stated in terms of SITC Revision 1 which contains less commodity detail than does SITC Revision 3. The various publications of the United Nations Statistical Office document these changes and the links between old and new revisions, and it can provide these concordances in electronic form.

Linked trade and production data

Some international agencies have sought to provide trade and production data classified by the ISIC. The UNIDO *Commodity Balance Statistics Data Base* reports exports, imports and apparent consumption (production *plus* imports *minus* exports) for commodities defined at the 6-digit level of the ISIC. The OECD COMTAP (Compatible Trade and Production) data base links the exports, imports and production flows of OECD member countries at the 3-digit ISIC level for the years 1970–86. As already noted, the OECD

STAN data base contains exports and imports for 49 ISIC-related sectors. Full information and pricing for these data bases is available at the World Wide Web site of each organization.

A.3 Country characteristics

Data on country characteristics are available from a wide variety of sources. For 'raw' data the principle sources are the *Yearbooks* and similar annual publications of the various UN agencies. These include the UN *Yearbook of National Accounts Statistics*, the ILO *Yearbook of International Labor Statistics*, and the FAO *Production Yearbook*. Other important sources of country data are the World Bank *World Tables* and the IMF *International Financial Statistics*. Most of these publications are available in electronic form at relatively low cost. The following briefly discusses the construction of some country characteristics commonly used in the analysis of trade patterns.

Physical capital stocks

The calculation of national capital stocks is typically made by summing a country's Gross Domestic Investment (GDI) flows over time while applying deflation and depreciation factors. GDI flows measure expenditures for the addition of reproducible capital goods by the private and public sector. Excluded are increases in natural resources and government expenditures for construction and durable goods for military purposes. There is considerable latitude in choosing a rate of depreciation. If disaggregated data on investment flows are available then allowance can be made for asset lives for different classes of assets (e.g. structures versus equipment). However, most studies adopt an average asset life of 15 years which corresponds to an annual depreciation rate of 13.3% using the double declining balance method of depreciation.

One issue to be confronted in computing national capital stocks is the conversion of national currency values into a common unit of account, typically the US dollar. Three alternative methods are discussed below.[5] Let

I_t = nominal GDI flow in units of home currency in year t
P_t^b = implicit GDI deflator at time t with base year b, $P_b^b = 1.0$
e_t = exchange rate at time t, dollars per-unit of domestic currency
δ = rate of depreciation

The first formula sums a country's GDI flows measured in domestic currency and then converts this value into dollars using the current exchange rate: The real capital stock at the end of year t measured in year b domestic currency is

$$K_t^b = \sum_{j=0}^{t} (1 - \delta)^{t-j}(I_j/P_j^b)$$

Multiplying this year t capital stock by the year t GDI deflator in domestic currency units and then the exchange rate in year t gives the current dollar value capital stock:

$$K_{1t}^\$ = K_t^b P_t^b e_t$$

A defect of this method is that any exchange rate changes not offset by domestic price changes can lead to large changes in the measured value of the capital stock. A second method uses the US implicit GDI deflator $(P(\$)_t^b)$ instead of the national currency GDI deflator and then converts the domestic currency values at the exchange rate of the base year:

$$K_{2t}^\$ = K_t^b P(\$)_t^b e_b$$

With purchasing power parity (PPP), differences in the exchange rates over time would exactly match the changes in price levels (i.e. $P_t^b e_t = P(\$)_t^b e_b$) and the above two measures would be the same.

A final possibility is to convert the investment flows year by year into dollars and then use the US GDI deflator to convert the capital stocks to constant dollar figures which are then summed and converted to current year t dollars:

$$K_{3t}^\$ = P(\$)_t^b \sum_{j=0}^{t} (1 - \delta)^{t-j}(I_j e_j/P(\$)_j^b)$$

This last method effectively uses PPP adjusted exchange rates and therefore implicitly assumes that the composition of investment goods in each country is the same. The second and third capital stock measures (i.e. K_{2t}^b and K_{3t}^b) are less sensitive to changes in the exchange rate.

In recent years a number of sources for country capital stock data have become available. One common source is the Penn World Tables which is available free via the Internet (www.nber.org). These capital stock data are disaggregated by major asset category and the capital stocks have been computed using PPP corrected exchange rates. Another recent data set containing capital stocks is Nehru and Dhareshwar (1993), available from the World Bank. The OECD data base publication *Flows and Stocks of Fixed Capital* contains annual data on the flows and stocks of fixed capital for 13 individual OECD countries. These data relate to the composition of gross and net capital stock, capital formation, and consumption of fixed capital shown both by kind of activity and type of capital good. Some series begin in 1950 but the complete set of data for all series begins in 1968.

Labor force and human capital

The ILO maintains internationally comparable data on countries' labor force which is operationally defined as the Economically Active Population (EAP). The ILO maintains breakdowns of countries' EAP by sex, industry and occupation.

A country's supply of human capital or 'labor skills' is measured by either occupational categories, wage differentials or educational attainment. As noted above, the ILO maintains internationally comparable data on employment by occupation. These data are classified according to the International Standard Classification of Occupations (ISCO). Table A.3 shows the 1-digit level of the ISCO. Studies using these occupational data typically measure 'high skilled workers' by ISCO 0/1 plus ISCO 2 or ISCO 0/1 alone. To avoid the possibility of simultaneity bias when conducting regression analyzes, analysts frequently measure other categories of 'labor skills' by subtracting ISCO 0/1 from a country's EAP and then classifying the remaining workers using some other criterion. For example, Leamer (1984) divides a country's EAP into 3 groups, workers belonging to ISCO 0/1, literate workers not belonging to ISCO 0/1 workers and illiterate workers.[6]

Wage differential measures of human capital are usually calculated on an industry-by-industry basis rather that at the national level. A common measure is an industry's average wage *minus* the national wage of persons with less that 12 years of education. The calculation of wage differentials supposes that higher wages reflect higher levels of human capital.[7] Although

Table A.3 *International standard classification of occupations (ISCO) (1-digit level)*

ISCO	Description
0/1	Professional, technical & related workers
2	Administrative & managerial workers
3	Clerical workers
4	Sales workers
5	Service workers
6	Agriculture, fishing & forestry workers
7–9	Production & related workers

not normally calculated at the national level, one could in principle add or average the calculated wage differences across sectors.

Measures of educational attainment – that is, the percentage of the population that has attained a given level of education – are also used to capture differences across countries in levels of human capital. A related set of measures are primary and secondary school enrolment ratios. Barro and Lee (1993, 1996) have recently assembled a number of these education based measures into 1 comprehensive data set covering 138 countries at various points in time between 1960 and 1989. These data are available for free from the NBER (http://www.nber.org).

One item to note about occupational and educational attainment data is that the base information often comes from 10-year population censuses or 5-year labor force sample surveys. Hence, observations for years other than census or sample years must be estimated by interpolation or extrapolation. The lack of annual data therefore precludes the use of such data for time series analysis (in the sense that no additional information is gained by having additional, non-census year, observations).

Land data

Measures of land – or more properly, the economic importance of land – derive from the data on land use maintained by the UN Food and Agricultural Organization (http://www.fao.org) and published in its *Production Yearbook*. Several studies use the FAO's measures of a country's land under cultivation and permanent crops, forest land, and pasture and grazing land to respectively denote arable land, forest land and pasture land. Again, to remove the possibility of simultaneity bias that can arise in a regression framework, analysts often use hybrid measures of the economic importance of land. For example, Leamer (1984) uses land area differentiated by climate.

A.4 Other data and sources

International data on tariff rates and measures of non-tariff barriers (NTBs) are complied by the World Trade Organization (WTO, http://www.wto.org) and the United Nations Conference on Trade and Development (UNCTAD, http://www.unicc.org/unctad/). UNCTAD maintains a data base of nominal tariff rates and NTB coverage ratios (see Chapter 2) for commodities classified by the Harmonized System. At complete listing of the Harmonized System can be found at http://www.igpweb.com/hs/index.html.

Data on import and export prices are available from the US Bureau of Labor Statistics (http://stats.bls.gov). The OECD *International Trade and Competitiveness Indicators* data base contains price deflators for four broad SITC commodity groups (basic materials, food, fuels and manufactures) of OECD member countries from 1975 onwards.

Finally, many universities have access to data bases held by the Inter-University Consortium for Political and Social Research (ICPSR) in Ann Arbor, Michigan (http://www.icpsr.umich.edu). Your university librarian can tell you how to gain access to the ICPSR system.

Notes

1. An important discussion of the use of international data in trade analysis is contained in Maskus (1991).
2. For other problems with imputing data values in this way see Yeats (1995).
3. In fact, it is not possible to request a full extract.
4. Nomenclature des Activités de la Communauté Européenne.
5. This discussion taken from Leamer (1984, Appendix B).
6. The data on highly skilled, medium skilled and unskilled workers in Chapter 1 used these definitions.
7. However, recent evidence on 'unexplained' interindustry wage differentials suggests caution in using this method. See Katz and Summers (1988).

References and additional reading

Data and data bases

Barro, R.J. and J.-W. Lee (1993), 'International Comparisons of Educational Attainment', *Journal of Monetary Economics*, 32(3), 363–94.

Barro, R.J. and J.-W. Lee (1996), 'International Measures of Schooling Years and Schooling Quality'. *American Economic Review, Papers and Proceedings*, 86(2), 218–23.

Feenstra, R.C. (1996), 'US Imports, 1972–1994: Data and Concordances', NBER, *Working Paper* 5515.

Feenstra, R.C., Lipsey, R.E. and Bowen, H.P. (1997), 'World Trade Flows, 1970–1992, with Production and Tariff Data', NBER, *Working Paper* 5910.

Feenstra, R.C. (1997), 'US Exports, 1972–1994, with Other US Data', NBER, *Working Paper* (forthcoming).

Goldsmith, R. and Saunders, C. (eds) (1960), *The Measurement of National Wealth*, NBER Research in Income and Wealth, 8 (Chicago: Quadrangle Books).

Katz, L.F. and Summers, L.H. (1988), 'Can Interindustry Wage Differentials Justify Strategic Trade Policy?', *National Bureau of Economic Research Working Paper*, 2739 (October).

Krueger, A.B. and Summers, L.H. (1988), 'Efficiency Wages and the Interindustry Wage Structure', *Econometrica*, 56(2), 259–72.

Leamer, E.E. (1984), *Sources of International Comparative Advantage: Theory and Evidence* (Cambridge, Mass.: MIT Press).

Maskus, K.V. (1991), 'Comparing International Trade Data and Product and National Characteristics Data for the Analysis of Trade Models', in Hooper, P. and Richardson, J.D. (eds), *International Economic Transactions, Issues in Measurement and Empirical Research* (Chicago: University of Chicago Press).

Sveikauskas, L, (1984), 'Science and Technology in Many Different Industries: Data for the Analysis of International Trade', *Review of Public Data Use* (June), 133–56.

Vikram, N. and Dhareshwar, A. (1993), 'A New Database on Physical Capital Stock: Sources, Methodology and Results', *Rivista de Analisis Economico*, 8(1), 37–59.

Yeats, A. (1995), 'Are Partner Country Statistics Useful for Estimating "Missing" Trade Data?', *World Bank Policy Research Paper*, 1501 (Washington DC: World Bank).

SITC system

United Nations Statistical Office (1961), *Standard International Trade Classification, Revised*, Statistical Papers, Series M, 34 (New York: United Nations).

United Nations Statistical Office (1966), *Classification of Commodities by Industrial Origin; Relationship of the Standard International Trade Classification to the International Standard Industrial Classification* (New York: United Nations)

United Nations Statistical Office (1971), *Classification of Commodities by Industrial Origin; Links Between the Standard International Trade Classification and the International Standard Industrial Classification*, Statistical Papers, Series M, 43, rev. 1 (New York: United Nations).

United Nations Statistical Office (1975), *Standard International Trade Classification Revision 2*, Statistical Papers, Series M, 34, rev. 2, Department of International Economic and Social Affairs, Statistical Office (New York: United Nations).

United Nations Statistical Office (1986), *Standard International Trade Classification Revision 3*, Statistical Papers, Series M, 34, rev. 3, Department of International Economic and Social Affairs, Statistical Office (New York: United Nations).

United Nations Statistical Office (1986), *Classification by Broad Economic Categories: Defined in Terms of SITC Rev. 3*, Department of International Economic and Social Affairs, Statistical Papers, Series M, 53 (New York: United Nations).

United Nations Statistical Office (1986), *Correspondence Table Between the International Standard Industrial Classification of all Economic Activities of the United Nations (ISIC) and the Classification of Branches of the National Economy of the Council*, Statistical Standards and Studies, 38 (New York: United Nations).

United Nations Statistical Office (1986), *Commodity Indexes for the Standard International Trade Classification, Revision 3*, Social Information and Policy Analysis, Statistical Division, Statistical Papers, Series M, 38, rev. 2 (New York: United Nations).

ISIC system

European Communities, Statistical Office of the (1990), *NACE Rev. 1*, Document NACE 200, Annex 1/Version 2.1.6 (Brussels: European Commission).

Organization for Economic Co-operation and Development (1961), *Cross Reference Between the National Commodity Nomenclatures and the Standard International Trade Classification*, Organization for Economic Co-operation and Development, Statistical Bulletins (Paris: OECD).

United Nations Statistical Office (1959), *Indexes to the International Standard Industrial Classification of All Economic Activities* (New York: United Nations).

United Nations Statistical Office (1981), *Bibliography of Industrial and Distributive-Trade Statistics*, Department of International Economic and Social Affairs, Statistical Papers, Series M, 36, rev. 5 (New York: United Nations).

United Nations Statistical Office (1988), *Final Draft of the Revised International Standard Industrial Classification of All Economic Activities (ISIC), Rev. 3*, Statistical Papers, Series M, 4, rev. 3, add. 2 (New York: United Nations).

United Nations Statistical Office (1990), *International Standard Industrial Classification of All Economic Activities*, Department of International Econimic and Social Affairs, Statistical Papers, Series M, 4 (New York: United Nations).

United States, Bureau of the Census (1969), *Correlation Between United States and International Standard Industrial Classifications* (Washington, DC: US Government Printing Office).

United States, US Dept. of Commerce (1979), *Correlation Between United States and International Standard Industrial Classifications*, prepared by Subcommittee on Statistics for Allocation of Funds, Federal Committee on Statistical Methodology (Washington, DC: US Government Printing Office).

ISCO system

International Labour Office (1990), *International Standard Classification of Occupations: ISCO-88* (Geneva: International Labour Office).

Bibliography

Abraham, F. (1990), 'The Effects on Intra-Community Competition of Export Subsidies to Third Countries: The Case of Export Credits, Export Insurance and Official Development Assistance', report prepared for the Commission of the European Communities.

Abraham, F., Couwenberg, I. and Dewit, G. (1991), 'Towards an EC Policy on Export Financing Subsidies: Lessons from the 1980s and Prospects for Future Reform', *International Economics Research Papers*, *11*, Centrum voor Economische Studiën, Katholieke Universiteit Leuven.

Aghion, P. and Howitt, P. (1992), 'A Model of Growth through Creative Destruction', *Econometrica*, 60(2), 323–51.

Anderson, J.E. (1979), 'A Theoretical Foundation for the Gravity Equation', *American Economic Review*, 69(1), 106–16.

Anderson, J.E. (1994), 'Tariff Index Theory', *Review of International Economics*, 3(2), 156–73.

Anderson, J.E. and Neary, J.P. (1994), 'Measuring the Restrictiveness of Trade Policy', *The World Bank Review*, 8, 151–70.

Anderson, S.P., de Palma, A. and Thisse, J.F. (1990), 'Demand for Differentiated Products, Discrete Choice Models, and the Characteristics Approach', *Review of Economic Studies*, 56, 21–35.

Aquino, A. (1978), 'Intra-industry Trade and Inter-industry Specialization as Concurrent Sources of International Trade in Manufactures', *Weltwirtschaftliches Archiv*, 114, 275–96.

Armington, P.A. (1969), 'A Theory of Demand for Products Distinguished by Place of Production,' *International Monetary Fund Staff Papers*, 16, 159–76.

Arrow, K.J. (1961), 'The Economic Implications of Learning by Doing', *Review of Economic Studies*, 29, 155–73.

Atsumi, H. (1971), 'The Long-Run Offer Function and a Dynamic Theory of International Trade', *Journal of International Economics*, 1, 267–99.

Auquier, A.A. and Caves, R.E. (1979), 'Monopolistic Export Industry, Trade, Taxes, and Optimal Competition Policy', *Economic Journal*, 89, 559–81.

Aw, B.-Y. (1983), 'The Interpretation of Cross-Section Regression Tests of the Heckscher–Ohlin Theorem with Many Goods and Factors', *Journal of International Economics*, 14(1–2), 163–67.

Aw, B. and Roberts, M. (1986), 'Estimating Quality Change in Quota Constrained Markets: The Case of US Footwear', *Journal of International Economics*, 21, 45–60.

Bagwell, K. and Staiger, R.W. (1993), 'Multilateral Tariff Cooperation During the Formation of Regional Free Trade Areas', *National Bureau of Economic Research, Working Paper*, 4364.

612

Bailey, M.J., Tavlas, G.S. and Ulan, M. (1986), 'Exchange Rate Variability and Trade Performance: Evidence for the Big Seven Countries', *Weltwirtschaftliches Archiv*, 3, 466–77.

Balassa, B. (1963), 'An Empirical Demonstration of Classical Comparative Cost Theory', *Review of Economics and Statistics*, 45, 231–8.

Balassa, B. (1965), 'Tariff Protection in Industrial Countries: An Evaluation', *Journal of Political Economy*, 73(6) (December), 573–94.

Balassa, B. (1965), 'Trade Liberalisation and Revealed Comparative Advantage', *The Manchester School of Economic and Social Studies*, 33, 92–123.

Balassa, B. (1966), 'Tariff Reductions and Trade in Manufactures among the Industrial Countries', *American Economic Review*, 56, 466–73.

Balassa, B. (1986), 'Comparative Advantage in Manufactured Goods: A Reappraisal', *Review of Economics and Statistics*, 68(2), 315–19.

Balassa, B. (1986), 'Intra-industry Trade Among Exporters of Manufactured Goods', in Greenaway, D. and Tharakan, P.K.M. (eds), *Imperfect Competition and International Trade*, 108–28.

Balassa, B. and Balassa, C. (1984), 'Industrial Protection in the Developed Countries', *World Economy*, 7, 179–96.

Balassa, B. and Bauwens, L. (1987), 'Intra-Industry Specialization in a Multi-Industry Framework', *Economic Journal*, 97, 923–39.

Baldwin, R. (1988), 'Hysteresis in Import Prices: The Beachhead Effect', *American Economic Review*, 78(4), 773–85.

Baldwin, R. and Krugman, P.R. (1988), 'Market Access and International Competition: A Simulation Study of 16K Random Access Memories', in Feenstra, R. (ed.), *Empirical Methods for International Trade* (Cambridge, Mass.: MIT Press).

Baldwin, R. and Krugman, P.R. (1988), 'Industrial Policy and International Competition in Wide-Bodied Jet Aircraft', in Baldwin, R. E. (ed.), *Trade Policy Issues and Empirical Analysis* (Chicago: University of Chicago Press), 45–71.

Baldwin, R. and Krugman, P.R. (1989), 'Persistent Trade Effects of Large Exchange Rate Shocks', *Quarterly Journal of Economics*, 104(4), 633–54.

Baldwin, R. et al. (1992), *Is Bigger Better? The Economics of EC Enlargement* (London: Centre for Economic Policy Research).

Baldwin, R.E. (1971), 'Determinants of the Commodity Structure of US Trade', *American Economic Review*, 61, 126–46.

Baldwin, R.E. (ed.) (1988), *Trade Policy Issues and Empirical Analysis* (Chicago: University of Chicago Press and National Bureau of Economic Research).

Baldwin, R.E. (1989) 'Measuring Nontariff Trade Policies', *NBER Working Paper*, 2978 (May).

Baldwin, R.E. (1991), 'The Uruguay Round and Beyond: Problems and Prospects', NBER, *Conference Report*.

Baldwin, R.E. (1992), 'Assessing the Fair Trade and Safeguards Laws in Terms of Modern Trade and Political Economy Analysis', *The World Economy*, 15, 185–202.

Baldwin, R.E. (1995), 'An Economic Evaluation of the Uruguay Round Agreements', *Annual Trade Review*, Clairmont–McKenna College.

Baldwin, R.E. and Hilton, S. (1983), 'A Technique for Indicating Comparative Costs and Predicting Changes in Trade Ratios', *Review of Economics and Statistics*, 105–10.

Baldwin, R.E. and Richardson, J.D. (eds) (1988), 'Issues in the Uruguay Round', NBER, *Conference Report*.

Ballance, R.H., Forstner, H. and Murray, T. (1985), 'On Measuring Comparative Advantage: A Note on Bowen's Indices', *Weltwirtschaftliches Archiv*, 121, 346–50.

Ballance, R.H., Forstner, H. and Murray, T. (1986), 'More on Measuring Comparative Advantage: A Reply', *Weltwirtschaftliches Archiv*, 122, 375–8.

Ballance, R.H., Forstner, H. and Murray, T. (1987), 'Consistency Tests of Alternative Measures of Comparative Advantage', *Review of Economics and Statistics*, 121, 346–50.

Bardhan, P.K. (1965), 'Equilibrium Growth in the International Economy', *Quarterly Journal of Economics*, 79, 155 64.

Baron, D.P. (1976), 'Flexible Exchange Rates, Forward Markets and the Level of Trade', *American Economic Review*, 66, 253–66.

Barro, R.J. (1990), 'Government Spending in a Simple Model of Endogenous Growth', *Journal of Political Economy*, 98, S103–125.

Barro, R.J. and Lee, J.-W. (1993), 'International Comparisons of Educational Attainment', *Journal of Monetary Economics*, 32(3), 363–94.

Barro, R.J. and Lee, J.-W. (1994), 'Losers and Winners in Economic Growth', *World Bank Economic Review* (Supplement), 267–314.

Barro, R.J. and Lee, J.-W. (1996), 'International Measures of Schooling Years and Schooling Quality', *American Economic Review, Papers and Proceedings*, 86(2), 218–23.

Barro, R.J. and Sala-i-Martin, X. (1992), 'Convergence', *Journal of Political Economy*, 100, 223–51.

Barro, R.J. and Sala-i-Martin, X. (1995), *Economic Growth* (New York: McGraw-Hill).

Basevi, G., Cocchi, D. and Lischi, P.L. (1985), 'The Choice of Currency in the Foreign Trade of Italy', *Research Paper*, 17 (University of Bologna).

Beghin, J.C. and Knox Lovell, C.A. (1993), 'Trade and Efficiency Effects of Domestic Content Protection: The Australian Tobacco and Cigarette Industries', *Review of Economics and Statistics*, 75, 623–69.

Belderbos, R. and Sleuwaegen, L. (1996), 'Japanese Firms and the Decision to Invest Abroad: Business Groups and Regional Core Networks', *Review of Economics and Statistics*, 28(2), 214–21

Bellis, J-F. (1990), 'The EEC Antidumping System', in Jackson, J. H. and Vermulst, E. A. (eds), *Antidumping Law in Practice: A Comparative Study* (London: Harvester Wheatsheaf).

Ben Zvi, S. and Helpman, E. (1992), 'Oligopoly and Segmented Markets', in Grossman, G. (ed.), *Imperfect Competition and International Trade* (Cambridge, Mass. and London: MIT Press).

Bergstrand, J.H. (1983), 'Measurement and Determinants of Intra-industry International Trade', in Tharakan, P.K.M. (ed.), *Intra-industry Trade: Empirical and Methodological Aspects* (Amsterdam: North-Holland), 201–62.

Bergstrand, J.H. (1985), 'The Gravity Equation in International Trade: Some Microeconomic Foundations and Empirical Evidence', *Review of Economics and Statistics*, 67, 474–81.

Bergstrand, J.H. (1989), 'The Generalized Gravity equation, Monopolistic Competition, and the Factor-Proportions Theory in International Trade', *Review of Economics and Statistics*, 71(1), 143–53.

Bergstrand, J.H., (1990), 'The Heckscher–Ohlin–Samuelson Model, the Linder Hypothesis, and the Determinants of Bilateral Intra-Industry Trade', *Economic Journal*, 100, 1216–29.

Bernard, A.B. and Durlauf, S.N. (1995), 'Convergence in International Output', *Journal of Applied Econometrics*, 10, 97–108.

Bhagwati, J. (1958), 'Immizerising Growth: A Geometric Note', *Review of Economic Studies*, 25, 201–5.

Bhagwati, J. (1964), 'The Pure Theory of International Trade: A Survey', *Economic Journal*, 74, 1–84.

Bhagwati, J.N. (1965), 'On the Equivalence of Tariffs and Quotas', in Baldwin, R.E. et al. (eds), *Trade Growth and the Balance of Payments – Essays in Honor of Gottfried Haberler* (Chicago: Rand McNally), 53–67.

Bhagwati, J.N. (1968), 'More on the Equivalence of Tariffs and Quotas', *American Economic Review*, 58, 481–5.

Bhagwati, J. (1971), 'The Generalized Theory of Distortions and Welfare', in Bhagwati, J.N., Mundell, R.A., Jones, R.W. and Vanek, Y. (eds), *Trade, Balance of Payments and Growth: Papers in International Economics in Honor of Charles P. Kindleberger* (Amsterdam: North-Holland), 69–90.

Bhagwati, J. (1982), 'Directly-Unproductive Profit-Seeking (DUP) Activities', *Journal of Political Economy*, 90, 988–1002.

Bhagwati, J.N. and Hamada, K. (1974), 'The Brain Drain, International Integration of Markets for Professionals and Unemployment: A Theoretical Analysis', *Journal of Development Economics*, 1, 19–42.

Bhagwati, J.N. and Srinivasan, T.N. (1983), *Lectures on International Trade* (Cambridge, Mass.: MIT Press), Chapters 2–4.

Bhagwati, J.N. and Srinivasan, T.N. (1983), *Lectures on International Trade* (Cambridge, Mass.: MIT Press), Chapters 5 and 6, 50–81; Appendix B, 384–96.

Bhagwati, J.N. and Srinivasan, T.N. (1983), 'On the Choice between Capital and Labour Mobility', *Journal of International Economics*, 14, 209–21.

Bilson, J.F.O. (1983), 'The Choice of an Invoice Currency in International Transactions', in Bhandari, J.S. and Putnam, B.H. (eds), *Economic Interdependence and Flexible Exchange Rates* (Cambridge, Mass.: MIT Press), 384–402.

Black, S.W. (1985), 'International Money and International Monetary Arrangements', in Jones, R.W. and Kenen, P.B. (eds), *Handbook of International Economics*, Vol. II (Amsterdam: North-Holland), 1153–94.

Blanchard, O.J. and Fischer, S. (1989), *Lectures on Macroeconomics* (Cambridge, Mass.: MIT Press).

Bliss, A. (1994), *Economic Theory and Policy for Trading Blocks* (Manchester: Manchester University Press).

Boadway, R.W. and Bruce, N. (1984), *The Pure Theory of Welfare Economics* (Oxford: Basil Blackwell).

Boltuck, R. and Litan, R.L (eds) (1991), *Down in the Dumps: Administration of the Unfair Trade Laws* (Washington, DC: Brookings Institution).

Bond, E. and Syropoulos, C. (1993), 'Trading Blocs and the Sustainability of Interregional Cooperation', *Department of Economics Discussion Paper*, 93-17, University of Birmingham.

Boorstein, R. and Feenstra, R.C. (1991), 'Quality Upgrading and its Welfare Cost in US Steel Imports, 1969–1974', in Helpman, E. and Razin, A. (eds), *International Trade and Trade Policy* (Cambridge, Mass.: MIT Press, 167–86).

Bourgeois, J., Vermulst, E. and Waer, F. (eds) (1994), *Rules of Origin in International Trade: A Comparative Study* (Ann Arbor: University of Michigan Press).

Bowen, H.P. (1983), 'Changes in the International Distribution of Resources and their Impact on US Comparative Advantage', *Review of Economics and Statistics*, 65(3) (August), 402–17.

Bowen, H.P. (1983), 'On the Theoretical Interpretation of Indices of Trade Intensity and Revealed Comparative Advantage', *Weltwirtschaftliches Archiv*, 119(3), 464–72.

Bowen, H.P. (1985), 'On Measuring Comparative Advantage: A Reply and Extensions', *Weltwirtschaftliches Archiv*, 121(2), 351–4.

Bowen, H. P. (1986), 'On Measuring Comparative Advantage: Further Comments', *Weltwirtschaftliches Archiv*, 122(2), 379–81.

Bowen, H.P. (1992), 'Data Transformations in Interindustry Regression Tests of Trade Theory', mimeo, Graduate School of Management, University of California at Irvine.

Bowen, H.P., Leamer, E.E. and Sveikauskas, L. (1987), 'Multicountry, Multifactor Tests of the Factor Abundance Theory', *American Economic Review*, 77(5), 791–809.

Bowen, H.P. and Sveikauskas, L. (1992), 'Judging Factor Abundance', *Quarterly Journal of Economics,* 107(2), 599–620.

Brada, J.C. and Méndez, J.A. (1988), 'An Estimate of the Dynamic Effects of Economic Integration', *Review of Economics and Statistics*, 70(1), 163–8.

Brada, J.C. and Méndez, J.A. (1988), 'Exchange Rate Risk, Exchange Rate Regime and the Volume of International Trade', *Kyklos*, 41, 263–80.

Brainard, S.L. (1993), 'An Empirical Assessment of the Proximity–Concentration Tradeoff between Multinational Sales and Trade', *NBER Working Paper Series*, 4580.

Brainard, S.L. (1993), 'An Empirical Assessment of the Factor Proportions Explanation of Multinational Sales', *NBER Working Paper Series*, 4583.

Brander, J. (1986), 'Rationales for Strategic Trade and Industrial Policy', in Krugman, P.R. (ed.), *Strategic Trade Policy and the New International Economics* (Cambridge, Mass.: MIT Press), 213–46.

Brander, J.A. (1995), 'Strategic Trade Policy', in Grossman, G. and Rogoff, K. (eds), Vol. III, *Handbook of International Economics* (Amsterdam: North-Holland), 1395–455

Brander, J.A. and Krugman, P.R. (1983), 'A "Reciprocal Dumping" Model in International Trade', *Journal of International Economics*, 15, 313–23.

Brander, J. and Spencer, B.J. (1984), 'Tariff Protection and Imperfect Competition', in Kierzkowski, H. (ed.), *Monopolistic Competition and International Trade* (Oxford: Oxford University Press).

Brander, J.A. and Spencer, B.J. (1985), 'Export Subsidies and Market Share Rivalry', *Journal of International Economics*, 18, 82–100.

Branson, W. and Monoyios, N. (1977), 'Factor Inputs in US Trade', *Journal of International Economics*, 7, 111–31.

Brecher, R.A. (1974), 'Minimum Wage Rates and the Pure Theory of International Trade', *Quarterly Journal of Economics*, 98–116.

Brecher, R.A. (1980), 'Increased Unemployment from Capital Accumulation in a Minimum-Wage Model of an Open Economy', *Canadian Journal of Economics*, 13, 152–8.

Brecher, R. and Choudhri, E. (1982), 'The Leontief Paradox, Continued', *Journal of Political Economy*, 90, 820–3.

Brecher, R. and Choudhri, E. (1988), 'The Factor Content of Consumption in Canada and the United States: A Two Country Test of the Heckscher–Ohlin–Vanek Model', in Feenstra, R.C. (ed.), *Empirical Methods for International Trade* (Cambridge, Mass.: MIT Press), 5–17.

Bresnahan, T.F. (1989), 'Empirical Studies of Industries with Market Power', Chapter 8 in Schmalensee, R. and Willig, R.D. (eds), *Handbook of Industrial Organization*, Vol. II (Amsterdam: North-Holland).

Brooke, A., Kendrick, D. and Meeraus, A. (1988), *GAMS, A User's Guide* (California: Scientific Press).

Brown, D.K. (1987), 'Tariffs, the Terms of Trade, and National Product Differentiation', *Journal of Policy Modeling*, 9(4), 503–26.

Brown, D.K. (1992), 'The Impact of a North American Free Trade Area: Applied General Equilibrium Models', in Lustig, N., Bosworth, B.P. and Lawrence, R.Z. (eds), *North American Free Trade: Assessing the Impact* (Washington, DC: Brookings Institution), 26–68.

Brown, D.K., Deardorff, A.V. and Stern, R.M. (1992), 'A North American Free Trade Agreement: Analytical Issues and a Computational Assessment', *The World Economy*, 15, 11–30.

Bulow, J., Geanakoplos, J. and Klemperer, P. (1985), 'Multimarket Oligopoly: Strategic Substitutes and Complements', *Journal of Political Economy*, 93, 488–511.

Burenstam Linder, S. (1961), *An Essay on Trade and Transformation* (New York: Wiley).

Burgess, D.F. (1978), 'On the Distributional Effects of Direct Foreign Investment', *International Economic Review*, 19, 647–64.

Burmeister, E. (1980), *Mathematical Theories of Economic Growth* (New York: Macmillan).

Burns, M.E. (1973), 'A Note on the Concept and Measure of Consumer's Surplus', *American Economic Review*, 63, 335–44.

Calvo, G. and Wellisz, S. (1983), 'International Factor Mobility and National Advantage', *Journal of International Economics*, 14, 103–14.

Campa, J.M. (1993), 'Entry by Foreign Firms in the United States under Exchange Rate Uncertainty', *Review of Economics and Statistics*, 75(4), 614–22.

Cantwell, J. (1994), 'The Relationship between International Trade and International Production', in Greenaway, D. and Winters, A. (eds), *Surveys in International Trade* (Cambridge, Mass. and Oxford: Blackwell).

Card, D. and Krueger, A.B. (1995), *Myth and Measurement: the New Economics of the Minimum Wage* (Princeton: Princeton University Press).

Carmichael, C.M. (1987), 'The Control of Export Credit Subsidies and its Welfare Consequences', *Journal of International Economics*, 23, 1–19.

Casas, F.R. and Choi, E.K. (1985), 'The Leontief Paradox, Continued or Resolved?', *Journal of Political Economy*, 93, 610–15.

Cass, D. (1965), 'Optimal Growth in an Aggregative Model of Capital Accumulation', *Review of Economic Studies*, 32, 233–40.

Caves, R.E, (1971), 'International Corporations: The Industrial Economics of Foreign Investment', *Economica*, 38, 1–27.

Caves, R.E. (1981), 'Intra-Industry Trade and Market Structure in the Industrial Countries', *Oxford Economic Papers*, 33, 203–23.

Caves, R.E. (1985), 'International Trade and Industrial Organization: Problems, Solved and Unsolved', *European Economic Review*, 28, 377–95.

Caves, R.E. (1996), 'Multinational Enterprise and Economic Analysis', *Cambridge Surveys of Economic Literature*, 2nd edn (Cambridge: Cambridge University Press).

Caves, R.E., Porter, M.E. and Spence, A.M. (1980), with Scott, J.T., *Competition in the Open Economy: A Model Applied to Canada* (Cambridge, Mass.: Harvard University Press).

Chacholiades, M. (1973), *The Pure Theory of International Trade* (London: Macmillan).

Chang, W. (1979), 'Some Theorems of Trade and General Equilibrium with Many Goods and Factors', *Econometrica*, 47(3), 709–26.

Chang, W., Ethier, W. and Kemp, M. (1980), 'The Theorems of International Trade with Joint Production', *Journal of International Economics*, 10 (August), 377–94.

Cheffert, J.-M. (1994), *Exchange Rate and Prices in Models of Imperfect Competition*, PhD thesis (University of Namur, Belgium).

Cheng, L.K. and Wong, K.Y. (1990), 'On the Strategic Choice between Capital and Labor Mobility', *Journal of International Economics*, 28, 291–314.

Chipman, J.S. (1965), 'A Survey of International Trade: Part I – The Classical Theory', *Econometrica*, 33, 477–519.

Chipman, J.S. (1991), 'Intra-Industry Trade in a Loglinear Model', University of Minnesota (mimeo).

Clarida, R.H. (1991), 'Entry, Dumping, and Shakeout', *American Economic Review*, 83(1), 181–202.

Coe, D.T. and Helpman, E. (1995), 'International R&D Spillovers', *European Economic Review*, 39, 859–87.

Coe, D.T., Helpman, E. and Hoffmáister, A.W. (1997), 'North–South R&D Spillovers', *Economic Journal*, 107, 134–49.

Coes, D. (1981), 'The Crawling Peg and Exchange Rate Uncertainty', in Williamson, J. (ed.), *Exchange Rate Rules: The Theory, Performance and Prospects of the Crawling Peg* (New York: St. Martin's Press), 113–36.

Collie, D. (1991), 'Export Subsidies and Countervailing Tariffs', *Journal of International Economics*, 31, 309–24.

Commission of the European Communities (1989), *Survey on State Aids in the European Community* (Luxembourg: Office for Official Publications of the European Communities).

Coneybeare, J.A.C. (1987), *Trade Wars: The Theory and Practice of International Commercial Rivalry* (New York: Columbia University Press).

Cooper, R. and John, A. (1988), 'Coordinating Coordination Failures in Keynesian Models', *Quarterly Journal of Economics*, 103, 441–64.

Cooper, C.A. and Massell, B.F. (1965), 'Towards a General Theory of Customs Unions for Developing Countries', *Journal of Political Economy*, 73, 461–76.

Corden, W.M. (1971), *The Theory of Protection* (London: Allen & Unwin).

Corden, W.M. (1972), 'Economies of Scale and Customs Union Theory', *Journal of Political Economy*, 80(3), 465–75.

Cornes, R. (1992), *Duality and Modern Economics* (Cambridge: Cambridge University Press).

Cuddington, J.T. (1992), 'Long-Run Trends in 26 Primary Commodity Prices: A Disaggregated Look at the Prebisch–Singer Hypothesis', *Journal of Development Economics*, 39, 207–27.

Culem, C. and Lundberg, L. (1986), 'The Product Pattern of Intra-industry Trade: Stability among Countries and over Time', *Weltwirtschaftliches Archiv*, 122, 113–30.

Cushman, D.O. (1983), 'The Effects of Real Exchange Rate Risk on International Trade', *Journal of International Economics*, 15, 45–65.

Cushman, D.O. (1988), 'US Bilateral Trade Flows and Exchange Risk during the Floating Period', *Journal of International Economics*, 24, 317–30.

Dam, K.W. (1970), *The GATT – Law and International Economic Organization* (Chicago: University of Chicago Press).

Danthine, J.-P. (1978), 'Information, Futures Prices and Stabilizing Speculation', *Journal of Economic Theory*, 17, 79–98.

Das, S.P. and Donnenfeld, S. (1987), 'Trade Policy and its Impact on Quality of Imports', *Journal of International Economics*, 23, 77–95.

Das, S.P. and Donnenfeld, S. (1989), 'Competition and International Trade: Quantity and Quality Restrictions', *Journal of International Economics*, 27(4), 299–318.

Deane, R.S. (1970), *Foreign Investment in New Zealand Manufacturing* (Wellington: Sweet and Maxwell).

Deardorff, A.V. (1979), 'Weak Links in the Chain of Comparative Advantage', *Journal of International Economics*, 9(2), 197–209.

Deardorff, A.V. (1980), 'The General Validity of the Law of Comparative Advantage', *Journal of Political Economy*, 88(5), 941–57.

Deardorff, A.V. (1982), 'The General Validity of the Heckscher–Ohlin Theorem', *American Economic Review*, 72, 683–94.

Deardorff, A.V. (1984), 'Testing Trade Theories and Predicting Trade Flows', in Jones, R.W. and Kenen, P.B. (eds), *Handbook of International Economics*, Vol. I (Amsterdam: North-Holland), 467–517.

Deardorff, A.V. and Stern, R.M. (1986), *The Michigan Model of World Production and Trade* (Cambridge, Mass.: MIT Press).

Deardorff, A.V. and Stern, R.M. (1990), *Computation Analysis of Global Trading Arrangements* (Ann Arbor: University of Michigan Press).

Deardorff, A.V. and Stern, R.M. (eds) (1994), *Analytical and Negotiating Issues in the Global Trading System* (Ann Arbor: University of Michigan Press).

Deaton, A. and Muellbauer, J. (1980), *Economics and Consumer Behavior* (Cambridge: Cambridge University Press).

De Grauwe, P. and Verfaille, G. (1988), 'Exchange Rate Variability, Misalignment and the European Monetary System', in Marston, R.C. (ed.), *Misalignment of Exchange Rates: Effects on Trade and Industry* (Chicago: University of Chicago Press), 77–103.

De la Torre, A. and Kelly, M.A. (1992), 'Regional Trade Arrangements', *International Monetary Fund, Occasional Paper*, 93 (March).

de Melo, J. and Messerlin, P.A. (1988), 'Price, Quality and Welfare Effects of European VERs on Japanese Autos', *European Economic Review*, 32, 1527–46.

de Melo, J. and Robinson, S. (1989), 'Product Differentiation and the Treatment of Foreign Trade in Computable General Equilibrium Models of Small Economies', *Journal of International Economics*, 27, 47–67.

de Melo, J. and Tarr, D. (1992), *A General Equilibrium Analysis of US Foreign Trade Policy* (Cambridge, Mass: MIT Press).

de Melo, J. and Urata, S. (1986), 'The Influence of Increased Foreign Competition on Industrial Concentration and Profitability', *International Journal of Industrial Organization*, 4, 287–304.

de Melo, J. and Winters, L.A. (1993), 'Price and Quality Effects of VERs Revisited: A Case Study of Korean Footwear Exports', *Journal of Economic Integration*, 8(1), 33–57.

de Meza, D. (1986), 'Export Subsidies and High Productivity: Cause or Effects', *Canadian Journal of Economics*, 19, 347–50.

Diamond, P. (1982), 'Aggregate Demand Management in Search Equilibrium', *Journal of Political Economy*, 90, 881–94.

Dick, A.R. (1993), 'Strategic Trade Policy and Welfare', *Journal of International Economics*, 35, 227–49.

Diewert, W.E. (1982), 'Duality Approaches to Microeconomic Theory', in Arrow, K.J. and Intrilligator, M.D. (eds), *Handbook of Mathematical Economics* (Amsterdam: North-Holland), 535–99.

Dinwiddy, C.L. and Tal, F.J. (1988), *The Two-Sector Equilibrium Model: A New Approach* (Oxford: Philip Allan).

Dixit, A.K. (1984), 'International Trade Policy for Oligopolistic Industries', *Economic Journal Conference Papers*, 94, 1–16.

Dixit, A. (1987), 'Strategic Aspects of Trade Policy', in Bewley, T.F. (ed.), *Advances in Economic Theory: Fifth World Congress* (Cambridge: Cambridge University Press), 329–62.

Dixit, A. (1988), 'Anti-Dumping and Countervailing Duties under Oligopoly', *European Economic Review*, 32, 55–68.

Dixit, A. (1988), 'Optimal Trade and Industrial Policies for the US Automobile Industry', in Feenstra, R. (ed.), *Empirical Methods for International Trade Policy* (Cambridge, Mass.: MIT Press), 161–65.

Dixit, A. (1989), 'Entry and Exit Decisions under Uncertainty', *Journal of Political Economy*, 97(3), 620–38.

Dixit, A. (1989), 'Hysteresis, Import Penetration and Exchange Rate Pass-Through', *Quarterly Journal of Economics*, 104(2), 205–28.

Dixit, A. (1992), 'Investment and Hysteresis', *Journal of Economic Perspectives*, 6(1), 107–32.

Dixit, A.K. and Grossman, G.M. (1986), 'Targeted Export Promotion with Several Oligopolistic Industries', *Journal of International Economics*, 21, 233–50.

Dixit, A.K. and Kyle, A.S. (1985), 'The Use of Protection and Subsidies for Entry Promotion and Deterrence', *American Economic Review*, 75, 139–52.

Dixit, A.L. and Norman, V. (1980), *Theory of International Trade* (Cambridge: Cambridge University Press).

Dixit, A. and Pindyck, R.S. (1994), *Investment under Uncertainty* (Princeton: Princeton University Press).

Dixit, A. and Stiglitz, J.E. (1977), 'Monopolistic Competition and Optimum Product Diversity', *American Economic Review*, 67, 297–303.

Dixon, P., Parmenter, B., Sutton, J. and Vincent, D. (1982), *ORANI: A MultiSector Model of the Australian Economy* (Amsterdam: North-Holland).

Domar, E.D. (1946), 'Capital Expansion, Rate of Growth and Employment', *Econometrica*, 14, 137–47.

Dornbusch, R. (1987), 'Exchange Rates and Prices', *American Economic Review*, 77(1), 93–106.

Dornbusch, R., Fischer, S. and Samuelson, P.A. (1977), 'Comparative Advantage, Trade, and Payments in a Ricardian Model with a Continuum of Goods', *American Economic Review*, 47(5), 823–39.

Dunning, J.H. (1981), *International Production and the Multinational Enterprise* (London: Allen & Unwin).

Dunning, J.H. (1992), *Multinational Enterprises and the Global Economy* (Wokingham: Addison-Wesley).

Eaton, J. and Grossman, G.M. (1986), 'Optimal Trade and Industrial Policy under Oligopoly', *Quarterly Journal of Economics*, 101, 383–406.

Eaton, J. and Panagariya, A. (1979), 'Gains from Trade under Variable Returns to Scale, Commodity Taxation, Tariffs and Factor Market Distortions', *Journal of International Economics*, 9, 481–501.

Eden, L. (1985), 'Microeconomics of Transfer Pricing', in Rugman, A.M. and Eden, L. (eds), *Multinationals and Transfer Pricing* (New York: St Martin's Press), 13–46.

Eden, L. (1994), *Multinationals in North America* (Eden, Calgary: University of Calgary Press).

Ethier, W. (1973), 'International Trade and the Forward Exchange Market', *American Economic Review*, 63, 494–503.

Ethier, W.J. (1979), 'Internationally Decreasing Costs and World Trade', *Journal of International Economics*, 9, 1–24.

Ethier, W.J. (1982), 'Dumping', *Journal of Political Economy*, 90(3), 487–506.

Ethier, W.J. (1982), 'National and International Returns to Scale in the Modern Theory of International Trade', *American Economic Review*, 72, 388–405.

Ethier, W.J. (1982), 'Decreasing Costs in International Trade and Frank Graham's Argument for Protection', *Econometrica*, 50(5), 1243–67.

Ethier, W.J. (1983), *Modern International Economics* (New York: Norton), Appendix I, 511–56.

Ethier, W. (1984), 'Higher Dimensional Issues in Trade Theory', Chapter 3 in Jones, R. and Kenen, P. (eds), *Handbook of International Economics, Vol. I* (Amsterdam: North-Holland), 131–84.

Ethier, W.J. (1986), 'The Multinational Firm', *Quarterly Journal of Economics*, 101, 805–33.

Ethier, W.J. (1987), 'The Theory of International Trade', in Officer, L.M. (ed.), *International Economics* (Boston: Kluwer Academic), 1–57.

Ethier, W.J. (1996), 'Regionalism in a Multilateral World', *Working Paper*, International Economics Research Center, University of Pennsylvania.

Ethier, W.J. and Fisher, R.D. (1987), 'The New Protectionism', *Journal of Economic Integration*, 2(2), 1–11.

Ethier, W.J. and Horn, H. (1984), 'A New Look at Economic Integration', in Kierzkowski, H. (ed.), *Monopolistic Competition and International Trade* (Oxford: Clarendon Press), 207–29.

Ethier, W.J. and Horn, H. (1990), 'Managerial Control of International Firms and Patterns of Direct Investment', *Journal of International Economics*, 28, 25–45.

European Communities, Statistical Office of the (1990), *NACE Rev. 1*, Document NACE 200, Annex 1/Version 2.1.6 (Brussels: European Commission).

Faini, R. and Heimler, A. (1991), 'The Quality of Production of Textiles and Clothing and the Completion of the Internal Market', in Winters, L.A. and Venables, A. (eds), *European Integration: Trade and Industry* (Cambridge: Cambridge University Press).

Falvey, R. (1979), 'The Comparison of Trade Within Export-Restricted Categories', *Journal of Political Economy*, 87(5), 1142–65.

Feder, G., Just, R.E. and Schmitz, A. (1980), 'Futures Markets and the Theory of the Firm under Price Uncertainty', *Quarterly Journal of Economics*, 95, 317–28.

Feenstra, R.C. (1985), 'Automobile Prices and Protection: The US–Japan Trade Restraint', *Journal of Policy Modeling*, 7(1), 49–68.

Feenstra, R.C. (1988), 'Quality Change under Trade Restraints in Japanese Autos', *Quarterly Journal of Economics*, 103(1), 131–46.

Feenstra, R.C. (ed.) (1988), *Empirical Methods for International Trade* (Cambridge, Mass.: MIT Press).

Feenstra, R.C. (1989), 'Symmetric Pass-Through of Tariffs and Exchange Rates under Imperfect Competition: an Empirical Test', *Journal of International Economics*, 27, 25–45.

Feenstra, R.C. (1989), *Trade Policies for International Competitiveness* (Chicago: University of Chicago Press and National Bureau of Economic Research).

Feenstra, R.C. (1993), 'Measuring the Welfare Effect of Quality Change: Theory and Application to Japanese Autos', *NBER Working Paper*, 4401.

Feenstra, R.C. (1995), 'Estimating the Effects of Trade Policy', Chapter 30 in Grossman, G. and Rogoff, D. (eds), *Handbook of International Economics, Vol. III* (Amsterdam: North-Holland).

Feenstra, R.C. (1996), 'US Imports, 1972–1994: Data and Concordances', NBER, *Working Paper* 5515.

Feenstra, R.C. (1997), 'US Exports, 1972–1994, with Other US Data', NBER, *Working Paper* (forthcoming).

Feenstra, R.C., Lipsey, R.E. and Bowen, H.P. (1997), 'World Trade Flows, 1970–1992, with Production and Tariff Data', NBER, *Working Paper* 5910.

Feinberg, R.M. (1989), 'Exchange Rates and "Unfair Trade" ', *Review of Economics and Statistics*, 71, 704–7.

Fels, J. and Gundlach, E. (1990), 'More Evidence on the Puzzle of Interindustry Wage Differentials: The Case of West Germany', *Weltwirtschaftliches Archiv*, 3, 544–60.

Findlay, R. (1984), 'Growth and Development in Trade Models', in Jones, R.W. and Kenen, P. B. (eds), *Handbook of International Economics, Vol. I* (Amsterdam: North-Holland), 185–236.

Findlay, R. (1988), 'Comparative Advantage', in Eatwell, J., Milgate, M. and Newman, P. (eds), *The New Palgrave: A Dictionary of Economics* (London: Macmillan), 514–17.

Findlay, R. and Kierzkowski, H. (1983), 'International Trade and Human Capital: A Simple General Equilibrium Model', *Journal of Political Economy*, 91, 957–78.

Finger, J.M. (1993), 'The Origins and Evolution of Antidumping Regulation', in Finger, J.M. (ed.), *Antidumping: How it Works and Who Gets Hurt* (Ann Arbor: University of Michigan Press).

Finger, J.M. and Kreinin, M.E. (1979), 'A Measure of "Export Similarity" and its Possible Uses', *Economic Journal*, 89, 905–12.

Finger, J.M. and Laird, S. (1987), 'Protection in Developed and Developing Countries: An Overview', *Journal of World Trade Law*, 21, 9–23.

Finger, J.M. and Olechowski, A. (1987), 'Trade Barriers: Who Does What to Whom', in Giersch, H. (ed.), *Free Trade in the World Economy* (Tübingen: J.C.B. Mohr), 37–71.

Fischer, R.D. (1992), 'Endogenous Probability of Protection and Firm Behavior', *Journal of International Economics*, 32, 149–63.

Fisher, E. (1989), 'A Model of Exchange Rate Pass-Through', *Journal of International Economics*, 26, 119–37.

Flam, H. (1987), 'Reverse Dumping', *European Economic Review*, 31, 82–8.

Flam, H. (1992), 'Product Markets and 1992: Full Integration, Large Gains?', *Journal of Economic Perspectives*, 6(4), 7–30.

Flam, H. and Helpman E. (1987), 'Industrial Policy under Monopolistic Competition', *Journal of International Economics*, 22, 79–102.

Ford, R. and Suyker, W. (1990), *Industrial Subsidies in the OECD Economies* (Paris: OECD Department of Economics and Statistics).

Francois, J.F., McDonald, B. and Nordström, H. (1995), 'Assessing the Uruguay Round', paper presented at the World Bank Conference, *The Uruguay Round and the Developing Economies* (January).

Francois, J.F. and Shiells, C.R. (1994), *Modelling Trade Policy: Applied General Equilibrium Assessments of NAFTA* (Cambridge: Cambridge University Press).

Froot, K.A. (1993), *Foreign Direct Investment* (Chicago and London: University of Chicago Press).

Froot, K. and Klemperer, P. (1989), 'Exchange Rate Pass-Through When Market Share Matters', *American Economic Review*, 79(4), 637–54.

Fukuda, S.-I. and Cong, J. (1994), 'On the Choice of Invoice Currency by Japanese Exporters: The PTM Approach', *Journal of the Japanese and International Economies*, 8, 511–29.

Gale, D. and Nikaido, H. (1965), 'The Jacobian Matrix and the Global Univalence of Mappings', *Mathematische Annalen*, 159, 81–93.

GATT (1990), *International Trade, Vols I and II* (Geneva: GATT).

GATT (1991) *Trade Policy Review Mechanism, European Communities* (March) (Geneva: GATT),

GATT (1994) *The Results of the Uruguay Round of Multilateral Trade Negotiations* (November) (Geneva: GATT).

General Agreements on Tariffs and Trade (1991), *European Communities. Report by the Secretariat* (Geneva: Trade Policy Review Mechanism).

Gersovitz, M. (1982), 'The Estimation of the Two-Gap Model', *Journal of International Economics*, 12, 111–24.

Gibbons, R. (1992), *Game Theory for Applied Economists* (Princeton: Princeton University Press).

Giovannini, A. (1988), 'Exchange Rates and Traded Goods Prices', *Journal of International Economies*, 24, 45–68.

Glejser, H., Goossens, K. and Vanden Eede, M. (1979), 'Inter-industry and Intra-industry Specialization Do Occur in World Trade', *Economics Letters*, 3, 261–5.

Glejser, H., Goossens, K. and Vanden Eede, M. (1982), 'Inter-industry versus Intra-industry Specialization in Exports and Imports (1959–1970–1973)', *Journal of International Economics*, 12, 363–9.

Goldberg, P.K. and Knetter, M.M. (1997), 'Goods Prices and Exchange Rates: What Have We Learned?', *Journal of Economic Literature*, 35(3), 1243–72.

Goldsmith, R. and Saunders, C. (eds) (1960), *The Measurement of National Wealth*, NBER Research in Income and Wealth, 8 (Chicago: Quadrangle Books).

Goldstein, M. and Khan, M.S. (1978), 'The Supply and Demand for Exports: A Simultaneous Approach', *Review of Economics and Statistics*, 60, 275–86.

Goldstein, M. and Khan, M.S. (1985), 'Income and Price Effects in Foreign Trade', in Jones, R.W. and Kenen, P.B. (eds), *Handbook of International Economics*, Vol. II (Amsterdam: North-Holland), Chapter 20, 1041–1105.

Gotur, P. (1985), 'Effects of Exchange Rate Volatility on Trade', *IMF Staff Papers*, 32, 475–512.

Graham, E.M. and Krugman, P.R. (1993), 'The Surge in Foreign Investment in the 1980s', in Froot, K.A. (ed.), *Foreign Direct Investment* (Chicago and London: University of Chicago Press), 13–36.

Graham, F. (1923), 'Some Aspects of Protection Further Considered', *Quarterly Journal of Economics*, 37, 199–227.

Grassman, S. (1973), 'A Fundamental Symmetry in International Payment Patterns', *Journal of International Economics*, 3, 105–16.

Greenaway, D. (1983), 'Intra-industry and Inter-industry Trade in Switzerland', *Weltwirtschaftliches Archiv*, 119, 109–21.

Greenaway, D. and Milner, C. (1983), 'On the Measurement of Intra-industry Trade', *Economic Journal*, 93, 900–8.

Greenaway, D. and Milner, C. (1986), *The Economics of Intra-industry Trade* (Oxford: Basil Blackwell).

Greenaway, D. and Milner, C. (1987), 'Intra-industry Trade: Current Perspectives and Unresolved Issues', *Weltwirtschaftliches Archiv*, 123, 39–57.

Greenaway, D. and Tharakan, P.K.M. (eds) (1986), *Imperfect Competition and International Trade: Policy Aspects of Intra-industry Trade* (Brighton: Wheatsheaf).

Greenaway, D., Hine, R. and Milner, C. (1995), 'Vertical and Horizontal Intra-Industry Trade: A Cross Industry Analysis for the United Kingdom', *Economic Journal*, 105, 1505–18.

Grinols, E.J. (1984), 'A Thorn in the Lion's Paw: Has Britain Paid Too Much for Common Market Membership?', *Journal of International Economics*, 16, 271–293.

Grinols, E.L. (1991), 'Increasing Returns and the Gains from Trade', *International Economic Review*, 32(4), 973–84.

Grossman, G.M. (1981), 'The Theory of Domestic Content Protection and Content Preference', *Quarterly Journal of Economics*, 96(4) (November), 583–603.

Grossman, G.M. (1986), 'Imports as a Cause of Injury: The Case of the US Steel Industry', *Journal of International Economics*, 20, 201–23.

Grossman, G.M. (1987), 'Strategic Export Promotion: A Critique', in Krugman, P.R. (ed.), *Strategic Trade Policy and the New International Economics* (Cambridge, Mass.: MIT Press).

Grossman, G.M. and Helpman, E. (1991), *Innovation and Growth in the Global Economy* (Cambridge, Mass.: MIT Press).

Grossman, G.M. and Levinsohn, J.A. (1989), 'Import Competition and the Stock Market Return to Capital', *American Economic Review*, 79(5), 1065–87.

Grubaugh, S.G. (1987), 'Determinants of Direct Foreign Investment', *Review of Economics and Statistics*, 69, 149–52.

Grubel, H.G. and Lloyd, P.J. (1971), 'The Empirical Measurement of Intra-Industry Trade', *The Economic Record*, 47, 494–517.

Grubel, H.G. and Lloyd, P.J. (1975), *Intra-Industry Trade, the Theory and Measurement of International Trade in Differentiated Products* (London: Macmillan).

Gruber, H., Mehta, D. and Vernon, R. (1967), 'The R&D Factor in International Trade and International Investment of US Industries', *Journal of Political Economy*, 75, 20–37.

Grubert, H. and Mutti, J. (1991), 'Taxes, Tariffs and Transfer Pricing in Multinational Corporate Decision Making', *Review of Economics and Statistics*, 79, 285–93.

Gruenspecht, H.K. (1988), 'Export Subsidies for Differentiated Products', *Journal of International Economics*, 24, 331–44.

Gruenspecht, H.K. (1988), 'Dumping and Dynamic Competition', *Journal of International Economics*, 25, 225–48.

Haberler, G. (1936), *The Theory of International Trade* (London: W. Hodge).

Hamilton, J.D. (1994), *Time Series Analysis* (Princeton: Princeton University Press).

Hamilton, C. and Svensson, L.E.O. (1983), 'Should Direct or Total Factor Intensities be Used in Tests of the Factor Proportions Hypothesis?', *Weltwirtschaftliches Archiv*, 119(3), 453–63.

Hansen, J.D., Heinrich, H. and Nielsen, J.W.-M. (1992), *An Economic Analysis of the EEC* (London: McGraw-Hill).

Harkness, J. (1978), 'Factor Abundance and Comparative Advantage', *American Economic Review*, 68, 784–800.

Harrigan, J. (1994), 'Scale Economies and the Volume of Trade', *The Review of Economics and Statistics*, 76(2), 321–8.

Harrigan, J. (1995), 'Factor Endowments and the International Location of Production', *Journal of International Economics*, 39, 123–41.

Harris, R. (1984), 'Applied General Equilibrium Analysis of Small Open Economies with Scale Economies and Imperfect Competition', *American Economic Review*, 74(5), 1016–32.

Harris, R. (1985), 'Why Voluntary Export Restraints are "Voluntary"', *Canadian Journal of Economics*, (4), 799–809.

Harris, R. and Cox, D. (1984), *Trade, Industrial Policy, and Canadian Manufacturing* (Toronto: Ontario Economic Council Research Study).

Harris, J.R. and Todaro, M.P. (1970), 'Migration, Unemployment and Development: A Two-Sector Analysis', *American Economic Review*, 54, 961–74.

Harrod, R.F. (1939), 'An Essay in Dynamic Theory', *Economic Journal*, 49, 14–33.

Hatton, T. (1995), 'A Model of UK Emigration, 1870–1913', *Review of Economics and Statistics*, 77(3), 407–15.

Hazari, B.R. (1978), *The Pure Theory of International Trade and Distortions* (London: Croom Helm), Chapter 1, 7–29.

Heller, W.P. (1988), 'Coordination Failure with Complete Markets in a Simple Model of Effective Demand', in Heller, W.P., Starr, R.M. and Starrett, D.A. (eds), *Equilibrium Analysis: Essays in Honor of K.J. Arrow*, Vol. II (Cambridge: Cambridge University Press).

Helpman, E. (1981), 'International Trade in the Presence of Product Differentiation, Economies of Scale, and Monopolistic Competition: A Chamberlin–Heckscher–Ohlin Approach', *Journal of International Economics*, 11, 305–40.

Helpman, E. (1984), 'A Simple Theory of International Trade with Multinational Corporations', *Journal of Political Economy*, 92, 451–71.

Helpman, E. (1984), 'Increasing Returns, Imperfect Markets and Trade Theory', in Jones, R. and Kenen, P. (eds), *Handbook of International Economics*, Vol. II (Amsterdam: North-Holland), 325–65.

Helpman, E. (1987), 'Imperfect Competition and International Trade: Evidence from Fourteen Industrial Countries', *Journal of the Japanese and International Economies*, 1, 62–81.

Helpman, E. and Krugman, P.R. (1985), *Market Structure and Foreign Trade, Increasing Returns, Imperfect Competition, and the International Economy* (Cambridge, Mass. and London: MIT Press), Section 2.7, 22–5.

Helpman, E. and Krugman, P.R. (1989), *Trade Policy and Market Structure* (Cambridge, Mass. and London: MIT Press).

Helpman, E. and Razin, A. (1983), 'Increasing Returns, Monopolistic Competition, and Factor Movements: A Welfare Analysis', *Journal of International Economics*, 14, 263–76.

Helpman, E. and Razin, A. (1991), *International Trade and Trade Policy* (Cambridge, Mass. and London: MIT Press).

Herberg, H. and Kemp, M.C. (1969), 'Some Implications of Variable Returns to Scale', *Canadian Journal of Economics*, 3, 403–15.

Hicks, J. (1939), 'Foundations of Welfare Economics', *Economic Journal*, 49, 696–712.

Hill, J.K. and Méndez, J.A. (1984), 'The Effect of Commercial Policy on International Migration Flows: The Case of the United States and Mexico', *Journal of International Economics*, 17, 41–53.

Hillman, A.L. (1980), 'Observations on the Relation Beween "Revealed Comparative Advantage" and Comparative Advantage as Indicated by Pre-Trade Relative Prices', *Weltwirtschaftliches Archiv*, 116, 314–21.

Hillman, A.L. (1989), *The Political Economy of Protection* (Chur: Harwood Academic).

Hillman, A.L. and Riley, J. (1989), 'Politically Contestable Rents and Transfers', *Economics and Politics*, 1, 1989, 17–39.

Hillman, A.L. and Ursprung, H.W. (1988), 'Domestic Politics, Foreign Interests and International Trade Policy', *American Economic Review*, 78, 729–49.

Hillman, A.L. and Ursprung, H.W. (1993), 'Multinational Firms, Political Competition and International Trade Policy', *International Economic Review*, 34(2), 347–63.

Hindley, B. (1994), 'Safeguards, VERs and Antidumping Actions', in OECD Documents, *The New World Trading System* (Paris: OECD), 91–103.

Hine, R.C. (1994), 'International Economic Integration', in Greenaway, D. and Winters, L.A. (eds), *Survey in International Trade* (Oxford: Basil Blackwell), 234–72.

Hinojosa-Ojeda, R. and Robinson, S. (1991), 'Alternative Scenarios of US–Mexico Integration: A Computable General Equilibrium Approach', *Working Paper*, 609 (University of California, Berkeley).

Hipple, F.S. (1990), 'The Measurement of International Trade Related to Multinational Companies', *American Economic Review*, 80(5), 1263–70.

Hirschleifer, J. and Riley, J.G. (1992), *The Analytics of Uncertainty and Information* (Cambridge: Cambridge University Press).

Hoekman, B. (1996), 'Trade Laws and Institutions: Good Practices and the World Trade Organization', *World Bank Discussion Paper*, 282 (Washington, DC: World Bank).

Hollander, A. (1987), 'Content Protection and Transnational Monopoly', *Journal of International Economics*, 23, 283–97.

Holthausen, D.M. (1979), 'Hedging and the Competitive Firm under Price Uncertainty', *American Economic Review*, 69, 989–95.

Hooper, P. and Kohlhagen, S.W. (1978), 'The Effect of Exchange Rate Uncertainty on the Prices and Volume of International Trade', *Journal of International Economics*, 8, 483–511.

Hooper, P. and Mann, C. (1989), 'Exchange Rate Pass-Through in the 1980s: The Case of US Imports of Manufactures', *Brookings Papers on Economic Activity*, 1, 297–337.

Horst, T. (1971), 'The Theory of the Multinational Firm: Optimal Behavior under Different Tariff and Tax Rates', *Journal of Political Economy*, 79, 1059–72.

Horst, T. (1974), 'The Industrial Composition of US Exports and Subsidiary Sales to the Canadian Market', *American Economic Review*, 62, 37–45.

Horstmann, I.J. and Markusen, J.R. (1986), 'Up the Average Cost Curve: Inefficient Entry and the New Protectionism', *Journal of International Economics*, 20, 225–47.

Horstmann, I.J. and Markusen, J.R. (1987), 'Licensing vs. Direct Investment: A Model of Internalisation by the MNE', *Canadian Journal of Economics*, 20, 464–81.

Horstmann, I.J. and Markusen, J.R. (1987), 'Strategic Investments and the Development of Multinationals', *International Economic Review*, 28, 109–21.

Horstmann, I.J. and Markusen, J.R. (1992). 'Endogenous Market Structures in International Trade (Natura Facit Saltum)', *Journal of International Economics*, 32, 109–29.

Horstmann, I.J. and Markusen, J.R. (1996), 'Exploring New Markets: Direct Investment, Contractual Relations and the Multinational Enterprise', *International Economic Review*, 37, 1–19.

Hotelling, H. (1929), 'Stability in Competition', *Economic Journal*, 39, 41–57; reprinted in Stigler, G.J. and Boulding, K.E. (eds), *AEA Readings in Price Theory* (Chicago: Richard D. Irwin, 1952), 467–84.

Hufbauer, G.C., Berliner, D.T. and Elliott, K.A. (1986), *Trade Protection in the United States: 31 Case Studies* (Washington, D.C.: Institute for International Economics).

Hummels, D.L. and Levinsohn, J. (1995), 'Monopolistic Competition and International Trade: Reconsidering the Evidence', *Quarterly Journal of Economics*, 799–835.

Hummels, D.L. and Stern, R.M. (1994), 'Evolving Patterns of North American Merchandise Trade and Foreign Direct Investment, 1960–1990', *The World Economy*, 17(1), 5–31.

Hunter, L. and Markusen, J. (1988), 'Per-Capita Income as a Determinant of Trade', in Feenstra, R.C. (ed.), *Empirical Methods for International Trade* (Cambridge, Mass.: MIT Press).

Hymer, S. (1976), 'The International Operations of National Firms: A Study of Foreign Direct Investment', PhD dissertation (Cambridge, Mass.: MIT Press).

Hwang, H. and Mai, C.-C. (1988), 'On the Equivalence of Tariffs and Quotas under Duopoly: A Conjectural Variations Approach', *Journal of International Economics*, 24, 373–80.

International Labour Office (1990), *International Standard Classification of Occupations: ISCO-88* (Geneva: International Labour Office).

International Monetary Fund (1984), 'Exchange Rate Volatility and World Trade', *Occasional Paper*, 28 (Washington, DC: IMF Research Department).

Intriligator, M.D. (1971), *Mathematical Optimization and Economic Theory* (Englewood Cliffs: Prentice Hall).

Irwin, D.A. and Klenow, P.J. (1994), 'Learning-by-Doing Spillovers in the Semiconductor Industry', *Journal of Political Economy*, 102(6), 1200–27.

Ito, T. (1990), 'Foreign Exchange Rate Expectations: Micro Survey Data', *American Economic Review*, 80(3), 434–49.

Jackson, J. (1969), *World Trade and the Law of the GATT* (Indianapolis: Bobbs-Merrill).

Jackson, J. (1989), *The World Trading System: Law and Policy of International Economic Relations* (Cambridge, Mass.: MIT Press).

Jackson, J.H. and Vermulst, E.A. (eds) (1990), *Antidumping Law and Practice: A Comparative Study* (London: Harvester Wheatsheaf).

Jacquemin, A. and Sapir, A. (1988), 'European or World Integration?', *Weltwirtschaftliches Archiv*, 124(1), 127–38.

Jacquemin, A. and Sapir, A. (1991), 'The Discipline of Imports in the European Market', in de Melo, J. and Sapir, A. (eds), *Trade Theory and Economic Reform: North, South, and East, Essays in Honor of Bela Balassa* (Cambridge, Mass. and Oxford: Blackwell).

Jacquemin, A., De Ghellinck, E. and Huveneers, C. (1980), 'Concentration and Profitability in a Small Open Economy', *Journal of Industrial Economics*, 29(2), 131–44.

Johansen, L. (1960), *A Multi-Sectoral Study of Economic Growth* (Amsterdam: North-Holland).

Johnson, H.G. (1953), 'Optimum Tariffs and Retaliation', *Review of Economic Studies*, 21, 142–53.

Johnson, H.G. (1958), 'The Gains from Freer Trade with Europe: An Estimate', *Manchester School*, 26, 247–55.

Johnson, H.G. (1962), 'The Economic Theory of Customs Union', in Johnson, H. (ed.), *Money, Trade and Economic Growth* (London: George Allen & Unwin).

Johnson, H.G. (1969), 'Minimum Wage Laws: A General Equilibrium Analysis', *Canadian Journal of Economics*, 2, 599–604.

Johnson, H.G. (1971), *Aspects of the Theory of Tariffs* (London: Allen & Unwin).

Jones, H.G. (1975), *An Introduction to Modern Theories of Economic Growth* (London: Nelson).

Jones, R.W. (1965), 'The Structure of Simple General Equilibrium Models', *Journal of Political Economy*, 73, 557–72.

Jones, R.W. (1969) 'Tariffs and Trade in General Equilibrium: Comment', *American Economic Review*, 59, 418–24.

Jones, R.W., Neary, J.P. and Ruane, F.P. (1983), 'Two-Way Capital Flows', *Journal of International Economics*, 14, 357–66.

Jones R. and Scheinkman J. (1977), 'The Relevance of the Two-Sector Production Model in Trade Theory', *Journal of Political Economy*, 85, 909–35.

Judd, K.L. (1985), 'Credible Spatial Preemption', *Rand Journal of Economics*, 16(2), 153–66.

Julius, D. and Thomsen, S. (1988), 'Foreign-Owned Firms, Trade, and Economic Integration', *Tokyo Club Papers*, 2(1), 151–74.

Kant, Ch. (1988), 'Endogenous Transfer Pricing and the Effects of Uncertain Regulation', *Journal of International Economics*, 24, 147–57.

Katrak, H. (1979), 'Multinational Monopolies and Commercial Policy', *Oxford Economic Papers*, 29, 283–91.

Katz, L.F. and Summers, L.H. (1988), 'Can Interindustry Wage Differentials Justify Strategic Trade Policy?', *National Bureau of Economic Research Working Paper*, 2739 (October).

Katz, L.F. and Summers, L.H. (1989), 'Industry Rents: Evidence and Implications', in Baily, M.N. and Winston, C. (eds), *Brookings Papers on Economic Activity: Microeconomics* (Washington, DC: Brookings Institution), 208–75.

Kawai, M. (1981), 'The Behaviour of an Open Economy Firm under Flexible Exchange Rates', *Economica*, 48, 45–60.

Kawai, M. and Zilcha, I. (1986), 'International Trade with Forward-Futures Markets under Exchange Rate and Price Uncertainty', *Journal of International Economics*, 20, 83–98.

Kemp, M.C. (1969), *The Pure Theory of International Trade and Investment* (Englewood Cliffs: Prentice-Hall), Chapters 1–4, 5–118; Chapter 5, 119–33.

Kemp, M.C. and Negishi, T. (1970), 'Variable Returns to Scale, Commodity Taxes, Factor Market Distortions and Their Implication for Trade Gains', *Swedish Journal of Economics*, 72(1), 1–11.

Kemp, M.C. and Wan, H.Y. (1976), 'An Elementary Proposition Concerning the Formation of Customs Unions', *Journal of International Economics*, 6, 95–7.

Kenen, P.B. and Rodrik, D. (1986), 'Measuring and Analyzing the Effects of Short-Term Volatility in Real Exchange Rates', *Review of Economics and Statistics*, 68, 311–15.

Kennan, J. and Riezman, R. (1990), 'Optimal Tariff Equilibrium with Customs Unions', *Canadian Journal of Economics*, 23(1), 70–83.

Khan, M.S. and Ross, Z. (1977), 'The Functional Form of the Aggregate Demand Equation', *Journal of International Economics*, 7, 149–60.

Kim, S. (1995), 'Expansion of Markets and the Geographic Distribution of Economic Activities: The Trends in US Regional Manufacturing Structure, 1860–1987', *Quarterly Journal of Economics*, 110, 881–908.

Klein, L.R. (1983), *Lectures in Econometrics* (Amsterdam: North-Holland), 21–36.

Klepper, G. (1990), 'Entry into the Market for Large Transport Aircraft', *European Economic Review*, 34, 775–803.

Knetter, M.M. (1989), 'Price Discrimination by US and German Exporters', *American Economic Review*, 79(1), 198–210.

Knetter, M.M. (1992), 'International Comparisons of Pricing-to-Market Behavior', *American Economic Review*, 83(3), 473–86.

Kohler, W. (1988), 'Modeling Heckscher–Ohlin Comparative Advantage in Regression Equations: A Critical Survey', *Empirica*, 15(2), 263–93.

Kohler, W. (1991), 'How Robust Are Sign and Rank Order Tests of the Heckscher–Ohlin–Vanek Theorem?', *Oxford Economic Papers*, 43(1), 158–71.

Kohli, U. (1991), *Technology, Duality, and Foreign Trade: The GNP Function Approach to Modeling Imports and Exports* (Ann Arbor and London: University of Michigan Press and Harvester Wheatsheaf).

Kohli, U. (1993), 'US Technology and the Specific-Factors Model', *Journal of International Economics*, 34, 115–36.

Kojima, K. (1964), 'The Pattern of International Trade among Advanced Countries', *Hitotsubashi Journal of Economics*, 5, 16–36.

Koopmans, T.C. (1965), 'On the Concept of Optimal Economic Growth', in *The Econometric Approach to Development Planning* (Amsterdam: North-Holland), reissue of Pontificae Academiae Scientiarum Scripta Varia, 28 (1965), 225–30.

Krauss, M.B. (1972), 'Recent Development in Customs Union Theory: An Interpretive Survey', *Journal of Economic Literature* (June), 413–36.

Krauss, M.B., Johnson, H.G. and Skouras, T. (1973), 'On the Shape and Location of the Production Possibility Curve', *Economica*, 40(159), 305–10.

Kravis, I.B. and Lipsey, R.E. (1992), 'Sources of Competitiveness of the United States and its Multinational Firms', *Review of Economics and Statistics*, 74(2), 193–201.

Kreps, D.A. and Scheinkman, J.A. (1983), 'Quantity Precommitment and Bertrand Competition Yield Cournot Outcomes', *Bell Journal of Economics*, 4, 326–37.

Krishna, K. (1987), 'Tariffs versus Quotas with Endogenous Quality', *Journal of International Economics*, 23, 97–122.

Krishna, K. (1988), 'The Case of the Vanishing Revenues: Auction Quotas with Oligopoly', National Bureau of Economic Research Inc., *Working Paper*, 2723.

Krishna, K. (1989), 'The Case of the Vanishing Revenues: Auction Quotas with Monopoly', National Bureau of Economic Research Inc., *Working Paper*, 2840.

Krishna, K. (1990), 'The Case of Vanishing Revenue: Auction Quotas with Monopoly', *American Economic Review*, 80(4), 828–37.

Krishna, K. (1990), 'Protection and the Product Line', *International Economic Review*, 31(1), 87–102.

Krishna, K. (1991), 'Making Altruism Pay in Auction Quotas', in Helpman, E. and Razin, A. (eds), *International Trade and Trade Policy* (Cambridge, Mass. and London: MIT Press), 46–65.

Krishna, K., Hogan, K. and Swagel, P. (1994), 'The Non-optimality of Optimal Trade Policies: The US Automobile Industry Revisited, 1979–85', in Krugman, P.R. and Smith, A. (eds), *Empirical Studies of Strategic Trade Policies* (Chicago and London: University of Chicago Press), 11–40.

Krishna, K. and Itoh, M. (1988), 'Content Protection and Oligopolistic Interactions', *Review of Economic Studies*, 55, 107–25.

Krishna, K. and Krueger, A.O. (1994), 'Implementing Free Trade Areas: Rules of Origin and Hidden Protection', in Deardorff, A., Levinhson, J. and Stern, R. (eds), *New Directions in Trade Theory* (Ann Arbor: University of Michigan Press).

Krishna, K. and Thursby, M. (1991), 'Optimal Policies with Strategic Distortions', *Journal of International Economics*, 31, 291–308.

Krueger, A.B. and Summers, L.H. (1988), 'Efficiency Wages and the Inter-Industry Wage Structure', *Econometrica*, 56(2), 259–93.

Krugman, P.R. (1979), 'Increasing Returns, Monopolistic Competition, and International Trade', *Journal of International Economics*, 9, 469–79.

Krugman, P.R. (1981), 'Intra-Industry Specialization and the Gains from Trade', *Journal of Political Economy*, 89, 959–73.

Krugman, P.R. (1984), 'Import Protection as Export Promotion: International Competition in the Presence of Oligopoly and Economies of Scale', in Kierzkowski, H. (ed.), *Monopolistic Competition and International Trade* (Oxford: Oxford University Press), 180–93.

Krugman, P.R. (1987), 'Pricing to Market When the Exchange Rate Changes', in Arndt, S.W. and Richardson, J.D. (eds), *Real-Financial Linkages Among Open Economies* (Cambridge, Mass.: MIT Press), 49–70.

Krugman, P.R. (1989), 'Differences in Income Elasticities and Trends in Real Exchange Rates', *European Economic Review*, 33, 1031–54.

Krugman, P.R. (1991), 'Is Bilateralism Bad?', in Helpman, E. and Razin, A. (eds), *International Trade and Trade Policy* (Cambridge, Mass.: MIT Press), 9–23.

Krugman, P.R. (1993), 'The Narrow and Broad Arguments for Free Trade', *American Economic Review*, 83(2), 362–6.

Krugman, P R. and Baldwin, R. (1987), 'The Persistence of the US Trade Deficit', *Brookings Paper on Economic Activity*, 1, 1–55.

Krugman, P.R. and Obstfeld, M. (1988), *International Economics: Theory and Policy* (Glenview: Scott, Foresman), Appendix to Chapter 2, 36–41.

Krugman, P.R. and Smith, A. (eds) (1994), *Empirical Studies of Strategic Trade Policies* (Chicago and London: University of Chicago Press).

Krugman, P.R. and Venables, A.J. (1995), 'Globalization and the Inequality of Nations', *Quarterly Journal of Economics*, 110, 857–80.

Kunimoto, K. (1977), 'Typology of Trade Intensity Indices', *Hitotsubashi Journal of Economics*, 17, 15–32.

Laird, S. and Yeats, A. (1990), *Quantitative Methods for Trade Barrier Analysis* (New York: New York University Press).

Laird, S. and Yeats, A. (1990), 'Trends in Nontariff Barriers of Developed Countries, 1966–1986', *Weltwirtschaftliches Archiv*, 299–325.

Lancaster, K. (1966), 'A New Approach to Consumer Theory', *Journal of Political Economy*, 74, 132-57.

Lancaster, K. (1979), *Variety, Equity, and Efficiency* (New York: Columbia University Press).

Lancaster, K. (1991), 'The "Product Variety" Case for Protection', *Journal of International Economics*, 31, 1–26.

Laussel, D., Montet, C. and Peguin-Feisolle, A. (1988), 'Optimal Trade Policy under Oligopoly: A Calibrated Model of the Europe–Japan Rivalry in the EEC Car Market', *European Economic Review*, 32, 1547–66.

Lavergne, R.P. (1981), 'The Political Economy of US Tariffs', PhD thesis, University of Toronto; partially reproduced in 'US Trade Policy Since World War II' in Baldwin, R.E. and Krueger, A.O. (eds), *The Structure and Evolution of Recent US Trade Policy* (Chicago: University of Chicago Press, 1984).

Leamer, E.E. (1974), 'Nominal Tariff Averages with Estimated Weights,' *Southern Economic Journal*, 41, 34–46.

Leamer, E.E. (1980) 'The Leontief Paradox Reconsidered', *Journal of Political Economy*, 88(3), 495–503.

Leamer, E.E. (1981), 'Is it a Demand Curve or is it a Supply Curve? Partial Identification through Inequality Constraints', *Review of Economics and Statistics*, 63, 319–27.

Leamer, E.E. (1984), *Sources of International Comparative Advantage: Theory and Evidence* (Cambridge, Mass.: MIT Press).

Leamer, E.E. (1988) 'Measures of Openness', in Baldwin R.E. (ed.), *Trade Policy Issues and Empirical Analysis* (Chicago: University of Chicago Press and National Bureau of Economic Research), 147–200.

Leamer, E.E. (1992), 'Testing Trade Theory', *NBER Working Paper*, 3957.

Leamer, E.E. and Bowen, H.P. (1981), 'Cross-Section Tests of the Heckscher–Ohlin Theorem: Comment', *American Economic Review*, 71(4), 1040–3.

Leamer, E.E. and Levinsohn, J. (1995), 'International Trade Theory: The Evidence', in Grossman, G. and Rogoff, K. (eds), *Handbook of International Economics, Vol. III* (Amsterdam: North-Holland), chapter 26, 1339–94.

Leamer, E.E. and Stern, R.M. (1970), *Quantitative International Economics* (Boston: Allyn and Bacon).

Lee, D.W. and Lee, T.H. (1995), 'Human Capital and Economic Growth: Tests Based on the International Evaluation of Educational Achievements', *Economics Letters*, 47, 219–25.

Leidy, M.P. and Hoekman, B.M. (1988), 'Production Effects of Price- and Cost-Based Anti-Dumping Laws under Flexible Exchange Rates', *Discussion Paper* 224, Research Seminar in International Economics (University of Michigan).

Leontief, W. (1953), 'Domestic Production and Foreign Trade: The American Capital Position Re-Examined', *Proceeding of the American Philosophical Society*, 97, 332–49.

Leontief, W. (1954), 'Domestic Production and Foreign Trade: the American Position Re-examined', *Economica Internazionale*, 7, 3–32.

Lerner, A. (1936), 'The Symmetry between Import and Export Taxes', *Economica*, 3, 306–13.

Levine, R. and Renelt, D. (1992), 'A Sensitivity Analysis of Cross-Country Growth Regressions', *American Economic Review*, 82, 942–63.

Levine, R. and Zervos, S.J. (1993), 'What We Have Learned about Policy and Growth from Cross-Country Regressions', *American Economic Review, Papers and Proceedings*, 83, 426–30.

Levinsohn, J. (1993), 'Testing the Imports as Market Disciple Hypothesis', *Journal of International Economics*, 35, 1–22.

Liesner, H.H. (1958), 'The European Common Market and British Industry', *Economic Journal*, 68, 302–16.

Linnemann, H. (1966), *An Econometric Study of International Trade Flows* (Amsterdam: North-Holland).

Lipsey, R.E. (1990), 'Foreign Direct Investment in the United States: Changes over Three Decades', in Froot, K.A. (ed.), *Foreign Direct Investment* (Chicago and London: University of Chicago Press), 113–72.

Lipsey, R.G. (1960), 'The Theory of Customs Unions – A General Survey', *Economic Journal*, 70, 496–513.

Lloyd, P.J. (1982), '3 × 3 Theory of Customs Unions', *Journal of International Economics*, 12, 41–63.

Loertscher, R. and Wolter, F. (1980), 'Determinants of Intra-Industry Trade: Among Countries and Across Countries', *Weltwirtschaftliches Archiv*, 116, 280–93.

Lucas, R.E. (1988), 'On the Mechanics of Economic Development', *Journal of Monetary Economics*, 22, 3–42.

Lucas, R.E. (1990), 'Why Doesn't Capital Flow from Rich to Poor Countries?', *American Economic Review*, 80(2), 92–6.

Lucas, R.E. (1993), 'Making a Miracle', *Econometrica*, 61, 251–72.

Lustig, N., Bosworth, B.P. and Lawrence, R.Z. (1992), *North American Free Trade: Assessing the Impact* (Washington, DC: Brookings Institution).

McCulloch, R. (1993), 'The Optimality of Free Trade: Science or Religion?', *American Economic Review*, 83(2), 367–71.

McGilvray, J. and Simpson, D. (1973), 'The Commodity Structure of Anglo–Irish Trade', *Review of Economics and Statistics*, 55, 451–8.

McMillan, J. (1993), 'Does Regional Integration Foster Open Trade? Economic Theory and GATT's Article XXIV', in Anderson, K. and Blackhurst, R. (eds), *Regional Integration and the Global Trading System* (New York: Harvester Wheatsheaf), 292–310.

MacDougall, G.D.A. (1951), 'British and American Exports: A Study Suggested by the Theory of Comparative Costs, Part I', *Economic Journal*, 61, 487–521.

MacDougall, G.D.A. (1960), 'The Benefits and Costs of Private Investment from Abroad: A Theoretical Approach', *Economic Record*, 36, 13–35.

MacDougall, G.D.A., Dowley, M., Fox, P. and Pugh, S. (1962), 'British and American Productivity, Prices and Exports: An Addendum', *Oxford Economic Papers*, 14(3), 297–304.

Magee, S.P. (1980), 'Three Simple Tests of the Stolper–Samuelson Theorem', in Oppenheimer, P. (ed.), *Issues in International Economics* (London: Oriel Press), 138–53.

Mankiw, N.G. (1995), 'The Growth of Nations', *Brookings Papers on Economic Activity*, 1, 275–326.

Marchese, S. and Nadal De Simone, F. (1989), 'Monotonicity of Indices of "Revealed" Comparative Advantage: Empirical Evidence on Hillman's Condition', *Weltwirtschaftliches Archiv*, 125, 158–67.

Markusen, J.R. (1981), 'Trade and Gains from Trade with Imperfect Competition', *Journal of International Economics*, 11, 531–51.

Markusen, J.R. (1983), 'Factor Movements and Commodity Trade as Complements', *Journal of International Economics*, 14, 341–56.

Markusen, J.R. (1995), 'The Boundaries of Multinational Enterprises and the Theory of International Trade', *Journal of Economic Perspectives*, 9(2), 169–89.

Markusen, J.R. and Melvin, J. (1984), 'Trade, Factor Prices, and the Gains from Trade with Increasing Returns to Scale', *Canadian Journal of Economics*, 14, 450–69.

Markusen, J.R. and Venables A.J. (1988), 'Trade Policy with Increasing Returns and Imperfect Competition: Contradictory Results from Competing Assumptions', *Journal of International Economics*, 24, 299–316.

Markusen, J.R. and Venables, A.J. (1995), 'Multinational Firms and the New Trade Theory', *NBER Working Paper*, 5036.

Markusen, J.R. and Venables, A.J. (1996), 'The Theory of Endowment, Intra-Industry and Multinational Trade', *NBER Working Paper*, 5529.

Marquez, J. (1990), 'Bilateral Trade Elasticities', *Review of Economics and Statistics*, 72, 75–86.

Marshall, A. (1890), *Principles of Economics* (London: Macmillan; revised edn 1972).

Marston, R. (1990), 'Pricing to Market in Japanese Manufacturing', *Journal of International Economics*, 29, 217–36.

Martin, J.P. (1976), 'Variable Factor Supplies and the HOS Model', *Economic Journal*, 820–31.

Martin, S. (1993), *Advanced Industrial Economics* (Cambridge, Mass. and Oxford: Blackwell).

Marvel, H.P. and Ray, E.J. (1995), 'Countervailing Duties', *The Economic Journal*, 105, 1576–93.

Maskus, K.V. (1985), 'A Test of the Heckscher–Ohlin–Vanek Theorem: The Leontief Commonplace', *Journal of International Economics*, 9, 201–12.

Maskus, K.V. (1991), 'Comparing International Trade Data and Product and National Characteristics Data for the Analysis of Trade Models', in Hooper, P. and Richardson, J.D. (eds), *International Economic Transactions, Issues in Measurement and Empirical Research* (Chicago: University of Chicago Press).

Melitz, J. and Messerlin, P. (1987), 'Export Credit Subsidies', *Economic Policy*, OECD (April), 149–75.

Melvin, J.R. (1969), 'Increasing Returns to Scale as a Determinant of Trade', *Canadian Journal of Economics*, 3, 389–402.

Melvin, J.R. (1970), 'Commodity Taxation as a Determinant of Trade', *Canadian Journal of Economics*, 3, 62–78.

Melvin, J.R. (1971), 'On the Derivation of the Production Possibility Curve', *Economica*, 38(151), 281–94.

Memedovic, O. (1994), 'On the Theory and Measurement of Comparative Advantage', *Tinbergen Institute Research Series*, 65 (Rotterdam).

Messerlin, P. (1990), 'Anti-Dumping Regulation or Pro-Cartel Law? The EC Chemical Cases', *World Economy*, 13(4), pp. 465–92.

Messerlin, P.A. and Becuwe, S. (1986), 'Intra-industry Trade in the Long Run: The French Case, 1850–1913', in Greenaway, D. and Tharakan, P.K.M. (eds), *Imperfect Competition and International Trade: Policy Aspects of Intra-Industry Trade* (Brighton: Wheatsheaf), 191–215.

Messerlin, P. and Reed, G. (1995), 'Antidumping Policies in the United States and the European Community', *Economic Journal*, 105, 1565–75.

Metzler, L.A. (1949), 'Tariffs, the Terms of Trade, and the Distribution of National Income', *Journal of Political Economy*, 57, 1–29.

Michaely, M. (1962), *Concentration in International Trade* (Amsterdam: North-Holland).

Michaely, M. (1977), *Theory of Commercial Policy* (Chicago: University of Chicago Press).

Miller, M.H. and Spencer, J.E. (1977), 'The Static Economic Effects of the UK Joining the EEC: A General Equilibrium Approach', *Review of Economic Studies*, 136, 71–94.

Mills, T.C. (1990), *Time Series Techniques for Economists* (Cambridge: Cambridge University Press).

Mundell, R. (1957), 'International Trade and Factor Mobility', *American Economic Review*, 47, 321–35.

Munk, B. (1969), 'The Welfare Costs of Content Protection: The Automobile Industry in Latin America', *Journal of Political Economy*, 77(1) (February), 85–98.

Mussa, M. (1979), 'The Two-Sector Model in Terms of its Dual: A Geometric Exposition', *Journal of International Economics*, 9, 513–26.

Mussa, M. (1984), 'The Economics of Content Protection', *NBER Working Paper*, No. 1457.

Neary, J.P. (1978), 'Short-Run Capital Specificity and the Pure Theory of International Trade', *Economic Journal*, 88, 488–510.

Neary J.P. (1991), 'Export Subsidies and Price Competition', in Helpman, E. and Razin, A. (eds), *International Trade and Trade Policy* (Cambridge, Mass.: MIT Press), 80–95.

Neary, J.P. (1994), 'Cost Asymmetries in International Subsidy Games: Should Governments Help Winners or Losers?', *Journal of International Economics*, 77, 197–218.

Neumann, M , Bobol, I. and Haid, A. (1985), 'Domestic Concentration, Foreign Trade and Economic Performance', *International Journal of Industrial Organization*, 3, 1–19.

Nguyen, T.T. and Wigle, R.M. (1992), 'Trade Liberalization with Imperfect Competition: The Large and the Small of It', *Journal of International Economics*, 36, 17–33.

Nogués, J.J., Olechowski, A. and Winters, L.A. (1986), 'The Extent of Non-Tariff Barriers to Industrial Countries' Imports', *World Bank Economic Review*, 1, 181–99.

Norman, G. and Dunning, J.M. (1984), 'Intra-industry Foreign Direct Investment', *Weltwirtschaftliches Archiv*, 120, 522–39.

Norman, V.D. (1989), 'Trade Policy under Imperfect Competition, Theoretical Ambiguities–Empirical Regularities?', *European Economic Review*, 33, 473–9.

Ohlin, B. (1933), *Interregional and International Trade* (Cambridge, Mass.: Harvard University Press).

Okuno-Fujiwara, M. (1988), 'Interdependence of Industries, Coordination Failure and Strategic Promotion of an Industry', *Journal of International Economics*, 25, 25–43.

Oniki, H. and Uzawa, H. (1965), 'Patterns of Trade and Investment in a Dynamic Model of International Trade', *Review of Economic Studies*, 32, 15–38.

Organization for Economic Co-operation and Development (1961), *Cross Reference Between the National Commodity Nomenclatures and the Standard International Trade Classification*, Organization for Economic Co-operation and Development, Statistical Bulletins (Paris: OECD).

Panagariya, A. (1981), 'Variable Returns to Scale in Production and Patterns of Specialization', *American Economic Review*, 71, 221–30.

Parry, T.G. (1978), 'Structure and Performance in Australian Manufacturing, with Special Reference to Foreign-Owned Enterprises', in Kasper, W. and Parry, T.G. (eds), *Growth, Trade and Structural Change in an Open Australian Economy* (Kensington, Australia: Centre for Applied Economic Research), 173–99.

Parsley, D.C. and Wei, S.-J. (1993), 'Insignificant and Inconsequential Hysteresis: The Case of US Bilateral Trade', *Review of Economics and Statistics*, 75(4), 606–13.

Pelzman, J. (1988), 'The Tariff Equivalents of the Existing Quotas under the Multi-fiber Arrangement', US Department of Labor, Bureau of International Labor Affairs, Washington, DC.

Perée, E. and Steinherr, A. (1989), 'Exchange Rate Uncertainty and Foreign Trade', *European Economic Review*, 33, 1241–64.

Perroni, C. and Whalley, J. (1996), 'How Severe is Global Retaliation Risk under Increasing Regionalism?', *American Economic Review Papers and Proceedings*, 86(2), 57–61.

Petith, H.C. (1977), 'European Integration and the Terms of Trade', *Economic Journal*, 87, 262–72.

Prusa, T.J. (1992), 'Why are so Many Antidumping Petitions Withdrawn?', *Journal of International Economics*, 33, 1–20.

Prusa, T.J. (1994), 'Pricing Behavior in the Presence of Antidumping Law', *Journal of Economic Integration*, 9(2), 260–89.

Pugel, T.A. (1978), *International Market Linkages and US Manufacturing: Prices, Profits and Patterns* (Cambridge, Mass.: Ballinger).

Pugel, T.A. (1980), 'Foreign Trade and US Market Performance', *Journal of Industrial Economics*, 29(2), 119–29.

Pugel, T.A., Kragas, E.S. and Kimura, Y. (1996), 'Further Evidence on Japanese Direct Investment in US Manufacturing', *Review of Economics and Statistics*, 208–13.

Qiu, L.D. (1995), 'Why Can't Countervailing Duties Deter Export Subsidization?', *Journal of International Economics*, 39, 249–72.

Ramaswami, V.K. (1968), 'International Factor Movement and the National Advantage', *Economica*, 35, 309–10.

Ramsey, F.P. (1928), 'A Mathematical Theory of Saving', *Economic Journal*, 38, 543–59.

Rangan, S. and Lawrence, R.Z. (1993), 'The Responses of US Firms to Exchange Rate Fluctuations: Piercing the Corporate Veil', *Brookings Papers on Economic Activity*, 2, 341–79.

Rebelo, S. (1991), 'Long-Run Policy Analysis and Long-Run Growth', *Journal of Political Economy*, 99, 500–21.

Reitzes, J.D. (1993), 'Antidumping Policy', *International Economic Review*, 34(4), 745–63.

Ricardo, D. (1821), *The Principles of Political Economy and Taxation* (London: J. Murray).

Richardson, J.D. (1989), 'Empirical Research on Trade Liberalization with Imperfect Competition', *NBER Working Paper*, 2883.

Richardson, M. (1991), 'The Effects of a Content Requirement on a Foreign Duopsonist', *Journal of International Economics*, 31, 143–55.

Riezman, R. (1982), 'Tariff Retaliation from a Strategic Viewpoint', *Southern Economic Journal*, 48, 583–93.

Riezman, R. (1985), 'Customs Unions and the Core', *Journal of International Economics*, 19, 355–65.

Riezman, R. (1991), 'Dynamic Tariffs with Asymmetric Information', *Journal of International Economics*, 30(3/4), 267–83.

Rodriguez, C.A. (1974), 'The Non-Equivalence of Tariffs and Quotas Under Retaliation', *Journal of International Economics*, 4, 295–8.

Rodriguez, C. (1979), 'The Quality of Imports and the Differential Welfare Effects of Tariffs, and Quality Controls as Protective Devices', *Canadian Journal of Economics*, 22(3), 439–49.

Rodrik, Dani (1988), 'Imperfect Competition, Scale Economies, and Trade Policy in Developing Countries', in Baldwin, R.E (ed.), *Trade Policy Issues and Empirical Analysis* (Chicago: University of Chicago Press).

Romer, P.M. (1986), 'Increasing Returns and Long-Run Growth', *Journal of Political Economy*, 94, 1002–37.

Romer, P.M. (1989), 'Capital Accumulation in the Theory of Long-Run Growth', in Barro, R.J. (ed.), *Modern Business Cycle Theory* (Cambridge, Mass.: Harvard University Press).

Romer, P.M. (1990), 'Endogenous Technological Change', *Journal of Political Economy*, 98, S71–102.

Romer, P.M. (1994), 'The Origins of Endogenous Growth', *The Journal of Economic Perspectives*, 8(Winter), 3–22.

Roussland, D.J. and Soumela, J.W. (1985), 'Calculating the Consumer and Net Welfare Costs of Import Relief', *Staff Research Study*, 15, United States International Trade Commission.

Roy, S. and Viaene, J.-M. (1998), 'On Strategic Vertical Foreign Direct Investment', *Journal of International Econnomics*, forthcoming.

Roy, S. and Viaene, J.-M. (1997), 'Preferences, Country Bias and International Trade', *Review of International Economics* (forthcoming).

Rubinstein, A. (1982), 'Perfect Equilibrium in a Bargaining Model', *Econometrica*, 50, 97–110.

Rubinstein, A. (1987), 'Perfect Equilibrium in a Market with Decentralized Trade and Strategic Behaviour: An Introduction', *Theoretical Economics Discussion Paper Series*, 87/147 (London School of Economics).

Rubinstein, A. and Wolinsky, A. (1985), 'Equilibrium in a Market with Sequential Bargaining', *Econometrica*, 53, 1133–50.

Ruffin, R.J. (1984), 'International Factor Movements', in Jones, R.W. and Kenen, P.B. (eds), *Handbook of International Economics*, Vol. I (Amsterdam: North-Holland), 237–88.

Ruffin, R. and Jones, R. (1977), 'Protection and Real Wages: The Neo-Classical Ambiguity', *Journal of Economic Theory*, 14, 337–48.

Rugman, A. (1988), 'The Multinational Enterprise', in Walter, I. and Murray, T. (eds), *Handbook of International Management* (New York: Wiley).

Ruland, L.J. and Viaene, J.-M. (1993), 'The Political Choice of the Exchange Rate Regime', *Economics and Politics*, 5, 271–83.

Sampson, G.P. (1996), 'Compatibility of Regional and Multilateral Trading Agreements: Reforming the WTO Process', *American Economic Review Papers and Proceedings*, 86(2), 88–92.

Samuelson, L. (1982), 'The Multinational Firm with Arms' Length Transfer Price Limits', *Journal of International Economics*, 13, 365–74.

Samuelson, P. A. (1953), 'The Prices of Goods and Factors in General Equilibrium', *Review of Economics and Statistics*, 21, 1–20.

Sapir, A. (1975), 'A Note on Short-Run Greek Labor Emigration to Germany', *Weltwirtschaftliches Archiv*, 111, 356–61.

Sapir, A. and Sekkat, K. (1995), 'Exchange Rate Regimes and Trade Prices: Does the EMS Matter?', *Journal of International Economics*, 38(1/2), 75–94.

Savosnick, K.M. (1958), 'The Box Diagram and the Production Possibility Curve', *Ekonomisk Tidsskrift*, 60(3), 183–97.

Saxonhouse, G. R. (1989), 'Differentiated Products, Economies of Scale and Access to the Japanese Market', in Feenstra, R.C. (ed.), *Trade Policies for International Competitiveness* (Chicago: University of Chicago Press and National Bureau of Economic Research).

Scharrer, H.E. (1979), 'Die Wahrungsstruktur im Welthandel', Wirtschaftsdienst.

Scherer, F.M. and Ross, D. (1990), *Industrial Market Structure and Economic Performance* (Boston: Houghton Mifflin), 3rd edn.

Schmalensee, R. (1989), 'Inter-Industry Studies of Structure and Performance', Chapter 2 in Schmalensee, R. and Willig, D. (eds), *Handbook of Industrial Organization* (Amsterdam: North-Holland).

Schuknecht, L. (1992), *Trade Protection in the European Community* (Chur: Harwood Academic).

Seade, J. (1978), 'Consumer's Surplus and Linearity of Engel Curves', *Economic Journal*, 88, 511–23.

Seade, J. (1980), 'On the Effects of Entry', *Econometrica*, 48, 479–89.

Shephard, R.W. (1953), *Cost and Production Functions* (Princeton: Princeton University Press).

Shibata, H. (1968), 'A Note on The Equivalence of Tariffs and Quotas', *American Economic Review*, 58, 137–42.

Shoven, J. H. and Whalley, J. (1992), *Applying General Equilibrium* (Cambridge: Cambridge University Press).

Smith, A. (1776), *An Inquiry into the Nature and Causes of the Wealth of Nations* (London: W. Straham and T. Cadell).

Smith, A. (1987), 'Strategic Investment, Multinational Corporations and Trade Policy', *European Economic Review*, 31, 89–96.

Smith, A. (1994), 'Strategic Trade Policy in the European Car Market', in Krugman, P.R. and Smith, A. (eds), *Empirical Studies of Strategic Trade Policies* (Chicago and London: University of Chicago Press), 67–81.

Smith, A. and Venables, A.J. (1988), 'Completing the Internal Market in the European Community: Some Industry Simulations', *European Economic Review*, 32, 1501–26.

Smith, A. and Venables, A.J. (1991), 'Counting the Cost of Voluntary Export Restraints in the European Car Market', in Helpman, E. and Razin, A. (eds), *International Trade and Trade Policy* (Cambridge, Mass. and London: MIT Press).

Solow, R.M. (1956), 'A Contribution to the Theory of Economic Growth', *Quarterly Journal of Economics*, 70, 65–94.

Spence, A.M. (1976), 'Product Differentiation and Welfare', *American Economic Review*, 66(2), 407–14.

Spencer, B.J. (1993), 'Capital Subsidies and Countervailing Duties in Oligopolistic Industries', *Journal of International Economics*, 24, 45–69.

Spencer, B.J. and Brander, J.A. (1983), 'International R and D Rivalry and Industrial Strategy', *Review of Economic Studies*, 50, 707–22.

Srinivasan, T.N., Whalley, J. and Wooton, I. (1993), 'Measuring the Effects of Regionalism on Trade and Welfare', in Anderson, K. and Blackhurst, R. (eds),

Regional Integration and the Global Trading System (New York: Harvester Wheatsheaf), 52–79.

Staiger, R.W. and Wolak, F.A. (1989), 'Strategic Use of Antidumping Law to Enforce Tacit International Collusion', *Working Paper*, 3016, National Bureau of Economic Research.

Stalhammar, N.O. (1991), 'Domestic Market Power and Foreign Trade: The Case of Sweden', *International Journal of Industrial Organization*, 9(3), 407–29.

Stark, O. (1992), *The Migration of Labor* (Oxford: Blackwell).

Stegemann, K. (1990), 'EC Anti-Dumping Policy: Are Price Undertakings a Legal Substitute for Illegal Price Fixing?', *Weltwirtschaftliches Archiv*, 126(2), 268–97.

Stern, R.M. (1962), 'British and American Productivity and Comparative Costs in International Trade', *Oxford Economic Papers*, 14(3), 275–96.

Stern, R.M. (1975), 'Testing Trade Theories', in Kenen, P.B. (ed.), *International Trade and Finance: Frontiers for Research* (New York: Cambridge University Press), 3–49.

Stern, R.M. (ed.) (1993), *The Multilateral Trading System: Analysis and Options for Change* (Ann Arbor: University of Michigan Press).

Stern, R.M. and Maskus, K.V. (1981), 'Determinants of US Foreign Trade, 1958–76', *Journal of International Economics*, 11(2), 207–24.

Straubhaar, T. (1988), 'International Labour Migration within a Common Market: Some Aspects of EC Experience', *Journal of Common Market Studies*, 27(1), 45–62.

Straubhaar, T. (1988), *On the Economics of International Labor Migration* (Berne: Verlag Paul Haupt).

Summers, R. and Heston, A. (1991), 'The Penn World Table (Mark 5): An Expanded Set of International Comparisons, 1950–1988', *Quarterly Journal of Economics* (May).

Sutton, J. (1986), 'Non-Cooperative Bargaining Theory: An Introduction', *Review of Economic Studies*, 53, 709–24.

Sveikauskas, L, (1984), 'Science and Technology in Many Different Industries: Data for the Analysis of International Trade', *Review of Public Data Use* (June), 133–56.

Swan, T.W. (1956), 'Economic Growth and Capital Accumulation', *Economic Record*, 334–61.

Tanzi, V. and Bovenberg, A.L. (1989), 'Is There a Need for Harmonizing Capital Income Taxes within EC Countries?' (Washington, DC: International Monetary Fund), mimeo.

Taylor, M.S. (1993), 'Quality Ladders and Ricardian Trade', *Journal of International Economics*, 34, 225–43.

Teece, D.J. (1977), 'Technology Transfer by Multinational Enterprise: An Assessment', *Economic Journal*, 87, 242–61.

Teece, D.J. (1986), 'Transaction Cost Economics and the Multinational Enterprise: An Assessment', *Journal of Economic Behavior & Organization*, 7(1), 21–46.

Tharakan, P.K.M. (ed.) (1983), *Intra-industry Trade: Empirical and Methodological Aspects* (Amsterdam: North-Holland).

Thursby, J.G. and Thursby, M.C. (1984), 'How Reliable are Simple, Single Equation Specifications of Import Demand?', *Review of Economics and Statistics*, 66, 120–8.

Thursby, J.G. and Thursby, M.C. (1987), 'Bilateral Trade Flows, the Linder Hypothesis, and Exchange Risk', *Review of Economics and Statistics*, 69, 488–95.

Tinbergen, J. (1962), *Shaping the World Economy: Suggestions for an International Economic Policy* (New York: Twentieth Century Fund).

Tirole, J. (1988), *The Theory of Industrial Organization* (Cambridge, Mass. and London: MIT Press).

Tornell A. (1991), 'On the Ineffectiveness of Made-to-Measure Protectionist Programs', in Helpman, E. and Razin, A. (eds), *International Trade and Trade Policy* (Cambridge, Mass. and London: MIT Press), 66–79.

Tower, E. (1975), 'The Optimum Quota and Retaliation', *Review of Economic Studies*, 42, 623–30.

Trefler, D. (1993), 'International Factor Price Differences: Leontief was Right!', *Journal of Political Economy*, 101(6), 961–87.

Trefler, D. (1993), 'Trade Liberalization and the Theory of Endogenous Protection: An Econometric Study of US Import Policy', *Journal of Political Economy*, 101, 138–60.

Trefler, D. (1995), 'The Case of the Missing Trade and Other Mysteries', *American Economic Review*, 85(5), 1029–46.

UNCTAD (1994, 1996), *World Investment Report, Transnational Corporations, Employment and the Workplace* (New York and Geneva: United Nations).

United Nations Statistical Office (1959), *Indexes to the International Standard Industrial Classification of All Economic Activities* (New York: United Nations).

United Nations Statistical Office (1961), *Standard International Trade Classification, Revised*, Statistical Papers, Series M, 34 (New York: United Nations).

United Nations Statistical Office (1966), *Classification of Commodities by Industrial Origin; Relationship of the Standard International Trade Classification to the International Standard Industrial Classification* (New York: United Nations)

United Nations Statistical Office (1971), *Classification of Commodities by Industrial Origin; Links Between the Standard International Trade Classification and the International Standard Industrial Classification*, Statistical Papers, Series M, 43, rev. 1 (New York: United Nations).

United Nations Statistical Office (1975), *Standard International Trade Classification Revision 2*, Statistical Papers, Series M, 34, rev. 2, Department of International Economic and Social Affairs, Statistical Office (New York: United Nations).

United Nations Statistical Office (1981), *Bibliography of Industrial and Distributive-Trade Statistics*, Department of International Economic and Social Affairs, Statistical Papers, Series M, 36, rev. 5 (New York: United Nations).

United Nations Statistical Office (1986), *Classification by Broad Economic Categories: Defined in Terms of SITC Rev. 3*, Department of International Economic and Social Affairs, Statistical Papers, Series M, 53 (New York: United Nations).

United Nations Statistical Office (1986), *Commodity Indexes for the Standard International Trade Classification, Revision 3*, Social Information and Policy Analysis, Statistical Division, Statistical Papers, Series M, 38, rev. 2 (New York: United Nations).

United Nations Statistical Office (1986), *Correspondence Table Between the International Standard Industrial Classification of all Economic Activities of the*

United Nations (ISIC) and the Classification of Branches of the National Economy of the Council, Statistical Standards and Studies, 38 (New York: United Nations).

United Nations Statistical Office (1986), *Standard International Trade Classification Revision 3*, Statistical Papers, Series M, 34, rev. 3, Department of International Economic and Social Affairs, Statistical Office (New York: United Nations).

United Nations Statistical Office (1988), *Final Draft of the Revised International Standard Industrial Classification of All Economic Activities (ISIC), Rev. 3*, Statistical Papers, Series M, 4, rev. 3, add. 2 (New York: United Nations).

United Nations Statistical Office (1990), *International Standard Industrial Classification of All Economic Activities*, Department of International Economic and Social Affairs, Statistical Papers, Series M, 4 (New York: United Nations).

US Department of Commerce (various years), *Survey of Current Business* (Washington, DC: US Government Printing Office).

US International Trade Commission (1990), *The Economic Effects of Antidumping and Countervailing Duty Orders and Suspension Agreements*, Investigation, 332–44, Publication 2900 (Washington DC).

United States, Bureau of the Census (1969), *Correlation Between United States and International Standard Industrial Classifications* (Washington, DC: US Government Printing Office).

United States, US Dept. of Commerce (1979), *Correlation Between United States and International Standard Industrial Classifications*, prepared by Subcommittee on Statistics for Allocation of Funds, Federal Committee on Statistical Methodology (Washington, DC: US Government Printing Office).

Uzawa, H. (1961), 'On a Two-Sector Model of Economic Growth', *Review of Economic Studies*, 29, 40–7.

Van Wijnbergen, S. (1986), 'Macroeconomic Aspects of the Effectiveness of Foreign Aid: On the Two-Gap Model, Home Goods Disequilibrium and Real Exchange Rate Misalignment', *Journal of International Economics*, 21, 123–36.

Varian, H.R. (1992), *Microeconomic Analysis* (New York: W.W. Norton), 3rd edn.

Vartia, Y. (1983), 'Efficient Methods of Measuring Welfare Change and Compensated Income in Terms of Ordinary Demand Functions', *Econometrica*, 51, 79–98.

Vaupel, J.W. and Curhan, J.P. (1973), *The World's Multinational Enterprises* (Geneva: Research Unit, Centre d'Etudes Industrielles).

Venables, A.J. (1985), 'Trade and Trade Policy with Imperfect Competition: The Case of Identical Products and Free Entry', *Journal of International Economics*, 19, 1–19.

Venables A.J. (1990), 'International Capacity Choice and National Market Games', *Journal of International Economics*, 29, 23–42.

Venables, A.J. (1990), 'Microeconomic Implications of Exchange Rate Variations', *Oxford Review of Economic Policy*, 6(3), 18–27.

Venables, A.J. (1994), 'Trade Policy under Imperfect Competition: A Numerical Assessment', in Krugman, P. and Smith, A. (eds), *Empirical Studies of Strategic Trade Policy* (Chicago and London: University of Chicago Press).

Vernon, R. (1993), 'Where are the Multinationals Headed?', in Froot, K.A. (ed.), *Foreign Direct Investment* (Chicago and London: University of Chicago Press), 57–84.

Viaene, J.-M. (1982), 'A Customs Union Between Spain and the EEC', *European Economic Review*, 18, 345–68.

Viaene, J.-M. (1987), 'Factor Accumulation in a Minimum-Wage Economy', *European Economic Review*, 31, 1313–28.

Viaene, J.-M. and de Vries, C.G. (1992), 'International Trade and Exchange Rate Volatility', *European Economic Review*, 36, 1311–21.

Viaene, J.-M. and de Vries, C.G. (1992), 'On the Design of Invoicing Practices in International Trade', *Open Economies Review*, 3, 133–42.

Viaene, J.-M. (1993), 'The Harrod–Johnson Diagram and the International Equilibrium', *International Economic Journal*, 7(1), 83–93.

Viaene, J.-M. and Zilcha, I. (1998), 'The Behavior of the Competitive Exporting Firm under Multiple Uncertainty', *International Economic Review*, forthcoming.

Vikram, N. and Dhareshwar, A. (1993), 'A New Database on Physical Capital Stock: Sources, Methodology and Results', *Rivista de Analisis Economico*, 8(1), 37–59.

Viner, J. (1937), *Studies in the Theory of International Trade* (New York: Harper).

Viner, J. (1950), *The Customs Union Issue* (New York: Stevens & Sons).

Vousden, N. (1987), 'Content Protection and Tariffs under Monopoly and Competition', *Journal of International Economics*, 23, 263–82.

Vousden, N. (1990), *The Economics of Trade Protection* (Cambridge: Cambridge University Press).

Walter, I. (1972), 'Nontariff Protection among Industrial Countries: Some Preliminary Evidence', *Economic Internazionale*, 25, 335–54.

Weinstein, D. (1989), 'Competition, Unilateral Dumping and Firm Profitability', *Seminar Discussion Paper*, 249, Research Seminar in International Economics, University of Michigan.

Weitzman, M. (1982), 'Increasing Returns and the Foundations of Unemployment Theory', *Economic Journal*, 787–804.

Willenboekel, D. (1994), *Applied General Equilibrium Modelling: Imperfect Competition and European Integration* (Chichester: John Wiley).

Williamson, O.E. (1985), *The Economic Institutions of Capitalism* (New York: Free Press).

Willig, R.D. (1976), 'Consumer's Surplus without Apology', *American Economic Review*, 66, 589–97.

Winters, L.A. and Venables, A.J. (1991), *European Integration: Trade and Industry* (Cambridge: Cambridge University Press).

Wolf, H.C. (1994), 'Growth Convergence Reconsidered', *Weltwirtschaftliches Archiv*, 130, 747–59.

Wong, K.Y. (1983), 'On Choosing Among Trade in Goods and International Capital and Labor Mobility: A Theoretical Analysis', *Journal of International Economics*, 14(3/4), 223–50.

Wong, K.-Y. (1988), 'International Factor Mobility and the Volume of Trade: An Empirical Study', in Feenstra, R.C. (ed.), *Empirical Methods for International Trade* (Cambridge, Mass.: MIT Press), 231–50.

Wong, K.Y. (1995), *International Trade in Goods and Factor Mobility* (Cambridge, Mass. and London: MIT Press).

Wonnacott, R. (1990), *US Hub-and-Spoke Bilaterals and the Multilateral Trading System* (Toronto: Howe Institute).

Wonnacott, P. and Wonnacott, R. (1981), 'Is Unilateral Tariff Reduction Preferable to a Customs Union? The Curious Case of the Missing Foreign Tariffs', *American Economic Review*, 71, 704–13.

Woodland, A.D. (1977), 'A Dual Approach to Equilibrium in the Production Sector In International Trade Theory', *Canadian Journal of Economics*, 10(1), 50–68.

Woodland, A.D. (1980), 'Direct and Indirect Trade Utility Functions', *Review of Economic Studies*, 47, 907–26.

Woodland, A.D. (1982), *International Trade and Resource Allocation* (Amsterdam: North-Holland).

Wooton, I. (1986), 'Preferential Trading Arrangements: An Investigation', *Journal of International Economics*, 21, 81–97.

World Bank (1990), *World Development Report: Poverty* (Oxford: Oxford University Press).

WTO (1995), *International Trade, Trends and Statistics* (Geneva: WTO).

Yang, X. and Heijdra, B.J. (1993), 'Monopolistic Competition and Optimum Product Diversity: Comment', *American Economic Review*, 83, 295–301.

Yeats, A. (1995), 'Are Partner-Country Statistics Useful for Estimating "Missing" Trade Data?', *World Bank Policy Research Paper*, 1501 (Washington DC: World Bank).

Young, L. and Romero, J. (1992), *Steady Growth and Transition in a Dynamic Dual Model of the North American Free Trade Agreement* (Austin: University of Texas).

Index